OFFICE SYSTEMS

PEOPLE, PROCEDURES, AND TECHNOLOGY

SECOND EDITION

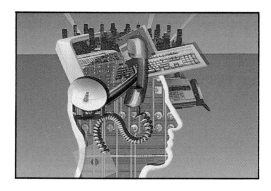

Rosemary T. Fruehling, Ph.D
Business and Office Education Consultant

Constance K. Weaver
Director, Investor Relations
MCI Communications, Inc.

Victoria R. Lyons
Instructor, Business Education Administrative Management Department
University of Wisconsin-Eau Claire

PARADIGM

PHOTO CREDITS

We acknowledge the assistance of the following sources which provided the photos used throughout this book:

Jules Allen; Apple Computer, Inc.; Ashton-Tate; AT&T Bell Laboratories; Borland International; Candee and Associates/Click Chicago; John Cavanaugh; Claris Corporation; Digital Equipment Corporation; Devoke Data Products; Will Faller; Gestetner Corporation; Richard Hackett; Hayes Microcomputer Products; Erich Hartmann/Magnum Photos; Hyundai Electronics America; IBM Corporation; Microsoft Corporation; Bob Rogers; Sperry Corporation; 3M Corporation.

This is the second edition of a text previously published as *Electronic Office Procedures*.

DEC is a registered trademark of Digital Equipment Corporation.

Hyundai is a registered trademark of Hyundai Corporation.

First Publisher, Harvard Graphics, and Harvard Project Manager are registered trademarks of Software Publishing Corporation.

Compaq is a registered trademark of Compaq Corporation.

Power Point, Microsoft Works, Microsoft DOS, Microsoft Word, Windows, and Excel are registered trademarks of Microsoft Corporation.

Symphony, Lotus, and 1-2-3 are registered trademarks of Lotus Development Corporation.

WordPerfect is a registered trademark.

SmartWare is a registered trademark of Informix Software, Inc.

dBase III+, dBaseIV, and Chart Master are registered trademarks, and FrameWork is trademark of Borland International.

IBM and DisplayWrite are registered trademarks of International Business Machines, Inc.

MultiMate is a registered trademark, and MultiMate Advantage is a trademark of South-Western Publishing Company.

Ventura Publisher is a registered trademark of Xerox Corporation.

PageMaker is a registered trademark of Aldus Corporation.

Micrografx is a trademark of Micrografx, Inc.

Hewlett Packard and LaserJet are registered trademarks of Hewlett Packard Company.

ProComm is a registered trademark of Datastorm Techniques, Inc.

Smartcom is a registered trademark of Hayes Microcomputer Programs, Inc.

VP Planner is a registered trademark of Paperback Software International.

Library of Congress Cataloging-in-Publication Data

Fruehling, Rosemary T.
    Office systems.
    Includes Index.
    1. Office practice—Automation.   2. Electronic office machines.
    3. Systems—Business office. I. Weaver, Constance K. II. Lyons,
Victoria R. III. Title.
1986   651   86-10326
1-56118-403-9

© 1992, 1987 by Paradigm Publishing Inc.
          Published by EMCParadigm
          875 Montreal Way
          St. Paul, MN 55102
          (800) 535-6865
          Email publish@emcp.com

Printed in the United States of America.

10 9 8 7 6 5

TABLE OF CONTENTS

About the Authors   vi
Preface   vii

**UNIT 1
WORKING IN THE ELECTRONIC
OFFICE   1**

Chapter 1
Today's Business Office   3
Levels of Office Automation   12
Organizational Structure   14
Summary   28
Vocabulary   29
Checking Your Understanding   29
Thinking Through Procedures   29

Chapter 2
Information Processing Technology   31
Stages of Information Processing   31
The Information Processing Cycle   37
Technology Applied to Office Functions   40
Choosing the Technology for the Function   52
Summary   54
Vocabulary   55
Checking Your Understanding   55
Thinking Through Procedures   56

Unit 1: The Workplace Problem   57

**UNIT 2
MANAGING THE OFFICE
WORKSTATION   61**

Chapter 3
The Electronic Workstation:
Hardware   63
Computer System Components   70
Other Workstation Components   81
Organizing the Electronic Workstation   84
Maintaining the Electronic Workstation   89
Summary   90
Vocabulary   91
Checking Your Understanding   92
Thinking Through Procedures   92

Chapter 4
The Electronic Workstation:
Software   94
Computers and Software   94
Types of Software   94
Learning to Use Software   114
Selecting Software   116
Summary   117
Vocabulary   118
Checking Your Understanding   118
Thinking Through Procedures   119

Unit 2: The Workplace Problem   120

**UNIT 3
MANAGING PERSONAL
PRODUCTIVITY   123**

Chapter 5
The Communication Process   125
Communication   125
Oral Communication Skills   132
Listening Skills   136
Nonverbal Skills   137
Business Communication Roles   138
Teleconferences   142
Summary   142
Vocabulary   143
Checking Your Understanding   144
Thinking Through Procedures   144

Chapter 6
Human Relations   146
Human Relations in the Office   146
Office Rules and Politics   156
Handling Stress   162

Summary   165
Vocabulary   165
Checking Your Understanding   166
Thinking Through Procedures   166

Chapter 7
Time Management Principles   169
Time Management   169
Using Time Management Skills   178
Summary   188
Vocabulary   189
Checking Your Understanding   189
Thinking Through Procedures   190

Unit 3 The Workplace Problem   192

UNIT 4
MANAGING ADMINISTRATIVE
FUNCTIONS   195

Chapter 8
Coordinating Office
Communication   197
Coordination Tools   197
Communications with Visitors and
   Clients   205
Organizing the Daily Schedule   209
Summary   210
Vocabulary   211
Checking Your Understanding   211
Thinking Through Procedures   211

Chapter 9
Coordinating Conferences and
Meetings   213
Meetings and Conferences   213
Types of Meetings   214
Planning and Scheduling Meetings   218
Special Meeting Considerations   229
Evaluation and Follow-Up   237
Summary   242
Vocabulary   243
Checking Your Understanding   243
Thinking Through Procedures   243

Chapter 10
Coordinating Telephone
Communications   245
Telecommunications   245
Telephone Systems   249
Telephone Techniques   257
Teleconferences   268
Summary   270
Vocabulary   271
Checking Your Understanding   272
Thinking Through Procedures   272

Chapter 11
Coordinating Travel Arrangements   275
Arranging Business Trips   275
International Travel   293
Managing the Office While the Supervisor is
   Away   297
Summary   301
Vocabulary   302
Checking Your Understanding   303
Thinking Through Procedures   303

Unit 4: The Workplace Problem   306

UNIT 5
PROCESSING WRITTEN
DOCUMENTS   309

Chapter 12
Creating Written Documents   312
Writing Skills in Today's Office   312
Dictating and Transcribing Written
   Documents   320
Types of Written Business
   Communications   322
Summary   343
Vocabulary   344
Checking Your Understanding   344
Thinking Through Procedures   345

Chapter 13
Processing Written Documents 347
Information Processing Procedures 347
Summary 377
Vocabulary 378
Checking Your Understanding 378
Thinking Through Procedures 379

Chapter 14
Distributing Written Documents 381
Output and Distribution 381
Electronic Distribution 390
Processing Mail 399
Summary 410
Vocabulary 411
Checking Your Understanding 412
Thinking Through Procedures 412

Unit 5: The Workplace Problem 413

UNIT 6
MANAGING BUSINESS
INFORMATION 419

Chapter 15
Information Management 421
The Need for Business Records 421
Information Management 422
Information Management Systems 424
Paper Filing Supplies and Equipment 436
Electronic Files 440
Electronic Supplies and Equipment 444
Microimage Media Storage 446
Summary 452
Vocabulary 453
Checking Your Understanding 454
Thinking Through Procedures 454

Chapter 16
Financial and Legal Information
Management 457

Financial and Legal Business Functions 457
Processing Financial and Legal
    Information 458
Basic Financial Functions 461
Specialized Financial Functions 480
Legal Functions 488
Summary 494
Technical Vocabulary 495
Checking Your Understanding 496
Thinking Through Procedures 496

Unit 6: The Workplace Problem 498

UNIT 7
MANAGING YOUR CAREER 501

Chapter 17
Management and Supervision 503
Managing Human Resources 503
The Functions of Managers 504
Managing People 508
The Functions of Supervisors 516
Planning an Automated Office 524
Managing Automated Office Systems 538
Summary 539
Vocabulary 540
Checking for Understanding 541
Thinking Through Procedures 541

Chapter 18
Advancing in Your Career 543
Building Your Business Career 543
Career Planning 546
The Job Application Process 556
Advancing on the Job 572
Summary 578
Vocabulary 579
Checking Your Understanding 579
Thinking Through Procedures 579

Unit 7: The Workplace Problem 581

Glossary 583
Appendix 1 595
Appendix 2 599
Appendix 3 602
Appendix 4 604
Index 607

ABOUT THE AUTHORS

Dr. Rosemary T. Fruehling is currently President of Paradigm Publishing International. An internationally known educator and lecturer in the field of business education, Dr. Fruehling has taught office education at both the high school and the postsecondary levels. She has also conducted business education teacher-training seminars in the United States, Europe, Australia, and the Far East. Dr. Fruehling has served as consultant to such business firms as International Milling, General Mills, Honeywell, and Warner-Lambert Pharmaceutical Company. Dr. Fruehling received her B.S., M.A. and Ph.D degrees from the University of Minnesota, St. Paul, Minnesota.

Constance K. Weaver currently serves as Director, Investor Relations, for MCI Communications. Ms. Weaver has a wide-ranging background and practical experience in business computer applications and office systems implementation in business and industry. In addition to her extensive experience in business, Ms. Weaver spent several years developing and marketing educational materials in the field of business education. As a marketing manager with McGraw-Hill Book Company, she conducted business education teacher-training seminars in the areas of office automation and microcomputer applications. She has also taught at the postsecondary level. Ms. Weaver received her B.S. degree from the University of Maryland, College Park, Maryland.

Victoria R. Lyons currently teaches technology education, business education methods, and records management at the University of Wisconsin-Eau Claire. Ms. Lyons has taught a variety of courses at both the secondary and postsecondary levels, including extensive technology training programs. She has also served as a business education consultant to secondary schools in the areas of curriculum development and technology integration. She has spoken nationally in the areas of computer technology and integration of technology into the curriculum. Ms. Lyons received her B.S. and M.S. degrees from the University of Wisconsin-Eau Claire, Eau Claire, Wisconsin.

ACKNOWLEDGEMENTS

We would like to acknowledge the assistance of Dr. William Mitchell, University of Wisconsin-Eau Claire and Roberta Moore, Editorial Consultant. For their reviews of the manuscript we thank Carol Cardone and Maryann Edelbach of The Cittone Institute, Princeton, New Jersey; Sharon Halsted, Green Bay, Wisconsin; Jo Nell Jones, Eastern Kentucky University, Richmond, Kentucky; Charlotte Montanus, Glendale Community College, Glendale, Arizona; and Neild Oldham, Oldham Publishing Services.

PREFACE

Problem solving skills include the ability to recognize and define problems, invent and implement solutions, and track and evaluate results.—America and the New Economy by Anthony Patrick Carnevale

Business organizations achieve their goals by striving for constant improvements in productivity that keep them competitive. Creative thinking and problem solving are the most important tools for maintaining a competitive edge. Industry needs workers who can solve problems and think constructively. *Office Systems: People, Procedures, and Technology* lets you practice and demonstrate realworld job skills—document processing, computer applications, human relations, communication, and information management. The ability to use these skills to adapt to the changing office environment and to solve business problems is critical.

Office Systems: People, Procedures, and Technology will help you understand business information systems and how technology can be used to create productivity in today's business office. The text emphasizes the interaction of people, equipment, and procedures, which provide the basic structure in any type of office, small to large, semi-automated to fully electronic. You will learn the job functions that are common to most offices and how specific skills are applied to accomplish tasks and procedures.

Technology makes it possible to process great amounts of information quickly and accurately. As you use this text, you will learn about procedures related to handling person-to-person and written communications, scheduling and organizing work activities, processing information, organizing and managing records, handling financial and legal tasks, supervising other workers, and managing your own career.

The successful office employee of the future will be expected to perform many different information processing tasks, to be able to solve problems, and to work cooperatively with others in a team atmosphere. Technology provides a means for employees to exchange information quickly and easily and creates an environment where all work activities are interrelated far more than in the past. This means that each task an employee does can have a direct and immediate impact on other functions in the office. Therefore, the successful employee must also be attentive to detail and, at the same time, be aware of the big picture or larger goals of the task at hand.

This text will help prepare you for entering a business world in which you will find may types of office environments as well as different types of management and human relations styles. It teaches the significant skills and knowledge you will need to function well in your chosen career and to handle the challenges you will face in the years ahead.

UNIT 1

WORKING IN ELECTRONIC OFFICES

POSITION DESCRIPTION

Job Title: Administrative Support Specialist

Department: Sales and Marketing

1. MAJOR FUNCTION:

   Responsible for performing administrative support functions for the manager of sales and marketing. Primary emphasis is on using the information processing network system to follow and establish procedures for processing documents; manage information storage and retrieval; coordinate office communications; and manage the office system technology to improve the efficiency of office functions.

2. SPECIFIC DUTIES:

   1. Manage procedures for the use and operation of microcomputer hardware, software, and other office equipment; develop procedures for updating hardware and software systems; maintain office supplies and supervise staff use; maintain a working knowledge of software programs and their application.

   2. Coordinate communication procedures for interaction among departmental staff and staff interaction with customers, vendors, and suppliers to maintain positive customer relations and maximize productivity of the department.

   3. Coordinate office communications: manage telephone and other electronic communication systems; coordinate and maintain staff schedules; coordinate business meetings; manage travel arrangements and expense records; develop procedures for effective time management; participate in staff meetings.

   4. Establish procedures for information processing functions: document creation, document processing, electronic file management, database storage and retrieval, manual document distribution, and electronic communication.

   5. Manage business information relating to departmental functions: manage manual and electronic filing systems; manage database information: update database regularly, analyze data fields using sort/search commands, prepare reports based on database analyses; manage record keeping functions for order processing invoice processing, and inventory control; process departmental budgets and other financial information; process and maintain confidential business records.

   6. Assist department manager in supervisory and managerial functions: process and maintain confidential and general records pertaining to departmental staff; gather information and prepare visuals for management presentations; establish departmental procedures; train new employees.

THE WORKPLACE SITUATION

MasterWorks, Inc. is a small company which purchases and sells original works of art and art reproductions. The majority of MasterWorks' clients are business firms which buy or lease paintings and pieces of sculpture to decorate their offices. MasterWorks' suppliers are art galleries, artists' agents, and individual artists.

Janice Hughes has just been hired as administrative support specialist in the Sales and Marketing Department of Master-Works. This is her first full-time position, after completion of her education. Janice was given a copy of the official job description for her position and was told that she would be given on-the-job training to help her in mastering all of her job duties.

MasterWorks, Inc. has just recently implemented an electronic information processing system. They are in the process of redefining office functions, tasks, and procedures, as well as the roles of the office staff, to achieve the maximum benefits of having an electronic office system.

DEFINE THE WORKPLACE PROBLEM
   Where in the business should automation be used and what hardware and software systems would increase worker or system productivity?

ANALYZE THE WORKPLACE PROBLEM
   What are the organizational structures that must be altered and what are the business functions that can be automated to improve productivity? How will the improvement be measured?

PLAN YOUR PROCEDURE
   How will current procedures change and what new procedures need to be implemented to achieve the productive automation of business functions?

IMPLEMENT YOUR PROCEDURE
   How and within what timeframe will the effects of the new procedures be determined?

EVALUATE YOUR RESULTS
   What is the outcome of the new procedures and what changes need to be made to improve the new workplace situation?

chapter 1

TODAY'S BUSINESS OFFICE

THE CHANGING OFFICE

Over the past two decades American business and industry have undergone many changes. In the postwar **Industrial Age** of the 1950s and 1960s, factories and their manufacturing processes were the central focus of American industry. Our economy was driven by the production of goods, such as cars and household appliances. In the 1970s these manufacturing industries began a period of decline. Our economy began to shift from a dependence on manufacturing industries to a dependence on service-oriented businesses, such as banking, insurance, medical and legal services, real estate, entertainment, and communications. During this same period, computerization entered the business office. These growing industries began using computer technology to process and distribute the massive amount of information that was generated by their expansion.

By the end of the 1980s we had moved from the Industrial Age to the **Information Age.** Today, more Americans are employed in jobs that involve processing information than are employed in jobs that produce goods. It is an exciting time to be in business, because information is the lifeblood of the business world. Every time a company makes a sale, purchases supplies, acquires new customers, expands its staff, introduces a product, or explores a new market, it generates information. We have more information at our disposal today than at any other time in history.

These changes have made the business office of today a far more challenging place than in the past. Along with computers came an "information explosion" that required workers to produce and exchange information at a vastly increased rate of speed. To cope with this information explosion, businesses have

3

Figure 1.1 The business office of today has a "high tech" look that reflects the impact of technology on all aspects of office work.

moved rapidly to enhance and replace the basic office equipment of the past—the telephone, typewriter, file cabinet, and photocopy machine—with computers, printers, software applications, scanners, and electronic communications devices. This new information processing technology is fundamentally changing the way office workers perform their jobs. Computers now handle many of the repetitive, tedious tasks that used to take up so much time. This leaves more time for office workers and their managers to handle more challenging responsibilities that require creativity, judgment, and the ability to make decisions.

In this chapter you will learn how Information Age technology is changing the very nature of office work. You will become familiar with the computer-related terminology used in the modern business office. And you will learn about the role you will play as an office worker in the Information Age.

TECHNOLOGY IN THE BUSINESS OFFICE

The need to find more efficient ways of handling a rapidly growing mountain of business information has been the driving force behind the development of office technology. When people talk about office technology or **office automation,** what they are really talking about is creating a workplace where sophisticated computers and other electronic equipment carry out as many of the office's routine tasks as possible. The basic reason for bringing electronic technology into the office is to increase **productivity.** In a narrow sense, increased productivity means that more work can be done by employees in the same period of time or that employees can do the same amount of work in a shorter period of time. It can also mean that fewer employees can perform the same amount of work. In a broader sense, increased productivity can mean that workers have greater flexibility in accomplishing their tasks. Thus, the quality of their work can be improved, as well as the efficiency.

Until the 1980s the major application of technology to improve productivity was in the shop or factory, not the office. One reason for this is that the need for efficiency in the factory was greater than in the office. But another important factor is that in the shop and factory it is easier to find and identify those jobs that are repetitive and can be broken down into steps or tasks. Assembly line jobs such as filling bottles with catsup and welding auto bodies are examples of factory jobs that lend themselves easily to automation. These are **labor-intensive** tasks that require many work hours to complete. It is not surprising, therefore, that the first computers to enter the office world were used to automate labor-intensive, routine business functions in accounting and financial operations. There is no question that electronic equipment can greatly speed up the performance of many specific office tasks. After all, using a computer to automate the typing of letters is in itself a time-saver. However, real increases in productivity are not realized unless technology is applied to the functions of the office as a whole.

AUTOMATING OFFICE FUNCTIONS, TASKS, AND PROCEDURES

An office **function** can be defined as a series of acts or operations expected from a person or group of persons; it is a set of responsibilities imposed by an occupation. A **task** is a specific work activity, often to be completed within a given time frame. A function is composed of a series of tasks. For example, dictation, transcription, keying, editing, proofreading, copying, mailing, and filing are the series of office tasks that make up the function of processing written documents. To perform each task in this series, the office worker must follow a **procedure,** which is a set of defined steps that compose the elements of a task and provide a framework for getting the job done. Office procedures define not only how a particular task is to be done but also the time frame in which it is to be accomplished, the materials and equipment to be used, and the individuals or departments with

Figure 1.2 Computers are used in every type of business and industry, as reflected in these photos of a factory, a laboratory, a hospital, and a musician's studio.

whom or with which the worker must interact to complete the task. Through the use of office procedures, a business can carry out its functions in a predictable and orderly way.

The ultimate goal in applying technology to the business office is not merely to automate various tasks such as typing, filing, and calculating but to help the company perform major functions such as planning, scheduling, communicating, negotiating contracts, receiving and filling orders, and making and receiving payments. It follows that the most efficient office is one in which office automation encompasses virtually all the routine information processing tasks and functions performed by the employees in that office. When the computer performs a function, or a whole series of tasks, it is being used in a much more productive and efficient manner.

OFFICE FUNCTIONS, TASKS, AND PROCEDURES

FUNCTION The broad acts, operations, or duties expected from a person (usually under a dozen individuals); a series of tasks or responsibilities imposed by one's occupation.

TASK A specific work activity, often to be completed within a given time frame.

PROCEDURE A set of defined steps, composed of the elements for completing a task.

EXAMPLE

FUNCTION	TASK	PROCEDURES
Schedule meetings.	Set up staff meeting.	Check boss's calendar.
		Contact staff members to reserve time and date.
		Reserve meeting room.
		Distribute memo confirming date, time, place.
		Prepare materials for the meeting.

Categorizing a job duty as a function or as a set of tasks sometimes depends on the level of the job. For a manager such job duties as planning, scheduling, and monitoring are functions. Tasks associated with the budget planning function might be forecasting expenses, analyzing previous years' expenditures, identifying budget items to cut or add, identifying areas of increasing costs, balancing the final budget figures, and preparing a draft of the budget for keying.

The administrative assistant to the manager might be respon-

Figure 1.3 Technology has changed the way managers and administrative assistants work together. The administrative assistant is able to take on more responsibility and works as a member of the decision-making team.

sible for several of the tasks that make up the budgeting function, such as collecting data, calculating the figures, and keying and editing the final document. Some of the procedures involved might include preparing the budget in a specified format, submitting it to upper management by a specific date, and getting a specified number of approvals before money can be spent. The administrative assistant would probably have some role in carrying out all of the budgeting procedures.

The goal of applying automation in this situation would be to improve the budget planning function as a whole. Using technology to improve the quality of information that goes into the planning stage—the analysis, forecasting, and identification of specific costs—would improve the quality and efficiency of the entire budgeting process. This broader goal would be more likely to result in an increase in productivity in the organization than would the goal of simply using technology to speed up isolated tasks, such as calculating the final figures or keying final copy.

KEY INFORMATION PROCESSING FUNCTIONS

FUNCTION	DEFINITION
Planning	Laying out a method for achieving a goal.
Scheduling	Laying out a time frame with specific milestones for achieving a goal.
Monitoring	Designing systems of reporting progress toward achieving goals.
Collecting data	Assembling facts from various sources.
Sorting and analyzing	Examining and judging facts.
Preparing drafts	Transferring thoughts, data, or information from one source to other sources to create new material.
Reviewing and revising drafts	Evaluating the rough draft of a document and making changes in content, grammar, and format.
Obtaining approvals	Requesting approval to proceed with an action.
Maintaining records	Organizing, coding, and preparing information so that it can be located at a later date.
Keying	Processing information through use of a computer keyboard or typewriter.
Dictating	Recording into a machine to speaking to someone else to take notes.
Transcribing	Reproducing handwritten notes or machine dictation.
Filing	Storing material for future retrieval.
Duplicating	Making copies.
Distributing	Sending or taking materials to designated recipients and files.
Printing	Producing printed pages of material.
Communicating	Using the telephone to transmit oral messages or automated equipment for electronic transfer.
Calculating	Using computers, calculators, or manual methods to compute financial information.

The **automation** of office functions, tasks, and procedures is done by restructuring the flow of work to take full advantage of the available technology. This means using technology to change the way in which information is processed. Figure 1.4 shows how the information processing work flow is handled in a nonelectronic office. The flow of work is linear, meaning that information processing tasks and functions are performed in a step-by-step fashion, beginning with the input of data and ending with the storage of processed information. Each step—input, processing, storage, output, and distribution/comunication—must be completed before the next step can take place. If you want to re-

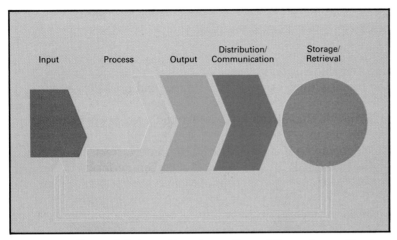

Figure 1.4 In the past, information always flowed through an office in a linear pattern.

use information that has already gone through the whole process —such as a list of sales figures or a description of your company's services— you have to repeat all five steps.

Figure 1.5 represents an **integrated information processing** system in which the steps in the information processing work flow overlap. This system, or what is called the electronic office, is more flexible and more efficient. It offers many new options and challenges to today's office workers.

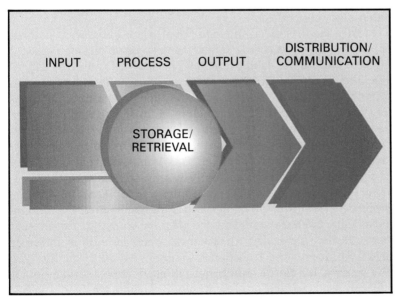

Figure 1.5 In an integrated information processing system, information flows in a dynamic fashion. This gives the worker more flexibility and a greater range of options for performing job functions and tasks.

INFORMATION PROCESSING WORK FLOW

Input is the entering of data into the computer or into one's mind to carry out a task.

Processing is the organization and calculation of words and numbers carried out by the computer; or the way the human mind works to recall facts and procedures to complete a task.

Storage is the saving of information so that it can be recalled and used again either in one's mind, on paper, or through the use of technology.

Output is the processed data, which can be displayed on the computer screen or printed out as a paper document, or the end result of the activities a person performs to complete a task.

Distribution/communication is the movement of data or processed information from one location to another by manual or technological means.

LEVELS OF OFFICE AUTOMATION

Today, offices vary widely in the extent to which they have adapted technology to meet their individual needs. Some offices can be categorized as nonelectronic, that is, they use almost exclusively traditional equipment and methods of carrying out office functions. Others are semiautomated, with widespread use of word processing, and still others are functioning as fully automated electronic offices.

Usually the first electronic equipment that a business acquires for information processing is electronic typewriters or personal microcomputers. As computers have become smaller, less expensive, and more sophisticated, more and more offices have begun to use them in some capacity. In this type of semiautomated office, work flow may be more flexible because the computer provides more options for processing, storing, and retrieving information. However, most semiautomated offices do not take full advantage of these options. Often the computers are used strictly for word processing tasks, usually taking the place of the typewriter. The computers are not connected to large mainframe computer systems or other desktop systems. Therefore, there is no capacity to share stored information or transmit information electronically. Typically, all documents are generated in paper form and filed in the traditional manner. An office of this type may have a **facsimile machine,** which is an electronic device that can scan printed documents and transmit them to another location over a telephone line. However, most distribution in such an office is handled through manual distribution services.

Figure 1.6 In the early stages of automation many organizations purchase computers which are used mainly to speed up document processing tasks.

If you work in an office at this stage of automation, you will be able to use many basic secretarial skills, such as taking dictation, processing documents, filing, and handling mail.

A fully automated electronic office makes maximum use of the input, processing, storage, and communication capabilities of computers. In an electronic office, text can be input into the system through a keyboard or the use of other electronic devices. Word processing is only one of many applications available to automate office tasks. Applications for processing numerical data and graphics are also utilized, opening up a range of options for the kinds of information that can be generated. In the electronic office, information storage occurs as information is input into the computer. Almost all information is stored electronically rather than in paper form. Therefore, all information is also retrieved electronically; that is, to get at information, an office worker keys in a command that instructs the computer to find the data, which is then displayed on a screen or printed out. Information is stored on electronic storage devices which can hold massive amounts of data. Information can be retrieved and reused at any stage of the process. The time required to search for information is greatly reduced in comparison to using manual filing systems.

In an electronic office, many new options are available for outputting information. Information can be output as **soft copy,** which means that it is put in final form and transferred through electronic communications to be read on the computer screen. Or, printers and other sophisticated output devices can be used to output multiple paper copies of documents, which are called **hard copy.** Documents can be printed with both text and graphics and in color or black and white.

Another difference in the electronic office is that computers are able to communicate with each other through **networking.** Networks link computers through special communications lines or through telephone lines. This allows workers to access information that is stored on centralized computer systems or on other microcomputer systems on the same network. Documents can be distributed in soft copy form, and information can be obtained from computers outside of the organization.

As an office worker you need a thorough understanding of electronic information processing systems, since you cannot predict the degree of automation you may find on a given job. Even if you work for a company that does not use much electronic equipment, your employer may decide to make changes at any time. In addition, office workers today are expected to bring to their jobs new ways of using the information processing system in order to increase office productivity. Secretaries and administrative assistants are then freed to carry out more administrative support activities and to become more involved in research, analysis, and decision making.

ORGANIZATIONAL STRUCTURE

Getting the right information to the right people is central to the success of a business organization. Organizations have historically been organized in a "top-down" fashion. Individuals at the top make the decisions, and individuals in the middle are responsible for carrying them out. Middle managers and administrative support workers produce the information needed by top management to make decisions. This organizational structure is known as a **hierarchy,** and it allows for complete control of all functions within the organization by top management. In this type of structure, work is organized around the major functions needed to operate the business. Every job is clearly positioned in the organizational structure, with a specific superior and subordinates. Authority is carried out through a "chain of command," with each management level having authority over a defined set of responsibilities. Management, research and development, product development, marketing, financial services, and legal

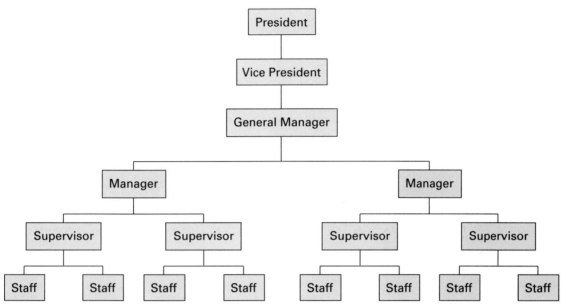

Figure 1.7 In a hierarchy, authority and information follow strict vertical lines moving in layers from the top of the organization to the bottom.

services are typical departments found in a large company. Each department works independently to manage its own information.

With the introduction of computer technology, offices work more interdependently. Since work no longer flows in a linear pattern, it is not necessary, nor is it always efficient, to make decisions in a linear, top-down path. The electronic office work flow has made more information available and created more options for using information. With so many factors to consider, top management no longer has the time or the resources to make all the decisions alone. In many companies managers are moving toward a pattern of organization that is known as **matrix management.** In this type of structure the staff is organized in project teams. Interdepartmental or departmental teams are set up to represent all facets of a project. Since information is shared by all departments, decisions are not made in isolation but rather with all facts available.

In this type of structure the administrative support staff is a major part of the decision-making team. Their functions include creating, analyzing, processing, and communicating information as a member of the project team. As management relies more on the office worker for decisions, it is necessary for workers to rely on one another to make the best decisions. This approach of team/project work is widely utilized in businesses today. Individ-

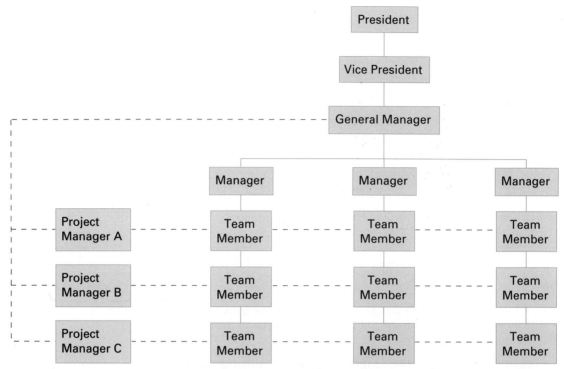

Figure 1.8 A matrix organization follows horizontal lines that relate to the needs of specific projects and goals. Authority is more flexible. Depending on the situation, the team member reports to either their department manager or the leader of the project.

uals from different departments join forces to accomplish set goals, whether the goal is to prepare quarterly sales reports or to develop a new product marketing plan. Individually a worker completes tasks related to a specific purpose, but the information created affects all parts of the organization. Information flows among departments and divisions so that management and supervisors can make decisions based on facts from all parts of the organization and not isolated from the whole.

With this new type of office structure comes a new type of responsibility. Each time an office worker from one division or department creates information, it can affect decisions made by other divisions. For example, an administrative assistant in marketing enters information in the central database concerning the sales quantities for a new product. (A **database** is a large collection of information stored electronically in a computer system.) The projections are entered incorrectly; the figure entered was 50 percent higher than it should have been. Production retrieves this information from the database and uses it to

Electronic Office

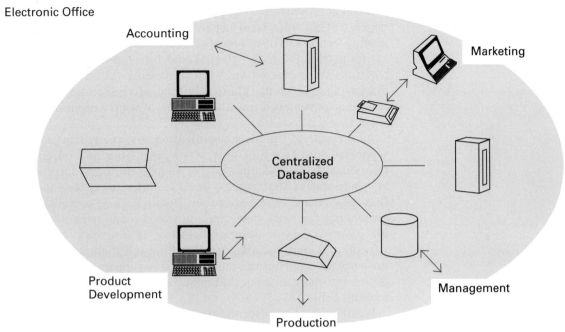

Figure 1.9 In an electronic office all departments have access to a centralized database.

plan production of the product. Production costs may exceed the budgeted amount because more of the product will be produced, there will be higher shipping and inventory costs, the budget analysis by the financial department will not be accurate, and the profit margin will be reduced because the demand for the product was not there. With this one data entry error, the organization can lose thousands of dollars. Therefore, it is important that all employees, including administrative assistants and other office workers, realize the importance of their roles within the organization and how they affect all divisions or departments in the company.

THE ROLE OF THE ADMINISTRATIVE ASSISTANT

As word processing technology became widespread, many people thought that automation of this office function was office automation itself. The first reaction to the influx of word processing equipment in the office was an increase in productivity in the area of document processing. In the late 1970s and even into the early 1980s, this was considered a very progressive use of automated office equipment.

As a result, organizations began separating the word processing/document production function from the traditional secretarial/administrative support functions. Large companies began setting up special departments, usually called word processing centers. These centers processed the majority of documents needed for both external and internal distribution. New positions were created for word processing operators and word processing specialists. Many administrative secretaries and office managers moved into the position of word processing supervisor.

As a result of this new organization, the secretarial role was separated into two functions: word processing and administrative support. The administrative support function incorporates all those duties that cannot be fully automated, that is, tasks that require individual attention. Duties such as organizing and controlling the work flow, making travel arrangements, gathering information, planning and setting up meetings, keeping financial and legal records, and handling telephone calls and visitors are all a part of the administrative support function. These duties incorporate tasks that require highly developed decision-making skills.

While special word processing departments are still found in

Figure 1.10 An administrative support specialist plays many roles and handles a variety of responsibilities in the electronic office.

some businesses today, the proliferation of microcomputers in the office in the early 1980s caused a shift back to combining the document production and administrative support functions in one job, with word processing centers used only for mass production of word processed documents. Now administrative support workers can use the power of technology for routine document production, and they still have plenty of time for other responsibilities, such as planning and scheduling meetings, maintaining appointment calendars, sending and receiving mail and messages, gathering information, setting up and maintaining information management systems, and handling expense accounts and other financial duties.

The role of the administrative assistant in today's electronic office can probably best be described with the title administrative support specialist. This title can incorporate word processor, executive assistant, secretary, personal secretary, corporate secretary, and correspondence secretary. As business offices increase their use of electronic technology to improve productivity, the role of the administrative assistant in the electronic office will increase in significance and responsibility. The administrative assistant today is more of an information processing specialist, with primary skills in administrative support and secondary skills in document processing.

IMPORTANT SKILLS FOR THE TWENTY-FIRST CENTURY

Not only does office automation increase the responsibilities of administrative support specialists, it also upgrades their stature as employees. In the electronic office, administrative support specialists are skilled operators of highly technical equipment. As more sophisticated computer systems are put in place, these individuals will use these systems to perform functions now carried out by special departments, such as accounting, inventory control, order entry, sales, and financial analysis. Therefore, the first requirement is a high level of technical skill, including the ability to operate the software applications programs used in offices today.

Because administrative support specialists are expected to perform a wide range of duties—such as researching, editing, and supervising and hiring other employees—that were once done by middle-level managers, many nontechnical skills are as important as technical skills for success in today's office.

The U.S. Department of Labor, Employment and Training Division, in cooperation with the American Society for Training and Development, conducted a nationwide study to identify the most important workplace skills of the future. The following section summarizes the skills that employers said they want.

Learning Skills

The report states, "Knowing how to learn is the most basic of all skills because it is the key that unlocks future success." Basic office skills—keying, computer applications, transcription, communications and language arts, and information management—will continue to be very much in demand. But added to these important skills is a need for adaptability. Never before have office workers been expected to learn so many new things as rapidly as in the past few years. And it is likely that this rate of change will continue. Many adults have difficulty learning new things because people tend to cling to the familiar and resist the unfamiliar. Until computers began to transform businesses, office work was fairly predictable. For years secretaries and other office personnel took dictation, typed letters and reports, answered

SKILLS FOR THE TWENTY-FIRST CENTURY

☐

Learning to Learn

☐

Basic Office Skills (Reading, Writing, Computation)

☐

Communication: Listening and Oral Communication

☐

Creative Thinking/Problem Solving

☐

Personal Management

☐

Group Effectiveness

☐

Organizational and Management Skills

Figure 1.11

the telephone, and maintained filing systems. Innovations such as electric typewriters and photocopying machines made their jobs easier, but generally, their work did not change much from year to year, and there was little opportunity to learn new skills or advance to higher positions.

There is no denying that automation has eliminated some jobs and required the redefinition of others. This trend will continue as new technology is introduced into the workplace. To be a successful office worker, you will have to develop the ability to view change as an opportunity to help your employer meet business goals and increase your own value as an employee. You must be willing to learn new ways of doing your job or possibly take on entirely new responsibilities.

Learning new skills and transferring skills already learned is the key to adaptability in a rapidly changing office environment. The first step in learning is being open to change. Then you need to develop an ability to recognize what you do not know and be willing to do what is necessary to gain the knowledge you need. Unless you can freely admit that you do not know some things, you cannot begin to learn new tasks and procedures. Learn to evaluate the old and welcome the new and the unexpected. Develop the habit of reading materials related to your business. This will help you keep abreast of changes and prepare you for new skills you will need to learn.

As you develop your ability to learn, be tolerant of errors. Try to accept them as a natural part of risk taking. A lack of tolerance for making mistakes causes some people to resist learning new things. Adults do not like to be embarrassed by "showing their ignorance." Those who learn to learn successfully are not ashamed to admit that they do not know something. The world is moving so fast that no one can remain an expert in anything for long. In today's changing office, a willingness to learn new things, even if it means giving up some personal time, is a key to your future success.

Basic Skills

The basic reading, writing, and math skills that you acquired in your earliest school days are essential in today's electronic office. Reading tasks on the job require you to be analytical, to summarize information, and to assess your own understanding of the material. Written instructions from a supervisor, technical manuals for operating equipment, and memorandums regarding policies and procedures are the kinds of materials you will read on a routine basis. In addition, many supervisors expect their administrative assistants to read all incoming mail, sort it, and compose responses on matters that are routine. Careful reading and attention to detail are essential in these circumstances. It is important to develop the habit of using a dictionary and asking questions when you do not understand something.

Writing tasks require a working knowledge of composition skills—writing, grammar, spelling, and punctuation. The abilities to follow instructions, to think abstractly, to think through a problem, and to organize material are also a necessity. In addition to composition skills, you need the skills to establish formats for various kinds of documents. Writing also requires good editing and proofreading skills. When storing written documents, either electronically or manually, you also need good organizational skills.

Even though computers process numbers, and electronic calculators perform basic math computations, math skills are essential for administrative assistants. As the example in the previous section showed, in an integrated electronic office, a single, seemingly minor mistake can affect not only your own business function but also others throughout the organization.

Figure 1.12 Excellent math, writing, and language arts skills are crucial to success in the electronic office.

When people talk about "computer errors," they are usually referring to mistakes such as the one just described. Computers do, in fact, provide incorrect information from time to time, but when this happens, it is almost always because people have input incorrect data or instructions. Computer technicians sometimes use the term **GIGO** when referring to this all-too-common occurrence. GIGO stands for "garbage in, garbage out." If what we put into a computer is wrong, what we get out will also be wrong. Office workers can prevent or correct many so-called computer errors by proofreading numbers and estimating arithmetic answers to see that the data they input is correct and that the output information makes sense.

Listening and Speaking Skills

A large part of every worker's job involves listening and speaking to others. Workers communicate about procedures and problems, they give and receive instructions, and they interact with customers, clients, or other business associates in person or on the telephone. According to the Department of Labor study mentioned previously, success on the job is linked to good communications skills. In fact, recent studies have indicated that only job knowledge ranks above communication skills as a factor in workplace success. One skill essential to successful communication is the ability to listen actively rather than passively. This means giving feedback to the speaker and taking notes if the information is complex or must be remembered.

Learn to recognize that people from different ethnic groups and different life-styles may have communication styles different from yours. You may need to adapt to the communication styles used by others. Paying attention to body language and voice inflection, both yours and other's, is an important aspect of being a good communicator. Many people will pay more attention to what you communicate in unspoken words than to what you are actually saying. A heightened awareness of different forms of communicating will help you avoid misinterpretation on both sides.

Technology has had an impact on interpersonal communication in the office. While electronic office technology saves time and helps you process information, it may also reduce opportunities for human contact. For example, sending interoffice messages through electronic mail cuts back on telephone calls, drop-in visits, and meetings. Similarly, if customers can order merchandise by electronic mail, employers' sales representatives will spend less time in face-to-face contact with them. Along with the technological advances in offices in the United States, the use of technology has allowed businesses to grow even faster into the global environment. Transfer of information internationally has placed even more demands on the communication skills of office workers. Electronic technology enables the employer to carry out business tasks more efficiently; however, when the amount of human contact in business is reduced, it is possible that business relationships will suffer. Every employee has an individual responsibility to prevent this.

Creative Thinking and Problem Solving Skills

The two main elements of creative thinking are creative problem solving and creative innovation. Creative problem solving is characterized by effective teamwork, looking at problems in new ways, and inventing new solutions to existing problems. Creative innovation refers to the ability to find new ways of doing things in order to achieve goals or get improved results.

Creative problem solving can be applied to any challenging task that you encounter on the job. When difficulties arise, a creative thinker will use analytical skills to look at all sides of the issue. As a creative problem solver you can make a list of possible solutions and try the one that seems to be the best alternative. If solutions are not readily at hand, seeking the advice of a co-worker, your supervisor, or some other knowledgeable person is a part of the creative problem-solving process. Suppose you are responsible for collecting all departmental expense reports, checking them for completeness and accuracy, and turning them over to the department manager by the fifth day of each month. You find that two people in the department consistently give you their reports a day or two late. As a result, you must interrupt your work to check their reports the minute they come in. Your other deadlines suffer and you are apt to overlook a mistake because you are rushing. In addition, the department manager has complained that you are not getting all the reports in on time. Do you say, "It's not my fault. They are not meeting their deadline, so how can I meet mine"? This response puts the burden of solving the problem on the manager's shoulders. It does not show a willingness on your part to accept responsibility and handle problems. A creative solution would be to ask the department manager (before he or she has had a chance to complain) to issue a memo stating that all expense reports are to come to you by the first day of the month. This way, those who have a tendency to be a day or two late will not make you miss your deadline on the fifth.

Creative problem solving skills give you more control over your job. Frequently you will find that when you take a problem to someone else to solve, you are not happy with the solution he or she offers. If you complain about too much work, your supervisor might assume you will be happy if he or she simply assigns some of the work to someone else. Consequently, you may find that the assignments you liked doing the best are no longer yours. Perhaps what you really wanted was a change in your job title, a salary increase, or an assistant to help you with the work. This example shows how not offering your own solutions can result in one problem being replaced by another.

Creative thinking is greatly enhanced by electronic technology. Technology presents us with new options for approaching job functions and tasks. A creative thinker understands that the real advantage of technology is not simply that more information is readily available, but rather technology offers the ability to produce, change, and manipulate information in many different ways. Technology allows more control over the factors of time, quality control, cost, and efficiency. Once you have a thorough grasp of computer systems and their capabilities, you will be able to use creative thinking to get the most out of the technology available to you on the job.

Personal Management Skills

Personal management involves three elements: self-esteem, goal setting/motivation, and personal/career development. **Self-esteem** is another term for confidence and pride in oneself. It means recognizing that your very existence makes you an important person. If you show others that you care about yourself and have confidence in yourself, they will reinforce these feelings in their attitudes toward you. On the other hand, if you have low self-esteem and project a negative self-concept, people will tend to react to you in a negative manner. Confidence is not inborn; however, it can be developed over time through focusing on the positive results of your endeavors and refusing to be defeated by setbacks. Avoid the tendency to compare yourself with others. Instead, set realistic personal goals and see if you can beat the expectations you set for yourself.

Motivation and goal setting are related; your motivation will be higher if you do not set goals beyond your reach. If you need to learn how to operate a new computer program, your motivation will be higher if you set a goal of working on it for an hour every day for two weeks, instead of deciding that you want to use it tomorrow to work on a big project. Impossible goals make you feel defeated before you begin. Your motivation will also be increased on the job if you learn to recognize your limitations and seek help to overcome them. Maintaining enthusiasm and a willingness to improve can usually offset moments when you may feel you have failed.

Setting personal and career development goals is another way to raise your self-esteem and level of motivation. If you look ahead to the future, you will be more inclined to seek opportunities to learn new things and accept new challenges. This, in turn, will bring you positive recognition from your co-workers and managers. Each aspect of personal management builds on the others, and together they form a foundation that is crucial to your success in the workplace.

Interpersonal Skills

Interpersonal skills, negotiation, and teamwork are the major components of group effectiveness. Interpersonal skills involve being able to interact easily with others and use good judgment about the appropriate behavior in a given situation. This means learning to cope with undesirable behavior in others without becoming angry, in addition to listening and responding to others with confidence and respect, handling stress positively, and being willing to cooperate with others and share responsibility. These skills are also essential for successfully negotiating con-

Figure 1.13 Project teams work closely together and rely on each other to meet each individual's goals and the goals of the project.

flicts. Conflicts are a fact of life in your personal life and at work. If you are willing to compromise and see a situation from a point of view other than your own, you will be able to negotiate satisfactory solutions in most conflict situations.

Each member of a team brings a different set of skills. Team members may also have different goals when working on the same project. One member may be most concerned with getting the project done on time, another may feel that quality is more important, and another may be worried about costs. Working with different personalities and motivations requires patience and insight into human behavior. It is often said that life at work would be wonderful if only people left their personalities at home. The fact is, however, that personal feelings and personality conflicts are an everyday part of any job. If you find that you are having problems with interpersonal skills on the job, you should seek help. There are many books, training programs, and short courses that can be useful in helping you to look at your own behavior and see how you can best deal with others.

Organization and Management Skills

In addition to the skills already summarized, you will need to learn how to manage your time and to plan and schedule your work so that high-priority tasks come first and less important tasks later. You must understand your particular job and also develop an awareness of how the processes involved in your work relate to the work of the organization as a whole. The automation of many administrative support and managerial functions is leading to a shift in responsibilities in the office. More administrative assistants are given the responsibility of retrieving and analyzing data, providing information to others who make decisions, and supervising other employees or temporary employees.

These responsibilities will give you the experience you need to move from position to position within an organization or to another organization. Since it is estimated that most individuals change jobs at least seven times in their lifetimes, an administrative assistant must be able to transfer the knowledge gained from education and experience to other work situations.

As you study office administration and office procedures in depth, you will gain an understanding of how the entire office functions. By the end of this course you will have acquired new skills that will give you the confidence to meet whatever challenges you face in the workplace.

SUMMARY

- We live in what is known as the Information Age. The use of computers in the business office has created an "information explosion," which has led to widespread use of computer technology.

- Office jobs are organized into functions, tasks, and procedures. The major reason for office automation is to increase productivity. This requires that technology be applied not only to office tasks but also to the broad functions of the office.

- Information processing takes place in five stages: input, processing, storage, output, and distribution/communication. Businesses have always processed, stored, and communicated information. The impact of technology on these functions has altered the flow of information from a linear process to a flexible process, with many options for accomplishing tasks at each stage.

- Technology has had an impact on how business organizations are structured. Organizations have moved from a top-down approach to decision making to a more expansive, team management approach. Now managers look to all members of the project team for their expertise in making decisions, as well as retrieving, analyzing, and communicating information.

- Each office (department or division) within an organization is interdependent with others. Information created in one area affects the decisions made in another. Therefore, it is very important that individuals are aware of information flow to ensure that accurate information is shared.

- The role of the administrative assistant in the electronic office encompasses document processing and a range of administrative functions, such as planning and scheduling meetings, maintaining appointment calendars, sending and receiving messages, gathering information, setting up and maintaining information management systems, and handling expense accounts and other financial duties.

- Working in an electronic office requires a high level of technical skill. In the twenty-first century workers will also need nontechnical skills that enable them to be flexible and continue learning. Other important skills are creative thinking and problem solving, personal management, group effectiveness, listening and written and oral communication skills, and organization and management skills.

VOCABULARY

- Industrial Age
- Information Age
- office automation
- productivity
- labor-intensive
- function
- task
- procedure
- integrated information processing
- input
- processing
- storage
- output
- distribution/communication
- facsimile machine
- soft copy
- hard copy
- networking
- hierarchy
- matrix management
- database
- GIGO
- self-esteem

CHECKING YOUR UNDERSTANDING

1. Explain the difference between the Industrial Age and the Information Age. What has been the impact of the Information Age on the business office?
2. What is the impact of technology on productivity? How can technology best be applied in the business office to achieve the greatest productivity gains?
3. Explain the difference between a task and a function. What are procedures and how do they help office workers perform their jobs?
4. What does the term *interdependent* mean when applied to the way information is shared in the electronic office? How does the sharing of information affect the way individual workers approach their jobs?
5. Think of an organization you have participated in recently— a job, a community group, a social club, for example. Draw a chart showing the organization of the group and the lines of authority that were followed to meet the organization's objectives.
6. Review the skills discussed in the section on business skills for the twenty-first century and list one or more methods you could use to improve your abilities in each area.

THINKING THROUGH PROCEDURES

1. Arrange a visit to a business in your area and observe the flow of work in the office. If possible interview a member of

the administrative support staff. Write a report answering the following questions:

a) What is the role of administrative support workers within the organization? What major functions do they perform?

b) What is the product or service offered by the company?

c) What types of documents are produced?

d) What type of equipment is used for information processing?

e) What methods of distribution are used?

Using the IPSOD chart as a model, draw a flow chart that depicts the work flow in the office you visit.

2. During your visit to investigate work flow, or on a visit to a second office, arrange to interview a manager or human resources director. Review with them the list of skills and abilities covered in this chapter and ask them to rate each category on a scale of 1 to 10 (or some other scale of your choosing). Report your findings to the class. Discuss differences in ratings found among the businesses visited and assess whether the differences are related to the type of business or if there are other factors involved.

3. Read a magazine or newspaper article and write a report on one of the following topics:

a) The use of computers in business—how and where they are being used; the effects on productivity in the office.

b) Current management approaches being used in business—matrix management, project teams, or some other approach to structure and staff roles.

Use word processing software to key and edit your report, if it is available to you.

chapter 2

INFORMATION PROCESSING TECHNOLOGY

STAGES OF INFORMATION PROCESSING

In this chapter we will look more closely at the information processing cycle and the impact of technology on information processing functions and tasks. In chapter 1 we talked about the processing of information in five stages: input, processing, storage, output, and distribution/communication.

These stages represent the broad functions that are performed when processing data into information. When we compare the information processing stages in the nonelectronic or semiautomated office with the electronic office, we find that the greatest impact of electronic technology has been in the areas of processing, storage, and distribution/communication. While the input and output functions have also changed, the significant advancements in these areas are really a part of the processing function. Input procedures such as the keying of commands and text are really mechanical tasks that are required to give the computer processing instructions. Similarly, it is advancements in the processing capabilities of the computer that have expanded the options available in the forms of computer output.

PROCESSING, STORAGE, AND COMMUNICATION

Human beings have been processing, storing, and communicating information for thousands of years. Goatherders who tied knots in lengths of rope to keep count of their flocks in ancient Greece were processing and storing information. Scholars who collected and stored papyrus scrolls in the great libraries of ancient Egypt and Greece were storing information for future generations. African tribes that used drums to send messages and Native Americans, who used smoke signals to talk to people from other tribes were communicating information.

As civilizations developed, the technology for processing, storing, and communicating information became progressively more efficient. In the earliest business offices, clerks used clay tablets and abacuses to note and calculate daily transactions. Later they progressed to pens and paper. But since all information is comprised of words and numbers, more modern devices such as the adding machine, the calculator, and the typewriter had a great impact on the processing of information in business offices. In today's electronic office, information is stored not only on paper in file folders but on microfilm, computer disks, and laser disks that can hold enormous amounts of data in a very small space. The telephone was the first big technological breakthrough to permit people to communicate information quickly and easily over long distances. Then came radio, television, and communications satellites, which link places throughout the world.

Processing

Automation was first applied to the processing function in the office because processing tasks could be more easily broken down into step-by-step procedures for computerization. In fact, it was the application of the computer to business data processing tasks that led to the "information explosion." Because computers can perform at astounding speeds, businesses could process more data and therefore generate much more information than before. Traditionally, processing in the business world has been divided into two broad areas: data processing and word processing.

The term **data processing** originally was used to describe what computers do. Its meaning has become so general that many people use it to describe any computer activity. Sometimes the term is modified as electronic data processing (EDP). This term was coined to stress the automatic as opposed to manual manipulation of data. EDP often means computing that focuses on business applications. Another term used for business applications is business data processing (BDP). Payroll, inventory control, accounting, and sales are typical activities for business data processing applications.

The next major use of processing technology was word processing, which is the manipulation of text. The term **word processing** was first applied to an electronic typewriter. Today, though,

Figure 2.1 Many large companies have centralized data processing departments. Large reports, like the one on the desk in the foreground of this photograph, are typical of the output from a centralized department that handles large volumes of information.

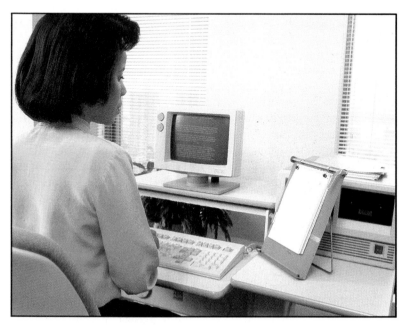

Figure 2.2 Word processing became the most common office use of computer technology in the 1980s.

the term has come to mean using a computer to create, edit, revise, format, and print out text.

A leading computer manufacturer, IBM, coined the term *word processing* in 1964 as part of a marketing strategy for a new kind of typewriter. This was the Magnetic Tape Selectric Typewriter, known as the MT/ST. The big difference between the MT/ST and other electric typewriters was that it could record words on a magnetic tape. In a sense, IBM combined a tape recorder and a typewriter. The MT/ST speeded the preparation of typed documents considerably by allowing the typist to make a limited number of corrections and revisions without retyping the whole document. Typists could also produce endless numbers of original or personalized letters, since different names and other information could be easily inserted and the new versions typed out by the MT/ST very quickly.

This was just the beginning. Modern word processing goes way beyond the MT/ST. It allows the user to make unlimited corrections and alterations before the final document is stored and produced. Paragraphs and pages can be lifted from one document and transferred to another. If a user is preparing a final report from a draft, he or she needs only to retrieve the draft from the computer disk and make the required changes without retyping the entire report. Scanning documents into the computer is also commonplace. A scanner can transfer a document into a word processing program, where it can be edited to create a revised document.

Today word processing is still the cornerstone of the electronic office. For a time many people thought that word processing was all there was to office automation. Now systems allow word processing, data processing, communication, and voice and imaging functions to be accomplished on one piece of equipment. This breakthrough in processing technology has allowed people to think in broader terms, and thus the concept of **information processing** as the major activity of the automated office is a reality. But processing is only one part of the information processing activity.

Storage

As discussed in chapter 1, when a document is processed on a computer, an electronic image is produced. When viewed on the screen, this image is called soft copy. This image can be stored temporarily in the machine's random access memory (RAM). Temporary files can be retrieved and used while information is being processed, or information can be stored permanently on a medium such as a tape, floppy disk, hard disk, or laser disk. The electronically stored documents are called **electronic files**. When the information is printed out on paper, it is called **hard copy.**

When technology was first introduced in the office, experts predicted that the electronic office would be a "paperless" office. In some industries, such as banking, this is almost true. In most businesses, however, the electronic office has generated more paper, not less. This is not surprising when you think about it. Computers have the ability to retrieve and process data with amazing speed. Consequently, more usable information is available for office workers and managers. Reading all of this information or working with it on a computer screen is not feasible. People still want to see hard copy.

Storage in the electronic office has broader implications than choosing between the use of hard copy or soft copy when retrieving information. Electronic storage technology makes it possible to store vast amounts of information in very small spaces. Stored information can be easily and quickly retrieved and used. And processed documents can be reused without rekeying them.

In many offices a **decentralized storage system** is used. This means that each worker stores his or her own electronic files. Users still often share files by making multiple copies of disks or borrowing them as needed. If a **centralized storage system** is available, workers can call up files stored on their own computers as well as those that are centrally filed. This means that information, such as sales information, client lists, or budget figures, that once had to be printed out as hard copy and distributed by a data processing department can now be accessed as soft copy by all workers connected to the system.

Anyone in an office who has the proper equipment can easily obtain information stored electronically. Managers and professionals with computers on their desks can retrieve information with the push of a button. Administrative assistants can store forms and documents that will be reused, thus reducing hours spent rekeying. And, more important, information that has been collected and stored can be retrieved quickly for use in making better business decisions and in enhancing business operations.

For example, consider a company that wants to improve health benefits for its employees but cannot afford to increase benefits across the board. One way to identify the areas where an increase would most benefit workers is to analyze the types of health-care services that employees have used most frequently in the past. If this information is stored only on paper documents, it could take weeks or even months to collect and organize the information for analysis. However, if employee insur-

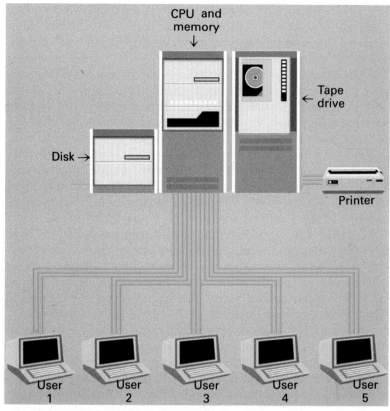

Figure 2.3 In a centralized storage system, users do not have to load programs individually. The programs they need are stored on the system and can be used simultaneously by different users.

ance claims are stored electronically, this information can be retrieved and printed out in a matter of minutes. Think what this would mean to the manager responsible for this business decision. He or she can collect the information quickly and with greater assurance of accuracy. Think also what it would mean to the company's employees, who would benefit from the manager's ability to retrieve and analyze the information and make the decision to increase benefits within a much shorter time frame.

Distribution/Communication

The ability to retrieve vast amounts of electronically stored information quickly would be limited if organizations had access only to information stored in their own electronic files. The ability is unlimited, however, when information can be transferred from computer to computer and retrieved from remote locations.

The impact of technology on the distribution and communication of information may be the most dramatic advantage of office automation and the one with the greatest capacity to increase productivity. Communications technology allows the linkage of information processing equipment both internally (within the organization) and externally (outside the organization). Documents can be electronically transferred from one location to another in soft-copy form. The receiver of a document can print out a hard copy, if desired. Information that is sent electronically, then held in storage until it is either read in soft copy form or printed as hard copy, is called **electronic mail** or **electronic messaging.** Today computers are often linked by telephone systems that allow individuals to receive and send electronic messages. These systems and other electronic communications equipment will be discussed in more detail in chapter 3.

Integrated Technology

The technological advancements in the areas of processing, storage, and communication are exciting when viewed separately. But it is the merging of these functions in today's electronic equipment that has resulted in a major impact on the office environment.

This merging, or integration, of computer technology into a single operating mechanism has changed the linear step-by-step functions of information processing into a dynamic, integrated process. Information is stored as it is being processed. The option is available to communicate information as it is being processed also. This integration, then, is the key to improving office productivity through the automation of business functions and tasks.

 # THE INFORMATION PROCESSING CYCLE

The flow of work in the office can be described as an **information processing cycle.** If you consider the functions of information processing technology outlined earlier—input, processing, storage, output, and distribution/communication—you will see how technological developments have changed the information processing cycle from a step-by-step linear flow to a dynamic, integrated process. For example, look at the job function of processing documents in the nonelectronic office. The tasks involved in processing a letter are to input the data, edit, proofread,

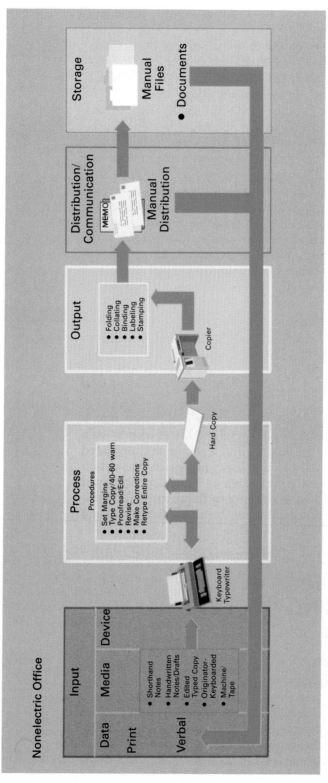

Figure 2.4 In a nonelectronic office, the typewriter is both the input device and the processor. After the information is typed and corrected, it is copied and made ready for distribution by hand or by mail. A copy is then filed by hand for office records.

The Electronic Office

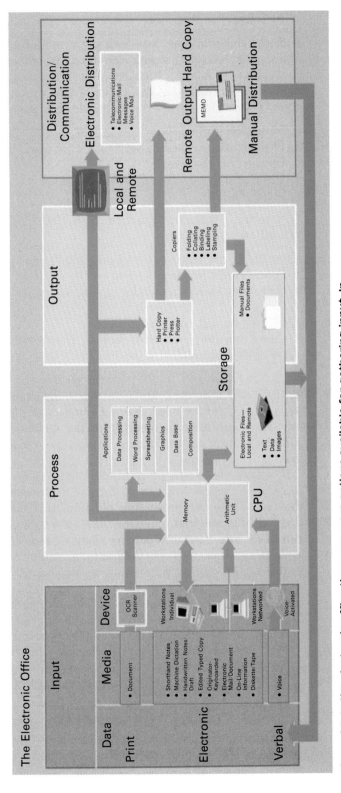

Figure 2.5 In the electronic office there are more options available for gathering input. In the processing phase a variety of applications can be accessed through the CPU. Storage is an ongoing part of the processing function and output can be in soft copy or hard copy form. Communication can be handled through electronic or manual methods of distribution.

and make photocopies. You then place the letter in an envelope and send it through the mail. You file copies of the letter in the appropriate file folders, which are kept in a file cabinet. These are distinct steps that you take, one after the other, until the job is done. You would think of these steps in this order:

1. Input (keying)
2. Process (edit/revise/retype)
3. Output (make copies)
4. Distribute (send through mail service)
5. Store (file)

Performing this same function in an electronic office, you may still follow these steps:

1. Input (key or retrieve file of previously stored document)
2. Process (edit/revise/proofread on the soft copy)
3. Store (key in commands for saving document as an electronic file)
4. Output (in soft copy or hard copy)
5. Communicate (send letter directly from your computer to the receiver's computer)

In this example you would perform all five phases of the information processing cycle almost at the same time, on one piece of equipment, and without leaving your desk. This merging of functions parallels the merging of the technology and has resulted in many major changes in the way office functions and tasks are carried out.

It is easy to see why office automation was first applied to the secretarial/clerical function of document preparation. The tasks that constitute the processing phase of this function—formatting, editing, and manipulating text—are tasks that can be broken down into a set of repetitive, logical steps for computer programming. Increases in productivity could be measured by faster, higher-quality production of documents. With the evolution and merging of processing, storage, and communication technology, however, many new options for increasing productivity were opened. Technology could be applied to higher-level functions in the office to achieve higher productivity goals.

TECHNOLOGY APPLIED TO OFFICE FUNCTIONS

Exactly how technology is applied to office functions varies according to a particular office's stage of automation. Today, it is more common to find a mixture of the traditional and electronic offices than to find offices that are functioning completely one way or the other. Therefore, we will look at the range of options for carrying out tasks at each stage, depending on the level of technology available.

INPUT

In an office where the basic processing tool is an electric or electronic typewriter, data for input is gathered from sources such as previously processed documents stored in traditional files. These may be in the form of letters, memos, reports, or other written documents. You will usually find data concerning customers or clients and names and addresses in organized filing systems, such as card files, or on lists that are updated periodically within the department. To obtain mailing lists or lists containing large amounts of numerical information, such as sales figures or inventory numbers, you may have to go to another department, such as the data processing department. Regardless of where you go to get the information, you will be getting it by hand out of files, by telephone, or by filling out requests for other people to get it for you.

With a paper filing system, it is the rare office that manages to keep its files absolutely accurate, up to date, and complete. More often, some files will be lying around outside of the file drawers, others will be misfiled within the file drawers, and still others will be missing altogether. Tracking down missing files is a time-consuming process that greatly interrupts the flow of information through an office.

Once the necessary data is gathered it must be prepared for keying. This data might include previously keyed documents, handwritten notes, machine dictation, lists of statistics, and so on. These must be assembled into a format from which they can be input for processing.

In an office that uses computers mainly for word processing, paper files are still the primary source for gathering data for input. In this type of office, it is common to find complete sets of both kinds of files. Individual workers organize and keep track of their own electronic files. Because information is not shared electronically, it is necessary to have paper files available for the general use of the staff.

In the electronic office, paper files are still kept, but most data is stored electronically. It may be stored on a disk at your workstation or on a centralized computer database file. You can retrieve it by giving appropriate commands to the computer. You

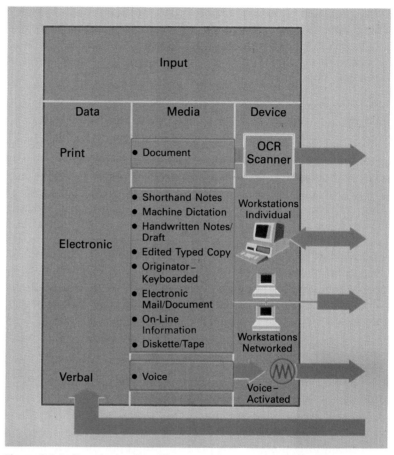

Figure 2.6 In the electronic office many types of input media and devices are available. The individual worker selects the option that best fits the task.

can then process the data according to your needs. In the electronic office machine dictation, notetaking, and longhand are also used to prepare data for input into the system using the keyboard of the computer.

Since all levels of office workers have computers at their desks in an electronic office, it is common for executives to key drafts of documents and then transfer them electronically to their administrative assistant's computer for final formatting, editing, and printing. Executives use this process to save time and be more productive. A more sophisticated technology that many companies may have in the future is voice-activated input. Systems that replace the keyboard by converting human speech into an electronic format are available today but are quite expensive. Another form of input is a system with a touch sensitive display screen for inputting and manipulating data. The user touches different parts of the screen or writes legibly on the screen.

PROCESSING

In a nonelectronic office, the typewriter is both the input and processing device. The processing function involves tasks such as setting format specifications—margins, tab stops, line spacing, and positioning of the first line of text. Once these preliminary steps are finished, you key the document at your best speed without making errors. Sometimes you may have to calculate numbers manually to be included in the document, or you may need to search other paper files for additional information. Your next step is to proofread and then, if necessary, edit the document. Minor mistakes can be corrected easily if you have a self-correcting or electronic typewriter. If not, each mistake must be corrected by covering over it with correction tape or correction fluid and then typing the correction over. If the errors are more substantial, you may need to retype one or more pages totally.

If you are either very lucky or very good at your job, the person for whom you prepared the document will not request any further changes. When further changes are necessary, however, you will have to retype part or all of the document. You must

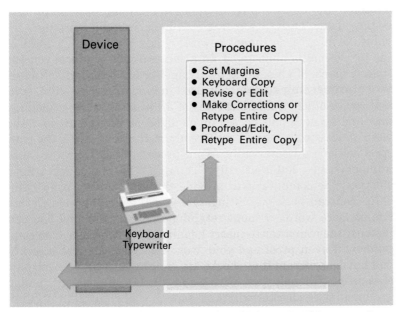

Figure 2.7 In the nonelectronic office formatting and editing procedures are done manually. Documents are retyped to make revisions.

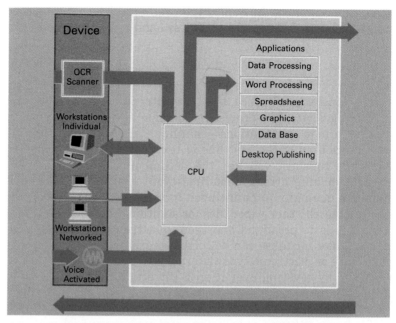

Figure 2.8 The various devices and applications available for processing require the administrative assistant in the electronic office to make the complex decisions.

then proofread again and resubmit the document for approval. Occasionally, more changes will be requested, and the process begins again. Thus, processing in a nonelectronic office may involve retyping a document several times, even though most of the text remains unchanged. In a semiautomated office, you are spared much of this work by using word processing software. **Word processing software** is used to input, process, store, edit, and revise office communications of all kinds. Margins, indents, and line spacing can be set or changed at any point, and the word processing program will readjust the text to fit the new specifications automatically. Word processing software can also number pages automatically. Then, if the document length changes, the computer will provide the new, correct page numbers. You can perform editing tasks such as adding or deleting one or more words without retyping whole pages. And you can instruct the computer to insert headings for each page. The computer will even proofread your work for typographical errors if you have a program that checks for spelling errors. An electronic thesaurus will help you with word variety and choice, and a grammar/style checker will point out some of your blatant grammatical errors. You will still need to read the work, however, because the computer cannot discriminate between homonyms such as *there* and *their*, nor can it know if you left out a word or misused punctuation.

After you have printed a hard copy of your finished document and submitted it for approval, you can easily make changes by editing the soft copy and then printing out a revised document. No matter how many changes you make, the new copy will be clean, with no evidence of the many revisions it has been through.

In an electronic office, in addition to word processing there are many other software programs to process information. These are often referred to as **productivity tools** or **decision support tools** because they allow complex, time-consuming tasks to be done in a fraction of the time it takes to do them manually. Following is a list of a few categories of software that are used abundantly in the electronic office:

- **Database Management** A database is a stored collection of data on a particular subject. For example, one company might create a database consisting of the selling prices of various competing products. Another might list the names, sizes, and locations of all its retail outlets in a database. Another company might have a database of all clients' addresses, phone numbers, company affiliations, product purchases, and account balances. You can use a database management program to assemble reports or other documents. The data can be reorganized in many ways to show different aspects of the same information. This is known as **data manipulation.** Tasks such as these take many hours of concentrated work in a traditional office.

- **Spreadsheets** Spreadsheets are software programs that calculate and recalculate numerical data. They are used to prepare budgets, forecast sales and revenues, determine prices, and perform general accounting functions.

- **Graphics** Graphics programs can be used to create charts, graphs, slides, and other types of pictorial images.

- **Desktop Publishing** These programs function as a desktop typesetting operation and are used for page layout of text and illustrations. They are used to create newsletters, announcements, brochures, complex reports, and many other types of documents.

- **Project Management** These programs are designed to schedule timelines for the completion of projects.

- **Personal Information Software** These programs include electronic notebooks for keeping track of day-to-day notes, personal calendars, and scheduling, as well as other features that may be individually designed, such as notebooks and reminder systems.

- **Integrated Software**   With a computer you can merge, or combine, information from different application files. For example, you must send the same letter to ten different people. Once you have keyed the letter using the word processing software, you can merge it with a file that contains a list of names, addresses, and salutations from the database software. The printer will then print the same letter ten times with the different headings. You are also able to merge data between software programs to avoid rekeying data. For example, you may choose to incorporate business graphics from a graphing program or data stored in a spreadsheet package into an annual report that was created in a word processing package.

- **Operating System Software**   This software operates the internal functions of the computer, such as organizing files and moving them from one place to another or activating the keyboard and printer. Operating system software is also referred to as the computer's **disk operating system (DOS)** because it controls all the basic computer operations.

STORAGE

In a nonelectronic office, the storage of information comes at the end of the cycle, after the data has been input, processed, output, and distributed. In a semiautomated or electronic office, storage is an automatic part of the input and processing stages. Whenever you input a document, it is stored by the computer temporarily in the electronic circuits of the system. By keying specific commands you can instruct the computer to save the document permanently. You can then easily retrieve it and reuse it for input. Today most electronic data is stored on magnetic disks, which may be **floppy disks** or **hard disks.** Information is

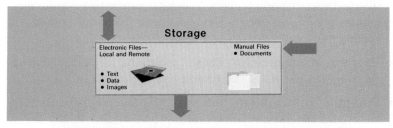

Figure 2.9 Most electronic offices still have manual filing systems.

also stored on **laser disks,** and some systems also store data on magnetic tape.

One major difference between storing information on disks and storing it as hard copy is in the amount of physical space required. A single 3.50-inch disk can hold hundreds of letters. You could easily file disks holding many hundreds of letters, memos, and reports in two small boxes that could sit on your desk. It would take several full-sized file drawers to hold the same amount of hard-copy information. There are disks larger (5.25 inches) and smaller (2.50 inches) in size, depending on the type of computer you are using.

Storage of information on hard disks or laser disks takes up even less space because the disks are usually a part of the computer system and the information is stored more compactly. Optical, or laser, disks are another medium to store information. These disks and disk drives attach to the computer as any other disk drive, but the information is not stored magnetically but rather by etching the information onto the disk.

Retrieval of stored information involves asking the computer to locate the appropriate file. A listing of files is located on the storage medium and can be accessed through a command to view the **directory** (designated storage area) on the disk. This step is similar to the retrieval phase in a traditional office, where the hard-copy document must be located in a file drawer. The main difference is that with disks you do not have to get up from your desk to retrieve information, but you must understand the electronic storage/filing system to retrieve the information.

Figure 2.10 This diskette can hold the approximate equivalent of 180 pages of text.

Electronic storage solves many of the problems associated with traditional files. For example, files stored on a computer's hard disk can be protected so that only certain people have access to them. Instead of locking file cabinets and signing documents in and out of files, users of a word processing system can secure their files by using a password system. Under this system, all individuals who are allowed to use the files are assigned a **password**. A password is a personal code known only to the individual and the technicians who set up the system. The user must key the password into the computer before he or she can gain access to any of the information stored there. A log is kept of who has accessed the file and how long it was kept to increase security and to track file locations if another person requests the file. To achieve additional security, some companies change user passwords regularly.

Figure 2.11 A hard disk is housed in the disk drive and cannot be removed.

Both semiautomated and electronic offices do keep paper records of many documents. Still, today 90 to 95 percent of records are stored on paper, with the remainder stored electronically or in film form. Electronically stored data is more fragile than data stored on paper. In a power failure, whatever is stored

Figure 2.12 Laser disks can store data, graphics, or sound.

in the temporary memory of a computer is lost unless it has been stored on a disk. Also, data already stored on a disk can become garbled if a power surge precedes a power failure. Many large companies that rely heavily on their computers have backup power generators and surge protectors for precisely this reason. One way to reduce accidental loss of electronically stored data is to make **backup copies** of all data and to update these regularly. Backups are copies of the original data stored on disks. All users of electronic equipment should make it a practice to copy their files for storage on other disks or media.

There is an important difference between storage in a semiautomated office, where computers are not able to communicate with each other, and an electronic office, where information can be transmitted electronically. In an electronic office where computers are networked, workers have access to centrally stored electronic files.

OUTPUT

In a nonelectronic office, the output is the finished document and the main output device is the typewriter. If you need dupli-

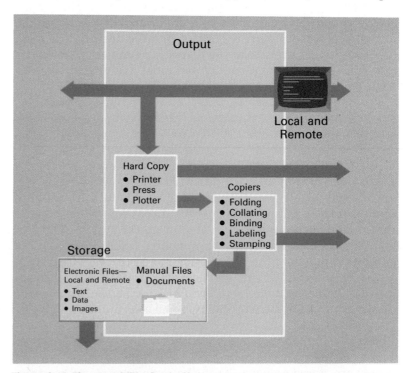

Figure 2.13 The capability for both local and remote output is a major change from the semiautomated to the electronic office.

cates of the finished product, you make photocopies. The output devices of computers are usually the printers to which they are connected. The kind of printer you use will determine the speed and quality of output.

In the electronic office, much of your output is originally generated in the form of soft copy before it is printed. The hard copy may be output at a local printer or it may be sent to a centrally located printer. The soft copy may be sent via electronic mail as well. The recipient will view the soft copy and may print out a hard copy or save the document on a disk. Lengthy documents are usually printed. Electronic messages are usually just deleted from the system, although they can be saved or printed, if necessary.

DISTRIBUTION/COMMUNICATION

The distribution and communication functions of information processing involve getting the information you have processed to those who need to receive it. The methods you use depend on the type of equipment available and the needs of the task you are performing. All offices still use traditional methods of distribution, which include the U.S. Postal Service, private courier services, and overnight services such as Federal Express.

In the electronic office, distribution also occurs through the use of data communications technology. Computers are linked to each other, allowing the output to be sent as soft copy to other computers. This is called a **networked system.** You will learn more about how networks are set up in chapter 3.

The computers within a networked system can share files and send messages and documents back and forth. Hard copies can be printed at the receiving end if desired. The advantage of this method is that distribution can be completed in minutes, and items are not delayed or lost as they may be in internal mailing systems. Communication of this sort can save at least several days and sometimes even weeks in the distribution/communication phase of the information processing cycle. Furthermore, it allows people to receive immediate feedback to help them make decisions. This time-saving dimension of the electronic office has the potential of revolutionizing how businesspeople make decisions that affect basic business functions. These links allow the people and equipment in the system to communicate with each other—and perhaps with outsiders—instantaneously through the use of electronic mail.

Electronic mail is a software application that sets up a mailbox for each user. Electronic mail can be received at any time, including when the user is involved in some other application on

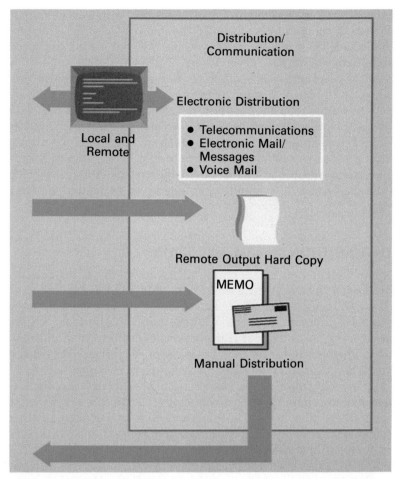

Figure 2.14 Communications technology has had a major impact on the way businesses function. Today, companies have access to networking on a global scale, opening up new opportunities to compete in the world market.

the computer. Most systems have a feature that notifies the receiver when a piece of mail has come in. They also notify the sender that mail has been received.

Electronic mail can be most useful when information is needed immediately. For example, you need the most recent sales figures from ten branch offices. In a traditional office, you would have to make ten phone calls or write ten memos requesting the information. Even if you used an express mail service, you would have to wait at least one day to get the information. But with electronic mail, you can send the requests for information to each office simultaneously. In seconds all ten branch offices would have your request. If no one is attending one of the machines to which the mail is sent, the computer will store the information until the person returns and turns on the system. The information you require will be sent back to you as quickly as the people on the other end can instruct their computers to supply it (probably in a matter of minutes).

Facsimile transmission is another method of immediate electronic communication. Facsimile machines allow transmission of documents over telephone lines. Thus, this machine may be used in any office, no matter what the level of automation.

Electronic offices do still need to use manual distribution methods of all kinds. It is up to the individual worker to determine what method is necessary and most cost efficient for the task he or she is handling.

Voice mail runs on a telephone system that is linked to a computer. Voice mail systems allow callers to telephone a business and leave a voice message on the telephone system. Basically, a voice mail system is a large answering machine that stores multiple messages. Telephone companies can supply this service to customers who may not have their own voice mail system.

Suppose that you work in the head office in New York, and it is 9 A.M. You need the latest projected sales figures from the branch office manager in San Francisco, where it is only 6 A.M. You are going to an all-day meeting, so you cannot make the call later. You can telephone the San Francisco branch now, where the computer answers the phone, takes your message, and alerts the San Francisco manager that a message is waiting. When the manager opens up the office, he or she will retrieve the message and respond immediately.

Electronic conferences enable several people in different locations to hold a conference. There are two types of electronic conferences: conference calls and teleconferences. A **conference call** links several people in different locations by telephone. This type of conference can take place in nonelectronic and electronic offices. During a conference call, the people involved may use a facsimile machine or some other device to exchange documents.

A **video teleconference** uses closed-circuit television and computers, telephones, and electronic devices to enable people to see as well as hear each other. Not only voice, but images and data can be transmitted. A video teleconference is possible only in an electronic office. It is perhaps the most sophisticated form of communication today, affording many benefits. It allows people in widely separated locations to hold discussions, see each other's facial expressions and gestures, look at charts and graphs together, exchange documents and data, and give demonstrations. It makes possible face-to-face meetings without the expense and time required to have all individuals travel to the same location for their meeting.

The video teleconference demonstrates how people and electronic equipment can work together to process information more quickly and more efficiently than ever before.

CHOOSING THE TECHNOLOGY FOR THE FUNCTION

How does an office worker choose the best way to do a particular job? Electronic technology has presented office workers with alternative ways for doing their work. Often they have to make a decision about the best equipment to use for a particular task. In order to make good decisions, they need to consider some important factors. Let's examine the five factors of capability, cost, speed, quality, and confidentiality to see how they interact to determine the best way to get a job done.

CAPABILITY

Each piece of equipment, whether it is a dot-matrix printer or a scanner, has limits on its capabilities. With software becoming

Figure 2.15 With all the different equipment that is available in the electronic office, workers must constantly make decisions that effect the quality and cost of the work they produce.

more powerful and the items people want to produce more complicated, equipment must be able to process the information you are requesting. You must be aware of what the piece of equipment and software can do to determine whether it will fit your need. For example, if you need a high-quality printout for the correspondence you send to your clients, a dot-matrix printer would not be suitable; however, a laser printer would. Microcomputer capability works the same way. Some software packages require certain amounts of computer memory and certain kinds of processors to run efficiently. If you do not have these capabilities in your microcomputer, you will not be able to use the software efficiently. Many organizations have information processing support services to help you determine if your equipment meets the requirements of the software you wish to use. Or, you may discuss your needs with a computer salesperson as well.

COST

As a responsible office worker, you will have to weigh the importance of a task against the costs involved. Usually, you will want to choose a method of accomplishing your goal at the lowest possible cost to your employer. However, cost must be considered along with quality and level of importance. For example, assume you are responsible for processing your division's three-year plan, which will be presented to the company's board of directors. Ordinarily, for a project such as this you would not want to skimp on expenses for artwork or binding of the report. You would want the quality of the plan to be reflected in the packaging. On the other hand, if the plan contains recommendations for cutting budgets and laying off workers, presenting an expensively produced report may make your boss look irresponsible. These are the kinds of cost-related decisions you may be confronted with on the job. As you can see, cost is not always a matter of spending the least amount of money. Other factors must be considered.

SPEED

In some instances speed is more important than economy. For example, if you had to get a document to a branch office in another city by the close of the business day, you would not use the normal services of the U.S. Postal Service, even though it is the least expensive means of external distribution in most cases. Electronic technology, while sometimes more expensive, usually offers the fastest means of communication and can provide time savings in all phases of information processing. Overnight mail service is also a way to send information quickly. Overuse of overnight mail is costly when individuals believe that every item is a "rush" item. You must be able to determine true "rush" items to keep costs at a minimum.

QUALITY

Many information processing tasks require that your output meet certain quality standards of appearance. Knowledge of these standards will help you determine which technology to use. For example, a computer system may include several printers, some of which are faster than others; however, the output from the dot-matrix printers may not be as presentable as the documents produced by the laser printers. You should choose the higher-quality printer for documents intended for customers and others outside your organization and the lower-quality printer for draft materials.

CONFIDENTIALITY AND SECURITY

Sometimes information needs special protection because it is confidential or because your employer's business would suffer if the information were altered or lost. The need for security might affect your decisions about how to process certain kinds of information. For example, if you were sending a confidential document to a branch office, you might want to send it electronically so that the recipient could read a soft copy on a computer screen. The document could not be lost in the mail, and you would retain a copy of it on the electronic storage medium in your office. The user's privacy would be protected by a security system, so using electronic communication could also reduce the chances of unauthorized personnel seeing the information.

When you are called upon to make decisions about various technologies, you will have resources available to help you. One important resource is the technical manuals that accompany software and hardware. These manuals provide an overview of the system and its capabilities. You will become familiar with these resources as you work with different kinds of equipment and software.

SUMMARY

- The most significant technological advancements in the use of electronic equipment have come in the processing, storage, and communications stages of technology use.

- The key functions in the information processing cycle have been changed by technology, providing many more options for accomplishing tasks at each stage in the cycle.

- The application of technology to office functions varies according to the stage of automation in a particular office.

- Electronic communication has made it easier and less time consuming for people and businesses to communicate using their computer systems.

- When using electronic technology you must decide the best way to apply technology to individual tasks. Such factors as capability, cost, speed, quality, and confidentialty must be considered.

VOCABULARY

- data processing
- word processing
- information processing
- electronic files
- hard copy
- decentralized storage system
- centralized storage system
- electronic mail
- electronic messaging
- information processing cycle
- word processing software
- productivity tools
- decision support tools
- database management
- data manipulation
- spreadsheet
- graphics
- desktop publishing
- project management
- personal information software
- integrated software
- operating system software
- disk operating system (DOS)
- floppy disk
- hard disk
- laser disk
- directory
- password
- backup copy
- networked system
- facsimile transmission
- voice mail
- conference call
- video teleconference

CHECKING YOUR UNDERSTANDING

1. Describe the five stages of information processing.
2. In what three areas of information processing has technology had the largest impact and why?
3. What is the difference between hard copy and soft copy? Give two examples of when it is appropriate to use each.
4. Describe the information processing cycle. Give an example of

how the information processing cycle works for processing a report in an electronic office.

5. For each of the stages of the information processing cycle, describe at least two ways the introduction of electronic processing has an affect on the process.

6. What are ways in which communications technology has changed how offices conduct business. Describe one instance of telecommunications being used in your school.

7. What factors must you consider when choosing technology for a function in the office? Give an example describing each factor.

THINKING THROUGH PROCEDURES

1. Given the following situations, list the hardware and software you would use to complete the project:
   a) mass mailing to clients
   b) budget preparation
   c) design a new form
   c) prepare a newsletter
   e) design a graphic for a newsletter
   f) keep track of a timetable for a project
   g) maintain your or your supervisor's daily schedule
   h) prepare a report using data from other documents.

2. Make a list of the software applications programs discussed in this chapter. Put a check mark next to the applications that you already have some experience with. Conduct some research to find out more about the applications with which you are unfamiliar. Read articles, visit a computer software store, or find someone who is using the product and ask them to demonstrate it for you. Provide your teacher with a list of the methods you used to get more information on each software application on your "unfamiliar" list.

3. Find out what types of hardware, software, and communications equipment is being used in your school or the place where you work. List each item and make a chart showing where it fits in the IPSOD cycle. What stage of automation is your school or office currently in—nonelectronic, semiautomated, or electronic? What are the major functions that have been automated, if any? Where could the organization benefit from additional automation?

UNIT 1 THE WORKPLACE PROBLEM

Part A:

MasterWorks, Inc. hired an office automation consultant to help them determine where in their offices automation could best be applied to improve productivity. The consultant asked each department to prepare a list of their five major functions and the tasks within each function. Using these lists the consultant prepared a chart summarizing her analysis of where automation could be applied to major office functions.

Using the problem solving process to guide you in making your recommendations, prepare a chart for the Sales and Marketing Department to submit to the office automation specialist. If you have word processing software available, use it to process the information. Part of the chart is shown below. Add two columns—**Can Be Automated** and **Cannot be Automated**—and beside each task place an "X" in the appropriate column.

Sales and Marketing Department

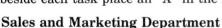

		Current Procedure
Function:	Purchase artwork from suppliers	
Tasks:	Contact suppliers	Make telephone calls
		Personal visit
		Process letters
		Maintain records
	Recommend purchase to manager	Calculate figures
		Process memo
	Purchase artwork	Process invoice
		Maintain records
Function:	Sell artwork to clients	
Tasks:	Contact clients	Make telephone calls
		Personal visit
		Process letters
		Create customer records
	Advertise to clients	Process newsletter
		Process brochures
		Maintain mailing list

Function: Service Customers

Tasks:	Entertain Clients	Schedule social activities
		Send invitations
	Handle complaints/	Retrieve customer files
	problems	Make telephones calls
		Process letters
		Process memos
		Maintain records

Part B:

When Janice began her job as administrative support specialist in the Sales and Marketing Department of MasterWorks, Inc., she found that she had a complete electronic office system at her disposal. Because the electronic office system was new, the previous administrative assistant had mainly used the equipment for word processing tasks.

On her first day on the job Janice's supervisor, Karen Cross, gave her a rough draft of a quarterly report that was being prepared for the president of the company. Attached to the draft was a set of instructions listing information that needed to be added to the report, the source for locating the information, and a summary of the procedure that Janice was to follow for processing each item.

1. **Information to add:** A list of departmental travel and entertainment expenses for the past three months.
   Source: Individual expense reports of the five professional employees in the department—get copies from each individual.
   Procedure: Add totals of each expense category from each report by month, then total the three months, key the numbers in chart form, and include the chart in the report.

2. **Information to add:** A list of names and addresses of new corporate clients acquired over the past three months.
   Source: Sales invoices for the past three months. These are filed alphabetically in a folder marked "Invoices." Each invoice has a column where the sales representative checks "new" or "repeat" customer.
   Procedure: Pull all the invoices for new customers from the file. Key a list of the new customer names and addresses. Refile the invoices.

Ms. Cross told Janice that the expense breakdown and new client list should be extracted from the finished report and distributed to the in-house staff in a memo. She asked Janice to draft the memo and give it to her to review the next day, along with the revised report. Ms. Cross also asked Janice to make a list of recommendations to improve the report writing task in the future by applying automation to some of the procedures. Using the problem solving checklist as a guide, compose a list of the procedures that can be automated and the equipment and software you would use.

PROBLEM SOLVING CHECKLIST

DEFINE THE WORKPLACE PROBLEM

Where in your office or in your procedures can automation be used?

ANALYZE THE WORKPLACE PROBLEM

Is this an area where automation would improve productivity? Will automation allow for improved decision-making, more timely information, and/or more accurate information?

Is the problem an efficiency problem or a communication problem or both?

PLAN YOUR PROCEDURE

To whom must you talk to implement the change or new procedure?

Who must you inform about the change in procedure?

With whom do you need to coordinate the procedure?

IMPLEMENT YOUR PROCEDURE

What will be the effects of the new procedures?

EVALUATE YOUR RESULTS

What criteria will you use to judge the benefits of the new procedure?

How will you identify additional changes that need to be made?

MANAGING THE OFFICE WORKSTATION

POSITION DESCRIPTION

Job Title: Administrative Assistant

Department: Vice President of Organization

1. MAJOR FUNCTION:

   Responsible for performing administrative support functions for
   the vice president of the organization. This assistant will oversee
   the office work flow procedures to include coordinating document
   processing, managing office communications, overseeing information distribution, and overseeing storage of insurance information.

2. SPECIFIC DUTIES

   1. Manage procedures for the flow of information within and outside
      of the office; manage the office equipment related to these pro-
      cedures.

   2. Coordinate communication procedures for interaction among of-
      fice workers, sales representatives, and clients to maintain
      positive customer relations and maximize productivity.

   3. Coordinate office communications by managing telephone system,
      coordinate and maintain staff schedules, coordinate business
      meetings, manage travel arrangements and expense records; de-
      velop procedures for effective time management; participate in
      staff meetings.

   4. Establish procedures for insurance processing function; docu-
      ment creation and processing, file management, client informa-
      tion, and document distribution.

   5. Manage business information relating to the functions of the or-
      ganization by managing manual and electronic filing systems;
      handle record keeping functions for insurance billing; process
      budgets and other financial information; process and maintain
      confidential business records.

   6. Assist vice president in supervisory and managerial functions;
      process and maintain records pertaining to office staff; gather
      information and prepare visuals for management presentations;
      establish office procedures; train new employees.

THE WORKPLACE SITUATION

North Central Crop Insurance Company is a medium-sized insurance company that sells crop insurance to agriculturists in the states of North Dakota, South Dakota, Minnesota, Kansas, Iowa, and Nebraska. Their main office is located in Iowa and sales representatives are located in regions throughout the area.

Michelle Jahnz works as the administrative assistant to the vice president of North Central, Jesse Barone. Up until this point North Central has been on a completely manual system, for writing and processing all their insurance policies and claims, using typewriters and calculators. Michelle has just attended a seminar on automating an insurance business and is excited to share her information with the vice president.

Since one of Michelle's duties is to oversee the work flow of the office, she is exploring the possibilities of automating North Central's office. After attending the seminar, Michelle has more questions about automation than answers. She knows that automating will enhance productivity as well as cut processing costs. How can she convince Mr. Barone that, overall, North Central will be able to serve their clients more efficiently?

DEFINE THE WORKPLACE PROBLEM
What type of hardware and software is available to automate routine tasks that are currently performed manually?

ANALYZE THE WORKPLACE PROBLEM
What workplace factors need to be considered when purchasing the hardware and software?
How will the new hardware and software increase productivity and efficiency in the workplace?

PLAN YOUR PROCEDURE
How will the workers be able to use the automated system quickly and efficiently?

IMPLEMENT YOUR PROCEDURE
How will the effects of the new hardware and software be determined?

EVALUATE YOUR RESULTS
What is the outcome of using the hardware and software?
What other changes need to be made to further improve the efficiency of the workplace?

chapter **3**

THE ELECTRONIC WORKSTATION: HARDWARE

THE ELECTRONIC WORKSTATION

Since the arrival of computer technology in the business office, desks have become electronic workstations and microcomputers have become the basic office tool. A **workstation** incorporates all the equipment, furnishings, and accessories needed to perform work in an electronic office environment. You may have an office job where you operate an electronic typewriter as a processing tool, but at some point in your career you will work at an electronic workstation. The technology for processing, storing, and communicating information is still changing rapidly. To keep up with these changes, you need a basic understanding of how the most up-to-date equipment works and how it is set up in the modern business office.

COMPUTER SYSTEMS

The computer equipment used in offices today is referred to as a **computer system.** Computer systems may be microcomputers, minicomputers, mainframe, or supercomputers. These classifications of computers are based on the amount of information they can process, the speed at which they operate, and the cost of the computer system.

Mainframe Computers

Mainframe computers have large processing and storage capacities that can accommodate many workers using the system simultaneously. They can process information faster than any other category of computers. These computers are also very costly, ranging from hundreds of thousands to millions of dollars. Because they are designed to handle large volumes of work, and because of their high cost, mainframe computers are usually found in large institutions, such as government agencies, universities, corporations, and hospitals. The largest mainframe computer is called a **supercomputer.** Supercomputers have the largest storage and processing capacity of all computers. They also have the highest speed, biggest physical dimensions, and greatest monetary cost, which is in the millions of dollars. Supercomputers use the most advanced technology available to solve engineering and scientific problems in fields such as medical research, space exploration, weather forecasting, and national defense.

Minicomputers

Minicomputers are also used by the government and by large- to medium-sized businesses. They are less expensive and

Figure 3.1 The AS/400 IBM mainframe computer.

easier to operate than mainframes, but they can perform the same types of operations. The main difference is that they are smaller and usually less powerful than mainframes, so they cannot accommodate as many users or process as much information at the high speed of a mainframe. However, their cost is significantly less than mainframes.

Microcomputers

Microcomputers are also called personal computers, desktop computers, or home computers. Their small size and relatively low cost revolutionized the computer industry in the 1980s. Today there are dozens of successful manufacturers, producing different types of machines with different storage and processing capabilities. Companies such as IBM, Apple Computer, and Compaq are among the leading manufacturers of equipment found in the business office. Microcomputers are becoming smaller in size and more transportable. **Laptop** or **portable computers** are small microcomputers that weigh six to fifteen pounds. They have many of the same capabilities as desktop-sized microcomputers but are small enough to carry. These computers are used widely among people who carry their work with them when they travel.

Figure 3.2 Hyundai's Super Notebook, a portable computer.

THE ELECTRONIC WORKSTATION

The electronic workstation is comprised of a computer system made up of the components needed to input, process, store, output, and distribute/communicate information. The equipment that forms a computer system can be set up in many different ways. The setup of electronic equipment is called its **configuration.** An electronic workstation is set up, or configured, as a stand-alone system or as part of a data communications system.

Stand-Alone Systems

Stand-alone systems are microcomputers that are not connected to any other computer. Stand-alone microcomputers are commonly found in semiautomated offices in which computers are used mainly for word processing and small accounting records. Documents and other information are processed, hard copies are printed, and distribution of the information takes place manually. Electronic transfer of information within the organization is not possible. If information stored on disks is to be shared, the disks are copied and transferred by hand or through the mail.

Data Communication Systems

A stand-alone microcomputer workstation may have a data communications capacity through the use of a **modem.** A modem is a device used to convert the **digital signals,** which are the individual electrical pulses read by a computer, into **analog signals,** which are the electrical waves that are transmittable over telephone wires. With a modem, a computer can send and receive data from another computer at a remote location. The only requirement is that a computer and a modem be available on the other end. For example, if you work for a newspaper in the home office, a traveling journalist would be able to transmit stories from a remote location back to you. All the journalist would need would be a computer, a modem, and an open telephone line.

A modem may be internal or external to the computer. An **internal modem** is a circuit board inside of the computer. It can be easily added or taken out of a computer, although once installed, it is usually kept in place permanently. An **external modem** is a separate device that is attached to the computer by a cable and to the phone outlet by a standard telephone cord.

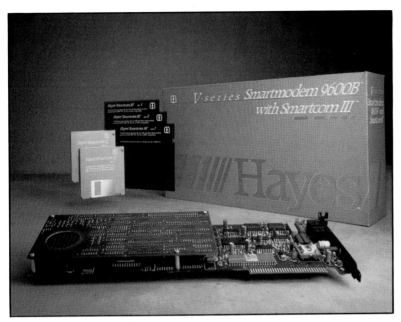

Figure 3.3 An internal modem is a circuit board that fits into the computer.

Figure 3.4 An external modem is connected to the computer by a cable.

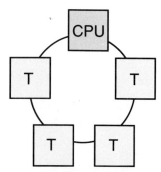

Figure 3.5A In a ring network configuration, each device is connected to another on either side. Information is communicated by being re- layed or handed off around the circle.

Networks are far more sophisticated data communications systems that allow the transmission of data in a variety of ways. Networked computer workstations, called **terminals** are con- nected through either a **local area network (LAN)** or through a **wide area network (WAN).** LANs are privately owned and are used to connect computers within a small area, such as a building or a group of buildings. Local area networks usually connect a group of microcomputers to one another. They may also connect a group of microcomputers to a minicomputer or mainframe system.

LANs are frequently used within a company to allow workers to share resources. This sharing reduces the cost of providing each individual user with certain types of costly equipment, such as printers. Workers also share centrally stored data that is used for processing information. Software applications, such as word processing programs or special programs designed for a compa- ny's individual needs, may also be shared on a local area net-

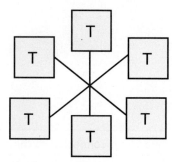

Figure 3.5B A star configuration gives each device direct contact to the central processing unit. Each device is not dependent on the operation of the others.

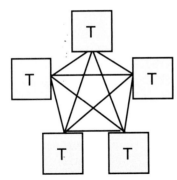

Figure 3.5C One alternative for multiple devices on a network is to establish a direct, point-to-point contact between each one. This is called a totally connected configuration. Because of the complexity of the cabling only a few devices can be handled on this type of network.

work. Users of a local area network may be able to share data stored on any other computer on the network if they have appropriate access rights.

A wide area network (WAN) covers a broad geographic area. WANs employ satellites, telephone lines, microwaves, and dedicated communications channels to transfer information from one computer network to another. A WAN connects mainframes, minicomputers, and microcomputers. Computers that are on a LAN can also be on a WAN.

Business offices use WANs to connect their offices all over the country and around the world. They also rely heavily on the commercial **on-line information services** that are available through wide area networks. These services have large collections of data in specialized subject areas, which they make available to users on a subscription basis. Some examples are NEXIS, which provides business information, LEXIS, which provides in-

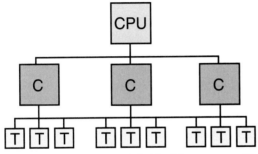

Figure 3.5D This hierarchical network is ideal for geographically dispersed units where all information does not have to be shared on a regular basis with the entire network.

formation to the legal profession, and many other services that provide information such as airline schedules, weather reports, and stock market reports. Hundreds of such services are available, and more are created each day.

Wide area network companies are public entities. The major telephone companies, such AT&T and MCI, are wide area network service providers. In addition to connecting business offices and on-line information services, WANs allow users to have access to a variety of other services, such as remote banking, home shopping, and electronic bulletin boards, which allow subscribers all over the world to communicate via their computers.

COMPUTER SYSTEM COMPONENTS

Every computer system, from microcomputers to mainframes, includes the components needed to input, process, store, and output information. A networked computer system also has communications components. To work with the equipment at your desk, you must first understand what type of system you have and how it is an integral part of the organization. Next, you must understand the individual components available and how they can be used to perform your job functions and tasks.

The components of a computer system parallel the steps of the information processing cycle. This overview will give you an understanding of the options available to you at each step of the process. In later chapters, you will have an opportunity to learn more about how these components are applied to specific administrative support functions and tasks.

Regardless of what functions they perform, all computers have the same basic physical components, which are called **hardware.**

The basic components of all computer systems are as follows:

- Input components
- Central processing unit
- Storage components
- Output components

In addition, systems configured to communicate with one another will have communications components.

INPUT COMPONENTS

Keyboard

The most commonly used input device is the **keyboard.** It is usually attached directly to the computer, although the keyboards on many models have detachable cords. This allows the keyboard to be moved around for comfort or detached if the system needs to be transported. The keys on computer keyboards vary among the different manufacturers' models, although all keyboards have the same basic alpha-numeric keyboard and most have a ten-key numerical pad. Different manufacturers provide different function keys and place them in different places on the keyboard. **Function keys** are special keys used to input commands that activate various system functions. Because the functions that these keys perform may be different from application to application, and because you can change the functions they perform, they are also called **programmable keys.**

Mouse

A **mouse** is a hand operated device available for attachment to a computer. It is a rectangular-shaped object attached to the

Figure 3.6 This hand operated mouse allows the operator to move the cursor to any point on the screen.

computer by a thin cable that resembles a mouse's tail. Frequently the mouse rests on a pad to the right of the keyboard. The ball on the bottom of the mouse rolls as the mouse is moved around on a pad or other flat surface, and this action moves the cursor on the screen. The mouse cursor is represented on the screen by an arrow or some other symbol that is typically referred to as the **pointer.** The pointer/cursor can be moved around the screen by rotating and sliding the mouse around on the pad or other flat surface; then a selection is made by tapping a button on the mouse.

The mouse may be used to scroll information on and off the screen, to move the cursor and change its shape, to locate a position for inserting information, to select functions, to draw graphics, and other graphic functions. Because of its flexibility and control, the mouse is second to the keyboard as the most commonly used input device. It cannot, however, be used to enter letters, numbers, or symbols.

Scanner

Scanners are electronic devices that can "read" text, images, and printed bar codes. The optical character reader (OCR) is a

Figure 3.7 A scanner reads characters, numbers, or graphics into the computer's memory and they appear on the screen. The scanned document can be manipulated and saved on an electronic file.

Figure 3.8 A light pen is used for input of graphics.

scanner that can "read" ink (text) on paper—written, typed, or printed—and convert it into a form that can be processed by a computer. Another type of scanner uses a laser beam. You have probably seen these scanners read the bar codes on products you buy in the supermarket. The checkout clerk passes an item over the scanner, which reads the price that corresponds to the bar code, rings it up, and adds it to the total. Scanners are also used to process checks and read price tags in department stores.

Other Input Devices

A pen containing a light beam connected to a computer is known as a **light pen.** It can be used to touch the monitor screen to input instructions or draw. A **voice input** device consists of a microphone attached to the computer that can record voice input electronically, process it as text, and output soft copy to be edited on the screen. The voice can also be used to activate commands for specific computer functions. **Handwriting recognition** involves a small device that can record handwriting in electronic form. The stored handwritten data can then be processed as text and edited. With a **video input** device, an image can be captured from a video camera, stored electronically, and processed by the computer to be placed into any type of document.

PROCESSING COMPONENTS

Many different types of computers do many different things, from controlling the heat in a microwave oven to flying an airplane. In the business office the computer is an extraordinarily efficient machine for processing information. A computer can add, subtract, multiply, divide, and make logical decisions, such as whether one thing is equal to, greater than, or less than another. If you were an administrative assistant in a registrar's office at a college, one of your job functions might be scheduling classes. You would need to answer students' questions when scheduling is not going smoothly. In an automated registration system, to schedule students' classes the computer could make the following decision: "The number of students signed up for a course equals the number of seats available in the lecture hall; therefore, the course is filled." It is the capability of a computer to perform these logical functions that makes it so much more than simply a super calculating machine.

Figure 3.9 A computer circuit-board.

The heart of the computer system is the central processing unit (CPU). The CPU is composed of **microprocessors,** which are the circuits or **computer chips** inside of the computer. These microprocessors receive data from the input devices, carry out the processing instructions, and send the results to output devices.

Computers "read" bits of information that are recorded as electrical or magnetic fields on magnetic tapes and disks. A computer looks at the electrical field and senses whether it is on or off, or it looks at the magnetic field and senses whether it is positive or negative. In effect, then, computers can make decisions only on the basis of answers to yes and no questions. To use the previous example, the computer would decide, "Yes, there is a seat left" and issue a course assignment, or it would decide, "No, there are no seats left" and issue a report that the course is filled. It is because computers can make hundreds of thousands of these yes/no decisions a minute that they can be instructed to perform complicated functions.

The CPU consists of three principal parts.

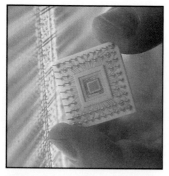

Figure 3.10 A microcomputer chip.

- **Control Unit** This is the part of the CPU that causes the system to carry out instructions. It is a kind of internal traffic cop that routes data within the computer for processing, storage, and communication.

- **Arithmetic-Logic Unit** This unit does the arithmetic functions of adding, subtracting, multiplying, and dividing. It can determine if a number is larger or smaller than another number and if it is negative or positive. In that way it is able to make logical decisions.

- **Memory** This is sometimes called **main memory** or **temporary memory** or **random access memory (RAM).** The memory in the CPU temporarily holds data that is input and sends it out as necessary to the arithmetic-logic unit or to output devices. It also holds the programmed instructions to carry out the functions. If the computer is turned off, information stored in temporary memory will be lost. Therefore, a permanent storage device external to the CPU is needed.

STORAGE COMPONENTS

The ability to store large amounts of data is essential to a computer. As just described, the computer stores data in its temporary memory. When the computer has finished processing the data, it must be given instructions to store, or "file," it permanently.

The most commonly used permanent storage media for computer files are floppy disks and magnetic tapes. In business offices, disks are used most often. The computer can transfer data electronically to these disks and tapes. Just as you can go to the file drawer and get the copy you filed, you can have the computer retrieve data stored on a disk or tape.

CPUs are equipped with **disk drives,** which house either hard disks or floppy disks. Floppy disks must be inserted into the computer's disk drive to be "read" or "written on" by the system. Floppy disks are not manufactured for specific machines. The user must perform a procedure called initializing or formatting to prepare a new disk to record data from the computer.

Hard disks are mounted inside the computer. They cannot be removed without special tools. Hard disks have a larger storage capacity than floppy disks. They are also less likely to be damaged; however, malfunctions can occur causing data to be lost. It is recommended that all data stored on a hard disk be copied onto floppy disks or tapes to avoid the loss of data.

Storage and retrieval are very important parts of any business office procedure. There is no sense in filing anything if you do not expect to look at it again. Computers are invaluable in the business office because they satisfy so well the three most important demands of a good filing system.

1. Computers have a large capacity and can store a lot of information in a small space.

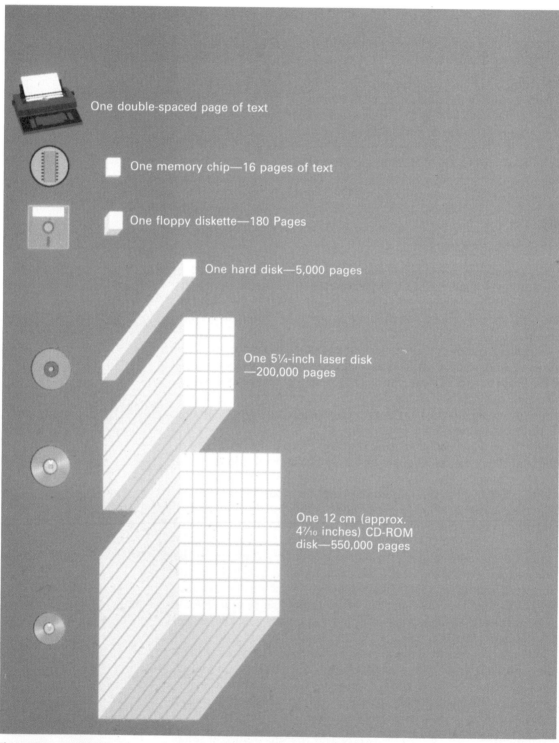

One double-spaced page of text

One memory chip—16 pages of text

One floppy diskette—180 Pages

One hard disk—5,000 pages

One 5¼-inch laser disk —200,000 pages

One 12 cm (approx. 4⁷⁄₁₀ inches) CD-ROM disk—550,000 pages

Figure 3.11 This illustration compares the storage capacity of different types of storage media.

2. They allow speedy access to needed data.

3. They store information relatively cheaply.

OUTPUT COMPONENTS

The most prominent output device in the computer system is the **monitor.** The computer processor does not need the monitor to process information; however, you need the monitor to display what the processor is doing, so it outputs its results to the monitor. But the monitor does not work by itself. A card is installed inside the computer that supports your specific monitor. This card provides the circuits and additional memory required for your monitor.

Monitors come in a variety of shapes, sizes, and characteristics that determine how much text or data they can display on the screen, the quality of the display, whether they can show graphics, and the number of colors in the display. Monochrome monitors show only two colors on the screen: a background color and a foreground color. The foreground color is the color in which text or other information is displayed. Monochrome monitors display black on a white background, white on a black background, or they may have one main color such as amber or green. Color monitors are able to display many different colors on the screen. Seeing color on the screen, however, does not mean you will get color on your printed output.

Some monitors display text only. A text monitor can display letters, numbers, and other standard typographical symbols, such as dollar signs. Graphics monitors display both text and graphics. They display such things as pie charts, line graphs, drawings, and photographs.

The second most commonly used electronic output device is the **printer.** A variety of printers are on the market, each offering different features related to print quality, speed, and choice of typefaces. The paper copy from a printer is called a **printout,** or hard copy. The kind of printer you use will determine the speed and quality of output. The printers used in most offices are dot-matrix, letter-quality, and laser printers.

Dot Matrix Printers

Dot-matrix printers produce either draft quality or near letter quality. This output does not have the clear, polished appearance of typewritten or typeset copy because the letters are formed from a series of dots with spaces between them. A letter-quality dot-matrix printer prints more dots per inch than a draft-quality printer. Therefore, the type will be closer to the ap-

```
Mr. William Chang
Personnel Director
The New Jersey Sentinel
315 Terrace Avenue
Hackensack, NJ 07004

Dear Mr. Chang:

       Your advertisement for a well-rounded student with organi-
zational skills for a summer word processing job was posted in
the guidance center of Carlton Business School, where I am a
student.  I believe I am the student for whom you are looking.
Let me explain why.
```

```
Mr. William Chang
Personnel Director
The New Jersey Sentinel
315 Terrace Avenue
Hackensack, NJ 07004

Dear Mr. Chang:

       Your advertisement for a well-rounded student with organi-
zational skills for a summer word processing job was posted in
the guidance center of Carlton Business School, where I am a
student.  I believe I am the student for whom you are looking.
Let me explain why.
```

Figure 3.12 The first document was produced by a draft quality printer. The second document is an example of letter quality output.

pearance of typewritten or laser copy. A dot-matrix printer will print text or graphics. Some dot-matrix printers can print basic colors, but the quality does not meet business standards.

Letter Quality Printers

Letter-quality printers are character printers. That is, they print each letter individually as does a typewriter. While the quality of print is better than dot-matrix printers, letter-quality printers tend to print more slowly and they do not print graphics.

Laser Printers

Laser printers use a narrow beam of light to form images on paper. They produce beautifully printed originals with great speed. These printers also print graphics and can print in color. The technology used in laser printers is the same as that used in photocopiers.

Plotters

Plotters are printing devices used in engineering and other design fields, such as construction and architecture. They can print oversized, intricate diagrams for documents such as blueprints or electrical diagrams. Plotters have a movable arm that holds colored pens, which draw the image on the page.

Many offices have more than one type of printer available. Due to the high cost of the higher-quality output devices, such as laser printers and plotters, it is more cost effective to have employees share these components. Workers may have dot-matrix printers at their individual workstations, with access to laser printers as needed. In this situation, workers must select the appropriate output device based on the needs of a particular job.

COMMUNICATIONS COMPONENTS

Since its invention the telephone has been an essential tool in the business office. Its importance increased as it became an essential part of the data communications industry. Since the breakup of AT&T in the early 1980s, many local and long distance telecommunications companies have begun to offer data communications services. Some of these services include the following:

- Dedicated telephone lines for computer transmissions

- Satellite transmission service

- Microwave transmission service

- Cellular or mobile phone service

In addition to using the telephone for these types of services, you will also use it as a basic communications device to transact business with people inside and outside of your organization. There are many varieties of telephone equipment and services. Telephone equipment and techniques for handling telephone calls will be covered in depth in a later chapter.

Your office may have a voice mail system in addition to basic telephone equipment. As described in Chapter 2, voice mail is a messaging system that is controlled by a centralized computer and is connected to the entire phone system. Through a computerized voice mail system, an individual can leave the same message for a number of people without calling each of them individually. All individuals in an organization can receive recorded messages without having their own answering machine.

Earlier we discussed networked systems—local area networks and wide area networks. If your computer system is not connected to a network, it can still communicate with other computers with a modem. Information is transferred or communicated between computers without the user seeing the process. Using a modem or a networked system, you need only follow a specific series of keyboard commands to carry out a communication procedure.

The data communications industry is growing rapidly. Through data communications systems, workers can communicate in many ways besides computer to computer. Facsimile (fax) machines are commonly used to transmit documents electronically. A document can be sent to another city or state in as much time as it takes to make a telephone call. Fax machines electronically scan a printed page and convert the image into analog signals, which are then sent over a telephone line to a receiving facsimile machine. The receiving machine reverses the conversion process and prints the image on blank paper.

One of the biggest advantages of facsimile machines is that

Figure 3.13 This Gestetner Plain Paper Faxstation is an example of state-of-the-art facsimile equipment with features such as storage capacity of up to 30 pages of information.

they can operate while unattended. A machine connected to an ordinary telephone line can send and receive documents automatically. Many models allow off-hours transmission using automatic telephone attachments. The machine has a built-in system for letting the sending location know that the documents have been received. This feature is very convenient for businesses that have a lot of interaction with branch offices or other businesses located in other time zones. Documents can be sent and received during hours when the office is actually closed.

A circuit board inside of a computer called a **fax board** will allow you to send and receive soft copy directly from your computer. This saves you from having to print the document before sending it.

Two of the oldest electronic systems for distributing messages over long distances are Telex and TWX. Both are operated by Western Union. When first invented, these machines transmitted information between machines called **teletypwriters,** which are keyboard devices with printers that can send and receive messages over telephone lines. Today Telex and TWX use computer, satellite, and microwave technology, which allows them to provide faster communication and higher-quality hard copies at a lower cost than in the past.

OTHER WORKSTATION COMPONENTS

We have just discussed the hardware computer components of the workstation and how information can flow between workstations. Let us now examine the other components of a workstation and how they combine to make workers productive and comfortable.

DICTATION/TRANSCRIPTION SYSTEMS

Dictation/transcription systems allow users to record data and have it transcribed at a later time. These systems consist of a dictation unit and a transcription unit. In a **decentralized dictation system,** each user has a dictation or transcription unit at his or her workstation. The **originator,** the person doing the dictating, records messages, instructions, memorandums, and letters into either a desktop or handheld dictation unit. The tape is then given to the individual who will transcribe the dictation, typically an administrative assistant. The administrative assistant transcribes the tape using a computer and word processing

Figure 3.14 Word processing operators in a centralized dictation system.

software. The rough draft is given to the originator for revisions, and it is returned for final editing and distribution.

Some offices, particularly those that have centralized word processing departments, have **centralized dictation systems.** In this case the originator has the option of using the telephone to call the dictation system to dictate letters or memos. A transcriptionist in the word processing center then transcribes the document and sends it, either electronically or manually, to the originator for approval.

In companies that have centralized dictation systems, a large volume of work is handled centrally, but day-to-day communications may require the use of notetaking and transcription skills at the administrative assistant's workstation. In a centralized system, an administrative assistant may also have the responsibility of dictating materials that are processed by the word processing center.

REPROGRAPHICS SYSTEMS

Since more than eighty million paper copies are made each day by individuals in organizations, **reprographics,** or copying systems, are an important part of an administrative assistant's work environment. Photocopiers, collators, shredders, and binders make up a reprographics system. Most of this equipment will not be located at individual workstations. Large companies have centralized reprographics systems to handle a high volume of work. However, every worker usually has access to the basic equipment needed to complete routine tasks.

• **Photocopier**   A photocopier machine duplicates information from an original page onto another page. Features of photocopiers include reduction/enlargement, two-sided copying (duplex), sorting, and stapling. Digital copiers print color copies, they connect to computers to duplicate electronic documents without printing a hard copy of the document, and they have multiple features as do regular photocopiers.

• **Collator**   Collators assemble multiple copies of pages in the order in which they are copied. Even though some copiers will collate up to fifty or more copies of one item, some publications require many more copies, such as quarterly reports or procedures manuals. The in-house photocopier can probably handle the amount of copies necessary but may not be able to collate all of them. A collator is necessary in this situation. Small- and medium-sized offices often use a printing service for large copying and collating jobs.

• **Shredder**   Shredders cut up or mulch paper, computer disks, or microfilm. These machines insure that confidential material cannot get into the hands of competitors or anyone who should not have access to it. In offices, shredding of materials takes place under the direction of the records manager because many items may be vital to the operation of the business.

• **Binders**   Binders fasten together collated documents into a book. These machines either glue the edge of the page together like a book or they place rings in the edge so the publication can lie flat.

ELECTRONIC CALCULATORS AND TYPEWRITERS

Electronic calculators add, subtract, multiply, and divide figures. Although you will have access to computer programs that perform mathematical calculations, more than likely you will perform tasks that require you to do "quick and easy" calculations. Many electronic calculators have an internal memory, allowing you to clear a figure you have just entered without erasing all the other figures you have input. Calculators are available with several sizes of displays, and some can print output on a paper tape as well as display it electronically.

Although computers are rapidly replacing typewriters of all

kinds in the office, many administrative assistants still use them as the main processing tool. It is also common to find offices that have both computers and **electronic typewriters.** Electronic typewriters operate with electronic circuit boards and microchips. Some electronic typewriters have video display screens, similar to those found on computers. They have a small memory capacity, which means that documents can be temporarily stored, edited, and revised without rekeying. Some electronic typewriters on the market today offer a combination of an electronic typewriter, word processor, and microcomputer all housed in one unit. This type of unit provides the text processing capability of a word processor and the data processing power of an inexpensive microcomputer. It offers the additional advantage of a direct key-to-paper typewriter mode, which secretaries need for many small typing jobs, such as envelopes, labels, and forms. If you have an electronic typewriter as well as a computer available, be sure you use the typewriter only for these kinds of applications. Processing documents on a typewriter is not an efficient use of your workstation.

ORGANIZING THE ELECTRONIC WORKSTATION

Office workstations are comprised of many parts. The individual using the workstation must make sure that all the components work together to achieve maximum productivity. In addition to the hardware components of the computer system, the workstation must have the proper supplies and must be organized to accomplish a smooth work flow.

A field of study called **ergonomics** is devoted to examining how the physical work environment affects the worker and his or her job performance. The focus of ergonomics is on the ways in which work surroundings can be modified to meet the needs of each worker. Ergonomists and most employers today know that people are most productive when they are physically and psychologically comfortable. Detailed attention is now being paid to designing work spaces, furnishings, and equipment with the workers' well-being in mind.

FURNITURE AND EQUIPMENT DESIGN

The placement of furniture, the lighting, the chair height, and the positioning of the keyboard and other computer system components are vital to an individual's productivity. When elec-

Figure 3.15 Ergonomically designed landscaped offices are more open than traditional offices. The modular furniture and layout of the office area can be changed easily to accommodate new equipment.

tronic equipment is brought into an office, it often requires employers to resdesign the layout of the work area. Many employers are turning to **office landscaping,** an approach to layout in which a large, open room is sectioned off by movable partitions into a number of workstations. Because landscaped offices have modular furniture and flexible wall partitions, office managers can reorganize work space to meet changing needs.

Ergonomics plays an important role in the design of modular office furniture. Specially designed tables for computers have several adjustable surfaces for arranging components at the level that is most comfortable for the user. Specially designed chairs can also be adjusted so that workers can change the height or the angle of the back and neck to reduce strain and fatigue.

Computer equipment itself is continually being redesigned to make it easier, safer, and more comfortable to use. On most microcomputers, the keyboard can be moved and the screen tilted to allow the user to adjust equipment to the most comfortable position. Many studies are being conducted to determine whether the radioactivity from computer screens has adverse health effects. Experts recommend that the user place the equipment two or more feet from the sitting position to minimize any radiation exposure. The keyboard should be placed at a comfortable height that does not cause any undue stress on the arms or shoulders. The monitor should be placed in a position that does not put a strain on the neck and where there is no glare from indoor or outdoor lighting.

To ensure your physical well-being and safety, direct lighting over the writing work area is necessary. Keep cables and electrical cords neatly arranged and out of the way of the walking space in your work area.

For physical comfort, and to protect your equipment, a static-free chair mat over the carpet will allow for easier mobility and less static electricity, which can interfere with the operation of electronic equipment.

AN ORGANIZED AND SECURE WORK AREA

The desk surface and surrounding area of a workstation should be kept clear of unnecessary items, such as pictures, novelty items, paper, and other office supplies. A light-colored desk surface is best for the eyes. Dark-colored surfaces provide too much of a contrast between the surface and the paper and can cause eyestrain. If your desk is made of dark wood or formica, use a desk blotter with light-colored paper.

Figure 3.16 No matter how small a work area you have, it can be safely and neatly organized to accommodate equipment and supplies.

The surface area, drawer space, filing cabinets, and bookshelves in a work area provide many places to store items. Personal belongings should not take up valuable drawer space or filing cabinets. Some items should be in secure (locked) areas, such as supplies inventory, backup copies of software and data, and petty cash. When arranging the desk work area, frequently used materials should be within easy reach. The telephone should be on the opposite side of the desk from your writing hand to permit writing while on the phone.

In the following box, you can see how individuals complete their workstations by using correct storage/organizational supplies. These items can greatly enhance your ability to complete your tasks.

STORAGE AND ORGANIZATIONAL SUPPLIES

In/out baskets	Filing baskets
Message tray	Drawer organization trays
Paper/envelope trays	Bulletin boards

Use security measures such as security cables to lock your equipment to the workstation to prevent theft. Files that contain sensitive or confidential information should be locked at the end of the day. Personal belongings should be kept in a secure place as well.

OFFICE SUPPLIES

The supplies you use to do your job will be time-savers and increase your productivity if they are the correct supplies. Think through the tasks you perform and select office supplies that meet your needs. Many office supply stores and vendors provide a large array of supplies to choose from. You may be asked to order and maintain an inventory of office supplies, or you might be in the position of requesting your supplies from another individual in the organization. Whatever your situation, it is important to keep an ample inventory at your workstation and periodically check that you have not depleted your inventory. If your supplies inventory is low, requisition or purchase supplies to have them on hand at all times.

Office supplies must complement your equipment as well as the tasks you must complete to ensure a smooth operational flow. Supplies must be placed where they are easily accessible and functional. For example, if you are continually clipping pa-

BASIC OFFICE SUPPLIES

GENERAL SUPPLIES
Pens/pencils
Line notebooks
Felt-tipped markers
Stapler and staples
Clear tape and dispenser
Masking tape and dispenser
Staple remover
Paper clips
Three-hole paper puncher

MICROCOMPUTER SUPPLIES
Disks
Disk labels
Disk cases
Disk mailers
Printer ribbons
Toner cartridges
Cleaning materials
Mouse pad

CORRESPONDENCE SUPPLIES
Letterhead
Plain white paper
Memo forms
Message reply forms
Company's preprinted forms

MESSAGE SUPPLIES
Telephone message pads
Telephone message holder
Self-stick notes

pers together, your paper clips should not be in a drawer but rather in a container on your desk. On the other hand, if you use disk labels infrequently, they should be stored neatly in a drawer. By analyzing your job duties and the tasks you perform, you can better better judge which office supplies you need and where they should be stored.

Office supplies are an expensive part of an organization's costs. Employee pilferage (or stealing) of office supplies is an on-going concern. Programs and procedures are put in place to help solve this problem, such as strict inventory control or imprinting the company's name on pens, pencils, envelopes, and other supplies. Even though an individual may accidentally take a pen or pencil now and then from the organization, other individuals believe it is part of their benefits to help themselves to an organization's office supplies. It is an employee's responsibility to help an organization achieve its goals of cutting costs. One way to do this is to be conscious of the supplies you use and to conserve whenever possible.

REFERENCE MATERIALS

Some of the most important items at your workstation are reference materials. They help you find information quickly and easily. You may create your own reference materials such as a notebook of procedures or frequently used information. After you have been on the job for a while, it may be useful to compile a book of forms or copies of certain materials.

Some reference materials should always be within your reach. These materials include the company policy manual, your job procedures manual, telephone books, a dictionary, a thesaurus, equipment and software manuals, travel scheduling information, and a secretarial handbook or reference book. Reference materials are a source for information. When you are called upon to make decisions about using technology, you will have resources you need to help you.

One important source is the technical manuals that accompany software and hardware. These manuals provide an overview of the system and its capabilities. You will become familiar with these resources as you work with different kinds of equipment and software.

MAINTAINING THE ELECTRONIC WORKSTATION

In a small organization, you will be involved with all aspects of the hardware and software at your workstation. In a large- or medium-sized organization you may work with technical support people who are responsible for the computer equipment throughout the organization. In either case, there are certain things you can do to control and maintain the valuable equipment at your workstation.

- Maintain a clean environment.

- Keep your equipment supplies on hand. This includes supplies for computers, printers, photocopiers, typewriters, and calculators.

- Keep your equipment clean and use dust covers.

- Maintain equipment by scheduling annual maintenance checks, reporting malfunctions to the appropriate department if you are in a large- or medium-sized organization, and keeping a log of the operating time and down time of equipment to help with maintenance or malfunction repair.

- Seek training or organize training for new employees on the use of the workstations and their components.

- Manage your hardware and software by keeping all contracts and maintenance agreements as well as warranty information. In a large organization an inventory may be kept by another department, but in a small organization, the administrative assistant needs to set up and maintain inventory records of hardware and software as well as other office products.

- Learn to install new computer programs and troubleshoot when your equipment malfunctions. If you do not do this, your organization may have to pay an outside consultant to handle minor problems. Or, in a large organization, you may waste valuable time of professional staff assigned to deal with all of the company's equipment. The more you can learn about your electronic workstation and maintain it yourself, the more productive you will be because you will not have to wait for others to maintain your station.

SUMMARY

- The three main categories of computers used by businesses are mainframes, minicomputers, and microcomputers.

- Workstations are configured as stand-alone or networked.

- Networked workstations may be part of a local area network, a wide area network, or both.

- Input components on workstations include, but are not limited to, the keyboard, mouse, scanners, light pens, voice input, handwriting recognition systems, and video input.

- Processing and storage components include microprocessors or the computer chips (circuitry) inside the computer, floppy disks, hard disks, tape, and paper.

- Output components include monitors and different types of printers that produce different quality output at varying speeds.

- All types of offices use manual distribution services, communications components, modems, and data communications services.

- Other components of the electronic workstation include dictation/transcription equipment, reprographics equipment, telephone systems, and electronic typewriters and calculators.

- Organization and maintenance of your workstation include maintaining adequate supplies, maintaining an organized and safe working environment, understanding how your workstation functions, seeking or providing training for yourself or new employees, and managing the hardware and software you use.

VOCABULARY

- workstation
- computer system
- mainframe computer
- supercomputer
- minicomputer
- microcomputer
- laptop or portable computer
- configuration
- stand-alone system
- modem
- digital signals
- analog signals
- internal modem
- external modem
- network terminal
- local area network (LAN)
- wide area network (WAN)
- on-line information service
- hardware
- keyboard
- function keys
- programmable keys
- mouse
- pointer
- scanner
- light pen
- voice input
- handwriting recognition
- video input
- microprocessor
- computer chip
- main memory
- temporary memory
- random access memory (RAM)
- disk drive

- monitor
- printer
- printout
- fax board
- teletypewriter
- decentralized dictation system
- originator
- centralized dictation system
- reprographics
- electronic calculators
- electronic typewriters
- ergonomics
- office landscaping

CHECKING YOUR UNDERSTANDING

1. Briefly describe how the processing capability of a computer system works.
2. What is the difference between temporary memory and permanent storage of information?
3. What equipment is necessary to turn a stand-alone system into a data communication system? How does this equipment work to allow communication to take place?
4. What storage media are available for storing electronic and nonelectronic information? Why do companies continue to use paper files for storage?
5. Describe the differences between floppy disks and hard disks. When would it be important to use each?
6. List the hardware components of a microcomputer system. Describe each component's function.
7. How is the administrative assistant's role in working with a decentralized dictation/transcription system different from a centralized system?
8. Besides a computer system, what other components will you find in an office that make up the workstation? List them and describe their function.

THINKING THROUGH PROCEDURES

1. A new employee has joined your department. You have been asked to explain to the new person how their workstation is connected to the WAN and how it will help the employee do his/her job. Write a short memo (or electronic mail message) to this person describing at least three things they should know about their networked workstation. Use word processing software, if it is available.
2. Your workstation has had an electronic typewriter as the major processing equipment. You are now about to get a completely equipped electronic workstation. Your job involves

processing important documents that go out to customers around the country. In addition, you have to communicate on a regular basis with sales representatives and others both inside and outside the company. Using word processing software, write a memo to your supervisor describing the basic components you need for your computer system. Include both hardware and software needs.

3. Get copies of the hardware and software manuals for the equipment and software you will use in this course. Examine their contents and the type of sections they contain. Design a mini-reference guide for yourself by listing the parts of each manual that would be used if you encountered the following problems while using your computer:

SOFTWARE MANUAL
    a. Loading a software program
    b. Knowing how to load, save, and print a file
    c. Formatting a document
    d. Printing a document
HARDWARE MANUAL
    a. Printer will not print
    b. Loading a new software
    c. You need to know the configuration of the system because you need to purchase peripherals
    d. You want to add a modem to the system

Place your notes in a three-ring binder and add to them as you solve hardware and software problems throughout this course.

4. Design an ergonomically sound workstation and desktop as discussed in this chapter. Include all the components of a workstation described in this chapter. Be sure to label each item. If you have graphics or other software available, you may use it.

CHAPTER 4

THE ELECTRONIC WORKSTATION: SOFTWARE

 ## COMPUTERS AND SOFTWARE

Computers can do many things, but without software, the computer is like a camera without film or a CD player without compact disks. To make a computer work, it must be given programs or instructions, known as **software.**

Recall that the ability to process text with word processing software is what brought computer technology out of the data processing department and into the mainstream of the office. Advances in computer technology, in combination with the development of a vast range of software programs, have greatly expanded the kinds of computer applications for office functions. With the right software, you can process text and numbers, record and sort data in different formats, analyze alternatives, and explore different approaches before making significant decisions. You can also create graphics, compose publications, and manage administrative support functions with the use of applications software.

In this chapter we will take a close look at the different kinds of applications software most commonly used in the business office and explore some important factors to consider when choosing the correct software for a task.

 ## TYPES OF SOFTWARE

Software programs are written, or coded, in special languages, called **programming languages,** which are sets of words and symbols that a computer can "read." **Computer programmers** are individuals who write these programs. Computer software programs exist in three broad categories: programming software, operating (or systems) software, and applications software.

PROGRAMMING SOFTWARE

Programming software consists of the instructions or programs implanted in the circuits of the central processing unit (CPU). These instructions make the computer operate, but the ordinary user does not interact directly with them. Most large organizations with automated systems have programmers or **systems analysts** on staff. Middle- and small-sized organizations may use outside consultants to handle these special needs. You may, however, work with a systems analyst to create special applications for your organization for which there is no software available commercially. A systems analyst specializes in working with programmers and office staff to determine the best

Figure 4.1 Computer programmers and systems analysts work with office staff to develop specialized programs for the company.

way to computerize specific office tasks. For example, if a company wishes to automate its inventory process, a systems analyst would discuss the inventory procedure with the workers and prepare an analysis of how the inventory process works. The analyst then creates a flow chart to show how the inventory data is generated, processed, and distributed. From this a program design is established and a programmer then codes the instructions for the program in a machine-readable programming language. Once the program is developed and put on the system, the user in the office is given instructions on how to operate it.

OPERATING SYSTEM SOFTWARE

The **operating system software** is a set of instructions that controls the running of other programs. Operating system software has two functions: to operate the computer equipment and to translate programs into machine-readable instructions. It performs such jobs as assigning places in memory, handling interruptions, and controlling input and output. Operating system software does most of its work behind the scenes. An example of systems software might be a program to schedule which of several waiting jobs the computer should carry out next. With some

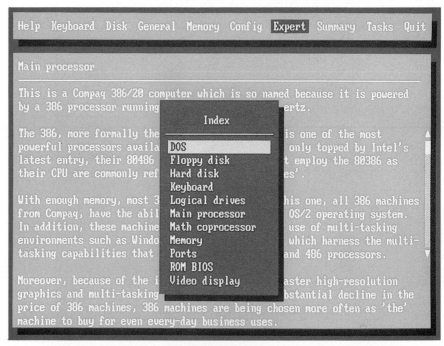

Figure 4.2 The disk operating system controls the interface between the user, the software application program, and the hardware.

computers, especially mainframes, office workers may not even be aware of the systems software. But they do need to know about the system in order to select applications software for it.

The operating system software of some computers is commonly called the **disk operating system (DOS).** Microsoft Corporation developed a disk operating system called **MS-DOS**®. The computers that use this operating system are manufactured by International Business Machines, Inc. (IBM), Zenith Corporation, Compaq, and Tandy Corporation, among others. Each manufacturer calls its disk operating system something slightly different, but the advantage of all these manufacturers using a similar disk operating system is that software designed for that system can be used on the different manufacturers' equipment. The ability to use the same disk operating system and software applications is called **compatibility.** Systems such as the Macintosh operating system and software applications are not compatible with MS-DOS. More and more manufacturers, such as Apple Computer, Inc., are developing disk operating systems that are compatible with MS-DOS and other manufacturers' disk operating systems. As a result, more compatibility is possible. Compatibility is an important factor for the end user because it expands the range of data that can be exchanged between one computer system and another.

The compatibility issue also reaches into the mainframe computer market, where companies such as UNISYS and IBM use mainframe disk operating systems that can understand and allow MS-DOS microcomputer software applications to be used on them. This creates an industry standard for operating systems so that all manufacturers' equipment can share information and applications.

APPLICATIONS SOFTWARE

Applications software programs are the software instructions that make computers execute specific tasks. These programs require the least amount of technical knowledge to run, and they are the backbone of the commercial computer industry. As an administrative support worker you may use many applications programs or only a few, depending on your job. For example, an administrative assistant in an executive's office might use word processing software for producing correspondence, communications software for distributing the correspondence, and a spreadsheet program for keeping track of expense reports and budgets. In an organization's order department, an office worker might use software for only two applications: for storing order information in the company's database and retrieving it and for

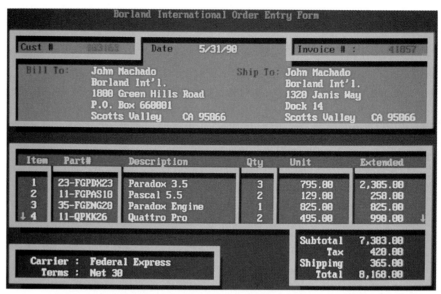

Figure 4.3 Specialized programs can be designed to record specific information in the format desired by the department manager.

sending and receiving electronic interoffice messages. Let's look at some of the applications software you might use in today's office.

There are thousands of specialized applications programs packages. Word processing, database, spreadsheet, presentation, desktop publishing, and accounting programs are some of the applications programs most widely used by administrative assistants. In legal and medical offices administrative assistants use specialized software programs for accessing information specific to their field, and many large organizations have specialized applications to carry out functions unique to their type of business. Generally, it is important to understand what types software to use for different office tasks. There are five basic categories of software applications or software tools:

1. Utility programs
2. Productivity tools
3. Planning tools
4. Communication tools
5. Specialized tools

More and more software programs are produced each day. You may find other applications in your workplace, but these five categories are the tools used most often in today's office setting.

Utility Programs

Software programs that assist you in using programs more efficiently are known as **utility programs.** These programs perform functions such as file management, allowing you not only to organize your data files but also to recover damaged files or "lost" information, delete files, and copy files. One very popular utility program is Norton Utilities for the microcomputer. This program interacts with your data files and applications to determine where information is and, if it is damaged, to repair it.

Another popular utility program allows you to check for viruses on your floppy or hard disks. **Viruses** are hidden programs that can cause random system malfunctions that can be carried from one system or disk to another. Viruses are sometimes hard to detect. Symptoms include random messages appearing on the screen, damage or loss of information, or other problems that cannot be corrected. Once viruses started to occur in computer systems they spread from system to system undetected (which is how they got their name). To counteract this spread, vendors have produced programs that can detect and wipe out common computer viruses.

Productivity Tools

Productivity tools include word processing, database, spreadsheet, graphics, desktop publishing, presentation, and integrated software applications. Let's look at each of these applications and ways you might use them.

Word Processing Word processing software is used for inputting, formatting, editing, and printing documents such as memos, letters, reports, manuscripts, and contracts. This software is particularly useful for repetitive documents such as form letters. It offers a wide range of functions, including alphabetizing lists, checking spelling, and setting up formats automatically. Perhaps you have heard of or used word processing programs, such as Word-Perfect®, Microsoft Word®, DisplayWrite®, or Multimate®, which are the four leading word processing programs. Although these programs vary in speed, power, and the range of functions they can perform, all perform the same basic word processing operations. While word processing has automated many document processing tasks, the user must still make formatting and editing decisions and proofread the work. When you use word processing software, you learn the commands for a particular package.

Figure 4.4 A WordPerfect word processing screen.

The **commands** are the keystrokes of menu selections that activate the program functions. For program functions that you do not use frequently, you must refer to the software manual as necessary.

Database Management Database management applications are used for entering, organizing, storing, and retrieving data in a specific format and order specified by the user (for example, alphabetically or chronologically). The data can be retrieved by names, account numbers, dates, and a variety of other identifying criteria. It is important to know that the same basic principles apply to all databases. The simplest way to understand the concept of database management is to visualize a large general filing department. The department collects all the company's sales figures, correspondence, accounts, personnel documents, and so on over the years. These are stored in file cabinets. The file cabinet drawers hold folders of let-

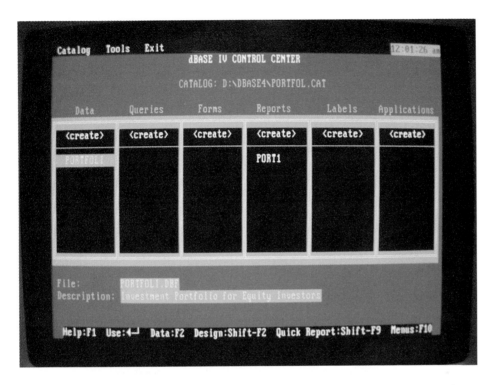

Figure 4.5 A dBASE IV Control Center screen.

ters, documents, periodicals, illustrations, and notes about where other documentation can be found. There are many directories to help users find the information they need.

Now imagine that all those files are stored within one computer system. In effect, database software emulates the work of the filing department: it stores the information and helps users find the information they need. The big difference is in the space needed to store the information and in the speed with which information may be found. Another major advantage is that the software enables the data to be retrieved in several different ways.

For instance, suppose you are an office worker in a medical office that uses a database. The physicians in the practice have learned of a new treatment for hypertension in people thirty-five or younger. They want you to write to all the patients who might benefit from the treatment and suggest that they make appointments to discuss this with their doctors. After you have keyed the necessary commands, the computer system can sort through the thousands of patient records stored in the database automatically and display or print the names and addresses of those patients under thirty-five who were diagnosed with hypertension. It would take you several days of tedious work to compile this information from typewritten or handwritten records. Once you have the list, you can use your program to merge the names with a letter informing patients of the new treatment.

Spreadsheets In many business offices spreadsheets have now surpassed word processors as the top-selling applications packages. In a nonelectronic office, a spreadsheet is a large piece of ruled accounting paper on which figures are entered in columns and rows. On an electronic spreadsheet, the figures appear in columns and rows on the computer screen instead. Spreadsheet software is used by office workers to produce budgets, profit plans, sales

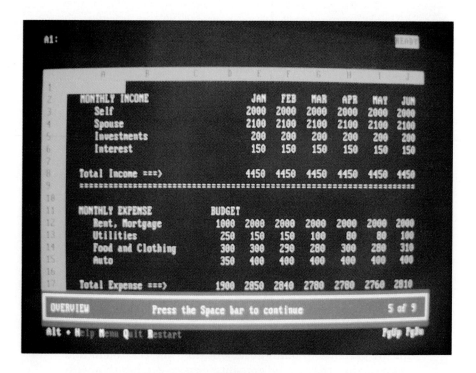

Figure 4.6 Lotus 1-2-3 spreadsheet screen.

forecasts, and so on. It allows them to calculate, recalculate, and present the results in a clear and flexible format.

To understand how electronic spreadsheets help in decision making, imagine yourself as the assistant to the manager of a large inventory control department. You want to find out how much you could afford to raise each staff member's salary. A spreadsheet would show each person's name and present salary. It would also show the total amount of money currently spent on all employees. With an electronic spreadsheet, the computer can recalculate each person's salary if it were raised 5 percent, 7 percent, 10 percent, or whatever percentage you choose. In this way, you could see how large an increase the company could afford. If the spreadsheet were not electronic, you would have to make the calculations by hand—a tedious and error-prone task.

Spreadsheets are set up on the computer screen in numbered and lettered columns and rows, which form a series of **cells.** Data is entered into a designated cell and can be changed cell by cell or recalculated automatically. Spreadsheets are usually too large to be displayed in their entirety on the screen, so most programs include a **scrolling function.** This enables the user to move copy vertically and horizontally and view different portions of the spreadsheet. The cursor on the screen becomes a cell pointer and enables the user to go to any cell in which an entry or change is needed.

Before electronic spreadsheets became available, managers and their support staffs developed spreadsheets by hand, using pencils, rulers, and calculators. If you wanted to change the number in any one cell, you had to erase, recalculate, and write new numbers in all the cells affected by that change. Since any one change usually affects dozens of cells, developing a spreadsheet by hand is time consuming. In fact, one key reason why managers first bought personal computers was so that they could use VisiCalc, the first electronic spreadsheet, which was introduced in 1979. Spreadsheets now used include Lotus 1-2-3® and Microsoft Excel®, as well as many others.

Graphics/Presentation Software Computers generate vast quantities of data, but for that data to be useful, it has to be converted into formats that people can understand. One way of translating lists of figures or other data into usable information is to convert them into charts or graphs using **graphics/presentation software.** Charts

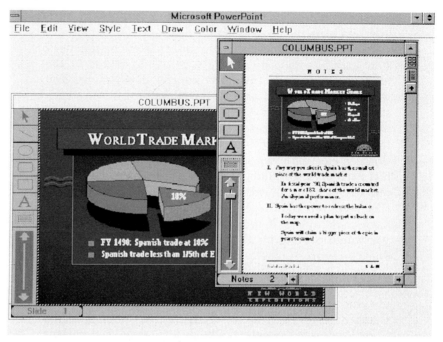

Figure 4.7 A presentation screen from the Microsoft Powerpoint program.

can be prepared by hand, of course, but a software program with a graphics capability will do the job faster and more accurately and will produce a professional looking result.

Charts and graphs are used in a variety of business situations. They are useful as a basis for slide presentations, for illustrations in reports, and for a variety of other situations in which a graphic illustration aids understanding. Wouldn't you prefer to see a breakdown of a company's budget expressed as a pie chart instead of reading and remembering rows of figures? Pie charts, along with bar graphs, line graphs, and flowcharts, are just some of the forms of graphic illustrations software can create.

As the use of business graphics grows, a wider variety of software packages is becoming available. Presentation software programs, such as Harvard Graphics®, PowerPoint®, and Morenot, produce only pie, line, and bar charts, but they also produce overhead transparencies and slides for graphic representations of information. Graphics software is used to create professional looking documents in-house for reports, newletters, and other communications.

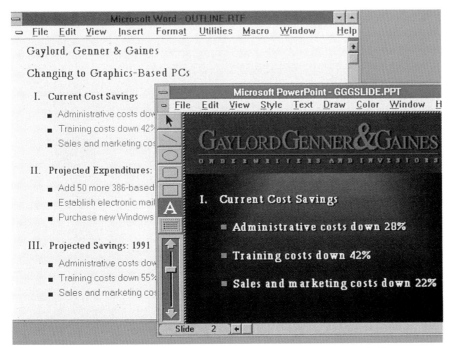

Figure 4.8 Microsoft Windows allows the user to develop a presentation slide from text that was prepared with word processing software.

Integrated Software Many software producers have concentrated on the development of **integrated software** applications, which combine programs for several applications in one software package. The purpose of integration is to bring the major business computing applications together so that data can be manipulated and coverted into different formats easily. A typical integrated software product includes spreadsheet, database, graphics, and word processing programs in a single package. Many products also include communications. With this kind of package, you can switch from one application to another quickly when the need arises. You can also move data from one application to another because different applications software programs are linked. For example, you can write and display the text of a sales report using the word processing program in the integrated package; then you can manipulate and analyze the same sales data by using the package's spreadsheet program; then you can show the results in a table; and finally, you can use your graphics program to produce charts from this data, which you can then transmit electronically.

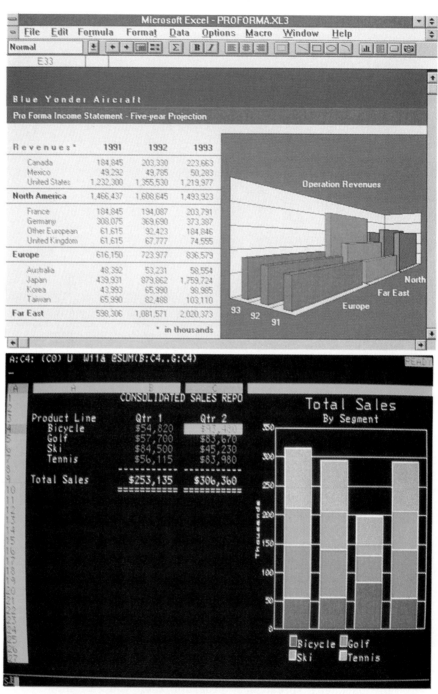

Figure 4.9 With integrated software, information from a spreadsheet can be converted to graphics.

All the programs in an integrated software package use similar menus and commands, thus enabling you to switch from one application to another without learning an entirely different set of procedures for operations such as deleting and inserting data. Well-known integrated microcomputer-based software packages include Lotus 1-2-3®, Microsoft Works®, Symphony®, Framework®, and Smartware®.

With many integrated software packages you can display data for several applications at once in different windows, or sections, of your screen. This enables you to switch among applications without changing screen displays. For instance, while writing a report with a word processing program, you could display part of a spreadsheet in another window and refer to it for data to include in your report. In a third window, you might create graphics to illustrate your report.

Individualized software packages can also share information. Basically, the user saves the file in a way that the other applications software programs can understand. The information can then be merged together into one file. However, the process to do this can be cumbersome because of the different commands between single-use software programs.

Microsoft Corporation developed Windows software to allow the MS-DOS-based microcomputer to operate with a mouse for selecting individual applications and intergrating them using icons. IBM has developed their own graphics-based integrated operating system called OS/2 (Operating System 2). A graphics-based tool provides a **graphic user interface (GUI).** A GUI lets the user select menu options from **icons,** which are pictures of the applications and commands. The Macintosh microcomputers have used a graphics-based interface since their inception. Because of their ease of use and interactivity with the user, other operating systems manufacturers have developed graphics-based interfaces as well.

With a graphics user interface (GUI) such as Windows® 3.0, users can integrate information from single-use programs in the same way that integrated software shares information. However, you must have the single-user application that is written to run under the Windows environment, such as WordPerfect for Windows, Microsoft Word for Windows, or Lotus for Windows.

If you are not using an integrated package, most major software programs on the market allow users to move files from one software application program to another. The software manuals provide specific instructions on how to do this.

PLANNING TOOLS

Planning tools are software programs used for administrative support functions, such as scheduling meetings, planning and monitoring projects, and keeping daily appointment calendars.

Calendaring software is used for maintaining daily schedules. It also allows users to make appointments or schedule meetings by checking the other calendars on the network. The user inputs the names of the individuals needed in the meeting, the length of the meeting, and possible dates for the meeting. The software then checks all the calendars of the individuals and responds with selections of dates and times. The user makes a selection and the software places the meeting on all the individuals' calendars for their approval. Individuals maintain privacy because the software picks up and reveals only the empty time slots. It does not reveal the appointments already listed on each person's calendar.

Project management software is a tool for long-term project

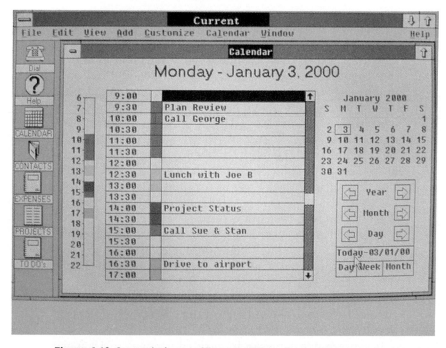

Figure 4.10 Current® is an office administration software program. This screen shows an electronic calendar which is designed exactly the same as a desk calendar.

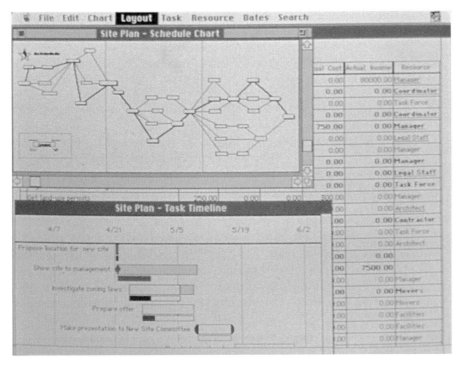

Figure 4.11 Project management software automates the planning, scheduling, and monitoring functions of long-term projects.

planning. The user enters project names, due dates, length of time needed to complete each project, and any other factors to be considered. The software then draws a timeline for reference as the project progresses. This saves much time because the timeline is now stored electronically. If the user needs to adjust a timeline, one entry is necessary and other factors are adjusted accordingly. In this way, the impact of a scheduling change on meeting the project completion date can be easily assessed. Project management software helps the user monitor the status of a project in general and the status of individual team members' contributions as well. It can also be used to make sure that schedules receive high visibility by issuing project status reports to project team members. Project management software is applicable to many kinds of projects, such as construction, product development, manufacturing, engineering, design projects, and computer programming.

COMMUNICATIONS TOOLS

In chapter 3 we discussed the hardware necessary for data communications. Like other computer operations, **communica-**

tions software is necessary for the communication process to take place. Electronic mail and voice mail are the most likely tools you will encounter in the workplace.

As you recall, electronic mail, or E-mail, is the electronic transfer of data through computer networks in either a local area network or a wide area network. In order for the data to be communicated, a software program must be provided on the network. All E-mail systems work basically the same. A worker can key in a message of a few lines or several pages. By keying in a code, the message can be sent to one person, a group of people, or the whole company. The workers on the receiving end get a message on their screens that indicates a message has come in. After reading the message they can usually choose to file it or delete it.

E-mail is one of the fastest growing computer applications in offices in recent years. One problem that has accompanied the widespread use of E-mail is a breakdown in privacy. In some companies management taps into E-mail messages between employees and uses the information to judge employee attitudes

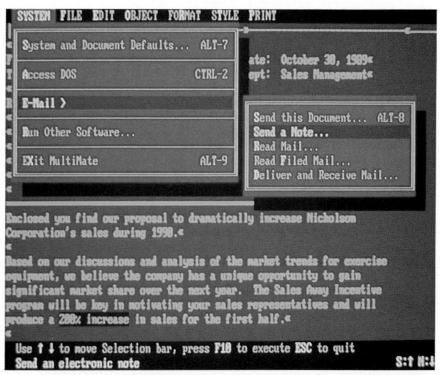

Figure 4.12 Electronic mail can be handled while the user is involved with a different software application. This screen shows both applications on the screen at the same time.

and performance. Another problem has been the use of E-mail among employees for socializing with co-workers. This is excessive in some companies and management has had to curtail it. Those who have studied E-mail systems in companies in which they have been in use for a long time report that employees tend to become "addicted" to the system and have difficulty adjusting if they move to a company that does not have a system.

Voice mail is controlled by a centralized computer in the workplace. Instead of sending a digital message, you are sending a voice message over the telephone. Your voice message is stored in the computer system until the receiver retrieves it. If you work in a company that has a voice mail system, each worker will have a recorded message that is automatically activated by the computer when the worker does not pick up the telephone. This is much like the telephone answering machines in use in private homes.

Communications software is necessary when you use a modem to connect to other systems via the telephone system. This software gives instructions to your computer on how to send and receive information from the remote computer. Some integrated software packages have communications software as part of their package, so that information you have created in any of the other applications can easily be electronically transferred to the host computer without ending one application session and starting another. Communications software also enables the user to send and receive data from on-line information retrieval services or public databases. Files can also be created on one computer system and sent directly to another system. Communications software can tell the computer to do such things as save incoming messages, dial a phone number for you, redial if the number is busy, or log you on or off of a communications network.

SPECIALIZED TOOLS

Many specialized software packages on the market are designed to take care of only one task. Some of these include desktop publishing, accounting software, and expert systems.

Desktop publishing is a composition software package used for designing and laying out items such as stationery, invitations, brochures, and newsletters. It offers the user a selection of different type sizes and type fonts. It can format text in double columns and integrate graphics, providing a finished publication. This software is widely used in advertising, marketing, and graphics departments, as well as by administrative assistants, to produce high-quality documents and other written communications.

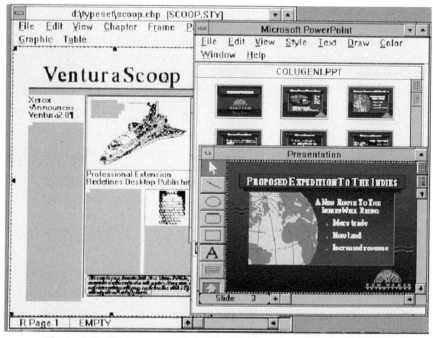

Figure 4.13 This screen shows how Windows is used for multitasking integration of text and graphics between Powerpoint® and Ventura.

The term *desktop publishing* as it is defined today in the microcomputer environment was coined by Paul Brainerd of Aldus Corporation in 1985. Aldus produced the first desktop publishing program for the microcomputer, Aldus PageMaker®. Since then many other manufacturers have developed layout programs, such as Ventura Publisher®, Quark Express®, and First Publisher®.

Desktop publishing allows the office user to create materials that used to be done by outside graphics and text composition services. In the printing industry, desktop publishing is used for magazine and newspaper layout as well as advertising layout and design. You may find yourself working in a situation where desktop publishing software is available for your use, or you may work in a department that specializes in handling this type of work.

Accounting software accomplishes all the tasks that are carried out in manual accounting systems. Accuracy is very important when working with accounting software because one entry can affect many transactions within the system. Users must be sure to enter the correct numbers in the correct accounts. If you work in a small office, your applications software may include either a general accounting program or one or more specialized accounting programs such as accounts receivable, accounts payable, payroll, inventory, and invoicing programs. In large organizations, accounting applications are used by specialists in departments such as payroll and accounts receivable.

Like spreadsheet programs, accounting software can save you work by having the computer recalculate old figures automatically as you enter new data. For example, if you enter data in the general ledger file about a $250 payment that customer Stephen Warner has sent in, the computer will send this information to other files automatically. When this information is sent to the accounts receivable file, the computer will reduce the outstanding total on Mr. Warner's bill by $250. That is, if the previous total was $800, the computer will calculate automatically that Mr. Warner now owes $550. All of this is done in one step. Without the computer you would have to make photocopies of the check, write in the numbers by hand, calculate the new amount on your calculator, file away the papers on Mr. Warner's account, and send memos about the account to other departments via interoffice mail.

There are hundreds of accounting software programs on the market. Many of these are full-scale accounting systems originally designed to run on large computer systems. These products have now been modified for microcomputers. The design of these products parallels traditional accounting subsystems: general ledger, accounts receivable, accounts payable, and payroll. Some also provide additional functions, such as job costing, inventory, and sales order entry. While the smaller-scale programs are easier to implement and run, most accounting software systems require some technical expertise so they can be tailored to the individual needs of a particular business. However, your job may require you to prepare data for entry into the system or even require that you enter data directly. For example, you may be asked to record the hours worked by each employee in your department on a computer input form. In some cases your manager may ask you to retrieve data from the accounting system to prepare a report. Or, perhaps you may be asked to obtain monthly sales or inventory figures.

Expert systems are software programs that simulate the human thought process. They are based on **artificial intelligence** programs, which program the computer to apply judgment and inference in addition to calculating factual data. Thus, the programs, to a limited extent, can factor in reasoning in a manner similar to the way the human mind functions. For instance, in the medical field, expert systems are used to diagnose medical problems, including psychological malfunctions. For this application the computer is programmed not only to analyze specific disease symptoms but also to interpret the symptoms in a variety of ways that take into account intuitive or judgmental factors that a doctor would use, in addition to factual data. For example, by asking a patient a series of questions, the computer could diagnose chronic headaches as a factor of stress rather than a symptom of a serious medical condition.

LEARNING TO USE SOFTWARE

Your first task with any new program is to learn how to use it. Learning to use a new spreadsheet or some other application is easier, of course, if you understand the underlying concepts and have already worked with similar programs. And using any program for the first time is easier if you are already comfortable with computer technology in general. Nonetheless, each program is unique, and everyone is a beginner when it comes to new software. There are many methods for learning how to use software.

- **Classes** One of the most effective means is through formal training, such as the education you are receiving now. Once you are on the job, you may find that the company provides formal training or that it encourages you to enroll in courses

Figure 4.14 The sales staff at computer stores are usually trained to help customers make purchasing decisions.

at the local two- or four-year college or technical school. You can also learn how to use popular microcomputer programs by attending classes run by computer dealers or businesses that specialize in teaching people to use computers and software. These classes may be intensive one- or two-day seminars, or they may meet for shorter weekly sessions. Computer software training classes are usually the fastest way to learn a program effectively. They may cost more than the software itself, but they are usually worth the time and money. Many companies offer such training free for staff members who will use the software regularly. The companies that sell computer systems to businesses sometimes conduct classes to teach office workers how to use their systems. It is wise to take advantage of these classes if they are available.

- **Tutorials** Another method of learning is to teach yourself using the tutorial package provided with the software or from a commercial vendor. Some software producers provide disk tutorials as well as instruction manuals. **Tutorials** are lessons recorded on a disk and displayed on the computer screen. These lessons take you step by step, at your own pace, through each procedure. Tutorials on how to use the most popular microcomputer programs have also been produced by publishers not connected with the software producers. These tutorials are sold in many computer stores.

- **Reference Materials** After you have learned the basics of the software, many times you will need to refresh your memory on how to accomplish a task or you will want to use the more complex functions of the software. In this case reference materials are very necessary parts of your workstation. **Documentation** consists of instruction manuals and other learning materials. Some software instruction manuals are clear and thorough; others are written in highly technical language and are organized so poorly that they are not much help to new users. These materials may include small cards, which you can consult quickly when you forget command codes, as well as thick volumes that include more details and technical information about the software. Books on how to use most of the popular microcomputer programs are available through your microcomputer classes or bookstores, computer stores, and libraries. These books are often easier to follow than the official instruction manuals and may explain how to solve common problems that the official manuals do not describe.

- **Electronic Manuals and Help Facilities** If the program you are using has a soft copy reference manual, you can look up information without thumbing through pages of text. You select a topic from an electronic index, and the information is brought to the screen. Many programs also include a help facility for solving problems while using the software. These electronic help facilities are slightly different from electronic manuals in that they provide you with help as you are working. You activate a "Help" command and get information immediately on a particular function.

- **Vendor Support**   Some software companies (vendors) provide a telephone information service at no extra charge. This is a way for you to talk with someone knowledgeable about the program. Other software vendors offer newsletters with information about bugs, or errors, and advice on using the programs more effectively.

- **Dealer Support**   Most of the sales staff at computer stores have been trained and are familiar with the different packages they sell. They can offer help in choosing and working with software.

- **User Groups**   These groups meet to discuss a certain computer or application. Individuals can provide help for new users and share what they have learned.

SELECTING SOFTWARE

When selecting software there are some general guidelines you can follow.

- Write down the tasks you would like to complete using the software, that is, document processing, graphics, financial reports, client information, or payroll.

- Talk to computer vendors about the types of software that will accomplish these tasks. To accomplish the tasks listed, you would look at word processing, presentation, and spreadsheet and database software, as well as an accounting package.

- After you have the names of software packages, refer to the manuals and find what hardware configurations the manufacturers suggest. This list will tell you what type of operating system to use, MS-DOS or Macintosh, how much memory is necessary, how much storage space is necessary on the hard drive, if you need a color monitor, and what size disk drive you will need. The list will also suggest a number of printers and discuss whether or not the software can be placed on a network.

- Compare the capabilities of the software to determine which has the appropriate functions for the task. (Ask for a demonstration because many people *think* the software can accomplish the task. You need to be able to *see* the task done to be sure the software will work for you.)

- Try out the software to determine ease of use.

- Compare software company support, such as toll-free technical support numbers or on-line support services. Many times software purchased from mail-order houses does not provide you with the technical support that the software company or a local dealer can.

- Compare prices of the same software from different vendors.

After comparing all these factors, you are now ready to make a decision and purchase the software and hardware you need.

SUMMARY

- Computers need software to accomplish their processing tasks.

- There are three broad categories of software: programming software, operating system software, and applications software.

- Office workers use applications software much more than they use the operating systems software. However, an understanding of operating systems software is necessary to use certain computers.

- Graphic user interfaces allow users to work with microcomputers using a mouse and icons.

- The main types of applications software include productivity tools, document processing tools, planning tools, and specialized applications. Each of these contains different applications.

- Utility programs are software tools that allow the user to work with the microcomputer more efficiently.

- Productivity tools are applications programs that allow users to more efficiently process all types of documents, from letters to graphics to budgets.

- Planning tools allow an individual to complete project planning and scheduling quickly with automated monitoring and adjustability.

• Specialized software tools are those applications that are for one specific task, such as accounting.

• Different methods to learn to use software are available, such as structured classes or the tutorial instructions sold with software. In addition, reference materials help the user answer questions when a task calls for a new function of the software.

• There are many factors to consider when selecting software for the office environment. The most important is for the user to determine what the software will be used for before it is purchased.

VOCABULARY

• software
• programming language
• computer programmer
• programming software
• systems analyst
• operating system software
• MS-DOS
• disk operating system (DOS)
• compatibility
• applications software programs
• utility programs
• viruses
• commands
• cells

• scrolling function
• graphics/presentation software
• integrated software
• graphic user interface (GUI)
• icon
• calendaring software
• project management software
• communications software
• desktop publishing
• accounting software
• expert systems
• artificial intelligence
• tutorials
• documentation

CHECKING YOUR UNDERSTANDING

1. What two pieces of software must any computer have before it can process information? What is the importance of each?
2. What makes programming software different from operating system software?
3. What is the IBM-compatible microcomputer operating software called? What manufacturers make computers that use this operating system?

4. Describe the main types of productivity tools. When would it be appropriate to use each of these tools?
5. Describe the main types of document processing tools. Give two examples of documents that would be produced using each document processing tool.
6. Describe the main type of planning tool. What functions of the tool make the office worker more productive?
7. Describe two types of specialized software tools. When would it be appropriate to use these tools in the office?

THINKING THROUGH PROCEDURES

1. You have been given the task of selecting software for the following applications in your organization. Determine which software discussed in this chapter would be the most productive for the application and describe why the software is most appropriate for this activity.
   a) Letter to clients describing a new product
   b) Annual report to stockholders
   c) Newsletter to internal members of the organization describing the activities of the department
   d) Second quarter budget using information from the previous quarter budget
   e) Mailing list of prospective clients
   f) Payroll application to provide payment to 500 employees
   g) Charts describing sales figures to be used in a quarterly sales report
   h) Report of clients who live in your area to be shared with sales representatives
   i) Memo to all users on the network describing an upcoming meeting
   j) Information from the on-line library service to gather data for a law case
2. Your employer has entrusted you with the job of buying desktop publishing software for you and your co-workers to use. You have some knowledge of what desktop publishing can do for you. What steps would you take to find out what the best software would be for your purposes? To whom could you talk? What factors would you have to take into consideration? On what factors would you ultimately base your decision?
3. Research to find specific vendors that provide software in each of the categories described in this chapter. You may need to check with vendors or gather the information from trade journals. Prepare a database that lists the category of software, type of software, name of software, vendor name, address, and

telephone number, and cost of software. Sort the database by category and type of software. Within each category put the names of the software programs in alphabetical order. Report the information in a format that provides a listing of the information you have found.

UNIT 2 THE WORKPLACE PROBLEM

Part A:

Mr. Barone, the vice president of North Central Crop Insurance, asked Michelle to research the computer hardware and software that is available to help them become more productive and efficient. As she began her research, Michelle determined that there were other systems besides computer systems that could increase their productivity such as reprographics, telecommunications, and dictation/transcription systems.

Michelle made a list of the tasks she thought could be automated in the office. She is preparing the list to be submitted to Mr. Barone before consulting with various vendors on what she needs to efficiently automate the office. Determine the software, hardware, and other office systems that would be appropriate for North Central. Using the problem solving checklist as a guide, make a list of the software applications programs, computer hardware, and any other electronic equipment that Michelle needs to effectively increase productivity in the office.

North Central Crop Insurance Company
Office Task
a) Write letters to clients
b) Maintain client list
c) Maintain client insurance data
d) Write interoffice communications
e) Communicate with sales representatives in the field
f) Bill customers
g) Pay employees and keep track of expense reports
h) Forecast sales and expenses
i) Prepare time schedules for examining damaged crops
j) Prepare company newsletters
k) Gather crop insurance information from agriculture reports (available in paper and from online database)
l) Prepare presentation overheads for the vice president
m) Prepare insurance forms
n) Prepare copies of company policies to be communicated to all employees

o) Handle incoming and outgoing calls

p) Destroy confidential information

q) Transcribe dictated information from three managers in the organization

Part B:

After Michelle made up the list of recommendations, her next job was to prioritize the implementation of the automation. Her immediate goals included being able to prepare correspondence more efficiently, communicate with the sales representatives, allow for communication within the office, and maintain an up-to-date client list and insurance information.

Given these goals, Michelle must prepare a memo to her boss, Jesse Barone, providing him with her list of recommendations and the priorities for implementing her automation plan. Using the problem solving checklist as a guide, write Michelle's memo to Mr. Barone. Include in the memo the stated goals, the short-term solution to the goals, and the long-term solution.

PROBLEM SOLVING CHECKLIST

DEFINE THE WORKPLACE PROBLEM

What hardware and software and other equipment is necessary to meet the immediate goals? What is needed in the future?

ANALYZE THE WORKPLACE PROBLEM

Is the hardware, software, and other equipment selected easy to implement?

PLAN YOUR PROCEDURE

In what order should the hardware, software, and other equipment be implemented to ensure continued productivity by the entire workforce?

IMPLEMENT YOUR PROCEDURE

What other factors must be considered during the implementation of the new equipment?

EVALUATE YOUR RESULTS

What ways will determine if the use of the hardware, software, and other equipment is meeting the stated goals of automation?

UNIT 3

MANAGING PERSONAL PRODUCTIVITY

POSITION DESCRIPTION

Job Title: Executive Legal Assistant

Department: Senior Partner

1. MAJOR FUNCTION:

   Responsible for performing administrative support functions for the senior partner of the organization. Primary emphasis is on assisting the Senior partner with overall office functions and policies relating to the organization. This assistant will oversee the office work flow procedures to include coordinating document processing, managing office communications, overseeing information distribution, and overseeing storage of information.

2. SPECIFIC DUTIES

   1. Manage procedures for the flow of information within and outside of the office; manage the office equipment related to these procedures.

   2. Coordinate communication procedures for interaction among office workers, lawyers, and clients to maintain positive customer relations and maximize productivity. Develop procedures for effective time management; participate in staff meetings.

   3. Coordinate office communications by managing telephone system, coordinate and maintain staff schedules, coordinate business meetings, manage travel arrangements and expense records.

   4. Establish procedures for document creation and processing, file management, client information, and document distribution.

   5. Manage business information relating to functions of organization by managing filing system, managing client information, analyzing client information, managing record keeping functions for billing; process budgets and other financial information, process and maintain confidential business records.

   6. Assist lead partner in supervisory and managerial functions; process and maintain confidential and general records pertaining to office staff; gather information and prepare visuals for management presentations; establish office procedures; train new employees.

THE WORKPLACE SITUATION

Krejci, Read, and Forson is a large legal firm specializing in corporate law. Their clients consist of service and manufacturing businesses. As the executive assistant to Kelly Krejci, senior partner in the firm, Thomas Perez's responsibilities include overseeing the work of the administrative assistants as well as working closely with Ms. Krejci in day-to-day decisions and actions.

Administrative assistants are assigned the duty of recording their supervisor's time for billing clients. They use an electronic scheduling system to record the amount of time spent in meetings with clients. The lawyers and legal assistants in the firm log in their own telephone calls and research time. These have to be turned in to the administrative assistants who are responsible for entering the information into the system by the end of each working day.

Mr. Perez has become aware that there is a breakdown in the processing of client billings. Not all billings are being entered into the system by the end of the business day and those that are entered on time frequently are in error and have to be corrected on later billings. The billing department which sends out the invoices to clients has complained about this situation. They blame the problem on the administrative assistants. The assistants feel they are doing the best they can. With all the other things they have to do, they are finding it impossible to keep up with the daily billing deadlines.

DEFINE THE WORKPLACE PROBLEM
What is the cause of this problem? How is it affecting office productivity and efficiency?

ANALYZE THE WORKPLACE PROBLEM
What factors are directly or indirectly contributing to the problem? Who is involved? What system is currently in place? Where does the breakdown occur? Which office procedures does the problem impact?

PLAN YOUR PROCEDURE
Do you have all the information you need to solve the problem? Who needs to be involved in changing the procedure? How will current systems be affected?

IMPLEMENT YOUR PROCEDURE
How should the new procedure be communicated to all departments and people involved?

EVALUATE YOUR RESULTS
What immediate effects were realized? Are there any negative effects after implementation? Did any new communication or human relations problem occur?

chapter 5

THE COMMUNICATION PROCESS

 ## COMMUNICATION

Communication is a process that involves the exchange of information. In the previous chapter you learned about communications technology. In this chapter you will learn about the planning and preparation necessary for successful communication. The main forms of communication used every day in the business office are oral communication and written communication. Oral communication—speaking and listening—is an important skill. In the business office it involves much more than just talking. Every time we make an appointment, answer the telephone, ask a question, make a presentation, or talk to a supervisor about an assignment, an important business transaction takes place.

In this chapter you will learn a little about the basic theory of the communication process—how people send and receive oral messages. You will learn the meaning of miscommunication—which occurs when something goes wrong in the communication process—and how to avoid it. And you will learn some basic techniques to improve your oral communication skills. These techniques will help you handle office visitors, address groups of people, and interact with office co-workers. In later chapters you will learn more about written communications, including document processing and other forms of written communication.

THE PROCESS OF COMMUNICATING

Communication is the process by which information is sent by a sender and understood by a receiver. All communication re-

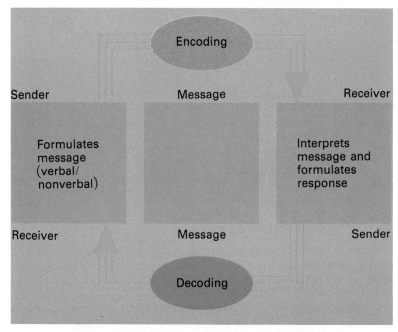

Figure 5.1 People communicate by encoding and decoding messages. The sender encodes the message; the receiver decodes it.

quires a **sender,** a **receiver,** and a **message.** The sender creates and sends the message, and the receiver detects and interprets it. In addition, for information to be exchanged, it is necessary for the receiver to respond. The terms given to this familiar dynamic of speaking, listening, and answering are **encoding** and **decoding.**

Keep in mind that people are the communicators. In the electronic office, with computers sending and receiving information, it sometimes seems that the machines are doing the communicating. In fact, the machines only distribute the message. There is always a person who prepares and sends the message and another who receives it, understands it, and responds.

Encoding takes place when a sender formulates the message to be sent. This form may be verbal, which is communication through the use of written or spoken words, or it may be nonverbal, which is communication through the use of symbols, pictures, or hand and body gestures. Nonverbal communication that depends on behavior—gestures, facial expressions, and posture—is called **body language.**

After the message is encoded, it is transferred from the sender to the receiver, where it is decoded, or interpreted. Messages are decoded when they pass through the receiver's **mental filters.**

These are all the ideas, facts, attitudes, emotions, experiences, and memories in the receiver's mind that determine the ways in which he or she detects and interprets a message. Each person's mental filters are different, so each person interprets a message in his or her own way. The decoding process triggers a response that starts the sender-message-receiver cycle all over again.

Miscommunication occurs when something goes wrong between the sender and the receiver. The sender may send an inaccurate or confusing message, or the receiver may mishear or misunderstand the message received. With so many messages coming and going and so many ways for our unique mental filters to interpret them, miscommunication is bound to happen once in a while. In a business situation, miscommunication can cause serious problems. A company might receive a wrong shipment or a busy executive might miss an important appointment because of miscommunication.

Good communication depends on messages being sent, received, and understood. Sometimes a situation in the office can interfere in the communication process. Ringing telephones, inattentive listening, failure to take down notes, malfunctioning equipment, a co-worker who interrupts others with unimportant information, and other activities can distract senders and receivers in the communication process. All of the things that stimulate us or change our mode of concentration are called signals. Let's take a close look at how this happens.

The normal, everyday routines of speaking, listening, reading, gesturing, and making facial expressions are all dependent on interactions between signals and sensory receivers. A **signal** is something in our environment that stimulates us—something we see, hear, taste, smell, or feel. A **sensory receiver** is a body organ that can detect and interpret signals—our eyes, ears, tongue, nose, or fingertips. Without being aware of it, our bodies are receiving and interpreting many signals simultaneously, often in combination. For example, it is possible for you to read a report, eat a sandwich, smell a visitor's cigar or perfume, and hear the phone ringing—all at the same time.

Normally, we can handle the bombardment our senses receive each moment because our mental filters tune out the effects of some of the signals on our sensory receivers. An example is the way we tune out some sounds so that they become background noises of which we are barely conscious. Miscommunication can occur when our mental filters tune out the wrong signal or when we try to handle two competing signals at once. If you were talking to one person on the telephone while another person was talking to you across your desk, for example, you could easily become too distracted to understand what either was saying to you.

Because miscommunication is quite common, especially in large organizations, the process of communication is studied by psychologists and sociologists to see what goes wrong and what can be done to prevent it. New theories and techniques are developed all the time. Some are well known and are used in the workplace. A company you work for may sponsor a seminar or workshop on communication in an effort to improve the exchange of information in the office.

It is easy to tell when successful communication has taken place. The message has been detected and interpreted the way the sender intended it to be, the receiver reacts appropriately to the message, and activities run smoothly and as expected. When miscommunication occurs, its effects may show up almost immediately, or they may not be apparent for quite a while. Sooner or later, something does not happen as expected, someone spots a mistake, or someone does the wrong thing. Ideally, the best time to detect and correct a miscommunicated message is as soon as it occurs.

There are some techniques you can use to improve message reception and minimize the possibilities of miscommunication.

Concentration

When there is a lot of activity in a business office—telephones ringing, intercoms buzzing, and people coming and going near your workstation—it can be difficult to read, listen, or respond accurately. Concentrating consciously on one thing can help you tune out distractions.

Awareness of Mental Filters

Mental filters vary in kind. An example might be a word with a special meaning in the region where you grew up or a long-standing fear, such as a fear of being criticized or of handling numbers. Sometimes we ascribe our mental filters to a "mental block"; we might claim, for example, "I never could spell very well." An awareness of your mental filters can help you overcome them.

Also be aware of other people's mental filters. You may discover, for example, that your supervisor does not remember messages unless they are written down. Using a combination of written and spoken messages with such people will help you work around their mental filters and communicate successfully with them.

Figure 5.2 Trying to concentrate on more than one thing at a time can interfere with the communication process.

Responding

Responding means providing feedback in some way to confirm that you have received and understood a message, or it may mean providing an opinion about something a person is doing. It might mean simply repeating what you have just heard to confirm that you understand a request, or it might mean writing the oral message or instructions down in the form of notes.

PREPARING FOR COMMUNICATION

Communication requires preparation. Whether you plan to speak or write to one person or a dozen, you need to perform a few basic steps in order to communicate effectively:

1. Create an idea.
2. Identify the audience.

3. Gather data.
4. Process the information.
5. Choose the method of communicating.
6. Send the message.
7. Make sure the message is understood.

In routine conversation these steps occur so quickly that you are not even aware of them. In the business office, however, oral communication requires thought and organization.

Know Your Purpose

To communicate effectively, you need to have a clear idea of what you want to say. Do you need to explain a procedure to a new employee? Do you want to send a memo explaining your company's new travel policy? Before you start, decide what you want to say: What points will you cover? In what sequence? In how much detail?

Identify the Audience

Before you gather information in support of your idea or decide how you will send your message, determine who your audience is likely to be. In a business setting, you might be communicating with your supervisor, your colleagues, or your subordinates. Ask yourself these questions:

1. Who needs to know this information?
2. What will they already know about this topic?
3. What will be the best way to send this message?
4. What response do I need from the receivers?

Gather Data

Data gathering is collecting information to add substance to and provide explanations for the idea you want to communicate. Typical data-gathering methods are reading files, records, and reference materials; reviewing computer data banks; and consulting with experts.

How involved the data-gathering process will be depends on the scope of the idea. It can be as simple as finding a telephone number in the Yellow Pages or as extensive as collecting the necessary figures for preparing an annual budget for your department. It is a good idea for you, as an office worker, to learn about all the sources of information at your disposal. Many companies have in-house libraries. With electronic technology you may also have access to computer files and on-line databases. Learn whom in your workplace you can consult for information. Once you have gathered your data, you can begin to create your message. Make notes of the sources you use in case you need to refer to them again or give formal credit for the information.

Process the Information

Processing the information means organizing it in a way that allows the listener to understand it. If you are sending a written message, prepare an outline and draft of the message before processing the final document. If you are going to have a meeting with someone or make a telephone call, make a list of topics or questions to cover. In some situations you may need to process some written information that will be referred to in the course of a discussion.

Choose the Method of Communication

Certain kinds of information require certain methods of communication. You would not choose to write a memo and send it through interoffice mail if a quick phone call would serve the same purpose. On the other hand, it would be hard to communicate highly detailed statistics by telephone, so you would choose

Figure 5.3 Hands-on practice can be the best way to show a co-worker how to operate a new piece of equipment. Choosing the right method for communicating information is an important office skill.

a written form of communication. In the office it is often necessary to have a written record of a conversation. For example, if you need to change the time or place of a meeting, it is a good idea to follow a phone call with a short memo of confirmation to avoid any misunderstandings.

Send the Message

There are many ways to send an oral message—face-to-face with one other person, face to face with a group, a telephone conversation with one other person, a conference call with a group, voice mail, or answering machines or services are the most common. Written messages may be sent via computer, fax, or interoffice or outside mail service. Depending on the type of message and the time frame involved, select the most effective means available.

Make Sure the Message Is Understood

Each time you communicate, you must evaluate to determine whether or not the message was understood. In person-to-person communication you can get immediate feedback, including directly asking the receiver if he or she understood you. In other situations you are able to evaluate whether the person received and understood a message when he or she follows up with some action or response after receiving the message.

COMMUNICATION CHECKLIST

Know your purpose for communicating.
Identify the audience.
Gather your data.
Process the information.

Choose the method of communicating.
Send the message.
Evaluate to be sure the message is understood.

ORAL COMMUNICATION SKILLS

The exchange of information through speaking, listening, and body language happens so frequently and so effortlessly that we do not often think of it as a skill at which we must become proficient. Yet it can become one of the most powerful skills on the job because of its immediacy. When you speak or listen, you are usually face to face or on the telephone. In your personal life, you soon learn that once you have spoken aloud to someone, you cannot take back your words, no matter how inappropriate they may be. It is the same way in the business office. Oral communication is the most important human relations skill because what you say to visitors and co-workers creates impressions and attitudes that are difficult to change.

One major factor influencing the impression you create in the business environment is your use of language. It is important to take note of the way you speak at home and among your friends. Would this same manner of speaking be understood and accepted by people who do not know you and whose expectations are that you communicate with them in a way that is generally considered to be the norm? For example, at home or at school when you greet your friends or are introduced to someone, it is acceptable to say "Hi" or "Hi'ya." In a business environment, however, this type of greeting would be considered inappropriate, particularly if you were speaking to someone outside the company or to someone at a higher level in the company. The appropriate greeting in this situation is "Hello, it is a pleasure to meet you." This is a common phrase, but it may sound and feel strange to hear yourself say it if you are not accustomed to speaking this way. Practice using this phrase and other more formal speech patterns until you feel comfortable with them. Remember that the goal of communication is to be understood. To be understood, it is sometimes necessary to adapt your way of communicating to the needs of the situation. Speaking standard business language will make your message clearer to others because the message will not get caught in the receiver's preconceived notions (mental filters) about people who do not speak the language of the business world.

CORRECT AND INCORRECT BUSINESS LANGUAGE

CORRECT	**INCORRECT**
I really enjoyed working with you on that project.	I, like, um, really like, it was great working with you on that project.
How are you today?	How ya doin? *or* What's happenin'?
It is a pleasure to meet you.	Nice meetin' ya.
Yes, I understand.	Right *or* Gotcha.
Sorry. I'm afraid I can't do that.	No way. I'm not doing that.

Oral communication can occur in both formal and informal settings. In the business office, however, even informal communication must be given more thought and care than casual, everyday conversation at home and among friends.

Here are some typical formal communications situations encountered most often by office workers:

- Presenting information or a report to a supervisor or colleagues.
- Conducting a job interview.
- Participating in a training program.
- Making a sale to a customer.
- Participating in meetings, seminars, or workshops.

Some typical informal communications settings are as follows:

- Talking on the phone.
- Greeting visitors or customers.
- Receiving instructions from your supervisor.
- Handling inquiries.
- Training a new staff member.

In addition to those discussed earlier, you, as the speaker, can use the standard guidelines described below to prepare and send messages in both formal and informal situations:

- **Have Something Worthwhile to Say** In the business office, time is money, and time that someone spends listening to you is valuable. Be sure that what you say is to the point, is timely, and has substance and value to the listener.

- **Be Sensitive to Your Audience** From the moment you begin to speak, be aware of your listeners. Make sure they can hear you; notice their expressions; be conscious of their body language. Adjust your speaking to meet their needs. If you are speaking before an audience, stop to get feedback by saying, for example, "Can you all hear me?" or "Are there any questions so far?"

- **Develop Voice Control and Quality** Your voice should be appropriately loud for your audience. The tone of your voice should be well modulated within your physical limitations. You do not have to sound like a radio or television announcer, but you do want your listeners to concentrate on what you say, not on how you sound. Your voice should be expressive, with emphasis in the appropriate places and with enough variety to maintain interest. Speak from your diaphragm and drop your voice an octave; that will give your voice more carrying power.

- **Avoid a Tentative Tone** Many pauses or filling in with "ums," "ahs," and "you knows" will erode your credibility.

Also, you should avoid ending your sentences with a questioning tone.

Page 190

- **Use Correct Language** Good grammar and a solid vocabulary will help you create an impression of authority and professionalism. Always be aware of whether you are speaking in the correct tense, with subject-verb agreement, and with the right inflection. Misuse of language can change the whole meaning of a sentence and result in a serious miscommunication. In today's global economy, English is the language of business around the world. Individuals who learn English as a second language learn very proper language skills. Words that are slang or have multiple meanings can change the message you are communicating. Therefore, it is very important to use the English language to facilitate communication with individuals who do not speak English as their first language.

  Incorrect pronunciation of words can also confuse your listener and erode your credibility. Take particular care with names. The correct pronunciation of names sends the message that you are sufficiently interested in those people to learn their names.

- **Be Sensitive to Timing** In informal communication, choose a time to speak that is not hectic or stressful for the listener. In formal settings, be aware of the time allotted for the topic you are addressing. Save questions for a question-and-answer period. If you are a member of the audience do not engage in a long dialogue with the speaker. Save comments and questions that might not be of general interest for a later time when you can approach the speaker. In any communication situation, avoid interrupting.

- **Maintain a Good Appearance** Dressing appropriately will make you more comfortable and confident when you speak and help establish your professionalism. There are many advice books on this topic, but remember that "image building" is only part of your effort to succeed in communication. You can look like an office superstar in your best suit or dress and spoil the image by using incorrect or inappropriate language.

SPEAKING CHECKLIST

Have something worthwhile to say.
Be sensitive to your audience.
Develop voice control and quality.
Avoid a tentative tone.

Use correct language.
Be sensitive to timing.
Maintain a good appearance.

LISTENING SKILLS

Receiving oral communication—listening—is also a useful skill in the office. Listening is a combination of hearing and understanding. Every day we hear things that do not make a distinct impact on our consciousness because we do not listen carefully. Here are some techniques that will help you build your listening skills:

- **Be Prepared** Familiarize yourself with the speaker's topic. This will give you a framework into which to fit new information and prepare you to ask intelligent questions.

- **Concentrate and Listen Actively** Consciously consider what the speaker is saying, and mentally sum up each major thought presented.

- **Interact with the Speaker** Look the speaker in the eye except when you are taking notes. Use appropriate body language, nodding or shaking your head. Make pertinent comments at appropriate times to give the speaker feedback.

- **Take Notes** Taking notes will help you remember what was said afterward. But be careful not to overdo it. Do not try to

Figure 5.4 Your body language lets the speaker know if you are listening actively. Direct eye contact and an alert posture signal that the speaker has your full attention.

write down everything; just put down the important points briefly. Otherwise, you might become so involved in writing that you lose track of what is said.

- **Try to Be Comfortable** Sit where you can hear and see the speaker. (His or her body language is information for you.) Try to avoid distractions such as glaring lights or humming air conditioners.

- **Avoid Anticipating What You Will Hear** Do you recall what you learned about mental filters? If you think you know what you are going to hear, you may not hear accurately what the speaker really says.

- **Make Time to Recycle the Message** If an opportunity to provide feedback and double-check for understanding does not present itself in the course of a conversation, consciously make time. It may save time in the long run if you can avoid a time-consuming follow-up phone call or, worse, an error.

- **Complete Follow-up Work Right Away** Except for your notes, your only record of the message is in your head. Do any follow-up work before you forget what you heard.

LISTENING CHECKLIST

Be prepared.	Try to be comfortable.
Concentrate and listen actively.	Avoid anticipating what you will hear.
Interact with the speaker.	Make time to recycle the message.
Take notes.	Complete follow-up work right away.

 # NONVERBAL SKILLS

During our discussion of speaking and listening, we have referred several times to body language. Body language is a powerful aspect of communication and miscommunication. Animated facial expressions, head movements, hand gestures, and posture can add meaning to your words, but you should be sure that they are coordinated with your speaking. For example, if you say "I am so glad to see you here this morning" but do not smile or look at your audience while you say it, your listeners will doubt your sincerity.

Always be conscious of your facial expression, and establish eye contact with your listeners whenever possible. Looking someone in the eye conveys authority, honesty, recognition, and self-confidence. Avoiding a person's eyes means just the opposite.

Figure 5.5 When your facial expression and gestures match what you are saying you come across as being sincere and self-confident.

When speaking on the telephone, use the same nonverbal skills you would use face to face. The receiver of your message will be able to tell if you are smiling or if you are having a bad day.

NONVERBAL SIGNALS

Eyes attentive to audience.
Pleasant facial expression.

Erect and alert posture.
Body positioned facing speaker or audience.

 ## BUSINESS COMMUNICATION ROLES

The speaking, listening, and body language skills you have learned will make you a better communicator in or out of the workplace. Let's take a closer look at some of the typical business situations you may find yourself in, and let's see what communication techniques you can add to those you have already acquired.

INFORMAL SITUATIONS

Most person-to-person communication in the business office is informal. The kinds of person-to-person situations you are likely to deal with include greeting visitors, handling telephone calls, responding to questions and requests for information, and giving and taking instructions.

When greeting visitors, familiarize yourself with the names, titles, organizations, and business relationship of frequent callers and visitors. Be sure to share this information with co-workers and supervisors so that they are prepared to communicate with and help visitors as well.

Always use a visitor's last name and his or her title—Mr., Ms., Dr., Senator, and so on—unless he or she specifically requests that you use a first name.

In offices in which a receptionist greets visitors in the reception area and notifies you of the arrival, let the receptionist know if you will be out immediately or, if not, how long the visitor will have to wait. If a visitor arrives early or if you are busy, take time to acknowledge the visitor's presence and assure him or her that you will be available as soon as you can. If a visitor arrives while you are on the telephone, smile and nod to put him or her at ease.

You will need to develop your interpersonal skills in the event you must converse with a visitor while he or she waits or partic-

Figure 5.6 In the office you will have to greet visitors and clients. Often these situations will require that you make introductions.

ipate in luncheons or other social occasions with clients. You may be required to introduce yourself to visitors or introduce them to others. Know how to shake hands firmly and formally introduce people. Offer a visitor refreshments if they are available, and be aware of the special needs of disabled visitors. These are all courtesies that convey your sense of professionalism.

MAKING INTRODUCTIONS

Introduce someone of lower status to a person of higher status.

"Ms. Casey, I would like you to meet Ms. Carothers, our president.

Ms. Carothers, Ms. Casey is a copywriter in the advertising department."

Use proper titles and names. Do not use first names until you are given permission to do so.

"Mr. Hernandez, I would like you to meet Ms. Jackson, the vice-president of sales." Ms. Jackson responds, "Please call me Bette." Mr. Hernandez responds, "Hello, Bette, please call me Joseph."

Address clients by their titles and formal names.

"Good afternoon, Ms. Lopez. Mr. Harrington will be with you shortly."

Clients are the most important persons in any organization.

Therefore, always introduce company personnel to the client.

"Mr. Harrington, I would like you to meet Ms. Lopez of Lopez Telecommunicatons, Incorporated."

Sometimes you may have to deal with an angry or upset visitor. For example, a visitor might show up without an appointment and demand to speak to the boss. Or, a visitor refuses to state his or her name or business. When you must communicate with such visitors, try first to find out who they are and the purpose of their visit. Second, try to protect yourself and your co-workers from unnecessary interruptions. The best way to achieve these objectives is to be as tactful as possible. **Tact** is the ability to avoid offending or embarrassing people. Remain objective, and do not take the visitors' tone or manner personally; courteously try to assist them. Avoid being abrupt or defensive. Once you have identified a visitor's problem, do your best to solve it yourself or refer the visitor to the most appropriate person. As a last resort, you may have to telephone the supervisor or co-worker your visitor is demanding to see. Do not say anything to commit your supervisor to a meeting. Instead, you might suggest that your supervisor and the visitor arrange a future meeting.

FORMAL SITUATIONS

Some person-to-person exchanges are formal and have a specific purpose. For example, if you were employed as a legal secretary, part of your duties might be to interview your employer's clients to collect information. All the general rules about oral communication and interpersonal skills apply here. Be courteous, be on time, and be prepared. That is, know the client's name and the purpose of the interview or meeting. During the meeting, have all materials prepared and questions written. When asking questions, be prepared to record the answers in writing or on your computer. When the meeting is coming to a close, take time to summarize the main points and verify the accuracy of the information. After the meeting is over, review your notes, think back over the conversation, and make any additional notes that may be required.

Many of your person-to-person communications will be by telephone. Perhaps it will be your job to screen your boss's telephone calls or to set up meetings by telephone. When using the phone, remember that you must compensate for the fact that you cannot see the person to whom you are speaking (and cannot, therefore, read his or her body language) and for the fact that you cannot be seen either. Techniques for using the telephone effectively are described fully in chapter 10.

Figure 5.7 When giving a formal presentation, preparation and the right image will help you feel comfortable in front of an audience.

Meetings are the most common formal communication situation in the office. Some meetings have an informal format, where the particpants speak randomly on topics as they are raised by the the person who called the meeting. Other meetings, such as staff meetings, seminars, or board meetings, are more formal. In a more formal meeting, you may be a listener or you may be asked to present information to the group. If you are a listener, read up on the topic to be discussed, review the agenda, and develop questions you may want answered to help you understand the message.

If you are presenting information, know your topic thoroughly and have your data gathered and carefully processed. When presenting complex information, you may want to put some of it in writing and hand it out to help your audience receive your message accurately. Sometimes you can make good use of visual materials, such as charts and diagrams, to make your point. After you have stated your message, briefly restate your main points; then answer any questions your audience may have. This is the time to get the feedback you need to make sure you have delivered your message accurately.

TELECONFERENCES

When you must participate in a telephone or video conference, all the techniques covered so far will help you communicate effectively in this situation. In addition, you must be especially aware of the limitations of the equipment you are using. For example, if the video is focusing on the graphics you have prepared, then the audience may not be able to see your body language at the same time.

If you are part of a teleconference without video, it may be necessary to identify yourself when you speak until everyone can recognize your voice. When involved in a telephone conference, it is very important that all the participants have been informed of what the conference will cover so that they are ready to contribute effectively. You will receive in-depth information on setting up meetings in later chapters.

To communicate well, you must think clearly, speak and write well, and demonstrate good interpersonal skills. Your main job in the business office is to be understood, and good communication skills make that possible.

SUMMARY

• Business communication is the sending and receiving of messages in the business office. Messages can be verbal or nonverbal. All communication requires a sender, a receiver, and a message.

- Sometimes in the business office, messages are miscommunicated because our sensory receivers fail to detect them clearly or because our mental filters misinterpret them.

- To ensure successful communication, messages should be prepared carefully. To prepare a message, the sender identifies the audience, gathers data, processes it into information, chooses the best method of communication, and makes sure the message is understood.

- Oral communication—speaking and listening—is our most powerful communication method because of its immediacy. In the workplace oral communication can take place in both formal and informal situations.

- To communicate orally, make sure you have something worthwhile to say. Watch and respond to your audience and speak clearly. Also, make sure you use the correct language for the situation.

- Listening is an important oral communication skill. Good listeners familiarize themselves with the speaker's topic, listen actively, and take notes.

- Body language, a form of nonverbal communication, refers to how speakers and listeners use facial expressions, gestures, and posture to communicate.

- In person-to-person exchanges it is important to be prepared and to be helpful and polite. Good interpersonal skills and using standard business language help you communicate effectively.

- Talking to a group is usually a formal communication situation. When you talk to a group, you need to know your material, provide visual or written material if necessary, and get feedback from your audience.

- When participating in a conference call or video teleconference you need to be especially aware of the limitations of the equipment you are using.

VOCABULARY

- communication
- sender
- receiver
- message
- encoding
- decoding

- body language
- mental filters
- miscommunication
- signal
- sensory receiver
- tact
- verbal
- nonverbal

CHECKING YOUR UNDERSTANDING

1. Define communication, and describe the communication process.
2. Explain the difference between verbal and nonverbal communication.
3. How does miscommunication occur, and what steps can be taken to avoid it?
4. What are the basic steps that have to be followed before you can communicate either orally or in writing? How would you use each step to prepare a five-minute presentation that would be delivered to your class?
5. Explain the differences between formal and informal communication situations. Use an example of each to demonstrate how you have encountered each situation.
6. Make a list of the listening situations you have encountered today. Describe the listening techniques you used in each of these situations.
7. List the typical business situations in which oral communication can occur, and give one example of each.

THINKING THROUGH PROCEDURES

1. You have just been hired as the executive assistant to Valerie Jefferson, the vice president of marketing in your firm. Michael Cates, a junior executive, was also hired at the same time and has made an appointment to meet with the vice president. The junior executive has now arrived and you are ready to introduce the junior executive to the vice president. Write out the dialogue as you could imagine it happening.
2. Attend a public lecture or talk at your school or in the community. Listen, using all the listening skills you have learned in this text. Take notes. When it is over, review your notes and memory. What was the speaker's main point? Did the speaker answer the questions Who? What? When? Where? Why? and How? Did the speaker interact with the audience? What kinds of body language did he or she use? Did you interact with the speaker? If you attend this lecture with a friend,

compare notes. Did you both come to the same conclusions about what was said?

3. "Rumor" or "Whisper down the lane" is a game that many people played when they were younger. It is based on the premise that if a message is repeated often enough, it is bound to be misinterpreted. Try to organize a half dozen to a dozen of your classmates to play a variation of this game. Put together a message that describes a meeting—where, what day, what hour, what will be discussed, who should attend— and have it passed orally from person to person during the class period. Have the last person to receive the message write it down, and compare his or her version with the original message. How do they differ? What other methods of communication would have ensured that the message would come back accurately?

4. A. It is hard to imagine how you appear when you speak. An audiotape or videotape of yourself can be very instructive. Research further one aspect of communication that was discussed in this chapter such as miscommunication, oral communication, written communication, or listening. Prepare an outline and notes, but do not write out verbatim what you wish to say. Locate a tape recorder or, better still, a video camera, and record your presentation of the information. Review the tape and note how you sound and/or look. Listen and watch especially for your tone of voice, verbal skills and habits, and body language. Then present your talk again, being conscious this time of anything you need to improve. Review the tape. How did you do this time?

B. Use a graphics, desktop publishing, or word processing program to design a presentation visual that supports the main point of your presentation.

chapter **6**

HUMAN RELATIONS

HUMAN RELATIONS IN THE OFFICE

When electronic technology became more widely used in the business office in the 1980s, the emphasis was on using it to increase productivity. With this emphasis the focus became saving time by processing and communicating information at an ever faster pace. One outcome of this focus was a reduction in human contact. For example, sending messages through electronic mail reduces telephone calls and "drop-in" visits. Developments such as teleconferencing reduce meetings in person. Similarly, when merchandise is ordered from a company by electronic mail, sales representatives spend less time in face-to-face contact with customers.

In each of these examples, electronic technology enables the employer to carry out business more efficiently. However, when the amount of human contact in business is reduced, human relations may suffer unless specific steps are taken to prevent this. Because people interact with machines more than with each other, they can lose sight of the importance of working with individuals and how to work together productively. Similarly, an overemphasis on high productivity has caused some business managers to place less emphasis on product quality and the needs of their customers.

HIGH TECH/HIGH TOUCH

Technological advances have been accompanied by an awareness of the need to examine their effects on people. John Naisbitt studied the phenomenon in his book *Megatrends,* in which he pointed out that every era of "high tech," or advanced technol-

Figure 6.1 Long hours of interaction with machines can lead workers to lose sight of the importance of human contact in business.

ogy, has brought a move toward "high touch," or sensitivity to human needs. This means that as a society becomes more technologically oriented, the need for personal contact does not diminish but, instead, finds new ways to express itself.

According to Naisbitt, "Whenever new technology is introduced into society, there must be a counterbalancing human response—that is *high touch*—or the technology is rejected." He cites examples such as advances in medical technology that created increased concern for issues such as patients' rights, the quality of medical care, and the "quality of death." Other examples are jet air travel, which created the opportunity for more face-to-face meetings, and communications technology, which made it easier and less costly to communicate with people in distant places.

Naisbitt predicted that technological developments that lead to less frequent contact between people and possible isolation will catch on very slowly or be rejected entirely. Among these he noted the **electronic cottage**—people doing secretarial/clerical work from home—electronic banking, and teleconferencing.

MANAGEMENT'S ROLE

The move toward a balance between high tech and high touch takes place almost automatically as new technology enters our lives. In the office, awareness of the human factors has led to new approaches to management.

The Participative Approach

One of the most successful techniques used is the participative approach to management. Using this approach, management involves workers in making decisions and implementing new procedures. The most prevalent factors behind people's resistance to change are fear of the unknown, insecurity, and the fear of being replaced by a machine. Here are some ways in which the participative approach can circumvent these problems:

- Employees are told in advance that the office will be automated. Individual job functions are reviewed, and employees are consulted on how to automate the tasks they perform before final decisions are made.

- The reasons for redefining jobs or reorganizing the staff are explained, and employees are given a clear idea of what their new duties will be.

- In some cases redefining job functions may result in more responsibility, a higher rate of pay, or greater opportunity for advancement.

- To avoid having people feel insecure and threatened by their lack of knowledge, equipment installation and training can take place simultaneously.

- Those who catch on quickly may be asked to help others so that there is a sharing of experiences, which reduces the level of tension.

- The office environment can be changed to ensure the physical comfort of employees.

Deming's Philosophy

Dr. W. Edwards Deming is a world famous management consultant whose philosophy is credited with the advantage the Japanese now enjoy in the world market of consumer goods. Dr. Deming's philosophy emphasizes product quality and customer satisfaction as the primary managerial focus needed to ensure a company's competitive advantage for both manufacturing and service businesses. He maintains that competitive advantage comes down to satisfying customers. Customers want value, which is measured by a combination of form, function, and price

Figure 6.2 Because people are the foundation of any business, it is important that they participate in the implementation of office automation and understand its effect on their contribution to the organization. Interviewing employees about methods and procedures used prior to automation is one way to get their support for a new system.

of the good they purchase. This combination is what Deming calls **quality.**

Deming's philosophy of managing people involves employees working together to understand and fine tune production processes. This working together is based on participation and teamwork as an absolute necessity to achieve the organization's goals. According to Deming, the move towards teamwork and employee involvement tends to be self-reinforcing. Work teams identify areas that need improvement and work together to solve problems. The success they experience becomes the incentive for cooperative problem solving as new needs arise. As this cycle continues, the process becomes smoother and better able to deliver quality or value on the basis of customer needs. Goals become more oriented to customer satisfaction than to the needs of an organizational system structure.

THE INDIVIDUAL'S ROLE

In the office, people, equipment, and information must work together to be productive. Equipment can be repaired, and information can be changed, but many times interactions with people cannot be repaired or replaced. All individuals in a business, as

Figure 6.3 According to Deming's management philosophy, project teams are essential to the type of creative problem solving that results in the highest quality products.

well as in their personal lives, must be aware of the effect their attitudes about work and the tasks they perform can have on people around them. The saying goes, "Your attitude is showing." Each time you speak with another person, your verbal and nonverbal communications skills are evident. Your words distinctly inform others what you are thinking, but your nonverbal signals also stress your attitude as well. Another saying is, "Your attitude is contagious." Think about the people you are in contact with every day. If their attitudes are pleasant, it is much harder for you to be unpleasant. But if their attitudes are unpleasant, then you have found someone with whom to complain. Constructive complaining is good, but constant complaining only depresses those around you; and if you are around others with negative attitudes, then yours will quickly become negative.

What, exactly, is an attitude? An **attitude** is the beliefs and feelings you have that cause you to react in a certain way to an object, a person, a situation, an event, or an idea. Your attitudes determine how you interact with others. Your human relations skills can be enhanced by your attitudes, or they can be limited.

A positive attitude makes effective human relations much easier. People respond to an enthusiastic person in a positive way. As a student, you may have found that the classes you looked forward to most were those in which the teacher was obviously enthusiastic about the subject. The teacher's excitement and interest in the topic were communicated to the class. In the work environment, a positive employee can raise the morale of a group of co-workers.

Negative attitudes limit your ability to get along with others. They may cause you to avoid dealing with certain types of situations or people. If you continually express negative attitudes about co-workers, office politics, or management, people will begin to view you in a negative way. It is usually more productive to project a positive attitude even when you do not really feel that way. If you are energetic, motivated, productive, alert, and friendly, your co-workers will respond positively to you.

WORKING RELATIONSHIPS

Any time two people have contact on a frequent basis, a relationship exists between them. It may be a good relationship; it may be not so good. Sometimes it may even be bad or destructive. But rarely will a relationship be neutral.

In your social life, you can usually choose those with whom you wish to have a relationship. In your working life, however, you have no choice. You will have a relationship with your co-workers, and it is in the best interests of your career and the productivity of your company that these relationships be positive.

Horizontal Relationships

What does a good working relationship involve? It does not mean that the people you work with need to become your best friends. It does mean that you interact with one another in such a way that your personal goals and company goals are achieved. Relationships with co-workers are called **horizontal relationships.**

The most important element in developing good horizontal relationships is free and open communication. Good communication allows the exchange of ideas and suggestions. Minor complaints and problems can be discussed and resolved before they become major ones.

You will also need to develop good horizontal relationships with people outside your company whom you contact in the course of business. Depending on the type of work your organization does, you may develop working relationships with people outside that are just as close and involved as your relationships with people on the inside of the business.

Figure 6.4 Positive relationships with co-workers are an important part of your working life.

Vertical Relationships

Establishing good horizontal relationships with your co-workers and outside contacts or clients also enhances your **vertical relationships.** Vertical relationships are those you have with supervisors and other managers. Developing a strong vertical relationship with your supervisor can be essential to your progress on the job.

The primary responsibility for creating a good vertical relationship lies not with you but with your supervisor. He or she will set the tone for the relationship. Realizing this, many businesses provide managers and supervisors with training in interpersonal relationships. However, like all relationships between two people, your relationship with your boss is a two-way street.

Vertical relationships are usually somewhat more formal than horizontal relationships. Some offices are casual—everyone is on a first-name basis. There may be a lot of chatting and friendly social engagement across levels of job responsibilities. Other offices are more traditional. You will be expected to refer to supervisors and managers as Mr. or Ms. They may address you the same way or by your first name.

The tone of your office may be influenced by the type of business conducted. The personality of the department manager will be a contributing factor also. Neither a casual nor traditional type of office is better than the other, but different people may work more effectively in one than in the other. You need to rec-

Figure 6.5 The kinds of relationships you have with clients, managers, and co-workers will vary, depending on the type of business you are in and the company atmosphere.

ognize what type of supervisor you have and the kind of office environment in which you are working. Verbal and nonverbal office communication will give you clues.

A good rule is to remember to respect the invisible line that separates employee from management, no matter how friendly or casual.

CONSTRUCTIVE AND DESTRUCTIVE ATTITUDES

Developing and maintaining a constructive attitude can mean the difference between success and failure on the job. Some people seem as if they are born with a constructive attitude. In any given situation, they look for new ways to help others solve problems. Their positive attitude makes them cheerful and friendly, and people are attracted to them because they are pleasant and also helpful. But a constructive attitude is more than just a smile. An important aspect of a constructive attitude is combining a smile with efficiency and knowledge.

Help Others

The best way to show a constructive attitude is a willingness to help others. Everyone wants to feel that he or she is important and not just another nameless face in the crowd. Your willingness to help someone will leave that individual feeling positive toward you. A willingness to help others leads to ties that bind.

Constructive attitudes bring positive responses. If your attitude says, "I'm here to help you as best I can," others will be more likely to approach you in a positive way. Even if you cannot help, they will remember your constructive attitude.

Leave Your Problems at Home

Everyone has bad days. Worries about family, health, or money, for instance, can interfere with your interactions at work. It is hard to smile at a customer or co-worker when you are worrying about something. If you have a constructive attitude, these days are the exception, however, and not the rule. Valued workers do their best to help others and in the course of doing so, they temporarily forget their own problems.

Destructive attitudes have a negative impact on everything you do. Destructive attitudes such as racism, sexism, and ageism profoundly influence our society. It is **racism** when people are denied basic human rights because of the color of their skin or their country of origin. The destructive attitude of **sexism** is exhibited by discrimination against someone because of their gender. An example of sexism is assuming wrongly that a person cannot perform some jobs simply because of his or her sex. **Ageism**—discriminating against others because of their age—affects attitudes toward older persons and senior citizens.

Racism, sexism, and ageism are examples of prejudices. A **prejudice** is an adverse or harmful opinion based on a generalization—often incorrect—about an individual or a group of people. Prejudices are obstacles to good human relations because they prevent us from seeing each person as an individual. They cut off communication between people. In the office prejudice can be responsible for destructive actions such as playing favorites. It can lead to arrogance or outright rudeness in dealing with others. It is possible to underestimate or overestimate those you work with if your negative attitudes about their race, age, or sex are allowed to influence your behavior.

Oversensitivity

Another destructive attitude that can limit your effectivenes on the job is oversensitivity—taking slights and mistakes personally. The overly sensitive worker may spend more time nursing wounded feelings than performing required tasks. Small gripes can become major upsets for people who are overly sensitive.

Selfishness

Selfish people have the attitude that their needs and concerns are more important than anyone else's. They are unable to put aside self-involvement for the good of another person or their employer. Workers with a selfish attitude arrive late, for example, without considering the effect on their co-workers who had to cover for them. Because they are primarily concerned with themselves, selfish people are often tactless and inconsiderate in their dealings with others.

Dale Carnegie's book *How to Win Friends and Influence People* lists several suggestions for how good human relations skills can help people in business succeed. Mr. Carnegie, a successful executive, developed methods to teach others how to improve their human relations skills. His successors present these methods to thousands of business executives through the Carnegie Institutes. The following list describes briefly some of Mr. Carnegies principles.

Techniques of Handling People
- Don't criticize, condemn or complain.
- Become genuinely interested in other people.
- Smile.
- Be a good listener. Encourage others to talk about themselves.
- Make the other person feel important— and do it sincerely.

Win People to Your Way of Thinking
- The only way to get the best of an argument is to avoid it.
- Show respect for the other person's opinions. Never say, "You're wrong."

- If you are wrong, admit it quickly and emphatically.
- Try honestly to see things from the other person's point of view.
- Be sympathetic with the other person's ideas and desires.

Be a Leader
- Begin with praise and honest appreciation.
- Call attention to people's mistakes indirectly.
- Talk about your own mistakes before criticizing the other person.
- Ask questions instead of giving direct orders.
- Let the other person save face.
- Praise the slightest improvement and praise every improvement.
- Give the other person a fine reputation to live up to.
- Use encouragement. Make the fault seem easy to correct.

(Carnegie, Dale. *How to Win Friends and Influence People*, Pocket Books, a division of Simon & Schuster Inc., 1230 Avenue of the Americas, New York, NY 10020, 1981; first published in 1934.)

Dissatisfaction

Dissatisfaction is a destructive attitude that can take the joy out of a job for yourself and those who work with you. Everyone knows at least one person who is never satisfied: salaries are too low, the working conditions are bad, the last raises were too small, or the customers are rude. This type of griping from one dissatisfied worker can reduce everyone's productivity.

Sometimes looking for the negative sides of people and situations can become a habit. You may not be aware of your destructive responses to people and situations because your attitude is often an unconscious reaction. When on the job it is necessary to take the time to examine your responses to co-workers, supervisors, and customers from time to time. Ask yourself if your attitudes are constructive or destructive.

 # OFFICE RULES AND POLITICS

One of the major challenges to good human relations and effective communications in the office is the informal communication system. You may have heard that in offices people "play politics" to get what they want. In reality, good human relations skills along with job knowledge and an understanding of others are more effective ways of working together and accomplishing objectives. **Office politics** is the interaction of individuals out-

Figure 6.6 Healthy competition among co-workers is good, but when it goes too far, office politics can result in serious problems.

side of the formal channels of communication. Unfortunately, the spirit of competition that makes a business thrive in the marketplace is sometimes turned inward, and competitive forces develop within the business itself. This is a destructive cycle leaving many individuals hurt, unmotivated, and frustrated when trying to meet objectives.

When office politics come into play, instead of individuals working together openly to accomplish objectives, they sometimes pursue individual goals or personal vendettas that conflict with the immediate goals of a project or with the goals of the entire organization. Sometimes, when individuals do not have good human relations skills or job knowledge, they may resort to "behind the scenes" tactics to achieve their objectives. The work then becomes a pawn in an individual's or a small group's game of achieving something separate from the whole. This separate goal may be recognition or credit for achievement at the expense of others. It may be an attempt to establish authority or power, or in extreme cases it may simply be to hurt others who are not liked or who are perceived as enemies for various reasons.

For example, as an administrative assistant, your supervisor, the department head, has asked you to assist one of the junior executives with the department's quarterly report. The junior executive delegates all of the work to you and expects you to complete it by the end of the week. You are an efficient assistant and comply. At the staff meeting the next week, the junior executive presents the quarterly report to the rest of the staff, including the department head, who lavishly praises the quality of the report. The junior executive accepts the praise and does not recognize the effort you provided in completing the report. How do you feel? Betrayed? Confused? Angry? Belittled? Will you willingly help the junior executive the next time a quarterly report is due? How do you handle the situation?

If you want to avoid playing office politics, you would not leave the meeting and then tell everyone in the department that you actually did the entire report and were not given credit. Nor should you approach your supervisor and discuss your involvement with the project so he or she knows what the junior executive is really up to. The first thing you should do is discuss your anger with the junior executive calmly. Without a defensive attitude, you would want to express your surprise that your contribution to the quarterly report was not mentioned. You would ask that when you work together on projects in the future, the junior executive please acknowledge all people who contribute to the project. If this problem persists, then discussing it with your supervisor can be helpful.

Office politics can also refer to the **chain of command,** which is the hierarchy of levels of management. The chain of command determines whom you approach with questions and when. For example, assume you have an idea to help improve the productivity in your office. Your first step is to write down your suggestions, covering all the pros and cons of the change and justifying why it would increase productivity. Your next step is to approach your direct supervisor with the project and discuss its merits. If your supervisor approves of the idea, you will be asked to present it at the next staff meeting or your supervisor will present the concept with you present. There you will be able to discuss the project with the individuals involved (other executives of the department or unit). The discussion will lead to acceptance or rejection of your plan.

The important point here is to be sure to go to your direct supervisor with ideas and problems. If this person does not act on your wishes, then you have to decide whether you will pursue the issue with the next person in the chain of command. Moving to the next level of management can cause human relations problems with your immediate supervisor; therefore, this should be done only after careful thought is given to the nature of the problem. Sometimes a supervisor may not appear to be doing something about a problem when, in fact, he or she is not at liberty to give you certain information. For example, someone in your work group is chronically absent. This is creating problems for you because you are asked to help out with that individual's work and are still expected to meet your own deadlines. If you complain to your supervisor about this, he or she may only be able to tell you that the problem will be taken care of. The supervisor is not able to tell you whether the person has been reprimanded or is about to be fired. Therefore, it may seem for a period of time that nothing is being done. In this kind of situation going over your supervisor's head will only aggravate your relationship. Unless you feel that your supervisor is being unfair to you intentionally or is putting you in a compromising position willingly, it is best to avoid carrying problems up the chain of command.

Working in teams can be another situation in which individuals put themselves ahead of the goal of the team. In this case, the team leader is responsible for identifying these "secret agendas" and must work with the individuals to bring about the goal of the team. In today's team approach to accomplishing objectives, it is imperative that you use good human relations skills and understand the importance of working within a structure to accomplish the company's goals.

DEALING WITH CONFIDENTIALITY

One of the most important traits of an individual working in an assistant or leadership role is that of confidentiality. **Confidentiality** refers to your ability to keep information private. This is particularly important when you work for a department head or executive. In this role you handle information about staff salaries, performance appraisals, and other sensitive information. You may overhear conversations or receive correspondence about confidential personal or company matters.

Your ability to be trusted with confidential information is vital to your success as an administrative assistant. By keeping information confidential, you show loyalty to your direct supervisor and to the corporation as a whole. Assistants who are able to work in a confidential setting are usually given more responsibilities and a higher salary to compensate them for their work.

For example, let's assume that you are the administrative assistant for the department head of a large manufacturing company. Your supervisor, who is head of production, receives a confidential memo from top management regarding a staff cutback in the next quarter due to falling sales. You are having lunch with another assistant, who says, "I have heard through the grapevine that there are going to be staff cutbacks next quarter." How do you answer? Do you breach the confidential nature of this information since the assistant seems already to know it anyway? Being the intelligent assistant that you are, you do not give out any information regarding matters that are deemed confidential by management. Instead you answer, "Oh, I have not heard that rumor. By the way, I saw a terrific movie last weekend." You have answered the person, but at the same time, by changing the subject, you are expressing the fact that you do not wish to discuss it. If pressed you would be obligated to flatly state that you are not at liberty to discuss what you know.

The purpose of an office will determine what types of information you must keep confidential. For example, by law you can not share medical records of a patient with other clinics without the permission of the patient. You cannot share educational records with any other adult or institution without the written consent of the student. Confidentiality of legal information is very important to uphold. However, if your supervisor is engaged in illegal activities, you do not have the obligation to remain silent. You should take some action when you have knowledge of illegal activity.

One trap you need to be aware of is the feeling of power that

Figure 6.7 Law offices are an example of a field where strict confidentiality is required at all times.

can come with working for a high-level executive and being privy to information that others do not have. Much of this information will not be labeled confidential. Some administrative assistants allow themselves to let the power of the office go to their heads. They use information as a way to manipulate people. For example, if you hear your boss criticizing a subordinate, and this person is someone you are not fond of, you can make matters worse by telling a few people that the boss "really let so and so have it." Some administrative assistants can also control who gets in to see their bosses, whose telephone calls get put through, and whose work gets to the boss's attention first. Avoiding the temptation to use this kind of power is what makes a mature, competent, and well-respected administrative assistant.

ETHICAL AND LEGAL ISSUES

Along with keeping certain information confidential, you also must be aware of your rights and responsibilities to use information and equipment in an ethical and legal way. Office crime is on the rise. Individuals believe it is acceptable to "borrow" supplies such as pens, pencils, paper clips, paper, envelopes, and other supplies as well as to use company equipment for personal activities. Information can also become a "supply" if individuals discuss new research or the development of products with clients or competitors. Many times this is unintentional, but sometimes employees feel they can "sell" information to others without repercussions. This is not true.

Organizations, both large and small, lose thousands of dollars a year from employees' pilfering of supplies from their inventory. Each person who does "steal" from an organization may think that this one pencil or one ream of paper will not hurt the company. But, if five hundred employees think the same thing, then a company could lose $5,000 because each employee stole a ream of paper.

Ethics relates to a value judgment of right and wrong in any given situation or circumstance. For example, you must evaluate your ethical behavior regarding company supplies. The only question you must answer yes to is, "Is the activity I am using these supplies for a company activity?" This same question must be answered when you are working with company equipment. It is ethically and legally wrong for individuals to work on personal projects during normal business hours; you are paid to produce for the company during this time. This includes working on equipment as well as using supplies. Making personal telephone calls (especially long distance) or sending out personal letters is not only ethically wrong (using company equipment and supplies) but also legally wrong if you do not have permission or you are completing the activity during your work hours. Many companies do allow their employees to use company services, such as copying, for a small fee. If you do this, be sure you ask to use the service when you are not obligated to be working.

Employees must avoid misuse of equipment and supplies, but they can also help the company to conserve its resources by taking part in supply control. For example, this may mean that you do not print out every rough draft of a document but instead use your software to analyze your writing and also to preview the page on screen before it is printed. Although you may not be able to read all the text in the preview mode, your software can make a small image of the layout of your page so that you can check for correct placement and extra lines at the bottom or top of the page. By using just this technique, you can save your company hundreds of dollars in paper, toner, and on-line costs as well as your time running to and from the printer to access your document. When the document is ready for final editing, then print out a copy for yourself and the originator to proofread.

As an employee of any organization, try to keep the costs of doing business to a minimum. When you do this, your organization will have more resources to devote to accomplishing company goals. In the long run this will ensure that you keep your job and get decent salary increases. Sometimes even greater rewards are given. Many companies give monetary rewards to em-

Figure 6.8 Carefully reviewing information in soft copy format saves both time and supplies.

ployees who come up with suggestions that save money for the company. For example, in 1991 an employee of the state of Massachusetts found new federal regulations that allowed her state to receive approximately $490 million in additional revenue from the federal government. Because of this windfall, the state was able to balance its budget, and she received a monetary bonus for her effort. Additionally, Massachusetts was able to fund other priority programs.

Your ethical and legal use of a company's information, supplies, and equipment shows you are doing your best to ensure that the organization succeeds. Unethical behavior and illegal activities in the workplace are no longer "secrets." Individuals mistakenly believe that they will not get caught or that if someone else gets away with something they might as well try it. This is not so. Questions about legal and ethical issues can be answered by your supervisor or by the legal department within your organization. Large companies are developing programs to assist individuals answer these and other difficult questions.

 HANDLING STRESS

As employees must deal with more and more human relations issues in the workplace (including office politics) and balance these with a constant state of change, the stress levels of job du-

Figure 6.9 Organizing and prioritizing can help you avoid feeling that pressure is closing in from all sides.

ties can rise to the point that they are no longer productive employees. **Stress** is the body's response to change and stimulation. High levels of unrelieved stress can cause physical and emotional problems for workers.

Job-related stress in the office occurs when employees perceive themselves as being controlled by outside forces rather than by themselves. For example, workers may experience stress when they are required to learn to operate complicated new machines or when they must meet unreasonable production quotas. Cases have been reported in the news media of overworked employees who shredded, threw out, or hid thousands of unprocessed documents in order to relieve the pressure of their work load. Being organized is one way to relieve the stress of feeling overloaded with work. This often means organizing your supervisor as well as yourself. By organizing and agreeing on the priorities of items, the feeling that everything is closing in is lessened. In most offices there are peaks and valleys in the work load. Some things you can do to avoid being stressed out during the peak periods are to keep a daily schedule with appointments and deadlines and set time aside every day to revamp it. Go over it with your boss or subordinates so that unmet expectations are avoided.

Workers who experience stress in the office may feel uncomfortable or threatened by changes in their routine, and they may react by underutilizing new equipment or ignoring new procedures. As discussed previously, it is best to stay productive on the job. Employees who feel that their jobs are taking over their lives may be experiencing the pressures of job-related stress. Some symptoms of job-related stress include the following:

1. Chronic fatigue
2. Unenthused about returning to work
3. Increased complaining about job duties
4. Negative attitude towards other parts of your life
5. Constantly thinking about the duties of the workplace with no relief
6. Deterioration of personal relationships
7. Weight gain or weight loss

EMPLOYEE ASSISTANCE PROGRAMS

To help employees deal with problems related to the office environment, ranging from the pressures of job duties to personal attitudes, companies offer **employee assistance programs.** Organizations have developed programs in the areas of job-related stress, personal counseling, job training, and investment counseling. These programs are offered either from within the company or through outside agencies. Usually the programs are run by individuals who have personnel, counseling, and physical fitness expertise.

Wellness Programs

The best way to overcome stress is to acquire skills and abilities to manage your time effectively and to live a well-rounded life that includes exercise, a good diet, and recreation. Part of a company's employee assistance program is often a wellness program. A **wellness program** helps employees analyze their lifestyles and find ways to enjoy work and play. These programs help individuals devise an effective time management plan and also teach employees how to live a healthy life. Studies have shown that individuals who eat a balanced diet, exercise regularly (anything from walking three to five miles a week to playing rugby), and have interests outside of the office are more productive when on the job because their energies are focused properly.

Most important, when developing your schedule of activities, you must be skilled in the area of time management. By taking control of your time, both personal and job-related, you will find that you have more time to enjoy yourself and your job.

SUMMARY

- The use of technology has had an impact on human relations. The participative approach and Deming's philosophy of emphasizing customer needs are management approaches implemented in electronic offices.

- Your relations with people in the office depend on whether the relationship is horizontal or vertical.

- It is important to develop constructive attitudes and be aware of the destructive attitudes that affect your ability to work well with others.

- Using Dale Carnegie's principles you can motivate yourself and others in a positive manner.

- Office politics can have a negative effect on employees. You must work within the structure of the organization and use good human relations skills to overcome any possible negative outcomes related to office politics.

- One of the most important traits in any employee is ability to keep information confidential.

- Pilfering of supplies can cost organizations thousands of dollars each year. Employees must be aware that this is stealing and causes the company unnecessary costs.

- Ethical behavior relates to a value judgment of right and wrong in any given situation or circumstance. In the office, ethical behavior can relate to how an employee uses company equipment and supplies.

- Previewing a document before printing can save many hours of printing time as well as supplies.

- Employee assistance programs within organizations help employees deal with problems related to the office environment, from the pressures of the job to personal attitudes. An outreach of these programs is wellness programs to eliminate the possibility of job-related stress before it occurs.

VOCABULARY

- electronic cottage
- quality
- attitude
- horizontal relationship
- vertical relationship
- racism
- sexism
- ageism

- prejudice
- office politics
- chain of command
- confidentiality
- ethics

- stress
- employee assistance programs
- wellness program

CHECKING YOUR UNDERSTANDING

1. Describe the participative approach to management. What are the most prevalent factors behind people's resistance to change? What are ways that this approach alleviates this resistance?
2. Describe Deming's philosophy of management. In what culture is this philosophy used widely? Describe an example that illustrates Deming's philosophy working in the office.
3. What are the two types of working relationships? How does an individual's attitude affect these relationships?
4. Attitudes have a lasting effect on communication. Using a constructive attitude will bring positive results. Describe ways that you can ensure having a constructive attitude and not having destructive attitudes while in the office.
5. What is confidentiality in the work place? Give at least two examples of when confidentiality is important.
6. What are ethics? Why is it important to practice ethical behavior in the office?
7. Working with people can often lead to stress in the workplace. Describe stress and the symptoms of job-related stress. What are organizations doing to help employees deal with job-related stress?

THINKING THROUGH PROCEDURES

1. Think about a job you have had—paying or nonpaying—and about the person who supervised you. How would you characterize your supervisor's human relations skills? Effective or ineffective? Write your thoughts in two columns, with the effective items in one column and the ineffective items in another. If you had been in your supervisor's position, what would you have done differently?
2. Write a section of a work appraisal form for an administrative assistant. The section should be related to the human relations skills that an administrative assistant must possess in order to be productive and effective on the job. List five cri-

teria that could be used to evaluate an employee's performance in the area of human relations.

3. If you were asked to "bring some paper home from the office"
   for a friend because he is a struggling student with a major
   paper due and no money to purchase paper, how would you
   deal with the situation? Write down your answers to this and
   the following situations and then discuss each situation with
   your classmates.

   a. You attend night classes to learn new techniques of time
      management. You have a research paper due concerning
      ways that people use time management effectively. You
      have not been able to get to school at night to use the
      equipment to key the paper. You consider the alternative
      of using the equipment at work, and you bring your ma-
      terials and outline to the office. What will you do next?

   b. Working in a small medical office you have the opportunity
      to view many patients' records, including those of friends,
      relatives, and acquaintances. On a Saturday afternoon you
      are spending time with friends. The conversation turns to
      a discussion about an acquaintance who is rumored to be
      sick. Your friends know where you work and that this per-
      son is a patient at the medical facility. They tactfully ask
      you if you know anything about this person's medical
      standing. How would you answer?

   c. As a level 3 secretary at a university, you are given the re-
      sponsibility of working as a private secretary to the chan-
      cellor. One of your duties is to interact with the personnel
      department regarding new faculty and staff. A new posi-
      tion has just been filled for a vice-chancellor of technology.
      You know who this person is, and so do all the members of
      the hiring committee—ten in all. A local reporter calls to
      ask if the decision has been made about whom to hire. You
      have been instructed by the chancellor that a formal an-
      nouncement will be made in the afternoon, and this is the
      answer you give the reporter. The reporter continues to
      talk with you and says, "If you give me the person's name,
      I will not divulge your identity. There are many other peo-
      ple who know who the hiree is; you would not be sus-
      pected." How will you handle this issue of confidentiality?

4. In your job you communicate with various insurance companies. Some of these are small firms that do not use much electronic equipment. You often speak on the phone with their
   representatives. But most of the insurance companies you deal
   with are large and technologically sophisticated. Most of your

communication with them is done electronically. Your supervisor, Ms. Rabinowitz, encourages you to get to know the people at the large firms by name and to conduct some business with them by telephone even when you could use the computer. Do you think that this is a good communications practice? Discuss the effect of electronic technology on human relations.

chapter 7

TIME MANAGEMENT PRINCIPLES

TIME MANAGEMENT

Employees often represent an employer's most valuable—and most costly—resource. One of the main reasons employers automate their offices, in fact, is to make better use of their human resources. Instead of doing tasks that can be done faster and better by machines, people who work in electronic offices can spend their time on tasks that require judgment, human relations skills, and other attributes that machines do not have.

Because time is money in business, office workers are expected to use their time carefully and economically. They need to schedule their assignments and plan their workdays so that they produce the most work possible in the time available to them.

There is more to working efficiently than knowing how to do each task. You also need to know when to perform each task, how to choose which job to do first, how long each project will take, and so on. This is called **time management.** Time management in the office involves planning and scheduling your work and avoiding wasted time. The behaviors that waste time in an office are failing to plan and budget time, giving in to interruptions, failing to carry through and complete a task, lack of privacy, slowness in reading and making decisions, performing unnecessary work, and desk clutter. We will discuss time management in two phases: first as a determining factor in what you accomplish each day and then how to use your time management skills to accomplish tasks.

DAILY TIME MANAGEMENT

Time management begins with assessing the way you currently work and then determining ways to use your time more effectively. The steps in an on-going time management plan include the following:

1. Record the way you currently spend your time.
2. Analyze how you spend your time.
3. Determine what activities can be adjusted or changed to be a more effective worker.
4. Schedule your activities daily, weekly, monthly, and long range.
5. Adhere to the schedule.
6. Periodically evaluate your schedule to determine if it is working.

Figure 7.1 depicts the flow of time management as a nonstop process; it is continually evaluated and changed as job duties change.

Evaluating how you currently spend your time on the job can determine how many distractions you have, the unnecessary steps you may take to accomplish a task, the times of the day

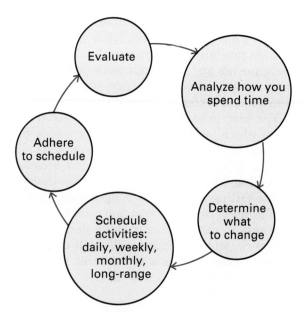

Figure 7.1 Time Management Flow Chart Reevaluation and rescheduling take place throughout the time management process.

you are most productive, and the amount of time within the day you have obligations.

You can evaluate your time by using a calendar with fifteen-minute blocks of time and recording when you finish a task, how long it took, and what the task was. You may think that this will simply take up more of your time. It will take a few more minutes during the time period you are evaluating, but it will save you many hours in the future. Figure 7.2 shows a sample of an evaluation calendar.

8:00	Gather mail, Sally stopped by
8:15	Open mail and prioritize, incoming phone call
8:30	Outgoing phone call, Ted wanted a file
8:45	Place mail on supervisor's desk
9:00	Gather documents from yesterday to revise, Alyssa stopped by
9:15	Continue revising, outgoing phone call
9:30	Continue revising, send documents to supervisor over network
9:45	Check for mail, duplicate documents
10:00	Break
10:15	A little extra for break; back at 10:25
10:30	Reorganize desk, outgoing phone call
10:45	Supervisor returns documents for final editing
11:00	Edit documents, reproduce final copies
11:15	Prepare outgoing mail for the finished documents, give copies to supervisor
11:30	Willie stops to ask for information on client, can't find file
11:45	Continue to look for file, find
12:00	Go to lunch
12:15	
12:30	
12:45	
1:00	Back at 1:05, supervisor resubmits document from morning for editing, edit document, prepare for mailing
1:15	Answer phone messages
1:30	Go to accounting to find out more about billing procedure
1:45	Still at accounting, person busy and had to wait for answer
2:00	Supervisor wants new documents edited, edit them
2:15	Prepare documents for mailing and give to supervisor
2:30	Break
2:45	Start to prepare materials for billing, incoming phone call
3:00	Schedule a meeting for next week for department heads
3:15	Continue making calls for meeting
3:30	Continue making calls for meeting
3:45	Go back to billing materials
4:00	Incoming phone calls about meeting, continue to work on billing
4:15	Judith interrupts with questions about billing
4:30	Still answering Judith's questions
4:45	Prepare to go home
5:00	Leave

Figure 7.2 A sample evaluation calendar.

As you can see, an evaluation calendar need not be completely detailed, but it should contain enough information so you know how you spend your time. This is not for your supervisor to evaluate your job performance. This activity is for you to evaluate yourself so you can improve.

After you have evaluated your work habits for at least one week, you are ready to analyze your habits and determine which of them are time wasters and then eliminate them. When you evaluate the use of your time honestly, you must look at time wasters, which plague all of us occasionally but should never become daily habits.

Now read figure 7.2 and analyze it against the list of time wasters. What time wasters did you identify as you read the figure? There are many time wasters, but a few of the major ones are as follows:

1. Failure to plan and budget time.
2. Giving in to interruptions from individuals who want to talk.
3. Placing outgoing calls at random times.
4. Extra long morning break.
5. Preparing outgoing mail before getting final, signed documents from supervisor, so had to redo some of the work.
6. Work area inefficiency, such as losing a file.
7. Walking to billing instead of calling to make an appointment; while there waited thirty minutes for a person before receiving information.
8. Failure to carry through and complete a single task (i.e., stopped billing activity to switch to scheduling a meeting).
9. Performing unnecessary work such as trying to answer Judith's questions about billing procedure when you just learned how to do it.
10. Walking to copier too many times.
11. Did not prepare a to do/did list for next day or use one on this day.

But not everything was bad. At the beginning of the day the mail was gathered, opened, and prioritized; documents were finished from yesterday; and the correct time was allotted for the afternoon break. Phone messages were answered as well. But the time wasters need to be dealt with and eliminated.

AVOIDING TIME WASTERS

If you have trouble sticking to your plans and schedules, you may have to change them. Perhaps you underestimated the time a certain task would take or were uncertain about its priority. Let's discuss ways you can eliminate time wasters.

TIME WASTERS

Lack of Goals   Do you arrive at your desk each morning waiting for things to happen, or do you have some control over what is done during the day? In other words, can you and do you plan your work?

Telephone Interruptions   Are you plagued by ringing phones? If answering the phone is part of your job, then organize your handling of calls. Do you have the information most often requested at your fingertips? Is there a possibility that another worker could share your phone calls?

Procrastination   Avoiding unpleasant tasks is only human. Yet sometimes, particularly when your supervisor is out of the office, this work can be completed. Putting off these tasks does not make them go away. Allow a few minutes each day to eliminate them from your schedule.

Disorganized Work Area   To work efficiently, your desk and its surface must be organized. Use desk organizers and in-out boxes. Keep reference works close at hand. Can you easily reach materials that you use often?

Trying to Do Too Much   Some lesser tasks should be delegated. For example, use other departments for their expertise, and if someone asks you a procedural question and you are not sure of the answer, refer him or her to the correct department.

Socializing   Do not be timid about telling co-workers that you have a lot of work to finish.

Communication Errors   Are your communications error free so that additional correspondence is not necessary to clarify your letters?

Too Many Written Communications-   Not every communication needs to be written and filed for historical purposes. Be selective in letter writing.

Lack of Future Plans   All offices have a slow period now and then. During slow periods do advance mailing lists, file, and prepare preliminaries for peak periods. Anticipate crises.

Incomplete Tasks   Do you find that you cannot complete tasks, and that many are left hanging for hours or even days? Reviewing this work hours later takes valuable time. It is much better to start and finish one task at a time.

Waiting for Information   You may not have control over this time waster. Avoid beginning a task involving incomplete data unless you are working with a long project. Are you waiting for people to give you information in person when you could have made an appointment to see them or they could send you the information?

Tired and Stressed   Start a wellness program so that you are fresh on the job each day.

Telephone Calls

Although answering the telephone will be an important part of your job, there will be times when telephone calls can get in the way of your other work. At such times, you can ask the caller if you may return the call, for example, "May I call you back with that information this afternoon?" Be sure to get the caller's name and phone number and the reason for the call. And do remember to return the call at the time you specified. If possible, share phone answering responsibilities with co-workers so that you can have certain hours of the day to work without phone interruptions.

Voice mail or answering machines can also help eliminate many of the disruptive telephone calls you receive. Messages can be stored in your computer terminal until you are ready to attend to them. You can set aside a block of time each day for responding to interoffice communications.

Interruptions by Co-Workers

Interruptions by supervisors and other co-workers waste time in the same way that telephone calls do. That is, when you are in the middle of a task and someone interrupts with a question or comment, you must stop what you are doing and answer. One way to reduce the number of interruptions is by exchanging some information in writing with your co-workers. Unless you urgently need the answer to a question, you can write a note and wait for the note to be answered either in person or in writing. Or if your office has an electronic mail system, you can send a note to your co-worker's electronic mailbox rather than interrupt while he or she is handling other priorities. Another way is to arrange in advance to talk with your supervisor or co-workers at specific times. You can save your questions for these times.

Socializing

Conversing with co-workers also steals time from your work. This problem is especially troublesome in open area offices. Because these offices have fewer doors and walls to serve as barriers between people, their layouts encourage conversation. Some socializing is acceptable and even desirable because it helps employees understand each other and work together better, but work must take first priority. You will probably find it necessary now and then to say to a co-worker, "Please excuse me. I've got to get back to my work."

Unnecessary Work

Your routine may include unnecessary tasks. One example of unnecessary work is filing papers that should be discarded. Another example is routinely filling in forms with details that your company already has in its database. Analyze the tasks you perform as well as the different elements of those tasks. When you suspect that a task or some part of it has no point, consult your supervisor to see if it can be dropped from your routine.

SOLUTIONS TO TIME WASTERS

TIME WASTERS	SOLUTION
Lack of goals	Use a to do/did list
Telephone interruptions	Use voice mail or an answering machine during your designated work time
Procrastination	Do it first
Disorganized work area	Follow procedures outlined in earlier chapters
Trying to do too much	Say no
Socializing	Avoid the situations and keep your socializing for breaks and lunch
Communication errors	Plan your message
Too many written communications	Determine which method is necessary to communicate the message
Lack of future plans	Short- and long-range planning
Incomplete tasks	Plan times for projects with no interruptions
Waiting for information	Use telephone or voice mail
Tired and stressed	Develop an overall wellness plan

Review the list of Solutions to Time Wasters. There are many options to help people manage time. Obviously, some workers need to block out time for project work as well as time for answering phone messages. Some work in desk organization could help and the ability to say, "I am in the middle of a project right now. Can we discuss this later?" The biggest item that has to be completed first is a calendar or schedule on a daily, weekly, and monthly basis.

A master schedule is needed to show the best time to accomplish tasks. Taking into account the list of time wasters, this person's master weekly schedule may look like the one in figure 7.3. This schedule should be placed in sight so that when adding activities to the day, the items listed are rescheduled for a later time. Long-term planning is effective with the use of wall calendars or desktop calendars. Following is a list of activities that might appear on a long-range three-month calendar:

Quarterly meeting; annual report due; seminar planning; seminar dates; supervisor vacation; your own vacation; attending a technology workshop.

After the master schedule is prepared the most important tool is a list of prioritized activities called a **to do.** Figure 7.4 gives

Time	Monday	Tuesday	Wednesday	Thursday	Friday
8:00	Check list mail	Check list mail	Check list mail	Check list mail	Check list mail
8:30	Collect materials for daily list	Collect materials for daily list	Collect materials for daily list	Collect materials for daily list	Collect materials for daily list
9:00	Project work	Project work	Project work	Project work	Project work
9:30	Project work	Project work	Project work	Project work	Project work
10:00	15-min. break	15-min. break	15-min. break	15-min. break	15-min. break
10:15	Answer phone mess.	Answer phone mess.	Answer phone mess.	Answer phone mess.	Answer phone mess.
10:30	Project work	Project work	Project work	Project work	Project work
11:00	Project work	Project work	Project work	Project work	Project work
11:30	Project work	Project work	Project work	Project work	Project work
12:00	1-hr. lunch	1-hr. lunch	1-hr. lunch	1-hr. lunch	1-hr. lunch
12:30					
1:00	Answer phone mess.	Answer phone mess.	Answer phone mess.	Answer phone mess.	Answer phone mess.
1:30	Project work	Project work	Project work	Project work	Project work
2:00	Project work	Project work	Project work	Project work	Project work
2:30	Duplicating	Duplicating	Duplicating	Duplicating	Duplicating
2:45	15-min. break	15-min. break	15-min. break	15-min. break	15-min. break
3:00	Prepare outgoing mail	Prepare outgoing mail	Prepare outgoing mail	Prepare outgoing mail	Prepare outgoing mail
3:30	Answer phone mess.	Answer phone mess.	Answer phone mess.	Answer phone mess.	Answer phone mess.
4:00	Filing	Filing	Filing	Filing	Filing
4:30	Evaluate day's activities	Evaluate day's activities	Evaluate day's activities	Evaluate day's activities	Evaluate day's activities
	Prepare to do/did list	Prepare to do/did list	Prepare to do/did list	Prepare to do/did list	Prepare to do/did list
5:00	Leave	Leave	Leave	Leave	Leave

Project time is for the following activities:
Document processing
Supervisor instructed activities
Daily duties
Special projects
Meetings

Figure 7.3 Master schedule.

TO DO		Date _8/28/91_		
				COMPLETED
ACTIVITY	NOTES	DUE DATE	Yes	No
Process and distribute monthly report	Mr. Ross wants to add a new section	Wed. 8/31		
Make reservations for Mr. Ross's Denver trip	Leave early a.m. on 8/25 return after 2 p.m. on 8/28	ASAP		
Write thank you notes to conference speakers	Send flowers to Lee Wright for doing keynote speech	Fri. 9/2		
Order supplies	Check to see what's needed	ASAP		

Figure 7.4 Part of a daily To Do List.

an example of such a list. You may find this example very usable or you may use another format. It is important, however, that a formal list be kept each day so that you set the plan; the list must be reviewed each evening before leaving to determine what has been completed and what needs to be finished the next day or can wait until later. A piece of scrap paper works when you do not have your formal list, but transfer the information to your schedule because these small pieces of paper often disappear. All information pertaining to each activity should be listed, such as telephone numbers or information that must be gathered, in order that you do not waste time looking for this information.

A schedule is made to be followed as much as possible. Compare your master schedule to your long-range calendar and your to do list to be sure all activities are completed. You may find that your schedule is thrown off with unplanned activities from your supervisor or others. If that happens, adjust your time and make up the time lost somewhere else. For example, if during your project time on Wednesday morning you are asked to attend an emergency budget meeting with your supervisor, you must put off what you were going to accomplish during this time. But the task will not go away. You may have to move other project work to a later time to finish the task at hand. It is best not to have too many projects started if it is impossible to finish even one of them. But flexibility in scheduling is a must. A rigid schedule can often prevent you from being valuable to your supervisor and others.

If you find that you cannot use your time after lunch for project work, you may need to adjust your master schedule. This is fine; however, do this only periodically. Otherwise, your schedule becomes ineffective because you have not been able to fit into a routine of activities.

These same steps can be applied to your supervisor's schedule. If he or she is unable to manage time well, you may suggest using this technique. After a while, a schedule becomes second nature, just as your class schedule is for you now. You do not have to look at your schedule every week to see where you should be next. You adjusted to your school schedule, and the same adjustment will be needed when you start a new job.

Although we have been discussing your overall time management skills, there are specific things you can do to accomplish individual tasks with more efficiency. Let's look at these now.

 # USING TIME MANAGEMENT SKILLS

 ## ORGANIZING INDIVIDUAL TASKS

Just as following a daily schedule can help you use your time more effectively, working according to a plan can help you perform individual tasks more efficiently. Planning the steps you will take to complete each task will save you time and effort and you will avoid mistakes. We discussed previously the use of daily, weekly, and monthly calendars, or **schedules,** which sets forth a timetable indicating the sequence of work and deadlines. Let's look at how we use them on a daily basis.

Daily Calendar

You may have a daily calendar on your desk or on your computer. Either calendar will divide the workday into segments of an hour or less, so that you can maintain a detailed schedule of appointments and tasks. If someone asks for an appointment, a quick look will tell you when you are free.

Weekly Calendar

Some calendars display a week's schedule at once. On these calendars, too, days may be divided into segments, and there

```
Msgs: New:  0           Feb 07,86  2:38 AM Document: MARKETING PLANS
       CALENDAR for Terry Smith                Date: Mon Feb 10,86
Ev        Time         Type      Location      Rem Rec    Subject
1      9:00 AM-10:30 AM Meeting  Conference Rm. 1         Staff Meeting
2     10:30 AM-11:30 AM Meeting  John's Office            Budget
3      2:00 PM- 4:00 PM Appoint  Starbright Offices       New Ad Campaign




Pick one: (1. Different date, 2. Change display, 3. View or Change, 4. Insert,
           5. Delete, 6. Confirm or Decline, 7. Print, 8. Scheduling) 1
Pick one: (1. Next, 2. Previous, 3. Specific) █
```

Figure 7.5 An electronic calendar for one day is shown here.

may be blank areas for general entries. Many weekly calendars are the size of a notebook, with pages large enough to allow room for detailed entries. Electronic calendars also provide weekly schedules. The advantage of a weekly calendar is that it allows you to see what you have planned for an entire week in one glance. If your boss asks when you can prepare a budget for your department, which will take three or four days, you can simply refer to your weekly calendar.

Monthly Calendar

A monthly calendar assists you in scheduling events such as vacations or long-term projects that occupy large blocks of time. They are also used for noting major events, such as conferences and training programs or time out of the office for vacation and business travel.

Yearly Calendar

A yearly calendar includes events that always occur at set times during the year. Holidays, the preparation of annual budgets and reports, employee evaluations, and conferences are just some of the events that might be listed on a yearly calendar. A yearly calendar is especially helpful to new staff members.

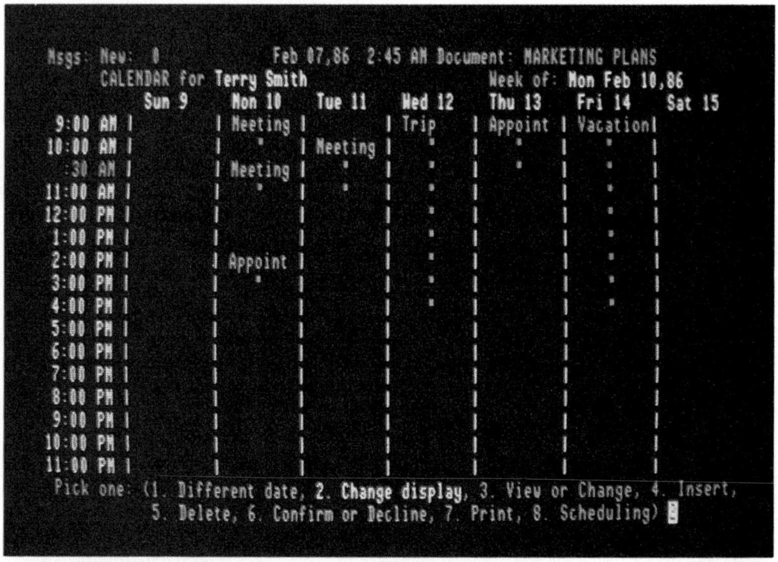

Figure 7.6 This is an electronic calendar for one week.

Tickler Files

Another kind of daily reminder system is the tickler file, which stores reminders and other notes until you need them. One type of tickler file uses file folders and divider guides in two colors. The divider guides in one color are labeled with the months, and one is labeled "Future Years." The divider guides in

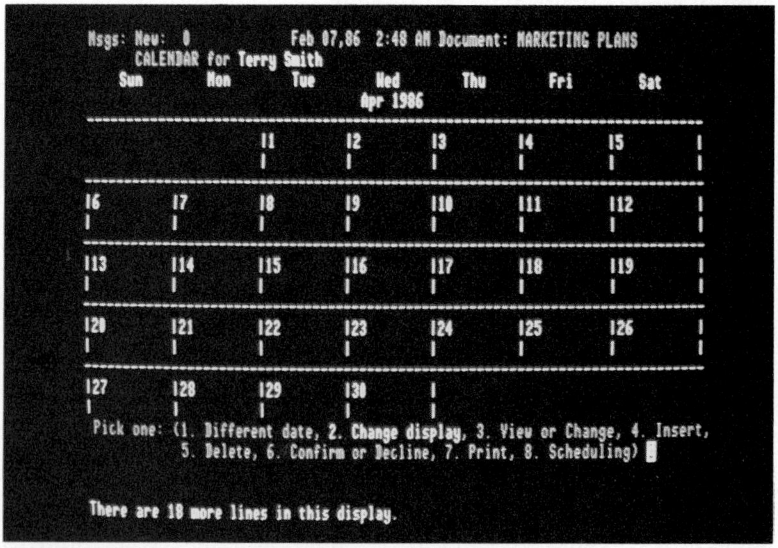

Figure 7.7 This is an electronic calendar for one month.

Figure 7.8 These are the different desk calendars you can use for daily and monthly scheduling.

the other color are numbered 1 through 31, for the days of the month. The divider guide for the current month is at the front of the numbered guide cards, and the other months are behind them.

To use this kind of tickler file, file pages of information under the appropriate dates. For example, if it is June 3 and you need to remind yourself to call a client on, say, June 20, you place a note in the file behind the guide card labeled "20." If you want to remember to make a follow-up call in October, you put a note farther back in the file, behind the card labeled "October." To remind yourself that you should begin to prepare for a conference in March of next year, file a note behind the "Future Years" card. Some tickler files are designed to hold originals or file copies of documents that need follow-up at a later date. These are larger so that they can hold letter- or legal-size documents.

Of course, tickler files are only useful if you remember to check them every day. Computer systems also have tickler files. The advantages of a computerized tickler file is that you do not have to set it up and you can delete items with by simply pressing a key. Figure 7.9 shows an example of an electronic tickler file.

Some more advanced features that may be part of an electronic time-management system are reminders and "things-to-do" facilities. A **reminder facility** automatically reminds the user of upcoming meetings, appointments, or projects. Scheduled items are entered, and on the scheduled day and time the computer screen will display the items automatically. This type of system can replace a manual tickler file. A **things-to-do facility** is an electronic to do list. Items can be prioritized, added, deleted, changed, and reprioritized quickly and easily. The list can also be printed out if desired.

MAINTAINING DAILY SCHEDULES

Whatever methods you use, your calendar and tickler file remind you of what needs to be done each day. To work most efficiently, you also need to create a schedule for the next day's work before you leave the office each evening.

Keep a Desk Calendar

The best manual tool you have for keeping track of your daily schedule is your calendar. In the office you can use daily, weekly, or long-term calendars to record appointments, deadlines for projects, and so on.

If you do not have an electronic calendar, write calendar entries neatly with a pencil so that you can change them easily. If your notes are clear and if your calendar is kept in a convenient place, your supervisor and co-workers can get any information they need about your schedule when you are away from the office. If you use an electronic calendaring system others on the

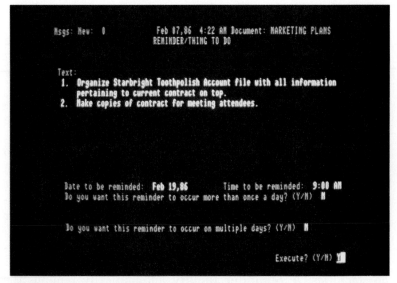

Figure 7.9 This is a reminder that describes what needs to be done to prepare for a meeting.

system will have access to your calendar. Do not make personal or confidential notes on a desk or an electronic calendar. Use it only for business.

Use To Do Lists

If you list all the tasks that need to be done, you can then estimate how much time each task will take. This helps you see how much work you can do in one day. List all pending tasks, not just those you must do that day, but you do not need to list daily routine chores, such as opening mail or sharpening pencils. Delete each task from your list as you finish it, and add any new assignments to your list. Any tasks you do not finish that day go on the next day's list. Keep your list in sight during the day to remind yourself of what needs to be done next and how you can best spend your time.

Set Priorities

Most of the time you will not finish all the tasks on your list in a single workday. If you rank each item on your list by its priority, or its level of urgency and importance, you can spend your time on the most important tasks (refer to the to do list in figure 7.4). To do this, divide the items on your list into these three categories: A for tasks you should do immediately, B for tasks you should do that day, and C for tasks that can be done whenever you have time. For example, arranging to have an important out-of-town visitor picked up at the airport tomorrow morning would get an A rating. Tasks you could postpone for a short time, such as transcribing shorthand notes for routine correspondence, are ranked B. Priority ratings of C go to tasks such as rearranging the books on your shelves, ordering supplies (unless you are running low on them), and putting new labels on file-folder tabs.

Be Flexible

You might have to change your plans during the day. Suppose that an unexpected visitor shows up or that your boss has a sudden "rush" project. You can cope with unexpected events if your schedule for the day is flexible. One way you can allow for flexibility is to rank your priority list by assigning numbers after the letters: A-1, A-2, B-1, B-2, C-1, C-2, and so on. Then you can choose easily among tasks that have the same urgency. Sometimes, however, you cannot be flexible with your schedule. For instance, your boss may need you to finish a special project in one day. In this case you could ask your co-workers if you could rely on them for help with some tasks.

Make Use of Slack Time

It is a good idea to keep a list of things you would like to do in the office when you have extra time. This could include tasks such as consolidating files, rearranging reference materials, and updating procedures manuals. Tasks like these are good for two reasons: they give you something interesting to do in slow times, and when they are done, your regular tasks are easier. Be sure to check with your boss before starting one of these jobs.

Consult Your Supervisor

Your supervisor may want to develop daily schedules with you, or he or she may prefer to check the schedules you make. In either case, consult your supervisor when you have schedule questions or conflicts. If you work for more than one person, it may be difficult to coordinate plans. In general, do the work of the highest-ranking person first unless another person's work is

Figure 7.10 You will need to consult with your supervisor daily and re-prioritize your workload to accommodate his or her needs.

more urgent. You might ask your supervisors to assign a priority to each task routinely.

ANALYZING DAILY TASKS

Each morning spend some time analyzing the tasks on your daily schedule. Make lists of the information, supplies, and other materials you will need to perform each task. Then think about where you will do the work, how long you expect it to take, and what steps are involved.

If a task is complex, write down the steps in the order you will carry them out. Then look at what you have written to see if you can simplify the task by combining some of the steps, performing them in a different order, or delegating some of them. For example, if you are arranging a business trip for an executive, perhaps you can delegate some tasks, such as reserving airplane seats and hotel rooms, to a travel agent. The following are some tips for analyzing and completing daily tasks.

Study Your Instructions

Unless you are thoroughly familiar with the job you are about to do, ask for instructions. Write these down, and study them until you understand exactly what you are to do and how you are to do it. Ask questions about anything you do not understand, but avoid interrupting your co-workers more often than necessary. If the task may be repeated in the future, keep the instructions for future use.

Group Your Tasks

Your plan for the day may include several tasks that involve similar steps or the same location. You can save time and effort by grouping these tasks and doing them all at once. For example, suppose that several tasks on your list involve looking up phone numbers and making calls. If you look up all the numbers and make the calls at the same time, you will spend less time and effort reaching for your telephone directory, address file, and telephone.

Gather Your Materials

Before you begin any task, gather all the materials you will need, and arrange them in the order that you will use them. You will concentrate better and finish each task faster if you do not have to stop in the middle of it to search for supplies, information, or equipment.

SCHEDULING BIG PROJECTS

Your job functions probably will include both small tasks that can be finished quickly and bigger projects that will take some time. Big projects may sometimes seem overwhelming and difficult to plan, but you can make them manageable. There are several ways that this can be done.

Break Big Jobs Into Segments

Divide a big project into segments, and think of it as several small tasks. For example, suppose that you work for an employment agency. Your supervisor wants you to write a report that will help her to do more business next year. The report must include a detailed account of the people the agency placed this year, the jobs they were placed in, and how each match was made. Because this is a large agency and you have other tasks to do as well, the report will take you several months to prepare. You will have to break this job into small segments. For example, first you can make the list of the people who were placed by the agency. Then you can put the list in a format that will allow you to fill in the additional information, such as the name of the company an applicant was placed in and the position the person filled. You can then go about finding and filling in this information. Finally, you can organize the report. When it is done, you will type it, proofread it, make a copy, and give the original to your boss. Each of these tasks is a segment you can handle one step at a time.

Set Short-Term Goals

You can set **short-term goals** for the individual segments of the task. Your success in reaching short-term goals on time will help you to determine how likely you are to reach your **long-term goal.** If you take more or less time than you had planned to reach a short-term goal, you will have to revise your plans. For the assignment to write the report for the employment agency, you might set short-term goals of finishing the first task in two weeks and the second task in another week. If you do not finish the first task at the end of two weeks, you will know that you need to devote more time to that task each day if you are to reach the next goal on schedule.

If you do not reach the first goal on schedule, figure out why. Then you can adjust your plan so that you can finish the work on time. You may need to give higher priority to this project and perhaps devote three hours each week to it rather than two. You may even decide that you are unlikely to finish the job, perhaps because you have more work than you can handle over the next few months. In this case you must decide whether to ask for help with the report or with your other work or for more time to finish the report. Without a plan you would have no way to determine how close you were to completing the report or whether you would need help to get the job done.

ESTABLISHING DEADLINES

Other people may have established **deadlines,** a specified date on which a task must be completed, for many of the tasks you perform in the office. For tasks that do not have deadlines already, set your own. Deadlines can push you to finish tasks that you might put off indefinitely. Also, deadlines help you plan and schedule work. For example, if you know that a letter must be written by next Friday, you can plan time for it more easily than if you do not know when it should be finished. When all your projects have deadlines, you can arrange your schedule so that you finish each one on time.

If you have a big project, you may need to set interim deadlines, which are dates for completing parts of the project, as well as a final deadline for others in your office. Interim deadlines can help you finish the parts of the project that involve other people. In other words, they function like the short-term goals you set for yourself, but they also apply to other people. For example, if you have a deadline of March 30 to complete a quarterly departmental report, you could ask the members of your department to submit interior reports on January 31, February 24, and March 15.

If you and your supervisor faced a November 16 deadline for submitting your division's proposed budget for the next year, you would note the final deadline on your long-term schedule. You would also schedule interim deadlines. For instance, you might set an August 30 deadline for reviewing this year's costs and your supervisor's plans for the division. You might also schedule an interim deadline for budget requests from managers who report to your supervisor. You would enter these deadlines on your long-term and daily schedules too.

Besides using manual methods of time management, there are many electronic time management software programs available to make you even more productive. We discussed these briefly in the chapter on software, but when you begin using time management skills and scheduling yourself and others, you will find these software tools to be very effective.

ORGANIZE WORK FLOW TO SAVE TIME

As stated in previous chapters, it is very important for you to maintain your work area in an efficient manner. If you find that your resource materials are hard to reach or even to find, you will spend many extra hours looking for things or taking extra steps to retrieve information.

Also, as you find yourself using procedures that take many steps, a procedures manual for your job duties would be helpful. If a procedures manual is provided for you, use it. As you are learning your job tasks, leave it open on your desk so you do not miss steps in any given task. After you become familiar with a task, you may no longer need to refer to the manual constantly; but always remember it is available if you need it.

If a procedures manual is not available, create one. It need not be elaborate; but it should contain step-by-step instructions on how to complete tasks in your job. As you complete a task, write down the steps you used. Label the list and place it in a three-ring binder. Then as you go through other tasks, you can add those to the manual as well. If you or the company changes the way a task is completed, you must change the steps in your procedures manual. If you do not, it is not an accurate account of how to complete a task. This reference tool becomes invaluable as new employees are hired or as temporary workers are hired during busy times of the year.

The techniques discussed in this chapter will make you an efficient office assistant. You will be an invaluable employee as you strive to be productive and help to make others efficient with their work schedules.

SUMMARY

- Doing your job well requires skill in organizing your time, your assignments, and your work materials.

- Careful planning is essential to managing your time well. It can help you finish assignments on time with a minimum of mistakes and frustrations. You will probably use a daily desktop calendar for scheduling, and you may also use weekly, monthly, or yearly calendars. Electronic calendars are also effective means of scheduling.

- Use a tickler file to keep reminder notes on events or responsibilities you must deal with in the future.

- To develop a daily schedule, list the tasks that need to be done, estimate how long each one will take, and then rank each task by priority. Try to develop a schedule that is flexible enough to allow for unexpected events.

- Consult your supervisor when you have schedule questions or conflicts. If you have slack time, use it for low-priority tasks. Avoid time wasters, such as phone calls, interruptions, socializing, and unnecessary work.

- A big project will be more manageable if you break it into segments and view each segment as a short-term goal on your way to the long-range goal of finishing the project. Your progress in reaching the goals on schedule can help you determine whether you can finish the project on time.

- If you set deadlines for tasks, you can manage your time better. For a long-term project, set interim deadlines in addition to a final deadline.

- Analyze the tasks on your daily schedule to see which ones you can simplify or delegate. Study your instructions before you begin each task. If tasks involve similar steps, save effort by grouping them together.

VOCABULARY

- time management
- to do/did list
- schedule
- reminder facility
- things to-do facility
- short-term goals
- long-term goals
- deadlines

CHECKING YOUR UNDERSTANDING

1. What are the steps you would use to set up a time management plan? Why is time management important?
2. How does time management help you to be a more productive worker?

3. What purpose does a to do/did list serve? What is the first step in developing a schedule for each day? Why is this important?

4. What purpose do daily, weekly, monthly, and long-term calendars play in time management?

5. Describe how you would use a tickler file to keep track of a reminder that you want to see on May 15 of next year.

6. If you do not reach a short-term goal on schedule, why is it important to determine the reason?

7. What are some steps you can take to help you get your daily tasks completed more efficiently?

8. Electronic calendaring or scheduling software packages serve a specific purpose in the office. What is this purpose and how do they make the office environment more productive?

THINKING THROUGH PROCEDURES

1. Starting today, write down your daily activities as you complete them. Do this for one week. Analyze your schedule to determine what your priority activities are and what activities are time wasters. Then develop a master schedule to help you organize your time now. Many of you probably already use a calendar to keep track of when assignments are due. This is a good start. Now add to this schedule time for classes, for study, for work schedules, to eat and sleep, and for recreation. After you have this schedule written down, adhere to it as much as possible. You may need to reevaluate your schedule later, especially when this course of study is over and you begin another. Although this activity may not seem important in the office setting, the process you will be using is. You are practicing good time management now so you can perfect it before entering the work environment.

2. You work for a small legal office with two lawyers. They have the following poor time management skills: procrastination of long-term projects, writing every request in memo form, not keeping calendars of upcoming appointments. Write a short memo to them explaining what they can do to improve their time management skills and what steps they need to take now to improve and then carry out their new-found skills.

3. It is your first week on the job. Your supervisor has asked for a status report of all of the activities you have completed this week. Since you now know how to manage your time, you are ready to put a time management plan into effect. The next week you write down your activities and keep all of your past to do/did lists. You are now prepared to write your status report. Given the information below, write a memo to your supervisor describing how you spent your week. Include those

items appropriate to your work hours, not the things you may
have done during your breaks or lunch hours. You decide on
the time spent on each activity that would account for all of
your time (forty work hours).

Monday Calendar and To Do List
Schedule seminar meeting
Prepare outgoing documents
Start billing
Phone friend
Meet with personnel
Meet with accounting department

Tuesday Calendar and To Do List
Answer calls
Work on billing
Staff meeting
Make doctor's appointment
Document processing
File historic documents

Wednesday Calendar and To Do List
Phone sister
Continue to work on billing
Sort mail
Document processing
Seminar planning meeting
Reorganize desk area
Reorganize reference area

Thursday Calendar and To Do List
Sort mail
Document processing
Schedule a new meeting for seminar
Continue to work on billing
Personnel meeting
Reorganize equipment on desk
Photocopying

Friday Calendar and To Do List
Phone Judy for lunch
Reorganize desk area
Finally finish billing (should have taken three
    days)
Meeting with supervisor
Sort mail
Answer phone messages
Document processing

4. A. Using an appropriate technology tool, create a schedule
form that you can use to keep your daily schedule. Enter
the fixed scheduled items and allow room for flexibility.
Once the template is created, you are now able to adjust
the schedule as needed from time period to time period.

B. Using the appropriate technology tool, prepare a timeline
for a long-term project you must complete for this class or
for another class. Begin by breaking the long-term project
into smaller tasks and then assigning completion dates. In
your timeline, include items to be completed, notes or reminders of things to complete for each item or task, and
dates each task will be completed.

UNIT 3 THE WORKPLACE PROBLEM

Part A:

For the past three years Krejci, Read, and Forson has been using the participative approach to management. When departmental problems occur, they form a committee of staff members to study the problem and recommend a solution to the manager involved. When the billing department made their complaint to Thomas Perez, he discussed the concerns at a staff meeting and appointed a committee to recommend a solution.

Put yourself in the position of an administrative assistant at Krejci, Read, and Forson. Mr. Perez has asked you to lead the committee to find a solution. You call a meeting of the committee and you hear the following complaints: the lawyers are inconsiderate and present the billing information at the last minute; frequently the lawyers are unavailable or too busy to answer questions, so the assistant is left alone to figure out discrepancies in billing information; the assistants find it difficult to organize their workday to ensure time for billing activities—sometimes they have to work late because they are overwhelmed with document processing, handling mail, and telephone calls during the day; some assistants say they did not know that the end-of-day billing deadline was "that important." Using the problem solving checklist outlined below, write a memo to Mr. Perez outlining the factors that are causing the problem, and the proposed solutions that you would like to pursue with the committee.

PROBLEM SOLVING CHECKLIST

DEFINE THE WORKPLACE PROBLEM

How does the current billing process work? Who participates in the process? What do they contribute to the billing process in either a productive or nonproductive way?

ANALYZE THE WORKPLACE PROBLEM

What factors are directly or indirectly contributing to the problem? Do all individuals who are involved in the process understand their part in the process? Where does the breakdown occur?

PLAN YOUR PROCEDURE

What information do you need to solve the problem? What is the best method of gathering information using the principles of good communications and human relations skills?

IMPLEMENT YOUR PROCEDURE

What should the new procedure be? Who will have to be informed of the new procedure? What method will be used to communicate the new procedure?

EVALUATE YOUR RESULTS

How will you determine whether or not the new procedure is working? How will you monitor the system to prevent another breakdown in the procedure?

Part B:

Part of the problem that was identified was that the administrative assistants were finding it difficult to organize their workday to ensure time for billing activities at the end of the day. Some of them found that they would have to stay overtime and their morale was not good when entering the data; others felt overwhelmed with the additional task of preparing the billing materials when they were just able to complete the daily document processing and telephone contact with clients during the day. After receiving this information, Mr. Perez felt that he needed to put more effort into helping the administrative assistants improve their time management skills. Using the problem solving checklist, prepare a detailed outline of the types of information and activities that the administrative assistants need to learn to manage time. The outline will then be used by Mr. Perez to set up a staff development workshop on time management.

PROBLEM SOLVING CHECKLIST

DEFINE THE WORKPLACE PROBLEM

What are possible causes of the time management problem?

ANALYZE THE WORKPLACE PROBLEM

Is there a common time management problem or are individuals faced with their own personal time management concerns? Besides the administrative assistants, who else may be involved in this process?

PLAN YOUR PROCEDURE

What options are available to help the employees manage their time better? What tools could be made available to assist employees in managing their time?

IMPLEMENT YOUR PROCEDURE

What is the best means of communicating good time management skills to employees?

EVALUATE YOUR RESULTS

Are the employees able to use the time management information to improve their productivity?

UNIT 4

MANAGING ADMINISTRATIVE FUNCTIONS

POSITION DESCRIPTION

Job Title: Administrative Assistant

Department: General Management

1. MAJOR FUNCTION:

   Responsible for performing administrative support functions for the president, vice president, and controller of the organization. Primary emphasis is on assisting with overall office functions and policies relating to the organization. This assistant will work with other administrative assistants in coordinating document processing, managing office communications, overseeing information distribution, and overseeing storage of workshop and seminar information.

2. SPECIFIC DUTIES

   1. Manage procedures for the flow of information within and outside of the office; manage the office equipment related to these procedures.

   2. Responsible for effective communication procedures for interaction among office workers, consultants, and clients to maintain positive customer relations and maximize productivity.

   3. Coordinate office communications by working with telephone system; coordinate and maintain staff calendars; coordinate business meetings; manage travel arrangements and expense records; develop procedures for effective time management; participate in staff meetings.

   4. Establish procedures for seminar/workshop processing functions, document creation and processing, file management, client database information, and document distribution.

   5. Manage business information relating to functions of organization by managing manual filing system, manage client information, analyze client information, manage record keeping functions for workshop billing, process budgets and other financial information, process and maintain confidential business records.

   6. Assist management in supervisory and managerial functions; process and maintain confidential and general records pertaining to office staff; gather information and prepare visuals for management presentations; help establish office procedures; help train new employees.

THE WORKPLACE SITUATION

Business Seminars National is a national firm that specializes in conducting seminars and workshops for lawyers. The topics of these seminars and workshops vary from new legal procedures to automated database online services available to lawyers. The seminars usually last one day. Business Seminars National organizes the seminars, hires consultants to conduct the seminars, and has employees at each seminar to attend to registration and evaluation materials.

Even though it is a national firm, the home office in Kansas City, Missouri, does not have a large office staff. The staff consists of the president, vice president, controller, and support staff made up of three administrative assistants. The support staff's duties include managing basic office workflow, processing documents (letters, memos, database input), preparing contracts for consultants, working with convention centers and hotels to reserve places to conduct the seminars, maintaining telephone communications, preparing travel arrangements, and serving as the first contact for walk-in clients.

The firm is planning to attend the next meeting of the American Bar Association. They will present workshops on how to conduct legal research using online information services. The administrative assistants are responsible for coordinating the arrangements for the workshops with the branch offices and making the travel arrangements.

DEFINE THE WORKPLACE PROBLEM
  What steps need to be taken to achieve the goal of setting up the workshops and planning for the staff's attendance at the convention?

ANALYZE THE WORKPLACE PROBLEM
  Who is responsible for making the arrangements? What is the deadline for completing the arrangements?

PLAN YOUR PROCEDURE
  What information is needed to complete the tasks involved? Who has the information?

IMPLEMENT YOUR PROCEDURE
  What resources and tools are available for completing the task? What information needs to be communicated? Who needs to receive the information?

EVALUATE YOUR RESULTS
  Was the deadline met? Were all arrangements made satisfactorily?

chapter **8**

COORDINATING OFFICE COMMUNICATIONS

COORDINATION TOOLS

Much of the communication that takes place in an office revolves around scheduled activities such as meetings, appointments, and luncheons. Coordinating these activities is a very important administrative support function, which requires a great amount of organizational skill on the part of the administrative assistant. Not only must you manage your own time, but you must also keep control of your supervisor's schedule and many times oversee the schedules of others around you.

Coordinating office communications also involves receiving and scheduling visitors and keeping individuals within the office informed of activities that pertain to them. There are many tools available to help you with these tasks. In the previous chapter we discussed tools to help you coordinate your time. Those same tools can be used to coordinate others' schedules as well. There are also additional ways for you to keep schedules quickly and easily.

As discussed in chapter 7, desk calendars, wall calendars, and calendars in daily, weekly, or monthly layouts, as well as magnetic and electronic calendars, can help you schedule your and your supervisor's time. You will find that people have different preferences for how they wish to maintain their schedules. Your supervisor will select a scheduling tool that best suits his or her style of time management. You may be asked to maintain your supervisor's personal calendar, but you must also keep a master schedule at your desk to manage schedule changes.

In today's office it is common for an administrative assistant to work for more than one person. For example, in a marketing department, you might work for three marketing managers. Each has a schedule of activities, and one of your duties would be to maintain their calendars, inform them of their scheduled activities, coordinate schedule changes, set up meetings for all of them to attend together, set up meetings for them to attend individually, and so on. When you work for more than one person you have to adjust to each individual's preferences. Most people have developed a way in which they feel comfortable dealing with their daily routine. One of the executives may want to keep her own calendar and inform you on a daily basis what is scheduled, and another may want you to control the entire calendar. Dealing with each of these situations requires organization, communication skills, and the knowledge of the best calendaring tools available today to help manage all of these schedules. One of the most effective of these scheduling tools is electronic scheduling systems.

ELECTRONIC SCHEDULING SYSTEMS

The two types of events that you will schedule most often are meetings and appointments. A **meeting** usually consists of a group of people discussing a common goal. This is different from an **appointment,** which is a time set aside for two people to discuss an issue. Suppose you had to schedule a meeting with ten individuals. The advantage of using an electronic scheduling system is that you can complete this scheduling task in only a few minutes. Using manual methods, you might expect to spend a good part of your workday determing a day and time when all can attend, and you may then need to schedule a meeting room and other resources such as audiovisual equipment. You might find that for the time you established as convient for all the participants, the conference room is unavailable. In this case you find yourself starting the scheduling process all over again—repeating telephone calls, playing telephone tag, and so on.

Electronic Calendars

Although each system differs in features, all **electronic calendar** systems make it easy to organize items and manage office resources. With such a system, you can record appointments, reserve office resources, and update and modify calendar events electronically. Some systems even have reminder facilities that can remind the user of upcoming events automatically.

With an electronic system, you indicate to the system the meeting's participants and the date, time, and length of the meeting. The system automatically surveys the electronic calendar of each individual, whether there are two or twenty. If a participant or resource is not available for the stated date and time, you are notified. You can then decide whether to go ahead and schedule the meeting or, if those unavailable are crucial to the meeting, request that the system determine the earliest possible date and time when all the participants and resources are available.

To illustrate this, let's assume that Patty Curran, administrative assistant to Jack Thompson, president of Thompson and Kelly Advertising, needs to schedule a meeting of the seven top executives of the firm. These include Jack Thompson, three vice-presidents, two assistant vice-presidents, and the controller. Mr. Thompson would like the meeting to be held in the executive conference room on Tuesday, February 18, from 2 to 5 P.M. He will need a slide projector and an overhead projector.

Using the electronic calendar on her system, Patty keys in the information as shown in figure 8.1. Different systems may display information in a different format and offer different options. After keying in the information, Patty asks the system to execute her request. The system checks the calendar of each individual and resource needed. If all are available, at the stated date and time the system indicates this, and Patty can schedule the meeting. However, as shown in figure 8.2, conflicts exist.

Patty sees that three of the seven individuals needed for the meeting are unavailable. In this particular case Patty knows that the presence of all seven individuals is required. If, how-

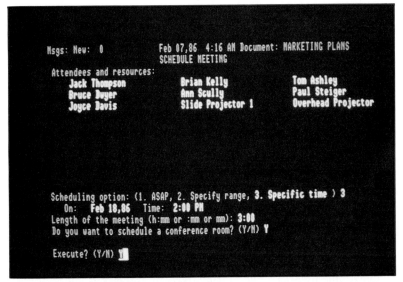

Figure 8.1 This screen shows the people and the equipment needed for the meeting to discuss marketing plans.

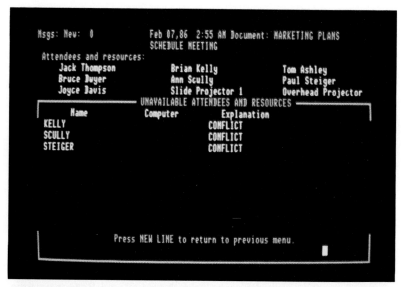

Figure 8.2 The program responds to the meeting request by indicating that three of the people who should attend the meeting have something else scheduled at the requested time.

ever, she was scheduling a meeting for twenty individuals and only three could not attend, she might decide to go ahead and schedule the meeting anyway if the unavailable individuals were not critical to the meeting. Conflicts should be evaluated on a case-by-case basis. Personal judgment is needed in making each decision.

Since Patty wants all seven individuals to attend, she requests that the system determine the earliest possible date and time when all seven are available for the meeting by choosing the ASAP (as soon as possible) scheduling option. After she does this, the system indicates the next available time period of three hours when all the individuals and resources are available. This is illustrated in figure 8.3. Now that the system has determined that February 19 at 1 P.M. is suitable for all the attendees and resources, Patty can continue the scheduling process. Keep in mind that everything illustrated from the beginning of this scheduling session takes only a few minutes to complete.

After she completes the scheduling session, Patty is given the option of providing a detailed description of the purpose of the meeting. This will serve as a reference for the attendees, and it can be accessed when each person views his or her own calendar entry for the meeting. Figure 8.4 shows what the description screen looks like.

Once the meeting description is completed, the calendar reserves the resources requested and inserts the meeting event in

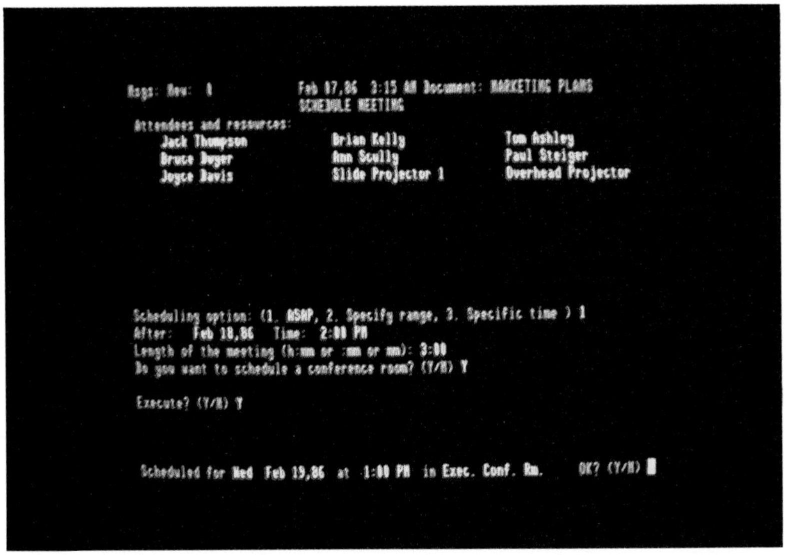

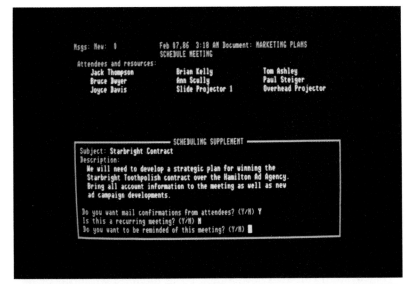

Figure 8.3 Since the meeting could not be held on February 18 at 2 p.m. the computer found the first available block of three hours when all the participants could attend.

each attendee's calendar automatically. Since Patty requested confirmation from the attendees, she will get a message in her electronic mailbox from each attendee as to whether he or she will attend the meeting. The meeting event in each attendee's calendar is a tentative notation until it is confirmed or declined.

Figure 8.4 A detailed message describing the purpose of the meeting is provided for the attendees.

If an individual must decline the meeting because of previous commitments not yet in his or her electronic calendar, Patty may then need to reschedule the meeting. It is important to remember, however, that whenever this happens, it takes a short time. There is no need for repeated telephone calls and follow-up.

Modifying Calendar Events

Often you will need to change the time of appointments, adjust meeting dates, or reschedule events to reflect the changing needs of your office. Electronic calendaring and scheduling systems make it easy not only to schedule events but to modify and update those events as well. All information pertaining to each event is stored electronically in the calendar, and so it is easy to make changes.

For example, individuals who spend much of their time out of the office will find it necessary to carry a pocket calendar for scheduling appointments. This is easier than calling the office to confirm free time on their electronic calendars every time there is a need to schedule an event. These individuals should be urged to provide you with their schedules on a daily basis so that you can update the electronic calendars accordingly. In this way, staff members in the office who need to schedule time with these individuals can still use the electronic calendar system without creating schedule conflicts.

USING PROJECT MANAGEMENT SOFTWARE

Many of the meetings that take place in the office involve the planning and monitoring of projects. **Project management software,** sometimes also called **groupware,** can be used to schedule projects as well as keep daily and monthly calendars. In the previous chapter we discussed planning your projects and completing them in small increments. Project management software keeps track of ongoing projects and allows you to integrate project management information into your calendar. Project management entails determining the beginning and ending point of a project and all the steps in between. You can keep track of who is responsible for specific project functions and tasks, procedures or documentation that accompany each phase of the project, notes on the progress of the project, and new information that may have an effect on the outcome of the project.

The system can also notify each team member when his or her component of the project is due and create reports on the status

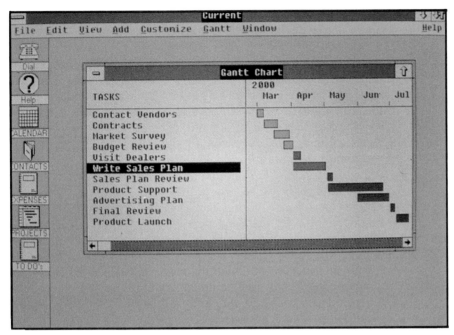

Figure 8.5 This is an example of a screen from a project management software program, listing the tasks and the target dates for completing each step.

of the entire project any time a team member accesses the project file. Figure 8.5 shows an example of a simple electronic project manager.

NONELECTRONIC SCHEDULING SYSTEMS

In a nonelectronic scheduling system, it is more likely that project management records are kept separately from daily or weekly calendaring systems. In a nonelectronic system, the team may schedule weekly meetings at which they will update printed forms used for scheduling and monitoring progress on projects. At these meetings the team will also discuss reponsibilities and make schedule changes. As administrative assistant in this type of situation, you may be responsible for updating and reissuing new schedules to the project team.

To understand how nonelectronic scheduling works, we can compare the scenario of the meeting that Patty scheduled electronically. In a nonelectronic system, there are a variety of ways that Patty can approach the task. One would be to discuss a convenient time and date with her supervisor and then send out a memo to the individuals requesting their presence at the meeting. She would ask for their response as to whether they can or cannot attend by a designated date. After receiving the responses, Patty would then decide whether to keep the meeting at the date set or change it. She may need to consult with her supervisor to find out whether those who cannot attend are essential to the meeting. If the meeting date needs to be changed, then the process starts over all again. This written process could take anywhere from one to several weeks, depending on how long it takes to arrive at a final date agreeable to everyone. Therefore, this procedure should only be used in situations where long-range planning is feasible.

A faster method would be for Patty to call each individual to get the days and times when they are available. Once she reaches everyone, she can select the best meeting time for all concerned. With this method it may take two or three days to reach everyone by phone and determine a date that is convenient for all. Patty should begin calling everyone at least one week ahead of an optimal meeting time, if possible, to make sure she has enough lead time to accommodate everyone's schedule. Once a meeting time and date are established, a follow-up memo should be sent to all participants for confirmation.

Some offices may have an electronic mail system even though they do not have a networked calendaring system. In this case, Patty could send an electronic message to the individuals, asking them to respond quickly to the suggested meeting time and date. Once again, this may require two or three rounds of communication, but if the individuals use their electronic mail daily, the meeting could probably be scheduled within one or two days.

MEETING CHECKLIST

Determine the goal of the meeting.
Determine the length of the meeting.
Determine the priority of the meeting.
Check your supervisor's schedule.
Select a few times when the meeting could be held.

Set the meeting time and date.
Inform the other participants of the meeting and its goals.
Receive confirmation from participants that they will attend.
Prepare materials needed for the meeting.

SCHEDULING FOLLOW-UP

After scheduling a meeting, you need to prepare any necessary materials. On the day of the meeting, make sure that your supervisor is prepared and has everything he or she needs to be most effective at the meeting. Some people like to be reminded about fifteen minutes before a meeting begins in case there are any last-minute things that they need to do. Some electronic calendars have a built-in reminder system, either a beep or a voice announcing the meeting reminder. If an automated reminder system is not available, you may simply step to the door to remind someone of a meeting. Keep in mind that it is very important to get your supervisor's permission to interrupt conversations or other activities. Some supervisors want to be reminded, and others do not. When discussing scheduling procedures, ask your supervisor if reminders are necessary, or if you notice that your boss tends to lose track of time, you might suggest instituting a reminder procedure.

COMMUNICATIONS WITH VISITORS AND CLIENTS

In any organization, good communication between the staff and clients is crucial to the success of business. Poor communication with those outside the organization can destroy a business or, at the very least, the loss of important clients. Many companies have specific policies their workers must follow to ensure that customers and workers are treated well. In some instances these policies are written in a policy manual and distributed to all employees. Other companies may discuss these policies with workers at the time of hire and on an ongoing basis through staff meetings and memorandums.

The competitiveness of today's business environment has caused business managers to reexamine their approaches to achieving success. Out of this reexamination has come a renewed focus on understanding customer needs as a primary aspect of doing business. Many companies are heavily reliant on repeat business and would, in fact, go out of business if they had to rely on a constant flow of new customers or clients. It is the responsibility of every employee to treat customers and clients with respect and to avoid any behavior that might offend. Greeting people with a smile, not keeping them waiting, and making sure they are comfortable may seem inconsequential, but they are not. How you treat people when they come into your company is an important part of their image of the company as a whole. If you are in a situation where no set policies are in place, you must be ready to exercise good judgment when working with clients or customers, making appointments, and communicating with visitors.

Figure 8.6 Taking notes is a good way to make sure that you are able to communicate the nature of a visitor's business.

GREETING VISITORS

Depending on your job and the type of company you work for, you will come in contact with different types of visitors to your establishment. They may be salespeople, community representatives, government inspectors, individuals seeking employment, customers purchasing products, or clients seeking your services. Each must be treated with respect and tact.

Some effective ways to ensure a pleasant interaction with visitors follow:

1. Address them immediately with a cordial greeting such as, "Good morning, may I help you?"
2. Listen closely as they say why they are there; take notes, if necessary, or ask for a business card to use when presenting the visitor to your supervisor.
3. If the person does not have an appointment, see if your supervisor or some other appropriate person has time to speak with the visitor. State the individual's name, the company he or she represents, and the purpose for visiting.
4. If your supervisor wants to see the visitor, take the visitor to the supervisor's office, introduce the visitor, and hand your supervisor the visitor's business card.
5. If your supervisor is not available and you cannot arrange for the visitor to see someone else at the moment, ask the visitor if he or she would like to make an appointment or, if you do not make appointments without your supervisor's input, ask the visitor to call for an appointment. If an appointment is made, gather the same information as if the visitor were meeting with your supervisor immediately.

Screening Visitors

If the individuals in your office normally see visitors only by appointment, you need to make sure that when visitors approach you without an appointment, they have come to the right place and that the purpose of the visit warrants finding someone to see them immediately. Remember that you may be giving them the first impression they receive of the company, and your attitude will determine how they view the organization from this point on. Even if you think the visitors' business is relatively unimportant, treat them with courtesy and suggest they schedule an appointment.

If you encounter a belligerent or nasty visitor to your establishment who has not made an appointment but wants to see your supervisor immediately, find out what the problem is, and try to solve the problem yourself. However, if the visitor shows any signs of remaining unhappy, offer to make an appointment for the person to see your supervisor. If you encounter a mysterious visitor who does not wish to reveal his or her identity, tactfully refuse to announce the visit unless the person gives you his or her name. If the person persists, notify security or someone else in a position of authority. When these situations arise, it is important to avoid becoming irritated or nasty to the visitor. This attitude will only make the situation worse and the problem will not be resolved.

Visitor's Log

In some organizations the policy is to keep track of all visitors by recording each visitor's name and the time, date, and purpose of the visit. Such a record is called a **visitor's log.** This may be done for security reasons or because the organization uses the information for its records or for other purposes. If you work in a department that does not have such a policy, you may wish to put one in place for your own use, particularly if you deal with many unscheduled visitors. A visitor's log is very effective as a historical tool to determine who has visited your organization, when, and why. An example of a visitor's log is shown in figure 8.7.

Vistors Log

Date	Time In	Time Out	Visitor's Name	Company Affiliation
5/5/xx	8:15 am	9:30 am	Suzanne Meinen	Meinen Artists
5/5/xx	10 am	10:45 am	Adam Marohl	ADMIKE Systems
5/5/xx	1:45 pm	3:00 pm	Michelle Chrystal	Chrystal Manuf.
5/6/xx	1:40 pm	2:55 pm	Arthur Johnson	AJ Editing
5/6/xx	3:45 pm	4:40 pm	Brent Kenneth	BK Designs

Figure 8.7 An example of a visitor's log.

MAKING APPOINTMENTS

When scheduling appointments with people outside the organization for yourself and for your supervisor, these appointments must be scheduled so as not to conflict with inside meetings, appointments, and hours that are needed to perform other job tasks. The following guidelines will help you perform this time management task efficiently and courteously.

GUIDELINES FOR MAKING APPOINTMENTS

1. When someone calls to set up an appointment with you or your supervisor, always look at your calendar before making any commitments. This means your calendar should be available at all times in a convenient location.
2. Make a note of the person's name, company, and purpose of the appointment.
3. Ask how long the appointment may take.
4. Schedule the appointment. Get the person's telephone number in case a change is necessary.
5. Identify any special information or materials that need to be gathered for the visitor or for your supervisor to read before the meeting.
6. Confirm the appointment with your supervisor; then write a confirmation letter to the visitor.

GUIDELINES FOR CANCELING OR RESCHEDULING APPOINTMENTS

1. Always call to cancel or reschedule an appointment as far in advance as possible. It is rude and inconsiderate to cancel at the last moment.
2. State the reason for the cancellation or rescheduling. You do not need to go into detail, and never say that something more important came up. Simply state that a conflict has occurred and you will need to reschedule the appointment.
3. Follow up the cancellation or rescheduling with a confirmation of the new date and time of the appointment.

Other scheduling considerations are as follows:

1. Find out your supervisor's preference for meeting times. Some people prefer to schedule important meetings and appointments in the morning hours (between 8 A.M. and 11 A.M.) because this is the time they are most alert and least distracted with the problems of the day.
2. Before you schedule each appointment for your supervisor, find out how much time the meeting is expected to take.
3. Leave some time (at least fifteen minutes) between appointments in case some last longer than expected.
4. When appointments are outside of the office, be sure to leave enough time to travel from one appointment to the next.
5. For outside appointments, record the contact person and phone number next to the appointment in case you need to reach your supervisor in an emergency.

GUIDELINES FOR REQUESTING AN APPOINTMENT

1. When you request an appointment, identify yourself (and the person for whom you are scheduling the appointment). Identify your employer, as well, if you are speaking to someone who is unfamiliar with you and your company.
2. State the reason for the appointment.
3. Indicate how much time you think the appointment will take.
4. Have your schedule (or your supervisor's) in front of you so you can suggest a time or respond to a suggestion from someone else without delay. If the time slot requested is not available, suggest an alternate time.
5. After making the appointment, you may have to confirm it. Do this as soon as possible, in case a change is necessary.
6. Enter the details of any appointment you make: date, time, location, purpose, and the other person's name and title in your calendaring system. Note any additional information that you need to prepare for the appointment, such as files to be reviewed.
7. Confirm the details with the other person to make sure you have communicated clearly.
8. Ask the other person to get in touch with you if the appointment must be changed.
9. If the person is outside of the company, send a confirmation letter to the individual you made the appointment with; if the person is inside the company, send an interoffice memo on paper or electronically.

ORGANIZING THE DAILY SCHEDULE

Your calendar and your supervisor's calendar should always be up to date. It is your responsibility to keep up with all schedule changes and make sure they are recorded. If you make changes when your supervisor is out of the office or away from his or her desk, leave a note about the change or mention it as soon as possible so that your supervisor will not be caught unprepared or waste time preparing for a meeting that has been canceled.

If you use an electronic calendar, you can help yourself and your supervisor to be organized by printing out a copy of the day's appointments and activities, including all notes and the necessary materials for the meetings. Your supervisor can then glance quickly at the schedule for the day when moving from appointment to appointment. All pertinent information (person, time, purpose of appointment or meeting, and notes) will be right there for perusal. If you are not working with an electronic calendar, keep a copy of your supervisor's schedule for the day as well as your own calendar.

Together with the calendar for the day, have all necessary materials gathered, label them for the proper meetings and appointments, and place them on your supervisor's desk. This allows you longer periods of time to work on other tasks, since you are not interrupted to gather materials each time a meeting or an appointment is about to occur.

Scheduling and keeping calendars for yourself and others is one of the most effective ways to manage time and stay organized. By planning ahead and keeping schedules current, you are saved the embarrassment of missed appointments or meetings that last too long because people must run out to make copies of documents or gather needed documents. Your ability to keep yourself and your supervisor organized and on schedule alleviates stress and makes you an invaluable member of the workplace team.

SUMMARY

- Coordinating office schedules is a very important task and requires a great amount of organizational skill on the part of the administrative assistant.

- Electronic calendaring systems save time by checking the schedules of individuals and calculating the earliest available date and time for all parties automatically.

- In addition to setting schedules, electronic calendaring systems have features that allow the user to send messages to all participants, and request answers, as well as attach notes and information to dates as reminders.

- Project management software offers the ability to manage projects and integrate project scheduling with daily, weekly, or monthly schedules of meetings and appointments.

- Project management software can be used to schedule long-term projects including deadlines and interim deadlines. Team responsibilities as well as materials and information necessary for each task are recorded electronically. Changes to the schedule are made easily because the software adjusts the rest of the schedule.

- Greeting clients, salespeople, community representatives, and customers requires tact and a pleasant attitude.

- The impressions visitors get of a company are influenced by the reception they receive when they arrive for an appointment.
- A visitor's log is a historical record of all visitors to the office.
- Visitors should be screened in a cordial and pleasant way. Find out the person's name, company, and purpose of the visit before introducing him or her to the individual to be seen.
- Appointments should be canceled or rescheduled as far in advance as possible.
- Organizing source material according to scheduled events each day contributes to overall organization and job performance.

VOCABULARY

- electronic calendar
- meeting
- appointment
- project management software
- groupware
- visitor's log

CHECKING YOUR UNDERSTANDING

1. Summarize the steps you should take when scheduling appointments for yourself or your supervisor.
2. What advantages does an electronic calendar system have over a manual system? What are the advantages of a manual system?
3. What is the difference between a meeting and an appointment?
4. What additional things can project management software do over just a calendar system?
5. Why is a visitor's log a good item to maintain?
6. What information must you gather when making appointments? Where should this information be recorded?
7. Why is it important to call when canceling or rescheduling appointments or meetings?
8. When is the best time of the day to schedule meetings and appointments for a busy executive? Why?

THINKING THROUGH PROCEDURES

1. As the assistant to the sales director, you have been asked to set up a meeting to discuss the quarterly sales reports. The

personnel involved include the sales director, the board of directors, the chief operating officer, the president, the chief financial officer, and the marketing director. Usually these meetings last one to two hours. List the steps you would take to set up the meeting. Use word processing software to write a memo to the stated personnel announcing the meeting.

2. You have just been hired as a receptionist at the main entrance at a power plant facility. They do not have a visitor's policy in place. Prepare a visitor's log form and attach it to a memo to your immediate supervisor, Edwardo Smith. The memo should describe the process for using the form and the reasons why the log would be useful at a power plant facility.

3. As the executive assistant to an account manager at Sartowski Manufacturing, one of your duties is to screen visitors. An angry client storms into your office demanding to see the account manager. She says that she has been billed incorrectly two months in a row for materials she purchased from Sartowski Manufacturing. Her repeated efforts to discuss the situation by phone were ignored and she wants to take care of the situation now. You are taken by surprise because you are not used to dealing with angry clients. Discuss with a partner how you would deal with this person. Describe your decision to the rest of the class to see if others would deal with the person differently or in the same way. As a group, decide on the best way to deal with an angry client.

4. Using the appropriate technology tool, create a calendar that would fit your scheduling needs. The calendar could be a template of just the days of the month, or it could contain times and areas to write information. Once the calendar is created, use a copy of the calendar and enter in your activities for the day. Each day you are able to use the computer, enter your upcoming activities and print a copy. Get in the habit of doing this on a periodic basis. This process will enable you to move to electronic calendaring systems easily when you are on the job.

chapter 9

COORDINATING CONFERENCES AND MEETINGS

MEETINGS AND CONFERENCES

Business executives spend about 50 percent of their work time in meetings. In fact, they devote more of their time to meetings than to any other single business activity. With so much executive time, and, therefore, so much corporate money, going into meetings, it is important that the time be well spent. In the last few years, companies have turned to outside services called **professional conference planners** (a new occupational title from the *Handbook of Occupational Titles*) to help with planning large-scale conventions or conferences. However, many organizations still use their in-house staff to organize meetings of all sizes.

Meetings come in many shapes and sizes; they range from two people talking informally in an office to two thousand or more people gathered in a hotel for a conference. If such widely differing events have one thing in common, it is that their success and usefulness depend largely on planning.

In this chapter you will learn how to use communication skills to obtain and convey the information you need to arrange a successful meeting. The chapter also discusses the kind of planning needed to ensure that meetings run smoothly. You will learn how to avoid last-minute aggravations that can cause people to lose both time and patience.

Preparation for a meeting involves such tasks as informing those who will attend, reserving rooms, arranging meals, and generally making sure that all the needed seating, tables, and equipment are in place and operational on the day of the meeting. This chapter helps you make sure you will not overlook anything in this important phase and in the other phases such as evaluation and follow-up.

TYPES OF MEETINGS

Companies function best when their employees hold meetings frequently. A carefully planned, orderly meeting is often the best way for members of a group to exchange information, solve problems, make plans, and accomplish their business goals.

Meetings range from informal talks to highly structured events involving panel discussions, exhibits, votes, and other activities. They can last for a few minutes or for several days, and they can involve two or three participants or several hundred. Meetings can be held in offices, conference rooms, auditoriums, restaurants, and conference centers. When people talk about **informal meetings,** they are usually referring to discussions of everyday business activities that take place in an office or conference room. Other meetings which are formal meetings, usually are longer in duration with a large number of people in attendance listening to numerous speakers.

INFORMAL MEETINGS

Most meetings held in the office are informal meetings. They generally do not involve complicated arrangements or scheduling. The three basic types of in-office meetings are staff meetings, project team meetings, and supplier/client meetings.

Staff Meetings

Perhaps the most common in-office meeting is the staff meeting. You may arrange informal staff meetings frequently, and you will probably participate in them from time to time. A staff meeting is generally held in a supervisor's office or in a conference room. It is attended by employees who report to that supervisor. The purpose of a staff meeting is to discuss and solve problems, make decisions, review progress, plan projects, or distribute assignments. Some supervisors meet with their staffs monthly, weekly, or even daily; others call staff meetings only when they need to deal with special problems or unusual circumstances.

Project Team Meetings

Another kind of informal in-office meeting is the project team meeting. Project teams may hold a series of meetings to plan a project and then meet less frequently as the project progresses through various stages of development. Exchange of ideas, monitoring of schedules, and approval of various design stages are among the frequent reasons for holding project team meetings.

Supplier/Client Meetings

An executive may also hold informal supplier/client meetings, either in the office or at a restaurant. A meeting between a law firm administrator and representatives of a company that supplies telephone equipment for the firm would be an example of a meeting in which the executive acts as a client. In the same firm, attorneys might meet frequently with their clients to discuss work the firm is doing for them.

FORMAL MEETINGS

Formal meetings may be held inside the office or at another location. These meetings involve more preparation than informal meetings. Sometimes a special setting has to be rented to accommodate the meeting. Formal meetings of groups such as professional associations or corporate boards of directors usually follow the procedures set forth in *Robert's Rules of Order, Newly Revised,* which is a guide that organizations use to conduct meetings in which they make decisions and set policies. The rules set forth in this book are known as **parliamentary procedure.** Parliamentary procedure is a method of conducting meetings to ensure each participant in the meeting has a voice and vote in the decision-making process. The Senate and House of Representatives at both the national and state levels follow parliamentary procedure. Stockholders' meetings are examples of where parliamentary procedure is used in business. Formal meetings can follow other formats as well.

The basic types of formal meetings are seminars, conventions, conferences, and official meetings.

Seminars and Workshops

Seminars usually are held to involve participants in learning the information presented. Seminars or workshops can last an entire day or even days. These may be training sessions for em-

LEADING AND PARTICIPATING IN MEETINGS

You can learn to conduct and participate in formal meetings by studying *Robert's Rules of Order, Newly Revised*. In addition, keep these guidelines in mind, whether your meeting is formal or informal:

- Every meeting should have a clearly defined purpose.
- A meeting should start promptly and be adjourned as soon as the group finishes its business.
- An agenda should be followed. Only one topic at a time should be discussed, and each discussion should be finished before discussion of the next topic begins.

- Discussions should focus on issues that are of concern to the group as a whole, not on personalities or subjects unrelated to business.
- Participants should speak one at a time and only when the leader of the meeting has called on them. The statements they make should be brief and to the point.
- The person who called the meeting should make sure that the appropriate amount of time is given to each topic and close the meeting on time.

ployees to learn new hardware or software, new techniques of layout and design for desktop publishing, stress management techniques, or any other topics in which the participants engage in active learning. The participants do not simply listen to a variety of speakers as they would in a conference or convention.

Conventions and Conferences

A **convention** is one kind of formal meeting at which members of a large professional group or organization elect officers, establish policies, and exchange information of interest to the membership. Examples of conventions are the annual Business Professionals of America and the Association of Information and Image Management meetings. A **conference or seminar,** on the other hand, is a meeting at which the primary objective is to exchange information rather than to make group decisions. The main difference between conventions and large-scale conferences is that conferences usually do not involve voting, committee meetings, and other official business, since the participants are not necessarily members of an association.

Conventions and conferences are usually held in hotels or in special convention centers, often in major cities or at resorts. The sites for these large-scale meetings often have exhibit halls where vendors display products and services they hope to sell to participants. The displays provide a convenient way for partici-

Figure 9.1 Large conventions are held in convention centers or hotels which offer convention planning support services.

pants to learn about new products in their profession. In smaller meeting rooms at a convention site, individual speakers present research papers or deliver talks on topics of interest to the profession. These smaller meetings may also feature panel discussions, films, slide presentations, and question-and-answer periods. Conventions and conferences help participants find out about technological, legal, political, and marketing developments in their field. For example, at the annual Office Automation Conference, office automation managers can attend panel discussions about new telecommunications technology and other current subjects, and they can view exhibits by information processing equipment vendors.

In addition to official business sessions, speeches, and panel discussions, conventions and conferences often involve social events, such as luncheons, cocktail parties, and dinners. The social events provide an opportunity for members of a profession to get to know each other and exchange useful business information.

Company Meetings

Some companies occasionally have official meetings that are open to their stockholders or, if they are nonprofit organizations, to their members. The elected officials of these groups also hold smaller official meetings more frequently. These meetings are formal, and discussion and decision making are generally carried out according to parliamentary procedure. The kinds of decisions that are made, however, vary according to the organization's purposes and **bylaws,** which are written policies and procedures. Official meetings may be held for special purposes, or they may be conducted annually, monthly, or on some other regular schedule.

PLANNING AND SCHEDULING MEETINGS

Each meeting you arrange will present you with a different set of tasks. Usually, though, the success of any meeting depends on five key elements: defining the purpose of the meeting, gathering information, planning, preparation, and evaluation/follow-up.

DEFINE THE PURPOSE

The first thing to consider when planning any meeting, formal or informal, is its purpose or goal. Once the purpose is defined, then the planning can take place. Usually the goal or purpose of a formal meeting is set by the officers of the organization or a committee designated to work on the convention or conference. The goal or purpose of an informal meeting is usually set by the person leading the meeting. In staff meetings, usually the supervisor of the department or unit determines the goal of the meeting and may ask for input from department members for items that must be addressed to meet the goal.

The next thing to consider when you arrange a meeting is when it will take place and the length of time that is necessary to accomplish the goals. As discussed in the section on time management, any informal meeting should not last longer than one hour. If the purpose of the meeting requires more time, be sure to schedule for that amount of time.

If the meeting is for a small group, you generally find a time when everyone can attend. But for larger conferences, stockholders' meetings, or other gatherings that involve hundreds or thousands of participants, you generally arrange a time that is convenient for the people who will lead them. Keep in mind that when scheduling dates for large conferences or conventions, you must reserve the dates at the location many months in advance (usually up to one year) because convention centers and hotels book these engagements one, two, or even up to five years in advance.

GATHER INFORMATION

You are now ready to gather more specific information about the meeting. These facts include such details as the number of participants, the general format of the meeting (formal or informal), the budget for expenses, and the desired location. Obtaining as much information as possible will make your planning more efficient.

As you begin to arrange a meeting, establish a file folder for any information that will help you plan, prepare for, or conduct the meeting. Or, you may find that scheduling software can help determine timelines for accomplishing all the facets that go into planning a large-scale meeting. Retain all information necessary to document the planning of the meeting, including contracts, or if it is an informal meeting include the correspondence between your supervisor and the client on the matter they will discuss. You may also include information that your supervisor wants to give to the client.

PARLIAMENTARY PROCEDURE

The usual order of business for a group following parliamentary procedure is as follows:

- The presiding officer calls the meeting to order by stating, "The meeting will now come to order."
- The secretary calls the roll (or notes silently who is present).
- The secretary announces whether the attendance constitutes a **quorum,** which is the number required by the group before a vote can take place.
- The secretary reads the **minutes** of the last meeting and asks whether members would like to offer any additions or corrections. If the minutes were distributed prior to the meeting, the secretary asks if the minutes that were distributed need any changes or corrections.
- The group votes on whether to approve the minutes of the last meeting. If

something is incorrect or has been left out of the minutes, the group may vote to amend them. If there are no additions or corrections, the secretary states that the minutes stand approved as read.

- The officers read their reports to the group and give copies of them to the secretary. These are followed by reports from standing committees and then reports from special committees, copies of which are given to the secretary.
- Items of unfinished business remaining from the last meeting are discussed.
- Items of new business are discussed.
- Any new committee appointments are made.
- The group nominates and elects people for any group offices that are open.
- The next meeting date is established.
- The meeting is adjourned.

When planning a large-scale meeting, make notes about conference room reservations, equipment, and supplies that will be needed during the meeting and include them in the folder or scheduling software as well. Check whether you will be asked to prepare handout materials, slides, or overhead transparencies to support a presentation. Make sure that you have an understanding of how expenditures for these items are to be handled.

For a small meeting, prepare a separate file folder for the day of the meeting that contains all the information your supervisor needs to conduct the meeting. Arrange these materials in the order of presentation.

PLAN THE AGENDA

After you have gathered all the information necessary for the meeting, you must put together an agenda or plan for the meet-

---

| UWC | UNIVERSITY OF WISCONSIN-CHIPPEWA
Chippewa, WI 55555-1234 | *Department of Business Education
and Administrative Management
(715) 555-4320* |

TO: BEAM Faculty

FROM: Jack Benson

DATE: April 18, 1992

SUBJECT: DEPARTMENT MEETING

There will be a department meeting on Wednesday, April 25, at 3:30 p.m. in SSS 219. The agenda is as follows:

1. Curriculum Committee recommendation for pass/fail – Dr. Wunsch

2. Summer Seminar – Dr. Hofacker

3. Goals and Objectives for 1992-93

4. Annual Report

Figure 9.2 An informal agenda for a departmental meeting may be a part of the notice distributed to meeting attendees.

ON-LINE INFORMATION SERVICES

Executive Committee Meeting

June 4, 1992

AGENDA

1. Review of marketing plans for ART INFO ON-LINE (Leslie Amato).

2. Review of second-quarter expenditures (George Johnson).

3. Production status report (Randolph Miller).

4. Review of third-quarter creative services budget (Fay Peterson).

5. New business.

Figure 9.3 A formal agenda is typed on a separate sheet which is used at the meeting as a guide for the group's discussion.

ing. An **agenda** is a listing of the activities or the order of business for a meeting. Figures 9.2 and 9.3 show example agendas for an information meeting (such as a staff meeting) and a formal meeting (such as a board of directors meeting). This listing should include all topics for the meeting in the order that they will be discussed. Agendas should be distributed in advance (at least one week) of the meeting to allow all participants the opportunity to prepare.

If the meeting group has bylaws, review them to see if they set forth a specific order for discussing business. If the bylaws do not specify the order of business, or if the meeting group does not have bylaws, check minutes and agendas from previous meetings to see if the group's agenda usually follows a set order.

RESERVE FACILITIES AND EQUIPMENT

If you are planning a large meeting, you will need to create a written schedule of events. This will guide you in planning how many meeting rooms or other kinds of facilities are needed before you reserve the conference site. The next thing to consider is where the meeting will take place. Some formal meetings or informal gatherings are too large to take place in an office. In this case you will need to reserve conference rooms or other meeting places, either on the company's premises or at a hotel or conference center. The meeting place should be large enough to accommodate the group comfortably but not so large that the group occupies only a small corner. A small group may feel uncomfortable in a room that is too large, and the participants may have trouble hearing each other.

If you are making arrangements for a meeting with a hotel or conference center, you may be able to obtain a conference planning guide from the facility. The guide will provide you with basic information, such as sample floor plans, dining and catering information, descriptions of rooms, price lists, and a variety of special information. This material can be very useful, especially if you are not able to visit the facility in advance.

If possible, visit the facility yourself to determine if it is appropriate for the meeting. This is especially true if you are planning a conference or seminar. Check that the room is appropriate for the equipment needed. For instance, if the meeting will include a technical presentation, make sure the room you reserve can accommodate computers, modems, or whatever equipment has been requested and that there are enough electrical outlets and a telephone line if necessary. Also make sure that the room can be made dark enough for presentations using slides, transparencies, or videos.

Your file notes on room reservations and other arrangements should include the following items:

- Descriptions of the rooms, services, and equipment you have ordered.

- The dates when you plan to use the facilities.

- The length of time you will be using the facilities.

- Fees and payment methods.

- The names of the people you made the arrangements with.

- A copy of the letter you sent confirming the reservations.

- Any signed contracts for use of the facility or equipment.

This information will be helpful if you need to make changes in the arrangements as plans for a meeting progress. And written confirmation helps prevent misunderstandings.

You may also have to reserve equipment for an individual presentation. To reserve a slide projector or other equipment that your company owns, follow company procedures. If your company does not have the equipment you need, you may be able to rent it from a dealer listed in the Yellow Pages. And if the meeting is in a hotel or a similar location, you may be able to rent a meeting room that is already equipped for audiovisual presentations.

NOTIFY THE PARTICIPANTS

You will need to notify each participant of the meeting's time, location, and subject. How you notify participants and how far in advance of the meeting you do so will depend on the meeting's size and purpose. There are three basic ways of notifying participants of meetings.

Telephone Calls

For small, informal meetings, notify participants by telephone. These meetings are usually scheduled only a few days before they occur, so make the calls as soon as you find out about the meeting. Voice mail can be used if the individual is not available to confirm the meeting. Ask the person in your message to call you to confirm the meeting. If you are not available, a voice message will be left for you as well. When time allows, meetings arranged by telephone should be followed up with a written confirmation.

Electronic Calendar

If your company has an electronic calendar system you may be able to set aside co-workers' time for your meetings automatically. After you keyboard information about a meeting, the computer will check the participants' schedules and either add the meeting to their calendars or let you know which participants already have plans for the proposed meeting time. When you have set the meeting, the participants will be notified. You may want to ask them to confirm by sending you an electronic mail message.

Written Notices

Because larger meetings involve many people, written notices are more efficient than telephone calls when the individuals are outside of the organization. You can compose a notice, process it, and distribute copies to two dozen participants in much less time than it would take to telephone all the participants. Written notices also reduce the chances of miscommunication. If all the participants are in-house, these notices could be sent to the individuals in the electronic mail system for more efficient use of your time and theirs. Instead of manually distributing individual notices, you would compose one memo and send it to an entire group of electronic mail users within the organization.

A meeting notice will do two things: give notice of a meeting and serve as a reminder. It should state the date, time, place, and purpose of the meeting and give an agenda. Figure 9.4 shows an example of a meeting notice displayed on an electronic mail system. If participants are invited to present items for discussion at the meeting, the notice should request that they notify you of their presentation topics so you can add them to the meeting agenda. Keep a copy for your own files and note the responses you receive from participants.

When you are preparing to send out a meeting notice, be aware of any group bylaws that might affect the content or tim-

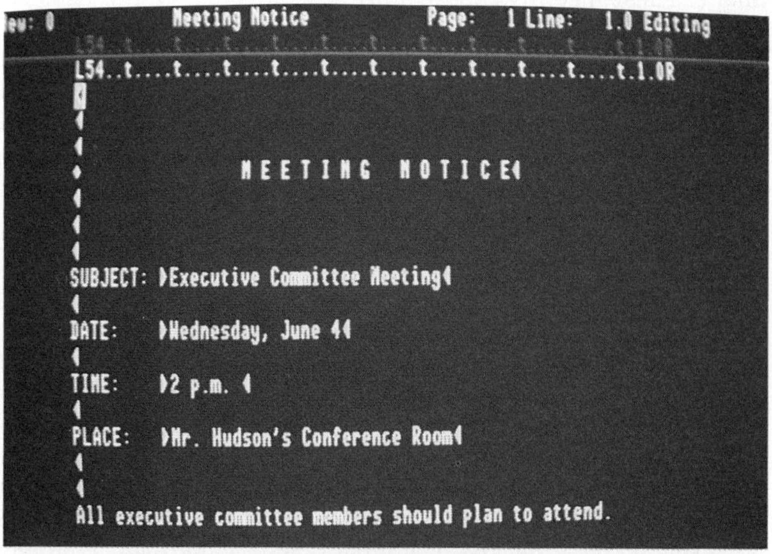

Figure 9.4 If you do not have an electronic scheduling system, you can create a notice form for regularly scheduled meetings. Include standard information and blanks for keying in the date, time, place, and any additional information. This form will save you the time it would take to compose a new notice for each meeting.

ing of the notice. Some groups, for example, have a bylaw that specifies how far in advance of a meeting notices must be distributed. If you are arranging a meeting at which attendance is voluntary, you might also want to ask people to let you know if they intend to come. Then you will be able to let caterers and other people involved in the event know the size of the group they can expect.

You will need to follow up on meeting notices. Some people will respond; others will not and you will have to telephone them. Keep track of all responses in your file. One way to do this is to use a database to prepare a listing of all the participants. Provide fields for the department each is from, when the notice was sent, and the response. As each activity is completed, you are able to indicate the correct information on your database. If a database is not available, divide a sheet of paper into four columns: use one column for the group members' names, one column for their departments or other relevant information, one column with the heading "Yes," and one column with the heading "No." Make a check mark in the appropriate column next to each member's name as you hear from that person.

For small, informal groups, you might follow up your meeting notices by calling the participants a few hours before the meeting and asking if they plan to attend. Explain tactfully that you are making a last-minute check on attendance. Your calls will serve as reminders for the participants, and the information you gather about who will be absent or late will help ensure that the meeting begins on time.

PREPARE FOR THE MEETING

As you plan the meeting, develop a checklist to be sure all activities that need to be completed for the meeting are accounted for. Figure 9.5 gives an example of a checklist.

The day before the meeting, be sure that you have all the materials collected and the necessary copies made, and double check on all other equipment reservations and meal reservations. All items should be gathered and prepared to be transported if necessary. On the day of the meeting, check to see that the room in which the meeting will be held is clean and tidy. Also make sure it has everything you need. Check the following items:

- **Atmosphere** The room should be a pleasant temperature, with sufficient light and ventilation.

SEMINAR CHECKLIST

_____

Meeting Title

Planning Schedule:

ITEM	DUE DATE	COMMENTS

Plan meeting
6 months to 1 year in advance:

    Determine meeting dates
    Prepare budget
    Develop meeting program
    Identify and reserve location
    Contact speakers/presenters
    Create database of participants

Begin the registration process
3 months in advance:

    Complete registration form
    Compile mailing list/print labels
    Determine equipment needs
    Reserve equipment
    Confirm location
    Plan meals

Begin final preparations
2 months in advance:

    Complete participant information
        Program
        Travel
        Accommodations

    Mail registration/information packet
    Reconfirm speakers/presenters
    Make any necessary travel arrangements
    Complete printing of all program materials

- **Furnishings** Make sure that there are enough tables and chairs and that they are set up so that the participants can see each other and projection screens, if used.

SEMINAR CHECKLIST (cont)

Handle final details 1 month in advance:

Prepare on-site registration materials
   Prepare convention "packets":
      Printed program
      Nametags
      Gifts (if any)
      Additional information
Prepare visuals/handouts for speakers

Final preparations 1 week in advance:

Reconfirm all reservations:
   Location/meeting rooms
   Equipment
   Food/entertainment
Prepare materials for transport to location

Notes for day of the meeting:

Figure 9.5 A typical meeting planning checklist.

- **Equipment** If you have requested special equipment, such as a tape recorder, a slide projector, or a computer, check to see that the equipment is in place and works properly.

- **Supplies** Be sure that you have provided paper, pencils, markers, and any special materials the participants need. If the meeting has many participants who do not know each other, provide name tags as well. If smoking is permitted, supply ashtrays.

- **Other Meeting Materials** You might also supply materials that relate to the meeting, such as a list of the names and affiliations of the people attending, copies of the last meeting's minutes, or the agenda for this meeting.

- **Refreshments** Often participants are offered coffee, tea, water, and simple refreshments such as fresh fruit or doughnuts. If tea and coffee are not available in your office, perhaps you can obtain them from the company cafeteria or have them catered.

USING SOFTWARE TO PLAN MEETINGS

You can use an electronic spreadsheet or integrated software to help organize the many separate details of a large-scale meeting. For instance, on a spreadsheet you can label the rows to represent individual expense items, such as the cost of an airline ticket for a speaker and the fee you must pay for a dinner-dance orchestra. The columns represent expense categories, such as entertainment and transportation. When you enter an expense item on the grid, the computer can recalculate automatically the other figures on the grid that are affected. For example, after you enter the cost of an airline ticket, the computer can recalculate the total expenditure for travel, the total expenditure for the conference, and the amount remaining in your budget for travel and for the entire conference. This can help you determine easily whether you are likely to stay within your budget for expense categories and for the whole event or whether you need to adjust your plans.

Also consider how the computer software you use normally can eliminate duplication of work when you organize a meeting. You can use word processing, list merging, database management, graphics, and communications programs to process and distribute the many notices and letters you will handle and record.

SUPPORT DUTIES DURING THE MEETING

You will probably be expected to perform a number of duties while a meeting is in progress. The first of these may be to greet participants as they arrive. Make sure they know where to leave coats and which room to go to. Unless somebody is hired to prepare a transcript of the meeting, you might be asked to take notes. Efficient notetaking requires some advance planning.

Taking Notes

Before the meeting begins, take time to study the agenda, review the previous meeting's minutes, and look over the other materials in your meeting folder to acquaint yourself with the items that are likely to be discussed. The more you know about what is going on, the easier it will be to take notes.

Sit next to the person who will lead the meeting so you can hear everything that is going on. If you miss something a speaker has said, ask the speaker to repeat it, or give the leader of the meeting a prearranged signal that will prompt him or her to ask for a repetition. If you miss a speaker's name, make a note to determine his or her identity after the meeting.

Note the names of group members who are present, who are absent, and who arrive late or leave the room during the meeting. This information may be important for the voting records of the group, especially if the group votes on a controversial issue.

Your notes should cover everything of consequence that occurs, but they do not need to cover everything that is said. If you are not sure if a statement is important enough to be included, take notes on it and decide later. If the meeting is tape recorded, your notes should include any data that are not on the tape, such as the names and titles of speakers and the times when the meeting started and ended. From your notes you will prepare a report or minutes of the information discussed. How to prepare minutes in final form is discussed later in the chapter as a follow-up activity to the actual meeting.

Using a Tape Recorder

Your duties may include operating a tape recorder during a meeting. If possible, set up two tape recorders before the meeting; then you will not have to interrupt the meeting or lose information while you change tapes. All you must do is remember to activate the second recorder when the tape on the first is about to run out. Keep tapes of meetings until the transcripts, minutes, or summaries have been signed by the group's secretary or approved by your supervisor.

Obtaining Transcripts

Stockholders' meetings and some other official meetings often require **transcripts,** which are word-for-word records of everything said during the meeting. Transcripts are generally prepared by specialists who transcribe from tape recordings of the meeting or use shorthand machines to record speeches and then transcribe the shorthand. Transcripts generally have to be approved and signed by the group's presiding officer.

SPECIAL MEETING CONSIDERATIONS

So far this chapter has focused primarily on meetings in which the participants gather in an office or in a conference room. However, some of the meetings you help to organize may take place under different circumstances. To arrange these meetings, you will need to make additional plans and preparations.

MEALTIME MEETINGS

Some meetings involve meals in restaurants, hotel dining rooms, or executive dining rooms. Most meetings such as these take place at lunchtime or in the evening, but breakfast meetings are becoming popular. A small, mealtime meeting usually involves three or more people from within the company who discuss a project among themselves or with outside clients or suppliers.

When you schedule a small, mealtime meeting, you need to make a table reservation. If you are asked to select a restaurant, choose one that offers privacy and where the food, service, and atmosphere are highly recommended by businesspeople. If the restaurant is especially popular, you may need to call days or weeks in advance. Otherwise, you can call an hour or two ahead of time to reserve a table. State your supervisor's name, the number of people who will be at the table, how the bill will be paid, and the time they will arrive. When you note the time of the reservation, include the name, address, and phone number of the restaurant as well as the name in which you made the reservation.

If you would like any special treatment, such as a table next to a window or a small, private dining room, request it when you make the reservation. If the group includes vegetarians or other

Figure 9.6 Luncheon and dinner meetings provide an opportunity to develop positive working relationships by mixing social interaction with business.

people with special diets, mention this to the restaurant staff in advance. Ask about the restaurant's policy on smoking; if it segregates smokers from nonsmokers, specify the area in which you want your table. Also, find out which credit cards the restaurant accepts.

For larger meetings, you must make more elaborate arrangements. For example, you may have to select a menu and organize place cards, flowers, and other decorations. The meeting may include a predinner cocktail hour and after-dinner entertainment, which you might also have to arrange.

Most hotels and restaurants with large dining rooms have employees who are trained in arranging mealtime meetings. They can help you plan the meal, choose the decor, arrange the seating, and deal with many of the other details. Usually they will offer you a number of options, depending on your budget. You would probably discuss the options with your supervisor.

CONVENTIONS AND CONFERENCES

If your supervisor attends a convention or conference, your responsibilities will probably include filling out registration forms, making travel and hotel reservations, and preparing a cash advance. At some point, though, you may be asked to help plan a convention or conference. Since no conventions or conferences are alike, there is no set formula for organizing one. When you plan one of these events, you perform many separate tasks. Because the job of arranging a convention is so complex, you need to be very well organized.

Most large-scale meetings include a number of smaller meetings. There may be exhibit rooms in which vendors display equipment or information about their services. There may also be various speeches or panel discussions in rooms adjacent to the main meeting place. The people who attend conventions and conferences generally divide their time between visiting the main exhibit rooms, or listening to the main speakers, and attending some of the smaller discussion groups and specialized meetings. They might also attend mealtime meetings and cocktail parties.

Planning a convention or conference is like planning several smaller meetings and coordinating them so that they fit together. But several additional considerations are involved.

Budget

You will probably be given a fixed amount of money to use for the convention or conference. Set up your budget on a spreadsheet and allocate amounts for each expenditure. Expenditures might include the rental of a site, speakers' fees, speakers' travel, duplicating costs, telephone costs, meal and refreshment costs, decoration costs, and entertainment costs. Be sure you are aware of each of the amounts allocated. You may have to charge a registration fee or charge for meals so you do not go over budget. Most organizations that hold conferences or conventions do charge a registration fee to cover costs.

Site Selection

Selecting a site for a convention or conference is much more complex than choosing a location for an ordinary business meeting. Conventions or conferences are generally held in resorts or large cities. The meeting sessions and accommodations may all be at a single location, or participants may stay at several hotels near a convention center that houses the meeting rooms and vendors' exhibits.

Most cities and resorts that are suitable for large-scale meetings have convention bureaus. Your first step in selecting a site is to write or call the convention bureaus or resort staffs at the places you are considering. The Chamber of Commerce in the city where you will hold the conference can also provide this information. When you contact the convention bureau or chamber, ask for the following information:

- The names, addresses, and phone numbers of hotels and descriptions of their facilities.

- Transportation between the hotels and the airport and between the hotels and the convention center.

- Weather conditions at the time of year the convention is scheduled.

- Sightseeing and other recreational opportunities.

- The sizes of the meeting rooms.

- Catering arrangements.

- The location of the hotels in relation to the convention center and the downtown area.

- The overall quality of the hotels.

- The number of hotel rooms available at the time you want.

Speakers

You may be involved in booking speakers or members of discussion panels. You can do this by writing letters or making phone calls that explain the nature of the meeting, the topics for discussion, and how long the talks should be. Sources of speakers include speakers' bureaus of colleges and universities, professional organizations, professional speakers' bureaus, and the local Chamber of Commerce or Toastmasters organization. A local library or convention center can also help you locate speakers. Ask each speaker for biographical data to include in publicity for the conference. Also, ask if the speaker will require any particular type of meeting room or equipment for the discussion. Follow up your phone calls with letters confirming the arrangements you have made. Just as with securing convention centers, you must ask your speakers well in advance (six to eight months) of the conference so that you are certain they will be able to participate. Also be aware of each individual's fee and include this in your budget.

Registration

There are several ways to register for a conference. Written notification of conference dates generally includes forms the recipients can use to register for the meetings by mail (see figure 9.7). You may be responsible for distributing or receiving these forms. And you will need to set up a registration desk at the entrance to the convention center for participants who did not register by mail. The people who staff the desk are responsible for collecting registration fees and distributing name tags and packets of information about the conference.

Conference Report

Academic and professional organizations sometimes publish the proceedings of important conferences so members and outsiders can obtain them. These publications are written and edited by specially trained reviewers, and they may contain copies of research papers presented at the conference. You may be asked to help prepare such materials for publication. You will need to obtain copies of speeches and papers presented at the conference, as well as the speakers' permission to publish them, and you may be expected to locate reviewers.

June 10, 1992

TITLE FIRSTNAME LASTNAME
ADDRESS

Dear FIRSTNAME:

The Sixth Annual Business Education Summer Seminar will be held July 11-12, 1992. The theme this year is "What is Business Education in 1992?" The three main topics to be addressed include cross-cultural communication, technology, and business education program definition. You will surely find something to assist you in your program.

Delta Pi Epsilon is once again assisting with the seminar. The DPE banquet on Thursday, July 11, will have an international theme. Pleased use the attached form to secure registration materials. You can also call Credit Outreach at 712-555-2538 to secure registration information. The seminar is available for graduate credit, or you can audit the seminar and secure continuing education units.

Thank you for your support of previous seminars, I look forward to seeing you at this year's program.

Sincerely,

Cynthia Hofacker

BEAM/DPE Summer Seminar – BEAM 796

[ ] Please send registration materials.

[ ] I cannot attend the seminar; but I will attend the DPE Banquet.
$9.25 payable to Credit Outreach is enclosed.

Name: _____

Address: _____

Phone: _____

Send to: University of Wisconsin Eau Claire
Credit Outreach
L1055
Eau Claire, WI 54702

Figure 9.7 For large meetings a registration form can be developed as part of the meeting notice, saving time and costs.

Recordings

There are companies that specialize in tape or video recording meeting sessions at conferences and producing tape or video cassettes to sell to members of the group. This service can be helpful to participants who cannot attend all the sessions that interest them, perhaps because two or more sessions of interest are scheduled for the same time. You may be responsible for arranging this service.

TELECONFERENCES AND COMPUTER CONFERENCES

As you have read, large-scale meetings are sometimes conducted as teleconferences or computer conferences rather than as

gatherings at single convention centers. This enables participants to sit in on meeting sessions without traveling great distances or being out of the office for several days.

Arranging a Teleconference

Even the simplest video teleconference involves complicated
equipment that must be operated correctly. If your company has
its own conference room with technicians and built-in equipment, your duties may be to make the same kinds of arrangements you would make for face-to-face meetings, such as setting
a time and assembling the documents the participants will need.
On the other hand, if you have to arrange a teleconference in
rented facilities, your duties will be more extensive. Always
check to find out if technical assistance is available on site.

If you rent a room at a hotel or conference center, make the
reservation as far in advance as possible, because rooms suitable
for teleconferences are usually in demand. The room you select
should be large enough to accommodate the participants and the
equipment. If you have to set up the equipment or assist in arranging it, be aware that color television requires more lighting
than black-and-white television, and that the lights should be
arranged so they do not reflect from the conference table or other
objects. You may have to experiment with lighting before you
arrive at an arrangement that creates a pleasant setting. Television lights give off a great deal of heat, so you may want to turn
down the room heat or increase the air conditioning before the
conference.

Check with the hotel to make certain there are enough telephone lines to handle your microphones and other transmitting
equipment. If there are not enough telephone lines, you may
have to lease lines from your local telephone company for the duration of the conference. Microphones should be placed in front
of each seat or between every two seats. Some teleconferences
use microphones that can be clipped to clothing or placed around
a person's neck. If loudspeakers are not already installed in the
room, you may have to place some on the walls so that the participants can hear the speakers at the other ends of the teleconference.

The television screen has to be set up so that all the participants in the room can see it. The seats should be arranged so
that participants can see both the screen and each other. The
best seating arrangement has the participants seated along the
outer curve of a crescent-shaped table, with the inner curve of
the crescent facing the screen.

If the camera setup is relatively simple, with only one preset video camera, it may be up to you to load and monitor the camera. You may be required to switch it from speaker to speaker during the course of the conference. If you do have to monitor or operate the camera, you will need special instructions prior to the conference. When several cameras are used at your end of the teleconference, they probably will be set up and operated by a trained technician, but you will need to discuss any special requirements. For example, you may require a camera with a zoom lens stationed so that it can focus on a chalkboard or on a slide projection screen.

A number of devices are available to transmit graphics during a teleconference, such as light pens and graphics tablets (which transmit images to television screens) and electronic blackboards (which transmit images written or drawn on them over telephone lines). If your company uses any of these devices, you will probably need to learn how to operate them. The simplest ways to transmit graphics at a teleconference are to send the materials beforehand; to have a television camera focus on the slide projection, chalkboard, or flip chart; and to use a facsimile machine or computer.

Arranging the scene and the equipment is important, but do not forget to consider the participants when you are arranging a teleconference. If a featured speaker has no experience with teleconferences or television appearances, you might offer to arrange a practice session. That way, the speaker can become familiar with the microphone system and learn where to stand or sit and where to look when different cameras are used. To arrange a teleconference, make sure that the facilities and equip-

Figure 9.8 Video teleconferences require complex planning for equipment needs and setup. Conference sites usually provide personnel with the expertise necessary to assist you in setting up this type of meeting.

ment are adequate and arranged properly and that the participants are well prepared.

If the meeting is an audio conference, your duties could include scheduling and placing calls and connecting all the participants through an operator or a computerized phone system. Also, you may be asked to listen to the conference and take notes.

Computer Conferences

Another way that people can hold meetings without leaving their offices is through a computer conference, in which participants use linked computers to send each other messages. All the participants may be at their terminals at the same time for a computer conference, or the messages can be stored in the computer and read at a participant's convenience. Your role in a computer conference might include keying messages and retrieving stored messages or scheduling the conference and organizing materials.

Teleconferences and computer conferences should be planned in advance so you can distribute background materials to the participants ahead of time. Sometimes you can send documents electronically while a meeting is going on.

EVALUATION AND FOLLOW-UP

After a meeting you generally perform follow-up tasks. Some of these tasks relate to the meeting itself; others may result from decisions that were made during the meeting.

One very important follow-up duty is to prepare a report about what took place at the meeting. The report may be in the form of a summary for the participants of an informal meeting, or it may be an official record of the meeting called the minutes. The minutes are kept in an organization's permanent files. When you transcribe your notes into a report, emphasize the actions the group took rather than what each member said.

PROCESSING THE MINUTES

Most groups keep **minutes,** which are an office recording of the meeting proceedings. In many offices this is not done for informal meetings, such as staff meetings, however, keeping minutes of meetings is always advisable. Even though the minutes may not be disseminated, a record of the proceedings can be kept on file, in case it is needed. If confidential items are discussed, the person conducting the meeting can request that they be left out of the minutes. For informal meetings the chair of the meeting may have the secretary take minutes or request that it be done by a member of the group. If you serve as the secretary of an ongoing group, one of your official duties will be to record its minutes. Figure 9.9 is an example of the minutes of a formal meeting. Figure 9.10 shows minutes of an informal meeting.

Begin the minutes by stating the name of the group, the date,

ON-LINE INFORMATION SERVICES

Meeting of the Executive Committee

June 4, 1992

ATTENDANCE

The monthly executive committee meeting was held in the office of J. R. Hudson, Vice President and General Manager, at 2 p.m. on June 4, 1992. Mr. Hudson presided. Those present were Leslie Amato, George Johnson, Fay Peterson, and Albert Sutton. Randolph Miller was absent.

AGENDA ITEMS COVERED

1. Leslie Amato presented the marketing plans for the new product, ART INFO ON-LINE. It was decided to move the launch date from June 1 to September 1, due to delays in getting the program up and running. The rest of the plan was approved.

2. George Johnson reviewed second-quarter expenditures. All departments were within or under budget for the quarter to date.

3. Randolph Miller presented the production status report. ART INFO is the only major project not on schedule. It was agreed to reschedule it as stated in item 1 above.

4. Fay Peterson reviewed the creative services budget for third quarter. It was estimated that an additional $30,000 would be needed to cover promotional plans for the launch of ART INFO. It was decided that Fay would meet separately with Leslie Amato and George Johnson to develop a strategy for implementing the original plan without going over budget. Mr. Hudson asked Fay to present a report and recommendation by June 15.

DISCUSSION

Judith Smith presented a proposal for a new product that would supply information to businesses on convention sites in the United States and throughout the world. Members of the committee were asked to review the proposal and prepare a response for next month's meeting.

Mr. Hudson requested that each department prepare a report on the status and utilization of microcomputers by all personnel within the department.

ADJOURMENT

The meeting was adjourned at 3:25 p.m.

Figure 9.9 An example of the minutes of a formal business meeting.

place, and purpose of the meeting, its starting time, the name and title of the person who led the meeting, the names of those in attendance, and whether a **quorum** was present. A **quorum** is an agreed upon number of members that must be present in order for a vote to be taken. Also indicate whether the meeting was held according to a regular schedule or if it was called for a special purpose. Next establish that the presiding officer called the meeting and notified members in accordance with the by-laws. The minutes should summarize the group's discussion of each topic rather than quote speakers verbatim. For formal meetings you must include the exact wording of each **motion,** or proposal for an action by the organization such as expending money, that was introduced as well as the names of the people who introduced and seconded it and how the group voted (or why it did not vote) on it. You should also give the details of any ac-

---

Department of Business Education and Administrative Management

Meeting Minutes
September 13, 1992

Faculty present: R. Witowsky, S. Lorenzo, B. Weston, A. Levine, G. Baker,
            L. Merriweather, J. Donaldson, F. Lopez

The meeting convened at 8 a.m. in Room 216.

Ron and Al presented costs and details for the proposed 1993 summer seminar in Scotland. The tentative agenda was distributed and discussed. A motion was made and seconded to proceed with making plans for the Scotland seminar. There was discussion on a minimum number of participants. It was decided that at least 20 participants would be necessary. A final decision on whether to offer this seminar will have to be made by April, 1993. A mailing to potential participants will be made as soon possible to initiate and determine interest.

There was discussion on the summer seminar for 1993. It was decided that we should do the preliminary planning, even though it may not be held if the 1994 summer seminar is definitely offered. It was suggested that an alternate group be contacted to see if they are interested in conducting the 1993 seminar. There was also a suggestion for a general policy change to offer the summer seminar every other year; no decision was reached.

The minutes of the August 28, 1992 meeting were approved as circulated.

The meeting adjourned at 9 a.m.

Linda Carlson
Departmental Secretary

Figure 9.10 An example of the minutes of an informal business meeting.

tion the group took. Acknowledge the efforts of individual members, and mention any correspondence the group received from former members.

Use a professional tone in writing the minutes, and be careful not to write them in a way that reflects your opinions. The purpose of the minutes is to provide an unbiased record of what occurred, so phrases such as "heated discussion" and "thorough and accurate report" are inappropriate.

Devote a separate paragraph of the minutes to each item discussed or acted on at the meeting. The minutes should reflect the activities listed on the agenda. You can group related discussions or actions together if this makes the minutes easier to follow. Transcribe your notes while the meeting is still fresh in your mind. Here are some guidelines to help you format the minutes or the meeting report:

- Capitalize and center the heading that indicates the group's title or purpose, and include subject headings to help readers find information in the minutes.

- Use either single-spacing or double-spacing for the final copy. (Double-spacing makes the report easier to read.)

- Leave generous margins, and indent one-half inch at the beginning of every paragraph.

- Number the pages at the bottom, use a footer in your software, and include the date and filename of the document. And if the minutes are likely to be used for reference at future meetings, include line numbers in the margin (this will make it easier for the group to follow the discussion involving the minutes).

- Capitalize business titles and words that refer to the meeting group or the organization that employs its members, such as *Committee, Company,* and *Corporation.*

- Keep a hard copy of the report on plain white paper.

You may be asked to distribute copies of the minutes before you read them aloud at the next meeting. The minutes of the last meeting are usually approved without comment, but occasionally someone may point out an error or omission. If this happens, use a pen to write in the correction and strike out the incorrect portion. A copy of each meeting's minutes, signed by the secretary, should be filed with the group's permanent records. The bylaws may also require that the minutes be signed by the president.

AFTER THE MEETING

After the meeting or conference is over and you have processed the minutes, there will still be some miscellaneous tasks that need your attention.

Paying Bills

Within a short time after a meeting or conference, you will have to process and pay the bills for meeting rooms, audiovisual equipment, transcripts, meals, and any other facilities or services that were rented or purchased for the meeting. It is a good idea to check these bills against the confirmation letters in your meeting folder.

Processing Correspondence

During a meeting, participants may make decisions or raise questions that require correspondence. Your follow-up work may include writing and processing letters that provide information requested during the meeting.

Processing Resolutions

During an official meeting, a group may adopt a **resolution,** which is a formal expression of opinion or intention it wishes to convey to another group or person. Resolutions are often written before the meeting by the participants who propose them, but sometimes a group will ask its secretary to compose one. The group's secretary—or a support worker on that person's office staff—is also responsible for processing the resolution, having it signed by the group's officers, distributing it, and incorporating it into the meeting minutes.

EVALUATING THE MEETING

An evaluation is another important task when you follow up on a meeting. Review the meeting file, and consider the ways in which the meeting was a success and how it might have been better. Think about any problems that arose and what you might do to prevent or solve them at future meetings. Also, keep notes on any people or businesses that helped to make the meeting a success. These might include speakers, hotels, restaurants, interpreters, and any other person or organization whose services you might wish to obtain again in the future. When you follow up each meeting with an evaluation, you give yourself information you can use to organize successful meetings in the future.

SUMMARY

- The success of any meeting depends on determining the purpose of the meeting, gathering information, planning, preparation, and evaluation/follow-up.

- Meetings range from informal to highly structured formal events. Informal meetings, which generally occur in the office, involve discussions of everyday business. Formal meetings include those that follow parliamentary procedure and large conferences in which participants exchange information.

- Staff meetings, committee meetings, and supplier/client meetings are usually informal. Conventions and conferences are formal, as are official gatherings of ongoing groups.

- Scheduling an informal meeting can be as simple as making a phone call and a calendar notation of the time when all the participants can attend. To schedule a large-scale meeting, you must reserve meeting rooms and other facilities months in advance.

- For each meeting you arrange, keep a file folder that includes copies of confirmation letters and any information that might help you prepare for it. Prepare a separate folder for the day of the meeting that contains all the materials needed for conducting the meeting.

- Notify participants through phone calls or written notices of the date, time, and place of the meeting and its topic or the fact that it is a regularly scheduled meeting.

- On the day of the meeting, check the room where it will take place. See that it is clean, orderly, and comfortable. Also, check any equipment and supplies that will be needed.

- Some meetings require special arrangements. For example, if a group is meeting over a meal, you may need to make a restaurant reservation. For a conference or convention, months of planning will be necessary.

- Meetings generally require follow-up work by office employees. This work may include processing the minutes of the meeting, writing summaries, paying bills, processing correspondence resulting from the meeting, and evaluating the meeting.

VOCABULARY

- professional conference planners
- formal meetings
- convention
- parliamentary procedure
- conference
- seminar
- informal meeting

- bylaws
- agenda
- transcript
- minutes
- quorum
- motion
- resolution

CHECKING YOUR UNDERSTANDING

1. What five elements are essential to the success of any meeting? Select one of the elements and describe what would happen if it was not present?
2. Describe the three types of in-office meetings. Explain how project team meetings can enhance communications skills.
3. What is the difference between a conference or seminar and a convention? Give an example of each.
4. What is the process used to set up any kind of meeting? Is the process like any other processes you have completed so far? What is the same and what is different?
5. To have an effective meeting notice, what information should be included? What actions must you take if you have not received notice from the participants that they are able to attend?
6. What is the purpose of an agenda? How are they used in formal and informal meeting situations?
7. Why are meetings tape recorded? Describe the most efficient way of tape-recording a lengthy meeting.
8. Describe the process used to set up a teleconference. Give specific examples on when a teleconference is appropriate.

THINKING THROUGH PROCEDURES

1. Using the information below, compose a meeting notice to inform members about the next meeting.
   The New Jersey Truck Dealers Association, which has its headquarters at 32 River Road, Stockton, NJ 08559, meets on the first Thursday of each month at 3 p.m. to hear a speaker or panel discussion. This is followed by a question-and-answer session, reception, and dinner. The January meeting will be

held at the headquarters. To make final arrangements for each month's meeting, you need to know a few days in advance how many of the group's members will attend. Your office phone number is 609-555-1017.

2. You have reserved a conference room down the hall from your office for a large staff meeting at 3 p.m. Another group is scheduled to meet there this morning. After lunch you go to the conference room to prepare it for your meeting and discover that it is a mess. The room smells of cigarette smoke and greasy food. The conference table is littered with coffee cups. Your meeting is set to begin in an hour. What are the best options for dealing with this situation? Share your answer with other members of the class.

3. Choose one of the major convention cities in the United States (for example, San Antonio, Atlanta, Chicago, San Francisco, or New York), and use reference materials from your school or public library to find out all you can about the facilities it has to offer. Prepare a report for your class in which you describe the convention center facilities, hotel accommodations, and restaurant and entertainment facilities.

chapter 10

COORDINATING TELEPHONE COMMUNICATIONS

■ TELECOMMUNICATIONS

Some experts estimate that as much as 90 percent of all business is conducted over the telephone. It is easy to see why this is so. It is a great deal faster and easier for an executive or a secretary to place a call than to go through all the steps required to process a letter. Moreover, telephoning allows business people to build and maintain interpersonal relations with people at other companies or branch offices. Now, some 116 years after its invention, the telephone has become the most common and most important communications device in the world, because using it is one of the fastest and easiest ways to transmit messages.

In this chapter you will learn more about how the technology that enables people to communicate with each other directly over the telephone is continually changing and improving. You will learn more about voice mail, which enables you to send and receive messages at any time, and other telecommunications technologies that enable people separated by great distances to share information as if they were in the same room.

In this chapter you will also learn about different kinds of telephone systems, such as key systems and private branch exchanges, and the many features that telephone technology can offer, such as cellular phones, conference calls, and answering machines that help people keep in close touch with their offices and homes. And, perhaps most important, you will learn the basic telephone techniques that office workers need to handle business telephone calls.

TELECOMMUNICATIONS COMPANIES

Telephones are such a familiar part of our lives that we generally do not give them much thought. Until a few years ago, we did not need to give much thought to purchasing telephone service either. Nearly everyone—businesses and individual consumers alike—rented telephones and telephone service from one of the many local Bell telephone companies that made up the American Telephone and Telegraph Corporation (AT&T). Bell was known universally as "the telephone company." If you wanted to call Australia, the telephone company put the call through and added the charge to your monthly bill. If something went wrong with your telephone, the telephone company sent someone to fix it. All that changed in 1984 as a result of a court order aimed at encouraging competition in the telephone industry. AT&T was obliged to give up its monopoly of the industry and divest itself of its local companies. The local phone companies became independent of AT&T, and consumers were allowed to buy their own phone equipment. Although AT&T continues to offer telephones and long distance service, it now has many competitors. Because of the changes brought about by the divestiture, businesses and consumers now obtain telephone equipment and services from a number of sources. They also use different companies for local service and long distance service. The benefits of AT&T's divestiture include many new telephone products and lower prices for some services. On the other hand, many people find it difficult to choose among the services and equipment available.

Figure 10.1A Rotary dial phones like this one are disappearing from offices.

Figure 10.1B Most companies use touch-tone phone systems. This is an example of a programmable touch tone phone with multiple lines.

Many businesses now obtain long distance service from companies other than AT&T. Companies such as MCI and Sprint are among AT&T's best-known competitors, but there are many others. Businesses can determine which of these companies can provide the best service at the lowest cost. They can compare such factors as longdistance rates, the quality of transmission, and the range of services offered.

In addition to purchasing services from AT&T or other long distance carriers, businesses purchase local service from the phone companies that serve their immediate area. The local phone company owns and maintains the service lines to which the telephone equipment is connected, but the local company may not own or repair the equipment itself.

TELECOMMUNICATIONS EQUIPMENT

Telephone equipment is changing along with telephone service. Although nearly everyone still speaks of "dialing" calls, the rotary dial phone has given way to push-button or touch-tone telephones with ten numbered keys plus additional keys labeled * and #, redial, memory, mute, and others used for dialing special codes that provide additional services. You can make calls much faster with push-button phones than with rotary dial phones. And tone telephone lines can serve as distribution/transmission devices for computers.

The connection of computer and telephone networks has increased the volume and the speed of information transmission to levels unthinkable in the past. The speed at which information can be exchanged has changed the way businesses function all

Analog waves or
voice signals

Digital or
Computer Data signals

Figure 10.2 Analog or voice signals. Digital or computer signals.

over the world. More companies do business internationally, and they are becoming dependent on a global marketplace for the growth and expansion of their operations. This is possible because of the telecommunications technology that links people instantaneously, no matter how many miles apart they may be.

Computer data can be transferred in two ways—directly, through cables that link one system to another, or indirectly, through data communications systems that use telephone lines. Computers transmit digital signals and telephone wires transmit analog signals. (See figure 10.2.) Digital signals can be sent directly to the receiving computer from the sending system instead of going through a telephone line. The signals do not have to be converted into an analog signal; they stay in digital format.

Computers can also communicate through the telephone lines with the use of a modem that changes the digital signal to an analog signal so the data can be sent via regular telephone lines. The receiving computer changes the analog signal back to digital information to read and manipulate. (See figure 10.3.) Businesses have the option of installing or renting direct lines for sending computer data or they can purchase the use of telephone data communication services by paying a monthly fee.

VOICE/DATA/VIDEO NETWORKS

The technology and engineering of the telephone cable (copper wire) has advanced to the point where we can send voice, com-

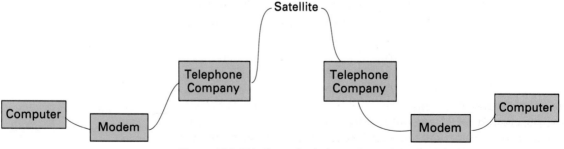

Figure 10.3 This flow chart shows how data flows between computers with the assistance of telecommunications equipment.

puter data, and video signals simultaneously. With a video phone you can see a picture of the person you are talking to, converse as though you were having a face-to-face conversation, and even send fax information during your discussion. **Fiber optic cable** makes this possible. Fiber optic cable consists of very small, thin glass or plastic tubes about the diameter of a single hair through which light signals move. Because light signals are much faster than any other type of signal, many digitized signals can be sent quickly. A regular copper wire can handle twenty-four phone conversations at one time, but fiber optic cable can deal with hundreds of signals at one time. Many telephone companies now use fiber optic cable between major cities, but local companies and homes are not wired with fiber optic cables. When this method of transmission is perfected, you will be able to pick up your telephone, watch a video transmission on your television, and fax data to the receiving party simultaneously.

Today several voice/data telecommunications systems are available that support teleconferencing, voice messaging, and data communications. This allows office workers to send and receive electronic mail and messages or to access central processing systems and databases by simply dialing a telephone number. Many experts believe that computer controlled digital telecommunications systems are or will be the hub of office communications.

TELEPHONE SYSTEMS

Some businesses continue to rent telephone equipment from telecommunicatons companies, but many purchase their own telephone systems. In either case, there are several systems you can use for directing the flow of incoming and outgoing calls, which is also known as switching calls. Two basic types of telephone switching equipment are available today: key systems and private branch exchange systems. As telephone systems are developed further, however, the differences between these systems are becoming blurred.

KEY SYSTEMS

In a **key system** the phones have several keys, or buttons, that represent different phone lines. When the phone rings, one of the buttons lights up. To answer the call, you press the lighted button and pick up the phone. Key system phones also have hold buttons. If you are talking on one line and another line rings, you press the hold button to put the first call on hold before answering the incoming call. If you answer a call for someone else, you can put the caller on hold while using an intercom or a separate telephone line to alert the person being called. A key system has the advantage of letting office workers use any phone in the system to answer calls.

Key system telephones come with a variety of features. One feature is an electronic memory that stores frequently called numbers. If you had to call a branch office several times a day, for example, you could assign a single digit to the branch's telephone number. Then you would only have to press the button for that one digit instead of dialing the entire telephone number each time.

Another feature offers distinctive ringing sounds so you can tell if the caller is telephoning from outside the office, from another office line, or over an intercom line. By pushing a button, you can also use the telephone as a microphone to summon coworkers over wall-mounted loudspeakers. Key telephone systems can be set up so that if one line is busy, a call coming in on that line will be switched to another line automatically. These systems can be programmed to provide background music to entertain callers on hold.

In an organization too small to need a switchboard, a key system may be the only means of directing telephone traffic. In a larger office, key systems may be linked with other switching equipment inside or outside of the organization. The system may, for example, be linked to the mainframe system to provide voice mail services.

PRIVATE BRANCH EXCHANGES

A **private branch exchange,** or **PBX,** can switch calls among the telephone extensions in an office. A switchboard controls the central switching station of a PBX. In a manual PBX system, an operator directs calls. Many offices today have automated private branch exchanges that utilize automatic switching operations known as digital PBXs. With digital PBXs you may reach a recorded message from an operator instructing you how to access other departments within an organization. Toll-free numbers and direct dial numbers provided by companies such as WordPerfect Corporation, Microsoft Corporation, Ford Motor Credit Company, and many others are usually answered by a recorded message directing the caller to press 1 for product information, 2 for technical information, etc., or to stay on the line to be connected with an operator. Each company has a different set of instructions. You must be ready to listen and take the next action necessary to complete your call.

Digital PBXs (as well as key systems or any phone system) can carry the digital signals from computers as well as the analog signals from human voices. A digital PBX can link computers and other electronic equipment into a network, in addition to directing telephone traffic. Digital PBXs offer several features not found on the manual switchboards. With one feature, **direct outward dialing,** you can make outside calls by dialing an access number first. In a manual PBX you have to call the switchboard operator to ask for an outside line. Some PBX systems also have centrex systems. A **centrex system** can work in two ways. If you know the extension number of the person you are calling, you can call that office directly, without speaking to the switchboard operator. On the other hand, if you do not know the extension number, or if you are calling for information and do not have a specific person you want to speak with, you call the company's number. Then the switchboard operator will transfer your call to the right extension. On systems without centrex, all calls go through the general number and the operator.

OTHER TELEPHONE FEATURES

Telephones offer a variety of special features in both key and PBX systems. The features your phone has will depend on the size of your company and how much business is handled over the telephone. Your phone could have computerized features such as call waiting, speed dialing, and call forwarding, which are explained below. Some telephone systems are relatively simple to use; others are more elaborate and may be difficult to use at first because their automated features require you to learn special dialing codes. For example, instead of simply pressing a hold button if a call you have answered is for a co-worker in another office, you may have to key in a code, such as "#4," and then key in another code and the co-worker's extension number to transfer the call. However, most users find phone systems convenient once they have learned their features. Telephone systems can offer more than three hundred features, but most companies use about forty of them. The following are a few of the most commonly used features.

Call Waiting

If you are using your telephone line when another call comes in, a special tone will inform you that you have a call waiting.

You can then either finish the call with your first caller or place that caller on hold while you answer the second call. Businesses ask for call waiting more often than for any other feature of computerized telephone systems. This feature, which is popular on home telephones as well, prevents people from missing important calls.

Speed Dialing

One convenient feature is an electronic memory that allows you to store the phone numbers you use most often. Once you have done this, you can call any of those numbers by keying in a one- or two-digit code rather than the entire number. A button for redialing the last number you called is also prominent on many phones today. This feature is especially handy when you are trying to reach someone whose number is busy.

Call Forwarding

Another convenient feature, call forwarding, allows you to key in a code that automatically forwards all your incoming calls to another number. If you are working in a conference room down the hall or a branch office across town, this feature enables you to receive your calls without imposing on your co-workers.

Conference Calls

Suppose you are talking with a regional manager in another city, and you want to have two other department heads participate in the conversation. One way to do this is with a **conference call,** which is a telephone call involving three or more people. If your telephone has a conference call feature, you can set up a four-way call in just a few seconds. You would ask the regional manager to hold while you dial the two department heads. When you have them on the line, you go back to the regional manager and all four of you can finish the conversation. You can also set up a conference call through the local telephone company by arranging it ahead of time. In this case the operator will set up the call for you.

Automatic Callback

This feature lets you call back somebody whose line is busy as soon as the line becomes free. To do this, you hang up, dial a command code, and redial the busy number. When the line be-

Figure 10.4 Conference calling, a popular feature of computerized telephone systems, allows office workers to confer with each other without having to meet face-to-face.

comes free, the telephone system first calls you. When you pick up your phone, it dials the number you are trying to reach. This feature is particularly useful when you need to reach a very busy office, such as an airline reservation office.

Automatic Route Selection

As you learned earlier, businesses may use several long distance services to save money on toll calls. Many computerized phone systems place long distance calls through the most economical service automatically. Office workers, as a rule, are not even aware that this is taking place.

Call Accounting

Some companies, especially professional offices such as law firms and accounting firms, bill each client for the time spent handling the client's business. Since they may handle a lot of business on the phone, they need to keep track of these telephone calls. Many professional offices are installing telephone systems with call-accounting features in an effort to keep track of phone calls. These systems can also provide the total time spent on phone calls to each client since the last billing and compute the total cost of the bill automatically.

Call Restriction

Some computerized phone systems require users to key in authorization codes before placing calls. This enables organizations to keep track of the calls people make, and it discourages workers from making personal long distance calls from the office.

OTHER EQUIPMENT AND SERVICES

Many businesses today use telephone-related equipment and accessories that add to the functions their phones can perform. Because individuals are very busy and many are out of the office much of the time, other means of communicating are needed. When placing phone calls, many times individuals must wait for the person they are calling. This can be very expensive and time consuming. Executives, for example, may spend up to sixty hours a year on hold on the telephone. This equals about seven working days. Some of the devices you may encounter are cellular mobile telephones, paging devices, answering machines, answering services, and voice mail systems.

Cellular Mobile Telephones

Telephones that use satellite/microwave transmission technology are known as **cellular mobile telephones.** These telephones can be carried in your briefcase. They transmit signals to a microwave station and not directly to a wire system. From the microwave station the signal is sent to the local telephone company, which connects the signal to the person being called. Cellular mobile phones can enhance the ability of a salesperson or executive to connect with clients and the office dramatically. Instead of taking days to make a sale, salespeople are concerned about minutes and hours. The accessibility of voice communications is a necessity.

Cellular mobile phones can be carried wherever the user goes. Antennae and power boxes are installed in cars to boost the signal while driving. These portable means of communications are found on trains and airlines for the convenience of travelers as well.

Paging Devices

Another way that businesses stay in touch with people who are traveling is with pocket-sized **paging devices,** sometimes known as "beepers." (See figure 10.5). A paging device emits a high-pitched sound that alerts the person carrying it that someone is trying to reach him or her. There are several types of paging devices. Some have tiny screens that display messages, such as telephone numbers to which calls can be returned. Others just beep, and the sound is a signal to call the office.

Answering Machines

If you work in a very small office, your employer may have an **answering machine** that answers calls automatically and records messages when no one is in the office. Your job may include recording the message the machine will play for callers when it answers as well as listening to the messages and screening them to determine whom the employer will call and when.

Individuals are often annoyed when they reach answering machines because they may be unprepared to leave a message. A cheerful but professional-sounding message delivered in a friendly tone of voice can help overcome this problem. Your message should identify the business, ask the caller to leave a name, telephone number, a brief message, and the time and the date the call was made. (Many answering machines insert a time and date message at the end of each incoming message.) Your message should assure the caller that someone will call back as soon as possible.

The procedures for recording a message for incoming callers depend on the machine you are using, as do the procedures for playing back messages left by callers. With most answering machines it is possible for the owner to play back messages received by calling the machine from another phone. This feature requires dialing the telephone number and using special codes that instruct the machine to play back the messages.

Answering Services

While some small companies use answering machines to collect messages from their customers, others prefer to use an **answering service.** Answering services are companies that serve as message-takers for other companies who do not have the resources to provide their own receptionist. For example, a one-person plumbing company does not want to miss calls for new jobs, and the plumber wants calls to be answered by a person, not a machine. The plumber would contract with an answering

Figure 10.5 Beepers can be used to transmit messages or to alert people to call their offices from wherever they are.

service and calls to the plumber's business phone number would be forwarded to the service. Periodically the plumber would call in to receive messages so that no business is lost.

Voice Mail

A much more sophisticated automatic answering system is voice mail, or voice messaging. More and more medium-sized and large companies use internal voice mail systems to communicate with traveling executives and with people at offices in other time zones. Voice mail is also used to intercept telephone calls when workers are away from their desks.

Voice mail is something like electronic mail, except that to send a message you use your phone instead of your computer, and the message is stored in the form of recorded words instead of soft copy or text in the computer's storage. A person gains access to his or her voice mailbox to receive messages or change the outgoing message by keying in certain prearranged codes on a touch tone telephone. Assume, for example, that you are a secretary in an office that uses a voice mail system. You will be away from your desk for several hours, so you key in a code on your telephone that sends all your incoming calls to a voice mailbox controlled by a computer to which the phone is linked. While you are away, the computer will answer your phone automatically with the message you recorded, instruct callers on how to leave a message, and record messages of any length. Messages can be left on the system by outside callers as well as by co-workers from within your own company.

When you return to your desk, you can check for messages on your voice mailbox by dialing your authorization code on the phone. You can also use the telephone keypad to instruct the voice mailbox to play your voice mail messages or store them for replay later, to erase the messages, or to forward them to others. When you retrieve a message, you can reply to it immediately, and the system will route your answer back to the sender automatically. You can also add something to a message you have received and send the entire package to one or more other people also on the voice mail network.

No one can listen to messages in your voice mailbox without using your identification code. Also, like electronic mail, a voice mail system can be an internal system, or it can be an external subscription service. Some telephone companies offer this service to their customers.

For employers who can afford a voice mail system, the major advantage is that it can put an end to "telephone tag," the time-wasting and frustrating situation in which two people, who are often away from their desks, repeatedly miss each other's calls. It is also a convenient way for workers who must be away from the office to communicate with co-workers or subordinates.

If your company has a voice mail system, it is important to remember that there is no substitute for the sound of a human voice to a customer or client, or even a co-worker, when trying to reach a company. In an earlier chapter we discussed how each worker is responsible for using technology in a way that does not have a negative impact on human relations. A voice mail system is one area in which it is easy to let the machine talk while you attend to other matters. A call could be just a routine matter— an annoying interruption that will take you away from a task that seems to be more important at the time—but on the other hand, it could be the president of the company frantically trying to reach your boss while transferring planes at a distant airport. It is up to you to exercise your best judgment as to when to use your voice mail system. Remember that it is a tool to help you do a better job, but it cannot and should not replace you on a routine basis.

ANSWERING MACHINE/VOICE MAIL ETIQUETTE

- Write and practice the recorded message before the actual recording.
- The recording should consist of the company name, your department, your first name (for a personal touch), a cordial request to leave a name and a message after the designated sound and the time and date if the system does not automatically record them. Assure the caller that someone will return the call as soon as possible.
- Listen to all recorded messages, manually record the message on paper, and route the messages. If you are using a voice mail system, you may route messages or answer calls electronically as well.
- Return all calls recorded on the system.

TELEPHONE TECHNIQUES

When callers telephone your office, they cannot see you. They judge you and the office or business you represent by the professionalism and courtesy you convey with your voice. This is why it is important to develop the oral communication skills we discussed in chapter 5.

It is also important for you to be familiar with your employer's telephone system so that you do not cut people off accidentally or transfer them to the wrong office. Before you begin using any telephone system, learn the procedures for transferring calls, putting calls on hold, and other operations. Then practice these operations with your co-workers until you can perform them without error.

ANSWERING CALLS

In any office you show courtesy and efficiency to callers by answering calls promptly, on the first or second ring. Answering quickly and with a pleasant and businesslike tone of voice makes callers feel welcome. It also inspires confidence in you and your employer. Always have notepaper and a pencil on hand to take down messages. There is a verbal process to use when answering telephone calls so you do not miss important information. The following guidelines will help you answer calls properly.

Identify the Office

Answer the phone by identifying the office the caller has reached. The way you answer will depend on the preferences of your supervisor. Many executives prefer that you answer with their names first and then your own, for example, "Dr. Bradley's office; Mr. Quinn speaking." Others prefer that you answer with the name of your department and your name.

You may be required to screen calls for a supervisor who does not want to answer every call he or she receives. You will learn quickly which callers should always be put through right away, which you should take a message from, and which you should handle yourself or direct to another office. If you have to screen callers, it may sometimes require tact to identify callers without giving them the impression that you are stalling them. You might say, "Ms. Reynolds is away from her desk at the moment. May I take a message or ask her to call you back?"

Monitor Calls on Hold

Sometimes you will put a caller on hold. You might have to check with a supervisor before putting a call through, or you might have to answer another call. Callers who are kept on hold too long will feel annoyed. So if you leave a caller on hold for more than a few seconds—while waiting for a supervisor to fin-

Figure 10.6 A client's first contact with a business office is often by telephone, so it is important for office workers to develop good telephone techniques and oral communication skills.

ish another call, for instance—keep the caller informed about the delay.

Never pick up the phone and immediately place a caller on hold before giving the caller a chance to identify himself or herself. Always courteously explain to the caller that you need to have him or her hold for a few moments and give them the choice of waiting or calling back.

Gather Information

Sometimes in order to handle a phone call you may need to pull a paper file or retrieve electronic information. If you need to put a caller on hold while you search for information, offer instead to call back when you find it. Then be sure to note the name and number. After you have gathered the information necessary to answer the caller, plan how you will present the information to the caller. Your tone of voice, the organization of your message, and how you answer additional questions will affect how the caller perceives you and the company.

For example, a customer calls to inquire about a bill she has paid recently but your company continues to send collection notices on this bill. You must retrieve her billing file from the database. Once these items are gathered, plan how you will answer her request. You might look over the billing and see that your company has not received the payment. You might also note that the last time payments were posted was two days ago. You are now ready to answer the customer by telling her that your records show that the payment was not received, but that payments have not been posted for the last two days. Therefore, you can request that she call again in two days to check the status of the billing, and if there is still a problem other action will be taken.

Forward Calls

If your supervisor is not available to answer a call, or if someone else can be more helpful to the caller, you might forward the call. This can irritate callers, however, especially those who have already described their requests to several people in your organization.

One way to avoid this is by explaining why another person can be more helpful. You might say, "Ms. Reeves handles inquiries about billing. May I transfer your call to her office?" It is also a good idea to ask if the caller would rather be called back than transferred. If so, get the caller's name and telephone number, try to determine the nature of the caller's request, and tell the caller the name and extension number of the person who will call back. This will save time for both of them, and it will help to ensure that the caller gets a satisfactory response.

If you must forward the call, state the name and number of the person to whom you are forwarding it. The caller can use this information if the call is cut off accidentally or if the number to which you forward it is busy or goes unanswered.

Take Messages

Offer to take a message from a caller when your supervisor is not available. Keep notepaper near your phone for taking messages. Write down the caller's name and telephone number (including the area code) as well as any additional information the caller wishes to leave. Take time to verify the information. Your boss may be embarrassed—and annoyed with you—if he or she returns a call using incorrect information. Always, put the date, the time, and your name or initials on each message so that the recipient knows whom to ask if he or she needs more information. Many offices use standard message forms that can be purchased in any office supply store. These forms remind you to take all the necessary information. Figure 10.7 shows a form with space for the time; the date; the caller's name, company, and phone number; the type of response desired; a short message; and your name.

Be Discreet

When answering a telephone call for someone else, it is extremely important to be discreet when explaining why that individual is not available and when the individual will be available. Some good examples are as follows:

"Mr. Ferraro is on vacation for two weeks. Mrs. Riviera is handling his calls. Would you like to speak with Mrs. Riviera?"

"Mr. Daniels is in a meeting until 2:30. May I take a message?"

"Ms. Wilson is on another call at the moment. Do you wish to wait or may I take your name and number and have her return your call?"

"Ms. Stover will be out of the office until Thursday. Is there anything I can do to help you?"

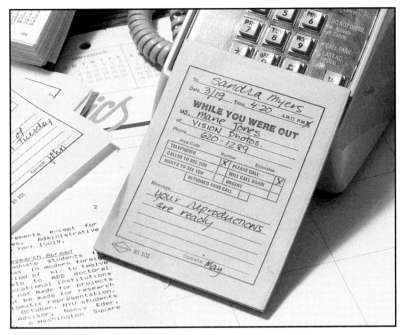

Figure 10.7 These forms remind you of what information you should ask for when taking messages.

Avoid remarks such as the following:

"She hasn't arrived yet." (two hours after the time she should be at work).

"He's left the office for the day." (early in the afternoon). "She is out for coffee." or "She hasn't come back from lunch yet."

These kinds of comments create negative impressions and do nothing to help the caller.

Handle Problem Calls

Some callers can be difficult to deal with or even unpleasant. For example, a caller may refuse to give a name, saying only that the call is personal. If you refuse to put through such a call, you run the risk of offending someone who is important to your company or your supervisor. In general, it is best to put a difficult caller on hold and check with your supervisor before putting the call through. Always be as courteous and tactful as possible with problem callers. There is no set formula for dealing with unpleasant calls, but with time and practice you will become skillful at handling them.

Evaluate and Follow Up

After you have received a call, many times you are expected to follow up on a message or pass the message on to another person. Evaluate to yourself how the call has gone: pleasant with the situation solved; pleasant with the situation unsolved; unpleasant with the situation solved; or unpleasant with the situation unsolved. When you have determined how the phone call went, you can then determine whether or not you need to change how you answer calls in the future.

If you take a message, be sure to transfer the message to the appropriate person. If you promise to forward someone information, be sure that you do follow through and send the information. Many times this is where telephone communications break down. A message is left by a client, but the person who should have received the message never does and the client never receives the requested information. When this occurs your company may lose a client due to neglect.

PLACING CALLS

Outgoing business calls require oral communication skills similar to those used for answering calls. In addition, you need to know how to place local and long distance calls using the public telephone system. We will deal with how to place calls first and then with the oral communication skills needed to make the best impression on the people you are calling. The process you will use to place a call includes the following:

1. Determine whom and why you are calling.
2. Gather the information necessary to complete the call.
3. Plan your call or message.
4. Place the call.
5. Evaluate and follow up if necessary.

Determine the Purpose of the Call

Before placing a call, know why you are calling and whom you are trying to reach. Many times your supervisor will ask you to place a call to a client, for example, so that the supervisor may talk with the client. In this case, you are receiving the "whom" from your supervisor and the "why" includes the fact that your supervisor would like to speak with the client. Sometimes your supervisor will tell you the purpose of the call as well.

When you make a call, sometimes you are not sure of the person's name, but you have a general idea of what department you want to discuss the situation with. For example, you are calling a supplier to check on an order that was to be delivered today. First you determine that you must call the supplier's shipping department, and the purpose of the call is to track down a shipment that your company was to have received. You are now ready to gather the information you need to make the call.

Gather Information

Check the Number   Be sure of the number before you dial. Consult your phone list, a telephone directory, or a phone company information operator. Phone companies usually charge for directory assistance, so if you must use this service, add the number you request to your telephone list so you will not have to ask for it again.

Check Time Zones   If you make long distance or overseas calls, you need to be aware of time zones. Most telephone directories include a map showing the time zones in the United States, as well as lists of overseas cities and their time zones (see figure 10.8). A complete listing of time zones can be found in your telephone directory. If you check the time zone, you will not waste time trying to reach an office before or after business hours. If you are calling someone's home, check the time zone to avoid disturbing people in their sleep.

Have Your Information in Front of You   After you have collected information, whether it is a phone number or a file folder or an electronic file depicting the information you need to discuss with the receiver of your call, you must have this information readily available. Usually you want the actual document such as a shipping invoice at your fingertips so you are able to discuss the situation. In the preceding example, you would gather the phone number of the supplier, the purchase order requesting shipment, and the confirmation you received from the supplier. With all of these documents, you are now ready to discuss with the shipping department how to solve the problem.

Plan Your Call or Message

Before you make a call, outline what you want to say on paper; then check off the items as you cover them in your telephone conversation. This way, you will not forget something im-

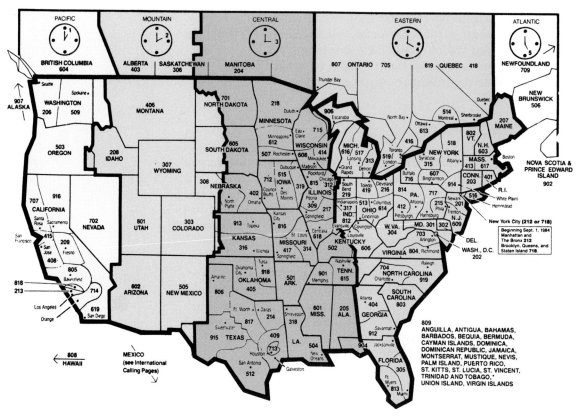

Figure 10.8 It is important to check time zones when making long-distance calls. This map shows the standard time zones for the United States and Canada.

portant. In our shipping scenario mentioned earlier, you would outline the fact that you are calling to check on a shipment and the purchase order number. Also list the shipping confirmation number and the dates of the documents. Check for the shipping terms and the promised ship date. You are now ready to dial the number of the supplier.

Make the Call

You have the number of the company and the information necessary, and you have planned what you will say. You are ready to place the call and respond according to how the person at the other end of the line answers the call and tries to solve the problem. There are a number of other things to consider when placing the call.

Long Distance Options   When you make long distance telephone calls, there are several different ways you can call. Some options are cheaper than others, so check with the company before placing your call. Choose the service that will complete your call most efficiently and economically.

If you wish to speak only to one person who may not be there to answer your call, place a *person-to-person call* by dialing "0" as the first digit of your call. When an operator comes onto the line, tell him or her that you want to place a person-to-person call, and identify the person you are trying to reach. The rates for these calls are higher, but the charges do not begin until you reach the person to whom you want to speak.

When you call *collect,* the person or office you are calling agrees to pay for your call. Again, dial "0" as the first digit. Tell the operator you are calling collect. The operator then checks that the person you are calling will accept your call and asks you to give your name.

Use *direct dialing* if you are willing to talk with anyone who answers. Calls that you place without help from a phone company operator are cheaper than calls that require an operator's assistance, but charges begin as soon as the phone is answered. You can direct dial calls to any place within the United States and to many foreign countries as well.

Telephone companies provide *calling cards* for people to use when they are out of the office but want to charge the call to the office phone. While traveling on business, using a calling card is less expensive than asking the operator to charge the call to a number. Bypassing the operator and letting the system read your card saves time and money and you are assured that it will be billed correctly.

When placing long distance calls, be brief and clear when you state your business. For example:

"Operator, I would like to place a person-to-person call to Ms. Marilyn Thomas, please."

"Operator, I would like to place a collect call to Ms. Marilyn Thomas, please. My name is Mary Smith, calling from Southwest Travel Services."

"Hello, this is Mary Smith from Southwest Travel Services. I would like to speak with Marilyn Thomas, please."

Identify Yourself Identify yourself and the executive for whom you are placing the call to the person who answers (unless you reach the switchboard of a large office). If you are placing the call for a supervisor, you might say, "This is Antoinette Jackson, Dr. Bradley's assistant. I am returning Mr. Black's call for Dr. Bradley." When calling on your own behalf, you might say, "This is Antoinette Jackson from Centercomp, Inc. May I please speak with Mr. Black?" If a switchboard operator answers your call at a large organization, simply state the name or extension number of the person you are calling.

Listen to Recorded Messages Many companies now use voice mail systems to answer telephone calls and switch the caller to the correct telephone extension. Be prepared to listen carefully to what the voice message tells you to do. Many times you will be asked to press certain numbers to access different departments. Each time you press a number, you may be asked a series of questions and you must respond by pressing another number. Businesses use these systems to help route calls automatically.

Avoid Sexism Many people make assumptions about the roles of men and women in the business world. Indeed, many people assume that executives are always men and secretaries are always women. These assumptions are incorrect. If your call is answered by a woman, do not assume that she is a secretary and ask to speak to her boss. Instead, ask for the person who handles what you are calling about. Address all office workers, not just managers, with respect and courtesy regardless of whether they are male or female. It is important to remember that terms such as *young lady* and *girl* or *boy* are offensive and condescending when used to refer to adults, even if you think of these terms as neutral or complimentary.

State Your Business When your call is put through to the person you wish to speak to, identify yourself again, if necessary, and state your business politely in as few words as possible. Depending on how well you know the person you are calling, you might say, "Good morning. This is Rebecca Lasker from Centercomp, Inc. I'm calling about a delivery we are expecting from your company tomorrow," or, "Hello, Mr. Jackson. This is Rebecca. I'm calling to confirm our delivery tomorrow." When you call people you know, of course, you may exchange pleasantries before getting down to business. The idea, though, is to get to the point and deliver your message without wasting anybody's time.

Leave Messages   If the person you are trying to reach is not available, you may want to leave a message. The message may contain all the information you wanted to convey in the call, or it may be a request for that person to call you back. The type of message you leave will depend, in part, on who answers the call. If you wish to leave a lengthy or very important message, try to determine whether or not this would be appropriate. You might ask, "Do you work for Mr. Jones?" or "Are you in Mr. Jones's department?" If the answer is no, it would probably be best to request that Mr. Jones call you back.

MORE ANSWERING/VOICE MAIL ETIQUETTE

- Always prepare your message before calling another person. If you do have the opportunity to leave a message, you will not forget what information you want to tell the person.
- Leave your name, the company you represent, the time and date you called, and a short message of why you are calling.

- Always leave a message. Even if you do not want to leave the reason you called, at least inform the person that you called and you will call later. By calling and not leaving a short message, you have wasted the person's time because he or she must listen to the messaging system beep and then nothing is recorded.

Evaluate and Follow Up

Just as you evaluate the calls you receive, you must evaluate the calls you make. Was the message received? Was the action taken appropriate? Did you solve the problem? Must you take some follow-up action or will the person you called follow up? In the case of our shipment, the supplier may have to trace the shipment with their cellular phone system and return your call immediately to solve the problem. If you do not hear from the supplier within a reasonable amount of time, you may need to follow up with another telephone call. However, be sure to stay with the situation until it is solved and all actions have been taken.

TELECONFERENCES

One use of telecommunications gaining acceptance among electronic offices is the **teleconference.** In a teleconference, people in separate locations use a variety of electronic communications technologies to conduct a meeting.

Increasingly, employers use teleconferences to cut the costs of business travel. Executives and other employees often travel long distances to attend meetings that last only a few hours. For each out-of-town participant in even a brief meeting, a company may have to pay for one or two nights in a hotel, several restaurant meals, and an airplane ticket. Moreover, the participants are taken away from their regular duties for a day or more. Even executives who take portable computers and dictation machines on business trips are less productive away from their files and support staffs.

In a teleconference, managers and other employees can participate in decision-making processes that might otherwise exclude them. For example, a manager might not be willing to send a supervisor to a meeting that would keep her or him away from the office for two days, but that same manager might not object to the supervisor's spending three hours taking part in a teleconference down the hall.

A teleconference can be as simple as a three-way telephone call, or it may involve the use of more sophisticated technologies for the exchange of visual, printed, and spoken information. Let's look at the different types of teleconferences and how they might be used.

AUDIO TELECONFERENCES

An **audio teleconference** is basically a conference call. However, audio teleconferences involving large numbers of people are generally conducted with speakerphones rather than with ordinary desk telephones. A **speakerphone** is a telephone device that amplifies a call for an entire room rather than for one person, and it can transmit voice messages from a roomful of people as well. An audio teleconference can be an economical and effective means of distributing information to large numbers of people and receiving instant feedback from them.

For example, suppose that the Zeppelin Automobile Corporation in Detroit has financial problems and must trim its budget immediately. Through an audio teleconference, Zeppelin's president explains the financial situation to executives at the company's plants and offices throughout the country. Then the president asks for questions and suggestions from the participants. Some of these questions and suggestions could result in ways of cutting costs. Finally, the president orders that several cost-cutting measures be put into effect immediately. As you can see, the teleconference enables Zeppelin's president to receive instant feedback and consider revisions for the cost-cutting plan.

VIDEO TELECONFERENCES

When people talk about teleconferences, however, they are usually referring not to conference calls but to **video teleconferences,** in which participants can see and hear each other over closed-circuit television. You may have seen this technology on television news shows where, for example, a senator in Washington, D.C., might debate with a professor in Boston. In video teleconferences, participants can demonstrate procedures, display new products, and exchange other kinds of information—visual as well as verbal. Using facsimile transmissions or computer communications, they can also exchange hard copies of documents.

A video teleconference may involve two-way video and two-way audio communication, or it may involve two-way audio but only one-way video. In a teleconference with one-way video, one video teleconference room has a television camera, but the video teleconference rooms in the other locations have only video screens. The people in the room with the camera cannot see the other participants, but the other participants can see them.

Some very large companies have teleconference rooms in their headquarters and branch offices. These rooms are equipped with television cameras, large video screens, and microphones, and they may be equipped with other electronic devices such as facsimile machines, computers, and printers.

Several companies rent video teleconference facilities to organizations that are too small to afford or need their own video teleconference rooms but that still want to hold occasional teleconferences. For example, some of the major hotel chains have equipped several of their hotels with teleconference facilities that corporations can rent for meetings and that trade associations and similar groups can use for televised conferences and conventions.

TELECOMMUTING

Telecommunications technology enables many employees to work from their homes using computers and modems to commu-

Figure 10.9 Telecommuting is working at a home-based computer which is linked to the company computer.

nicate with their offices. This phenomenon is known as **telecommuting.** Telecommuters are often more productive workers because they tend to work more hours and experience fewer distractions at home than workers in offices. They also do not expend energy traveling to and from work. Businesses find that they can save on office and parking facilities, and they can recruit workers from among the physically impaired and from distant geographic areas.

Telecommuting does present some problems. At-home workers do not have any social contact with co-workers. Some telecommuters do not have the self-discipline to work without supervision. Even superior workers may be overlooked for promotions and advancement because they have less contact with their supervisors. As more and more businesses turn to telecommuting to keep down business costs and increase productivity, employers and workers will have to deal with these issues as well as with other important issues such as union representation and insurance coverage for employees who work at home.

SUMMARY

- Businesses and consumers used to rent telephones and services through subsidiaries of AT&T, but since 1984 many other companies provide telephone systems and long distance services as well.

- Businesses can purchase key systems with buttons or private branch exchanges with manually operated or automatic switchboards to route company calls.

- Computerized telephones provide many specialized services, such as speed dialing, call forwarding, conference calling, and call accounting.

- Other telephone equipment and accessories include cellular mobile telephones, paging devices, answering machines, and voice mail systems.

- Voice mail is a sophisticated message system that allows users to leave, receive, answer, and reroute recorded messages at any time because the system is controlled by a computer.

- Each time you place or answer a call, you follow a process that includes determining the purpose of the call, gathering information, planning your message, and evaluation/follow-up of the call.

- You need to be courteous and efficient when screening and forwarding calls, placing callers on hold, and taking messages.

- When office workers place calls, they need to be sure of the number, check time zones, plan their calls, and use the most efficient and economical means of placing long distance calls.

- Office workers making business calls should identify themselves clearly, avoid sexism, state their business promptly, and leave clear messages.

- Teleconferences allow people in separate locations to hold a business meeting without traveling.

- Audio teleconferences involve the use of speakerphones so that groups of people at each end of a conference can hear the entire conversation.

- Video teleconferences let participants see and hear each other over closed-circuit television.

- Telecommuting means using computers and telephone equipment to work at home instead of at the office.

VOCABULARY

- digital signal
- analog signal
- paging devices
- answering machine

- modem
- key system
- private branch exchange (PBX)
- direct outward dialing
- centrex system
- conference call
- cellular mobile telephones

- answering service
- teleconference
- audio teleconference
- speakerphone
- video teleconference
- telecommuting

CHECKING YOUR UNDERSTANDING

1. Explain how information is transmitted from one telephone system to another.
2. What are the two main types of telephone systems? Describe their main differences.
3. Name and describe four features a business can purchase with a telephone system.
4. Explain how a voice mail system works.
5. What makes a cellular phone system so attractive to executives?
6. Describe the process you would use to place a call. Answer a call.
7. What is the difference between a conference call and an audio teleconference? When would it be appropriate to use each?
8. Explain the difference between a one-way video teleconference and a two-way video teleconference.

THINKING THROUGH PROCEDURES

1. As the assistant to the international sales vice president of Viking International Hotels in New York, you will make many international telephone calls. All Viking offices are open from 9 a.m. to 5 p.m. in their time zones. The vice president has asked you to set up a conference call with the regional sales directors in the following cities:

    Dallas
    San Francisco
    Mexico City
    Rome
    Minneapolis
    Hong Kong
    Perth
    New York

Write a memo to the vice president informing her of the best time of day to hold the conference call as well as which of the regional sales directors will not be able to participate due to differences in office hours across time zones. Check the phone book and other library references (such as a world atlas) for time zone information.

2. Rose Sanchez is the administrative assistant to sales manager James McFarlain, and it is part of her regular duties to place and take telephone calls for him. On a separate sheet of paper, write a summary of how she should handle each of the following situations.

   a. Mr. McFarlain is attending a sales meeting at a branch office, and he receives an urgent long-distance telephone call from his boss, who is calling from an airport pay phone while waiting between planes.

   b. While she is attempting to transfer a call to Mr. McFarlain, Ms. Sanchez accidentally hangs up on an important client. Ms. Sanchez did, however, record the client's name before transferring the call.

   c. Ms. Sanchez receives a call from a disgruntled client threatening legal action if not allowed to speak with Mr. McFarlain immediately. Mr. McFarlain is in, but with a client and will be for another 45 minutes. He has asked not to be disturbed.

3. Role-play answering and placing phone calls with another person in your class. Take turns being the caller and the receiver as you enact each scenario listed below. Use the process described in the chapter for placing and answering telephone calls.

   a. Caller: You are an angry customer of a department store who has not received satisfactory service on a defective appliance.
      Receiver: You are the customer service representative unaware of the history of this client's situation.

   b. Caller: You are a potential customer calling to receive ordering information on new project management software.
      Receiver: You are a sales representative but your company does not carry this type of product.

   c. Caller: You are a salesperson calling to speak with a purchasing agent.
      Receiver: You are the administrative assistant to the purchasing agent who has instructed you to screen all calls and not disturb her during the next two hours.

4. Using a tape recorder or writing in a notebook, construct messages you would leave in the following situations if your call were answered by a voice mail system or an answering ma-

chine. You are the executive assistant to the president of Konopski Manufacturing. Before you begin, look over the steps in the chapter on how to prepare and leave good messages.

a. You are calling for the president of the company, Marilee Konopski, to set up a meeting with Thomas Creger of Creger and Company. The purpose of the meeting is to discuss the upcoming stockholders' meeting. She would like the meeting to take place as soon as possible.

b. Michael McCormick is the legal partner of McCormick Auto Parts. Ms. Konopski would like to talk to him about the upcoming merger of Konopski Manufacturing and McCormick Auto Parts. Leave a message for him to return the call so that a meeting time can be scheduled.

c. Elsie Graff of Atlanta Charities called inviting Ms. Konopski to the annual charity dinner. Please inform her that Ms. Konopski will have to decline the invitation to the charity, but that she will be donating a monetary sum to the charity.

chapter 11

COORDINATING TRAVEL ARRANGEMENTS

ARRANGING BUSINESS TRIPS

Science fiction writers used to imagine a future in which traveling from place to place would no longer be necessary. People would talk to each other with picture phones instead of flying cross-country to meet face to face. Computers, satellites, and telephones would make it possible for people around the world to communicate with each other without stepping out of their living rooms or offices.

This technology exists now, and some electronic marvels, such as teleconferences and electronic messages, have become familiar tools in the office. But businesspeople still travel a great deal. Company professionals still go to conventions. Real estate dealers still travel to inspect factories and offices internationally. Sales representatives and managers attend regional sales meetings. And company executives take contracts and plans to clients in far away cities.

It will probably be an important part of your job to help businesspeople reach their destinations. You will be expected to make arrangements for your supervisors' hotel rooms, rental cars, and meals and to get them back home again—all with a minimum of confusion. You will prepare lists of travel arrangements and business appointments, and you will make sure your supervisors have the proper business documents to take with them.

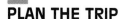

PLAN THE TRIP

The process you will use to plan for travel includes the following:

1. Determine the purpose of the travel.
2. Gather all the information needed.
3. Plan how you are going to make the arrangements.
4. Make the travel arrangements.
5. Evaluate and/follow up on the trip.

It is up to you to keep the office running smoothly while your supervisors are away and to help them evaluate their trips once they return. To do these things, you need to use information-gathering, communications, and decision-making skills. In this chapter you will learn about the many details to take into account when planning a business trip. And you will learn how computers and other electronic equipment can make your trip planning more efficient.

Determine the Travel Situation

Any time a person travels, the situation is different. The person may be traveling for a short business trip or for a long conference. The trip may be a local car drive or it may require international accommodations. Whatever the case, you must first determine the travel situation.

Gather Information

The next step in planning any trip is to gather information and record it accurately. As you gather the information you need, place it in a file folder or store it in an electronic file. If you are arranging a trip for some of your company's executives, you will need to ask them many questions before making their arrangements. A personal **traveler profile questionnaire** will help you determine what type of arrangements each person likes and how he or she likes to travel. The traveler profile questionnaire should include questions such as the following:

- At what time of the day does the individual prefer to leave and return?

- If the person will fly on an international flight, does he or she prefer smoking or nonsmoking section?

- Does the traveler prefer an aisle or window seat?

- Does the traveler require a special meal (for example, vegetarian) on the plane?

- Does the traveler prefer one airline over another?

- Should you reserve a rental car at the destination? any specific company?

- Does the individual prefer a particular hotel?

Gather the information far in advance of planning any business trips. You can then keep this information on file for future reference. When planning a specific trip, other questions need to be answered. You may ask these orally or ask your supervisors to fill out a **travel preference form** for this one trip. Some of these questions might include the following:

- How many days will the individual be gone?

- Will he or she travel by plane, train, car, or a combination?

- What time does the traveler need to arrive?

- How many sleeping rooms or suites will be needed; smoking or nonsmoking rooms; any preference for where in the hotel the individual wants to stay; any meeting rooms necessary?

- What facilities/services must be at the hotel; conference calling, teleconferencing, fascimile, dedicated telephone lines?

- Should you make restaurant reservations? How many people?

- What materials will the individual need to take along? Should you mail materials ahead of time to the hotel? (materials may include files, data disks, slides, transparencies, handouts, computer printouts, and so on.)

- Does the individual need any special equipment, such as a tape recorder or slide projector?

MAKE TRAVEL ARRANGEMENTS

Once you have gathered the information you need, you are ready to make all the travel arrangements, from transportation to sleeping accommodations to local transportation needs. The information you have gathered may be fragmented. Organize it in a manner that allows you to tell the travel agent or airline and hotel clerks exactly what you want. Be sure to have several options if your first plan is not possible. Being organized will save you many hours of recalling.

When making travel arrangements, you have several options to pursue. For example, you may use a travel agency, you might work with your company's travel department, you could use your computer to access an electronic on-line reservation service, or you can contact the airlines, hotels, and car rental agencies yourself. What you do usually depends on the size of your company and the kinds of arrangements you are asked to make. Some companies are too small to have their own travel departments, while others maintain contracts with travel agencies. Even if your company uses a travel agency routinely, you might prefer to arrange simple trips yourself. Or you would use the services of a specialized travel agency to arrange for a complicated trip such as a company trade mission to China.

Travel Agencies

Travel agents can make airline, railroad, rental car, and hotel/motel reservations for you easily. They use computerized databases to find the lowest fares and most convenient flight schedules. They also use printed guides and schedules to determine hotel room rates and facilities. Travel agents are paid commissions by the airlines and hotels they book. They usually do not charge a client.

Selecting a Travel Agent   Your company may require you to use a particular agency, or you may have to pick one yourself. If you choose the agency, be sure to pick an agency that specializes in business travel. These agencies usually deliver tickets and other documents to your office at no extra charge.

Working with the Agent   Call the travel agent as soon as you are prepared to make flight and hotel reservations. By making reservations as far in advance as possible, you can save your company money and make certain that your travelers get the flights and hotels they want.

When you have gathered and prepared the information for the trip, pass this information on to the travel agent for reservations. For example, if you are arranging for two company executives to go from Los Angeles to Detroit, you might provide the travel agent with the following information:

- They plan to fly to Detroit on March 3 and return on March 5. They do not plan to make any other stops, and they will spend two nights in Detroit.

- They have no preference for any particular airline, but they want to fly nonstop to Detroit in the morning and return to Los Angeles on an evening flight.

- They both want to fly first class, and they both prefer aisle seats.

- They want a rental car to be waiting for them at the airport in Detroit, preferably a large four-door sedan.

- They require separate rooms in a downtown hotel for the nights of March 3 and 4.

- They prefer double, rather than single, rooms.

If your company will pay for the airline tickets, car rental, and hotel rooms by its authorized credit card, you need to give the agent the credit card number and expiration date. The travel agent could also bill the company directly.

Some companies may require their employees to fly in coach or business class or to use certain airlines or hotel chains that offer special corporate rates or discounts. If your company has such policies, inform the travel agent. Once the agency makes the arrangements, it will mail or deliver the tickets and an **itinerary,** which is a document that lists departure and arrival times, flight numbers, hotel addresses and telephone numbers, and other details of the trip (see figure 11.1). Examine the tickets and the itinerary carefully to make sure that the arrangements they describe are the ones you requested and that the information they contain is complete and correct.

Corporate Travel Departments

Some large companies have their own travel departments for booking business trips. They function just like travel agencies and may even receive the same commissions from hotels and airlines. If your company has a travel department, provide it with the same information you would give a travel agency. The travel department will then give you a choice of flights and hotels so you or the traveler can pick the most convenient schedule. The travel department will also provide tickets and a travel itinerary.

Arranging Trips Yourself

If you work for a small company, or if you have to arrange a trip at the last minute, you may have to make all the arrangements with airlines, hotels, and car rental agencies on your own.

July 10, 1992

TO: Ellen Cole

FROM: Elaine Fowler

SUMMER INSTITUTE, SEATTLE, WASHINGTON

SUNDAY, JULY 28, 1992

Leave: Minneapolis   Northwest #7   9:30 AM
Arrive: Seattle   11:04 AM

HOTEL: Airport Hilton
              $65 per night
              Contact, if needed, is Gary Collins, Sale Manager

CAR: Dollar Rental (at terminal)
              $139.75 weekly rate
              compact car
              Confirmation #: R520136

FRIDAY, AUGUST, 2, 1992

Leave: Seattle   Northwest #156   2:30 PM
Arrive: Minneapolis   7:40 PM

YOU WILL RECEIVE A MAP FROM GARY COLLIN'S OFFICE.

Fare = $886.00 (100% refundable). Tickets booked and charged to your credit card 7/3/92 by Justine, Mainline Travel.

c: Gary Collins

Figure 11.1 A travel itinerary.

Let's discuss the procedures to follow when making travel arrangements on your own.

Transportation When arranging transportation for company executives, first obtain the information from the travel profile questionnaire that the executives filled out some time ago. You are now ready to gather the information for this particular trip. Ask how they will travel. Will they take a train or plane to their destination? Will they take cabs or limousines to and from the airport or train station? Will they require rental cars? Most people fly when they have to go three hundred miles or more because flying is the fastest way to get there. Large airlines can take travelers to any major city in the United States. **Commuter airlines** travel from major airports to smaller

```
HOUSTON, TEXAS                                   CST  HOU
     H-HOU  I-IAH  E-IWS  C-JWH  Q-JGQ  T-JTC  A-JLC
     P-JPT  G-JTG
2345  4:18a I    6:30a O   EA   220     T     AB3     0
167   4:18a I    6:30a O   EA   220    AT     AB3     0
      7:00a I    9:11a O   AA   174  FYBQM   72S B    0
      7:00a H   12:46P O   AA   190  FYBQM   72S SB   3
                          AA 190 EFFECTIVE  17JAN
      7:05a H    9:21a O   AA   580  FYBQM   72S B    0
                 AA 580 DISCONTINUED AFTER   5JAN
X67   7:40a H   11:15a M   WN   761     S     73S     2
6     7:40a H   11:15a M   WN   761     K     73S     2
      8:08a I   10:19a O   UA   744  FYBQM   727 B    0
                          UA 744 EFFECTIVE   6JAN
      8:10a I   10:21a O   UA   744  FYBQM   727 B    0
                 UA 744 DISCONTINUED AFTER   5JAN
```

```
                  CONNECTIONS
2345   4:00a I      5:42a MCI   EA  1696     T      AB3      0
          8:30a MCI   9:45a O   EA   227   FYHQK    D9S B/S  0
167    4:00a I      5:42a MCI   EA  1696    AT      AB3      0
          8:30a MCI   9:45a O   EA   227   FYHQK    D9S B/S  0
       6:45a I      7:55a MEM   RC   256   CYBQM    D9S B    0
D- 5JAN   8:30a MEM  10:04a O   RC   471   CYBQM    D9S B    0
       6:45a I      7:55a MEM   RC   448  CYMBnQn   DC9 B    0
E- 6JAN   8:30a MEM  10:04a O   RC   471   CYBQM    D9S B    0
X7     6:45a H      8:00a MEM   RC   830   CYBQM    DC9 S    0
D- 4JAN   8:30a MEM  10:04a O   RC   471   CYBQM    D9S B    0
X7     6:45a H      8:00a MEM   RC   830  CYMBnQn   DC9 S    0
E- 6JAN   8:30a MEM  10:04a O   RC   471   CYBQM    D9S B    0
X7     7:00a I      8:12a MEM   DL  1100   FYBQM    D9S B    0
          8:40a MEM  10:05a O   DL  1114   FYBQM    D9S B    0
       7:00a H      7:53a DFW   DL  1003   FYBQM    73S S    0
          8:31a DFW  10:30a O   DL   690   FYBQM    D9S B    0
X67    7:00a I      7:51a DFW   AA   490   FYBQM    72S S    0
          8:45a DFW  10:43a O   AA   470   FYBQM    72S B    0
67     7:00a I      7:51a DFW   AA   684   FYBQM    72S S    0
          8:45a DFW  10:43a O   AA   470   FYBQM    72S B    0
       7:00a H      7:53a DFW   AA   524   FYBQM    72S S    0
```

Figure 11.2A A sample entry from the printed *Official Airline Guide*.

airports or between major airports that are not far apart. Or you may charter a special flight just for this business trip. **Charter airlines** handle special flight requests. Usually the planes are smaller, but the departure and arrival times are very flexible. If you have many executives flying to the same meeting, a charter flight may be less expensive than a major airline. Your company policy and the travel preferences of the executives will determine what type of airline you use.

Airlines If your company frequently makes airline reservations, it may subscribe to the ***Official Airline Guide (OAG).*** This directory, published every two weeks, lists airline routes and schedules between major American cities. The *OAG* can also be accessed on-line through public database services. Figure 11.2 provides a sample listing

```
FROM-NEW YORK,NY;NEWARK,NJ,USA
# TO-SAN FRANCISCO;OAKLAND,CA,USA
1* 1000A  EWR  110P  SFO PE   5 747 F 0
2  1040A  LGA  300P  SFO RC 343 72S L 1
3* 1100A  JFK  140P  SFO UA  25 767 L 0
4* 1200N  JFK  240P  SFO AA  17 767 L 0
5* 1225P  LGA  535P  SFO AA 491 D10 L 1
6  1220P  EWR  617P  SFO EA 201 757 L 2
 * THOMAS COOK TICKETING ONLY
ENTER +,-,CX,X#,F#,RS,B#(#=LINE NUMBER)
!!  ◄

          DIRECT FLIGHTS      TUE-01 APR
FROM-NEW YORK,NY;NEWARK,NJ,USA
# TO-SAN FRANCISCO;OAKLAND,CA,USA
1*  200P  EWR  510P  SFO PE  21 747 F 0
2   335P  LGA  850P  SFO DL  99 L10 S 1
3*  355P  EWR  840P  SFO TW 171 L10 S 1
4   400P  EWR  910P  SFO WO  79 D10 D 1
5*  415P  JFK  720P  SFO PA  85 747 D 0
6*  530P  JFK  835P  SFO AA  19 767 D 0
 * THOMAS COOK TICKETING ONLY
USE +,-,O,CX,X#,F#,RS,B#(#=LINE NUMBER)
!!  ◄
► Receiving B:OAG  (ALT-R or PgDn to Terminate) ◄
```

Figure 11.2B A sample screen from the electronic *Official Airline Guide*.

from the *OAG* showing flights from Houston, Texas, to Chicago, Illinois.

The first line of the table tells you that Houston is on central standard time and that the official airport code for Houston is HOU. The second line provides one-letter abbreviations for airports; for example, *1-IAH* means that *I* stands for the International Airport in Houston. Reading from left to right across the next line of the table, you learn the following:

- Column 1 indicates flight frequency. Each number represents one of the seven days of the week. *2345* means the flight is every Tuesday, Wednesday, Thursday, and Friday; *X67* means every day except Saturday and Sunday.

- Column 2 shows the time the flight departs. The plane leaves at 4:18 A.M.

- Column 3 is the one-letter abbreviation for the airport from which the flight is leaving.

- Columns 4 and 5 indicate the time the flight will arrive and the airport at which it will land. In this case, the first flight lands at 6:30 A.M. at O'Hare Airport.

- Column 6 indicates the name of the airline. The letters *NW, AA,* and *UA* stand for Northwest Airlines, American Airlines, and United Airlines.

- The numbers in column 7 are the flight numbers.

- The letters in column 8 are codes for the classes (*T* is coach economy discounted, *A* is first class discounted, *F* is first class, *Y* is coach economy, and so on).

- Column 9 shows the kinds of planes used on the flight: *AB3* means the plane is an airbus industrie, *72S* means the plane is a 727, and so on. The letters *B, L, S,* and *D* in the next column mean that breakfast, lunch, a snack, or dinner will be served on the flight.

- The *0, 2,* or *3* in column 11 means either that the flight is nonstop or that it will make two or three stops.

- If nonstop flights are not available, consult the part of the table labeled "Connections." This shows where and when connecting flights can be caught. For example, the first entry shows that a traveler can take a Northwest Airlines flight from Houston at 4 A.M. and arrive in Kansas City, Missouri, at 5:42 A.M. He or she would then leave Kansas City at 8:30 A.M. and arrive in Chicago at 9:45 A.M.

The *OAG* used to list fares between cities, but airlines today have become very competitive and offer too many different kinds of fare plans. Many companies subscribe to the *Official Airline Guide* through on-line database services that allow a computer operator to call up flight information and airfares on a computer. Companies can also subscribe to an electronic database, such as CompuServe, that provides access to detailed information about flight schedules and airfares.

Selecting an Airline Most big cities are served by several major airlines. Choose the airline with the most convenient schedules and the best fares. If you were arranging a trip by plane from Houston to Chicago, for example, start by choosing three or four possible flight times after consulting the *OAG,* an electronic database, or individual airlines.

It is part of your job to obtain the lowest fares available for the required flights. Fares vary according to how far in advance reservations are made, how many days passengers intend to spend at their destinations, and which days of the week or hours of the day they intend to fly.

In order to attract repeat business, some airlines offer "frequent flier bonuses" to business customers. One airline, for example, offers free round-trip tickets between any two of the North American airports it serves to individuals who have traveled twenty thousand miles or more on that airline. If your employer is enrolled in an airline's frequent flier program, book flights on that airline as often as possible to earn credits toward free flights. Hotels, telephone services, rental cars, and other travel services now offer free frequent flyer miles to those individuals who use their services while flying with a certain airline.

Making Reservations Airlines have either toll-free numbers or local telephone numbers you can call to make reservations. Again, you will be passing on much of the information you collected when you interviewed your employer about his or her trip. The reservations clerk will need to know the traveler's destination and the desired dates and times of day for traveling. The clerk may then offer you a choice of flights that more or less fit your requirements.

When you make reservations, try to choose a nonstop flight or one that does not require a change of planes. Most business travelers do not want to waste time with stopovers or risk missing a connecting flight. Travelers who are flying long distances or overseas may want to arrive a day or so in advance of their appointments so they have time to recover from **jet lag,** the fatigue and confusion that result from flying across several time zones.

The reservations clerk will need to know whether the traveler intends to travel first class or coach. First-class travel is more costly but provides extra comforts and conveniences. Some companies may require all their employees to fly coach or business class, while others expect high-level employees to travel first class so they can arrive at their destinations rested and ready to work.

Many travelers prefer to fly on airlines that allow seat selection when reservations are confirmed, because this saves them time at the airport. If the airline you have chosen permits advance seat assignments, the reservations clerk will ask whether the traveler prefers an aisle or window seat. Be sure to inform the clerk if the person would like to sit in the front or rear of the plane. If your supervisor requires a special kosher, vegetarian, or salt-free meal, this is the time to inform the airline clerk.

Finally, the airline clerk will want to know how your company will pay for the tickets and whether the airline should send them to your office or hold them for the traveler to pick up at the time of the flight. Make careful notes about the flight numbers, the dates and times of arrival and departure, the seat numbers, and other details. Repeat this information to the clerk to make sure you have noted it correctly. Find out whether the airline can confirm the arrangements immediately or whether you must call again to confirm. It is usually necessary to confirm overseas flights three days before departure.

You might have to cancel or postpone a trip at the last minute or make some other changes in the reservations. If so, telephone the airline as soon as possible. Some airlines may charge your company a higher fare or a penalty fee for changing the reservations. If you book your supervisor on a flight that will require additional payment if the reservation is changed, be sure he or she is aware of this before you confirm the reservation. If your employer decides during the trip to change the return reservation, you can usually do that with a call to your local airline office. Major airlines keep reservation information in a central database that is accessible to all their reservations clerks. You can obtain a refund or credit card adjustment on unused tickets by submitting them to the airline or your travel agent.

When suitable airline flights are not available, companies may charter planes or helicopters to take employees to their destinations. Some companies also use air taxis, which are small planes and helicopters that carry a few passengers at a time on frequent flights between nearby cities. These services are generally more expensive than regular airline flights, but sometimes they are the only way to get from one place to another in a hurry.

Railroads Businesspeople traveling from one nearby city to another may find it more convenient to take a train than to fly. In many cities business offices and train stations are centrally located, while the airports are located miles away, so taking a train is a more convenient way to travel. For example, you can fly from New York to Washington, D.C., in about an hour, but it may take an hour or more to get from an office in midtown Manhattan to an airport and another hour to get from a Washington airport to a downtown office. A three-hour Metroliner train ride between the business districts of the two cities may be easier and more relaxing. It may also be cheaper because on heavily traveled routes, train fares are usually less expensive than airfares.

You can reserve seats and sleeping accommodations in advance on many trains, but some travel agents will not

Figure 11.3 Some executives prefer to travel by train when they take regional trips.

book train trips within the United States, so you may have to make the arrangements yourself. To find out about train service between cities, call Amtrak or look under *Railroads* in your local Yellow Pages. Your company may also subscribe to the *Official Railway Guide,* a directory similar to the *Official Airline Guide,* which includes the schedules of all railroads in the United States and Canada.

Traveling by Car   In some cases the best way for a businessperson to get from one place to another is by car. Some firms provide company cars or pay employees per mile for the use of their own cars. Others rent cars from rental agencies. Car rental agencies usually charge either a flat daily, weekly, or monthly fee or a flat fee plus an additional amount for each mile driven. They also charge for insurance, and they may charge a drop-off fee when a driver picks up a car at one place and leaves it at another.

Most airports and cities offer a wide choice of rental agencies. Your company may have a long-term contract with an agency that provides discounts for frequent use, or your supervisor may belong to an automobile club or airline frequent flyer club that provides car rental discounts at specific agencies. If you have to choose an

Figure 11.4 When making rental car arrangements it is important to get information on any available discounts.

agency yourself, compare the fees and services of several firms. Some companies encourage their employees to avoid big agencies and deal with smaller companies that offer lower rates.

When you telephone the car rental company, give the reservations clerk your supervisor's name, and specify when and where he or she will pick up the car. If the car will be picked up at an airport, give the clerk the traveler's flight number so the rental agent can hold the car if the flight is late. Describe the kind of car your supervisor prefers, including the model and size. Big cars with extra features cost more than smaller, standard models but may be worth the extra cost. If your supervisor has to spend much time driving, a larger, comfortable car will be less tiring.

Ask the reservations clerk what the fees will be and whether there are additional charges for dropping the car off at another agency office. Tell the clerk whether to charge the fees to a personal or company credit card or bill the company directly.

People who drive to their destinations must know what routes to follow, what signs to look for, where to stop for the night, and so on. If your supervisor asks you to prepare driving instructions, you will need a road map. Always get directions from the clients your supervisor will be meeting. Use the map to locate the final destination and any stops along the way. Then you can determine the best road and the shortest, most direct routes to take. You can give written directions, or you can highlight the routes with a transparent marker so that the traveler can easily consult the map during the trip.

Those who frequently drive long distances find it helpful to pay an annual fee to join an automobile club such as the American Automobile Association (AAA). These clubs can help you plan a car trip and provide you with maps marked to show the recommended routes. Usually the maps show the locations of restaurants and motels along the way. Automobile clubs also provide emergency road services, such as free towing, for their members.

If you work for a company whose employees travel by car a great deal, your employer can purchase travel planning software to help you plan an automobile trip. To use such a program, you enter the trip's starting point, the destination, and any stops along the way. The program then chooses the fastest, most direct route. If you were mapping a trip for a regional sales representative, you could use this program to work out a route that included calls on customers in several different cities.

Business professionals often use company cars or their own cars for business trips within a state or region. If they use company cars, the company may provide them with a gasoline credit card, or they may pay for gas themselves and then submit expense accounts for reimbursement. When people drive their own cars, the company usually pays them so much per mile to cover wear and tear and insurance. Customarily, the company also pays all tolls and parking fees. Be prepared to keep records and expense accounts for supervisors who use their own cars or company cars extensively for business trips.

Some travelers find it cheaper and easier to get around a strange city by using taxis or public transit rather than by driving. If your supervisor plans to get around without a car in an unfamiliar city, learn as much as you can about these alternate methods of travel. You may be called upon to provide a list of taxicab company telephone numbers in San Francisco, a map of the Philadelphia subway system, or bus schedules for Seattle. You can obtain this information by talking to your travel agent, by looking at tourist guidebooks for the city your supervisor intends to visit, and by questioning hotel clerks.

Airport limousine services carry passengers between the airport and various downtown terminals or hotels. Limousine rates are usually lower than taxi fares. In most cities there are private limousine services that provide cars and drivers for local trips. These services require reservations, which you can make by telephone a day or two in advance. Some companies based in big cities have long-term contracts with limousine services that entitle them to discounts. If your employer does not use a service regularly, you may have to choose a limousine service. As with car rental companies, compare the rates and services of different companies. Limousine services may charge an hourly fee or a flat fee for drives they make often, such as trips to the airport.

BOOKING HOTEL ROOMS

Now that you have arranged to get your supervisor to Houston, or Cincinnati, or London, you must reserve a hotel or motel room where he or she can stay. If the traveler has no personal preferences and your company does not require you to use a specific hotel chain, choose the hotel yourself.

Cost and Location

Cost and location are the two most important factors to consider in selecting a hotel for your supervisor. Suppose, for example, that you have arranged for two company executives to fly to Detroit. If they were planning to drive from the airport to a suburban office for a one-day business meeting, it probably would be more convenient for them to stay at a hotel near the airport. But, in fact, they are going to have a series of meetings over two days with clients at a downtown office. In that case it is more convenient to reserve rooms at a downtown hotel close to the meeting place.

Hotel Guides

If you make hotel reservations frequently, your company should subscribe to a directory such as the *Official Hotel and Motel Guide,* the *Hotel and Motel Redbook,* or Leahy's *Hotel-Motel Guide.* These directories give the names, addresses, telephone numbers, room rates, and services of hotels in most cities.

Hotel directories usually indicate what services a hotel offers, such as room service, garage service, laundry and valet services, secretarial services, and transportation to and from airports. Most large hotels and motels have toll-free 800-numbers you can call to make reservations. If no 800-number is listed for a hotel in your hotel directory, call (800) 555-1212 to find out if the hotel has one.

When you make a room reservation, tell the hotel clerk when your supervisor will be arriving and departing. Also tell the clerk whether you want to reserve a single or double room or a suite. To hold a room for a traveler who will arrive late in the day you need to make a **guaranteed reservation.** This means that the hotel will hold the room as long as necessary. You may have to provide a credit card number and agree to pay for the room whether or not the traveler shows up. If the hotel provides transportation from the airport, ask for information on how the service operates. If there is time, ask the hotel to send you a written confirmation specifying the date of the reservation, the length of stay, and other details.

PREPARING FOR THE TRIP

Once you have made all the transportation and hotel arrangements, you still have a number of tasks to perform to help your employer prepare for the trip. A day or two before departure, confirm all flight and room reservations unless they were confirmed earlier. Also confirm arrangements for getting the traveler to and from the airport. In some cases you may have to make some last-minute changes in the airline or room reservations. Always make such changes as soon as possible, and always ask how a change will affect the cost. If your supervisor wants you to make restaurant reservations or arrange for theater or concert tickets, it is a good idea to make these arrangements just before departure, when all the other details have been worked out.

Preparing an Itinerary

Your travel agent or travel department has already provided you with an itinerary showing all the flight and hotel arrangements that have been made. Now you will use that information and all the other data that has been accumulating in your trip folder to prepare a more detailed itinerary. This itinerary includes not only travel and hotel information but also all business appointments, speaking engagements, entertainment events, and other activities planned for the trip.

Prepare an outline of the itinerary using all the reservation confirmations, calendar notations, letters, and appointment notes you have collected as you have planned the trip. The outline should list all activities in chronological order. It should be organized in a clear, logical format with separate heads for each day or for each scheduled activity. Figure 11.5 shows an example of a complete itinerary.

When preparing an itinerary, try to include as much information as possible to show where the traveler should be at all times. Be sure to list the names of companies and individuals the traveler will visit as well as their addresses and telephone numbers. If your supervisor is delayed, he or she can then call ahead without looking up numbers.

Make several copies of the itinerary. Your supervisor should keep a copy handy in a jacket pocket, briefcase, or purse. You should keep a copy, and key co-workers and members of the traveler's family may also receive copies.

Appointment Schedules

Some managers prefer to have their business appointments listed separately from travel and hotel arrangements. You can easily prepare a separate schedule containing the same information that you would have included in a complete itinerary.

October 25, 1992

TO: Michael Framingham

FROM: Rebecca Sanchez

Itinerary for Trip to Miami Florida, Nov. 1-2

SUNDAY, November 1

6:30 p.m.   Pick-up by Harvard Limosine service at your home
            for trip to Logan Airport (Boston)

7:40 p.m.   Leave Delta Flight #240, direct to Miami

10:15 p.m. Arrive at Miami International Airport
            Confirmed reservation for rental of full-size car

            Guaranteed reservation at Downtown Mariott
            (travel instructions provided by Hertz)
            Hotel reservation #J648910011

MONDAY, November 2

7:30 a.m.   Breakfast with Lillian Obermeyer and Joseph Hernandez
            of Universal Data Corp. to discuss training seminar.

            Meet in Mariott hotel lobby.

9:00 a.m.   Meeting with Leslie Phillips, Vice President, Miami
            Branch Office. Leslie will present you with the day's
            itinerary.

4:15 p.m.   Leave Miami on Delta Flight #452, direct to Boston.

8:05 p.m.   Arrive at Logan. Harvard Limosine driver will meet
            you at the arrival gate.

Figure 11.5 This is an example of a complete itinerary that includes a schedule of appointments.

TRAVEL FUNDS

Another part of your job is to see that your supervisor has cash, traveler's checks, and credit cards to cover expenses during the trip. Some expenses may be billed directly to the company or to company credit cards, but travelers still have to pay for such things as meals, cab rides, parking, and tips.

Credit Cards

Some companies give their employees credit cards for most of their trip expenses. Other companies expect their employees to use their personal credit cards and then submit receipts for reimbursement. Credit cards make it easier for companies and their employees to keep track of travel expenses. Your supervisor is responsible for carrying the credit cards, but you may be asked to keep all credit card numbers on file so that you can notify the credit card companies if the cards are lost or stolen.

Cash Advances

When travelers must pay for tips, cab fares, highway tolls, and other such expenses in cash, many employers issue cash advances for business trips. To obtain a cash advance, you probably will have to fill out a request form and submit it to the company cashier. Most forms require authorized signatures, an explanation of the request, employee identification numbers, and other details. Keep copies of cash advance requests for your expense records.

Traveler's Checks

It is usually a good idea for the traveler to carry only a small amount of cash and the bulk of his or her travel funds in the form of **traveler's checks** (sometimes spelled *cheques* in foreign markets). Traveler's checks can be spent almost as easily as cash, but they are insured against theft or loss. The checks are available from banks and American Express offices. Some banks issue their own checks, while others sell checks issued by companies such as Visa or American Express. They come in denominations of $10, $20, $50, and $100. The person who will use the checks must pick them up and sign each one in the presence of a teller or bank officer. Traveler's checks come with a receipt that is a record of the checks' serial numbers. Keep one copy of this receipt in your files and give one to the traveler so that if the checks are lost, he or she can be reimbursed. (Remind the traveler that the receipt should be kept separately from the checks.)

ORGANIZING THE TRAVELER

Shortly before your supervisor leaves for a business trip, organize all the information, documents, and materials he or she will need on the trip. Your supervisor can use your checklist to organize the materials in his or her briefcase. The briefcase should contain all the files and documents your supervisor must read or distribute at meetings while away. Include background information on the companies and individuals your supervisor will visit, as well as any correspondence relating to the trip.

On your checklist include any guidebooks, maps, and directories that will help the traveler find public transportation, entertainment, and restaurants at his or her destination.

TRAVELER'S CHECKLIST

Keep a checklist such as the following, and use it each time you need to prepare materials for your supervisor to take on a business trip.

- Tickets
- Itinerary
- Appointment record
- Hotel confirmations
- Rental car arrangements
- Travel funds and traveler's checks
- Equipment and supplies
- Address book
- Files, documents, slides, materials
- Miscellaneous items (maps, city guides, and so on)

EVALUATE AND FOLLOW UP

When your supervisor returns from a trip, you need to perform some follow-up tasks. One task is to return to your files all the materials your supervisor took along on the trip. You also need to help your supervisor prepare an expense account and return any unspent funds to the cashier's office.

Another follow-up task is to handle correspondence arising from the trip. This may include notes to thank hosts or letters confirming sales orders, contracts, or other such business deals.

Also talk to your supervisor about the trip itself. Discuss any problems he or she encountered with airlines, accommodations, and other aspects of the trip. Then try to determine how your planning and preparations contributed to the trip and what you should do differently the next time you plan a trip.

INTERNATIONAL TRAVEL

More and more people make business trips to other countries as companies seek to open new markets and purchase raw materials abroad. Some corporations, such as IBM and Exxon, are called **international companies** because they have manufacturing plants, and other properties in several different countries. Lawyers, accountants, and consultants who provide professional services for international companies, also have foreign offices. You may be asked to arrange international as well as domestic trips. When you plan an international trip, follow the same steps as for planning a domestic trip, but you must do more research, planning, and preparation as you gather information and plan the trip.

RESEARCH AND PLANNING

When planning a trip to a foreign country, you need information about its customs and cultures. For example, if you did not know that July 14, Bastille Day, is a national holiday in France, you might try to schedule business meetings on a day when all French business offices are closed. Information about social customs can help the traveler avoid offending people in other countries. It would be highly offensive, for example, for your supervisor to offer a bottle of wine to a Moslem business associate in Saudi Arabia, where Islamic law prohibits the use of alcohol.

The U.S. State Department publishes a series of pamphlets entitled *Background Notes on the Countries of the World*. There is a pamphlet for every country in the world, and each pamphlet describes the geography, history, social customs, economy, and trading patterns of the country it covers. Check your local library and bookstores for other reference works and guidebooks about the country your supervisor will visit.

TRAVEL DOCUMENTS

People traveling outside their own countries may be required to carry documents such as birth certificates, passports, visas, and papers that identify them and their employers and state the purposes of their trips. They should carry these documents at all times and be ready to produce them upon request.

Figure 11.6 This is a page from a passport. Each time the traveler enters a different country, an official stamps the page with the date and place of entry.

Passports

For international travel, the traveler needs a **passport,** which is an official identification document. U.S. passports are issued by the U.S. State Department. Passports identify travelers by photograph and prove their citizenship in their country.

A traveler applying for a passport in the United States must appear in person at the passport office with an application, photographs, and some proof of citizenship, such as a birth certificate. It sometimes takes several weeks to obtain a passport, so travelers should apply as soon as they know they are going abroad.

Visas and Other Documents

Visas are permits granted by governments that allow foreigners to enter their countries. Most Western countries do not require American travelers to obtain visas, but Eastern European, Asian, and African countries usually do. A visa sets a time limit on how long the visitor can remain in the country and states his or her purpose in being there, such as for work, travel, or study. To find out whether a country requires a visa, ask your travel agent or contact the country's nearest consulate. The consulate can also tell you whether your traveler needs to obtain a special permit to work in the country.

Currency

A traveler visiting another country will need some money in that country's currency, even if only to buy a cup of coffee during an airport stopover. You can purchase currency for each country the traveler will visit from a currency exchange office, your travel agent, or a large bank. Generally, however, travelers can exchange American money and traveler's checks for foreign currency at currency exchange offices in banks, hotels, and airports in the countries they visit. Find out what the current rate of exchange is between foreign currency and American dollars to help your employer calculate tips and other expenditures abroad.

Vaccinations

Travelers are often required to be vaccinated against diseases that are prevalent in the countries they visit. Travel agents and consular offices can tell you which vaccinations are required. Travelers can obtain vaccination records from the physicians who vaccinate them. They must also obtain International Certificates of Vaccination and submit them to their local or state health departments. These certificates can be obtained from a travel agent, a passport office, or the traveler's doctor.

LOCAL INFORMATION

Climate

Climate can vary dramatically from one part of the world to another. When it is summer in the United States it is winter in Australia. In order for the traveler to know how to dress appropriately, it is important that you check weather conditions. You can do this by checking with the United States embassy in the country to be visited; or you can look at weather maps such as those found in a world atlas. An almanac is also an excellent source to use.

Customs

You can also help your supervisor be ready for international travel by offering information on customs in the country to be visited. There are many materials and books available in public and private libraries about the correct protocol for business and pleasure travel in foreign countries. Once such publication, *Do's and Taboos From Around the World,* published by Parker Pen Company, gives a short synopsis of cultural differences in different countries.

Traveling

It can be a trying experience for travelers to find their way from airports to hotels or meeting places in a foreign country, especially if they do not know the language. In addition to gathering information about local transportation, as you would for any domestic business trip, you can help your supervisor cope with this situation by making some transportation arrangements in advance.

Many foreign countries, particularly in Europe, have excellent train service, with passenger trains running frequently to all big cities and most smaller cities and towns. European railroads usually offer different classes of service. A first-class ticket costs more but ensures the traveler a comfortable seat in an uncrowded compartment. First-class tickets usually require reservations. You may be able to make reservations through your travel agent. If not, the traveler can make reservations through a travel agent overseas.

Most major American car rental agencies have toll-free numbers to make reservations for overseas rentals. Car rental rates in foreign countries can differ substantially from American rates, so be sure to ask the reservations clerk about rates in advance. Also ask whether your supervisor will need an international driver's license. Many countries accept United States driver's licenses, but if an international license is required, it can be obtained from the American Automobile Association (AAA).

MANAGING THE OFFICE WHILE THE SUPERVISOR IS AWAY

Most supervisors delegate major business decisions to other managers before they leave on a trip. But they also expect you to be responsible for handling day-to-day decisions and for seeing that the office runs smoothly while they are away.

HANDLING LETTERS AND TELEPHONE CALLS

Your responsibilities will probably include answering calls and mail that your employer would ordinarily answer. If mail cannot wait for your supervisor to return, you can handle it in one of three ways:

1. Forward it to the appropriate person.
2. Refer it to another supervisor who can handle it.
3. Answer it yourself.

For example, a letter to your supervisor regarding a real estate transaction probably could be handled by your company's real estate manager or by another supervisor. On the other hand, you could easily handle a letter requesting an appointment with your employer yourself. Handle telephone calls the same way you handle the mail. Help the callers yourself when you can, or refer them to someone else who can help. If the callers must speak to your supervisor, take messages and tell them when you expect your supervisor to return. Keep the originals and copies of letters you receive while your employer is away. Place all letters, telephone messages, and documents that your supervisor must handle personally when he or she returns in a file folder labeled "Important." Place copies of all materials you have already handled or directed to someone else in a file folder labeled "Information Only." Always arrange the materials in order of importance. If your employer will be away for a long time, he or she may want you to forward copies of any materials that require immediate attention.

HANDLING PROJECTS AND PROBLEMS

Your supervisor may have specific tasks or assignments for you to handle while he or she is away. If you are not busy, you can complete projects for which you do not normally have time, such as updating the office files.

Some supervisors place daily telephone calls to the office when they are away. Others expect their employees to call them at scheduled times or when problems arise. Ask your supervisor how often he or she intends to telephone the office. Keep notes on matters you need to discuss, and have your notes handy when your supervisor calls.

Many office workers keep daily logs of all office activities while their supervisors are away. In these logs they record all visitors, incoming letters, and telephone calls as well as their own projects and activities. These logs help them keep track of all information regarding what transpired during the supervisor's absence.

EXPENSE REPORTS

Executives generally submit expense reports when they return from traveling. **Expense reports** or **travel and entertainment (T&E) reports** are forms that businesspeople fill out in order to be reimbursed for using their own money to meet business expenses or to account for any airline tickets, travel vouchers, or cash advances they have received from their employer. It may be part of your job to process expense reports for your supervisor.

Most companies require employees to submit monthly expense reports, but some require the reports immediately after business trips. Expense report formats differ from one company to another, but figure 11.7 depicts two sides of a typical expense report form. All business expenses are listed on one side, and entertainment and miscellaneous expenses are explained on the other.

Expense Records

Because of federal tax regulations, employees must submit receipts for reimbursable expenditures over the amount of $25. Some employers may require receipts for other expenditures as well. One reason for the popularity of credit cards among businesspeople is that cardholders get receipts automatically when they use them. In most places, though, receipts for cash payments are available. In addition to obtaining receipts, most travelers keep notes or logs of expenses for which they do not have receipts. Since employers generally reimburse a set amount per mile for business use of personal cars, drivers may use mileage logs to keep track of their mileage. You will need to obtain your supervisor's receipts and log in order to prepare the expense report.

Reporting Expenses

Before you begin filling out an expense form, sort the receipts and logged expenses by day, and determine the nature of each expense so you will know where to insert the information about it on the form. Note that the form includes separate columns for different kinds of transportation and living expenses.

BUSINESS CONFERENCES, MEALS, ETC.

If business expenses are incurred under circumstances not normally conducive to business discussions (athletic events, theatre, etc.) state, in addition to the information requested below, the date, hours, place and subject matter of the related meetings.

DATE	DESCRIPTION OF EXPENSES	MEETING PLACE AND CITY	NAME, FIRM AND TITLE OR OCCUPATIONAL DESIGNATION OF PERSONS PRESENT	BUSINESS PURPOSE	AMOUNT

OTHER EXPENSES

SUPPLEMENTARY DATA
(Explanation of other items as required)

DATE	TYPE OF EXPENSE		AMOUNT

INSTRUCTIONS

GENERAL
(a) Report only expenses actually incurred on company business. Enter each day's expenses separately. (b) Submit reports weekly. (c) Attach all receipted bills. All items of $15 or more must be supported by receipts. Hotel: All hotel expenses must be supported by itemized bills or charge slips. Personal Meals: Show cost of personal meals only and include tips. Telephone: For long distance telephone, show name of person contacted under Supplementary Data above. Other Expenses: Expense of a personal nature such as barber, beverages, hotel, laundry, magazines, movies, valet, etc., are not reimbursable.

Figure 11.7 A typical company expense report form.

(Continued.)

NAME _____ LOCATION _____
PURPOSE OF
EXPENDITURE _____ CHARGE TO _____

| DATE | CITIES VISITED | | TRANS. Attach Recpt | HOTEL Attach Recpt | Breakfast* | Lunch* | Dinner* | TELEPHONE | BUSINESS CONFERENCES* | OTHER EXPENSES* | TOTAL |
	To	From									
TOTAL											

*Explain all items except meals for employee only on reverse side.   Total expense reported _____

I certify I have incurred all of these expenses on behalf of the Company and that they are directly related to the Company's business.

1. Total paid by employee _____
2. Less Advance applied _____

EMPLOYEE SIGNATURE _____

Balance returned _____ 2 greater than 1

DEPT. APPROVAL _____

Balance due employee _____ 1 greater than 2

DATE _____ MGT. APPROVAL _____

APPROVAL (For Accounting Use) _____

Figure 11.7 (cont.).

When you fill out an expense report form such as the one in figure 11.7 follow these procedures:

- Next to the date, write the departure point and destination of each trip.

- Enter the expenses for each day in the appropriate columns following the destination. On the reverse side of the form, provide details of entertainment and miscellaneous expenses.

- Total each expense column, and enter each monthly total at the bottom of the column.

- Total the rows, and enter the totals at the far right, in the TO-TAL column.

- Record the "Grand Total" on the "Total expense reported" line.

- Check the grand total by adding the monthly totals that appear at the bottoms of the columns. You should get the same grand total that you got by adding the daily totals.

Reconciling Expense Reports

At the bottom of the expense report form there is a section that is used to reconcile the amount of money that the company owes the traveler or vice versa. To reconcile an expense report, follow these steps:

- Enter the total month's expenses.

- Enter the amount of any cash or transportation advances the employee has received during the reporting period.

- If any portion of an advance was returned to the company during the month, enter it on the next line.

- Subtract the smaller total from the larger one, and enter the closing balance.

Automating Expense Reports

With the right software, you can use a computer to prepare expense reports and store them electronically. For example, with a spreadsheet program, you could prepare an expense worksheet as a template. Then at the designated time, after the trip or at monthly intervals, input expense items on the worksheet as you obtain them from your supervisor throughout the month. At the end of the month, you would retrieve the worksheet, which has been totaled automatically. Be sure to include on the electronic expense form your supervisor's name, department, and account number. Then print a hard copy of the filled-in form to be signed by your supervisor and submitted to your employer's accounting department.

You can also use the computer to keep running totals of expenses for a longer period, such as a budget year. Then, with a few keystrokes, you can find out how much remains in your department's budget for a particular category, such as travel.

SUMMARY

- Making travel arrangements requires you to answer these questions: Where is the individual going? What information must you collect to prepare for the traveler? How do you arrange the information to make the necessary arrangements? When making the arrangements, have you covered all the traveler's needs? When the arrangements are made, did you go over them to be sure they were all correct; and when the traveler returns, did you evaluate the trip itself?

- Travel agents or travel departments of large companies can make arrangements for you, or you can make reservations yourself. You can use airline, railroad, and hotel directories to assist you in making reservations.

- Schedules and connections are two main points to consider when making airline reservations. Others include which airline to use, seat assignments, frequent flier bonuses, and special food requirements.

- Car rental companies will ask about dates and times, the place where the traveler will return the car, and the size, model, and special features of the car. You will have to compare rates and mileage fees and ask about insurance and discounts. Make sure your employer knows the best route to take.

- People traveling to other countries need passports, visas, and other documents. When you plan an international trip, follow the same steps as for planning a domestic trip, but you must do more research, planning, and preparation.

- Cost and location are the two most important factors to consider when selecting a hotel for your supervisor. Hotel directories usually indicate the services a hotel offers.

- Use all the trip information you have gathered to prepare a detailed itinerary for your employer. The itinerary should include travel and hotel arrangements, business appointments, and all the other activities planned for the trip.

- While your supervisor is away, you will handle correspondence, telephone calls, projects, and problems. Deal with these according to their priority, and take notes about what to do.

- Most people have to submit an expense account after a business trip. Gather and save all receipts and logged expenses before filling out an expense report form.

VOCABULARY

- traveler profile questionnaire
- travel preference form
- itinerary
- commuter airline
- charter airline
- *Official Airline Guide (OAG)*
- jet lag

- guaranteed reservation
- traveler's checks
- international company
- passport
- visa
- expense reports
- travel and entertainment (T&E) reports

CHECKING YOUR UNDERSTANDING

1. Describe the basic steps in the procedure for arranging business trips. What details must be included in each step as they pertain to arranging a trip?
2. If your supervisor is planning a business trip, what information do you need to gather before you can begin making travel arrangements? Why is this important?
3. What services do travel agencies and corporate travel departments usually provide? How can these services help you when you need to arrange a business trip?
4. If your supervisor intends to drive to a client's offices, use the process of planning a trip to describe how you would go about planning his or her car trip.
5. Name the documents your supervisor might need to carry on an international trip, and explain how to go about getting them.
6. What information would you include in an itinerary? Where would you get the information for the details of the itinerary?
7. Describe what software is available to record business expenses and how it can be used to prepare an expense report.

THINKING THROUGH PROCEDURES

1. Using the information below, prepare an itinerary for your supervisor, Ms. McGuire.

   Ms. McGuire is leaving from the Los Angeles airport at 6 p.m., Wednesday, on American Airlines flight 79, and she will land in Seattle two hours and ten minutes later. Roger Stern of CCL Industries will meet her at the arrival gate at the airport and take her to dinner with several CCL executives. Ms. McGuire has a guaranteed reservation at the Seattle Hyatt Regency, 4335 Pines Parkway, (206) 555-7500. The hotel confirmation number is 67524FX. She will spend the entire next day in meetings with the marketing staff at CCL, including Mr. Stern. The address of CCL is 331 Pacific Avenue, Seattle, and its phone number is (206) 555-6000. She has a reservation for that evening on American Airlines flight 112, which leaves Seattle at 8 p.m. and arrives in Los Angeles at 9:50 p.m.
2. Describe how you would handle each of the following situations that occur during Ms. McGuire's absence.

a. An interoffice memo arrives; it asks your supervisor to provide some urgently needed confidential information. The due date is two days prior to your supervisor's return.

b. You receive notice of a meeting that your supervisor should attend, but the meeting is scheduled to take place while he or she is away.

c. You receive a phone call from a client whom your supervisor will visit at the end of his or her trip. The client wants to change the time of the meeting.

d. An unscheduled visitor, Mr. Allen, comes to the office to talk to your supervisor about a matter he describes as "urgent." He refuses to divulge the nature of the matter.

3. Decide which, if any, of the above items Ms. McGuire should be aware of and describe the method you used to solve the situation. Prepare a memo using word processing software.

4. Ms. McGuire and three other executives from your company have planned an international business trip that will take them from Phoenix, AZ to Glasgow, Scotland via Chicago, IL. Using the information from the sample airline schedule below, prepare an itinerary going to Glasgow. Include departure times, flight numbers, arrival information and lodging information if necessary.

Prepare a cover memo to Ms. McGuire for the itinerary. Include information about the type of climate they can expect as well as changes in time zones (check a world atlas.) If there are any other international travel tips you can offer, do so in this memo.

Freq.	Leave	Arrive	Flight	Class	Eq	MI	S
Phoenix to Chicago							
6	1:30 p	5:45 p	AA	612 FYBMV	72S	D	0
	3:00 p	7:15 p 0	UA	1510 FYBMQ	757	D	0
Chicago to Glasgow, Scotland							
	10:00 a	8:15 a (next day)	UA	321 FYBM	763		1
	6:00 a	4:15 a (next day)	AA	546 FYBM	763		1

Chicago Lodging:

Marriott Hotel
O'Hare Way
Chicago, IL 47893-9083

Blue Top Hotel
Midway Street
Chicogo, IL 47895-9065

Chicago Inn
Southside Parkway
Chicago, IL 47896-8790

UNIT 4 THE WORKPLACE PROBLEM

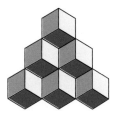

Part A:

Lauren Artin, the administrative assistant to Alexis Bartow, the company president, has been given the job of overseeing the arrangements for Business Seminars National's attendance at the American Bar Association convention.

On July 6, Lauren received the following memorandum from her boss:

April 6, 1992
TO: Lauren Artin
FROM: Alexis Bartow
American Bar Association Convention

Please handle arrangements for BSN's involvement in this year's ABA convention. The convention is scheduled for May 20-23 at the Moscone Convention Center in San Francisco. I will be attending along with Walter and Al.

BSN has been invited to provide two convention speakers to conduct workshops. Please contact our two speakers who conduct workshops on "Communications Technology and Legal Research" and "Computerizing Juror Profiles." See if they are available, and if so, include them in all the arrangements you will be making.

I would like you to handle the following:
1. Make travel and hotel arrangements for staff and speakers.
2. Coordinate the workshops with the speakers and with the ABA convention planners.

Please see me if you have any questions.

Using the problem solving checklist as a guide, prepare the following materials:
a. Make a list of the information Lauren needs in order to complete the two tasks listed in the memo.
b. Make a list of the telephone calls Lauren will need to make in order to get the information. State to whom the call will be made and what questions Lauren will need to ask.
c. Create a traveler profile questionnaire for Lauren to use in making travel arrangements for the five people who will be attending the conference.

Part B:

Lauren called the two speakers and they have agreed to conduct the workshops. Lauren promised to get back to them with the information they need concerning the workshops.
a. Make a list of the information Lauren will need to send the

speakers regarding their presence at the workshops and their travel arrangements.

b. Make a list of the questions Lauren will want to ask the speakers concerning their needs at the meeting and conducting the workshops.

c. Make a list of the questions Lauren will need to ask the convention planners concerning the two workshops that the speakers will conduct.

Part C:

Beginning with the date Lauren was first notified to plan for BSN's participation in the ABA Convention, create a project management plan with goals and timelines for completing all arrangements before the convention.

PROBLEM SOLVING CHECKLIST

DEFINE THE WORKPLACE PROBLEM

What processes and procedures should be followed for coordinating travel arrangements and planning for seminars and workshops?

ANALYZE THE WORKPLACE PROBLEM

What information is needed to complete the arrangements for the convention?

What sources are available for obtaining the information?

PLAN YOUR PROCEDURE

What methods should be used for obtaining the information from the available sources?

What deadlines must be met for each step in the process of completing the arrangements?

What methods of communication should be used for each step in the process?

IMPLEMENT YOUR PROCEDURE

Do the travel plans meet the needs of those who will be attending the convention?

Are the workshop arrangements clear to everyone involved?

EVALUATE YOUR RESULTS

Did the staff and speakers have any problems with the travel or hotel arrangements?

Did the workshops go according to plan?

UNIT 5

MANAGING DOCUMENT PROCESSING

POSITION DESCRIPTION

Job Title: Executive Assistant

Department: Marketing Manager

1. MAJOR FUNCTION:

Responsible for performing administrative support functions for the marketing manager of the organization. Primary emphasis is on assisting the marketing manager with overall office functions and policies relating to the organization. This assistant will oversee the office work flow procedures to include coordinating document processing, managing office communications, overseeing information distribution, and overseeing storage of documents.

2. SPECIFIC DUTIES

1. Manage procedures for the flow of information within and outside of the office; manage the office equipment related to these procedures.

2. Coordinate communication procedures for interaction among office workers, sales representatives, and clients to maintain positive customer relations and maximize productivity.

3. Coordinate office communications by managing telephone system; coordinate and maintain staff schedules; coordinate business meetings; manage travel arrangements and expense records; develop procedures for effective time management; participate in staff meetings.

4. Manage creation and distribution of marketing documents and sales information. Coordinate document creation and processing; create and process customer information and sales support materials; manage sales information; handle distribution of documents and sales information.

5. Manage business information relating to functions of organization by managing manual filing system; manage client information, analyze client information; manage record keeping functions for marketing department; process budgets and other financial information; process and maintain confidential business records.

6. Assist marketing manager in supervisory and managerial functions; process and maintain confidential and general records pertaining to office staff; gather information and prepare visuals for management presentations; establish office procedures; train new employees.

THE WORKPLACE SITUATION

Neil Simonson has been executive assistant to Roger Connelley, the Marketing Director for Computer Systems, Inc., for five years. During this time, Neil has learned to use many different types of equipment for processing documents. He has worked with typewriters, standalone microcomputers, and now uses a microcomputer that is connected to the company's mainframe through a local area network. Available to him are word processing, database, spreadsheet, graphics, desktop publishing, communications, scheduling, electronic mail, and electronic calendaring software.

Roger Connelley relies on Neil for his outstanding ability to adjust to new situations and learn to use the tools that make him most productive. Computer Systems started as a local company building and selling MS-DOS microcomputers 10 years ago. Since that time they have grown into a multimillion dollar company with branch stores in Palm Beach, Minneapolis, New Orleans, and Portland, ME. The corporate office is located in Minneapolis, home to the marketing, administrative, research and development, and financial departments. The production and sales of the computers take place at the branch stores in the four cities named.

The marketing staff is responsible for processing daily correspondence and reports, preparing product information and visuals for presentations by sales representatives, creating advertising copy, and preparing promotional brochures. They handle distribution of sales information to customers, and must maintain a system of storage and retrieval for this information.

DEFINE THE WORKPLACE PROBLEM
What is the purpose of each document?
Who is the audience for each document?
Who is the originator of the documents?
ANALYZE THE WORKPLACE PROBLEM
What types of messages need to be created?
What are the sources for gathering information needed to create documents?
What tools are available for processing the information most efficiently?
PLAN YOUR PROCEDURE
What are the priorities for processing documents on a daily basis?
What steps are necessary to process different types of documents?
What means of output and distribution are most appropriate for each document?

IMPLEMENT YOUR PROCEDURE

Is each document being processed on time?

Does each document meet the quality standards set by the company?

Does each document reach the intended receiver on time?

EVALUATE YOUR RESULTS

Are the sales representatives satisfied with the information their customers are receiving?

Are customers getting the information they need in order to make good buying decisions?

What feedback has been received about distributed documents?

chapter **12**

CREATING WRITTEN DOCUMENTS

WRITING SKILLS IN TODAY'S OFFICE

In chapter 5 you learned about the communication process, which is the exchange of information between a sender and a receiver. In oral communication, messages are encoded and decoded through the dynamics of speaking, listening, and answering. The exchange of written information involves equivalent processes. The difference is that the message is encoded by the sender through the development of a written document and decoded by the receiver when the message is read. The dynamics of this process involves the input, processing, storage, output, and distribution/communication stages of the information processing cycle (see figure 12.1).

Basic communication skills and excellent writing skills are necessary for success in the workplace. No matter what kind of company you work for, or what type of work your particular office handles, you will find that written communication is an important part of the information flow. In business offices today you have a variety of tools available to create and process documents. Various input, processing, storage, and output hardware are available, as well as many types of software programs. Your hardware choices may range from an electronic typewriter to a computer networked to a mainframe and ultimately to a wide area network. Your software choices may range from word processing to desktop publishing, to electronic mail linked to an international market.

With all the choices of hardware and software, and the different methods of communicating and distributing information, ad-

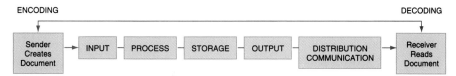

Figure 12.1 When the communication process involves a written message, encoding occurs at the document creation stage and decoding occurs after the distribution/communication stage of the information processing cycle.

ministrative assistants are asked to write original correspondence and to process documents that require complex planning, writing, and editing. As an administrative assistant you can also expect to transcribe and edit your supervisor's first drafts of written material, as well as write your own communications or first drafts of letters, memos, and reports for your supervisor to put into final form.

When creating written documents, there are many ways to create and input the information. In this chapter we will discuss the procedures used to create written documents. Documents can be stored and distributed in electronic form almost as soon as they are created. Therefore, the procedures discussed here for creating documents introduce formatting concerns as well.

Writting skills can be improved with knowledge and practice. You will be introduced to a writing process that can be applied to the major types of written communications you will encounter on the job.

THE WRITING PROCESS

The written word is one of civilization's most distinguishing characteristics. Without it, civilization as we know it would not exist. Written communication, however, does lack the immediacy of oral communication. When you speak to someone, the information is sent and received instantaneously, and you also get immediate feedback in the form of a reply. Immediate feedback helps you determine if your communication was successful.

While written communication does not have this advantage, it does have its own advantages: it is an effective way to present large amounts of information; it does not require the receiver's immediate attention; and it provides an effective, accurate, and permanent record of business information. When you communicate in writing, you have more time to think about what to say and how to say it. Your message is more accurate. In any office one factor that influences how much time you have to prepare or edit is the accepted **turnaround time** (the time from when a task is given to when it is expected to be completed) for typical business correspondence. The longer the acceptable turnaround time, the more time you have to prepare your written communication.

If you work in an electronic office, you have an advantage over your counterpart in a nonelectronic office. The technology available in an electronic office enables you to edit and revise your written communication much more quickly and easily. Since it takes less time to input, process, store, retrieve, and distribute information, you will have more time available for the actual creation of written documents.

When you communicate in writing, you have a permanent, verifiable record of the information exchanged. If anyone challenges the record, forgets it, or remembers it incorrectly, the written communication is available to correct and refresh memories. Because they are permanent, written communications should be carefully and thoughtfully prepared. They should reflect your best efforts, since they are a permanent record by which not only you but also your company is judged. An inaccurate, poorly organized, unclear, incomplete, or sloppy letter with misspellings and incorrect grammar is evidence of a poorly run company. Many people avoid doing business with such companies. They reason that the quality of a company's correspondence reflects the quality of the company's work, and to a large extent, this is a valid assumption. Always keep this in mind when preparing written correspondence.

THE WRITING PROCESS CHECKLIST

Analyze the problem.
Identify your audience.
Determine the best method for preparing the
  document.
Determine the format of the document.
Plan your message.

Write the first draft.
Edit and revise the document.
Proofread for errors.
Reread the final draft.
Distribute the message.

Writing is a skill that can be acquired and, with practice, improved. The importance of this skill is attested to by the amount of time schools spend teaching writing and fundamental language arts skills, such as spelling, grammar, and punctuation.

Many of the techniques to improve oral communication apply to written communication. Preparation is one important technique, and getting comfortable, chosing the right tools or instruments, and matching your message with the situation are others. There are also general techniques that can be applied specifically to improving writing skills.

When you create any type of document, whether it is a note to a co-worker, a memo to be sent through electronic mail, a letter of inquiry, or a formal business report, you follow a process. This process helps ensure the message you send is complete, correct, precise, and formatted for business correspondence. At times you may do one step more than another, but never shortcut the process or you will leave out steps necessary for effective written communication. By following the basic steps, you can be sure the message is complete and you will have a professionally written document for distribution.

Analyze the Situation

Analyzing the situation to determine your purpose is the first step in writing. Without this step, you have no direction for planning your message. In the business office, there are different kinds of writing tasks for different purposes. Your purpose may be to leave a phone message for someone, to give instructions or work assignments, to write a letter of acknowledgment or request, or to present information to someone through a memorandum or business report.

Identify Your Audience

You must know what you want your message to achieve. Is your audience a customer, a co-worker, or a newspaper reporter? If you have an image of the reader(s) in mind, you are better able to aim your message accurately. Although courteousness is important you might adopt one tone when writing a valued client about a missed payment and another tone when writing to a problem client who often misses payments. Your audience determines whether you use a conversational tone or a more formal tone. Most important, the tone of your letter should match the message of your letter.

Determine the Best Method for Preparing the Document

Determine the best choice of hardware and software to prepare your document. Is there stored information that can be used to prepare the document? Are there sources of information to be consulted before preparation can begin?

Determine the Format of the Document

Is the document a memo, a letter, an electronic mail message, or a report? The type of document determines the format you will use. Shorter, informal announcements are usually prepared in memo form. Detailed business analysis is usually prepared in a report.

Plan Your Message

Organize your source material and then prepare an outline of your message by listing the points logically and following this general format:

- Begin your communications with the most important information or facts.

- Follow up with details.

- Close with a tone of goodwill.

Follow these guidelines when writing:

1. *Be clear and specific.* Give the reader as much information as you can while avoiding unnecessary detail. For example, if you have the responsibility for arranging a conference and must write to the convention site about your needs, it is better to write, "We will need a room that will hold at least 50 people," rather than "We will need a large room."
2. *Keep to the point.* Without sacrificing courteousness, focus on your topic and be concise. Being too short can seem rude, but a wordy, rambling message wastes the receiver's time, which is the ultimate rudeness. A well-written message exhibits a skillful balance.
3. *Be yourself.* This is as true in writing as in any interpersonal activity. Writing is a more structured and formal exchange of information than is oral communication, which means you have more leeway in using a higher level vocabulary and more eloquent sentences. Nevertheless, be yourself and sound natural, and make sure your writing has a businesslike tone.
4. *Exercise empathy.* Empathy is the ability to understand and feel what others feel. Identify your readers, and then put yourself in their shoes as you read over the message you have prepared. Ask yourself if they will receive the message as you intend them to receive it, or could they misinterpret it?
5. *Be courteous.* Although writing is not a direct person-to-person activity, human relations are important. Being businesslike does not mean being brusque or short. A written business message should quickly reach the point, but not so fast that it strikes the receiver(s) as rude. Studies indicate

that when people communicate via computer, either interactively or by leaving messages, they tend to be brusque and less polite. This is something to watch, if you are in a position to communicate via computer.

6. *Avoid jargon.* **Jargon** is specialized technical language not normally used in everyday communication. In this book we have talked about hard copy and soft copy, for example. These terms represent the jargon of the electronic office. Avoid such terms in written messages to people outside your office unless you are certain they will understand them.

Write the First Draft

Following your outline, write a first draft of your message. Your goal at this point is to get the information into usable form. Follow the rules you know for sentence structure, grammar, punctuation, and spelling, but do not worry too much about fine tuning the grammar and punctuation at this stage. You will do that in the editing/revising stage.

Edit and Revise the Document

After writing the first draft of the message, edit and revise the content—check the completeness and accuracy of information,

Figure 12.2 Using the keyboard to compose documents is a different mental process from transcribing copy that someone else has written.

organization, sentence clarity, word choice, and tone. Keep in mind the items mentioned in planning your message. Use the following as a checklist to ensure your message is complete, clear, and to the point.

1. *Read the message from the recipient's point of view.* Have you given enough information or too much? Are you making assumptions that the reader may not make?
2. *Be complete.* Include all pertinent information. Journalism's who? where? when? what? and why? are good guidelines to follow. Not all your messages will require answers to each of these questions, but checking your message against them will ensure that you have included everything.
3. *Be organized.* Your message should be presented in a clear and logical order. Do not jump from idea to idea.
4. *Use the active voice.* Experts recommend using the active voice as much as possible in writing. The active voice is direct and to the point: "We appreciate your order" is better than "Your order is appreciated." The former is the active voice; the latter the passive. When you use the active voice you are writing in the third person. Many writers of business messages begin sentences with the word *it,* as in "It is found that. . . ." This is a weak way to state something, and you should avoid it when possible. Instead, be more direct by using the first person, "We have found that. . . ."
5. *Be concise.* Avoid using long sentences and many words. Use "because" instead of "due to the fact that"; "the consensus" instead of "the general consensus of opinion." Watch for useless modifiers, redundant expressions, and phrases used in place of single words.
6. *Do not overexplain.* Many details will not necessarily make the subject matter clearer to the reader. Too much detail or explanation can confuse rather than clarify, especially in a business communication.
7. *Use positive expressions.* Instead of writing "We do not have a need for your products," say "We are satisfied with our current supplier."
8. *Be definite and firm in your statements.* Instead of writing "We do not believe that we can accept your offer at this time," write "We are not able to accept your offer at this time."

Anyone preparing written messages should have on hand reference manuals such as *The Elements of Style,* by William Strunk Jr. and E. B. White. This slim volume is packed with good advice for all writers.

PROOFREAD FOR ERRORS

After your message is complete, well organized, and effectively written, you are ready to proofread for other errors: typographical errors, grammatical mistakes, and punctuation and formatting inconsistencies. If time allows, ask another person to proofread your long documents as well. Often another person's viewpoint can reveal blatant errors and also determine whether the message is clear and understandable.

1. *Proofread for accuracy.* Check the accuracy of your facts. Compare the information in your document against your source documents. Research any information when you are not certain of it.
2. *Proofread against source.* You must know grammar, punctuation, and spelling, as well as have a good vocabulary for the editing and transcription functions of writing. Your software may have an automatic spellchecker, grammar checker, and thesaurus to help you find mistakes. These software features are described in detail in the next chapter.
3. *Proofread for consistency.* Make sure that your format is consistent throughout the document. For example, if you decide to indent the first line of paragraphs, do so throughout. Will you capitalize abbreviations, such as A.M. and P.M., or write them in lowercase? Either way is correct, as long as you use only one way throughout.

REREAD THE FINAL DRAFT

Read once again for any errors that may have slipped through. Sometimes when you make changes to your original document, you introduce new errors. Return to your source information and double check the information in your document. Be sure material recently introduced to your document is worded and formatted in the same manner as the rest of the information.

DISTRIBUTE THE MESSAGE

Decide on the best method of distribution for the document and send it to the intended receiver. Be sure to evaluate all of the options available to you. Do you or the receiver need a hard copy or is an electronic mail message sufficient? Are there others who would benefit from seeing a copy of the message? Should the document be in a sealed container so others do not have access to the information?

DICTATING AND TRANSCRIBING WRITTEN DOCUMENTS

Dictation is often used in the document creation process in place of keying or writing the first draft in longhand. You may have the opportunity to create documents by dictating to a person or by using a dictation machine. When you dictate a document you follow a process that is the similar to the writing process. After all, you are preparing a written message; the only difference is that you prepare it by speaking and not literally writing it at this point.

The basic process for dictating a document includes the following:

1. *Determine your audience.*
2. *Plan your message.* Write a short outline or list of topics to be covered. If someone else will transcribe the dication, state any special notes or instructions to assist the transcriber.
3. *Dictate the message.* Inform the transcriptionist of the following:
   - Type of message (letter, memo, report, news release, etc.)
   - Whom the message is to; their address or department
   - When the document has to be distributed
   - Any special spellings or unclear information
   - If you are not sure of numbers, ask the transcriber to verify them

   Speak clearly and in a conversational tone. If you make corrections, tell the transcriber what to correct. End the message with a statement to the transcriber such as "end of document."
4. *Edit the transcribed message.* Make corrections or return the edited document to the transcriptionist for a final draft.
5. *Sign the final draft for distribution.*

Transcription is a different function because, in the transcription process, you do not create new documents; you listen to another person's words or read your shorthand notes and transcribe what was recorded.

Transcribing a dictated document accurately requires your writing skills: make sure the message is complete and accurate. Since transcription is part of processing documents, we will revisit this process in the next chapter.

1. *Know the originator's purpose and audience.* The originator gives you this information.

Figure 12.3 Technology has increased the options available for creating documents, but dictation and transcription are still important functions in the data creation process.

2. *Plan how you will transcribe the document.* What format should be used? Is a rough draft necessary? When does it have to be completed? What hardware and software should be used?

3. *Transcribe the notes or the recorded material.* Listen to the dictated tape or read your notes, then proceed with the transcription.

4. *Edit the transcribed document.* Be sure the originator has made the message clear and organized it well.

5. *Edit and proofread for grammar, punctuation, spelling, and formatting.* Look for things such as accuracy of the date and any other numerical information, fact accuracy, and grammar, punctuation, and spelling consistency. Check the spelling of the names and addresses. If there are enclosures or attachments, be sure to include them when you give the document to the originator for final signature or approval.

6. *Present the document for signature.*

7. *Make necessary revisions.* If changes were made by the originator repeat the process and submit again for the signature.

8. *Print the final copy and distribute.*

READING WRITTEN COMMUNICATION

As with writing skills, practice will improve your reading skills. Here are some techniques to practice or keep in mind when you read:

- **Sit in a comfortable position.** The more comfortable you are, the better you can concentrate.
- **Have adequate lighting.** The company you work for is required by law to provide adequate and safe working conditions, which includes adequate lighting. Position your computer screen away from any light that causes a glare.
- **Have a noise-free environment.** Again, your company is responsible for providing an environment that is relatively noise free; however, some noise cannot be avoided in large offices. Do what you can to minimize it.
- **Highlight important points.** In letters and memos, highlight with a colored marker or by underlining the important points so you can see them at a glance. For long reports or books, make notes of the important points.

- **Improve your vocabulary.** You will have to learn the jargon of your particular business. If your job is in a highly technical field, you can learn through practice to read technical material. Make a practice of asking someone or looking up unfamiliar words in the dictionary.
- **Learn to read material.** A good reading technique in any situation is scanning. Look through the material quickly, reading the table of contents and subheads and formulating a picture of what the material is about and how the information flows. Then look for summary paragraphs at the ends of the chapters. Review the material for help sections such as the table of contents, glossary, index, and troubleshooting sections. After you have the general idea, go back and read more closely.

TYPES OF WRITTEN BUSINESS COMMUNICATIONS

In the business office, most written documents take one of four forms:

- **Memorandums (Memos)**—brief, direct, sometimes informal communication among people who work for the same organization.
- **Letters**—more formal communications with people outside the organization.
- **Reports**—documents used to communicate information in depth to people both inside and outside the organization. Usu-

ally they are lengthy, but sometimes reports are written in memo form.

- **Public Relations Publications**—newsletters, news releases, speeches, presentations, or publications.

You will encounter these typical forms of written communication on the job, both in hard copy and in soft copy. Because you will be involved in writing as well as reading them, you should be familiar with each one.

MEMORANDUMS (MEMOS)

Most business memos are written to convey short messages or provide brief reports on routine matters. Staff announcements, project status reports, meeting notices, agendas, and minutes are all common subject matter for interoffice memorandums. Like all other written communications, memos serve two basic functions: they transmit information, and they provide a record of the information and the fact that it was transmitted.

Memos are most useful in the quick exchange of information among co-workers. In some organizations, people send memos about everything they do. They do this for a good reason—to avoid being misunderstood—and sometimes for another reason—to protect themselves by having a record. Then they can prove exactly what their actions were in any situation. One good reason for writing a memo is to avoid interrupting co-workers with telephone calls for business that is not really urgent. For messages that are complicated or where a record is needed, memos are usually the best medium to use.

All memos must contain the date, the sender's name, the receiver's name, and the purpose or subject of the message. This simple format allows the reader quickly to see what it is about. To speed up the writing of memos, some companies provide forms with preprinted headings for the date, the names of the writer and the recipients, and the subject. Some companies may have their own memo format to follow, and E-mail systems also may have a standard *To, From, Date,* and *Subject* format. Figures 12.4A, 12.4B, and 12.4C show different memo formats that are considered standard. The simplified format is recommended by the Professional Secretaries International organization as the fastest and least cumbersome to use.

The content of a memo needs to be focused and concise. The main purpose of the memo should be stated first, with details and a closing or the action for the reader to take after the main purpose. Normally, a memo covers only one subject. Rather than

Simplified Memo (Blank Paper)

```
February 9, 19--

To: Bill Walczak, Educational Consultant

Ron Decker, Editorial Department

SEMINAR OUTLINE


Ron, attached is the revised seminar outline for the program on
Organizational Communication.

Ned Ostenso, Bill Sleep, Randy Smith and I collaborated on this
revision.  Please note that we changed the name of the program.
We feel that this is really a better description of the content
of the seminar.

Please let us know when you are ready to review the program.

kw

Attachment

c:  Mark Mitchell
    Ned Ostenso
    Bill Sleep
    Randy Smith
```

Figure 12.4A Simplified memo format.

Preprinted Memo Format

WALCZAK CONSULTING CO.
MEMORANDUM

```
date:    February 9, 19--

to:      Ron Decker, Editorial Department

from:    Bill Walczak, Educational Consultant

subject: SEMINAR OUTLINE


Ron, attached is the revised seminar outline for the program on
Organizational Communication.

Ned Ostenso, Bill Sleep, Randy Smith and I collaborated on this
revision.  Please note that we changed the name of the program.
We feel that this is really a better description of the content
of the seminar.

Please let us know when you are ready to review the program.

kw

Attachment

c:  Mark Mitchell
    Ned Ostenso
    Bill Sleep
    Randy Smith
```

Figure 12.4B Preprinted memo form.

Keyed Memo Form

```
date:      February 9, 19--

to:        Bill Walczak, Educational Consultant

from:      Ron Decker, Editorial Department

subject:   SEMINAR OUTLINE


Ron, attached is the revised seminar outline for the program on
Organizational Communication.

Ned Ostenso, Bill Sleep, Randy Smith and I collaborated on this
revision.  Please note that we changed the name of the program.
We feel that this is really a better description of the content
of the seminar.

Please let us know when you are ready to review the program.

kw

Attachment

c:  Mark Mitchell
    Ned Ostenso
    Bill Sleep
    Randy Smith
```

Figure 12.4C Keyed memo form.

putting two unrelated topics in the same memo, write two separate memos, even though they are both going to the same person at the same time. This allows the recipient to deal with each subject separately and maintain accurate files.

The writing process is the same for a memo as for all other written documents: define the purpose and audience, plan the message, write the message, edit and revise the content, proofread, and distribute. Hard copies of memos are distributed by hand. You might deliver a memo personally if you needed an immediate response. Otherwise, use interoffice mail. Most large companies have special envelopes for this purpose. With electronic mail the memo is sent directly from your computer to the recipient's computer in soft copy form.

In the following example, Rita has been asked by her supervisor to write a memo to two employees to check the status of a project. Rita first determined that the purpose of the memo was to request information for her supervisor. The audience was Craig Xang and Emma Walters. Her plan consisted of the following notes:

- Skylight Window, Project #458, due August 12

- Small-paned Window, Project #873, due August 18

- Information due within two days

After writing the memo, Rita revised and edited it, checking for the accuracy of the project numbers and due dates. Her next step was to proofread it for errors in grammar, punctuation, and spelling. Rita's completed memo is shown below.

August 2, 199-

TO: Craig Xang
       Emma Walters

FROM: Rita Roeser, Assistant to Department Manager

PROJECT COMPLETION DATES

Ms. Shelton would like a report on your progress to date on the following projects:
  • Skylight Window, Project #458, due August 12
  • Small-paned Window, Project #873, due August 18
Please give her a brief written report within two days.

LETTERS

When you or your supervisor must communicate in writing with someone outside your organization, the most common method would be by letter. Letters are usually more formal than memos because they most often go to people outside your company. For this reason, it is essential that they create a good impression.

Like memos, letters have standard parts or sections. Since most people are familiar with and expect to see these parts of a letter, using them helps the process of communication. Not using them or using them incorrectly can hinder communication. Figure 12.5 shows the standard parts of a letter.

Although the general rule is to keep letters short—no more than one page—sometimes that is not possible. When letters consist of two or more pages, you need a format for the pages after page 1. Chapter 13 contains more processing and formatting information.

Typical types of letters that you may be asked to write as an administrative assistant are as follows:

• Request and inquiry letters

• Response letters

• Confirmation letters

FORMATTING GUIDELINES

Letters and Memos:
- Always use the writing process for creating communications.
- Use a consistent format.
- Use word processing or E-mail for processing.
- Identify the document with the electronic filename for ease of storage and retrieval.
- Use plain paper for rough drafts.
- Use plain paper for memos unless the company provides preprinted forms.
- Use the company's letterhead for letters.

Multiple Pages:
- Use plain paper without a letterhead but of the same size and quality as page 1.
- Have the same side margins as on page 1.
- Start the first line at least 1 inch, but no more than 2 inches, from the top.
- Have a heading on each page after page 1 that includes the addressee's name, the page number, and the date. These can all be on one line, which saves space; or each element can be on a separate line.

Letters that your supervisor may write and that you will edit into final form include the following:

- Goodwill letters

- Refusal letters

- Claim letters and adjustment letters

- Credit and collection letters

Following are some examples of the writing style and content for each of these types of letters.

Request and Inquiry Letters

Along with response letters, request and inquiry letters make up the bulk of most business correspondence. Businesses generate a constant flow of letters seeking information, requesting goods or materials, and asking for services or reservations. These letters should be brief, to the point, and worded to encourage a fast response. Unless the specific situation suggests otherwise, the general flow of information in the letter is to start with stating the request, then state the action you want the reader to take, and close with a courteous statement.

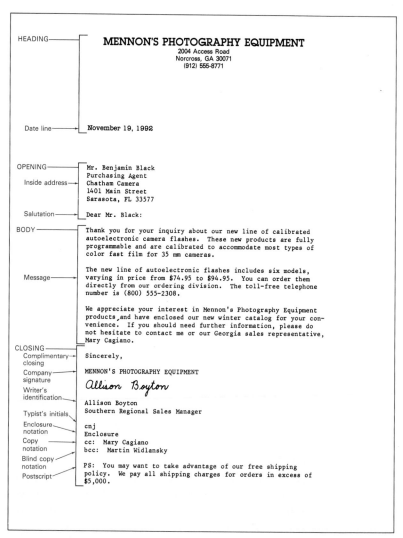

Figure 12.5A The block style is a standard letter format because it is the easiest and fastest to key.

ILLINOIS OFFICE TECHNOLOGIES, INC.
3200 South Michigan Avenue
Chicago, IL 60611
(312) 555-8700

August 22, 1992

Ms. Diane Nelson
Advertising Manager
Business Network Supplies Center
220 Delaware Avenue
Buffalo, NY 14202

Dear Ms. Nelson:

Would you please send me your current office supplies catalog
and price list? I am in charge of our company's reference
center and receive requests from my coworkers for office
supplies and equipment catalogs.

May I be put on your mailing list so that I will receive new
catalogs as they are available?

                    Sincerely,

                    ILLINOIS OFFICE TECHNOLOGIES, INC.

                    David P. Weinstein

                    David P. Weinstein
                    Reference Center Associate

pd

**Figure 12.5B The modified block format is a frequently used format in
business correspondence.**

Weinstein & Associates
1400 East Alpine Avenue
Topeka, KS 99178

Business Network Supplies Center
23 East 45 Street
New Haven, CT 78263

REQUEST FOR MATERIALS

In the last *Information Today*, you advertised a free supply
kit for users of your products. As a devoted purchaser of
your supplies, I would like to receive this kit. I know that it
will contain many of the same quality supplies I purchase regularly.

You may send the kit to me at the above address. I look forward
to receiving it soon.

Sincerely,

Alan Weinstein
President

Response Letters

Often letters are written in response to a request or inquiry.
Response letters should answer the request or question directly,
and they should be prepared and sent promptly.

Organizations that receive many similar request letters usually have preprinted **form letters** or **boilerplate** paragraphs
that are electronically stored so there is no need to create original letters for each response. A form letter could easily be used
by the Business Network Supplies Center to reply to customers'
requests. Because customers prefer to get personalized attention,
you could personalize the response by adding information aimed
specifically at Mr. Weinstein's company.

Dear Mr. Weinstein:

(blank)

The enclosed summer catalog includes the latest product

and price listings from Business Network Supplies Center.

You may find the information about our new telecommuni-

(blank)

cations equipment on pages 49 to 61 especially interesting.

Your complimentary supply kit has been mailed as you

(blank)

requested. You will receive all our new-product announce-

ments automatically as well as our seasonal catalogs. The

next one will be available in September.

Thank you for writing Business Network Supplies Cen-

ter. We are proud of our products and look forward to serv-

ing your company.

Cordially,

Confirmation Letters

Confirmation letters confirm an action that has been agreed on or the outcome of a discussion that has taken place. Examples of confirmation letters include those to confirm appointments, meeting dates and times, or contract terms. As an administrative assistant, you will make appointments and plan meetings routinely. Confirming these arrangements is necessary to ensure that all parties have the same understanding. Assume you have been asked to set up an out-of-town appointment for your supervisor, Jonathan Winchester. You have made all the necessary travel arrangements, but you want to confirm the time and place of the meeting with the person Mr. Winchester is scheduled to see. You would begin by determining the name of the person handling arrangements at the firm Mr. Winchester will visit and listing the information you have about Mr. Winchester's travel plans and the meeting schedule:

- Arrive September 1—London—7:45 P.M.

- Hotel: London Hilton

- Breakfast with Mr. Bentley, Director of London Operations, 8 A.M., September 2. Mr. Bentley's assistant is Alicia Walker.

- Meeting room at London Hilton reserved for September 2 and 3. London staff exptected to arrive by 10 A.M. September 2 to begin meeting.

You are now ready to write the letter.

August 5, 199-

Ms. Alicia Walker
Assistant to C. Bentley
Mass Transit International
8907 Lighthouse Road
London, England

Dear Ms. Walker:

This is to confirm that Mr. Winchester will arrive in London on Sunday evening, September 1. He will go directly from the airport to the London Hilton Hotel by taxi.

The arrangements for the staff meeting at the London Hilton Hotel have been confirmed. The two-day general staff meeting is scheduled to begin at 10 A.M. on Monday, September 2. Mr. Winchester is looking forward to having Mr. Bentley meet him at the hotel for an 8 A.M. breakfast prior to the meeting.

We are completing the final agenda and expect to send it to you for confirmation within a few days. I have enjoyed working with you on setting up this important event and know that this trip will be as satisfactory as Mr. Winchester's previous trips to the London office.

Sincerely,

Your name
Assistant

Goodwill Letters

All letters should have a friendly tone and serve as goodwill builders. Some letters are written specifically to generate goodwill for a company. Such letters include announcements, invitations, and messages of sympathy, appreciation, congratulations, and praise.

Goodwill letters should be written promptly, and they should be enthusiastic, somewhat informal, and—most important—sincere. If the sincerity is forced, the letter may seem hypocritical and do more harm than good. Here is an example of a simple goodwill-building letter:

Dear Michael:

The seminar you organized, "Living with Automation," was the best of its kind. I want you to know how thoroughly my staff enjoyed it.

All your speakers were excellent, but my staff identified Jonah Stonington, who covered voice-activated input, as the best. He reportedly presented a very technical topic with ease and humor—not an easy task, as I am sure you know.

Attending seminars like yours is time well spent. My staff and I look forward to the next seminar in your series on office automation.

Cordially,

Ryan Manning
Human Resources Manager

Refusal Letters

The purpose of a refusal letter is to tell someone no. Few people react well to negative news, which makes tact of utmost importance when you are writing refusal letters. You will write refusal letters when you do not have the information requested, or when you are out of stock on an item, or when, for any reason, you cannot comply with a request.

While you may not be able to build goodwill with a refusal letter, the objective is to avoid destroying goodwill as much as possible. A well-written refusal letters is a real test of writing skills. You must find a way to phrase a negative response in a positive way. The following refusal letter says no in a helpful and tactful tone. It also sets a positive note by suggesting a course of action that would result in the *no* becoming *yes*.

Dear Mrs. Rios:

Thank you for your letter asking for a special discount on your quarterly copier-paper order. As a valued customer, you know that our prices are quite competitive and that under certain circumstances we have a discount policy. Our discount policy is explained on the back of the invoices included with your orders. That policy allows a 10 percent discount on orders exceeding 500 sheets.

We noted in a review of your account, Mrs. Rios, that you order quarterly in amounts of about 250 sheets, which unfortunately does not qualify Rios Hardware for the discount. May we suggest that instead of ordering for a quarter, you anticipate your paper needs for longer periods. If you combine your fall and winter or spring and summer orders, they will probably exceed the 500-sheet minimum, which will qualify your order for the discount.

We appreciate your business and hope our suggestion will help our valued customer, Rios Hardware.

Sincerely,

Samuel P. Schwartz
Marketing Agent

Claim Letters and Adjustment Letters

A claim letter usually contains a complaint about something, such as slow service, faulty or wrong merchandise, invoice errors, or even discourteous service. A claim letter is an attempt to get satisfaction from a company in the form of an explanation, a compensation, or a replacement.

The receiver of a claim letter responds with an adjustment letter, which explains how the mistake can be rectified or suggests some other means for providing satisfaction for the person who has lodged the complaint.

When writing or editing a claim letter, keep it short, direct, and specific. If you are writing or editing an adjustment letter, be sure you are familiar with your company's policies on claims and adjustments. You must also keep customer satisfaction as your primary objective.

The following are examples of claim and adjustment letters:

Claim Letter

Dear Customer Service:

The digital AM/FM clock radio that I ordered from Ridgeway Electronics arrived yesterday. It was poorly packed, and the plastic shelf over the radio call numbers was smashed.

I used your mail-order toll-free number for out-of-state residents to order this product. I ordered it on January 25 and charged it to my MasterCard credit card, number 5183-0005-0992-8554. The clock radio model number is AX 411.

I am returning the damaged product in this package and would like you to replace it with an undamaged one. If possible, please send me the replacement within the next two weeks.

Sincerely,

(Mrs.) Dorothy Marceau

Adjustment Letter

Dear Mrs. Marceau:

A new digital AM/FM clock radio is being shipped to you today. You should receive it within two weeks.

We appreciate your detailed explanation and prompt return of the damaged product, which made it possible for us to make the replacement quickly. We are sorry for any inconvenience this has caused you. Enclosed is a copy of Ridgeway's monthly listening guide to local radio programming. We hope it increases your listening pleasure.

We look forward to serving you again.

Cordially,

Peter Levertov
Claims and Adjustments Manager

Credit and Collection Letters

The clock radio referred to in the previous letter was purchased with a credit card. Credit cards and charge cards are used extensively for personal and business expenses. To obtain a credit account, you apply to the sponsoring store or bank with an application form. The store or bank then checks your financial record and responds favorably or unfavorably.

The response letter telling you whether or not your application has been accepted is often a form letter or boilerplate. If you work in a word processing or electronic office, all you need to do to write a credit letter is retrieve the file containing the boiler-plate paragraphs on the computer and insert the specific information, such as the applicant's name and address.

Use a positive, warm tone in credit letters either approving or rejecting an applicant. Here are samples of both:

Credit Letter (Approving)

Dear Miss Lauro:

Congratulations on joining the Halls family of credit customers. Your charge card is enclosed, and we are certain that its use will make your shopping more convenient.

As a valued credit customer, you are entitled to special treatment at Halls. Your charge card can be used to purchase all our services and merchandise. In addition, you will receive our monthly catalogs announcing sales before they are publicly advertised! You will be invited to our bi-annual fashion shows featuring the latest styles from New York, Paris, Milan, and Tokyo. And bring a friend to our exquisite dining facilities on our seventh floor—you will both be offered a complimentary dessert of your choice.

Terms for your charge card use are explained in the enclosed contract. We hope you enjoy the privileges of our special family of Halls charge-card holders, Miss Lauro. We welcome you and look forward to serving you.

Sincerely,

Danielle Watson
Credit Supervisor

Credit Letter (Rejecting)

Dear Miss Lauro:

The Halls Department Store staff always appreciates-hearing from a customer. Thank you for submitting a credit application.

As is our policy, we reviewed the information on your application form carefully. Since you do, at this time, have a number of outstanding credit commitments, may we suggest that you continue to allow Halls to serve you on a cash basis.

The personnel at Halls look forward to continuing their present association with you, Miss Lauro. Should you resubmit your application for credit when you have fewer financial commitments, we will welcome the opportunity to reconsider it.

Sincerely,

Danielle Watson
Credit Supervisor

Despite careful checking, department stores and banks always encounter some credit customers who do not pay promptly. When a customer has defaulted on several payments, a collection notice is sent. Again, these notices are often form letters or boilerplate. When a person first fails to pay on time, the first notice is usually a polite reminder. If payment is not made over a period of time, the collection letters become increasingly stern. The final collection letter is a stern demand for payment, often threatening legal action. Here is an example of such a letter:

Collection Letter

Dear Miss Lauro:

This is our fourth and final reminder that your payment of $149.95 on your Halls account is overdue. If payment is not received by October 15, we will unfortunately be forced to turn your account over to a collection agency.

We realize that such a drastic step might damage your credit reputation, and we sincerely hope that it will not be necessary for us to do this. We take this action only when we believe that a customer has no intention of paying. You can prevent this action, Miss Lauro, by sending your payment of $149.95 by the above-stated date.

Sincerely,

Danielle Watson
Credit Supervisor

REPORTS

Business reports are written to communicate several facts and ideas to people inside or outside the company. Because reports usually cover a topic in depth, their preparation requires more time and effort than the preparation of most business letters and memos. When you compile a report, take the following steps:

1. Determine the purpose of the report.
2. Prepare an outline listing all the sections of the report, including the topics in each section (see figure 12.6).

```
            REPORT OF THE OFFICE EQUIPMENT COMMITTEE


    I.   PURPOSE OF STUDY - PHOTOCOPIER NEEDED


   II.   SCOPE OF STUDY

         A.  Copying needs - by department
         B.  Equipment available


  III.   PROCEDURES

         A.  How much copying do we do?
             1.  Volume
             2.  Paper sizes used
             3.  Capabilities used
             4.  How many machines?  What kinds?
             5.  Changes projected?
         B.  Machines tested
             1.  Capabilities
             2.  Performance
             3.  Costs for leasing or buying
             4.  Service contracts available
         C.  User reactions - by department


   IV.   FINDINGS


    V.   RECOMMENDATIONS AND CONCLUSIONS
```

Figure 12.6 An outline is an invaluable guide in helping you to prepare a report.

3. Conduct any necessary research.
4. Write the report in draft form.
5. Edit and revise the content of the report.
6. Proofread the report for errors in grammar, punctuation, spelling, and formatting.

Formal Reports

Formal reports can be a few pages or many. Some reports are divided into sections and may require special printing and binding. Following are the standard parts of a formal report:

- **Title Page** The first page of the report, which includes the report's title, receivers, author, and submission date.

- **Preface** An introductory statement of what the report contains.

- **Table of Contents** A list of the various sections of the report.

- **List of Illustrations** A list of pictures and graphics with page numbers.

- **Synopsis** A brief summary of the main points and conclusions.

- **Body of Text** The main message of the report.

- **Appendix** A supplementary section containing supporting documents or data.

- **Bibliography** A list of the books and periodicals used as sources. Each entry in the bibliography includes the author's name, title of source, publisher, place of publication, and date of publication. The entries should be listed alphabetically by author's last name.

- **Index** An alphabetical list of significant topics.

- **Letter of Transmittal** Usually correspondence accompanying the report that explains the report and provides background on any research that was conducted. If the report is for distribution within the organization only, the letter of transmittal is in the form of a memo; if the report goes outside of the organization, it is in letter format.

Each part of a formal report has standard formatting requirements. The preliminary materials, or frontmatter, include the title page, table of contents, preface, and list of illustrations. These pages are numbered consecutively with small roman numerals, except for the title page, which is not numbered. A report includes the body of the text, the appendix, the bibliography, and the index. These pages are numbered consecutively with arabic numbers. Usually the report begins with an introductory section, followed by a synopsis of the general findings or summary of the research. The body of the report contains the details of each topic. A closing section contains additional documents, lists, or tables that support the information in the body.

There are many different formats you can use to arrange a formal business report. Use a style manual such as the *Paradigm Reference Manual* to choose the best style.

Memo Report

A memo report is usually a short report that does not contain all the parts needed in a formal report. Figure 12.7 shows an example of a memo report.

GUIDELINES FOR USING BUSINESS GRAPHICS

Integration of graphics into a business report can greatly enhance the message being delivered. Follow these general guidelines for using business graphics in business reports.

Graphs

- Line graphs usually show the relationship of information or data to a timeline. The bottom portion of the graph usually represents time (days, weeks, months, hours, years, etc.) and the side represents other measures or items.
- Bar graphs show relationships between two sets of data and are constructed either vertically or horizontally. The bars should be of equal width and wider than the space between the increments.
- Pie graphs represent simple data for comparison such as percentages of a whole. The largest portion of the graph usually begins at the 12 o'clock position and then the other portions are presented in order of descending size. You can shade a part of the graphic you want to highlight or separate a section from the rest of the pie.

- Other charts such as organization charts, schematics, or room layouts may enhance the message of the business report.

Positioning of Graphs

- Always position the graph after the text explaining what it is.
- Title the graph with the name of the graph, subtitle if necessary, and figure name or number to be referred to in the text.
- A graph should always illustrate the information explained in the text.
- A graph should be able to stand on its own and not need full explanation.
- Position graphs appropriately for their content.
- Do not skew the numbers in the graph to make information appear what it is not.
- Always use software or other professional techniques to put graphics in a publication. Hand drawings and handwriting are not appropriate for business publications.

Example of a Memorandum Report

Current Date

TO: You, the Student

Business People of America

MEMORANDUM REPORT PREPARATION

Reports in business are frequently prepared in different forms from those in
education. You are looking at a very popular example, the memo report.
Rather than prepare both a report and an accompanying letter or memo, the two
are combined. This method is usually used for reports that are fairly short,
fewer than three pages. You will notice that the style is the same as shown
in the memorandum section of this text.

Many times you will find that the report content lends itself to the use of
subheadings as shown below.

Summary. The findings of the survey of advertising at Old London Square Mall
are similar to the national trends. All the mall stores use, in addition to
local cooperative advertising, some type of outside media. The choice of outside media compares quite closely with national trends, since newspaper is
listed most effective and used most frequently, followed by radio, television,
direct mailing, and magazines.

Background. Our organization entered into an agreement three months ago with
the merchants of the Old London Square Mall to investigate avenues of approach
to effective advertising. We assigned methods currently in use throughout the
nation, and especially those methods utilized by businesses in some type of
physical location arrangement (shopping centers, malls, and so on). After
gathering the evidence used throughout the country, a questionnaire was prepared and administered to all the merchants located in the Old London Square
Mall. The results of both the nationwide survey and the mall survey were then
compared.

Findings. Nationwide merchants agree that individual firms must do more
advertising than the cooperative efforts the mall association makes. Cooperative efforts seem to be quite effective when the entire mall conducts some
type of sale (usually seasonal), but for the remainder of the time it is the
individual firm which must generate sales by individual advertising efforts.
The Old London Square Mall merchants agree with this 100%. The national use
and popularity of various types of advertising media is somewhat different
from what the Old London Square Mall merchants now use.

You, the Student
Page -2-
Current Date

Types of Advertising Media

Nationwide	Old London Square Mall
newspaper	newspaper
television	radio
radio	television
direct mail	direct mail
magazines	magazines

Ranked according to frequency of utilization

Conclusion. The use of advertising media by merchants at the Old London
Square Mall closely follows what is being done on a national scale. The only
difference found was in the ranking of television and radio. Television is
second in popularity nationwide, and radio is third. At the Old London Square
Mall, radio is second in popularity and television is third.

Recommendations. Our agreement called for both a written report and an oral
presentation of the findings. This information was given to the merchants at
their last monthly meeting. A recommendation was made that the merchants
utilize television more than radio in the future. After discussion, it was
decided by the members in attendance to follow this recommendation for the
next six mothes. Accordingly, the mall manager was instructed to change the
mall cooperative advertising campaign. We were give another agreement to
provide a research follow-up report at the conclusion of the trial period.

Follow-up. Jim Lane will be in charge of the follow-up research project.
Alice Barnes, June Folton, Bob Arterburn, and Leslie Barth will work with him.

**Figure 12.7 Memorandum reports are used frequently in most business
offices.**

After determining the purpose and audience for your report, you can then choose whether your report needs to be formal or a memo report. You are then ready to write your outline. You should be able to put your information in correct order for writing. After writing the report, edit for content, proofread for errors and formatting, and print the final report.

PUBLIC RELATIONS INFORMATION

More and more, administrative assistants are being asked to write public relations information. With the use of desktop publishing capabilities, secretaries are being asked to write such materials as announcements and newsletters. We will not cover the particulars of planning and creating the various kinds of public relations materials offices produce, but by taking a closer look at the creation of a newsletter, we can provide a good example of the kind of material you may be required to handle as a part of your document creation responsibilities.

Newsletter writing is different from the type of writing used in a business letter. The same writing process is used, but the message has to be presented differently. You are not requesting or collecting information but passing on information in a public forum. Therefore, you use a news style or a journalistic style. Some general guidelines for this type of writing include the following:

• Write as simply as possible.

• Be short, be friendly, and be specific.

• Use a variety of verbs, especially action verbs.

• Arouse the reader's interest in the first sentence (lead in) of a news story.

• Place the important information early in the article with detail reported later.

• The tone should be professional, but including a bit of humor at appropriate times can make your report more readable.

• Use quotes to give authenticity to your information. But be sure they are not taken out of context or give the wrong impression.

• Stay away from clichés, for example, "as happy as a lark;" "shedding an image."

• Shun racial, gender, or religious bias.

Following is an example of a newsletter article.

Business Council Installs New Leadership

At the January meeting Kay Magadance was installed as president of the Business Council for 1991.

Kay is currently the Assistant Manager for Records and Data Systems at Data Tech, Inc. She has served the Business Council as historian, recording secretary, and vice president. She is a member of the Indianhead Data Processing Organization and a volunteer for the Los Angeles Service League.

Kay has made numerous presentations at the conferences of the American Association of Business Leaders and other professional organizations. Her main goal for this year is to increase the involvement of both current and past council members. She encourages the members to provide comments and suggestions, and to become involved.

Besides writing articles, there are other formatting and stylistic considerations when creating a newsletter. These will be discussed in the next chapter.

Written communication will fill a large part of your working day in the office. You will be a valued worker if you can write effective communications and adapt your writing to cover a variety of situations. Use appropriate tools to help you in the writing process. But always follow the process; it may be shorter or longer depending on the type of document, but you must always know your purpose for writing, plan your message, write the message, edit and revise the content, proofread, and prepare the final copy.

SUMMARY

- Written communication does not have the spontaneity and immediate feedback of oral communication. But it has the advantages of giving you time to prepare a message and a permanent record of it. Well-written communications are a characteristic of a well-run company.

- Writing is a skill that can be improved with practice. The basic steps in the writing process can help you improve writing skills. These steps include analyzing the problem, identifying the audience, determining the best method for preparing the document, determining a document format, planning the message, writing the first draft, editing and revising, proofreading, and distributing.

- Some general writing techniques to remember are to be yourself, know your reader, exercise empathy, be courteous, and keep to the point. A good writer is results-oriented; organizes the message; is clear, specific, complete, and accurate; avoids jargon; and proofreads.

- Techniques to improve your reading skills include being comfortable in a noise-free environment with adequate lighting, highlighting important points in the text, learning the language of your field, and scanning the material.

- Most written communications in the office are in the form of memos, letters, reports, or public relations materials. Memos, the briefest and least formal of the three, are used for internal communication.

- Letters are most frequently used to communicate with people outside the company, and they have standard parts and accepted, traditional formats. In an electronic office, the computer can set up letter formats automatically, but you need to know which format to choose.

- Most business letters fall into these categories: request and inquiry, response, confirmation, goodwill, refusal, claim and adjustment, and credit and collection. Each type of letter requires its own tone.

- Some companies have standard form, or boilerplate, letters. With electronic technology, graphics can be produced easily and added to written communications.

- Reports are the longest form of written communication in the office. The writer must state the objective, prepare an outline, do research, write the report, and proofread. Like letters and memos, reports have specific parts and formats.

- Newsletters are becoming a widely used medium for public relations in many departments and offices. Writing in a news style is different from writing a business letter or memo. Your audience will determine how the message is written.

VOCABULARY

- turnaround time
- jargon
- form letters
- boilerplate

CHECKING YOUR UNDERSTANDING

1. What is the writing process? What general steps must you follow for each piece of communication you write?

2. What are the most frequently used types of written communications in a business office? Give an example of a business situation that would require each type of document.

3. Explain the goals of a goodwill letter and an adjustment letter. How are they alike? How are they different?

4. Decide whether a formal report or a memo report would be most appropriate for each of the situations below:
   a. a new fire drill procedure needs to be explained to the staff
   b. a review of expense records for the past six months
   c. the market performance of a new product that was released one year ago
   d. a monthly status report on project goals and milestones.

5. Describe when it is appropriate to use a memo and when it is appropriate to use a letter when a written document is required.

6. Describe the formatting guidelines for multiple page letters and memos. Why is the heading important?

THINKING THROUGH PROCEDURES

1. Wordiness—using more than one word to say something when one word will do—is something that is difficult for writers to avoid. There are many phrases which we tend to use almost automatically and which add to the number of words without adding anything to the meaning. A common example is *due to the fact that*. It is much better to write *because* or *since*. On a separate sheet of paper write one or two words that could replace each of the wordy phrases below.
   a. at this point in time
   b. if you would be so kind as to
   c. during the time that
   d. destroyed by fire
   e. do not pay any attention to
   f. came into contact with

   Think of other wordy phrases that you often hear or read. Make a list of them, and include the one or two words that can replace each one.

2. Write the appropriate type of correspondence for each of the following situations. Follow the writing process and turn in your plan or outline, and your edited rough drafts of the materials along with your final draft. Use word processing software if it is available to you.
   a. Roberta Nims's Tool and Dye sells Outa Sight all the hardware for its window production—brackets, window locks,

and so on. On April 24, Bob Cheney, the production manager at Outa Sight, says to you, "we ordered ten thousand window locks from Nims five weeks ago. We don't have them yet. You usually fill our orders in a month. We can get by for another two weeks without the order, but no longer. I would like to get in writing your response to this situation. Please tell your shipping foreman that he must get the order to me ASAP and put a copy of the purchase order in with it." Write a response to Mr. Cheney, stating that you have tracked down the order and have discussed the shipment date with the shipping foreman. The shipping date is within one week. Nims's Tool and Dye is located at 1589 Western Wind Industrial Park, San Jose, CA 43596; Outa Sight is located at 89 Starr Avenue, Berkeley, CA 20034.

b. Marge Walker has asked you to check the files and prepare a list of everyone who has signed delivery receipts at the warehouse in the last year. You should also note how often each person has signed. You find that five people signed delivery receipts in the last year: Kurt Vanderheiden, 27; Al Dugan, 100; Ann Rice, 13; Bill Feckner, 6; Gene O'Connel, 4.

3. Research the latest information on electronic mail by contacting businesses or by locating articles in telecommunications and office automation magazines. Using the correct technology tool, write a memo report to your instructor describing your findings and why e-mail is a productive tool for written communication.

4. As a class, determine what information would be appropriate in a newsletter to people within your school. You select the topics and write the articles for a 2-3 page newsletter. Store your files electronically so you can share these files for processing the newsletter in the next chapter.

chapter **13**

PROCESSING WRITTEN DOCUMENTS

INFORMATION PROCESSING PROCEDURES

Electronic technology makes office work easier in many ways. It allows you to spend less time on routine tasks such as correcting and retyping documents or storing and retrieving information. Many offices are at some stage of transition—moving from traditional equipment to semiautomated to fully electronic procedures. Even those offices that are already fully automated continue to change as new equipment and procedures render the activities of two or three years ago obsolete.

Change, then, is a fact of office life. The office worker of a few decades ago who was able to learn office skills and then consider himself or herself trained for life has also become obsolete. Office workers today must be prepared for a lifetime of learning. Once you acquire the basic processing skills, you will be able to transfer them to new technology as it becomes available. Each new development in the field of office technology enables you to add to your store of knowledge.

In the previous chapter, you learned how basic skills are applied to the writing process. This document planning and creating stage of document processing is far less subject to change—the technology tool will vary, but the process remains the same. In this chapter we will apply the technology to the input and processing functions in the information processing cycle.

Most of your processing time will be spent on the preparation of documents. The term *documents* here means more than letters and memos. The process of preparing documents applies to all types of documents, letters, memos, reports, presentation visuals or support materials, product lists, price sheets, and forms. To process documents you must choose from a variety of sources for gathering information, select the appropriate software and hardware tools for the task, and choose the best method of output and distribution.

Just as you follow a process to write a document or solve a business communications problem, you also follow a process to prepare a document after writing it: to prepare the input through the final output for distribution. This process includes these steps:

1. Prioritize the processing.
2. Determine the appropriate input procedures.
3. Format the document.
4. Edit and proofread for errors.
5. Prepare the final copy.

Let's examine each of these steps and how you can process a document efficiently in a professional manner.

PRIORITIZE THE PROCESSING

At the start of each workday your first task is to analyze the things you have to do and make decisions about priorities. Your processing tasks will have to be scheduled in conjunction with all the other job functions you perform. Some priority decisions are easy because they are dictated by routine. Routine tasks can be scheduled ahead of time and placed on your calendar or "To Do" list with a notation of the deadline for each. Some processing tasks fall into the "routine" category and others are "special projects."

Routine Processing

The documents that typically need to be processed on a daily basis include memos, correspondence, informal reports, and forms. These items can be classified in order of importance and placed on your daily "To Do" list. On days when you have a heavy work load of such items, it is important to set aside a period of time in which you can complete them without interruption. Your "A" priority items are those left over from the previous day or any documents that need to be distributed as soon as possible. Your "B" priority items are those that need to be distributed by the end of the day. Keep in mind that the order of importance is based on the time or date by which the document objective is met. Your judgment on this matter must be considered along with the importance of the document itself. Therefore, it is important that you read all documents given to you for processing and assess their relative priority before you proceed with your processing tasks.

Special Projects

Those documents that are more complex, and therefore more time consuming, are termed special projects. They include such items as formal reports, presentation visuals or documents, unique contracts, or any other documents that do not occur on a regular basis. Such documents require special planning to allow for the possibility of more than one revision stage. They might also require more research time for information or other documents that may need to be incorporated or used as resource materials. In many cases the processing of such documents has to be segmented over more than one day to allow for other tasks to be accomplished. In other instances, you may have to set all other work aside in order to complete such a task on a short deadline.

Frequently, special projects are "rush jobs" because they are not started far enough in advance to accommodate all the steps required to complete them. This situation can affect the quality of a document negatively and cause a great deal of stress, frustration, and additional work hours. You can play a significant role in heping your supervisor avoid this kind of circumstance. Once you are aware of a deadline, estimate how much time is needed and then plan the steps that need to be taken to complete the work by the target date. In order to keep as much control over your schedule as possible, there may be times when you need to prod your supervisor to initiate work on a big project. In such instances, a plan for meeting the deadline will encourage your supervisor to give you enough lead time to complete the processing part of the project.

In many offices today administrative assistants report to more than one person. In some cases each supervisor does the same type of work; however, in many instances the type of work varies from one person to the next. Or, to make the situation even more complex, one person is the manager of the others. In this case you must learn to prioritize the work assignments given to you by different individuals. You may also have to balance the perception of a higher-ranked individual that his or her work comes first by virtue of position. This situation can be a true test of your judgment and human relations skills. Communication is the best tool you can employ to ensure that the needs of each supervisor are met with the least amount of stress on yourself. At first it may be necessary to meet with the group to establish mutually acceptable priorities for each individual's work. Once you become more familiar with the daily work load, you will probably be able to resolve conflicts with one-on-one conferences. When the work load is exceptionally heavy, you may need to ask each individual to label his or her documents as an A, B, or C priority to assist you in balancing the work load. You also have to learn to schedule your time.

DETERMINE THE APPROPRIATE INPUT METHODS

Methods of gathering data vary, depending on the form of the data and the hardware available. Traditionally, the most common method of gathering and organizing data has been taking dictation and transcribing the dictation notes as a document. Before data can be input, however, it must be gathered and organized. In this case processing the document involves translating data from one form into another. In the electronic office, data for input can come from a variety of sources in addition to dictation. (See figure 13.1) The data may be stored on a floppy disk, on a hard disk, or on a networked system. It may be contained on a document that will be scanned into the system and then processed, or it may be retrieved from an on-line information service. Voice input directly into the computer is another method, and this will become more widely used in the future. The next few pages explain the basic forms of input you will work with in an electronic office.

NOTETAKING/SHORTHAND

Today there are different systems of shorthand, such as the traditional symbol shorthand and others such as alphabetic shorthand, or notetaking systems. **Notetaking** is a system based on the alphabet or a combination of alphabetic and symbolic shorthand.

Notetaking/shorthand remains in demand for several reasons. The language arts skills learned in a notetaking/shorthand system make an individual even more marketable because he or she is able to edit and perfect someone else's work. Some executives prefer to dictate to a secretary because they may feel uncomfortable dictating to a machine. And there are many executives who are simply accustomed to giving dictation directly to

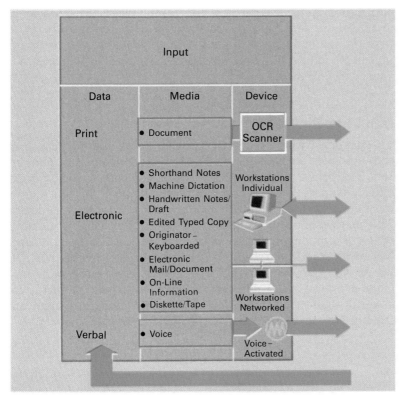

Figure 13.1 Data that is to be input can come from a variety of sources and appear in different formats and in different media.

another person and do not want to change their working methods.

Personal dictation has a number of advantages. It offers office workers an opportunity for human contact, which they may welcome as they spend more and more time working with electronic devices. Many supervisors find that face-to-face dictation helps them organize and verbalize their ideas. And if they change their minds about something they have dictated, it is easy to go back and make corrections.

Another important reason why notetaking/shorthand is still valued is that it can help preserve confidentiality in offices where executives and office workers deal with sensitive information. Until information is processed into a letter or report, it exists only in the minds of the executive and assistant or in notes. It is not on a dictation tape, which anyone might hear, or in a draft form, which anyone might read.

Notetaking/shorthand is also an invaluable tool to the office worker who must carry out a wide variety of administrative support duties. He or she may use notetaking while doing research, to take down telephone messages accurately and quickly, or to take the minutes of meetings. For all of these reasons, notetaking/shorthand remains an essential skill, even in the most advanced electronic office.

Machine Dictation

Companies utilize machine dictation more today because of the savings in personnel costs. With dictation machines, supervisors can dictate when no one is available to take notes. For example, managers can dictate while away from the office on a business trip or after working hours at their own convenience. This method of originating data provides a great deal of flexibility for the manager. The machines record the dictation on tape, just as a home tape recorder records music or other sounds. Office workers use similar machines, or sometimes the same machines, to play back the recordings and transcribe the dictation. Several types of machine dictation/transcription equipment are used in the electronic office.

TRANSCRIBING NOTETAKING/SHORTHAND DICTATION

- Assemble all your materials and information before you begin transcribing so you will not have to interrupt your work to look for things.
- Establish the priority of each item you must transcribe, and begin with top-priority items that must be processed immediately.
- Check the instructions for each item before you begin to transcribe, and always make at least one copy of each item you transcribe.
- Check spellings, addresses, technical terms, and any other important details before you begin.
- Transcribe directly from your notes. Check each segment of your notes for grammatical errors, incomplete sentences, and any changes and additions in the editing process.
- Avoid making paragraphs too long or too short.
- Before you print the document, check it over for errors.
- Cancel each item in your notebook with a diagonal line after you transcribe it. Keep a rubber band around the last page you have transcribed so you will know where to begin again.
- Always check your notebook at the end of each day to make sure that you have transcribed all your notes. If any work remains undone, do it the next day after you have transcribed that day's priority items.

TAKING DICTATION

SUPPLIES Always keep a plentiful supply of pads and pens or pencils handy, and mark off the used area of your notebook with a rubber band.

SPECIAL TOOLS Have a red pencil handy to note down instructions, and carry a folder and paper clips to hold and mark any papers you may have to take away with you. Some secretaries use editor's clips, which are brightly colored, triangular plastic clips used for color coding related notebook pages and documents. Rush items should be marked with a paper clip or by a turned-down corner of a notebook page.

SEPARATING ITEMS The first notebook page you use should be dated at the bottom of the page and marked "A.M." or "P.M." so you can locate a specific segment of the notes later on. Also leave a space between each item of dictation so you can add instructions in red about how to mail the item or how many copies to make.

CHANGES You can insert small changes as you go along or add a long change at the bottom of the item and indicate where to insert it. If your supervisor tends to make frequent changes, leave one column on the notebook page free for them.

SPELLING Spell out names and technical terms in longhand. You should also copy names and addresses from incoming documents to avoid misspellings and mistakes.

END MARKS Mark the end of each item with some distinctive symbol so that you can tell at a glance where each item begins and ends.

NUMBERING One way to organize your shorthand notes is to number each letter or memo requiring an answer and then number each corresponding item of dictation.

QUESTIONS If a question occurs to you while you are taking dictation, mark a large "X" in your notebook so that you can find it easily when the dictation is finished.

COMPLETE RECORDS If you are asked to take dictation when a notebook is not available, date the paper you take the notes on and staple it in your notebook so that you will have a complete record of all your dictation.

PRINTED FORMS If the dictation is material to be inserted on a printed form, number each item in your notes to correspond to each item on the form. If possible, obtain a copy of the form and attach it to your notebook.

Desktop dictation machines record dictation on minicassettes or somewhat larger standard cassettes much like those used for music. Desktop machines are used primarily by executives who dictate frequently while working in their offices. Some desktop units can record dictation but cannot play it back for transcription. Others can be used for transcribing but not for recording. Combination units can be used for both purposes. Some desktop machines have automatic controls that can be used for indexing the dictation, scanning to find a particular spot on the tape, and other operations.

Portable dictation machines are small and lightweight and run on batteries. They can be used in automobiles and in other places where there are no electrical outlets. These machines record dictation on minicassettes or on smaller microcassettes. Portable machines are ideal for executives who want to dictate at home or on business trips. Figures 13.2A and 13.2B show a portable and a desktop dictation machine.

Centralized Dictation Systems

Organizations in which hundreds of employees originate documents may have a centralized dictation system. In such a system, originators use the telephone to call a central recording device to dictate.

In some centralized systems, dictation is recorded on endless loops. An endless loop is a long tape, joined at the ends, that stays inside the recording device and stores the dictation for hundreds of documents. As the device records the newest dictation, it erases the oldest input automatically. Many operators can transcribe different documents from an endless loop simultaneously.

In other systems, input from many originators is recorded on multiple-cassette machines. These machines also display information about how much dictation has been recorded on each cassette, whether each cassette is still receiving dictation or can be

Figure 13.2A Portable dictation machine.

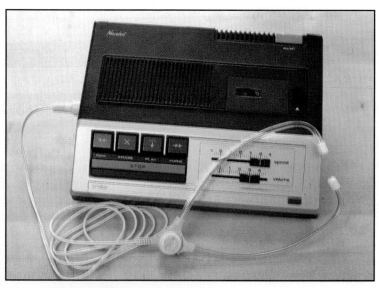

Figure 13.2B Desktop dictation machine.

transcribed, and so on. Unlike endless loops, cassettes can be removed from the machines and distributed, so transcribers do not need to work together in one central location.

There are also dictation systems controlled by a mainframe computer system, allowing many individuals to dictate and many to transcribe. Companies use this type of centralized dictation system to establish individual control of the transcription process. This centralized dictation system gives confidentiality and security to the dictation as well as more control over when the dictation is completed and ready for signature.

Shorthand Machines

Conventional shorthand notes and tape recordings are the media most often used for dictation, but some situations call for shorthand machines. A shorthand machine is a portable device with keys that are pressed in combinations to produce several letters of each word. Shorthand machine operators, who have special training in using these devices, can record up to 250 words a minute, which is more than twice as fast as most people can take shorthand notes by hand.

Shorthand machines are especially useful in situations where many people are talking. They are used to record what people say during trials, public hearings, and some special business meetings when participants require official records of the proceedings. If you make arrangements for such a meeting, you might obtain the services of a shorthand machine operator from a court reporting service, which you could find in your telephone directory. Or you may tape record the meeting for transcription later.

Rough Drafts

Sometimes you might process documents from drafts that have been typed, written in longhand, keyed, or printed out from a computer, shorthand machine, or computer-aided transcription machine. A **rough draft** is a preliminary rough copy on which you can write corrections and editing changes to guide you in preparing a final, finished document. Rough drafts may be in the form of hard copy or soft copy.

As more and more executives use computers, keyed drafts have become a common form of input. When the originator's computer is networked to the assistant's computer, drafts can be transferred in soft copy form for editing and formatting.

Many people still compose in longhand for convenience. Exec-

TRANSCRIBING MACHINE DICTATION

- To transcribe machine dictation without disturbing others in the office, you need a transcription machine or combination unit with earphones.
- Many transcription machines have hand or foot controls that enable you to stop, start, or play back dictation. If you are using hand controls, place the control unit near your keyboard so that you will not waste time or effort moving between the keyboard and the controls.
- Follow the procedures outlined in your machine's operating manual on how to insert the recorded medium. Also consult the manual for other information about operating your particular machine. Each type of transcription machine has its own procedures.
- Place the slip for the tape you are transcribing in the space provided for it on the front of the machine. An indicator slip, also called an index slip, is a specially marked piece of paper on which the originator notes where each dictated document ends and any special instructions for processing it.
- If your equipment has a digital dial instead of an indicator slip, the originator should note the numerical starting point for each document.
- If your transcription machine features electronic scanning, use this feature to scan for any special processing instructions the originator may have included.
- From the originator's instructions, determine the priority of each dictated document. Transcribe the highest-priority items first.
- The first time you input you are transcribing a draft. Mark the draft with the date and the word *draft*. Give the draft to the originator for changes; make the changes and print out a final copy for signature.
- Try to estimate how long each item is so you can plan the margins, line lengths, and spacing.
- Coordinate your keying with your listening. If you do not hear part of the dictation, or if you do not remember it, stop keying and use the playback control to listen to it again. As you develop your listening skills, your memory span will increase, and you will be able to type longer phrases without pausing.
- Listen to complete sentences or clauses so that you can understand the context in which words that sound alike are used. Examples of words that sound alike but are used in different contexts are *their* and *there*, *billed* and *build*, and *air* and *heir*.
- Sometimes the originator indicates punctuation, but if not, listen to pauses in the dictation so you can determine where to insert punctuation marks. The voice should indicate when you have come to the end of a sentence or a clause, whether to end a sentence with a period or a question mark, and so on.
- Ask another office worker to listen to any part of a recording that you cannot hear distinctly. If that does not resolve the problem, key the dictation as it sounds to you, or substitute a word that you think will be appropriate. If you do this, however, always check with the originator when you submit the draft copy to see if the word you used is correct.
- Always review each page for errors before you print it out, following the edit for content and proofreading stages of the process.

utives can compose memos on airplanes and in other public places without disturbing others and being overheard as they might if they used dictation machines. The biggest disadvantage of longhand is that it is not always legible to others. The reader may need to check what he or she cannot read, causing the loss of valuable time. It is expected that as more executives become accustomed to using keyboards, the use of longhand will decline in the electronic office.

Some of the drafts you work with may be keyed and then printed instead of written in longhand. Supervisors sometimes key rough drafts and print them out or provide hard copies of old documents that they have edited for new purposes.

Printed drafts may contain editing marks that have been made in pen or pencil. They may also include handwritten additions or inserts. Figure 13.3 shows a longhand draft that has been edited and is ready for inputting. You may sometimes have to work with messy drafts that have been cut into sections, reorganized, and taped or pasted back together. Whether a draft is handwritten copy or printed or keyed copy that has been heavily edited, the amount of time it takes to transcribe it depends on how legible it is. If copy is difficult to read, it might save time in the end to do another draft, especially if the document is long.

To process information from edited typewritten drafts, you will need to be familiar with editing and proofreading symbols. Basic proofreading symbols are shown in figure 13.7.

Electronic Files

Documents already processed by you or by someone else in your office may serve as input for new information. For example, instead of writing a new memo you might retrieve a similar one from your electronic files and modify it for a new purpose. Or you might reply to a customer inquiry by substituting a new address and salutation on a stored letter you have already sent to many other people.

Once you have the soft copy of the original document on your screen, you can revise it to create the new document. If you want to save an electronic copy of the original document as well as the new one, you must give the new one a different name.

Electronic Notebooks

The newest technology in inputting information is the ability to write in longhand on **electronic notebooks.** The handwriting on these tablets is then converted to machine readable data

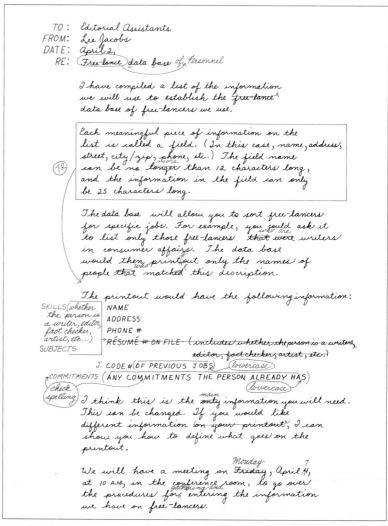

Figure 13.3 Handwritten drafts are one of the most popular ways of originating data in the business office. This sample of a handwritten draft has been edited to indicate changes and corrections.

and sent to software for processing. The handwriting can be placed in word processing, database, spreadsheet, or any other kind of software. Electronic notebooks allow for handwriting recognition and are currently used in the shipping industry to provide electronic records of shipping and delivery instead of paper copies. Handwriting technology has not yet been perfected, but companies are excited about its potential for on-site information in the insurance claims industry, law enforcement industry, and others.

Databases

As you learned in previous chapters, a database is a collection of information stored in a computer. Examples of databases are a list of customers or an inventory of a company's stock.

Each company has its own procedures for inputting data or gathering information from its internal databases. These procedures depend on the kind of electronic equipment the company uses, the nature of the data, and the company's policies regarding data security. In some instances it may be possible to obtain information from an internal database just by keying a few computer commands. In others you may need special clearance from a data manager before you can gain access to the data.

On-line Information Services

In addition to maintaining their own databases, many companies subscribe to external data banks that offer a variety of information to meet different business needs. These data banks are called on-line information services. They are owned and operated by companies that offer information to outsiders for a fee. If you work for a law firm, your firm may subscribe to Westlaw, a database of law cases.

The data is accessed through a telecommunications system using a modem, and then downloaded, or saved, to a local media. Once the information is saved locally, it can then be brought into a word processing package or other software for additional processing. Usually this data must be converted into a format the software program you use can accept before you are able to process it efficiently. Figure 13.4 shows an example of downloaded information.

The opposite of downloading is uploading, which is the process of transferring large amounts of information already created in another software package to an electronic mail or bulletin board service. More information on uploading will be discussed in the next chapter on distribution.

Uploading and downloading information saves the company telecommunications charges and additional keying time. The administrative assistant's production increases because no rekeying is necessary; only editing is needed.

Electronic Mail Messages

Data for input can come from an electronic mail or message system. To see how you might use an electronic message as input, suppose you have been asked to prepare a report detailing

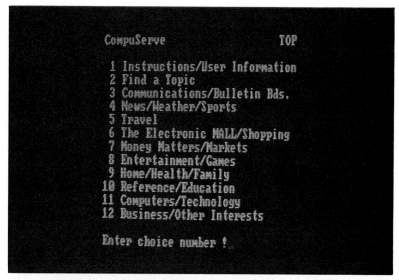

Figure 13.4 On-line data bases provide many different types of information for businesses that subscribe to their services.

the personnel needs of each of five departments in your company. You can ask each department head to send you an electronic message about his or her personnel needs. Once the messages are sent to your terminal, you can incorporate part or all of each message into your report just by entering a few commands. This will save you the trouble of obtaining a hard copy of each message and then keying the parts of the messages you want to use.

Scanned Images

Optical character reading (OCR) software scans typed or printed pages and converts the text into electronic signals the computer can understand. A flatbed scanner connected to a micro- or mainframe computer is usually used. The software determines what the scanner will do with the information it obtains during the scan. As the software scans the page, the typed or printed contents are transferred to storage. The text is then brought into a word processing program for text editing. This software is still not 100 percent accurate and so much editing is necessary. As the software is perfected, the accuracy rate will climb and its use will become more effective.

OCR software eliminates the need for keying data that has already been typed or printed. Most OCR software can convert a wide range of typefaces into electronic signals. Some very specialized OCRs can even read handwritten numbers and letters.

Graphics can also be scanned for use in publications by using a graphics scanning package and a graphics editing package. In scanning images, both text and graphics, you must not infringe on **copyright laws.** Basically, this means that you are not to use published material without quoting, acknowledging, or gaining the permission of the author to print it in your materials. With the use of desktop publishing software and graphics and text editing software, it is very easy to "lift" or "steal" another person's creation. You, as the individual creating the document, are responsible for observing the copyright law. Therefore, be very certain that you follow this law accurately.

Digital Facsimile

Some facsimile systems can be linked to computers so that they function as long distance OCRs. A standard facsimile machine scans a document page and transmits signals to a receiving facsimile machine, which produces a duplicate. With newer digital units, the sending machine can transmit the signals to a computer instead of to another facsimile machine. The receiving computer displays the signals as soft copy, which can be stored on a disk or printed. The hardware necessary for this transaction is called a fax board. This is a circuit board that is placed inside of the microcomputer and acts as a facsimile system.

Data Forms

Another kind of stored information found in most business offices is the preprinted form, such as an employment application or a purchase order. Forms can be hard copy, to be completed in longhand or with a typewriter, or soft copy, to be displayed on a computer screen and filled in by keying the information.

You may sometimes use data from one form to process another. For example, you may use data from an invoice to prepare a customer's bill. Some computer systems can fill in parts of a form for you automatically. Suppose you are responsible for taking telephone orders for an office supply company. When a customer calls, you call up an order form on your computer screen and key the customer's name and address and the quantity, description, and price of each item being ordered in the spaces provided. Once you have entered all the prices and handling costs, you can instruct the computer to add up the items and provide a total.

Boilerplate

Another kind of soft copy you might work with is boilerplate or electronic copies of frequently used paragraphs. To produce documents containing these paragraphs, you retrieve the boilerplate and combine it with new data. For example, to process a contract you might retrieve some standard paragraphs that go into all of your employer's contracts. You do not have to key these paragraphs, which might make up the bulk of the contract, but you would key new data that relates to the specific intent of the contract.

Merging

Merging allows you to send a form letter or document to hundreds of people by merging it automatically with a mailing list that contains all the names, addresses, and salutations for the letters and perhaps other information as well. This merging process results in a personalized letter or document for each recipient. It is more efficient than making photocopies of a form letter and filling in the blanks with a typewriter. The end result is also more pleasing to the eye. With list processing software, every letter in a mass mailing will look as though it has been individually typed.

When merging, you first input the letter or document using your word processor. You provide the appropriate commands for each bit of information (such as name, address, and salutation) that will be merged from the mailing list. After completing the letter, you input the mailing list, sometimes called the merge document, and give the commands for the parts that will be inserted. Refer to figure 13.5 for examples.

As discussed previously, you must determine the source of input and the best way to organize and gather data for processing. Once these decisions are made, you are ready to process the document.

WORKSTATION DATA INPUT GUIDELINES

Whether you are transcribing shorthand notes, machine dictation, or hard copy such as a rough draft, the following guidelines will help you do the job more comfortably and efficiently.

POSTURE   Correct posture helps prevent the back strain and fatigue that can result from working at a keyboard and terminal for several hours.

FURNITURE   People who do a lot of keying generally use adjustable chairs like those used by typists in traditional offices. Adjust your chair to suit your height and the position of your keyboard (unless the keyboard itself is movable). Your chair is properly adjusted and your sitting posture is correct if your feet reach the floor and rest there without pushing up your knees, if your spine is straight, and if your hips are placed firmly against the back of the chair. You should not have to move your upper arms away from your sides in order for your hands to reach your keyboard.

COMPUTER TERMINAL   A well-placed keyboard and terminal can also help you avoid poor posture and the fatigue and tension that result from it.

You may work with a keyboard and terminal that are housed in a single unit. If so, you may not be able to adjust either the tilt of the screen or the placement of the keyboard in relation to it, but you can place the entire terminal at a height that allows you to reach the keyboard comfortably and look at the screen without slumping in your chair or straining your neck. The screen should be below your eye level so that you look slightly downward at it.

Some offices use computer equipment with screens and keyboards that are separate from each other. If you work with one of these computers, you can place the keyboard wherever it is most comfortable. The screen may be mounted on an adjustable platform so you can tilt it to a comfortable angle.

COMPUTER TABLES   Your keyboard and terminal (and perhaps other system components) may all be on a special-purpose table. On many computer tables, terminals and keyboards sit on separate surfaces, and you can adjust the heights of these surfaces individually. You may also be able to adjust the tilt of the keyboard surface.

COPYHOLDER   A copyholder positions copy at an angle that enables you to read it comfortably while you are keying. You can place a copyholder so that you do not have to move your head back and forth constantly to shift your eyes between the screen and the hard copy. This also helps to prevent fatigue and back strain.

LIGHTING   Proper lighting contributes to your comfort and productivity when you are keying. In the electronic office, you need lighting that enables you to read both your screen and your hard copy without eyestrain.

Your notes or hard copy should be illuminated by an overhead light or a desk lamp, but the lamp should be placed so that it does not cause glare or reflections on your screen. If your room is lighted by windows, place your screen so that the windows are behind it. This way, the screen will not reflect light from them.

Adjusting the brightness and contrast on your screen can also help prevent eyestrain. Turn up the brightness as much as you can without hurting your eyes; then adjust the contrast so that the bright soft copy appears against a dark background.

```
                                        7463 State Street
                                        New Orleans, LA  89712




        August 12, 19--



        <first name> <last name>
        <company name>
        <address>
        <city>, <state> <zip>

        Dear <first name> <last name>:

        After reading about your exciting new product line, I would like to
        receive a copy of your latest catalog.  You may send the catalog to me
        at the above address.

        Sincerely,


        Kit Marcher
```

Figure 13.5 This is an example of a form letter that can be merged with a list of names and addresses from a mailing list stored in a different file.

FORMAT AND PROCESS THE DOCUMENT

The processing procedures you use depend on the type of equipment you have on the job. You are most likely to have an electronic typewriter and a stand-alone or networked microcomputer system. Once you understand how to operate one type of equipment, it is generally easy to transfer that knowledge to another type. So if you understand the similarities and differences among various types of equipment, as you learned in previous chapters, you can easily learn to use different types of equipment.

Information Processing Equipment

In an electronic office, different kinds of start-up procedures are used, depending on the type of computer system. With a networked system, there is a specific log-on procedure that probably involves a password security system. A **password** is a name you key in when you get on the system. This name is known only to you and the person responsible for the maintenance of the network. The password ensures that no unauthorized person can gain access to the computer files stored on the centralized system.

You will learn specific procedures for retrieving stored files and other data files. These might include mailing lists, software applications programs, and other data that is available to everyone who uses the central files.

On a networked or on a stand-alone system, you will also work with floppy disks and possibly a hard disk drive on your equipment. Remember to keep backup copies of all stored files on floppy disks in case of problems with the hard disk or central storage files, which could result in loss of data. Whatever storage devices you use, become familiar with the necessary ways to access them and store information on them.

When using electronic equipment for processing information, you must also be careful that you do not inadvertently bring viruses into the computer system. A **virus** is a software program that can destroy data or cause a computer system to malfunction in other ways. Sometimes these viruses can cause damage to your data disks by eliminating the formatting commands that tell the software where to go to find information on the disk. If this happens, you may see the filenames on your data disk, but the software will not be able to access the files and your data is lost.

Viruses attach to the executable files on your software and then spread from one file to the next. An **executable file** consists of the commands written into the software to make a program run. Once a virus gets into a system, it can be spread from computer to computer by exchange of disks or software files. Another way to get a virus into your company's computer system inadvertently is by using on-line services such as bulletin boards. Later in this chapter we will discuss the process for using on-line services. Just be sure that any information you gather from using an on-line service is checked by using a virus

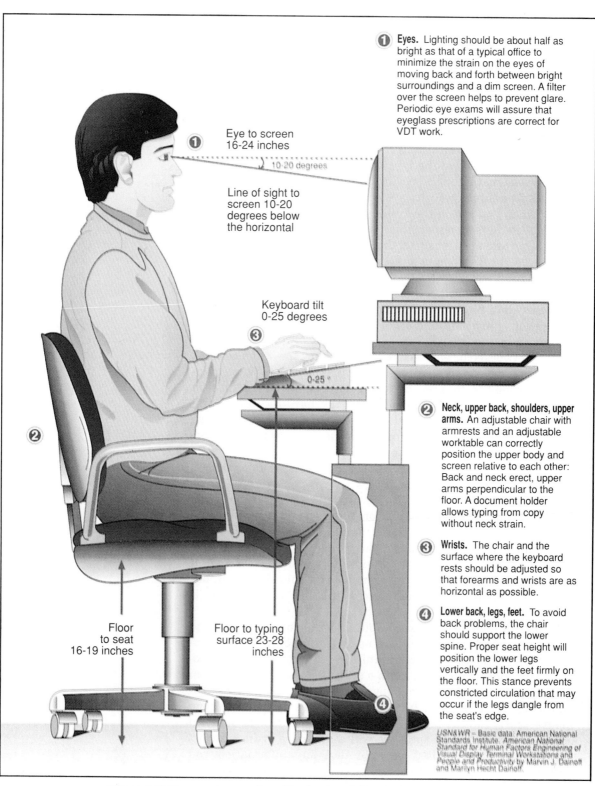

① **Eyes.** Lighting should be about half as bright as that of a typical office to minimize the strain on the eyes of moving back and forth between bright surroundings and a dim screen. A filter over the screen helps to prevent glare. Periodic eye exams will assure that eyeglass prescriptions are correct for VDT work.

Eye to screen
16-24 inches

10-20 degrees

Line of sight to screen 10-20 degrees below the horizontal

Keyboard tilt
0-25 degrees

③

0-25°

②

Floor to seat
16-19 inches

Floor to typing surface 23-28 inches

② **Neck, upper back, shoulders, upper arms.** An adjustable chair with armrests and an adjustable worktable can correctly position the upper body and screen relative to each other: Back and neck erect, upper arms perpendicular to the floor. A document holder allows typing from copy without neck strain.

③ **Wrists.** The chair and the surface where the keyboard rests should be adjusted so that forearms and wrists are as horizontal as possible.

④ **Lower back, legs, feet.** To avoid back problems, the chair should support the lower spine. Proper seat height will position the lower legs vertically and the feet firmly on the floor. This stance prevents constricted circulation that may occur if the legs dangle from the seat's edge.

④

USN&WR – Basic data: American National Standards Institute, American National Standard for Human Factors Engineering of Visual Display Terminal Workstations and People and Productivity by Marvin J. Dainoff and Marilyn Hecht Dainoff.

Figure 13.6 Your posture and positioning in relation to the equipment help you to maintain a high level of productivity.

protection software program before you save the file into the system. These are available through software vendors.

Companies avoid viruses by installing virus protection software and by allowing only internal media to be used on company equipment. If the company you work for does not have virus protection, suggest getting it to your supervisor. Making backup copies of your data is also a way to protect your data from a virus invasion.

CARE AND HANDLING OF DISKS

- Handle a disk only near the label at the top of its rigid protective cover. Never remove a disk from its protective cover, and never touch the parts of the disk that are exposed through openings in the cover.
- Do not fold, crease, or bend a disk. Always keep disks in carrying cases, even those that have hard plastic jackets.
- Do not use pens, pencils, or erasers on the surface of the protective cover of a disk. Instead, write on an adhesive-backed identification label before you apply it to the disk cover. Remove any old labels, if possible, instead of adding new labels on top.
- Apply write-protect stickers to *new software disks* and to any disks containing data that should not be changed. A box of blank disks usually includes a package of write-protect stickers. Computer supply dealers also sell them.
- Keep disks out of direct sunlight and away from radiators, lamps, and other heat sources.
- Keep disks away from the power source of your computer.
- Store disks at room temperature.
- When they are not in the disk drive, keep disks in protective jackets.
- Store disks so that they are standing on their edges, not in stacks, in specially designed containers. These are available from computer supply dealers.
- Keep magnets away from disks, because magnetism can erase data. Keep metal paper clips away from disks too, because many office workers use magnetic paper-clip containers that magnetize the clips themselves.
- A ringing telephone can create a magnetic field, so do not leave your disks near telephones or set a telephone on top of a disk drive.
- Follow the procedures for handling disks outlined in your computer's instruction manual, and be careful when you insert disks into disk drives.
- Keep disks away from water and other liquids. If they should get wet for some reason, dry them with a lint-free cloth.

Information Processing Software

Document processing requires you to use different types of software applications. The more proficient you become at using software, the more valuable you are as an employee. In the course of processing a single document you may retrieve information from a central database; use a spreadsheet program to calculate figures from the data you gathered in the database; use a word processor to combine all of the information into a report; and use a desktop publishing package to add graphics and a professional look to your document.

Understanding the capabilities of the hardware and software available to you is an important skill for document processing. The ability to make judgments concerning the appropriate processing tool will make a major difference in your ability to be as productive as possible when processing different types of documents.

As you have seen, there are a variety of different methods for obtaining and organizing data for processing. You have made the decisions as to what hardware and software to use, and you have gathered all of the data necessary to complete the task. You are ready to begin processing.

Arrange your workstation so that it is comfortable. Adjust the screen and keyboard, and place your data where you can see it comfortably. Some of your data may be in hard-copy format, and other data may be in electronic format.

In a stand-alone microcomputer system, you first need to load the software program onto your system. You may load it from the hard drive or from floppy disks, depending on your system. You either enter commands or make a menu selection to begin creating a document. If a new disk is necessary, it must be formatted or initialized before you can save information. Formatting just tells the computer where to store information and how to retrieve it. If your media is not formatted, you will receive an error or the system will ask if you want to format the disk.

With a networked system you log on to access the software you need. If you have electronic files you are working from, make a short list of the filenames and their stored location so you can retrieve the files easily when appropriate. In any case, you may have an integrated system that allows you to select a multitude of software programs simultaneously. With a **graphics user interface (GUI),** such as Microsoft Windows, you are able to open multiple files and software applications at once so you can retrieve the information you need to process the document easily. A GUI basically is a software program that allows you to access multiple software packages at once and cut and paste information from one document to another without quitting one software package and starting another. The information from one application is stored in the system's RAM in an area called the clipboard. Once the information is placed in the clipboard, the user opens another document and places it into this document. This process saves many hours converting documents into formats that unlike software packages can understand.

Whatever type of system you have, you will probably select a word processing function from the system menu to create a letter, a spreadsheet application for a budget, a database to find names and addresses of clients, or a graphics program to create presentation documents. If you want to edit a stored document, enter the filename of the document you wish to work on. To save a document, depending on the software, you name the document either when you create it or when it is completely input and you are ready to save it.

Determine the Format

When you have decided on the type of equipment and software to use, and you have gathered all of the data you need, decide the formatting of the document in general. If you spend too much time trying to figure out the intricate details, it will slow down your processing speed. The final formatting is done after all the editing is completed.

You learned some standard formats for letters, memos, and reports in previous chapters. You must find out which formats your company uses. If there are no preferred formats, consult a style guide, such as *Paradigm Reference Guide*. Here are the general settings you use when you format a document:

- **Set the Margins** Use the standard margins according to your style guide. Make adjustments if the document will be put in a binder.

- **Select the Font** The typeface you choose will have a direct effect on the tone of the document. For example, a serif font (one that has "feet" attached to the letters) such as Times Roman is readily accepted as a newsletter or public relations font. A sans serif font (straight with no "feet") such as Helvetica is readily accepted as conservative and good for large type in headlines.

- **Tabs** If you do not want to use the paragraph settings in your software package, use the tab settings to set appropriate paragraph indentations. Do not try to set the tabs for tables within the document at this time. Use the preset tabs in your software and then select the section later for final spacing attributes.

- **Line Spacing** Select the spacing for the document: single-spacing, double-spacing, or a different amount of space between lines. Draft documents are easier to proofread with additional spacing such as double-spacing. When the editing process is finished, change your spacing back to the type you want for a professional-looking document. Some software programs, such as desktop publishing programs, allow you to change the **leading,** or space between the lines, in smaller or larger increments than single-, double-, or triple-spacing. If your software allows for this, learn to use it; adjusting leading can enhance the look of your document and give it a typeset quality.

- **Page Size** Define what size your paper is for the final draft. For example, you may use letter size 8.5 $\times$ 11 or legal size 8.5 $\times$ 14. Or you may want to print in tall (portrait, 8.5 $\times$ 11) mode or wide (landscape, 11 $\times$ 8.5).

Input the Data

After setting up the format, you are ready to input information into the document. Organizing your data becomes crucial at this point. You may be inputting a combination of keying, conversion processes, retrieved electronic data files, downloading, or scanned information into the document. As you retrieve or input the data, it should be organized as closely as possible to how the document will appear when finished. Once all the data has been input, you are ready to edit. Remember, always save your document periodically during the input stage so that information is not accidently lost due to a power surge or some other reason.

EDIT AND PROOFREAD THE DOCUMENT

After you have input the information, edit for content. It is important that you do the editing in stages so that you do not accidentally miss organization or language usage errors.

Use Software Editing Features

You can use the editing features of your software program as you key in the document to ensure it is organized properly and that the content and facts are accurate. Some of the functions you may use include the following:

- **Load or Retrieve** Brings a saved file into soft-copy format for editing or printing.

- **Convert** Converts the electronic file into a format that is readable by the software package. Many software packages do this automatically if the file was saved properly.

- **Copy** Designates a block of text, such as a paragraph, that needs to be duplicated in another place or several places within the document.

- **Move** Designates a block of text to be moved from its original location to another place in the document.

- **Delete** Designates a block of text to be removed from the document. This type of delete function requires fewer keystrokes in removing large portions of text than the two following delete functions.

- **Search/Replace** Replaces every occurrence of a selected word or phrase in a document with new text. For example, if the words "United States of America" appear in many places in a document and you decided to change them in each place to the abbreviation U.S.A., you would use the global replace function.

- **Search** Locates a specific text sequence that you wish to get to quickly.

- **Help** Provides an electronic manual of functions and details on how to use them.

- **Insert or Paste** (Usually used with the copy/move functions.) Allows more text to be inserted in the middle of existing text without altering any of the text that was originally there.

- **Merge.** Inserts another document that was previously stored or filed into the current document. Usually means taking information from word processing, spreadsheets, and databases and placing it in other documents.

- **Save** Stores or files a portion of the current document as a separate document.

Proofread a document on the screen before you print it, but still you will need to proofread the hard copy as well. And, al-

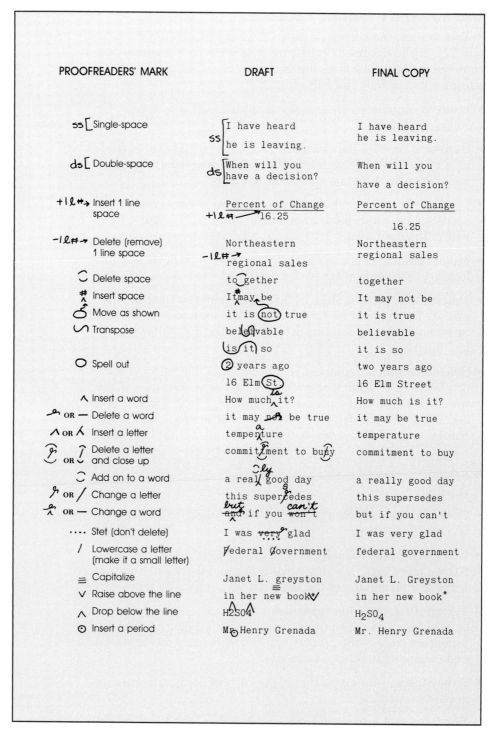

PROOFREADERS' MARK	DRAFT	FINAL COPY
ss[Single-space	I have heard he is leaving.	I have heard he is leaving.
ds[Double-space	When will you have a decision?	When will you have a decision?
+1l#→ Insert 1 line space	Percent of Change 16.25	Percent of Change 16.25
−1l#→ Delete (remove) 1 line space	Northeastern regional sales	Northeastern regional sales
⌒ Delete space	to gether	together
# Insert space	It may be	It may not be
Move as shown	it is (not) true	it is true
⌢ Transpose	believable	believable
	is it so	it is so
○ Spell out	2 years ago	two years ago
	16 Elm St	16 Elm Street
∧ Insert a word	How much it?	How much is it?
OR — Delete a word	it may not be true	it may be true
∧ OR ∧ Insert a letter	temperature	temperature
OR Delete a letter and close up	commitment to buy	commitment to buy
⌒ Add on to a word	a real good day	a really good day
OR / Change a letter	this supersedes	this supersedes
OR — Change a word	and if you won't	but if you can't
.... Stet (don't delete)	I was very glad	I was very glad
/ Lowercase a letter (make it a small letter)	Federal Government	federal government
≡ Capitalize	Janet L. greyston	Janet L. Greyston
V Raise above the line	in her new book	in her new book*
∧ Drop below the line	H2SO4	H_2SO_4
⊙ Insert a period	Mr Henry Grenada	Mr. Henry Grenada

Figure 13.7 Standard proofreader's marks.

PROOFREADERS' MARK	DRAFT	FINAL COPY
⌃ Insert a comma	a large, old house	a large, old house
⌄ Insert an apostrophe	my childrens car	my children's car
⌄⌄ Insert quotation marks	he wants a loan	he wants a "loan"
= Insert a hyphen	a first=rate job	a first-rate job
	ask the coowner	ask the co-owner
OR ⅟M Insert a dash or change a hyphen to a dash	Success at last! Here it is cash!	Success--at last! Here it is--cash!
___ Insert underscore	an issue of Time	an issue of Time
Delete underscore	a very long day	a very long day
( ) Insert parentheses	left today May 3	left today (May 3)
¶ Start a new paragraph	¶ If that is so	If that is so
⨞ Indent 2 spaces	Net investment in tangible assets	Net investment in tangible assets
⊐ Move to the right	$38,367,000	$38,367,000
⊏ Move to the left	Anyone can win!	Anyone can win!
= Align horizontally	Bob Muller TO	TO: Bob Muller
‖ Align vertically	Jon Peters Ellen March	Jon Peters Ellen March

Figure 13.7 (cont.).

ways save your document periodically during the editing stage so that information is not accidently lost due to a power surge or some other reason. Figure 13.7 shows standard proofreader's symbols you can use when proofreading hard copy of documents.

Proofread for Transcription Errors

After you have finished editing the document for content accuracy, you will need to proofread it for errors in keying, spelling, grammar, and syntax. Your software may have some of the following electronic proofreading tools:

• **Spellcheckers** Many software packages have electronic dictionaries, or **spellcheckers.** These electronic dictionaries compare the words in the document being processed with those in the dictionary. When a word does not match one in the dictionary, it is highlighted so that the user can correct it if necessary. Since the electronic dictionary cannot possibly contain all words, it will sometimes highlight correctly spelled words, such as proper names. But you can usually add frequently used proper names and industry-specific terms to the dictionary so they are not continually highlighted. Spellcheckers also help you find keying errors. For example, if a space is missing between two words, the dictionary will consider the error as one misspelled word rather than as two words with a missing space. You can also use some electronic dictionaries to "look up" words you are not sure of as you are inputting the document. This reduces the number of corrections needed later. Refer to figure 13.8 to see how a spellchecker works on a typical document.

A spellchecker cannot tell the difference between singular and plural forms of words or words with different verb endings unless they are included in the dictionary. For instance, both phenomenon and phenomena must be on the dictionary's list for them to be checked. But even if both of these words are on the list, the spellchecker cannot tell if you have used the words correctly. You must still proofread your document to check word usage. With most programs you will also have to check that you have hyphenated words correctly, although there are programs that will check word breaks for you too.

- **Grammar Checkers** Some packages include a grammar checker. A **grammar checker** helps you avoid common grammatical errors, such as split infinitives and the use of plural nouns with singular verbs. You still have to check your work to make sure that you have not made other grammatical errors, such as run-on sentences, incomplete sentences, and misplaced modifiers.

- **Thesaurus** An electronic **thesaurus** allows you to check if you used one word too many times, and, if so, it gives you word options. The thesaurus functions just like a spellchecker but gives additional words for use instead of correct spellings.

Once you have used these electronic tools to check your work, it is imperative that you do a final proofreading yourself. If it is a lengthy document, ask a co-worker to proof the document for errors as well.

Edit for Layout

The last editing job you have is to check for layout consistency. Are the margins even? Is the indentation consistent? Are the font styles (bold, italic) used appropriately and consistently?

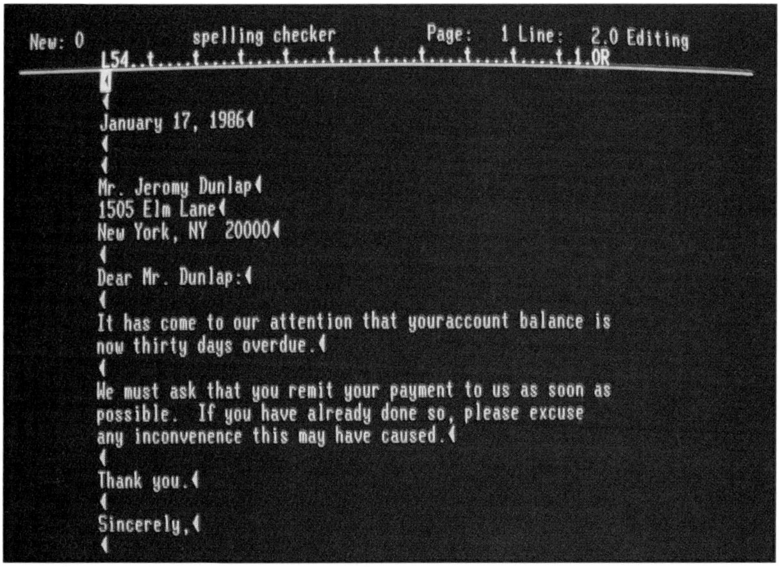

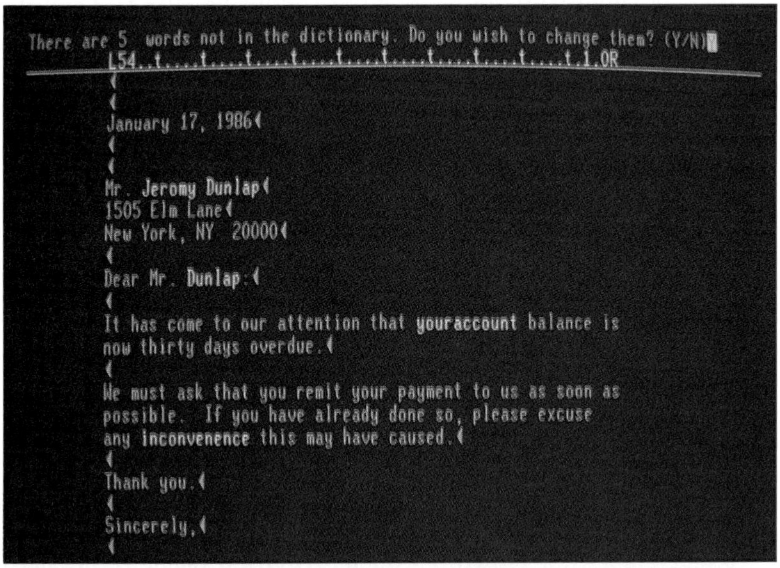

Figure 13.8 A spellchecker highlights words that are not entered in its dictionary. In this example, the first three words highlighted are proper names and do not need to be corrected. However, if they are words that you will use frequently, you should add them to the dictionary. The fourth word highlighted, "youraccount," is simply a typing error of two words without the separating space between them. To correct the error, you insert the space. The last word highlighted, "inconvenence," is misspelled. It can be looked up in the electronic dictionary and corrected in the document.

Did you change the font size, and if so is it consistent? You may at this point want to print out a rough draft of your document on plain paper to determine whether the layout is appropriate. Items to check include the following:

- **Indent** This feature sets up a temporary left margin automatically for keying indented text.

- **Justification** This item allows you to center, right, left, or full justify text.

- **Page Breaks** A page break should appear at the bottom of every page; do not leave incomplete lines at the top or bottom of multiple-page documents.

- **Page Numbering** Pages can be numbered automatically by many word processing programs. The numbers can be placed at the top or bottom of each page and printed at the center or at the right or left side of the page. If you delete a page in the middle of a document, the computer will change the numbers of the remaining pages so they are again in sequence.

- **Hyphenation** Many software packages hyphenate automatically; but many do not always use the formatting rules of hyphenation, only the dictionary rules. Therefore, be sure you do not have proper names hyphenated or too many hyphens (three or more) in a row in one paragraph. See your reference manual for specific guidelines.

- **Headers and Footers** In addition to page numbers at the top or bottom of every page, insert other information, such as the author's name or the title of the document. If the information is placed at the top of the page it is called a **header;** at the bottom it is referred to as a **footer.**

PREPARE THE FINAL COPY

Before the final copy is printed on letterhead or high-quality paper, read through the document one last time to be sure you have not missed any errors. Many times in an office we are pushed to complete documents under tight deadlines; however, any document that is printed for distribution needs to project a professional appearance. Errors in a document, however small, are sometimes enough to turn off a potential client. Accuracy errors may cost the company many dollars in litigation. This is why you should always follow the five-step process for processing documents. You will make fewer errors, and as you become comfortable with the process you will find it efficient as well.

Once the document is in final form, it is ready to be output and distributed. We will discuss these stages of the information processing cycle in the next chapter.

SUMMARY

- The steps to process any type of document include the following: prioritize the processing task, determine the appropriate input procedures, format and process the document, edit and proofread the document for errors, and prepare the final copy of the document.

- It is an important part of an office worker's job to gather and prepare data for processing. Office workers need to be knowledgeable in language arts, researching techniques, and office procedures.

- The major types of processing equipment you are likely to find at workstations in an office are microcomputers in a stand-alone or networked situation, terminals connected to a mainframe, and in some offices you may find electronic typewriters.

- Taking and transcribing dictation require that you follow several basic rules so that your materials are quickly at hand, so that you can organize them efficiently, and so that you can perform your work with a minimum of delays and errors.

- Dictation machines are convenient because they don't require you to be present when your supervisor wants to dictate. Some dictation machines are portable or desktop units, while others are large centralized units.

- Drafts are preliminary or working copies of documents from which you produce finished documents.

- If you use a standalone microcomputer to input copy, you have to load the appropriate software and prepare a storage disk to accept soft copy. With a network, you have to enter a password before you can use the system.

- When you are gathering data for processing, you may use handwritten, printed, electronic, or integrated files.

- A GUI (graphic user interface) speeds the integration of information from unlike formats because of its ease of copying information into a clipboard and retrieving it in another application.

- Without a GUI, you must convert information from one software format into a generic format such as ASCII to bring the information into a different software package.

- Downloading and uploading information from and to bulletin boards and on-line databases can save the company money and make the administrative assistant much more productive.

- The main settings you can choose when formatting a document are margins, font, paragraph indents, and line spacing.

- The most common editing for content functions are load/retrieve, convert, copy, move/delete, search/replace, search, help, insert/paste, merge, and save.

- Editing for transcription errors includes using electronic tools such as spellcheckers, grammar checkers, and thesauruses.

- Editing for layout includes determining consistency in indents, justification, page breaks, page numbering, hyphenation, and headers and footers.

- Even after using the electronic tools, it is imperative that you use the human eye to proof for the last time.

VOCABULARY

- notetaking
- rough draft
- electronic notebook
- copyright law
- password
- virus
- executable file

- graphics user interface (GUI)
- leading
- spellchecker
- grammar checker
- thesaurus
- header
- footer

CHECKING YOUR UNDERSTANDING

1. Describe the different formats in which data may be presented, and give examples of each one.
2. What are the most popular methods of creating data and why? List the advantages and disadvantages of each.
3. Compare and contrast desktop dictation machines with portable units and centralized dictation systems.
4. What tasks should you complete in the editing-for-content stage of the process? the editing-for-transcription errors stage of the process?
5. What tasks should you complete in the editing-of-layout stage of the process? Is this the last step you take before printing the document? If not, what else is necessary to complete the process?

6. Describe the reasons it may be necessary to have to convert from one software storage format to another.
7. Describe when you would use downloading and the process you would use.

THINKING THROUGH PROCEDURES

1. You are Edward Ringle's administrative assistant, and your job includes processing documents for him. Mr. Ringle sometimes dictates these documents to you in person, and sometimes he prepares longhand drafts. In both his dictation and his drafts, Mr. Ringle frequently makes grammatical errors and uses words incorrectly. Some of his documents have organizational problems or lack clarity. However, Mr. Ringle thinks of himself as a good writer, and he does not like it when you edit his drafts. In fact, just yesterday he was upset with you for rewriting a paragraph in an attempt to clarify it. This morning he has given you a draft of a letter in which he uses the word *infer* where he really means *imply*. Moreover, you think the letter would be easier to understand if the second and third paragraphs were transposed. What will you do? Be ready to discuss this with the class.

2. You are Margaret Wilson's secretary. While Ms. Wilson is away on a business trip she sent an important memo from her portable computer to your computer terminal. While you are editing the memo for transmittal to the company president, you accidentally erase it from the computer's memory. What should you do? What could you have done to prevent this from happening?

3. Review the procedures for transcribing machine dictation and the procedures for dictating. Use a tape recorder to dictate the section in this chapter on procedures for transcribing machine dictation. Exchange tapes with a classmate. Transcribe the tape as a memo to your instructor.

4. Using the steps outlined in this chapter, complete the activities listed below:

   a. Use an on-line service, and find out all you can about the service. Download some information if possible. If this technology is not available in your school, visit a library or some other public source that has it.
   b. Prepare a memo report using the information you gathered from the on-line service. Bring the information into a word processing package and edit accordingly.
   c. Prepare your monthly budget in a spreadsheet. Save the spreadsheet for integration into a word processing package.

Prepare a small report describing how your budget is beneficial to you and how you plan to change it in the future. Be sure to include your budget from the spreadsheet in the report.

d. Using the articles you wrote in Chapter 12, use them to prepare a newsletter for the department you are taking this class in. Use desktop publishing software if it is available, or use a graphics program to create an attractive display.

chapter 14

DISTRIBUTING WRITTEN DOCUMENTS

OUTPUT AND DISTRIBUTION

There is no point in processing information unless it is going to be sent somewhere. That would be like cooking a meal and then not serving it. The output and distribution/communication phases are important steps in the information processing cycle. Without them, all the other steps would be useless.

This chapter explores the many different ways people can output and distribute information in the office. Traditionally, the most common way office workers distributed information was by placing a hard copy in an envelope and mailing it. In the electronic office, a vast number of computer-based methods of sending information are available. We have already mentioned a few of these, such as electronic mail and facsimile machines.

Electronic communication allows all the offices of a company to interconnect, or integrate, their information processing systems so they can communicate with each other and with other companies. This enables businesses to output soft copy and send and receive information instantaneously instead of waiting hours or days for telegrams or mail delivery. Using electronic communication equipment, for example, a teller at a bank branch can record a transaction instantly on the main office computer, and a multinational corporation can send a contract from Zurich to New York in a matter of minutes.

Of course, even if you work in a fully electronic office, you still have to know about manual methods of distributing information, since you will sometimes communicate with people who work in traditional offices. And no matter what type of office you work in, you will have a number of output and distribution methods to choose from. This chapter explains these choices and looks into the advantages and disadvantages of each type of system.

OUTPUT METHODS

Determining the best method of distribution is directly affected by your choice of output. After processing information, you can output it in one of three ways: soft copy, hard copy, or a combination. In the last chapter we discussed that part of the planning stage of preparing documents is to determine how the document will be output. By knowing this, you are able to determine what type of processing to do. Will the end result be an electronic file only such as E-mail? Or will the end result be hard copy such as a letter to be sent overseas? Or will it be a combination of sending a hard copy and retaining the document in soft-copy form as an electronic file? Answers to these questions in the planning stage of preparing a document allow for ease of output after the document has been processed. If these questions are not answered, you may need to reprocess the document because you have not chosen the correct output method. Figure 14.1 provides a review of the output stage of the information processing cycle.

Soft-Copy Output

Soft copy is the electronic file or the file you are looking at on your monitor as you key. Soft copy is also the small electronic file you may be working on with an electronic typewriter if your typewriter has a display function. After processing the document, you must decide whether to keep the file as soft copy for distribution, as through E-mail, to print out a hard copy, or to store the file on your system for later retrieval.

Hard-Copy Output

Hard copy is the printed output of soft copy. When you have decided that hard copy is necessary for distributing the processed document, you have choices as to how this hard copy will be printed. Do you use the laser printer, the dot-matrix printer, or a letter-quality printer? These printers and their functions were described earlier. For professional-looking documents that represent the company well, only laser printed or letter-quality printed documents should be used. A drawback of letter-quality printers, however, is that you are limited to the element or type style that is installed in the printer and you are not able to print

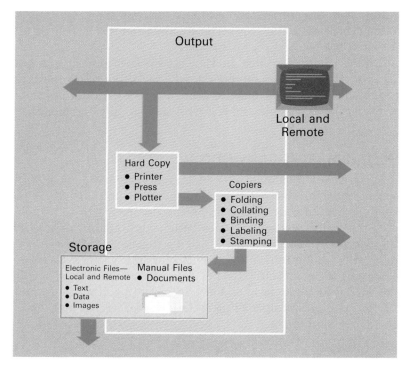

Figure 14.1 In the electronic office information is output in both electronic (soft-copy) and hard-copy form.

graphics. Therefore, most companies today purchase laser printers or ink-jet printers for versatility and professional-looking documents. Laser printers are very cost effective and are becoming more inexpensive as the technology advances. Many dot-matrix printers work well for rough drafts but should *not* be used for documents sent outside the office. Depending on the type of dot-matrix printer available, you are able to produce letter-quality, near-letter-quality type, print graphics, and print in different type styles. Dot-matrix printers that have letter-quality type are required for professional-looking documents.

Printers have various functions and capabilities. Some allow for formatting changes by pushing a button on the printer; others require formatting changes to be handled by the software. You must understand the capabilities of your printer to output hard copy efficiently and effectively. For example, some desktop publishing programs, such as Aldus PageMaker in the MS-DOS environment, output data in the Postscript Language. This output language must be read by a printer that is capable of understanding this language in order to print out various type styles and sizes. If the printer cannot understand the Postscript Language, then the only output available through the desktop publishing software is the type styles available on the cartridges inserted in the printer.

Printer companies such as Hewlett Packard and Canon are adapting their printers to understand a multitude of printer languages. Users will not have to change cartridges continually to print various type styles or deal with compatibility problems.

Hard- and Soft-Copy Output

In preparing documents for electronic distribution, you will output them in electronic or soft-copy form only. There is no need for a hard copy. When preparing documents to be distributed manually, you will prepare both a hard and a soft copy of the document. The hard copy will be distributed and the soft copy will be maintained as an electronic file. Businesses utilize electronic files as their record of documents rather than saving the file in electronic form and also in hard-copy form. In chapter 15 you will learn proper filing techniques for saving both hard- and soft-copy formats.

MANUAL DISTRIBUTION METHODS

When you pick up the day's mail after your letter carrier has dropped it in your mailbox, or when you walk across the hall to deliver a copy of a letter to someone in another office, you are using a manual distribution system. **Manual distribution,** or traditional mail, refers to any system in which people, rather than electronic machines, carry information from one place to another. It includes not only the U.S. Postal Service but also private couriers and delivery services, such as Airborne and Federal Express. It also includes office messengers, mail rooms, and interoffice mail systems.

The electronic communication methods already discussed are usually the most efficient and cost-effective ways to deliver messages between fully automated offices that can connect electronically. Even fully automated offices, however, still need manual delivery services to communicate with other businesses or offices that cannot communicate electronically. Sometimes an automated office may need to use a manual delivery system because its electronic equipment does not have the capability to transmit certain kinds of graphics or text or because the receiving equipment does not have the capability to receive the transmission. In addition, traditional methods are still needed to deliver periodicals and parcels.

The method you choose to distribute a document will depend on several factors. What kind of a document is it? Where is it going? Who will receive it, and how urgently is it needed? If it is a big, bulky report consisting of several hundred pages, it may be best to send it by regular mail, but if it consists of only a few pages of text or graphics, you could send it by facsimile transmission. If a document is to be delivered to a rural area or a foreign country, some delivery methods may not be available. In addition, the recipient may not have electronic equipment available to receive a document sent by computer or facsimile machine. If a branch office must have a copy of a contract for a meeting in an hour, you should send it by the fastest available means. But if you are mailing copies of the company's annual report in preparation for a stockholders' meeting next month, regular mail service will do.

U.S. Postal Service

The U.S. Postal Service faces growing competition from private courier and delivery services, but it remains the most widely used system for delivering mail between companies and individuals. One reason for this is that in most cases the U.S. Postal Service still offers the least expensive means of manual distribution despite rising postage costs. It also usually offers the most convenient means, and it is by far the most familiar delivery service.

CLASSES AND SERVICES OF MAIL

The cost and speed of U.S. Postal Service delivery depend on the class of mail sent. Here is what you should know about the classes of mail and the special services available.

FIRST-CLASS MAIL. You generally use first-class mail to send letters, personal notes, and payments. Any item can be sent by first-class mail if it weighs less than 70 pounds and if its combined length and circumference do not exceed 108 inches. First-class mail usually reaches its destination in less than a week. The U.S. Postal Service ships first-class mail by the fastest means available, but it is not overnight or priority mail. First-class postage assures that letters will not be opened for postal inspection, so they are private. First-class mailings that are not letter-size should be clearly marked "First Class."

PRIORITY MAIL. Priority mail is designed for sending small packages that require ensured delivery within two days. Fees are set by zone as well as by weight, but they are usually lower than those charged by private couriers.

Priority mail can be used for items weighing up to 70 pounds and measuring no more than 108 inches in length and circumference combined. The minimum weight for priority mail is 13 ounces. All priority mail should be clearly marked on all sides. There are also specially marked envelopes and labels to use from the Postal Service.

SECOND-CLASS MAIL. You may use second-class mail, which is less expensive than first-class, for mailing copies of newspapers and magazines. Publishers of periodicals are the biggest users of second-class mail.

THIRD-CLASS MAIL. For bulk mailings, especially advertisements, you might use third-class mail. Third-class mail can include printed materials and parcels that weigh less than a pound.

FOURTH-CLASS MAIL. For packages that weigh a pound or more, you might use fourth-class mail, which is also known as parcel post. A fourth-class parcel can weigh up to 70 pounds and can measure up to 108 inches in combined length and circumference. For books, records, materials for the blind, catalogs, and some other parcels, the Postal Service offers reduced rates.

EXPRESS MAIL. Express Mail is the Postal Service's fastest manual delivery system, and you can use it for any urgent letter or package weighing up to 70 pounds. The Postal Service guarantees that an item sent by Express Mail from a designated post office before 5 P.M. will reach its destination by 3 P.M. the next day (unless the destination is in a rural area classified as a two-day delivery zone). Express Mail is more expensive than other Postal Service options, but it is less costly than most similar private services. To send letters or parcels by Express Mail, you use special envelopes or address stickers from post offices.

SPECIAL DELIVERY. Special delivery, which you can obtain for any class of mail, assures that your letter or parcel is delivered as soon as it reaches the post office nearest its destination. Otherwise, it would go out with the next regular mail delivery, which might not be until the next weekday morning. Special delivery mail should be labeled with stickers that are available from the post office.

SPECIAL HANDLING. Special handling speeds up the sorting and transportation of third- or fourth-class mail but does not provide special delivery. The fee for special handling depends on the weight of the item. Packages for this service should be clearly marked with the words "Special Handling." For especially urgent mail, you can specify both special handling and special delivery.

CERTIFIED MAIL. The Postal Service will provide a record that certified mail has been delivered to the addressee. Your employer may need such a record for documents such as contracts. For an extra fee, the Postal Service offers restricted delivery, which means the mail will be delivered directly to an individual rather than to anyone at the delivery address. Only first-class mail can be certified.

REGISTERED MAIL. Valuable first-class mail or priority mail can be registered or insured. Registered mail is used for items such as stock certificates, cash, and precious metals. To register mail, you must declare its full value. For an additional fee, you can obtain restricted delivery of registered mail.

INSURED MAIL. Because registration is available only for first-class and priority mail, post offices offer insurance for mail of other classes sent to destinations in the United States. Insurance fees are based on the declared value of the item.

COD MAIL. You can send an item COD, which stands for "Collect on Delivery," if the addressee has bought the item from you but has not yet paid for it. The mail carrier collects the amount you specify (up to $200) and returns it to you in the form of a postal money order.

Courier and Messenger Services

Couriers and messengers generally guarantee that they will deliver documents and packages manually overnight. They can often make deliveries over short distances quickly. Couriers and messengers usually make pickups and offer other services not available from the U.S. Postal Service.

Some courier services operate only in the United States or within a smaller geographic area, while others make pickups and deliveries internationally. Most large courier services will pick up envelopes or packages from your office, but with others you drop off your materials at their offices. Courier services may also require that you use specially marked envelopes. If your employer uses couriers frequently, it may have a contract with one of the courier services. There are special procedures, such as getting authorizations or setting special pickup times, for using each service. Some private couriers offer other services, such as facsimile transmissions that they deliver within a few hours.

Messenger services may operate only within a city and its suburbs. Many offices in large cities have contracts with messenger services that they call on when they need to rush documents or parcels to other offices nearby. Messenger service within a city generally costs less than Express Mail and is much faster. Many large- and medium-sized offices employ their own messengers to make pickups and deliveries at nearby offices or other locations. For example, a typesetting company might employ a messenger whose job is to deliver documents to and pick up documents from publishing houses and design studios.

Overnight Mail

Some companies now specialize in overnight mail and ensure that your package will be delivered anywhere overnight. This is the same service as provided by the U.S. Postal Service, but it is offered by private companies such as Federal Express, United Parcel Service, and others. You contract with them as you do with courier or messenger services for their overnight mail service.

The company provides special envelopes or packaging along with labels to be used for their service. Many of the companies will come directly to your office or to a mail room to pick up and deliver packages.

Mail Rooms and Interoffice Mail

All large offices, including those with electronic mail systems, have mail rooms. These mail rooms are staffed by employees who sort and deliver **interoffice mail,** which includes all mail exchanged between people who work in the same location or at the company's branches. An example of interoffice mail is a memo from a supervisor to managers in other departments.

In a large office, each floor usually has a location for depositing interoffice mail as well as letters and parcels that will be mailed through the U.S. Postal Service. This mail drop may have separate bins for interoffice and outgoing mail. Mail-room employees generally make several pickups from these locations during each workday, and office workers should be aware of pickup and delivery schedules.

Some companies use an interoffice mail system called **mailmobile.** A mail cart follows a magnetic track on the floor automatically and is programmed to stop at various points and ring a bell to remind office workers to pick up and deposit mail. The layout of the track can easily be altered if the office floor plan is changed. Mail is also delivered through systems on tracks or through air chute systems. Many companies are also using robots for mail drop-off and delivery.

In addition to collecting, sorting, and distributing interoffice mail, mail-room employees sort outgoing mail and may be responsible for delivering it to post offices. Incoming mail is generally delivered to the mail room, where the mail-room staff sorts it for delivery to individual offices and employees along with interoffice mail.

U.S. Postal Regulations

The U.S. Postal Service recommends certain formats for addressing envelopes to ensure that mail is delivered effectively. Since the Postal Service now uses optical character and bar code readers to sort mail, they are able to sort mail addressed prop-

```
ADAM JOHN ROESER
ROESER FARMS INC
ROUTE 1 BOX 57
SARATOGA WI  54702-4001
```

Figure 14.2 An example of an address label output from a database.

erly for their scanners much faster. If the address is not correctly formatted, it must be sorted by hand, which takes longer.

The general format for addressing envelopes is to prepare the copy in all capital letters with no punctuation, as shown in figure 14.2. Formatting labels and envelopes this way is easy when using a database of mailing addresses. With some word processing software the information for each client must be entered in all caps for it to print appropriately. When using this same database for merging the address with a form letter, the inside address of your letter will appear as that on the envelope. With other word processors you can enter the addresses for the mailing labels in uppercase and lowercase, merge them with the letters, and then input a command that will change the labels to all uppercase before printing.

If you do not have the latter kind of software, a simplified letter format allows for database address merging without the use of capital letters in the salutation of the letter. Another alternative is to prepare another field in your database for upper- and lowercase first and last names and company names to be used within the text of a form letter.

ADDRESS PREPARATION GUIDELINES

Address Format

- Machine or typewritten.
- All capital letters.
- Uniformly aligned at the left margin.
- Without punctuation.
- In black ink on white background.
- Clear and sharp without overlapping characters.
- Clearly visible in window envelopes.
- Parallel to the bottom edge of the envelope.

Address Content

- Always use preceding format.
- Include floor, suite, and apartment numbers whenever possible.
- Use directionals such as north (N) and east (E).
- Use the two-letter state abbreviations.
- When addressing mail to a foreign country, the country should always be on the bottom line by itself.
- Always use the zip code or zip+4 code.

(See the appendix for state abbreviations.)

ELECTRONIC DISTRIBUTION

One early way to distribute information over long distances was by mail, though not in the way we think of the mail service today. From the Middle Ages, when commerce began to flourish, until the nineteenth century, camels, horses, sailing ships, and stagecoaches carried the mail between the cities and ports of Europe and America. It often took weeks or months to send mail from one place to another by stagecoach or ship, and even today with trains, trucks, and airplanes to speed mail on its way, it can take several days for a letter to reach its destination.

In the 1830s Samuel Morse perfected the first practical electronic communications system: the telegraph. The telegraph was a great boon to business and government because it was the first communications system to provide nearly instantaneous transmission of messages across hundreds or thousands of miles. In the early twentieth century, other electronic advances, such as the telephone and Telex, continued to improve business communications. Then, in the 1960s and 1970s, the electronic revolution brought a new array of machines that could send hard or soft copies at astonishing speeds. Today electronic offices can choose from electronic mail systems, computer-to-computer communications, time-sharing systems, facsimile transmission, and computer-based mail services. And, of course, electronic offices also have the option of sending mail by traditional manual delivery systems such as the U.S. Postal Service and private couriers (see figure 14.3).

ELECTRONIC MAIL SYSTEMS

The use of computers and other electronic equipment to send and receive documents instantaneously is known as electronic mail. Companies can use electronic mail among their own departments and to send messages to other companies or to distant branch offices and plants. You may recall that when a company's computers and peripheral equipment are all connected, they make up a network. To use electronic mail internally, a company has to have a local area network (LAN) that can communicate within several hundred yards or several miles.

A company generally uses its internal electronic mail system to send one message to an individual employee, to send the same message to several employees at once, and to gather comments and ideas from various employees at the employees' convenience. When you send a message by means of an electronic mail system, you key the message at your computer. Then you key a se-

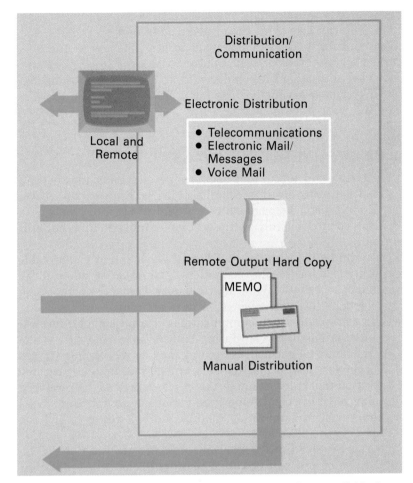

Figure 14.3 In the electronic office the variety of options available for distributing and communicating information requires the office worker to select the appropriate method for each task.

ries of special commands that tells the computer where to send the message.

Electronic mail permits computers to send, store, and receive messages. The messages you send go to the recipient's **electronic mailbox.** To receive electronic mail, you key in special commands that instruct your electronic mailbox to display a list of your messages. This list will indicate who sent each message, what time it arrived, its subject, and whether or not it is urgent. Some electronic mail systems require that a user identification code be entered prior to displaying messages. A recipient's identification code is usually known only to the recipient (and perhaps one or two others who work closely with the individual). This allows electronic mail to be kept private. You can leave messages in your electronic mailbox until you are ready to read them. You can also print them, make additional soft copies, add notes, and forward them instantly to other people in the network. You can transfer soft copies of messages to be electronically filed with other files on disks, tapes, or other electronic media. If you have no further use for a message, you can erase it from the computer's memory.

WIDE AREA NETWORKS (WANS)

We have been discussing short-range electronic information distribution using electronic mail and LANs. But companies also use E-mail between companies through wide area networks (WANs) communicating with on-line databases and bulletin boards.

Data can be transmitted in different ways and over many different kinds of media. Two computers sitting side by side can use simple copper wires. Wide area network transmission may be via telephone lines, microwave, or even satellite.

With some computer communications it is possible for formatting instructions to be lost during transmission, and part of the document may be garbled. Sentences may be received as strings of meaningless letters and symbols, or every comma may become a quotation mark, for example. An office worker at the receiving end may have to spend some time restoring the soft copy to its original form, and this may require some discussion with the sender over the telephone.

To avoid garbled messages, computer manufacturers have devised rules or procedures called **protocols** that allow different models of computers to communicate with one another. These rules, incorporated into various kinds of hardware and software, can identify and correct errors, control the speed and sequence of events during a transmission, establish and terminate transmissions, and edit and format transmitted documents. One set of protocols, for example, prescribes exactly how a person may ask a computer terminal to call up a database; another dictates the commands a person can key on a word processor to edit text.

Sometimes a message is garbled because the sending computer transmits a control code that the receiving computer cannot interpret. Computers usually use one of two **control codes,** or kinds of binary language to represent each letter, number, and symbol—the American Standard Code for Information Interchange (ASCII) and the Extended Binary Coded Decimal Interchange Code (EBCDIC). Computer operators can correct the problem of incompatible codes by using a software program to convert from one code to another.

When computers in distant locations send messages to each other, the messages usually travel through the telecommunications networks set up by the telephone companies. Telephone lines generally carry analog signals, which are continuous but variable electrical waves. Computers, on the other hand, produce digital signals, which are discrete electronic units transmitted in very quick succession like rapid-fire Morse code. Computers cannot send or receive analog signals, and most telephone lines cannot carry digital signals. Therefore, in order for two computers to communicate over long distances, a signal converter must convert the transmitted signals from digital to analog and back to digital as they are carried from computer to computer.

Modems

One device that performs these conversions is the modem. The term *modem* was made up from parts of the words *mo*dulate and *dem*odulate. The speed at which a modem transmits data is known as its **baud rate.** A modem with a baud rate of 1,200 can transmit roughly 120 characters a second. Most modems used in offices with microcomputers are either 2,400 or 9,600 baud. Some modems can operate at several baud rates, and if you are using such a device, you may have to select the baud rate yourself, either by flipping a switch or by keying a command (see figure 14.4). The baud rate you select must match that used by the receiving modem.

Many on-line data services offer users a choice of receiving data at either 1,200, 2,400, or 9,600 baud. The faster the modem the more money saved in on-line computer time and telephone connection time.

Communications Software

In addition to modems, communicating computers need communications software. These software programs perform several communications functions. A communications program connects one terminal to the other, transfers files from one terminal to another, repeatedly dials busy telephone numbers, and takes the user through the proper log-on sequence when he or she calls an external database. It can also store information about the computers with which you communicate most frequently, such as their telephone numbers, passwords, and baud rates, so that you do not have to rekey the information each time you call. Different communications programs have different capabilities.

A communications program like ProCom® can allow you to ac-

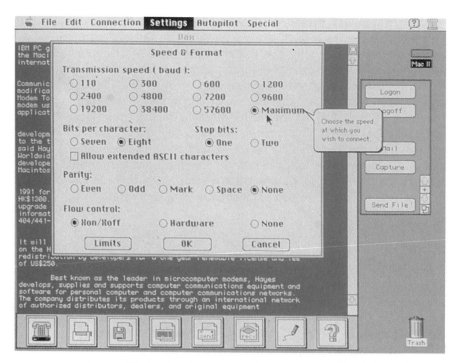

Figure 14.4 This is an example of a communication software program that asks the user to select the baud rate for transmission.

cess specific external databases and bulletin board services, such as Compuserve®, Prodigy®, or Dow Jones®. Your company may subscribe to these databases to access a wide variety of information, such as stock market reports, airline schedules, and research services. Communications between educational institutions internationally can be accomplished by subscribing to INTERNET, which is an international academic bulletin board service.

Transmission Media

While most long distance communication between computers involves sending signals over telephone wires, some offices also transmit information over microwaves and by satellite (see figure 14.5). When you use electronic communications equipment in an office, you probably will not even know which transmission medium you are using, but you should know something about them.

Microwaves travel invisibly in straight lines through the air, carrying data and voices between dish-shaped antennas. Because microwaves cannot bend or pass through obstacles such as

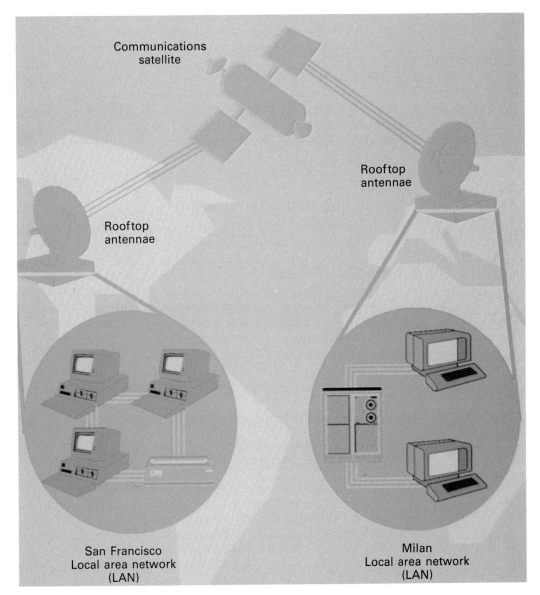

Figure 14.5 Communications satellites can transmit data over very great distances.

buildings, the antennas must be placed at high altitudes—on top of buildings or hills. Microwave transmission is used by companies to link facilities that are scattered over a limited area. It might be used by a bank in a city, for example, to communicate with its suburban branches. The Federal Communications Commission regulates microwave channels and assigns them to users.

Communications **satellites** orbit about 22,000 miles above the earth. They are equipped with transmission devices that receive signals beamed to them by an earth station. They amplify the signals and relay them back down to another earth station. Satellites permit communication between companies separated by very long distances or located on different continents. Poor weather and electrical interference occasionally affect satellite communications, but despite this drawback, satellites are very useful for transmitting not only data signals but also voice and video signals.

Uploading and Downloading

As discussed in chapter 13, when working with communications systems, you may find it necessary to upload or download information to save on-line time and processing time. **Uploading** refers to processing text or other information in a word processing, spreadsheet, or database, saving it as an **ASCII** file (American Standard Code for Information Exchange, the most widely used coding system to represent data), and then reading it into the communications package to send it through the wide area network. **Downloading** refers to the process of capturing information from bulletin boards or on-line services by saving the file as an ASCII file and then bringing the information into another software package for processing. Each of these processes is important for communicating electronically.

FACSIMILE MACHINES

Facsimile machines use telephone lines to transmit exact duplicates of entire pages of text and graphics over long distances. Like communication by telegraph, facsimile transmission is another form of electronic communication that began in the nineteenth century. The first facsimile machine was invented by a Scottish clockmaker in 1842. This machine used an electric wire to translate a document into an electrical signal. In 1907 a German inventor introduced photoelectric scanning, which used reflected light to translate light and dark areas on a page into electrical signals. By the 1920s RCA, AT&T, and Western Union had all developed commercial picture transmission systems, which were used mainly by newspapers to send and receive news photos and copy. Facsimile transmission did not become practical in most business offices until the late 1960s, when Xerox brought out a line of telecopiers that could access public telephone lines.

Today's facsimile machines operate by using a photocell or laser beam to scan a printed page and convert the image into analog signals, which are then sent to a receiving facsimile machine. The receiving machine reverses the conversion process and prints the image on blank paper, using much the same methods as coated paper and plain paper copiers or laser printers. The newest and most sophisticated machines convert images into digital signals and then send the signals to a computer through a faxboard rather than to another facsimile machine. The computer can then produce hard or soft copies of the pages and store them on magnetic tape or disks.

You will probably operate a facsimile machine if you work for a company that sends a large number of documents from one office to another on a regular basis. Facsimile machines allow offices to send exact duplicates of complicated drawings and statistical charts, but some machines produce only low-quality copies that many companies would not want to distribute to outsiders.

TELEX AND TWX

Two of the oldest electronic systems for distributing messages over long distances are Telex and TWX, both now operated by Western Union. TWX began as a competitor of Telex, but Western Union purchased it and merged the two systems. Originally, these systems transmitted information between terminals called **teletypewriters,** which are keyboard devices with printers that can send and receive messages over telephone lines. Today Telex and TWX use computer, satellite, and microwave technology for faster communication and higher-quality hard copies at lower costs. Most of the time-shared electronic mail subscription services are integrated with Telex, TWX, or both to allow for communication with nonsubscribers. You are most likely to use Telex or TWX if you work for an organization that has branch offices in distant cities or that communicates frequently with offices overseas.

Many offices now use computer terminals to send and receive electronic mail through TWX and Telex, but some still use teletypewriters, especially for communicating with branch offices. Teletypewriters are generally slower and noisier than computer terminals and printers. They receive messages by printing low-quality hard copies, so the messages have a crude appearance; however, teletypewriters are less expensive than computer terminals, and many organizations find them quite adequate for internal communications.

Most teletypewriters have keyboards and can send documents

as well as receive them, but some have no keyboards and are used only for receiving. TWX teletypewriters print faster than Telex terminals and have keyboards arranged somewhat differently, but the two systems are very similar.

Telex and TWX have a store-and-forward feature that allows you to send a message to a teletypewriter even if it is busy. The system's storage unit holds the message until the receiving unit is free. Since teletypewriters print messages automatically and operators do not have to be present when the messages arrive, they are very useful to organizations that communicate with distant offices in different time zones.

At one time only a Telex machine could communicate with another Telex machine, only a facsimile machine could communicate with another facsimile machine, and only a computer could communicate with another computer. But, as we have seen, electronic technology makes it possible for different kinds of equipment to communicate with each other. For example, computers can send messages to Telex machines, and facsimile machines can send messages to computers. This enables fully automated companies to communicate electronically with companies that have achieved only a certain level of automation. Western Union has a network service that allows you to use your office computer terminal to send telegrams, Mailgrams, or Telex messages to people who do not have computers. An office worker in Houston, for example, could use a computer terminal and modem to access Western Union and send messages that might be received on a Telex machine located in Kenya or hand delivered to an office in Singapore. This service can be cheaper than traditional telegram or Mailgram distribution because you type the message yourself. Your company would have to pay an access fee, however, so this service may not be worthwhile unless your office sends a large number of messages regularly.

MAILGRAMS

The **Mailgram,** which was developed jointly by the U.S. Postal Service and Western Union, is a combination of a telegram and a letter (see figure 14.6). To send a Mailgram, you can either telephone or hand deliver a message to a Western Union office, or you can send a message directly to Western Union by computer or Telex machine. A Western Union operator then transmits the message electronically to a post office near its destination. At the post office, another operator prints out a copy of the message and inserts it into a distinctive blue and white envelope. The message is delivered the business day after it is received by a regular U.S. Postal Service letter carrier.

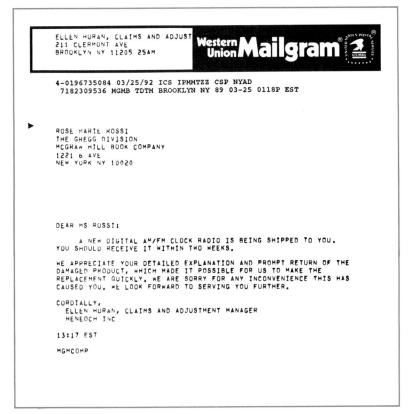

ELLEN HORAN, CLAIMS AND ADJUST
211 CLERMONT AVE
BROOKLYN NY 11205 25AM

Western Union Mailgram

4-0196735084 03/25/92 ICS IPMMTZZ CSP NYAD
7182309536 MGMB TDTM BROOKLYN NY 89 03-25 0118P EST

ROSE MARIE ROSSI
THE GREGG DIVISION
MCGRAW HILL BOOK COMPANY
1221 6 AVE
NEW YORK NY 10020

DEAR MS ROSSI:

A NEW DIGITAL AM/FM CLOCK RADIO IS BEING SHIPPED TO YOU.
YOU SHOULD RECEIVE IT WITHIN TWO WEEKS.

WE APPRECIATE YOUR DETAILED EXPLANATION AND PROMPT RETURN OF THE
DAMAGED PRODUCT, WHICH MADE IT POSSIBLE FOR US TO MAKE THE
REPLACEMENT QUICKLY. WE ARE SORRY FOR ANY INCONVENIENCE THIS HAS
CAUSED YOU. WE LOOK FORWARD TO SERVING YOU FURTHER.

CORDIALLY,
ELLEN HORAN, CLAIMS AND ADJUSTMENT MANAGER
HENEOCH INC

13:17 EST

MGMCOMP

Figure 14.6 Mailgrams are faster than regular mail delivery, but they lack the impressive appearance of business stationery.

Mailgrams have several advantages and disadvantages. They are delivered much faster than regular mail, and they can be sent to people who have no computers or other electronic communication devices. This makes them useful for sending urgent messages to places that cannot be linked electronically to the equipment in your office. The disadvantages of Mailgrams are that they can be sent only to destinations in the United States, and they lack the impressive appearance of messages printed on high-quality business stationery. You are more likely to send Mailgrams to branch offices or company sales representatives than to customers or clients.

PROCESSING MAIL

You now know the methods for outputting and distributing mail. The process you use to distribute the mail is dependent on each situation for delivery. And the process you use to prepare incoming mail is also dependent on what type of mail you are receiving.

INCOMING MAIL PROCEDURES

Most office workers process incoming mail every day. If you work in an electronic office, you will probably handle both traditional and electronic mail. This will include the letters and parcels that are hand delivered by mail-room employees or postal workers as well as the soft copy you receive in your electronic mailbox (or perhaps your supervisor's electronic mailbox). In the next few pages we will look at the procedures for handling each kind of mail.

Traditional Mail

If your company has a mail room, the people who work there will separate and sort your mail. They may also use a machine to open all envelopes that are not marked "Personal" or "Confidential." If your company does not have a mail room, one of your duties may be to sort the incoming mail.

Step 1: Sorting First sort the mail according to addressee and then according to priority. Personal and confidential mail gets top priority, followed by telegrams, Mailgrams, special deliveries, and registered or certified mail. Next comes first-class mail, then interoffice mail, then parcels. The lowest priority goes to second- and third-class mail, which normally consists of magazines, advertisements, and catalogs.

Step 2: Opening Mail Open traditional mail according to priority: first telegrams and other special mail, then first-class letters, and so on. Do not open confidential or personal mail addressed to others unless you have clearance from your supervisor. If you open such a letter mistakenly, return it to its envelope without reading it, and mark the envelope with the words "opened by mistake" and your initials.

Letters that are not confidential should be opened with a letter opener to ensure that the envelope and its contents are not damaged. Mail rooms are generally equipped with electric letter openers, but unless you handle huge quantities of mail, you will probably use a manual opener. If you cut a letter by accident while opening the envelope, tape it together immediately.

Step 3: Checking the Contents Remove letters from the opened envelopes, and attach any enclosures to the letters with paper clips. (Remember to use plastic clips if you keep magnetic storage media such as disks at your workstation. You must avoid the risk of demagnetizing them.) If a letter indicates that enclosures were sent but you do not find them in the envelope, attach a note that says the enclosures are missing, or mark on the letter that the enclosures are missing, and initial it. If appropriate, call the correspondent and request the enclosures. If a letter does not include the sender's full name and address, clip it together with its envelope, or note the information on a separate piece of paper and attach it to the letter.

Step 4: Date and Time Stamping After the mail is sorted and opened, each piece of correspondence must be marked near its top edge with the date you received it. Most offices have a rubber stamp for this purpose, but it can also be done by hand with a pen or pencil. Many employers want both the date and the time stamped on each piece of mail. This provides a record of when the mail was received, which helps in planning response time and serves as proof of receipt in the event of a dispute. Your employer may also want you to keep a log in which you note the date and time each letter arrives. Some offices keep logs as an added precaution in case there is disagreement over when documents reach them.

Step 5: Reading and Annotating Mail Read each piece of correspondence. If a letter refers to another document, retrieve that document and attach it to the letter. In some cases you may be able to call attention to important passages in a letter by underlining or highlighting them, making notes in the margins, or making notations on a separate sheet of paper (see figure 14.7). A temporary way to annotate a letter is to use self-sticking notes. They come in a variety of sizes and colors and are neat and easy to use. Simply make your notation on a self-sticking note and stick it to the margin of the letter next to the passage to which you want to call attention. The notes can be peeled off and discarded when you and your supervisor are through with them. If a letter will be photocopied and the copies forwarded to others, notations can be made on the letter with a nonreproducing pencil or pen. Notations made with this kind of pencil or pen are invisible on photocopies. How you annotate your supervisor's mail de-

---

Westport University

School of Business Administration
1500 Western Way
Westport, California 91432
(213) 555-6200

January 31, 1992

Mr. William Santos
Rockford Publications
1600 South Avenue
Minneapolis, MN 55302

Articles sent 12/5
Deadline for review
was 1/15 — *P.S.*

Dear Bill:

Attached is my review of the two articles you sent me (last
month), "Managerial Effectiveness in the Eighties" and "Success
is More than Luck." I found them to be interesting and well
written. My notations are brief, but I think they will help
your writers in sharpening the focus for your audience.

My fee for these two reviews is $500.00. *Check request attached*
for your signature.

Please let me know if you have any questions. I enjoy doing *P.S.*
this kind of work and hope you will call on me again.

Sincerely,

Paul

Paul L. Watson
Professor, Business Administration

PW/ps
Enclosures

Figure 14.7 This is an example of an annotated incoming letter. Marking key passages helps supervisors process their mail quickly and efficiently.

pends on his or her preferences and on the nature of the correspondence.

The mail you process will include professional journals and other magazines as well as correspondence, and you can annotate them in much the same way that you annotate letters. Instead of reading them from cover to cover, however, check their tables of contents for items that might be of particular interest to your supervisor. When you find such an article, you might scan it and highlight the key points. Then attach a note to the magazine's cover to call your supervisor's attention to it. Some managers prefer that their support staffs prepare written summaries of important articles to save reading time.

Step 6: Presenting Mail Try to anticipate what materials your supervisor might need in order to respond to the mail, and attach them to the incoming correspondence. For example, if you have written a margin note on a letter saying, "See Invoice 233807-B," give your supervisor a copy of the invoice.

Most executives keep in-boxes on their desks for depositing incoming mail. Others prefer to have it presented in a folder, with personal and confidential correspondence on top followed by the rest of the mail in order of priority. In any case, confidential mail should never be left on a desk for inspection by passersby. It should always be placed in a folder. If there is a lot of mail, divide it into categories, and place each category in a separate folder.

Step 7: Routing Mail If you want to bring a letter or journal to the attention of other people in the office, you can circulate it by stapling to it a **routing slip,** which is a piece of paper with a column of names (see figure 14.8). When you drop the item in the interoffice mail, the mail room routes it to the first person on the list. That person then reads the item, checks off his or her name, and returns the item to the interoffice mail so that it will be delivered to the next person on the list. Circulating mail with routing slips can take several days. Therefore, it is best to use this procedure for periodicals and other items that cannot be duplicated. When you are in a hurry for people to read an item, it is faster to photocopy it and address the copies individually.

ROUTING – REQUEST

Please
- ☑ READ
- ☐ HANDLE
- ☐ APPROVE

and
- ☑ FORWARD
- ☐ RETURN
- ☐ KEEP OR DISCARD
- ☐ REVIEW WITH ME

To *Richard Lam*
Angela Pendleton
José Vargas

Date __10/5/92__   From *Diane Brienza*

Figure 14.8 Routing slips enable you to circulate one document to several people within your office or company. Crossed out names indicate which co-workers have seen the document and passed it on.

Step 8: Responding to Mail Prompt responses to letters are necessary for good relations between correspondents, so reply as soon as possible to inquiries and requests addressed to you or to your office in general. This includes forwarding payment checks or invoices to appropriate departments and forwarding any letters that have been addressed to your office by mistake. If your supervisor is away from the office for more than a day or two, you may also be expected to read your supervisor's mail thoroughly and respond to it with appropriate actions.

When you are sure you have the information and the authority to do so, answer any requests or inquiries that arrive in your supervisor's absence. Otherwise, you can simply acknowledge many letters with notes explaining that your supervisor is away and stating when you expect him or her to return. Keep copies of all the responses and acknowledgments you write, and pass these copies on to your manager along with the incoming letters when he or she returns.

Electronic Mail

Procedures for receiving electronic mail are very similar to those for receiving traditional mail; however, an electronic mail system can do many of the things you would do manually with traditional mail automatically, such as date stamping and time stamping. In addition, an electronic mail system can prioritize items automatically so that the most urgent messages always appear first on the screen.

Each user on the electronic system has an electronic mailbox, which is a private receptacle for messages to which only the "owner" has access. Most electronic mail systems, however, allow users to give other people access to their in-boxes. Your supervisor will probably give you access to his or her mailbox.

Viewing Electronic Mail Each morning when you read through the mail, also check your electronic mailbox. Then set times to check your E-mail throughout the day.

Imagine that you have been away from your office for a couple of hours. During that time several of your colleagues used the electronic mail system to leave messages for you. When you return to your office, your computer will list for you all the messages that came in, indicating the time each was received, the sender, the classification (such as "urgent" or "classified"), and the subject. Figure 14.9 shows the kind of information that might appear on

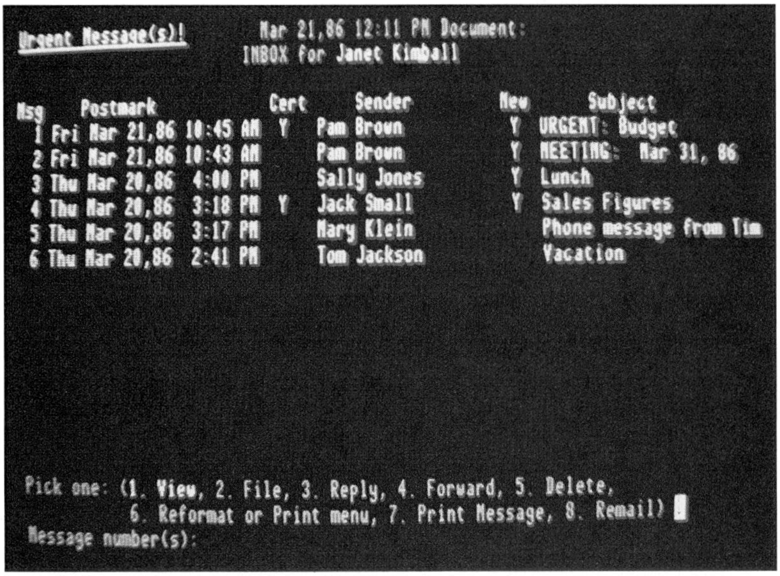

Figure 14.9 An electronic mailbox lists all the incoming messages, placing the urgent ones first.

an individual's screen. In this case Janet Kimball can see at a glance who has contacted her. Notice that the computer has placed the urgent message at the top of the list automatically, even though it was received later than some of the other messages.

Once you have read the list, you can use the view option to read the messages in any order you choose. Do this by indicating the number or numbers of messages you wish to view. Some systems allow you to select only one message at a time; others number the entries and allow you to select by keying in the numbers or through commands (such as ALL for all messages or NEW for only new messages).

Once you have read your electronic messages, you will need to act on them. Depending on the type of message you receive, you might want to forward it to someone else, file it, send a response, or delete it from your in-box.

Forwarding Electronic Mail Most electronic mail systems have a forwarding feature that allows you to send a message you have received to somebody else, with your comments attached. We will continue to use Janet Kimball's in-box to illustrate how electronic mail is processed. The urgent message listed as number 1 on her in-box is shown in figure 14.9. When Janet reads the message, she knows that she does not have the information that Pam Brown has asked for, but she knows that Sally Jones has a copy of the budget. Instead of sending a message back to Pam telling her that Sally is the one to ask for the documents, Janet can simply forward Pam's message to Sally. Janet selects option 4, the forward option. She indicates the person to whom she wishes to forward the message and can then key any comments or instructions she might want to give the person receiving the message. Figure 14.10 shows what Janet's screen displays when she forwards the message. Figure 14.11 shows what appears, seconds later, on Sally's screen. As you can see, the system attached Janet's comments to Pam's original message automatically.

Filing Electronic Mail Any time you receive information in your in-box that you might need to refer to again in the future, you should file it. To file information, use the file option (listed as number 2 in figure 14.9). Once you select the file option, you need to indicate where within the electronic filing system the information should be placed. You will also need to give the information a document name so that you can access it in the future.

Replying to Electronic Mail When you receive any type of mail, traditional or electronic, you often need to

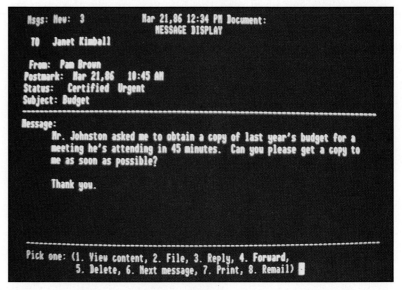

Figure 14.10 This screen shows the forward option highlighted because Janet decided to forward the message.

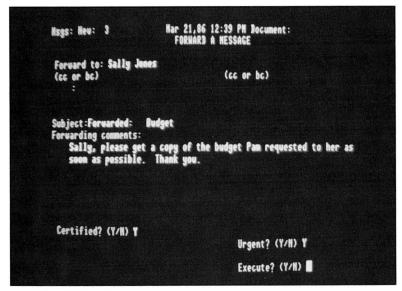

Figure 14.11 This screen shows how the forwarded message would appear on Sally's screen.

respond. With traditional mail, you respond by mailing back your answer, which may take several days, or by using the telephone or some form of express mail. With electronic mail, you can respond immediately.

Most electronic mail systems include a reply function. This sends your response to the person who sent you the message automatically. Suppose that Janet Kimball has viewed message 2 on her in-box. She learns that Pam Brown has scheduled a one-hour secretaries' meeting for March 31 at noon. Janet wants to let Pam know that she will attend, so she selects the reply option. Figure 14.12 shows what might appear on Pam's screen. Notice that the original message is included on the screen for easy reference. Electronic mail systems vary, and not all of them include this capability.

Deleting Messages As you process electronic mail and take the appropriate action, such as replying to a message or filing important information, clean out your in-box. Just as you would not keep the mail you processed yesterday in the in-box on your desk, you should not do so in your electronic in-box either. After each mailbox item is processed, it should be deleted. Then go on to process the next item. Deleting processed messages is the final step in electronic mail processing.

```
Msgs: New: 2                Mar 21,86  1:00 PM Document:
                            REPLY TO A MESSAGE
To: Pam Brown
(cc or bc)                                    (cc or bc)
         :
Subject: Reply to MEETING:  Mar 31, 86
Original message text:
         A one-hour secretarial meeting has been scheduled for March 31 at
         noon.  Please let me know if you can attend.



Reply Text:
         I will be attending the secretarial meeting.



Certified? (Y/N) N
File this reply? (Y/N) N        Urgent? (Y/N) N        Execute? (Y/N)
```

Figure 14.12 Electronic mail allows the receiver to send an immediate response.

PROCESSING OUTGOING MAIL

If you work in a large office where outgoing mail is processed by mail-room employees, you can still expect to be responsible for wrapping packages and for stuffing, addressing, stamping, and presorting envelopes. Keep a zip code directory among your reference materials to make sure outgoing envelopes bear the proper zip codes. Your post office can tell you how to purchase a zip code directory from the Government Printing Office.

If your office is too small to have a mail room, you may be responsible for the following processing operations.

Distributing Traditional Mail

Traditional mail can be distributed in a number of ways. You may choose from the U.S. Postal Service, messenger or courier service, overnight mail services, or hand delivering letters yourself. Each of these has its place according to the type of document. You must determine the most efficient yet cost-effective method of distribution. Planning for the time lag of the Postal Service or even using two-day priority mail can save your organization $10 to $20 per letter in distribution costs. Procrastination in finishing a project is not justification to send a letter or report in overnight mail for a cost of $15 to $20 when mailing it two days prior would have cost $5 or less. Or sending it by fax may cost as little as 50¢.

The importance of such items as sales contracts, bids, and accounting information may be reason to send them by overnight mail or by fax. Annual reports and requests for routine information may not justify overnight or even priority mail. If your company has a wide area or local area network system with E-mail capabilities, it may be faster and easier to upload a document to the E-mail system and distribute in that manner.

No office is paperless yet, and they may never be. Working with paper and traditional distribution methods can be very time consuming, but certain tasks allow for more cost-effective distribution.

Step 1: Prepare Addresses Use the U.S. Postal Service suggestions for correct addressing and prepare mail accordingly. Also double check to be sure that the address is correct and that the document inside the envelope is addressed correctly. Sending the incorrect document to an individual can not only be embarrassing but it is also a breach of confidence on your part towards your clients and can cause great delay in distributing the information to the correct person.

Step 2: Sorting Outgoing mail should be sorted according to destination and service class. When processing many outgoing envelopes, you can save money for your employer by sorting them according to zip codes, because the Postal Service offers discounts on sorted mail. Some employers have OCR devices that scan zip codes and sort envelopes automatically. If you do not have an automatic sorter, sort the mail manually.

Step 3: Weighing Unless you are certain how much postage a letter or package requires, you must weigh outgoing mail on a postal scale. A postal scale, which may be mechanical or electronic, shows the weight of an item in ounces and pounds. The postage is determined by both the weight and the class of mail.

Step 4: Stamping Once you determine the amount of postage, affix a stamp to each envelope or parcel. Depending on the quantity of mail you handle, you may do this by hand with ordinary stamps or you may use a **postage meter.** A mail room that processes large quantities of mail routinely generally uses a postage meter, which prints postage fees on gummed strips of paper that are used as stamps. A company purchases a postage meter from an office equipment company, but the meter must be licensed by the Postal Service, which also supplies a meter record book. Before using a new meter, take it to a post office and purchase a specific amount of postage. A postal worker records the amount of the purchase on the meter's dials. At the end of each workday, you record in your meter record book the amount of postage you have used that day and the amount that remains on the dials. When the amount remaining on the meter runs low, you go to the post office again to buy more postage and have the dials reset. With newer, more sophisticated postage meters, postage can also be purchased electronically.

Distributing Electronic Mail

We have discussed at great length the process used to prepare electronic mail. To distribute electronic mail you only need to know the proper commands of your software. To distribute electronic mail efficiently, learn the procedures for distributing mail to more than one person or to a group.

Working on-line in databases or bulletin board services allows you to gather great amounts of information and share a wealth of information with others. Processing your messages in a word processor, for example, and uploading them to the on-line service or E-mail system, allows you more time for the writing process. You can be sure the message is clear and will not be misunderstood by the receiver.

Choosing the correct method of output and distribution/communication makes the information processing cycle complete. You are now ready to work in an office setting, where you will be asked to write, edit, process, store, output, and distribute many types of messages. Even though we have discussed storage of electronic media, there are other means of storing information. Chapter 15 discusses these methods and how to use different storage techniques.

SUMMARY

- Traditional, manual delivery systems include the U.S. Postal Service; private courier and messenger services, including overnight mail; and company mail rooms and interoffice distribution systems.

- Workers in automated offices can choose from among a wide range of electronic equipment to transmit messages, or they can use traditional, manual methods such as the U.S. Postal Service system or courier services.

- Electronic mail utilizes computers to send and receive messages. Electronic mail can be sent to people within a company by means of computers linked together in a local area network or sent to people outside of the company when all are connected by a wide area network.

- Computer-to-computer communications refers to the transmitting of messages between computers using telephone lines, microwaves, or satellites. Modems and communications software make computer-to-computer communication possible.

- Other kinds of electronic communication include subscribing to large external computers with bulletin board, database, and E-mail services and facsimile transmission.

- It is efficient to prepare documents for electronic distribution in software other than communications software and to upload them to the communications package for transmission.

- Downloading files from bulletin boards, on-line databases, or E-mail services for further processing saves on-line and telephone charges.

- To handle traditional incoming mail, you must sort and open it, check it for missing enclosures, read and annotate it, and present it to your supervisor.

- To handle electronic incoming mail, you view what is in the electronic in-box and then process each item by using the appropriate functions of your system, such as forwarding messages, replying electronically, and filing or deleting processed messages.

- To handle outgoing mail, it is necessary to address, sort, weigh, and stamp it. Company mail rooms handle many of these chores for office workers.

VOCABULARY

- manual distribution
- interoffice mail
- mailmobile
- electronic mailbox
- protocol
- satellite
- uploading
- ASCII
- downloading
- teletypewriter

- control codes
- baud rate
- microwave

- Mailgram
- routing slip
- postage meter

CHECKING YOUR UNDERSTANDING

1. What advantages do private courier services offer over the U.S. Postal Service?
2. What is the most widely-used means of distributing mail to outsiders? Why?
3. How would you go about choosing a method for distributing a document in an electronic office? What factors would enter into your decision?
4. Describe an electronic mailbox, and discuss how it is used.
5. When is a modem used and why?
6. What is the purpose of communications software? Describe some of the functions it performs.
7. How do you send a message from your computer terminal to a co-worker in the same electronic mail system?
8. Describe the major differences and similarities in procedures for handling incoming traditional mail and incoming electronic mail.

THINKING THROUGH PROCEDURES

1. Suppose that you work in an office in Dallas. What class of U.S. mail or what special service offered by the U.S. Postal Service would get each of the following items to its destination on time and without unnecessary expense?
   a. A letter to an organization in New York City requesting information about a convention that is being held in two months.
   b. One routine invoice.
   c. Eight thousand routine invoices mailed at once to destinations around the country.
   d. A manuscript that has to reach an office in Chicago before that office closes tomorrow.
   e. A stock certificate.
   f. A sales contract.
   g. A personal note to a business acquaintance in another organization.
   h. A box containing a new supply of product brochures for a sales representative in Wisconsin.

   i. Five thousand copies of your employer's latest merchandise catalog.

   j. An item costing $175 for a customer in Maine who has not yet paid for it.

2. Carol Zeitz is a receptionist in a small office. One of her duties is to process all incoming mail. After opening a letter addressed to a supervisor one day, she was embarrassed to discover that its contents were personal, although its envelope was not marked "Personal" or "Confidential." Today a letter with the same return address has arrived for the same supervisor. Again, it is not marked to indicate that it is personal. How should Ms. Zeitz handle the letter?

3. Prepare a database of at least 10 people that you know, using the U.S. Postal Service Guidelines for addressing. Prepare mailing labels for these 10 people. Using the database you just prepared, write an invitational letter to these people asking them to attend an open house in the department where you are taking this class. Use the merge capabilities of your word processing and database software and merge the names and addresses of four of these individuals into your letter to make a personalized letter to each one. Prepare them for distribution using the mailing guidelines for addressing envelopes in this chapter. Turn in one letter, envelopment, and your electronic files to your instructor.

UNIT 5 THE WORKPLACE PROBLEM

Part A:

In his job as executive assistant to the marketing director of Computer Systems, Inc., Neil Simonson receives many letters and electronic mail messages from the sales representatives requesting marketing materials for use in their stores. Neil sorts through these suggestions and summarizes them for the marketing director and together they decide how documents should be developed for the purpose of supporting the efforts of the sales staff.

Neil has just looked at his electronic mail. Two sales representatives have sent him information regarding a new product. One needs some presentation materials that can be used as overhead transparencies; another needs a brochure describing a product; a third needs a letter introducing the product to prospective clients. From the information in the messages below, prepare the text that would be used for each sales tool. Use the software you

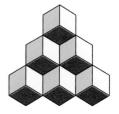

have available to create the materials. Use the problem solving checklist as a guide to make sure you have covered all aspects of the process.

Message #1
TO: Neil Simonson
FROM: Marta Jefferson
Presentation Materials Needed

These materials should introduce the new product, Classic System II. The system configuration includes 80 megabyte hard drive, operating system version 7.0, VGA graphics, 6 megabytes of RAM, optical disk storage, multimedia capabilities. Options include mouse and voice input, laser output, scanner with OCR software, and graphic user interface. Its software applications range from word processing to integrated software systems, to communications of voice, video and data, to multimedia uses with optical disk capabilities. The market for the system includes the higher education institutions and media centers in business.

Please make up about four or five transparencies. I need them a week from today.

Message #2
TO: Neil Simonson
FROM: Marta Jefferson

On second thought, it would be great if I had a brochure outlining this same information. I will leave it with customers (about 10 people) after the presentation. Please include my name, address, phone number, and fax number as follows: Marta Jefferson, Sales Representative, Computer Systems, Inc., 3490 Leslie Lane, Portland, ME 46372-9876 (325) 555-5748, FAX (325) 555-2626.

Message #3
TO: NEIL
FROM: SCOTT

I need a sales letter outlining the features of Classic System II. This product is really hot! My clients include higher education institutions and media centers in businesses. Please develop a letter I can use to introduce the product. I need it as soon as possible. Include my vital statistics: Scott Overmeyer, Sales Representative, Computer Systems, Inc., NW75T47 West 67th Avenue, New Orleans, LA 89234-0012 (698) 555-2869 FAX (698) 555-2828.

PROBLEM SOLVING CHECKLIST
DEFINE THE WORKPLACE PROBLEM

What formats are necessary to prepare presentation materials, brochures, and letters?

ANALYZE THE WORKPLACE PROBLEM

Who is the audience of these materials?

Is there enough information provided to prepare these materials?

What processes should be used in preparing the materials?

PLAN YOUR PROCEDURE

Which tools should be used to prepare each document?

How should the publication information be organized?

IMPLEMENT YOUR PROCEDURE

Were the correct tools used?

Were the correct processes for creating the materials used?

Is the information presented in a logical, attractive format?

Were all formatting options considered?

EVALUATE YOUR RESULTS

Are all materials error free?

Do the materials communicate their message appropriately?

Do they meet the audiences' needs?

Are they formatted appropriately for a businesslike, professional appearance?

Part B:

Neil has finished developing the sales materials and Roger has approved all of them for distribution. Neil wants to let each sales representative know that he has followed up on each request and that he will be sending the materials out tomorrow. Create two e-mail messages, using your e-mail system or using word processing software. Let each sales representative know what materials you have developed for him or her and how you will be sending it.

PROBLEM SOLVING CHECKLIST

DEFINE THE WORKPLACE PROBLEM

What information must be communicated to the sales representatives?

ANALYZE THE WORKPLACE PROBLEM

How should the message be formatted?

What process must be used to distribute the materials?

PLAN YOUR PROCEDURE

What is the most cost efficient way to send the materials?

What method will ensure that the materials arrive on time?

IMPLEMENT YOUR PROCEDURE

Were the messages sent and received?

Were the materials distributed?

EVALUATE YOUR RESULTS

Did the materials arrive on time?

Did the materials suite the purpose?

Part C:

It is the end of the quarter and Neil must now prepare the quarterly activities report for the department. The report was completed by a temporary worker and is not formatted or organized correctly. Key in the following report as it is and save the report. Then make the changes necessary to format the report correctly. If you do not have word processing software, you will need to create two reports, one for the existing quarterly report and one for the updated report. If they are available to you, you may use desktop publishing software and graphics integration to make the document communicate the message more effectively.

REPORT CONTENT

Marketing Department Activities Quarterly Report

1st Quarter, March, 1992

During the last quarter, we have completed major research projects in the areas of new hardware and new software. The results of these projects are as follows:

Determine the market need for a new multimedia computer system. Through our nationwide research of media departments in business, we have found that there is a need to provide DOS-based equipment to help media department staff work with training and development to provide adequate training materials. The results of the survey showed that 69 percent of the businesses surveyed were very interested in working with this type of product. Of the 69 percent, 43 percent were interested in using multiple systems; and 26 percent were interested in using one system. The results of this survey proved important for the production department to continue research and development of the new product.

Determine the needs of the sales representatives in terms of marketing materials support.

All the sales representatives in all branches were surveyed to determine the types of marketing materials that were most effective for them to use in promoting their product lines. Through this study, it was determined that all representatives use product flyers or brochures, 63 percent use presentation materials (the other 37 percent said they foresee using these materials in the future), 100 percent use product information letters introducing new product, and 49 percent use newsletters on a monthly or quarterly basis to keep their clients informed of new information and workshops they are providing.

Future plans include creating presentation templates and developing multimedia presentations with the new equipment to be used in marketing efforts. Marketing personnel are anxious to continue working with sales and production to provide the best computer systems possible to our clients.

The marketing department of Computer Systems, Inc. works closely with the sales and production departments to meet corporate goals. Our activities include doing market research, preparing marketing materials, supporting sales with specialized materials request, and working with production to get specific product information.

The budget for the department includes the following:

PERSONNEL	$125,000/year
SUPPLIES	$50,000/year
MAILING	$25,000/year
TOTAL	$175,000/year

PROBLEM SOLVING CHECKLIST

DEFINE THE WORKPLACE PROBLEM

What is the best way to present information in a report format?

What organization and layout is necessary?

ANALYZE THE WORKPLACE PROBLEM

Who is the audience for this report?

Is this a formal or informal report?

What needs to be included in the report?

PLAN YOUR PROCEDURE

What format is appropriate for the material in this report?

What technology tools will be useful in completing the report?

IMPLEMENT YOUR PROCEDURE

Does the report format reflect the appropriate organization of the information?

Is the content of the report presented clearly?

Have all sentence structure and grammar errors been corrected?

Were the correct tools used?

Has the report been proofread?

EVALUATE YOUR RESULTS

Does the report communicate its message appropriately?

Does it meet the audiences' needs?

Does the completed report present the information with a businesslike, professional appearance?

UNIT 6

MANAGING BUSINESS INFORMATION

POSITION DESCRIPTION

Job Title: Law Office Secretary

Loomis Legal Services

1. MAJOR FUNCTION

Responsible for managing the office work flow and setting up procedures for document processing, office communication systems, and
information management systems. Primary emphasis is on processing
legal forms and documents; organizing and managing records; and
maintaining communication with clients.

2. SPECIFIC DUTIES

1. Manage procedures for the flow of information within and outside
of the office; manage the office equipment related to information
processing and management functions.

2. Coordinate communications with clients: handle telephone calls;
schedule appointments; distribute correspondence using manual and
electronic methods.

3. Establish procedures for document creation and processing: use
electronic and manual sources for gathering information; use stored
documents and boilerplate information to create contracts, letters, and other documents; process legal forms and distribute by appropriate methods; process financial documents.

4. Establish records and information management systems for files
stored manually and electronically; analyze records and organize
storage systems; maintain client database; use microimaging technology to retrieve records and gather information.

THE WORKPLACE SITUATION

Sarah Loomis operates a small private law firm in Fort Lee, New Jersey. Leslie Taylor has recently accepted a position as secretary to Ms. Loomis. The Loomis law practice handles many different types of cases. Leslie is responsible for processing documents, handling telephone calls, and keeping appointment calendars and daily schedules up-to-date, as well as performing specific functions related to handling law cases. Because the law office just opened, Leslie will need to organize the business records and set up systems for keeping track of the cases, correspondence, and legal forms. Leslie is excited about starting this new job and she is looking forward to working in a small office where she will have the opportunity to be involved in many aspects of the firm's business.

DEFINE THE WORKPLACE PROBLEM
   What information management systems are needed in order for this office to function efficiently and cost effectively?
ANALYZE THE WORKPLACE PROBLEM
   What types of business records are generated in this office?
   What systems are available for managing the business records?
   What are the tools available for processing the financial and legal documents created in this office?
PLAN YOUR PROCEDURE
   What types of planning and scheduling systems will work best in this office?
   What types of information management systems will work best in this office?
IMPLEMENT YOUR PROCEDURE
   What are the daily, weekly, and monthly work goals?
   What meetings and appointments need to be scheduled?
   What information should be stored electronically? What information should be stored manually?
   What short term goals need to be established for processing financial and legal information?
   Are there long-term projects that need to be scheduled?
EVALUATE YOUR PROCEDURE
   Have the established deadlines been met?
   Is work proceeding without delays or conflicts? missing or lost materials? client complaints?
   Is processed information accurate, complete, and on time?
   Is stored information organized and classified correctly?
   Is information easily retrieved when needed?

chapter 15

INFORMATION MANAGEMENT

THE NEED FOR BUSINESS RECORDS

Most of us have personal experience in filing and records management. Bank accounts, car loans, and insurance policies, for example, generate information that we must keep. And most of us soon discover the importance of organization in managing our personal records. That is the only way we can be sure of finding the documents we need when making an insurance claim or completing a tax return.

Good organization is also essential when managing important information in the business world. Without it, any records/information system—whether it consists of file cabinets or stacks of computer disks—is useless. People must be able to retrieve the information stored in the system. And unlike your personal file system consisting of maybe ten or twenty files (not too many to search through should you misplace something), an office system might consist of literally millions of business records. A **business record** is any documentation of a business transaction— from an original copy of a contract to a handwritten telephone message. The records may be in the form of paper documents, computer disks or tapes, optical media, or various types of miniaturized film called microforms.

Businesses retain records for a number of important reasons. They need some documents as legal records of business transactions. Some financial records must be kept by law for a stipulated number of years. And many documents are kept so that people can refer back to them when necessary.

Information management involves the creation, distribution, use, storage, protection, retrieval, and disposal of records. This chapter examines the equipment and procedures used to set up and maintain a records/information management system. You will see where procedures for handling manual filing and electronic filing systems overlap and where they differ. Finally, you will gain an overview of the field of records/information management that covers handling records on a broad scale.

INFORMATION MANAGEMENT

You already know that businesses run on information. They create it, process it, store it, print it, and distribute it in many forms. With so much information and so many records, businesses would find themselves drowning in paper, microforms, and computer disks if they did not have a way of managing their records. To run efficiently, businesses must establish logical and usable systems for storing and retrieving information. This need has given rise to the field of records management, or what is now referred to as records/information management. **Information management** is the function of organizing and controlling all aspects of business records, from their creation and use to their storage and ultimate disposal. Most businesses manage their own records. But some large corporations turn to outside companies that specialize in setting up information management systems for other organizations. Whether your company manages its own records or uses specialists, you will inevitably be involved in information management tasks that require you to decide which records to keep, how to organize and store them, and when to dispose of them.

Any record goes through a life cycle, beginning with its inception and ending with its disposition (see figure 15.1). The life cycle of a record includes the following:

- **Creation** The origination of data and information. Creation may take the form of processing a document, sending an electronic message, or writing notes or telephone messages. At the time of creation, a decision is made as to the necessity of retaining a record of the information and the format in which the record will be maintained.

- **Distribution** In this stage, the data or information may be manually distributed or electronically sent to one or more receivers.

- **Use** The information received by another now has to be used. It must be either read and acted upon, read for information, or read to be referenced later.

- **Maintenance** This stage of the cycle involves determining if the information should be retained. If it is retained, what is

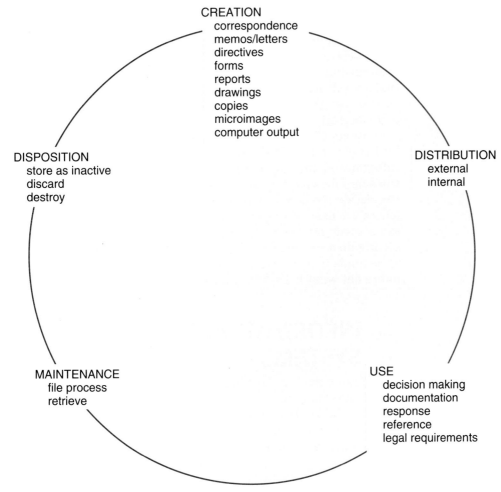

Figure 15.1 Life cycle of a record.

the best way to store the information, how long should it be stored, and how should it be stored for effective retrieval? These questions must be answered.

- **Disposition** In the last stage of the life cycle of any document it must be determined if it should be destroyed or disposed of because it is no longer valuable to the company or if it should be stored forever as an important document for the company.

All documents and information go through this cycle. It may mean that the document is created in electronic mail, distributed to fifteen users, and then deleted from the system. Or it may mean that confidential information is distributed to notify a person of some information and then shredded to ensure its confidentiality. Once the user receives the information, then the user decides whether to retain the information or dispose of it. The originator of the information must also decide whether or not to retain a copy of the distributed information and, if so, on what medium and for how long. This never-ending cycle requires that records/information management be set up in a systematic way so that the company's information can be retrieved quickly and efficiently at very low cost.

A system of information management can be applied to all the business records of a department or organization. The **records/ information management system** consists of procedures and rules for following the life cycle of a business document. How can you decide the best way to store any given record? Since no two offices are exactly the same and no two people have exactly the same needs for their files, there are no hard-and-fast rules for setting up a records/information management system. There are some guidelines, however—factors to consider that will help you figure out what is best for your work situation.

INFORMATION MANAGEMENT SYSTEMS

Let's assume that in your current position, you are put in charge of setting up an information management system. There are some basic steps to follow. If the task involves many hundreds or thousands of records, you may want to consider outside professional help. Setting up a major information management system is a time-consuming task requiring specialized knowledge, and you must make sure that you have enough time and training to do the job well.

RECORDS INVENTORY

The first step in setting up an information management system is to survey the records in question and conduct an **inventory.** An inventory determines what files exist, how many exist, who uses them, where they are stored, and in what form or what type of medium: paper, electronic, optical, or micrographic. Figure 15.2 shows an example of an inventory form for gathering this information.

Go through all the files, baskets, boxes, shelves, and other places where the records you will include in your system are currently stored. Talk to people in the office, and find out where they keep their files. Have respect for people's personal files.

INVENTORY FORM

Record Type/File and Dates Covered	Inches for Paper and Microfiche/Com; Volume for Floppy Disks and Cartridges	Retention Times	Special Handling Codes*	Could be: 1) Microfilmed 2) Moved to Archival Records (Indicate No.)	Location
(a) File: Job Description Material: Application for part-time position ('84) Description for full-time position Notes on benefit meeting Job Description - 4 Positions	1 sheet 1 sheet 1 sheet 16 sheets	None Until Superceded None Check with Records Analyst	Dispose Dispose		Section A Drawer 2
(b) Purchase Orders (Series) 1/5/83 to 1/1/84:	24" paper	6 Months beyond receipt of merchandise (dept. decision)			Drawer 20 Section C

> *CODES
> P = PRIVATE
> V = VITAL
> QA = QUALITY ASSURANCE
> C = CONFIDENTIAL

Figure 15.2 An example of a records inventory form.

Most likely these will not be included in your system. It is up to workers to establish their own management systems for their personal files.

This first step requires you to examine the records and the needs of the people who will be using them. You must identify the kinds of materials to be filed and then decide if they are a homogeneous group of records. That is, do they relate to each other in some way so that it makes sense to group them together? If they do, you only need one classification or filing system. If there are many different types of records, you may have to consider making several different filing systems.

APPRAISAL OF RECORDS

Once you have located and surveyed the records, you are ready to analyze their worth to the company. You must determine what type of records they are and how they are used by an **appraisal of records.** There are four major types of records in an organization: vital, important, useful, and unimportant. These records define how and why the record is used in the organization.

Vital Records

Vital records are essential documents that cannot be replaced. They must be kept permanently. Records in this category include the corporate charter; the deed, mortgage, or bill of sale for the company's place of business; minutes of all meetings of the company's directors or stockholders; stocks and bonds; trademark registrations and patents or other proprietary records; and tax records. Vital records should be kept in a fireproof, theft-proof vault or safe. Copies are often retained in another protected location off-site. Most office workers will not come in contact with these documents, and if they do, they should be instructed not to destroy them.

Important Records

Many records are extremely important to the operation of a business, but they are not vital. Generally, **important records** should be retained for five to seven years. Important records include accounts payable and accounts receivable, invoices, canceled checks, inventory records, purchase orders, payroll records, and employee time sheets and expense vouchers. These records may be needed if there is a question regarding financial transactions. Most companies have a policy that allows these kinds of records to be destroyed after approximately seven years.

Useful Records

Useful records are usually retained for one to three years, depending on the company. These include general correspondence, bank reconciliations, employment applications, stenographers' notes, expired insurance policies, and petty cash vouchers. The identity of vital records such as the company charter, or an important record such as a canceled check, is usually clear, but the identity of useful records is often unclear. What one company considers a useful record, another may consider garbage. It is always best to check with your employer before throwing away any useful record.

Unimportant Records

Common sense can help you figure out when to discard some records, known as **unimportant records.** These include papers that only you use, such as reminders of meetings, notes to yourself regarding tasks to be done (discard only if the tasks are done!), out-of-date announcements and pamphlets, duplicates of filed material (make sure the originals are filed before discarding the duplicates), rough drafts of documents that are now finished (and filed), and so on. Experience will tell you which records in this category you can dispose of safely. But if you have any doubt, check first with your supervisor.

Active and Inactive Records

Once you have determined the type of records you have, you must also determine how often they are used or retrieved during any given time period. **Active records** are those that must be kept in the office. They are used regularly, that is, more than once per month or at least often enough to justify the amount of space they take up. Active records include recent correspondence, proposals, accounts receivable and payable files, purchase orders and invoices, and any records that relate to ongoing projects. Active files should be located conveniently for the person or people using them.

Active files do not necessarily remain active indefinitely. When a record is no longer used regularly, it becomes an inactive record. **Inactive records** are those referred to once a month or less. Active records should be reviewed periodically to select those that should be moved to inactive storage or discarded.

Inactive records may be housed on- or off-site. The decision about where to store inactive records depends on how many records there are and what kinds of facilities are available. A company with only a few boxes of inactive records will find it cost effective to keep the records on-site in a protected, out-of-the-way place. On the other hand, a company with many inactive records to store should consider an off-site location such as a warehouse. As with active records, inactive records should also be reviewed and eventually discarded.

TYPES OF STORAGE SYSTEMS

Records, whether active or inactive, electronic, paper, or microfilm, can be filed in a centralized or decentralized system. In a manual **centralized system,** there is usually an area or room designated as the **records center.** With the exception of personal files, the records center houses all records that people within the company use. Depending on how large the company is and how many records the company has, the records center may operate on a self-serve basis or have trained personnel in charge of maintaining the records. The main advantage of a records center is that all the records you might want are located in one place. If you want a record, you go to the records center and ask for the record or find it yourself, depending on the procedure. In an electronic centralized system, the records are stored on a centralized computer. An individual accesses the records by logging onto the network from his or her office and retrieves the proper electronic record (see figure 15.3). There are other media that centralized records are stored on such as microfilm and optical media. These media will be discussed later in the chapter.

A **decentralized system** has records stored in different places, either near the people who use them most often or where they fit best in the office. The advantage of this type of system is that those who are most likely to use a given record are located near it. The disadvantage is that it is not always easy for people in other areas or departments of the office to locate the files. Decentralized systems can be made up of paper records, electronic records on stand-alone systems with floppy disks or hard disks, optical disks, or micrographics records. The point of decentralized systems is that usually one person maintains the station and others can have access to the information only if they work at that particular station.

Figure 15.3 In a centralized electronic filing system, workers can access files located in the central database by keying in a simple command and a password.

RECORDS RETENTION SCHEDULES

After appraising the records you are ready to draw up a **retention and disposition schedule.** You document how long the records should be kept, why they should be kept, their type, where they are stored, and on what medium. This is the retention aspect of the schedule. The disposition schedule covers who is responsible for the maintenance of the records, the way the records should be disposed of, and who is responsible for disposal.

All of us have had the experience of throwing something away and later realizing that we really needed it. Similarly, sometimes the things we keep are of no use. Today, good records/information management procedures are critical, particularly when both electronic and manual or paper files are being managed. Office workers must determine which files should be saved in electronic form and which should be stored as hard-copy documents. In many cases, the same document is stored in several forms unnecessarily. Documents that should be maintained in electronic form include only items such as monthly reports or other documents that may be used frequently or used to generate other documents. Hard copies should include items such as reports or correspondence with attachments or documents that will never be used to generate future documents. To make these decisions, it is necessary to understand the importance and future use of all documents. Studies have found that more than half of the documents on file in offices are not needed. To avoid adding to the mountains of unnecessary paper, film, and disks that waste space, you need to make careful decisions about which records to store, which to discard, and which to transfer to storage or **archives,** which are often off-site storage locations for inactive files.

Since making the wrong decision about records retention can be very costly, most businesses have strict guidelines regarding what records must be kept and what records can be disposed of. Each company has different requirements that will affect specific records, given the laws pertaining to what records must be kept for that industry. If you work in a small office, make sure you consult with your supervisor and co-workers on retention and disposal decisions. If you work in a large company, the development of retention and disposition schedules requires the input of individuals in the records and information management area, accounting and tax departments, legal department, and data processing department, along with input from all departments on how many, what kinds, and how long records should be kept. Figure 15.4 shows an example of a records retention form.

RECORD IS	SUBJECT TO	THIS RECORD IS		RECORD USE		
☐ VITAL	☐ TAX AUDIT	☐ RECORD COPY	☐ INTER-DEPT			
☐ HISTORICAL	☐ INTERNAL AUDIT	☐ DUPLICATE	☐ INTRA-DEPT			
☐ MICROFILMED	☐	☐	☐			
☐	☐	☐				

MICROFILM	REFERENCE IS	REMARKS	RECOMMENDATIONS
☐ ROLLS	☐ < 1 YEAR		RETENTION PERIOD
☐ CARTRIDGES	☐ 1-2 YEARS		
☐ FICHE	☐ 3-4 YEARS		
☐ APERTURE	☐ ≥5 YEARS		
☐	☐		

EQUIPMENT SAVINGS				RECORDS TURNOVER						DOLLARS	
TYPE	QTY	TYPE	QTY	OFFICE DESTRUCTION	TRANSFER TO STORAGE FROM OFFICE	SUB-TOTAL	DESTROY STORAGE ON-SITE	DESTROY STORAGE OFF-SITE	SUB-TOTAL	EQUIP	SPACE

Figure 15.4 An example of a records retention form.

CLASSIFICATION SYSTEMS

Next, look at how you can organize records. Can they be organized alphabetically? geographically? numerically? Would it make more sense to organize them by subject and have a different file for each subject? Who will use the files? Some files contain confidential material that should not be available to most people. Will clerical personnel or managerial personnel use the files? Depending on the answer, you may organize files differently. A sales manager might find files that are organized according to geographic region to be most helpful. An inventory clerk, on the other hand, might find it more useful to have them organized alphabetically by product name. If both of these individuals will use the same files, you may need to cross-reference the material or have two separate files. Classifying includes determining how paper, electronic, optical, and micrographic records will be filed. The same principles of alphabetic, numeric, subject, or other classification systems can be applied to electronic, optical, and micrographic media as well. Refer to the boxed procedures list for a description of how to prepare records to be placed in their classification area. Following is a general description of the types of classification systems.

Alphabetic Files

Most files are organized alphabetically. This is true whether the captions are names of people, geographic names, or names of forms. There are standard rules for alphabetizing correctly. Following these rules helps everyone who uses files to find records quickly and efficiently. See the list of rules from the Association of Records Managers and Administrators (ARMA). This is a worldwide professional organization of records managers that is striving to help standardize records management procedures. You may find this organization very helpful when on the job in gaining insight into ways to organize records, restructure existing records systems, provide training, and provide new technological information.

ARMA RULES FOR ALPHABETIC FILING

These rules are adapted from the Association of Records Managers and Administrators (ARMA) Simplified Rules.

Alphabetic order. Alphabetize names by comparing the first units of the names letter by letter. Consider second units only when the first units are identical. Consider third units only if the first and second units are identical, and so on.

Each filing unit in any given code is to be considered. When using the units or items in the code such as last name, first name, etc., also use prepositions and conjunctions; however, do not use *the*. *The* should be the last unit in the filing sequence.

Nothing comes before something. A name consisting of a single letter comes before a name consisting of a word that begins with the same letter (that is, *H* comes before *Hancock*). Similarly, a name consisting of one word comes before a name that consists of the same word plus one or more other words (that is, *Harley* comes before *Harley House*).

Ignore all punctuation when you alphabetize. Hyphenated words are to be considered as one unit, and periods, commas, dashes, hyphens, apostrophes, and all others should be ignored.

Use the most commonly used name or title. You may choose to cross-reference under items that may be referred to for ease of access.

Numbers, including Roman numerals, are filed before alphabetic information. All Arabic numerals, however, come before Roman numbers.

Treat acronyms, abbreviations, and television and radio call letters as one unit, and file company names as you see them. Treat each word in the name of an organization as a separate unit, and consider the units in the same order as they are written.

For a complete listing of ARMA rules, you can request a copy of Alphabetic Filing Rules, ARMA International, Association of Records Managers and Administrators, 4200 Somerset, Suite 215, Prairie Village, Kansas 66208.

Subject Files

When the subjects of records are more important to your office's use than the names on them, file the records alphabetically by subject. A record labeled "Proposals" would be filed between records labeled "Organizations" and "Questionnaires."

Like subject files, subject files can be subdivided into categories to allow for more efficient storage and retrieval. For example, if your records include dozens of files relating to insurance policies of different kinds, your main subject file would be labeled "Insurance." Subcategories would be "Hospitalization," "Malpractice," "Fire," "Theft," and so on. The subjects you choose as captions or key words in filing will depend on your office's business and the kinds of records it keeps. The more familiar you are with your employer's records and the way they are used, the easier it will be for you to classify records as subject files that allow for the most efficient storage and retrieval.

While subject filing is generally regarded as an efficient method, locating records in a subject file can be frustrating and time consuming. This is because people often use different words to identify the subjects. For example, you might file a document under "Automobiles," and someone else might look for it under "Motor Vehicles," "Cars," or "Transportation." The solution to this problem is to use cross-references. Another method is to maintain an alphabetic listing of all the subjects that are included in the system. This allows for a quick review of all the listings, if necessary, prior to locating the materials in the files.

Geographic Files

Geographic filing is useful when the records apply to particular geographic locations. For example, a large company might want to break down its operations by country, by region, by state, or even by town. Branch offices, real estate firms, government agencies, and public utilities frequently use geographic filing systems.

When organizing a geographic file, first break down the categories into the largest or most important geographic divisions relevant to your company's operations. Use these as the primary guides. Divide these major geographic regions into subdivisions, and then alphabetize the files within each subdivision. Figure 15.5 illustrates how a geographic file drawer might look. The drawer is divided into sections of the United States: Northeast, Southeast, Northwest, Southwest. The part shown in detail, the Northeast, is divided into subdivisions: the states of Connecticut, Maine, Massachusetts, New Hampshire, and so on. Note that the

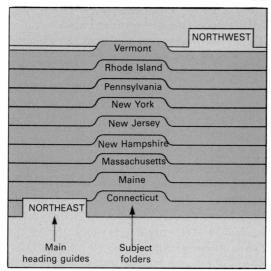

Figure 15.5 These files are classified geographically and indexed alphabetically.

states are listed in alphabetic order within the section. Within each state, the files are broken down into towns and cities. The companies within those folders are alphabetized according to the rules for alphabetic filing.

Numeric Files

Sometimes records can be retrieved more easily if they are filed by number rather than by name or subject. For example, a bank has thousands of customers, and some may have savings accounts as well as checking accounts, retirement accounts, mortgages, and personal loans. Rather than mix up the records on all of a customer's accounts under the customer's name, a bank files them according to account numbers.

Unlike records that are filed alphabetically according to name, subject, or geographic region, numeric files also generally require office workers to keep separate indexes or lists that show the files alphabetically by name or subject and indicate their corresponding numbers. Thus, if you worked in a bank and were handling a transaction for a customer who had forgotten his or her savings account number, you would look in the index under the customer's name to find that number so you could retrieve the file for the account.

Numeric filing offers several advantages that make it the most productive method in many situations. It is very useful when the files themselves are numbers, as in the example of bank accounts. Beyond this, however, there are other advantages. One is that you can add unlimited numbers of new records and files without running out of captions. Another advantage of numeric filing is that you can use it to conceal the names and subjects of confidential records. Still another advantage is that with numeric filing you never have to make decisions about what captions to use or how to label folders.

Offices use two systems of numeric filing. One is the **consecutive numeric system,** which uses consecutive numbers: 1, 2, 3, and so on. In a consecutive numeric system, a record labeled "97334" would go between those labeled "97333" and "97335." In a **terminal-digit system,** numbers are assigned for the purpose of classifying records into groups, and the last number in a caption indicates where to start looking for a record. For example, in the caption 97334, "34" might refer to a drawer number, "73" might refer to a folder number, and "9" might refer to the sequential position of the record within the folder. To make terminal-digit index numbers easier to read, offices may use hyphens, spaces, or periods to separate the components. In the terminal-digit system just described, 97334 might be written as 9-73-34.

Chronologic Files

Chronologic classification systems are those you code and store by date of the record, with the most current record on the top of the pile or the first record in a binder. Chronologic systems are used for current correspondence or projects in process. Once the project is completed, the records can be stored in the regular alphabetic, numeric, or subject classification system and then moved to inactive storage when necessary.

Tickler Files

Another type of chronologic classification system is a **tickler file** or follow-up file. The most common tickler file contains the days of the month and months of the year. You place items to complete in the future in the slot of the day you plan to accomplish the task. Then each day you look at your tickler file to see what activities you must complete. Electronic scheduling systems also have this capability, and you can supplement your manual tickler file with an electronic reminder of the task as well.

The captions on tickler files are usually the days of the month—1 to 31. Within such a file, arranged by day of the month, are forms or other papers that need to be attended to on particular days. Each day, time is set aside to review the tickler file. If there is something in the file that must be done that day, the task is attended to. If the task indicated in the file has been postponed to another day, the paper is moved to the appropriate day, where it will again be reviewed and attended to.

For an example of how a tickler file is used, let's look at the following situation. You are a secretary in a real estate office. On the morning of the tenth, you look in the tickler file and find a form that tells you that the Petersons will be closing the deal on the sale of their house on the eleventh. You must type up the necessary forms today and have them ready; however, when you go to the Peterson file to get the information you need, you find that the closing has been delayed until the twentieth. You return the Peterson folder to its file and then move the reminder to a new slot in the tickler file. You put it in the slot for the nineteenth—a day ahead of the closing date—to remind yourself again to prepare the appropriate documents. Then, on the twentieth everything will be prepared and organized. Note that in a tickler file, you must pay attention to what day of the week any given day of the month falls on. If something is filed in the slot for a weekend day or a holiday, that task will not be attended to.

PREPARING RECORDS FOR FILING

Set aside a time each day or every few days for filing paper records. Keep papers to be filed in a designated place—a basket marked "To Be Filed" or an "Out" box will do. File electronic records immediately as you input them on a floppy disk, a hard disk, or a networked system. Make backup copies of all files as you complete them.

There are five basic steps in filing, and they are generally done in this order: inspect, index, code, sort, and store.

Inspect   Review each record to make sure that it is something you must file. If you are sure it can be disposed of (check the retention schedule), throw it out. If your inspection tells you that it must be filed, move to the next step.

Index   Determine under which caption or title within your classification the particular record should be filed. Index-

ing records is really a mental process requiring you to make a decision. If the record is incoming or outgoing correspondence and your records are classified by names, you might file it under the name of the corresponding person or organization. If your files are organized by subject, you might file the letter under the subject it pertains to. If your files are geographic, you might file the letter under the geographic location it pertains to. If you have a cross-referencing system, you might file one copy under the name of the person and one copy under the subject. (Cross-referencing is explained following.) Electronic records are indexed by determining on what disk and directory the file should be located and by following a uniform procedure for naming the files. It is inappropriate to name electronic files with characters or words that do not identify what the subject of the record is.

Code   Once you have determined the caption or title of the record to be filed, you must assign a code before filing it. **To Code** is to highlight or write the caption on a paper record or give the electronic file a name. On an electronic record this is done by creating a descriptive filename and including it on the document under the initials of the creator. If an electronic file is also in paper form, the filename on the document allows for quick and easy retrieval. On a paper document you can underline or highlight the name under which the paper will be filed. The underlining or highlighting serves as a permanent reminder to anyone using the file in the future to refile the record under that name. Another method is to write the caption in the upper-right corner of the paper. This is necessary when the caption name or subject does not appear anywhere on the page and therefore cannot be underlined or highlighted.

Sort   Once you have properly coded the records to be filed, you are ready to sort records. Arrange them in the order in which they will be placed in the file. If your file is alphabetic, put them in alphabetic order. If your file is numeric, put them in numeric order, and so on.

Electronic files are sorted by you as you save the files in the correct directory on the correct disk. The system then sorts the files for you alphabetically by filename, by date, by type, or by size; whichever you designate.

Store   Finally, you are ready to store the records. When placing records in the paper folders in file drawers, be careful to check and double-check that you are filing them correctly. Be sure you place your floppy disks or other media such as microfilm in the correct place as well.

Cross-referencing   A **cross-reference** notifies people looking for a record in a particular place that it is stored elsewhere. One way to provide a cross-reference is to make an extra copy of the record and then file the copies in the referenced files, noting in the upper-right corner of the paper that it is cross-referenced material. Another way is to use a cross-reference sheet and file this instead of an actual copy. The sheet contains the name of the individual and/or organization found on the original record, the date it was filed, a brief description of the subject of the record, and the place(s) in which that record can be found. If you have ever used a library card catalog, you have probably seen a cross-reference card, which refers you to other places where the book you want is listed.

PAPER FILING SUPPLIES AND EQUIPMENT

Almost all offices still keep paper records. Because of their volume and size, physical storage is an important issue when handling paper records. Records management supplies and equipment vary from office to office, but there are standard items found in most offices.

STORAGE SUPPLIES

File-drawer guides are used to separate a file drawer into sections and to make it easier to locate records. They are usually made out of thin but rigid cardboard, and each guide has a tab that extends above the top when the guide is placed in a drawer. Some of these guides have hooks that allow them to hang from the sides of the drawer. The purpose of the extending tabs is to separate groups of records. File-drawer guides are described according to the width of the tab. The positions on the tab are referred to as first cut, second cut, third cut, and so on. A one-fifth cut means that the tab takes up one-fifth of the horizontal width of the guide; a one-fifth cut guide can have five tab positions. When the positions of tabs are staggered, each tab is readily visible, as shown in figure 15.6. You should have no more than ten guides in any given drawer.

File-guide captions go on the tabs of the file-drawer guides. A caption indicates what lies between the guide you are looking at and the one directly behind it. If a guide caption says "A," then all records beginning with the letter A are found behind that guide. A caption that reads "Ban–Baz" tells you that only names falling alphabetically between these groups of letters are found behind this guide.

File folders are used for organizing papers in file drawers and cabinets and also for keeping papers neat, clean, and together when carried from one place to another. You might, for example, carry a freshly typed letter from your desk to your supervisor's desk in a folder. But the main use of file folders is to keep papers arranged in order in file drawers. Like file-drawer guides, folders have tabs on them for identifying captions. Many people like to stagger the positions of the file-folder tabs as they would the positions of the file-guide tabs, but others like to have the tabs of all file folders in a category in the same position. This can be an aid in categorizing files and can help you locate a given folder more quickly.

File folder labels are already gummed and come attached to a special paper backing that allows you to peel them off when you are ready to use them. The headings should be typed on the labels while they are still attached to the backing. Then they can be peeled off and placed on the folders. Labels are available for use with word processors and also in many sizes, shapes, and colors. Depending on your filing system, you might want to use a color code or simply white labels.

MANAGING WORKSTATION RECORDS

Almost all office workers spend some of their time filing. Even if their filing duties are limited to organizing their own files, they need to develop and follow a simple system. The first step in easy retrieval is to use a storage method that fits the kind of record being filed. Here are some of the methods that workers use to store records at their workstations:

Paper Records

1. Organize incoming and outgoing papers in an in/out box. This is a device with two or three stacked metal or plastic trays labeled "in," "out," and perhaps "hold." The purpose of the in/out box is to organize and temporarily store papers coming in to you and going out from you for further action. The "hold" tray is for papers that do not have to be acted upon immediately.

2. Desk drawer files can be used for your own personal records or to store blank forms, stationery, time sheets, company policy handbooks, and similar items that are routinely used. The filing system for this drawer should be set up using appropriate classification rules.

3. Log books may be kept at the workstation for recording recurring events, such as long phone calls, visitors, and petty cash outlays. The log shows the date, time, and description of each event, as well as the personnel involved in the transaction. It also usu-

ally contains a place for comments regarding the transaction in case it varied in some way from the usual procedure.

4. File copies of correspondence may be kept in a loose-leaf binder, called a chronological file or correspondence book. This is an easily accessible place to store a copy of each piece of outgoing correspondence in chronological order. This will give you a record of all correspondence pertaining to any given transaction and makes it easy to retrieve. It also provides you with an easy way to check quickly on what happened in response to specific actions or look up information you may need while talking on the phone.

Electronic Records

Disks that hold electronic files can be difficult to organize. The following points can aid you in filing the disks at your workstation.

1. Label each disk with a general classification.

2. Print out an index of the documents currently on disk each time a new document is added. The index can be folded and placed in the jacket with the disk or kept in a notebook.

3. Store disks in a file box especially designed for this purpose.

4. If one disk is full and you want to use the same label for a new disk, number the disks consecutively—for example, "Letters 1," "Letters 2." Mark each new disk with the date it was first used.

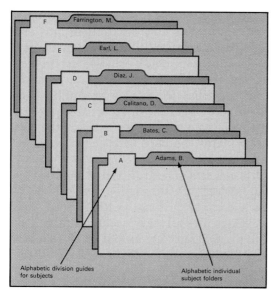

Figure 15.6 File guides separate groups of files for easy retrieval.

STORAGE EQUIPMENT

Filing equipment refers to the actual structures in which files are stored. While manufacturers offer many different models at different prices and in different colors, most equipment has basic features in common. Let's look at some of the more common kinds of manual filing equipment.

Until recently, the most common kind of file was the vertical file. **Vertical files** come in two-, three-, four-, and five-drawer models. The drawers are stacked one on top of the other and frequently have locks. They are designed to accommodate either 8½- by 11-inch (letter-size) files or 8½- by 14-inch (legal-size) files. The cabinets are usually made of metal and provide sturdy, often fireproof protection of files. Documents are placed in the vertical cabinet with the heading or top of the document located at the left. These are not the best file cabinets to use for saving space. Not only must you allow room for the cabinet but also for the pullout drawer space. You need approximately double the space of the vertical cabinet.

A **lateral file** is similar to a vertical file except that the longest side opens, and the files are stored as if they were on a bookshelf. Lateral files have the added advantage of providing a countertop for reviewing files removed from the cabinet or for displaying books and other materials. Like vertical files, lateral files are designed to accommodate letter- or legal-size files. Less actual floor space is necessary because these cabinets can store more files and require less floor and pullout drawer space.

Open-shelf files are lateral files, but they do not have drawers. Their main advantages over enclosed cabinets are that they take up less space and you can change them easily. They are also useful for files that are in use constantly. You may have seen open-shelf files in a doctor's office, where each patient's folder is pulled when he or she goes in to see the doctor. This arrangement eliminates the need to open and close drawers each time a record must be pulled or refiled.

A **rotary file** consists of a large, round shelf with a hole in the middle through which the supporting post passes. The shelf can be moved in a circular fashion to locate files. Because of the round shape, rotary files are very useful for filing loose-leaf binders, which have a wedge shape and fit on the shelf like pieces of a pie. Rotary files also make sense when workers are seated around the files.

Shelves of files on tracks are usually called **movable storage.** The shelves can be placed together so that less aisle space is necessary in the storage area. When an individual wants to retrieve a file, he or she manually turns levers on the shelves or uses an automated system to move the shelves to open up an aisle space. The individual then walks down the aisle to retrieve the necessary file. Archives and records centers with many documents and records use movable storage to save space.

A **tub file,** which is usually a small container that opens at the top, can be moved from one location to another. When files must be used by people in many different locations, a tub file may be the answer to carrying individual folders back and forth, for these actions risk loss and create traffic problems within the office.

Card files come in an assortment of styles and sizes, depending on how the cards are used. All of the types of filing equipment mentioned are available in scaled-down versions for use as card files.

ELECTRONIC FILES

Electronic storage of records requires not only your knowledge of computer systems and storing of word processing, database, or spreadsheet files, but it may also require you to use a database with indexed information to sort, search, retrieve, and print reports. The specific equipment and software you use depends largely on what is available to you and on your company's needs. At your workstation, you will probably use a manual filing system, but you may also use at least one type of electronic storage system: floppy disk, hard disk, or centralized network storage and retrieval (figure 15.7).

In many offices, particularly if stand-alone microcomputers make up the primary computer system, a decentralized electronic storage system is used. This means that each worker stores his or her own files on floppy disks or tapes. Users still often share files by making multiple copies of data files or borrowing disks as needed.

If the workstations in a system are part of a network, users can call up files stored in any part of the network, including the central storage area. This is known as a centralized electronic storage system. In a system like this, a user may also use a modem to retrieve files from a remote location. After gaining access to the central database, you enter your request and the computer finds where the file is stored, calls up the file, and sends the information to you. The file may be a word processed document or it may be an image of a check or contract that was stored digitally. The office you work in may use electronic and manual storage systems that are completely centralized, completely decentralized, or a combination of centralized and decentralized.

Let's assume you are just beginning a new position. The person before you did not have an accurate electronic filing system. The first thing you must do is inventory the files stored on disks or in directories to determine what is there. Then you must create an index of the files, including type, content, and their location on a certain disk or in a certain directory. You may choose to set up a new directory system that follows ARMA rules. You are now able to find information because you are familiar with the stored files.

In a decentralized system, one way to keep track of which files are on which disks is to label each disk with its own identifying

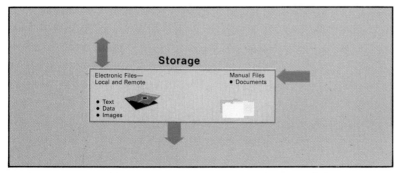

Storage

Electronic Files—
Local and Remote

• Text
• Data
• Images

Manual Files
• Documents

Figure 15.7 Most offices today have a combination of electronic and manual filing systems.

number or code. A separate index stored in a database can then list all the filenames and the numbers or codes of the disks on which they may be found. When you want to retrieve a certain file, you can search your index for the file by filename. The index will tell you what disk or directory the file is located in.

When setting up your electronic filing system, you can file the disks alphabetically or numerically, according to how you have indexed them. For example, you might want to arrange your disks alphabetically by primary person. The choice should be based on the way you usually file hard-copy documents. Or, you may use a file reference label and write the list of files stored on the disk for quick reference if a database is not available to you.

Many centralized electronic filing systems allow you to file your documents just as you do in your manual filing system or your decentralized electronic system. If you are working with one of these systems, you may encounter different terms for directories or areas of storage, such as the following:

• *Cabinet* Your collection of files is called a cabinet. Electronic cabinets can store data for private use only or for the entire department to share. If a user creates a personal cabinet, only

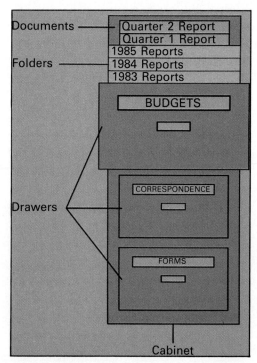

Figure 15.8 Some electronic filing systems are set up in much the same way as manual files, using the same terminology and levels of organization.

he or she can access information stored there. Generally, a
password is used when signing onto the system.

- *Drawer* Within each cabinet the user can create sections, or
  drawers. In most cases these can be named to duplicate your
  manual filing system.

- *Folder* Within each drawer users can create smaller sections,
  or folders, as found in manual systems. As with the drawers,
  the user can generally name the folders in any way desired.

Not all centralized systems work precisely this way, but they
all ease the burden of indexing your files by doing much of this
task for you automatically in one way or another. To illustrate
more clearly how these systems can assist you, let's look at how
the type of system described would work.

Figure 15.8 shows how this type of electronic filing system is
set up. Jennifer, Tracy, and Mark work in the Corporate Training Department. They all need to edit and update training manuals. Jennifer is also the department manager and works closely
with Phil, director of corporate training. Jennifer and Phil need
to work together on some upcoming programs that should be
kept confidential. Jennifer also maintains a personal file, to

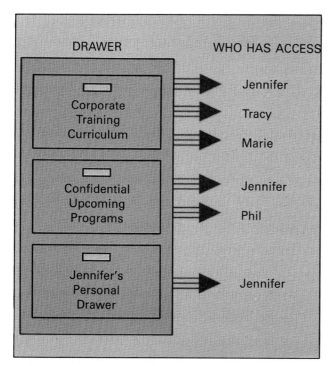

Figure 15.9 In a centralized system, access to files is limited. Employees
must use a password to access records.

which nobody, including Phil, has access. Figure 15.9 shows what the filing system might look like. As you can see, there is great flexibility and security in filing documents with a centralized filing system. There is so much flexibility because *any* type of document can be filed electronically, including scanned or digitized documents.

There is a huge amount of storage space in a centralized system, but it is a good filing habit to be aware of what space is left. Another thing to consider when using a centralized system is that in many cases files are shared. This means that you must be careful when you delete files. You will need to follow a procedure for reviewing files regularly and comparing them to the retention schedule to suggest which ones to discard. Consult the other users to find out if they will need the files you intend to delete. You may wish to transfer the files to backup tapes.

ELECTRONIC SUPPLIES AND EQUIPMENT

When organizing records on electronic files, follow the rules for filing paper documents, but the procedures and equipment are different. Follow the five steps of filing — inspect, index, code (give a filename), sort, and store—but your computer can speed up these functions. As discussed, inspect the file for storage, index it according to your floppy disk, hard disk, or networked setting, and code it by giving it a proper filename. The system sorts the file to be placed accurately on the electronic media, and of course the storage function occurs when you complete the save function of your software.

Office supply dealers sell several kinds of specially designed storage units for floppy disks. These include plastic and wooden desktop boxes (see figure 15.10), rotary files, and ring binders with vinyl pages that have pockets. Dealers also sell panels and racks to adapt your existing file cabinets for storing floppy disks safely and conveniently. The storage equipment you use will depend on your office design and preference as well as on cost. Optical storage supplies are also available in the same forms.

Figure 15.10 Desktop storage cases for disks come in many varieties.

DOCUMENT-BASED MANAGEMENT SYSTEMS

Document-based management systems (DBMS) are now used for the storage of active or inactive centralized files. DBMSs use optical disks as the storage medium. These disks (also known as laser disks) have a large storage capacity. One

5½-inch laser disk can hold up to 200,000 pages of copy. A laser disk is nonmagenetic and is far more durable than magnetic media. CD-ROM disks (compact disk—read only memory) are optical disks that have the capability of storing vast quantities of data (see figure 15.11).

The software in a document-based management system rearranges the information in the files so that it can be retrieved in a number of ways. For example, a manufacturing company may want to store all of its active and inactive invoices in a document-based system. The information is transferred to an optical disk system and stored. The software indexes all of the data from the invoices so when a customer calls to check on an invoice, the operator can sort the database for the customer name and retrieve the correct invoice. If the customer's name is not available but the invoice number is, then the search can begin for the invoice number. Once the document is found, it can be printed or downloaded to another station for additional processing.

Figure 15.11 Laser disks can store text, graphics, and sound.

The power of a document-based system is that it allows for flexibility when using information that has already been stored in another medium. A document-based management system can be installed on a mainframe, or in many medium-sized businesses the documents are stored on a powerful microcomputer with an optical disk drive(s) attached. The advantages of this type of system are that the operator is probably familiar with using a microcomputer, the software can be customized for the businesses' proprietary use, the stored information can be accessed quickly and easily through the use of the database, and the information can be updated when necessary. The common feature is the use of a database for indexed information.

Paper files can be part of a DBMS if they contain bar codes. The code number is placed on the file and the index information such as type of records, location, filename or code, and media stored on is entered into a database. When the file needs to be retrieved, the user accesses the database, searches for the correct file, determines its location, pulls the file, and then scans the bar code to input into the system that the file is out and who has the file. This allows for tracking of files.

The advantage of a DBMS is that the files can be transferred from other systems. This allows a company to create a centralized electronic storage system from a decentralized system that used manual or electronic files, or both. The files that have been stored as paper are scanned into the system, or the files that have been stored on disk or tape are read into the system. The type of optical disk system used is either a **WORM** (write once read many) system, which allows the storage of information once on the optical disk and then the information can be retrieved many times, or a **WMRM** (write many read many) system, whereby information can be stored, deleted, or changed. The types of files stored on WMRM systems, as well as electronic files stored on disks, must adhere to the legal implications of using this information. As long as electronic or optical files are stored and used in the day-to-day operation of a business, they are allowed as legal documents; however, check your company's retention schedule to see what type of media the document should be stored on and adhere to company policy.

DIGITAL IMAGING SYSTEMS

Another breakthrough in the storage of paper media is digital imaging systems. With these systems, businesses can store all the paper documents in an imaging system quickly and easily without investing in optical disk technology. Basically the system works by inserting flat paper documents into the scanner of the system. The documents are scanned and only an image is stored and placed in the appropriate "file folder" or "cabinet." The software of the system, once again, indexes the document for easy retrieval. The document can then be retrieved, viewed, and printed; however, the document cannot be changed or edited as it is only a "photocopy" of the original.

Digital imaging systems may take the place of microimage systems if they become less costly and accept other types of materials besides paper.

MICROIMAGE MEDIA STORAGE

Some companies have invested in **microimage technology** to store inactive files. Microimage technology is also called micrographics. Before electronic technology allowed for the scanning of documents, businesses used microimage technology. Since the 1920s, when the banking industry first started using negatives, or film, of pictures they had taken of checks, business has been using microimaging. The banking industry needed a way to keep a copy of the checks that were written by customers. When check-writing services first began, banks relied on the honesty of their clients to document that checks were written on their accounts because the bank returned the canceled checks to the client. This, obviously, did not work because the bank found it necessary to keep an audit trail of all the canceled checks written on accounts. Therefore, when photography was introduced, the Kodak Company introduced the banking industry to film, a reduced picture of the original check, for auditing.

Microimaging requires cameras, processors, readers, and printers to be able to use the documents stored on film. You will be trained on these specific machines when you enroll in a records management course or receive on-the-job training.

USES OF MICROIMAGES

Microimages are read by inserting them into a machine called a **microform reader**. Reading information through a machine means that originals of important documents are not subjected to the damage that results from frequent handling of paper documents. If the microimage is damaged, a new copy can be made from the original. Because micrographically reproduced material is so small, many documents can be reproduced on a single microform. A **microform** includes the different ways you can use microimaging technology to store images. This means that all the information related to one topic can be contained on a single microform, making it less likely that one piece of information will become separated and perhaps lost. These are distinct advantages over the use of paper, which is frequently misplaced, lost, damaged, or destroyed.

Microimaging also has some advantages over the process of electronic or optical records. For one thing, the images are exact duplicates of the original documents. Some electronic records are not the documents themselves but edited versions. Errors can be introduced in the rekeying. And since microimaging produces an exact duplicate in miniature (just as a digital imaging system does), handwritten data, engineering drawings, graphics, and color pictures can be stored as well. This is not always possible with electronic records. In general, the conversion of documents into microforms is easier than conversion to computerized files because of standardization in the microimage field. Developers of electronic imaging devices are still working on complete standardization.

MICROIMAGE MEDIA

The term *microform* refers to a variety of microimage media. These media make is possible to record miniature images of documents on film negatives. They all have advantages and disadvantages, as well as specific uses for which they are best suited. The following is a list of the types of microforms used by businesses.

The oldest micrographic medium is the microfilm **roll,** which is a continuous roll of film that can hold the images of hundreds of pages of documents. Microfilm rolls come in two sizes. The smaller size, 16 mm, is used for photographing pages that are 8½ by 11 inches or smaller. These include letters and invoices. The larger size, 35 mm, is used for photographing blueprints, newspapers, and other large documents or it is used for storing smaller images back to back. Figure 15.12 contains a picture of document storage orientation on film. All microfilm rolls, regardless of size, are stored on reels or in cassettes or cartridges. These holders, in turn, are generally kept in specially designed file cabinets or desktop files. Microfilm is especially useful when many pages of information relating to the same topic or document must be kept together. With microfilm all the information can be stored on one roll of film, eliminating the possibility of losing part of a file.

A microfilm **jacket** consists of two sheets of clear plastic that are sealed together to form horizontal slots for holding strips of microfilm. Microfilm jackets come in several sizes, but the most common is 4 by 6 inches. The top of each jacket has a strip of tape on which you can write labeling information. Microfilm jackets can be stored in ring binders, folders, or file drawers. Because they hold only short strips of film instead of the entire roll, microfilm jackets are most useful when many different docu-

Figure 15.12 The miniature images on this roll of microfilm will be a readable size when they are projected through a microfilm reader.

ments that should be separated are reproduced on one roll of film. Many times personnel files or information that needs to be added to on a regular basis are stored in jackets.

An **aperture card** has a rectangular hole that holds usually only one image. You can write on the cards to label them or they can contain optical characters read by scanners. Some of the older cards contain holes that are scanned by computer systems to access retrieval information. Aperture cards are a convenient medium for storing one-page documents and drawings. Because of this, one common use is for storing engineers' drawings.

A **microfiche** is a sheet of film, usually 4 by 6 inches, that can hold the images of several hundred letter-size pages (see figure 15.13). These images are smaller than the images on microfilm. This medium takes its name from the French word *fiche,* which means index card. A microfiche takes up less space than a microfilm roll bearing the same number of document images. Because they are flat, microfiche sheets are easier to file and mail than microfilm rolls. A sheet of microfiche is also easier to use than microfilm because you can find what you are looking for more easily. The images recorded on a microfiche are arranged in rows and columns. The columns are numbered across the top of the microfiche, and the rows are labeled with letters along one side. An index of the information on the fiche is usually found in the lower right-hand corner. After finding where the document is located on the fiche from the index, you can use the numbers and letters as guides and locate the image of a specific document the way you would locate a town on a map.

Another advantage of a microfiche is that one type of fiche, up-

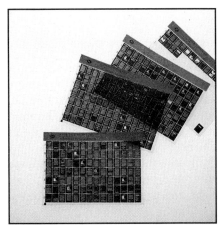

Figure 15.13 This piece of microfiche contains many pages of material. When seen through a viewer, the pages are a normal size that can be read easily.

datable fiche, can be updated by adding pages. This is not possible with microfilm except by splicing the roll of film, a risky and time-consuming process. A microfiche sheet can also be edited by blacking out portions of the sheet photographically. Fiche are also very economical to duplicate and distribute. Companies put directory information or parts and inventory information on fiche and then send copies of the fiche to distributors. It costs about three to five cents to duplicate a fiche that contains hundreds of pages and only one stamp to mail it. Duplicating and mailing the information on paper would cost much more.

The smallest micrographic images are stored on an **ultrafiche**, which resembles a microfiche, but a single sheet can hold the images of 4,000 letter-size pages. An ultrafiche is a very expensive micrographics medium because it can be processed only in photographic laboratories. Nonetheless, it offers a practical way of storing catalogs, directories, encyclopedias, and other documents that may have thousands of pages.

Advantages and Disadvantages

The main advantage of microforms is that they take up very little storage space. If microimage readers are available and documents will not be edited much, microforms provide a good way to store large amounts of information. Other advantages are that documents can be retrieved quickly and duplicated when necessary. One disadvantage of microforms is that a reader is necessary to enlarge the images for the naked eye, and an output device such as computer storage, network system, or printer is necessary to print and distribute the retrieved information.

Microimage Storage and Retrieval

Because records stored on microforms are too small for the naked eye to read, retrieval of records from microforms involves three steps. The first is to use an index to find out where a given document is located. Then you must find the microform. Finally, you use special projection equipment to locate the document on the microform itself.

How you find documents on microforms depends on the kinds of microforms used and how they have been indexed. Let's look at some equipment and procedures that you may find.

Microimage Readers

A microimage reader is a device that enlarges the images on microfilm media and projects them onto a screen so that you can read them or, with some models, print a hard copy. Manual readers may have a crank to advance the film. Computerized readers might use input, processing, and output devices to help you find documents automatically.

Computer-Assisted Retrieval (CAR)

Computers can be linked with micrographics equipment to retrieve information from microforms automatically. This application of computer technology is called **computer-assisted retrieval (CAR).** Computer-assisted retrieval of microimages provided an automated approach to retrieval by combining the mass storage capabilities of film with the indexing and retrieval capabilities of a computer and database software. To understand how CAR works, imagine that you have been asked to locate an invoice that has been filmed. An index stored on the system's database contains the retrieval information about the invoice. You access the database, key in the number of the invoice, and the system searches for the information. Your screen displays that the invoice is located on roll 67, frame number 1,002. You then instruct the system to retrieve the roll and start searching for the frame. The system uses robotics to retrieve the roll, inserts it into the reader, and forwards the roll to the correct frame. You are now able to read, print, or send the information to another station. Many CAR systems do not use robotics. In this case, you would have to find the roll manually and insert it into the system. Then by entering the frame number, the system would scan the roll until it came to frame number 1,002.

Computer Output Microfilm

Besides retrieving microimages through computer aided means, technology also allows companies to microfilm electronic images before they are printed. Many companies use **computer output microfilm (COM)** for filming documents from computer tapes to be used as working copies of inactive files. Basically COM involves using computerized readers to read electronic files and display them on a small screen inside the COM device. Once displayed, the documents are photographed and placed on fiche. An index is developed to determine what documents are stored on what fiche. Once the documents are filmed, they are processed and used as any other type of microimage would be used.

Computer Input Microfilm

Another way film can be used is as a source of input for electronic- or document-based management systems. The film is displayed on a screen, a picture of the image is taken, and instead of being placed on film it is digitized for storage in either an electronic- or document-based management system.

Using these methods of microimage control gives companies many options to choose from for their records/information management needs. Companies are now able to choose from a **media mix:** paper, film, electronic, or optical means for storage. As you enter any size of business, you will encounter one or more of these media. As an administrative assistant, it is part of your job duties to develop and maintain accurate records/information management systems so that you are able to get the right information to the right person at the right time.

SUMMARY

- Information management is the function of organizing and controlling all aspects of business records through the entire life cycle of a document.

- Records must be organized so that people can retrieve them quickly and easily to get the right information to the right person at the right time.

- Records/information management consists of storing, sorting, searching, and retrieving information whether it is through computerized means or through manual means.

- When starting a new position, you may be asked to help set up a records management system. First inventory the records, appraise their value, set up a retention schedule, determine the classification systems to be used, and store the records.

- Records can be classified in a number of ways. The most common are alphabetic, subject, numeric, geographic, and chronologic.

- The steps for getting a record ready for storage are to inspect, index, code, sort, and store. A fixed time every day or every few days should be set aside for filing. Special care must be taken to avoid misfiling.

- There are standard supplies and equipment for records/information management. The most frequently used supplies for manual systems are file folders, file-drawer guides, and labels.

Filing equipment comes in many shapes and sizes, including lateral files, open-shelf files, movable storage, and vertical files.

- Centralized and decentralized records systems are used throughout organizations. Centralized systems usually include a records center for storage of centralized electronic, paper, film, and optical files. Decentralized systems usually consist of stand-alone microcomputers. Combination systems are now evident as some records are centralized in a records center and others are centralized in document-based management systems through centralized databases.

- Microimages are photographically reproduced records in miniature. Microforms include microfilm, microfiche, jackets, and aperture cards.

- Computerized retrieval of film is accomplished through CAR systems.

- Computer output and input microfilm are used to help use microimages more efficiently as a means of input and output into computer systems.

VOCABULARY

- business record
- information management
- records/information management system
- inventory
- appraisal of records
- vital record
- important record
- useful record
- unimportant record
- active records
- inactive records
- centralized system
- records center
- decentralized system
- retention and disposition schedule
- archives
- consecutive numeric system
- terminal-digit system
- vertical files
- lateral files
- open-shelf files
- rotary files
- movable storage
- tub files
- card files
- document-based management system (DBMS)
- Write once read many WORM
- Write many read many WMRM
- microimage technology
- microform reader
- microform
- roll
- jacket
- aperture card
- microfiche

- code
- cross-reference
- file-drawer guides
- file-guide caption
- file folders
- file folder labels
- ultrafiche
- computer-assisted retrieval (CAR)
- computer output microfilm (COM)
- media mix

CHECKING YOUR UNDERSTANDING

1. Draw a simple flow chart depicting the life cycle of a document. Beneath each section list the tasks that are completed in that stage of the life cycle.
2. Conducting an inventory and appraising records are two of the things a person must do in establishing a records management program. Which of these must be completed first? What tasks do you do in each step?
3. Describe the difference between active and inactive records. Where are each stored? Are they usually stored centralized or decentralized? What types of records are stored as active? as inactive?
4. What are the four types of records classification systems? Describe the way records are stored in each type of system.
5. What are the five steps to follow in proper filing procedures? Describe what is completed in each step.
6. In what ways are centralized and decentralized manual files the same or different from centralized and decentralized computer systems?
7. Electronic imaging systems include electronic storage, document-based management systems, and digital imaging systems. Make a list of the similarities and differences between these systems.
8. Microimaging systems include the use of microfilm and storage and retrieval equipment. Describe the two types of automated microimage storage and retrieval. When would it be appropriate to use each?

THINKING THROUGH PROCEDURES

1. Gerald Hansen is one of four secretaries on a team that shares a filing system. He is the newest member of the team. Frequently the folders he wants to retrieve from the files are missing. All of the team's members except one, Betty Bowman, spend a few minutes each day filing. Ms. Bowman seems

always to be behind in her work, and the file tray on her desk is always overflowing. It has become routine to have to go in Ms. Bowman's tray or look on her desk to find folders that should be in the file drawer. Mr. Hansen has begun to resent the amount of time he spends looking for the folders Ms. Bowman has failed to return to the files. Discuss with your classmates the options Gerald has for solving this situation.

2. Kathi Mausserman has just started a new position in a small chiropractic office. The files are mostly paper-based, with some stored on a standalone microcomputer. Kathi is replacing a person who has moved out of state and she did not receive any training from this person. Kathi must evaluate the current records system to determine what records are stored, where they are stored, and what classification system is used. She knows that this will take some time and so she wants to inform the doctor of her activities. Describe, in a memo report format, the process Kathi would use to accomplish her goal of being able to use the current records and possibly improve the system if necessary.

3. When using microimages, it is always advisable to prepare an electronic index of where the images are stored so that retrieval is efficient. Using the information below, prepare an electronic index using a database program. Print reports containing the information requested.

Roll Number	Frame Number	Document
10	6958	invoice # 564
12	234	invoice # 1200
14	3450	invoice # 7500
13	700	invoice # 2500
5	2500	index for roll 5
13	2000	invoice # 3800
12	1001	invoice # 1927
5	1	invoice # 1
14	450	invoice # 4500
10	3500	invoice # 922

Prepare two reports: one sorted by roll number, the other sorted by invoice number. Prepare to discuss in class why you would want to sort by roll number and by invoice number. What purposes would each report have?

4. Inventory the electronic or paper files you use to store your class activities or personal records. Create a filing system for

these records so that you are able to better retrieve the information you need in a timely fashion. Use the classification systems described in this chapter. Label the disks and/or folders appropriately. If you have a lot of files on disks, you may want to create a printed index of the files you have stored on each disk for easy retrieval.

chapter **16**

FINANCIAL AND LEGAL INFORMATION MANAGEMENT

FINANCIAL AND LEGAL BUSINESS FUNCTIONS

All companies—from a tiny roadside diner to a giant corporation—must handle financial and legal matters. As an office worker, you can expect to perform many tasks related to the financial and legal functions of your organization. These might include sending and receiving bills, paying for materials and supplies, processing contracts, analyzing balance sheets, preparing a payroll, maintaining budget expenditures, keeping expense records, and so on. Secretaries and administrative assistants perform many of these functions, but the extent of their involvement depends on the size and nature of the business. For example, if you were an administrative assistant in a small company, you might be responsible for processing the entire company payroll each week. In a large corporation, you would not be responsible for the payroll, but your supervisor might require you to maintain time sheets for the employees in your department and provide that information for the payroll department.

When processing financial and legal documents accuracy is essential. Verification of data and attention to detail are necessary to ensure the processed information is correct. Incorrect data can mean improper sales forecasts, erroneous contract commitments, or inaccurate budget and expense figures. All of these can have very serious negative repercussions for the entire business.

In this chapter you will study the major types of legal and financial information that must be processed and managed in today's business office. You will learn how technology is applied to the financial and legal operations of companies to make them more productive.

PROCESSING FINANCIAL AND LEGAL INFORMATION

As with all written documents, a process must be followed to input, process, output, and distribute financial and legal information accurately. As you study the different types of financial and legal documents you will encounter in the workplace, keep in mind that accuracy is the most important aspect of dealing with this information. Gathering the correct information from the appropriate sources, using the most effective software tool, inputting the information correctly, using verification procedures, storing the data in the right place, and distributing the data in the most cost effective and timely way will ensure that quality information is available to support the decisions made by management.

STEP 1: GATHER INFORMATION

Frequently, putting together financial and legal documents requires gathering data from one or more source documents and then combining it with word processing documents. Source documents may be previously processed documents or they may be collections of data from which you extract information to create financial or legal documents. Examples are centralized databases, departmental spreadsheets (see figure 16.1), paper documents, active or inactive files, processed documents, forms, meetings, one-to-one conversations, outside businesses, clients, internal departments such as legal, tax, or accounting departments, or outside agencies such as the Internal Revenue Service (the federal government's taxing agency). The level of automation and the type of business your company is involved in will determine the types of data sources you use.

STEP 2: FORMAT INFORMATION

After gathering the necessary information, you need to select the tools to process the data. Spreadsheets are one of the most common software applications used to process financial information. There are also database management programs with the

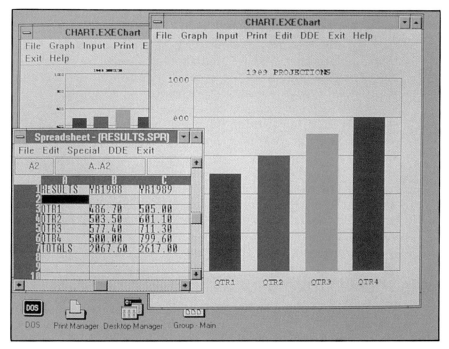

Figure 16.1 A spreadsheet that was previously processed may become a source for a graphic that could be used in a report.

capability of performing mathematical operations. Many payroll and general accounting systems are programmed databases. Working with financial information to create a finished document may require you to input information into a spreadsheet, combine it with information from a database, and integrate it all in a word processed document.

Most legal documents consist mainly of text, but frequently legal information must be supported with documents that contain supporting facts. These facts may be integrated into the text of the document or they may be presented as supporting documents. The type of factual data included in legal documents may include such items as schedules of timelines or monetary amounts, specifications, or financial data.

Many types of financial and legal information are standardized; therefore, forms, stored documents, and boilerplate paragraphs are frequently used in these types of documents.

STEP 3: VERIFY INFORMATION

The importance of accuracy in financial or legal information is so great that companies spend thousands of dollars training employees to use verification and proofreading techniques. After you have finished entering information, you must verify its accuracy. Do this by proofreading your entered data against the source information. Where mathematical calculations are involved, be familiar with the types of figures you are working with so that typographical or other errors will be apparent. Look for transposition errors, and if balances and other results do not seem correct, bring them to the attention of your supervisor for verification (after you have done a thorough verification yourself).

Other things to look for in the verification step are as follows: numbers referring to the same items or repeated in different parts of the document must match; names must be spelled correctly and consistently at each use; addresses must be correct; and dates must be accurate.

STEP 4: STORE INFORMATION

When using automated equipment, storage takes place as you are processing. If you are working with financial data or boilerplate paragraphs that are stored on a centralized system, you will have to download the original copies to your own files before you begin processing. Your completed document may or may not be one that should be stored on the centralized system. Many financial and legal documents contain senstive and/or confidential information. Make sure you have a clear understanding of how such documents are to be stored.

STEP 5: OUTPUT AND DISTRIBUTE INFORMATION

You will have several output decisions to make in regard to financial and legal documents. Frequently you may have to output several drafts in soft copy or hard copy so that revisions, additions, or deletions can be made. In most cases you will probably need to output hard copy of the final version, because many documents are too lengthy for the recipient to read on the monitor. Because contracts cannot be altered without the consent of all parties, it is a standard procedure to issue only original contracts to the signing parties. When the typewriter was the major processing tool, the typist had to type multiple originals. With electronic equipment, producing multiple originals is simply a matter of issuing a command to print out the number of copies required.

Issues of sensitivity and confidentiality are a major concern in the distribution of financial and legal documents. Make sure that you understand the procedures for handling the distribution of each type of document. In many cases financial and legal documents concern matters that are vital to business. Learn where these documents should be distributed and distribute accordingly in a prompt manner. Allowing finished documents to sit on your desk hinders your and your supervisor's productivity.

BASIC FINANCIAL FUNCTIONS

As mentioned, the kinds of financial and legal documents you work with and the level of your involvement as an administrative assistant vary widely depending on the type and size of the business for which you work. In this section we will review some general functions that can be found in almost every business and how they are handled at the administrative assistant level.

BUDGETS

A **budget** is a company's financial plan of operations for a given period of time, commonly a year. Usually the company has an overall budget that dictates the expected income and expenditures for each division and department. Each division and department of the company has its own separate budget that governs only its operations. A department manager's budget (see, for example, figure 16.2) will describe the department's expected expenditures for salaries, supplies, furniture, and so on. As an administrative assistant within a department, it may be your responsibility to set up and maintain records of the department's budget.

The purpose of a budget is to set the company's financial goals. **Expenditures,** the amount of money spent to operate the business, must be kept in line with **revenues,** the amount of income received by the company, in order to achieve an acceptable level of profit. What is acceptable as a level of profit is determined by the company's officers and, in some cases, a board of directors. Company executives and department managers are responsible for making sure that expenditures do not exceed the budgeted amount or for making cuts, if necessary, to achieve the company's financial goals. For example, if the company you work for decides that it has to cut its salary expenditures by 10 percent in the coming year, that reduction will be reflected in the budget section marked "Salaries." Then each department manager must work to achieve the reduction, perhaps by leaving vacant positions unfilled, by withholding merit raises and bonuses, or by laying off workers. If the company cannot achieve a 10 percent

DEPARTMENT BUDGET JANUARY–MARCH 19_				
EXPENSE	JAN.	FEB.	MARCH	TOTAL
SALARIES	6,300	6,300	6,300	18,900
EMPLOYEE FRINGE BENEFITS	1,660	1,660	1,660	4,980
TRAVEL & ENTERTAINMENT	600	600	600	1,800
PHOTOCOPYING CHARGES	100	100	100	300
LEGAL FEES	0	0	500	500
TELEPHONE & TELEGRAPH	125	125	125	375
MAILING EXPENSES	100	100	100	300
STATIONERY & SUPPLIES	300	50	50	400
MAGAZINES & BOOKS	100	100	100	300
FURNITURE & EQUIPMENT	200	600	200	1,000
MAINTENANCE & REPAIR	50	50	50	150

Figure 16.2 Budgets help managers see at a glance how much money will be spent in each area during the budget year.

salary reduction, its executives must revise that goal or look for some other area to cut. Your role in the budget process is to gather the budget information from the department head and enter it into a spreadsheet for use.

Preparing a Budget

When company managers prepare a budget, they include all the available information about both income and expenses under separate headings, such as "Raw Materials," "Revenues," and "Labor Costs." Under each heading they list all the line items for that heading. A **line item** is a category of expenditure or income (similar to an account) that is given a separate line in a budget so that anyone can tell at a glance how much is received or spent in that area during the budget year. Examples of line items are salaries, fringe benefits, supplies, equipment, office space, and postage.

A budget can be prepared for any aspect of a business, but the two most common types of budgets are the operating budget and the capital expense budget. The **operating budget** spells out the expected income and costs of the day-to-day operations of a company. It is broken down into a revenue or sales budget, showing income, and an expense budget, showing expenditures for such items as salaries, supplies, and raw materials. The **capital expense budget** shows long-range expenditures for such items as new facilities, equipment replacement, land purchases, and mortgages. Another type of budget is a project budget. A **project budget** shows money allocated for the development of a specific project. A marketing department might use this kind of budget to plan the expenses for production and promotion of each product. If you work in an office that operates according to project budgets, you might be asked to log expenses, process invoices, and monitor expenses for each project.

Departmental budgets include the items from the operating and capital budgets that pertain to an individual department. Items such as departmental salaries, benefits, equipment purchases, supplies, travel, and other items are included. A department must keep track of its budget to be sure that expenditures do not exceed the budgeted amounts. Some companies store department budgets in centralized database/spreadsheet programs. In this case, top management can peruse all department budgets to see that operations are on target. In other cases the department managers report periodically to top management on the status of their budgets. You would be responsible for updating these periodic printouts of the budget.

Making changes to the budget as they occur may be your responsibility. This is referred to as maintaining the budget. As the source documents come through, usually invoices, you must deduct the expenditure from the budgeted item. If you do this on a regular basis, the budget will always be up to date.

Budgeting Software Tools

Companies use spreadsheet software to develop their budgets so they can plan more thoroughly and in less time than with paper and pencil methods. Spreadsheets enable planners to see how a change in one calculation affects all the related calculations. For example, assume that a budget planner anticipates that the company will spend more for fuel oil in January and February of next year than it spent in the same months of this year. When you change the January and February fuel oil figures on the spreadsheet, the totals are automatically adjusted for the entire year, and the planner can tell at once how much to budget for fuel oil for the year. If your supervisor makes these decisions, he or she may ask that you provide copies of these different budgets so that a comparison can be made. Or your supervisor may ask you to note the differences and report to him or her the results.

You may use graphics, database, desktop publishing, or word processing software to help you perform many budgeting chores, such as developing charts to show how much of the budget is devoted to each income or expense category; keeping a running tally of expense data that you can store, retrieve, and sort in various ways; and preparing reports to explain how your department is meeting its budgetary goals.

Whatever type of budget your company uses, you are most likely to participate in the budgeting process at the department level. Budgets are usually set up on an annual basis and monitored quarterly (every three months, usually March, June, September, and December). Your department manager may ask you to gather information and documentation about various departmental line items such as office supplies or equipment maintenance costs. If you pay the bills or order office supplies regularly, you may be able to suggest ways to reduce these expenses.

EXPENSE REPORTS

One major category of departmental budgets in most companies is travel and entertainment. When budgets are set, individuals with expense accounts or their managers are responsible for determining how much travel is expected and what the expenses are. You have learned how to complete an expense report when the traveler returns from the trip. Figure 16.3 shows an example of a portion of an expense report prepared by a conference planner who recently returned from a trip.

Preparing a separate spreadsheet for travel expenses helps with monitoring the department's travel and entertainment budget. Some companies have centralized budgeting systems that allow you to enter the expense report information once and the software will update the departmental budget automatically.

CREDIT TRANSACTIONS

Companies often have to borrow money, or obtain credit, to purchase expensive goods or raw materials or to pay bills while they wait for payments from customers. They can obtain that credit from banks, finance companies, retail stores, and credit card companies.

In a small company, you may be responsible for processing credit documents and handling the company's credit card accounts. Big companies usually have credit departments that investigate loan applications from customers, develop credit terms, process applications for credit cards, and so on. Even in a com-

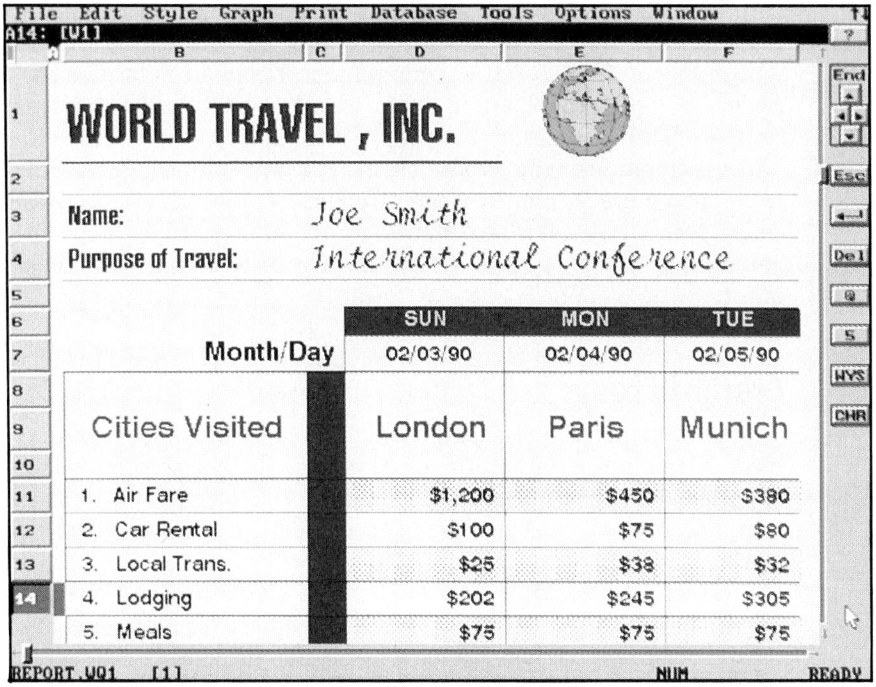

Figure 16.3 This is an example of an employee's expense report showing the cities visited and a partial list of expenses incurred on each part of the trip.

pany with a credit department, you may still be responsible for receiving and forwarding your supervisor's credit card statements and receipts, so you should have a general understanding of credit transactions.

Credit Agreements

Before a business extends credit to a customer, it usually checks the customer's credit rating to ensure that the customer will pay the debt. Once the loan application is approved, the borrower and the lender must agree on the credit terms and repayment schedule. Credit terms establish how much the borrower is seeking, how much interest the lender will charge, and what penalties the borrower will incur if the credit terms are violated. The interest rate is a percentage of the loan, and it represents the lender's charge for the money. The federal Truth-in-Lending Act is a law that requires businesses to explain these credit terms to the borrower.

Repayment schedules specify how the borrower will repay the loan. One common business arrangement is for a company to ship merchandise or raw materials to a customer with the understanding that the customer will pay for the goods in full within thirty days. Another common arrangement is for the borrower to repay the loan in installments—that is, in portions that are paid at regular intervals. For example, many stores, finance companies, and credit card companies collect payments from customers in monthly installments. The borrower, in most cases, has to pay a finance charge, an amount based on a specific percentage of the unpaid balance, with each installment payment.

Credit Cards

One form of credit is the credit card. Your supervisor may have a company credit card to charge meals, hotel rooms, office supplies, and other legitimate business expenses. Credit card companies, such as American Express and Visa, issue cards to businesses. When an employee uses a company credit card at a restaurant, for example, the credit card company pays the restaurant and then bills the employee's company for payments and interest charges. When companies do not provide credit cards, employees may use their personal credit cards for both personal and business expenses. The credit card company bills the employee, who is then reimbursed by the company for the business expenses.

If your supervisor uses a credit card for business, it may be part of your job to maintain credit card records. For example, you may have to keep receipts, check credit statements, and then use the information to fill out expense vouchers. You may also have to keep a record of credit card numbers in case they are lost or stolen.

Just as banks provide bank statements each month, credit card companies provide credit card statements that show when and where each purchase was made during the billing period, the total amount of outstanding charges, and the amount of interest owed on the account. If you are responsible for maintaining credit card records for your supervisor, keep copies of all the receipts of expenditures to compare with the monthly statement. If your supervisor cannot account for an expenditure on the statement and you do not have a receipt for it, you may have to contact the credit card company to determine whether an error in billing was made.

INVENTORY RECORDS

The term **inventory** has different meanings, depending on the business. An inventory can be goods purchased to run the business, such as office supplies; capital purchases, such as desks and computers; goods purchased to produce the goods for sale; or the products for sale. Keeping track of inventory is necessary for businesses to function efficiently. As an office worker you may be responsible for maintaining inventory records and processing information on the inventory of particular items.

If a company keeps a large inventory consisting of products that are sold or other items, the inventory may be stored in warehouses or storerooms; small office supply inventories may be stored in cabinets in offices.

An inventory may also be referred to as **stock.** Support staff in stockrooms or inventory storage areas are usually required to help process the receipt and delivery of goods to and from the stockroom. Inventory duties may include physically counting the inventory or processing shipping orders, invoices, and purchase orders. Sometimes it is necessary to check purchase orders against shipping orders and invoices to ensure that no errors are made in filling a customer order or in the billing. This process may be done through the use of bar codes and automated systems, or it may be done by a manual check.

Whenever any item is delivered to a department or a stockroom, the support staff in charge of deliveries must check the contents of the shipment and sign for the delivery. Usually the delivery person will request a signature on a shipment form to verify receipt of the shipment.

Another duty of support personnel is to keep an ongoing account of what is in inventory. An automated inventory system set up in a centralized database allows workers simply to enter the shipment data into the system and print new inventory reports. The system enters the correct inventory numbers in the correct account automatically, as long as the information entered is correct. The inventory count is adjusted automatically, and a requisition form is filled out. The computer program asks for the name of the person removing the goods, the type of goods removed, how many, and the date. Then the inventory system is updated automatically.

Another type of automated system uses bar codes on the items as the main identification number. A light scanner reads the bar code, and the inventory is updated automatically when the item is scanned.

PETTY CASH FUNDS

Most offices keep **petty cash,** which is a cash fund used to pay for small day-to-day expenses that cannot conveniently be paid for by check or credit card. If you are responsible for maintaining the petty cash fund, keep cash on hand to cover about two weeks' worth of expenses. It is not a good business procedure to keep large amounts of cash in the office, and be sure to lock up even small amounts of petty cash each night in a cash box stored in an office vault or safe. Figure 16.4 shows how to fill in a petty cash voucher.

Recording Petty Cash Withdrawals

The best way to keep a record of each withdrawal from the petty cash fund is to use a petty cash voucher. A petty cash voucher is a preprinted form with spaces to fill in for the date, amount, and purpose of the withdrawal, the name of the payee, and the signature of the person making the withdrawal. You may also be required to keep a register in which you record each petty cash transaction.

Replenishing the Fund

A petty cash fund should have a fixed amount of money. The total of the cash in the fund and the withdrawals noted on

---

No. _28_   Amount $ _12.30_

PETTY CASH VOUCHER

Paid to _Fleet Equipment Co._

For _Index cards_

Charge to _Office Supplies_

Approved by   **Received by**

Susan Berman   _Mark Schaeffer_

vouchers should equal the fixed amount. When the fund runs low on cash, replenish it to the full fixed amount. How you go about this will depend on your employer's policy.

Keeping track of petty cash can be a time-consuming task. Developing a spreadsheet to record activity in the petty cash fund saves time. You will also have an ongoing record to track how the expense funds are used. This way, decisions can be made if it is determined that the petty cash fund is being overused or used inappropriately.

PAYROLL PROCESSING AND DISTRIBUTION

A large company probably has its own payroll department, and you may be responsible only for providing the department with weekly time cards or for distributing paychecks to the employees in your department. In a smaller company you may be responsible for using a computer system to process the payroll, and in some small businesses, you may even have to process the payroll by hand. We will discuss each of these situations in more detail later in this section.

Payroll Deductions

Every pay period employers provide their workers with a statement detailing **gross pay** (the salary before any deductions are made), the amount of and reason for each deduction, and the **net pay** (the amount remaining after the deductions have been made). Usually a pay statement is in the form of a stub or voucher attached to your paycheck, which you can detach and keep for your personal records (see figure 16.5).

Employers are required to withhold a percentage of your gross pay as advance payment on your annual federal income taxes. In some states, employers are required to withhold state and local income taxes as well. The Internal Revenue Service provides employers with tables for calculating the amount to be withheld for federal income taxes. The amounts vary according to marital status and the number of exemptions individuals can claim. The method of computing the amount of the withholding for state and local taxes varies from place to place. Employers are required to forward these tax payments to each government agency periodically.

Employers are also required to withhold federal social security tax and, in some states, state unemployment insurance tax. You may authorize your employer to withhold voluntary contribu-

EARNINGS	HOURS	CURRENT	YEAR TO DATE	DEDUCTIONS	CURRENT	YEAR TO DATE
REGULAR PAY	70 00	692 30	2 076 90	FICA	55 38	166 14
TOTAL PAY	70 00	692 30	2 076 90	FEDERAL	96 92	290 76
				STATE	34 62	103 86
				CITY	2 77	8 31
				NET PAY	502 61	1 507 83

SOCIAL SECURITY NUMBER	DEPT.	CO.
306-26-0210	WP20	01

PERIOD ENDING	FED. EX.	STATE EX.
03/31/-	02	02

Figure 16.5 This pay statement taken from a payroll check shows gross pay, net pay, and deductions. FICA stands for Federal Insurance Contributions Act, and that deduction is the employee's contribution to the social security fund.

tions to pension plans, contributions to charities, contributions to payroll savings plans, and monthly union dues.

Payroll Records

For the payroll staff to process a company payroll, it has to maintain certain permanent information on each employee, such as the employee's name, salary or hourly wage, and social security number. Your duties may include forwarding changes in this data to the payroll department when new employees are hired, when employees resign or retire, or when they receive raises, promotions, or transfers. The payroll staff can then call up the payroll records, stored in databases or in manual files, and update them with the new data. In large companies this updating must be done every pay period.

When employees are paid by the hour, they usually either punch in and out on a time clock or fill out time cards to indicate how many hours they worked during the pay period. Most hourly employees are covered by the federal Fair Labor Standards Act, which sets a minimum wage and requires employers to pay one-and-a-half times the regular wage for overtime, or time worked beyond forty hours a week.

To calculate an hourly employee's gross pay, the hourly wage is multiplied by the number of hours worked. Overtime pay is calculated separately and added to the regular wages. Database systems with calculation abilities are used to prepare payroll on a timely basis. Accurate payroll information is necessary to ensure that employees are paid on time and paid accurately.

Processing the Payroll

Businesses usually designate one day each week or every two weeks as payday. On that day each employee receives a check for the amount of his or her net pay for the last pay period and a pay statement detailing all the deductions. If your company has its own payroll department, the department and its automated system will perform all the processing, and your only duty may be to distribute paychecks to your co-workers.

If, however, it is one of your duties to help process your company's payroll, you need to key in the hours of work for each hourly employee and add any changes in the payroll records since the last pay period. If you work in a small office you may use payroll accounting software that has the formulas for computing income tax, social security deductions, and so on. The software calculates wages, deductions, and net pay, stores all this information for tax and accounting purposes, and prints each check and stub automatically.

Very few small offices still process the payroll manually; however, if you work in this type of office, keep a payroll register, which lists each employee by name, the number of exemptions, regular and overtime pay for the pay period, and each deduction in separate columns. To compute deductions, use withholding tables provided by the Internal Revenue Service, the Social Security Administration, and the state and local taxing authorities. Once you have computed each employee's gross pay, deductions, and net pay, you must total each column to determine your employer's total costs and the amount of taxes to be sent to each taxing agency. Then you must fill out and distribute checks and pay statements for each employee and record the payments in the accounting system.

Many companies offer employees the option of transferring their pay directly from the company's bank account to the employee's account. This procedure is called **direct deposit transfer** and is convenient and efficient for both the company and the individual. Employees still receive pay statements showing their gross and net pay and deductions so they can maintain their personal records. Whatever your role may be in processing or distributing the payroll, keep in mind that salary information is private and not to be shared with anyone.

BANK ACCOUNTS

All businesses deal with banks; your level of involvement in your employer's banking will depend on the size and nature of your company. Banking tasks carry a high level of responsibility because they involve money and confidential information. Some of the banking tasks handled by administrative assistants include making deposits and payments, reconciling account balances, dealing with dishonored checks, and transferring funds.

Making Deposits and Payments

Companies use banks, savings and loans, and credit unions to help them transact business. Setting up savings accounts and other investments with a financial institution can help a company earn more money than when using simply a checking account for cash flow.

Financial institutions have a variety of accounts for saving money. These include money markets, certificates of deposit, and interest-bearing savings and checking accounts. Each institution offers different services. As support staff in a small company, it may be your responsibility to maintain records of company savings accounts.

In an office that receives payments from customers, you may be responsible for endorsing checks and making deposits in the company's bank accounts. Other banking duties may include writing checks and reconciling savings and checking accounts.

Before you deposit any checks, examine them to see that they are written correctly. Each check you deposit must have an **endorsment,** which is a signature, on the back. The endorsement must be signed by the **payee**—the person or organization to whom the check is written. The endorsement is a legal procedure that transfers ownership of the check from the payee to the bank so that the bank can collect payment from the drawer or from the person on whose account the check is drawn. Make sure that the date, the amount, and the signature are correct. Otherwise, the bank may return the check uncashed and charge your company a handling fee. To make a deposit, you fill out a **deposit slip,** which is a bank form on which to record the date and the amount of checks or cash you are depositing. (Traveler's checks and money orders are considered cash.) The amount of each check is filled in on a separate line. If you have more checks than the deposit slip can accommodate, you can attach a list of the amount of each check and write only the total on the deposit slip. (See figure 16.6 for an example of a deposit slip.)

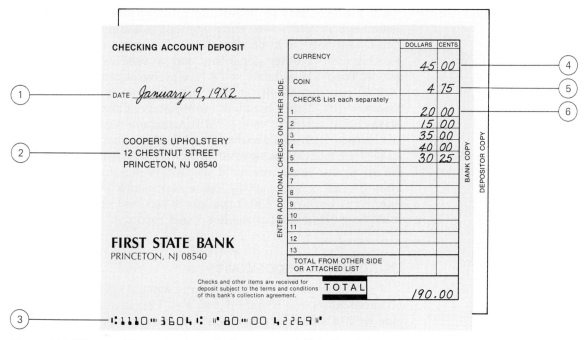

Figure 16.6 When making out a deposit slip, you must fill in the date (1), the account name and number if they are not preprinted on the slip (2 and 3), the amount of currency (4), and coins (5), and the amount of each check (6).

If you deposit currency and coins frequently as well as checks for your company, you will need a supply of coin rolls and bill wrappers from the bank. Before you wrap the coins and bills, mark the wrappers with your employer's name and account number so that the bank can notify you if the wrappers contain too much money or too little. Some banks do not accept large amounts of currency or coins if they are not already wrapped. Others charge businesses a fee for separating and counting loose bills and coins.

Using Automatic Teller Machines (ATM)

Automatic teller machines (ATM) allow you to deposit and withdraw funds by using a special access card and identification code. An ATM has a computer terminal with a keypad that enables you to instruct the machine about the types of transactions you require and the amounts and a display screen that tells you how to proceed with a transaction. ATMs permit you to make deposits and withdrawals after banking hours, and they can save you long waits on bank lines during the day. You should, however, take a few precautions when using an ATM.

Use an ATM only for depositing checks with a restrictive endorsement. A **restrictive endorsement** sets conditions such as "for deposit only" to a specific account. Never use an ATM for depositing cash or other items that can be used by unauthorized people. The ATM will give you a receipt, but it cannot give you a copy of your deposit slip so that you can prove you deposited a specific check. Notify the bank immediately of any discrepancies between its records of your ATM transactions and your employer's records, such as a deposit you made that is not listed on your employer's monthly bank statement. Also notify the bank immediately if your company's ATM access card is lost or stolen. If an unauthorized person uses the lost or stolen card, your employer's liability is limited to $50 if the loss is reported promptly, but it could be much greater if the loss is not reported.

Using Night Depositories

If your company must deposit large amounts of currency after business hours, use a night depository. This is a slot on the outside wall of a bank through which customers can drop their deposits after banking hours. Businesses that collect money after banking hours often use night depositories as a safety precaution. Then they do not have to keep money on the premises overnight. Banks provide deposit bags with locks for customers who frequently use night depositories. Bags containing deposits are dropped through the night depository slot and opened the next day.

Banking by Mail

Mailed deposits, like those made in ATMs, should include only checks with restrictive or special endorsements. Never send currency through the mail unless you use registered mail. Most banks provide special envelopes and deposit slips for banking by mail. The bank will send you a validated copy of your deposit slip as well as a new deposit slip and envelope by return mail.

MAKING PAYMENTS BY CHECK

Businesses generally use checks rather than cash to make payments. In large companies, these checks are handled by the accounting or payroll department. If you work in a small office, though, it may be your responsibility to prepare checks and maintain records of them. You may also be responsible for ordering new checks when your supply is low.

CHECK WRITING TIPS

The signature on a check authorizes a bank to remove money from one account and give it to someone else. The check indicates how much is to be transferred and to whom the money should be paid, (see figure 16.7). These guidelines can help you issue checks properly:

- Date each check and stub.
- Number checks and stubs consecutively if they do not already have numbers printed on them.
- Give the payee's full name, and make sure that it is spelled correctly and legible.
- Begin the amount close to the dollar sign on the check, and use bold, clear figures. If you are writing, write the figures close together so that no one can insert new figures between the ones you have written.
- On the next line write the amount of the check in words. Begin at the left end of that line, and capitalize the first letter only. Express cents as fractions of 100; that is, 38 cents would be $^{38}/_{100}$. Use hyphens, periods, or a line to fill any blank space on the line.
- Indicate the purpose of the check in a corner of the check. Some checks include a "memo" line for this purpose.
- If you make a mistake on a check, write the word *void* in large letters on the check and on its stub. Do not try to correct a mistake on a check by erasing or crossing out what you have written. Save any checks that you void, and file them in numerical order with those that are cashed by the bank and returned to you.

Banks issue books of checks with stubs or check registers in which you record the number, date, and amount of each check as well as the payee's name and the reason for payment. Relatively inexpensive software is available for you to use for printing checks for payment and keeping a check register. In a manual system you subtract the amount of a check from the checking ac-

NO. 122 $58 00/100
DATE March 27, 19 87
TO N. Y. Utility Co.
FOR Electricity

	DOLLARS	CENTS
BALANCE	1041	05
AMT. DEPOSITED	360	00
3/26 TOTAL	1401	05
AMT. THIS CHECK	58	00
BALANCE	1343	05

No. 122
5-350
110
March 27, 19 87
PAY TO THE ORDER OF New York Utility Company $58 00/100
Fifty-eight and 00/100 DOLLARS
National Bank
Rye, New York
Joseph Adams
⑆0100⑈0110⑆ 119⑈0430⑈

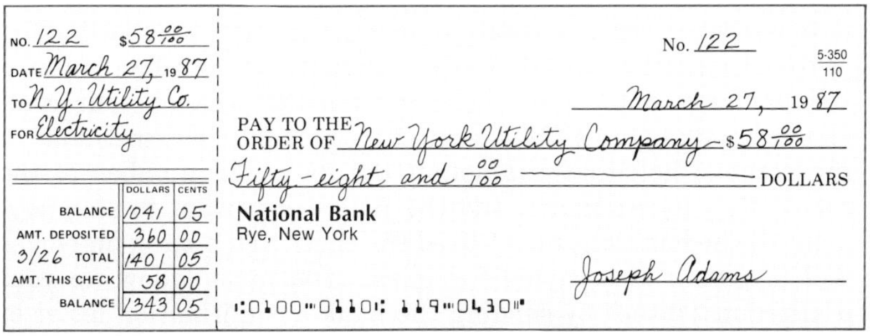

Figure 16.7 Here is how a properly written check and check stub should appear. Always make out the check stub first so you do not forget what the check was for.

count's **balance,** which is the amount of funds contained in the account, and write in the new balance. If a deposit has been made, you enter the date and the amount, and then you add that amount to the account balance. If you use software to maintain the account balance, when you enter the data for the check the register will be updated automatically; entering a deposit amount will do the same. Keeping accurate account balances is necessary for efficient business practices.

Types of Checks

Most payments processed by office workers are in the form of checks drawn against company checking accounts, but companies sometimes use other kinds of checks as well.

A **certified check** is drawn against a company checking account and certified by a bank teller. The teller immediately subtracts the amount of the check from the account. People use certified checks when the payee requires a guarantee that the check will be honored. They are most often used in transactions involving large sums of money, such as a real estate sale.

Banks issue **cashier's checks** for the amount of the check plus a small fee. Like certified checks, cashier's checks are guaranteed by the bank and are most commonly used in transactions that involve large sums of money. Cashier's checks are also called official checks, teller's checks, or treasurer's checks.

A **bank draft** is similar to a cashier's check except that it is drawn against one bank's account in another bank. Bank drafts are used to transfer large sums of money quickly between banks in distant cities.

Money orders are similar to cashier's checks, but they are usually issued for $250 or less. People who do not have checking accounts may buy money orders from a bank or post office and send them through the mail to pay for goods or services.

If a check that your company has issued is lost or stolen, or if it was written for the wrong amount, you may be able to stop payment on it by issuing a **stop-payment order**. To request a stop-payment order, call the stop-payment desk at your company's bank and give the checking account number, the name of the account holder, the amount, the date, the number of the check, the payee's name, and the reason you want to stop payment. If the bank has not cleared the check yet, a bank employee will process a stop-payment request. You must follow up your oral request either by sending the bank a confirmation letter or by filling out and returning a form that the bank supplies. Most banks charge a fee for issuing a stop-payment order.

AUTOMATIC PAYMENT/ELECTRONIC FUNDS TRANSFER

Banks now have services that allow you to use your computer terminal or the telephone to pay bills. Using these services requires less time and effort on your part and automates the payment process.

Customers of savings and investment funds routinely use **telephone transfers** to switch their investments from one fund to another. Certain bills can also be paid in this way as well.

Computer Transfers

If you use a computer terminal and modem to bank electronically, you can keyboard instructions for a **computer transfer** of funds from the company account to pay bills.

Point-of-sale transfers means that customers use bank identification cards called debit cards instead of credit cards or checks to pay for goods and services. The store clerk inserts the card into the store's register, which is a terminal for the centralized system, and links up with the bank's computer, which immediately transfers the amount of the sale from the customer's account to the store's account. Point-of-sale transfers are listed on the monthly bank statements of both the customer and the store.

RECONCILING AN ACCOUNT BALANCE

Each month banks send their customers statements of all activities involving their accounts, including deposits, withdrawals, checks that have cleared, interest paid to the accounts, and fees charged against them. With these statements, banks generally return the last month's canceled checks or checks that have been cleared against the account. Or, banks issue carbons of checks to allow the individual to keep a copy of the check immediately upon writing it. If you keep your employer's checkbook, your duties may include reconciling the balance, which involves comparing the balance reported on the bank statement with the balance recorded on the check stubs or in the check register and accounting for any difference between them (see figure 16.8).

If you use software for your bill paying, the computer reconciles the balance after you enter the numbers and amounts of the checks returned. Even if you do not bank electronically, you

NATIONAL BANK

JOSEPH ADAMS
12 MONEY ST.
RYE, NEW YORK 10580

Checking Account Number		Statement Closing Date
119 0430		02-22-87

Statement Savings Account Number	Page	Enclosures
	1	6

CHECKS   6 DEPOSITS   1

1646

4
A

Checking Activity

Previous Balance	Total Deposits & Credits	Total Checks & Debits	New Balance	Available Credit
296.44 +	1,579.97 −	1,028.64 −	847.77	.00

TRANSACTION DESCRIPTION	AMOUNT	Date	Balance
OPENING BALANCE		01-21	269.44
		02-03	46.44
		02-11	3.56 OD
	1,579.97	02-15	1,276.41
		02-16	1,212.50
		02-17	1,182.77
		02-22	847.77

DATE	CHECKS		DATE	CHECKS
0908 02-03	250.00	0911	02-16	63.91
0909 02-11	50.00	0912	02-17	29.73
0910 02-22	335.00	0913	02-15	300.00

To Reconcile Your Statement and Checkbook

1. Add to your checkbook balance any loan advances or other credits appearing on the statement which you have not previously recorded.

2. Deduct from your checkbook balance any bank charges or other debits appearing on the statement which you have not previously recorded.

3. **If your checks are serialized,** examine the listing on the front of this statement and check off the items against the entries in your checkbook. An asterisk

in the listing indicates a gap where one or more checks are not on this particular statement.

If your checks are not serialized, arrange them by date or number and check them off against the entries in your checkbook.

4. List any checks or debits issued by you and not shown on the statement, and any bank charges since the statement date, in the area provided at the right.

Outstanding Checks and Debits

Number	Amount
0914	74.10
0915	17.00
0916	237.00

5.

	List last balance shown on statement	847.77
+	Plus: Deposits and credits made after date of last entry on statement	350.02
	Subtotal	1197.79
−	Minus: Total of outstanding checks and debits	328.10
=	Balance: Which should agree with your checkbook	869.69

Bank charges since statement closing date	0.00
Total	328.10

Figure 16.8 A monthly bank statement shows all of the deposits, withdrawals, and service charges that have been made in each account during the month. Many banks also provide a convenient form on the back of the statement to reconcile the balance.

might be able to use your computer terminal to reconcile the balance by using a special program. The procedure for reconciling the balance, manually or electronically, is as follows:

• Arrange the canceled checks according to the check numbers.

• Compare the amounts of the checks with the amounts listed for them on the bank statement.

• Compare the checks with the checkbook stubs, and place a check mark on the stubs to indicate that the checks have cleared. On the reconciliation form, list the numbers and the amounts of any checks still outstanding, and add their amounts.

- Compare the deposit amounts shown on the check stubs or in the check register with those listed on the statement. List any deposits not reported on the statement, and add the amounts.

- Add the total of unlisted deposits to the balance shown on the bank statement, and subtract the total of outstanding checks. The resulting figure is called the adjusted bank balance.

- Examine the statement for service charges or interest payments. Subtract the service charges from the balance recorded in your checkbook, and add the interest payments.

- The resulting figure should equal the adjusted bank balance. If it does, record the service charge and interest payment amounts in the checkbook, and write in the new balance.

If your new checkbook balance and the adjusted bank balance do not agree, you need to determine the reason for the difference. First, look for mistakes in the calculations on the reconciliation form or mistakes in your data entry. If the calculations are correct, go through the check stubs to verify that each check is listed either among the cleared checks (on the bank's statement) or among the outstanding checks (on your reconciliation form) and be sure you have not entered them in the wrong columns. Then check the bank's list to be sure that you have a stub for each of the checks on the list and that the amounts agree. Also, make sure that no deposits have been omitted from the lists. Each deposit recorded in your checkbook should be listed either on the bank statement or on your reconciliation form. Then see that each deposit listed on the bank statement is also recorded in your checkbook.

If you still have not found the error, look at your checkbook to be sure that the balance you brought forward to each new page is correct. Or look at your last reconciled bank statement stored on the system. Then, if you find no errors in the forwarded balances, verify your calculations in the checkbook. When you find a check stub with an error on it, circle the error and write on the stub "True figure is $. Correction is on stub # ." Make the appropriate adjustment on the stub where the current balance appears. Enter the amount of the error on the reconciliation form, showing where the error occurred and the number of the stub where you corrected it. When you have reconciled the balance, write on the last stub covered by the bank statement "Agrees with bank statement" and the date of the statement.

After you reconcile the balance each month, file the bank statement, reconciliation sheet, and canceled checks. File all statements and reconciliation sheets in chronological order. Either fold the checks inside the statements on which they are listed, or file them numerically in a separate place. Canceled checks have legal importance as proof of payment. Your company's retention schedule will determine how long you should keep bank statements and canceled checks.

You should also trace what happened to any outstanding checks that have still not cleared when the next month's bank statement arrives. If a check has not cleared, the payee may not have received it, or it may have been lost. Call or write to the payee to find out. If the check has been lost, request a stop-payment order and issue a replacement check.

Finally, if you are also responsible for maintaining the general journal, which will be discussed later, make the same corrections in the journal as you made in the checkbook, if necessary. For example, if you have made a miscalculation on a check stub, the chances are that you also listed the same incorrect figure when you made the journal entry regarding that transaction.

Sometimes you may deposit a check that the bank cannot collect on, either because the check was altered, misdated, or made out incorrectly or because there were not sufficient funds in the drawer's account to cover the check. When a check can not be paid, it is called a **dishonored check.** The bank will return the check to the depositor and subtract the amount of the check from the depositor's account. Some banks will also charge the depositor a fee for handling the check. If the bank dishonors a check made out to your company, you will have to notify the drawer. The drawer may then deposit additional funds in his or her account and either issue a new check or instruct you to redeposit the dishonored check.

SPECIALIZED FINANCIAL FUNCTIONS

No matter how big or small a company, its managers need to have certain financial information to make decisions about the company and to evaluate its performance. They have to know how much money the business has, how many goods or services it has sold over the course of a month or a quarter, how much money the business owes to its suppliers, and so on.

Accounting is a means of gathering financial data and processing it into information that managers can use to analyze their financial situations and make decisions. In a large company, accounting may be done by a special department. A small business may pay an outside accounting firm to do its accounting, but office workers perform many day-to-day accounting tasks. If you are an administrative assistant at a small company, for example, you might be asked to keep the **accounts receivable** records, which list money owed to the company by customers, and the **accounts payable** records, which show money owed by the company to suppliers and creditors.

Accounting is a form of data processing, so accounting procedures generally follow the information processing cycle. First, the unprocessed data that is required to produce accounting information is organized and input into manual or electronic journals and ledgers. When accountants input data, the first thing they do is gather all the necessary source documents that serve as records of business transactions. Source documents consist of purchase orders, bills, checkbook stubs, invoices, credit agreements, and so on. Accountants also gather any other financial records that have been kept during the accounting period, such as accounts receivable records, accounts payable records, payroll records, tax records, facilities and equipment inventories, and credit records. These records are some of the kinds of data that reflect the company's financial condition. Figure 16.9 shows an example of a computer screen showing data on customer credit.

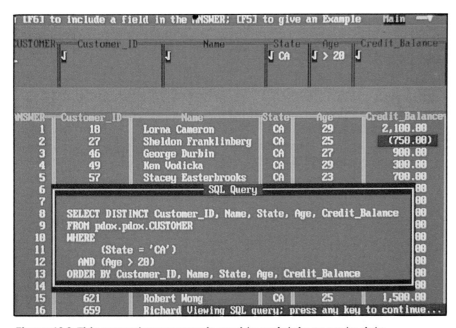

Figure 16.9 This computer program is used to maintain an up-to-date record of customer credit balances.

Next the data is processed or reorganized to produce useful information. For example, by totaling all of its individual weekly payroll expenditures, a company can determine how much it spends on employees' salaries and benefits in a month or a year. Similarly, when a company breaks down its yearly sales figures by month, it can determine when it makes the most or fewest sales each year, and it can then plan its advertising and sales campaigns accordingly.

In accounting, processing the data involves transferring it from the source documents to journals and ledgers, where items can be grouped in a logical order and manipulated mathematically. We will discuss ledgers in more detail later in this chapter. The process can be completed manually, or as in most businesses today it is completed automatically through the use of accounting software.

Once the data is processed and stored, it can be output in the form of financial statements. Usually the financial statements consist of an **income statement,** which shows the business's net income or loss for the accounting period, and a **balance sheet,** which shows the company's total assets and liabilities (debts). (See figure 16.10 for an example of a balance sheet.) This document is called a balance sheet because the total of a company's assets always equals the total of its liabilities and owner's equity. **Owner's equity** is the owner's financial interest in the company.

Just as with any other kind of data processing output, accounting records can be stored on paper or on electronic or optical media, and they can be printed out, reproduced, and distributed.

Accounting information is distributed to managers and business owners, who make decisions such as whether to build a new plant, drop a line of products, or hire or lay off employees. It is distributed to stockholders so that they can evaluate the financial health of their company; to banks, which decide whether to approve a loan to a company; to the Internal Revenue Service, which determines taxes; and to investors, who decide whether to buy shares in a company.

ACCOUNTING PROCEDURES

One accounting task that you may be asked to perform is to maintain a journal. Accountants use several different kinds of journals, but you would most likely keep a general journal. A **general journal** is a list in chronological order of each business

```
                        JULIA'S BOUTIQUE
                         Balance Sheet
                      December 31, 19XX
                    (in thousands of dollars)


                            ASSETS

     Current Assets
        Cash                              $100
        Accounts Receivable               175
        Inventory                         250
        Prepaid Expenses                   25
            Total Current Assets                   $  550

     Fixed Assets
        Land                              $150
        Building                          300
        Furniture                         100
           Total Fixed Assets                        550
           Total Assets                            $1,100

                 LIABILITIES AND OWNER'S EQUITY

     Current Liabilities
        Accounts Payable                  $160
        Taxes Payable                      25
        Other Accrued Expenses             75
           Total Current Liabilities               $  260

     Long-Term Liabilities
        Notes Payable                                350
           Total Liabilities                       $  610

     Owner's Equity
        Julia Bond, Capital               $400
        Net Income                         90
           Total Owner's Equity                      490
           Total Liabilities and Owner's Equity    $1,100
```

Figure 16.10 A balance sheet is a document that is used to analyze a company's financial situation.

transaction that a firm is involved in (figure 16.11). Each entry in the journal shows the date, the names of the accounts that must be debited and credited to record the transaction, a brief description of the transaction, and the amount of the transaction. The description would identify the nature of the transaction—a cash sale, a purchase of goods on credit, the payment of employee salaries, and so on.

An **account** is a grouping of similar transactions. Accounts can be assets (showing items of value owned by the business)

ACCOUNTING TERMS

These are some of the terms you will need to become familiar with if you work with financial information:

- **Account.** A grouping or classification of similar transactions, such as accounts payable or payroll.
- **Account balance.** The difference between the total debits and the total credits in an account.
- **Accounting period.** The period of time covered by the analysis of a company's financial records, usually quarterly (every three months) or annually (once a year).
- **Assets.** Money and other items of value owned by the company.
- **Balance sheet.** A financial statement that sums up a business's assets, liabilities, and owner's equity. On a balance sheet, the total of the assets always equals the total of the liabilities plus the owner's financial interest in the business.
- **Credit.** An amount that is entered on the right side of an account.
- **Debit.** An amount that is entered on the left side of an account.
- **Journal.** A record in which each business transaction is listed in chronological order.
- **Journalizing.** Maintaining the journal or making entries in the journal.
- **Ledger.** A record of each business transaction organized according to account.
- **Liability.** A debt or obligation owed by a company to its creditors.
- **Owner's equity.** The owner's financial interest in the business.
- **Posting.** The process of transferring data from a journal to a ledger.

such as cash, equipment, and accounts receivable, or they can be liabilities (showing debts owed by the business) such as accounts payable and loans payable. Accounts can also represent owner's equity, revenue, and expense items.

You may also be asked to keep a **general ledger,** which is a record of all the business transactions, grouped according to account (figure 16.11). Each account is recorded on a separate page of the ledger. You would use the journal as a guide to list each item in its appropriate account. Transferring items from the journal or a source document to the ledger is known as **posting.** Usually each item is posted in the ledger as a debit in one account and as a credit in another. For example, if you have a journal entry showing that a customer made a $3,000 payment to your company, you would list it as a debit on the ledger page designated "Cash" and as a credit on the ledger page designated "Accounts Receivable." In other words, since the payment has been received, it is no longer part of the money that the company is owed. Instead, it is added to the actual cash the company has on hand. The general ledger is, in effect, a master file of every business transaction, classified by account. It is a useful tool that

GENERAL JOURNAL   **Page 2**

DATE	ACCOUNT TITLE AND EXPLANATION	POST. REF.	DEBIT	CREDIT
19—				
May 30	Cash	101	3000 00	
	Accounts Receivable	102		3000 00

Cash   **GENERAL LEDGER**   **Account No.**   101

DATE	EXPLANATION	POST. REF.	DEBIT	CREDIT	BALANCE DEBIT	BALANCE CREDIT
19—						
May 30		J2	3000 00		3000 00	

Accounts Receivable   **GENERAL LEDGER**   **Account No.**   102

DATE	EXPLANATION	POST. REF.	DEBIT	CREDIT	BALANCE DEBIT	BALANCE CREDIT
19—						
May 30		J2		3000 00		3000 00

Figure 16.11 Journal entries (top) are made chronologically as each transaction occurs. Ledger entries (bottom) are listed according to categories called accounts.

accountants and business owners use to analyze a company's performance and financial health.

Another accounting procedure that you may be asked to perform involves adding and subtracting transactions. For example, you might be asked to total each day's receipts or keep a running total of the balance in each account. You can use computers and calculators to perform many of these functions, but you should also be able to perform basic arithmetic operations yourself. The accuracy of computer or calculator output depends on the accuracy of your input. If you enter a decimal point in the wrong place or key in a number incorrectly, you will get an incorrect answer. You should always check the calculator tape or computer entries against your source documents. Another way to guard against errors is to round off your input figures and estimate what the output should be. If the output is very different from your estimate, redo the calculation.

Accounting Software

There are hundreds of accounting software programs on the market. Many of these are full-scale accounting systems that were originally designed to run on mainframes. But the packages today run successfully on microcomputers as well as minicomputers. The design of these products parallels traditional accounting subsystems: general ledger, accounts receivable, accounts payable, and payroll. Some also provide additional functions, such as job costing, inventory, and sales order entry. While the smaller-scale programs are easier to implement and run, most accounting software systems require some technical expertise so that they can be tailored to the individual needs of a particular business. Your job, however, may require you to work with a vendor to set up the system and to prepare data for entry or even enter data directly. In some cases your manager may ask you to retrieve data from the accounting system to prepare a report. Or, perhaps you may be asked to obtain monthly sales or inventory figures.

Analyzing Accounting Documents

With an understanding of the types of accounting functions you may be asked to do, we will discuss your specific role in working with these functions and transactions. As mentioned, you may be asked to provide your supervisor with accounting information to make decisions; however, you also may be asked to analyze some accounting transactions and summarize their contents to your supervisor.

Previously we said that balance sheets are used to show the company's total assets and liabilities. Looking at a balance sheet, you should determine whether the assets do equal the liabilities, what liabilities seem too high or too low, and what assets the company is holding. If anything on the balance sheet looks out of line, you must go back and check your input and the accounting figures.

You may also be asked to compare balance sheets from different time periods and give a short summary of the accounts that have increased or decreased or those that stayed the same. What new, if any, accounts have been added or which ones have been deleted. Summarizing this type of information can give your supervisor a more efficient approach to making decisions.

To help your supervisor with income/loss decisions, you may also be asked to analyze the information on the latest income statement. Once again, you need to look for irregularities in the statement, verify the information, and summarize which account balances have risen and which have decreased. Determine the percent of loss or percent of income. Pull a previous income sheet from the files and compare the profit/loss line. Have profits increased or decreased? Have losses increased or decreased? With this information your supervisor can now focus on why the losses or increases occurred and how to continue.

Preparing Accounts Receivable Invoices

When clients or customers order merchandise from a company, they issue a purchase order to inform a company what they want to order. After a company fills the purchase order and sends the goods to the customer, the shipping company prepares an invoice or form to receive payment for the goods.

Office support staff has the responsibility for using purchase order information to prepare invoices. Use of automated accounting systems allows for invoices to be prepared from information entered into the system when the purchase order is processed. Some companies, however, do not have this type of software and so more manual processes must be incorporated to ensure an invoice is sent to a customer.

If you are responsible for preparing invoices, the process begins when you receive a copy of a purchase order from the accounting department. After verifying the accuracy of the amounts and the accuracy of the order numbers, you send one copy to shipping and keep the other for your records. At this time, you enter the purchase order information into the database. Now the shipping department has both a copy of the original purchase order and can access the information from the database. The software issues a shipping order, and the stockroom gathers the items from inventory, packages them, and sends the shipping order with the package.

Your responsibility is to send the invoice to the customer. When purchase orders are received, they act as a form of credit for the client. As credit, they are now classified as an accounts receivable at your firm. After you have sent the invoice to the customer, they return payment with a copy of the invoice. You double check the amount of the invoice with the purchase order, verify that the amount on the check equals the amount of the invoice, and endorse the check for deposit. You enter the amount paid on the customer's account record, and the customer is no longer in your active accounts receivable file.

Without an automated system, each of these steps would be completed separately by using a typewriter or handwriting the invoices. All posting of the accounts receivable information would be done by hand as well. By taking an accounting course, you can learn the total manual procedure used for posting receipt of accounts receivable.

PREPARING ACCOUNTS PAYABLE PURCHASE ORDERS

When your organization decides to purchase goods from another company, a procedure is necessary to ensure accountability of the authorization of the purchase. Let's assume your company is purchasing parts for the assembly of your product. When the inventory for that part is getting low, the inventory manager authorizes purchase of more parts. When you receive that authorization, you prepare a purchase order, which acts as both an ordering form and a credit form.

Filling out a purchase order requires that you verify the accuracy of the information on the form, double checking for account numbers, amounts, balances, and item descriptions. Other information on a purchase order is the correct address of the company you are sending it to, an account number if you have one with the company, and the complete address of the person who should receive the goods.

After you send the purchase order, you will receive shipment of the goods along with a shipping label. Then you will receive an invoice for payment of your purchase order. At this point, compare the original purchase order with the invoice and shipping label to determine the accuracy of the invoice. When you are satisfied with the accuracy, you can send the invoice to accounting for payment. Automated systems allow you to read the purchase order from a database to verify the invoice information and then authorize payment through entering a command after you have entered the invoice information into the system.

Once authorization is made, a check may be written or automatic transfer of funds may occur. More and more companies are connecting their shipping and billing systems to allow for faster transfer of funds at a lower cost.

LEGAL FUNCTIONS

Companies need to protect their interests and be able to show compliance with local, state, and federal laws. Each industry has a set of regulations to follow for trade agreements, employee contracts, and many other agreements. Industries must comply with environmental laws, zoning ordinances, and tax law.

Many laws involve important issues of civil rights, environmental protection, and malpractice. To comply with these laws, businesses often need to input, process, store, output, and distribute various kinds of legal information. If your company purchases a factory, for example, it would need to file a copy of the deed and mortgage with the county recorder in the county where the factory is located.

Businesses also use many legal documents, such as sales and credit agreements and contracts, to carry out routine financial transactions. These documents spell out the terms of a transaction and protect the company if the terms are violated. In addition, businesses occasionally are involved in litigation to resolve a debt or disagreement or for any number of other reasons. Such litigation always involves the preparation of a number of legal documents.

Recorded information related to legal matters must be stored in a medium as determined by law and listed in the company's retention schedule. Before we talk about specific legal documents, let's see how to process them.

▪ PROCESSING LEGAL DOCUMENTS

Legal documents are those used to protect a company in a court of law. They range from contracts to real estate deeds. Legal documents can be prepared from scratch, from standard legal forms and formats, and, many legal documents can be purchased from stationery stores as printed legal forms. Legal forms are also available on software. Many of these forms contain the same standard legal language, because the legal provisions of the transaction do not vary; only the specific details differ from one transaction to another. Examples of printed legal forms include mortgages, deeds, real estate sales contracts, office leases, and various litigation forms, such as notices and subpoenas. Because these documents are legal, binding agreements, they must contain no errors. When you process a printed legal form, sometimes called a **law blank**, you must first obtain the information to be filled in from your supervisor or from source documents. Then study the form to make certain you have all the information you need to fill in every space. If you are missing some of the information, gather it from your supervisor or from other sources.

When you process legal documents, whether on a word processor or on a typewriter, you must observe several basic formatting rules. Traditionally, legal-size paper is used, that is, 8½ by 13 or 14 inches. In the 1980s the Association of Records Managers and Administrators put on a national campaign to eliminate legal-sized files call ELF. As a result, many government agencies and others are switching from legal-sized paper to letter-sized paper (8½ by 11 inches) for uniformity and ease of storage.

RULES FOR PROCESSING LEGAL DOCUMENTS:

- Use a plain typeface or font. Do not use styles such as italic or bold.
- Double-space legal documents. If you are using paper with preprinted margins, leave one or two spaces blank on each side within the margins. If you are using blank paper, leave a 1½-inch margin on the left and at least a ½-inch margin on the right. Use a 2-inch margin at the top of each page and a 1-inch margin at the bottom.
- Indent each paragraph 5 spaces, and number each paragraph with a roman numeral and a period followed by two blank spaces.
- Set off quoted material by indenting each line of the material five to ten spaces from the left margin. This material can be single-spaced.
- Page numbers should be centered at the bottom of each page. Each draft should also be numbered, dated, and labeled "First Draft," "Second Draft," and so on.
- Numbers are usually written in both figures and words—for example, "Ten thousand dollars ($10,000)" or "Twenty (20) acres of land."
- Insert signature lines for all the parties to a legal document at the end of the document. Never place signature lines by themselves on a separate sheet of paper. Always include two or more lines of text on the same page. You may type either the name of each signer under the line or the designation of each signer, such as "Buyer," "Seller," "Lessor," or "Lessee." If the parties are companies, you can also include the names and titles of the persons who are representing the companies, such as "President," "Vice-President," or "Sales Representative."

Photocopies of legal documents are usually not acceptable. Each copy must be an original, so you must determine the number required. You may cover or block out portions of a legal document, or you can use *x*s, hyphens, or lines drawn through words and sentences to cross out portions of printed legal forms. Using software, you can have a clean original each time you prepare the document.

Blank spaces should not be left open on legal forms. If the information you are adding is short and the space allotted for it is long, draw a *z* in ink to fill up the unused space. You can also use an *x* to cross out paragraphs or blocks of preprinted legal language that do not apply to the transaction you are recording. If the space is short and the material you are adding is long, you can key it on a separate sheet of paper called a **rider.** Cut off any unused portion of the paper, and paste the rider onto the appropriate space on the form. Then fold the rider to fit neatly into the form.

As an administrative assistant your main responsibility in most legal matters will be to process legal documents. The extent of your involvement will depend on the nature and size of your company. You may work for a large corporation that has its own legal department to prepare documents and represent the company in legal matters. Nevertheless, even in a large organization, you may prepare certain legal documents routinely, such as contracts and credit agreements, that are commonly used by your department.

In a small organization, you may also be responsible for preparing other kinds of routine legal documents, such as leases and employment contracts. Of course, if you are employed in a law office, the bulk of your work will be processing a wide variety of complex legal documents, and you may decide to seek additional training to become a legal secretary, a paralegal, or a lawyer.

There are several types of commonly used legal documents that you may be asked to prepare. Stored legal documents are a convenient way to produce legal documents when the same language is used frequently (see figure 16.12).

Contracts and Agreements

Contracts and **agreements** are the most common kinds of legal documents used in the business world. They are legally enforceable understandings or arrangements between two or more parties. They are used most often to state a company's intention to buy or sell specific goods or services and to set the terms of the sale. A contract or agreement can be a sales slip, a memo, a letter, or even an oral promise made by one person to another.

When a contract is a formal written agreement, the person who prepares it should gather and include the names of the parties to the agreement, the date and place of the agreement, the purpose of the contract, the responsibilities of each party, a description of the goods or services to be sold, the amount of payment expected, the duration of the agreement, and the signatures of all parties to the agreement.

Affidavits

Affidavits can be required in many business situations. Affidavits are sworn, written statements of fact. When a person makes an affidavit, he or she swears under oath, before a judge or some other public officer, that the facts contained in the affi-

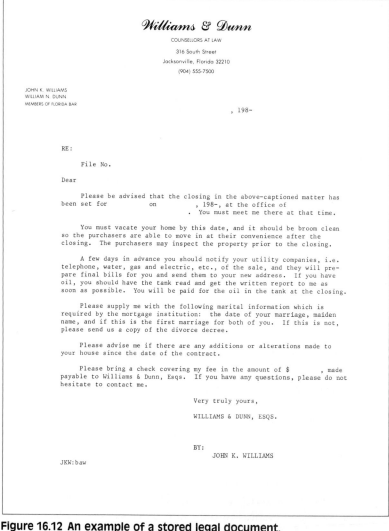

Figure 16.12 An example of a stored legal document.

davit are true. For example, people sometimes have to make affidavits to prove their citizenship or to prove that there are no financial or legal judgments pending against them.

Power of Attorney

A **power of attorney** is a legal authorization for one person to act as an agent for another. The power of attorney may apply to all of a person's business, financial, and legal matters or only to certain specific matters. For example, a corporate executive might give a lawyer in another state the power of attorney to carry out all the transactions necessary for the corporation to purchase a building in that state.

Litigation Documents

Lawsuits usually involve the preparation and filing of several different kinds of legal documents. These documents are often complex and usually require the preparation of one or more drafts. You are not likely to be responsible for preparing litigation documents unless you are employed in a corporate legal department or by a law firm.

Some of the more common litigation documents include **complaints** and **answers**—that is, the actual filing of a lawsuit by the complainer, or plaintiff, and the written response to the lawsuit by the opposing side, or the defendant. Either side may also make a number of motions to the court, which ask that the suit be dismissed, or that other parties be added, or that the judge make an immediate judgment, and so on. In addition, both sides are likely to file notices stating the time and place of a trial or pretrial conference, announcing the withdrawal of an attorney, and so on. The judge may issue a **court order,** which is a formal instruction to one side or the other to either do or stop doing a specific action. Finally, a witness may receive a **subpoena,** which is an order to appear at a trial or hearing to testify. Sometimes the subpoena also orders the witness to bring certain documents or records to the hearing.

PROCESSING REAL ESTATE INFORMATION

When a company purchases a piece of land or a building, it usually must process several legal documents. The buyer and seller have to draw up a contract of sale that details the sales price, the down payment, and other terms of the sale and that describes the property being purchased. The buyer will also have to enter into a mortgage agreement, which is an agreement between the buyer and a financial institution describing how the property will be paid for. The buyer will receive a copy of the title, which affirms ownership of the property, and will file copies of the title and mortgage with the county recorder. Another kind of real estate document is a lease, which is an agreement between the owner of a building and the renter. The lease gives the renter the right to occupy the building for a specific period of time in exchange for a stated rental fee.

NOTARIZING DOCUMENTS

Legal documents usually become valid when they are signed. A **notary public** is a person commissioned by a state government to verify signatures on documents for legal purposes. A notary witnesses the signing of documents and attests to the authenticity of the signatures. The notary then notarizes the documents by stamping and signing them. Property titles, assignments of mortgages, wills, deeds, partnership agreements, and affidavits are some of the kinds of documents that usually must be notarized.

Many companies find it convenient to have one or more office workers commissioned as notary publics so that employees do not have to travel to a notary's office every time a signature needs to be notarized. If your employer asks you to apply for a notarial commission, you can obtain an application at most stationery stores. You or your employer may have to pay a fee, and you may have to take a test. The state office that commissions notaries will inform you of the requirements. If no one in your office is a notary, keep the names and addresses of a few nearby notary publics on hand.

Financial and legal information play a vital part any organization. Not understanding the processes that are used to gather, process, verify, distribute, and store this information can hurt a company's chances for survival. Integrated accounting systems are used everywhere for the instant input, processing, output, and distribution of accounting information from departmental budgets to income statements. Your role in working with financial and legal information is to be consistently aware of the need for accurate information and the need to verify data if a question arises.

SUMMARY

- A process of gathering information, entering data, verifying data, and distributing and storing the information appropriately is necessary to prepare financial and legal documents accurately.

- A budget helps a company set financial goals and acts as a standard of measurement so that the company can determine if it is meeting its goals.

- Administrative support personnel are often required to help prepare and monitor departmental budgets.

- When companies borrow or lend money, they make credit agreements that describe the interest rates and repayment schedules of their loans.

- Petty cash funds pay for small expenditures that cannot be paid for conveniently by check or credit card.

- Payrolls can be processed by computer or by hand. A payroll check usually includes a statement of the employee's gross pay, deductions, and net pay.

- Office workers who process payrolls by hand must know how to compute taxes and other deductions.

- Banking chores include depositing checks and currency and using automatic tellers, night depositories, or bank-by-mail services.

- If an office worker is required to pay the company's bills, he or she must know how to write checks and how to reconcile a checking account balance.

- Electronic funds transfer is the transfer of funds from one bank account to another by means of the telephone, computers, direct deposit, or point-of-sale transfer.

- Secretaries and administrative assistants may be required to keep journals and ledgers to record business transactions.

- Accounting is a form of information processing; it follows the information processing cycle.

- Accounting is a means of recording financial data and processing it into information that managers can use to evaluate a company's performance.

- Businesses deal with many legal documents such as contracts, affidavits, real estate documents, and litigation documents.

VOCABULARY

- budget
- expenditures
- revenues
- line item
- operating budget
- capital expense budget
- project budget
- departmental budget
- inventory
- stock
- petty cash
- gross pay
- net pay
- direct deposit transfer
- endorsement
- deposit slip
- Automatic Teller Machine (ATM)

- restrictive endorsement
- balance
- dishonored check
- certified check
- cashier's check
- bank draft
- money order
- stop-payment order
- telephone transfer
- computer transfer
- point-of-sale transfer
- accounts receivable
- accounts payable
- income statement
- balance sheet
- owner's equity

- general journal
- account
- general ledger
- posting
- invoice
- legal documents
- law blank
- rider
- contracts
- agreements
- affidavits
- power of attorney
- complaint answer
- court order
- subpoena
- notary public

CHECKING YOUR UNDERSTANDING

1. Explain the importance of accuracy of financial and legal information in the business office. How will your role as an administrative assistant affect the accuracy of information?
2. Describe the five steps for processing financial and legal documents. What is the importance of the verification stage?
3. Budgets are an integral part of a company's ability to plan. Describe the three types of budgets discussed in this chapter and give an example of how each one might be used.
4. What deductions must be considered when preparing payroll? How do these affect the amount of money an employee receives?
5. Describe the difference between accounts payable and accounts receivable. List the steps used to process each.
6. What items must you look for in analyzing balance sheets and income statements? Why is it important to analyze these documents?
7. Describe at least four types of legal documents. What will be your role as an administrative assistant in the preparation of these documents?

THINKING THROUGH PROCEDURES

1. Suppose that you are reponsible for a petty cash fund. In the cash box there is $11.84 in bills and coins. You have vouchers for withdrawals of the following amounts: $.83, $1.98, $3.50,

$20, $4.75, $6, and $1.10. What is the total amount of the petty cash fund? Describe the process you used to determine the total amount of the fund.

2. What is the total amount of the cash deposit that includes the following bills and coins?

57 pennies

Four $10 bills

One $20 bill

37 quarters

18 dimes

Four nickels

Twelve $5 bills

One $50 bill

3. Roberta Jensen, the only secretary in a small real estate company, pays the company's bills and reconciles the monthly bank statement. One month she discovers that the company check register shows a balance of $698, while the bank statement indicates that the balance should be $935. Mrs. Jensen has checked and rechecked all the checks, stubs, outstanding checks and deposits, and service charges, but she cannot find the error. What should she do?

4. Interview a manager at a bank in your area. Using the information in this chapter as a starting point, ask questions to determine what type of automation is used to record the financial transactions of the bank. What automated services does the bank provide? Prepare a memo to your instructor reporting your findings.

5. A few legal documents were described in this chapter, but there are many others used in legal offices. Talk with a lawyer, a district attorney, or a legal secretary to find out what other types of legal documents are used. How are they processed? What skills or abilities are required to process the documents? What automated processes are being used? Prepare a memo to your instructor reporting your findings.

UNIT 6: THE WORKPLACE PROBLEM

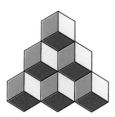

Leslie Taylor has been on the job as secretary to Sarah Loomis for only a few days. Already he has found that no day can be classified as "routine." Each case is unique and requires following different procedures. He has decided to take it a step at a time, getting as much work done as possible while setting up information management systems. The first thing Leslie did was make a list of the current cases and what needed to be done on each one within the next week, which was June 2 to 6. His list follows:

1. Schedule an interview with George Dorsey for 10 a.m., June 2. Auto accident case. Call for police and department of motor vehicles report. Have retainer contract and request forms for hospital and doctor's reports ready for client's signature.
2. File pre-trial motions on the Dr. Bettie Wilson malpractice case by June 3. Ms. Loomis will prepare a motion to dismiss and a motion to amend. Have motions processed and copied.
3. Interview with Samuel Lewis, filing business incorporation papers on June 6, 9 a.m. Need incorporation papers and notary stamp. Call Mr. Lewis to remind him to bring $50 filing fee.
4. Pre-trial interview with Matthew Corey, June 3, 9 a.m. Inmate, Sussex County Jail, assault charges. Get police report, evidence list, D.A. records, prior conviction record. Need Subpoena forms for Corey witnesses. Remind Ms. Loomis trial starts June 12, so that she can prepare for it.
5. Real estate closing, Morton and Phillips, Inc. 11 a.m., June 4, State National Bank Bldg. Check beforehand to make sure all papers are in order and all required information has been supplied—bill of sale, credit check, homeowner's insurance policy, deed, title search, mortgage agreement. Remind client to be prepared for closing fees. Remind Ms. Loomis to review the title search prior to closing.
6. Gregory Whalen divorce hearing, Courtroom 1, 2 p.m., June 4. Process final decree, custody agreement.
7. Alice Miller's suit against CBA Manufacturing Co. to be filed June 5. Ms. Loomis needs to research legal citations and write the complaint. Process the complaint and have summons ready to serve.

Using the problem solving checklist as a guide, complete the tasks listed below.

PROBLEM SOLVING CHECKLIST

DEFINE THE WORKPLACE PROBLEM

What procedures need to be implemented in order to complete the work on schedule?

ANALYZE THE WORKPLACE PROBLEM

What tasks need to be completed for each case?

What types of information management systems will make it easier to complete the tasks?

What types of information management systems will be useful for handling similar tasks in the future?

PLAN YOUR PROCEDURE

What planning and scheduling tools will be most useful in meeting the deadlines?

What information needs to be communicated?

IMPLEMENT YOUR PROCEDURE

What is the best way to communicate the information?

What document processing procedures should be used?

What records need to be created and stored?

How should information be stored for easy retrieval?

EVALUATE YOUR RESULTS

Was each deadline met on schedule?

Were the appropriate documents prepared and ready?

Were clients informed of what they needed to do?

Were records available for easy retrieval when needed?

Part A: Use index cards to create a tickler file for taking care of these items. File the card on the appropriate date, giving Leslie enough time to meet the scheduled dates. Also include notes for reminders that need to be given to Ms. Loomis, calls to clients, and other necessary tasks.

Part B: Make a "To Do" list that prioritizes Leslie's tasks.

Part C: Create a records management system for these and future cases. Make a list of the types of records that will be generated for each case. Decide what type of system would be most appropriate for organizing the case files. You may also decide to create a system for filing the forms that are used or you may want to classify some documents according to the type of case involved. Explain the types of filing systems you would create and make a list of the file captions you would use for each system.

MANAGING YOUR CAREER

POSITION DESCRIPTION

Job Title: Office Supervisor

Department: Public Relations

1. MAJOR FUNCTION:
   Responsible for performing supervisory functions for the management of the administrative support operations of the department.
   Primary emphasis is on coordinating overall office functions and
   policies relating to the organization. This supervisor will oversee
   the office work flow procedures to include coordinating document
   processing, managing office communications, overseeing information distribution, and overseeing storage of documents.

2. SPECIFIC DUTIES

   1. Manage procedures for the flow of information within and outside
      of the office; manage the office equipment related to these pro-
      cedures.

   2. Coordinate communication procedures for interaction among of-
      fice workers, sales representatives, and clients to maintain
      positive customer relations and maximize productivity.

   3. Coordinate office communications by managing telephone system;
      coordinate and maintain staff schedules; coordinate business
      meetings; manage travel arrangements and expense records; de-
      velop procedures for effective time management; lead staff meet-
      ings.

   4. Establish procedures for communication functions, document cre-
      ation and processing, file management, client information, mar-
      ket research, and document distribution.

   5. Manage business information relating to functions of organiza-
      tion by managing filing system; manage client information; ana-
      lyze client information; manage record keeping functions; pro-
      cess budgets and other financial information; process and
      maintain confidential business records.

   6. Supervise the office administrative support staff; process and
      maintain confidential and general records pertaining to office
      staff; establish office procedures, hire new employees; train
      new employees; fire employees if necessary.

THE WORKPLACE SITUATION

Hofaker Telecommunications Company is a medium-sized business which offers telecommunications consulting services to educational institutions and businesses. The company specializes in developing teleconferencing capabilities. Recently the human resources department posted a new position for office supervisor in the technology services department. The position involves supervising the technical support staff, including hiring, training, and evaluating employees. One of the new goals set by the management of the department is to automate the client services procedures in order to track the kinds of technology support services that are most in demand and gather other essential data.

The department manager is looking for a person who has administrative support experience, human relations skills, communication and problem solving skills, and who possesses the ability to analyze current procedures and policies.

DEFINE THE WORKPLACE PROBLEM
  What types of skills and abilities are necessary for success in this position?
ANALYZE THE WORKPLACE PROBLEM
  What previous job experience is necessary for this position? Is it beneficial to the company to promote from within or bring in someone new?
PLAN YOUR PROCEDURE
  What measures should be taken to recruit qualified candidates? What is the time frame for filling the position? Is there a written position description?
IMPLEMENT YOUR PROCEDURE
  What interview questions would be appropriate? How are in-house employee interviews to be handled?
EVALUATE YOUR RESULTS
  Does the person hired meet the requirements specified in the job description? What on-the-job training will be required?

chapter **17**

MANAGEMENT AND SUPERVISION

 ## MANAGING HUMAN RESOURCES

Corporate managers spend about half of their workdays in meetings and the rest of their time talking on the telephone, using executive information systems to gather information, and making decisions. In previous chapters we have seen how electronic innovations such as teleconferencing, electronic mail, and networking have enhanced a manager's capability to carry out all of these tasks dramatically.

Administrative assistant, secretarial, and other types of work in the office can lead to management careers. It is possible that you may become a manager someday, or at least you may find yourself performing many of the same functions as a supervisor or manager. To succeed as a manager, you will need to be well versed in all the basic office skills, you will need a good working knowledge of computers and other electronic equipment, and you must be able to work with and manage people.

As a manager you will be asked to make decisions, train employees, supervise their work, and assist in updating office functions. This chapter gives you an overview of these skills. It shows you how managers plan, carry out, and evaluate a business operation. You will also see how executives use different kinds of leadership styles to run their operations and how supervisors train, motivate, and evaluate their employees.

THE FUNCTIONS OF MANAGERS

The difference between managers and supervisors is that managers decide what has to be done and supervisors determine how to do it. In a small company, one person may do both jobs, but in a large company, these functions are often distributed among varying levels of personnel.

PLANNING

Managers and supervisors are responsible for planning, implementing, and evaluating the operations of a business. They are concerned with both long-term and short-term planning. **Long-term planning** refers to projects that take a year or more to implement, while **short-term planning** refers to proposals that can be carried out within a few weeks or months.

Assume, for example, that a soft-drink company decides to introduce a new kind of beverage that it hopes will capture 10 percent of the total soft-drink market within two years. First, the company must set the long- and short-range goals and objectives it needs to accomplish before it can produce the new soft drink. Its long-range goals will be to develop the new flavor and to construct a new plant to produce and bottle the drink. These goals are likely to take a year or more to complete.

To begin the project, the company must find a site for the new plant and obtain financing from the banks. These are short-term goals. They can be accomplished quickly, and they represent separate, small steps that need to be carried out to accomplish the long-term goal of producing the new drink. Planning can also include mid-range goals. In this case mid-range goals might be to hire a construction company to build the plant and to engage an advertising agency to begin planning a sales campaign.

To make long-term plans, managers need to gather and analyze a variety of information. Before deciding to produce a new drink, the soft-drink company will probably want to know the size of the market, what its competitors are planning to do over the next two years, whether it can obtain the financial resources needed to carry out the project, whether it can hire or train enough skilled workers to produce the new soft drink, and so on.

Managers also need similar kinds of data to carry out short-term planning. The soft-drink company's financial officer may want to know, for example, whether the company might save money by waiting a month to borrow the money for the new plant, or the manager of the research department may consult the department's work schedules to determine whether a particular team of chemists can be reassigned to begin working on the new formula. Management often delegates such short-term planning to supervisors and their staffs.

Today, more and more managers are using on-line computer systems to carry out the planning function. The computer gives the manager direct access to information that would take hours (or even longer) to acquire in a traditional office environment. In addition to having access to internal files, many managers use telecommunications to access external databases, which provide up-to-date information about events in the market, competition, and many other topics.

IMPLEMENTING THE PLAN

Implementing a plan involves carrying out the company's long- and short-term objectives. Several steps and tasks are involved.

Organizing

Organizing involves determining how the company can best use its employees, plants, materials, information, and money to carry out its plans. If you were the manager of a department that was assigned the task of producing a new product, you would have to assign supervisors to the job of hiring and training new employees, and you would probably also promote some existing employees to supervisory positions and reassign others so that they could begin work on the new project. In business management, **organization** usually refers to the way in which a business divides responsibilities among its departments and divisions. It also refers to how the business assigns various tasks and functions to employees and to the way it structures its chain of authority or command. This structure is usually spelled out in the company's organization chart.

Controlling

Companies establish standards to control the costs and production of each product or service they offer. If you were a manager, it would be a major part of your job to control the costs for such things as supplies and employee overtime within your department. You would also be responsible for making sure that your employees produce the expected number and quality of goods they have been asked to deliver. Production control is most common in assembly line operations using computer integrated manufacturing systems. At General Motors, for example, computer integrated manufacturing systems are used to monitor how cars are assembled. In offices, production can be determined by the number of projects completed, deadlines met, or many other factors.

Directing

To succeed with any project, a company needs to provide direction or leadership. In other words, it needs to assign managers who are authorized to make the decisions that ensure that a project runs smoothly. Managers must make decisions that will affect their companies' profits. A manager may have to decide whether to cease production of a product line, whether to close a plant, or whether to acquire another company. Leadership and decision making will be discussed in detail later in this chapter.

EVALUATING THE OPERATION

Evaluating means reviewing plans and their implementation to determine whether they have been successful. In the case of the soft-drink company, an evaluation of the new drink project might seek answers to questions such as these: Was plant construction completed on schedule? Did the plant start production and make its first shipments according to the plans? Did consumers like the new soft drink? Did it capture 10 percent of the market? Should the advertising campaign be changed?

Competent managers informally evaluate their projects continually as well as at the end. Ultimately, the evaluation process provides a way of comparing the actual results with the original long-term goals. If a project did not return enough profits, if it cost too much, or if it took too long to complete, the managers can reconsider their plans and goals and make new decisions about the project.

The processes of planning, implementing, and evaluating are repeated, often in overlapping sequences, as managers and supervisors fulfill their responsibilities. They may revise a plan midway in its implementation to meet new goals or circumstances. They may also formulate new plans and make new decisions to put their plans into action. In fact, making decisions is probably the most important function a manager performs.

DECISION MAKING

At the beginning of this chapter you read that managers spend most of their time attending meetings, talking on the telephone, using executive information systems, and making decisions. In essence, what managers are doing when they hold meetings, talk on the telephone, and read documents is gathering and analyzing information. They then use that information to make the decisions they are required to make to keep their businesses running smoothly and profitably.

Managers could not perform their jobs without making dozens of decisions every day, but they are not the only decision makers in the business office. Virtually everyone who works in an office has to make any number of decisions over the course of any given workday. Some decisions are complicated and difficult to make, while others are trivial and easy, but all decision making involves the same basic steps, as depicted below.

THE BASIC STEPS IN DECISION MAKING

1. **Defining the problem.** First, you need to determine what must be done. We have called this defining the problem, but the word *problem* does not necessarily mean something negative. It can mean an opportunity, a choice, or a project. Your "problem" may be to decide whether to accept a promotion that requires that you transfer to a company branch office.
2. **Gathering Information.** Next, you must gather all of the information necessary to generate options to solve the situation. This may mean interviewing people, developing and administering questionnaires, or analyzing workflow processes.
3. **Generating Options.** Then you must think of the possible solutions to the problem or the methods for arriving at the solution. You might want to discuss some of the possibilities with one or more of your colleagues.
4. **Evaluating Options.** Once you have thought of several solutions, you need to consider the possible outcomes of each one and weigh the advantages and disadvantages of each.
5. **Choosing an Option.** Finally, you must select the option that you are going to try. Be aware that you may change your mind at any stage by redefining the problem and generating new options.

Of course, each of us makes hundreds of decisions every day. The vast majority of these decisions are so routine and trivial that we are not even aware that we are going through the decision-making process. For instance, when you decide what to wear to work, what to have for lunch, or what assignments to work on for the day, you define the problem, gather information, and evaluate and choose options in each case, even though you are not conscious of each distinct step.

In an active, growing organization, managers and supervisors are constantly making decisions. Here are some examples of the kinds of decisions they need to consider:

- **New Products and Services**   Should we make the new automobile part out of plastic or metal? Which would be safer, more durable, or less costly?

- **Improved Procedures**   Should we set up a toll-free, twenty-four-hour hot line to take customer orders and complaints?

- **Changes in Policies**   Should we adopt staggered work hours for our employees?

- **Changes in Automation**   Should we change our computerized accounting system to a new system?

- **Sources of Materials**   Should we buy our supplies from a discount supplier who is cheaper but farther away?

- **Methods of Control**   Should we computerize our accounting procedures?

Effective decision making is a skill that you can develop just as you develop the clerical and interpersonal skills you need to work in a business office.

MANAGING PEOPLE

PEOPLE AND MACHINES

For a long time after the start of the Industrial Revolution, factory owners looked upon their workers as extensions of the machines they operated. They were just one component of an array of tools and materials the manufacturer could use to produce a product, and they were as interchangeable as the machinery. If a worker could not perform well, he or she was replaced by another worker who could do a better job. Workers' rights were nonexistent, and most factory owners had little regard for their employees' needs or desires.

At the beginning of the twentieth century, worker productivity and motivation became an issue for management. As businesses left the Industrial Revolution and moved into the Information Age, it became apparent that people and their abilities to problem solve were an integral part of a productive business.

The effect of good human relations on production was discovered almost accidentally in a famous experiment at the Hawthorne, New Jersey, plant of the Western Electric Company. While experimenters were studying the effects of improved working conditions, such as better lighting, on worker productivity, they had frequent contact with the workers and paid them a good deal of attention.

One startling discovery was that the increased attention alone resulted in higher productivity—regardless of any other factors in the study. When working conditions were improved (good lighting, music, frequent breaks), the workers' performance improved. But when all those improved conditions were removed, the workers still continued to better their performance. The workers had been made to feel special, and the attention that was paid to them was as important as or more important than any specific working conditions.

Different management styles are appropriate in different settings. Sometimes there are direct decisions that a supervisor or manager must make regarding the workplace, such as safety issues and legal requirements. Motivation of employees, however, always results in better work from employees.

MANAGEMENT STYLE

One of the most important jobs of management is to manage people competently. Although managers can also manage procedures and equipment, they are always involved with people. A manager's or supervisor's main concern is that the employees are productive, motivated, and do their best work. Different techniques are used by managers and supervisors to encourage and motivate people to produce and improve on the job. Most companies today use a team approach to management. A **team approach** means that managers and supervisors do not make decisions in isolation. They ask for input from members of their staff, receive their ideas and concerns, and then weigh all of the factors to make some decisions. Team management can also mean that managers and supervisors form a team to make some decisions as well. Managers and supervisors use different techniques to help the decision-making process work in a team management situation. Two of these techniques include brainstorming and modeling.

Brainstorming

The most efficient managers communicate with their staffs constantly to gather new ideas and learn about problems that interfere with productivity. This process is called **brainstorming.** When a manager brainstorms, he or she discusses a problem with an employee or with a group of employees who are affected

Figure 17.1 Brainstorming sessions are an important part of project team management.

by the problem and who will benefit from the solution. For example, a manager might pose the question, Should we have staggered work hours? When one member of the group proposes an option, others may think of the advantages and disadvantages of the option, or they may offer alternative ideas. Employees may know of obstacles of which the manager is unaware, or they may offer ideas that are cheaper and easier to implement than any solutions that the manager has proposed.

The manager's role in a brainstorming session is to make sure that the brainstorming is done in a positive atmosphere so that no proposals are ridiculed or dismissed out of hand. The manager must also evaluate each idea carefully to arrive at the best solution.

Sometimes the best solution to a problem generates a different set of problems. For example, when an office staff is placed on staggered hours, the office can be kept open longer, employees can select the hours they want to work to some extent, and rush hour commuting is reduced. New problems may include not having a full staff during certain hours, increased expenses for lights and heat, and the inability to give everyone his or her first choice of working hours.

Modeling

Part of the decision-making process may include modeling or testing. **Modeling** involves setting up a formula or model that can be used to forecast the possible outcome of a decision. For example, the soft-drink company might set up a mathematical model that could predict whether producing a new drink would be a profitable undertaking when projected costs and sales figures are factored in.

Mathematical models can be very useful in making decisions about manufacturing, retailing, financial planning, or any other kind of business for which statistics—objective, quantitative data—are available. Electronic technology has proved to be particularly valuable in modeling because computers can process a large quantity of data over and over again. New software is continually being produced to help managers make decisions in many different kinds of business situations. These programs allow managers to pose "what if" scenarios to determine the outcomes of various options. Spreadsheets are one kind of software that can be used this way.

Although modeling is very useful in making decisions about products, sales, and profits, it is less useful for predicting how people will act or react. Instead, businesses use various testing and surveying techniques to gauge the impact of a product on potential customers or users. For example, before going ahead with full-scale production, our hypothetical soft-drink company might test market its new drink in one geographic area, or it might employ a market research company to conduct taste tests or shopper interviews in different parts of the country.

Whether managers use brainstorming, modeling, or testing to gather data and ideas, as a general rule, the more information they have about a problem, the better able they are to make useful decisions. Once a manager makes a decision, it usually falls to supervisors to decide how to carry it out.

MANAGEMENT LEADERSHIP ROLES

Managers and supervisors develop different leadership styles, or ways of carrying out their functions and dealing with their employees. Each manager's style is a blend of his or her experience, training, and personality. Some managers are friendly and outgoing; others prefer to maintain a distance between themselves and their employees. Some are intuitive and creative; others are methodical and plodding. Managers develop their own leadership styles as they move up through the ranks by imitating those above them and by trying out different ways of doing things until they find the methods that best suit their own temperaments and circumstances.

A manager's leadership style can have a great impact on how well he or she motivates employees. Social scientists have been studying management theory and human behavior in the workplace for decades, and they have developed several different theories about how managers motivate their employees.

Team Approach to Management Using MBO

Management by objectives (MBO) is a team management style that seems to succeed very well in actual practice. MBO brings managers and employees together periodically to set specific goals or objectives. After deciding what the goals should be, managers and workers decide how to go about achieving those goals, setting deadlines, and agreeing on the standards to be met. They put their plans into writing and then meet from time to time to review objectives and evaluate progress. In effect, this is nothing more than involving employees in the management functions of planning, implementing, and evaluating. For management by objectives to succeed, managers and employees must develop realistic goals. They have to agree on how the goals will be met, and when the deadline has passed, they must evaluate the actual outcome against their expectations.

MANAGEMENT BY OBJECTIVES

This simplified statement of goals shows the essential ingredients of objectives that a worker and a manager would establish. Goals for increasing skills are combined with tasks and standards needed to get the job done. After each statement is a suggestion of how achievement is evaluated.

Goal Statements	Evaluation Method
1. To learn to use the new electronic mail system efficiently	Use of system every day
2. To maintain a telephone log	Have the log available for review
3. To have document turnaround of four hours	Check with users
4. To improve electronic filenames	Check ease of retrieval

To help an employee set objectives effectively, managers must know what the employees are doing on a daily basis. One way managers and supervisors accomplish this is by being available to employees and walking through their area often. Communication takes place constantly with employees, and managers see and hear for themselves how things are going instead of relying on information processed by other managers within the organization.

The benefits are obvious. No matter how good communication may be in a business, direct observation is a very reliable way to gather information. The complaint "you never see the boss around here" is never heard with this approach; the supervisor gets seen, and the supervisor sees. More and more, a leader's personal interest and enthusiasm are being recognized as important ingredients in a company's success.

A Leadership Style for You

As you develop your own leadership style, it is important to understand the different management techniques and to be able to use them to devise ways of motivating your employees. Your leadership style should be a good "fit" between your personality, the composition of your staff, and the kind of business you are involved in. You need to know your own strengths and weaknesses. You might be the kind of manager who relies on past experience and intuition when making a decision. You may rely on your business sense or on your personal likes and dislikes. Or you may like to gather a lot of information and make objective, intellectual analyses of each problem before making a decision. Most managers have a mixture of all of these attributes, but some elements are much stronger than others. If you can integrate all of these attributes, you will have a great advantage over managers who must always be compensating for their weaknesses.

CHARACTERISTICS OF A SUCCESSFUL MANAGER

As you become more experienced in your role as a secretary, office worker, or administrative assistant, you will have an opportunity to develop many work habits and skills that will help you become a good supervisor or manager. For example, when you perform administrative support tasks such as accounting and budgeting, you are already participating to some degree in the management functions of planning and evaluating. In addition, if you are required to train or oversee other employees, you are already learning the major function of supervisors.

Leadership style, as we have said, is a highly individual trait, but there are also some common characteristics that help identify people who are likely to become successful managers.

Basic Job Skills

If you want to become a manager, you need to develop good basic skills. These include technical skills and communication skills. They also include such personal traits as punctuality, dependability, good personal appearance, ethical behavior, loyalty, good organizational skills, and a solid knowledge of and interest in the company you work for.

Good Self-Image

In addition to basic job skills, you need to have self-confidence and a good perception of yourself. Do you have a good feeling about yourself? Do you approach new challenges with enthusiasm and an eagerness to learn rather than with fear and anxiety? Potential executives say yes to these questions.

Good Communication Skills

Managers often have to speak before large groups of people. They serve on boards and committees, where they try to persuade others to adopt certain courses of action. They write letters and reports, and they deal constantly with subordinates. All of these activities require good communication skills. This

Figure 17.2 Successful managers maintain close contact with their employees on a daily basis.

means learning to write concisely and to the point, learning to plan speeches and telephone conversations, and learning to communicate effectively with employees who may come from many different social, economic, and educational backgrounds.

Ability to See the Big Picture

You need to be able to see how each job contributes to the company's overall goals. Some employees are concerned only about their own jobs or their own departments. They may feel that they are in competition with other employees or offices within the company, and they fail to realize that all employees are, or should be, working toward the same goals. The employee who has a broad perspective and who promotes the interests of the company as a whole stands a better chance of being offered a management position.

The introduction of office automation offers an illustration of how the ability to see the big picture can contribute to a company's efficiency and productivity. Some companies have electronic equipment that is not fully utilized because the managers who planned for it failed to take an overall view. One office may have one kind of computer equipment, and another office may have another, incompatible system. In one office, microcomputers may be used only to improve the production of secretaries, while other offices remain unautomated or unnetworked and employees must carry out time-consuming tasks by hand.

In companies where management took a look at the big picture, the managers planned for computer systems that would enhance the entire company's operations. Terminals, printers, and copiers can communicate with one another, and secretaries can use their workstations not only to process documents but also to send electronic mail and to search databases. And each office can use the computer system for its own needs: to process purchase orders, take inventory, perform accounting and budgeting tasks, and so on. This kind of overall planning can save a company enormous amounts of time and money.

Initiative and Self-Motivation

The ability to start and complete assignments on your own and the willingness to look for new undertakings are probably the most important characteristics you can possess if you are interested in being promoted to a management-level job. These traits demonstrate that you are capable of making decisions and that you are comfortable with responsibility.

As you gain experience on the job, you will acquire many of the skills that managers need. Your self-confidence, for instance, will grow as you learn your job and become comfortable in it. You will develop good judgment, which will enable you to exercise your abilities at the right time and in an appropriate manner. Initiative may be perceived as aggression or ambition in some circumstances, and it will be up to you to recognize when and how to assert yourself. This in itself is another qualification for management responsibility. Once you have measured yourself against these characteristics and decided that you have the desire and ability to become a manager, you need to do some career planning. Chapter 18 will explore office-related careers and show you how you can plan for your own future.

 # THE FUNCTIONS OF SUPERVISORS

The primary responsibility of supervisors is to implement, or carry out, management's plans. Supervisors usually work directly with the materials and employees of the company, and their main functions are hiring, training, assigning, motivating, and evaluating the people who work under them.

 ## PARTICIPATING IN HIRING

Hiring includes recruiting, interviewing, and making job offers. In small companies, supervisors may do all of these things themselves. In large companies, a human resources department (personnel department) is responsible for performing many of these tasks. But more often, a group of supervisors or managers work together in the hiring process.

What commonly happens when an opening occurs in a large company is that the supervisor informs the human resources department and provides a job description, which defines the duties and the qualifications needed to fill the opening. The human resources department then advertises the opening in newspapers, posts announcements within the company, contacts job placement companies, or contacts postsecondary placement departments on campuses.

The human resources department may do the preliminary screening and interviewing of applicants. Then the supervisor interviews applicants, selects the finalists, and makes the job offer. Once the new employee begins work, he or she will probably undergo some kind of training program to learn how to operate equipment or follow procedures used by the company.

TRAINING EMPLOYEES

Employees on the job as well as new employees need training from time to time. Employees usually need to be trained when new equipment is installed or when new production procedures or techniques are adopted. Sometimes companies also retrain workers so that they can perform new tasks when their old jobs become obsolete. Usually, supervisors have the responsibility for training and retraining employees. **Initial training** refers to the training of new employees, and **in-service training** refers to the retraining of existing employees.

Initial Training

New employees need to know everything from where to hang their coats to how to run the computer terminal. They also need to know about such things as company work rules and vacation and sick leave policies. Orientation sessions are designed to fill these needs.

Some orientation programs, designed for large groups of incoming employees, use films, lectures, multimedia systems, and employee handbooks to do the job. But an orientation can also be

Figure 17.3 One-on-one training sessions with new employees is part of a manager's responsibility.

an informal session in which a supervisor or another employee shows the new worker around and answers his or her questions. In some cases a supervisor may simply stay with new employees to teach them how to perform their jobs until they feel comfortable on their own. Supervisors sometimes delegate this role to another employee, but most responsible supervisors prefer to work closely with new employees while they are learning a new job.

In-Service Training

Supervisors are also usually responsible for training or retraining on-the-job employees when they need to learn about new equipment or work methods. In-service training can be conducted for large groups, using films and lectures, training manuals, and multimedia systems, or it can be one-on-one, with the supervisor working with the employee until he or she learns the new skill.

Training Techniques

Assume that you are a supervisor responsible for training a group of employees to operate a new piece of equipment. Whether you are teaching one employee or a hundred, you should follow a structured training program that covers these four basic steps:

1. **Prepare the employees.** Put the trainees at ease. Explain the purposes and advantages of the new equipment or task. Let them know that you will be available to help them for as long as it takes them to learn how to use the new equipment. Start with what they know, and teach them how the new system fits in with the old and why the change was made.
2. **Present the task.** If you are training workers to operate new equipment, provide them with a training manual and visuals of the task on video or through computer programs. If you are training employees to perform a new job, provide a written job description. Explain the equipment or job, giving clear, complete instructions at a speed the trainees can absorb. Then demonstrate the job, emphasizing the major points.
3. **Provide practice.** Have the trainees walk through the job until they feel comfortable with it. Be patient and encouraging. Provide feedback for each employee, and reexplain any steps that seem unclear until they understand why they are an important part of the whole process.

4. **Put workers on their own.** Let the trainees do the job themselves. Be available to help, and provide written sources of help if necessary. Check on the trainees with decreasing frequency.

Always invite questions at every step. This way, you can tell whether you are providing clear, comprehensible instructions. And listen carefully to the types of questions trainees ask. Do the questions indicate a misunderstanding of the process or a lack of knowledge of how the system works? Knowing the types of questions asked can help you evaluate the training process to see if you can change it in any way.

WRITING JOB DESCRIPTIONS

Job descriptions are a key element in training, assigning, and evaluating employees. They spell out what employees are expected to do, what knowledge and skills they are expected to possess, and what criteria will be used to evaluate them. Supervisors are usually responsible for writing job descriptions or for helping the human resources department prepare them.

Often employees help refine or revise their own job descriptions, usually as part of their annual evaluations. For example, photocopying may be listed as a task in a job description, but employees may no longer be responsible for photocopying because the company has established a copy center; but the employee must understand the process to have items photocopied. In addition, frequently employees are assigned responsibilities over the course of the year that were not included in their job descriptions. These responsibilities should be added to the job descriptions when they are revised.

Written job descriptions are typically divided into three categories:

- **The Description Itself** This includes a summary of the overall functions of the position and a detailed list of the specific tasks and responsibilities the employee is expected to perform.

- **Knowledge and Skill Requirement** The job description spells out the minimum education or training requirements for the job.

- **Accountability** This part of the job description tells employees who their supervisors are and whom they are expected to supervise. It may also describe any equipment, expenditures, or areas of operations the employee is expected to oversee.

For example, a job description for an administrative assistant might read as follows:

Position functions: Provide support services for general manager of division; maintain and prepare records; schedule appointments, meetings; screen calls and visitors; retrieve, synthesize necessary information.

The job description then specifies the tasks required for carrying out the position function. A sample list might include the following:

- Update appointment calendar daily; review with manager.
- Make all travel arrangements as required.
- Answer telephones; greet visitors.
- Retrieve information as necessary from electronic or manual files.
- Take dictation; process correspondence.
- Use database to compile retrieved data into monthly reports.
- Set up electronic meetings (telephone conferences or video conferences).
- Receive, review, and prioritize both electronic and traditional mail.

DEVELOPING STAFFING PLANS

One skill that supervisors need to develop is the ability to match their employees' training and capabilities to the work that needs to be done. Supervisors also need to be aware of their employees' preferences in work assignments. One employee may have a talent for research and writing, while another may prefer to work with numbers. A good supervisor tries to make assignments in accordance with such preferences whenever possible. Of course, there are times when it is not possible to match an employee's preference to a task at hand, and it is up to the supervisor to make assignments based on the best interests of the company and the strengths of the individual.

MOTIVATING EMPLOYEES

Since supervisors work most closely with the work force, it is an important part of their jobs to **motivate** employees. Employees who are motivated perform their jobs as enthusiastically and energetically as possible. They try to solve problems, they show ini-

DELEGATING—A FINE ART

In many situations the work to be performed by employees is clearly identified. For example, the data-entry people enter data, and the supervisor makes assignments and oversees the work flow. Often, though, the division of labor is not so clear. A supervisor is given authority over a group of employees and is responsible for achieving a particular goal—producing the weekly payroll, for example—but it is not spelled out how the supervisor is to go about meeting that goal. The most skillful supervisors perform only the most complex and critical tasks themselves, and they **delegate,** or assign, routine and time-consuming tasks to members of their staffs.

Generally, the more duties and responsibilities supervisors have, the more likely they are to delegate individual tasks to others. This frees the supervisors to concentrate on management functions—planning, implementing, and evaluating—and it gives their employees the kinds of additional experience they need to develop into more productive and self-reliant workers.

Some inexperienced supervisors find it difficult to delegate. They are afraid to depend on other people, and they believe it is easier simply to do a job themselves than explain it to someone else. These supervisors end up trying to do everything themselves and quickly become bogged down. Other supervisors err in the other direction and try to assign all the work to subordinates. The art of delegating lies in the supervisor's ability to strike a balance between the two extremes—to identify and do the important jobs and to leave the routine work to others.

tiative, and they have a positive attitude about their work and their company. They are the kinds of workers who are willing toput in the extra effort or time that is sometimes required to get a job done.

How does a supervisor motivate an employee? No one knows all the elements that contribute to developing a well-motivated worker. If you become a supervisor, you can help motivate employees by treating them fairly and equally when making schedules and staffing decisions, by making them feel that they are important members of your team, and by listening to their complaints and suggestions. Make requests rather than demands, and issue clear, comprehensible instructions. Also make sure that you recognize your employees' efforts and accomplishments, and let them know frequently how well they are performing their jobs.

PARTICIPATING IN EMPLOYEE EVALUATION

Normally supervisors are responsible for evaluating employees, and they do this in one of two ways. They can evaluate workers informally, on a day-to-day basis, simply by saying

"Good job on that report" or "There are some problems with this. Can you straighten it out?" This kind of evaluation should occur constantly.

The other kind of evaluation is the formal performance review, which occurs annually in most companies. The supervisor and staff member sit down to discuss the employee's progress during the past year and to plan for the coming year. The annual review usually includes a written report or evaluation form that rates the employee on such traits as work habits, dependability, appearance, accuracy, decision-making ability, efficiency, and so on (see figure 17.4).

Supervisors often use an employee's job description as the basis for evaluating his or her work. For example, a secretary's job description might require a number of clerical duties. The performance evaluation will determine whether the secretary has been performing those duties adequately.

In some companies, supervisors supplement the job description with a written **statement of objectives** as a basis for evaluating employees. The statement of objectives is a description of the goals or objectives that the employee will accomplish during a set period of time, usually a year. Objectives are usually set in conjunction with the employee to make them real and attainable. Goals set by a supervisor are dictatorial and will not be effective. Together, supervisor and employee can develop a statement of objectives that is fair and attainable. And because the employee basically sets his or her own goals, more ownership of the goals is experienced and as a result more success is realized.

A formal performance review can be a positive and motivating experience for employees. It provides an opportunity for a supervisor and an employee to discuss the company's goals and the employee's goals. In addition, they can try to resolve any work problems the employee may be experiencing. All too often, however, employees come to dread the performance review because they are surprised by negative comments about their work. Supervisors who practice constant informal constructive criticism throughout the year can eliminate this element of unpleasant surprise.

One of the greatest weaknesses of supervisors and managers is their tendency to avoid formal performance reviews with their employees. The review process should be viewed in a positive light. When supervisors conduct performance reviews, their basic goals should be to identify and reinforce each employee's strengths and to identify where the employee can improve. In addition, the review should include programs and plans for the coming year that will help the employee grow and correct his or her weaknesses or enhance a strength.

Office Employee Performance Evaluation

Soc. Security No.	Employee Name		Division	Grade Level	Department	How Long Under Your Supervision?	Wk. Location	Date of Hire
Position Title						Postpone This Appraisal Until (Date)		

Performance Analysis

In the appraisal, focus on the key aspects of job performance. Check only those factors that are applicable to the employee's job. Space is provided for you to add any other job-related factors you think are important. Be sure to complete this section as fully as possible; it will help you determine the employee's overall performance rating.

JOB RESULTS
- Thoroughness of work
- Accuracy-lack of mistakes
- Quantity-output of meaningful work
- Coverage of total job responsibility

JOB KNOWLEDGE
- Understanding work procedures, methods and techniques
- Learning and adapting to new methods and techniques
- Understanding equipment

DEPENDABILITY
- Adherence to instructions and directions
- Consistency and reliability of work habits
- Efficiency under pressure
- Supervision required
- Ability to get things done

RELATIONSHIPS
- Cooperation with other in group
- Respect and consideration for others
- Acceptance of constructive criticism
- Impressions created outside department

INITIATIVE
- Efforts to improve own qualifications
- Efforts to improve the way work is done
- Coping with problems as they arise
- Willingness to assume responsibility

OTHER JOB RELATED FACTORS
- ....
- ....
- ....

ATTENDANCE

	IN A 6-MONTH PERIOD	IN A 12-MONTH PERIOD
Poor	☐ Absent 4-5 Days	☐ Absent 7-8 Days
Excessive	☐ Absent 6 or More Days	☐ Absent 9 or More Days

PUNCTUALITY

Poor	☐ Late 7-8 Times	☐ Late 11-12 Times
Excessive	☐ Late 9 or More Times	☐ Late 13 or More Times

Performance Comments

What aspects of the employee's duties are handled in an exceptional or commendable manner? _____

What aspects of the employee's duties are not handled as well as should be expected? _____

Performance Rating

Considering all the employee's performance factors, please check the statement that most nearly fits this employee's overall performance on the current job in the last twelve months.

1 ☐ Exceptional	Superior performance. Consistently exceeds job standards.
2 ☐ Commendable	High standard of performance. Consistently meets, and occasionally exceeds, job standards.
3 ☐ Good	Performance normally expected of qualified employee.
4 ☐ Needs improvement	Performance not up to desired standard, should show improvement.
5 ☐ Unacceptable	Poor performance. Cannot be retained on job without immediate improvement.

Development Plans

The employee's career objectives and your department's staff needs will dictate the development plan. The plan should help to improve the employee's skills, increase job knowledge, or provide a means of correcting problems. Use the following code list to identify the appropriate training programs:

State your plans and objectives for improving the employee's performance (consider increased responsibility, coaching, on-the-job training, etc.).

If formal training programs will help the employee, please code (using the course list in the instructions) those programs that the employee needs:

1 ____ 2 ____ 3 ____ 4 ____ 5 ____ Write in other ____

A. Business Writing & Editing	I. Business Math
B. Copy Editing & Proofreading	J. Business Correspondence
C. Make-up & Production	K. Business English
D. Graphics, Art & Design	L. Shorthand Refresher
E. Advertising & Marketing	M. Shorthand I
F. Promotion	N. Typing Refresher
G. Research & Statistics	O. Typing I
H. Office Practices Seminar	P. Telephone Techniques

Q. Receptionist Training
R. Supervisory Training
S. Accounting
T. Word Processing
U. Computer Technology
V. Language Arts
W. Other (specify):

Employee's Comments

Appraised By _____ Date _____

Appraisal Approved By _____ Date _____

Employee's Signature
(Your signature indicates only that you have read this appraisal.)

FORM 09-873 (30) (Rev. 7/85)

Figure 17.4 Evaluation forms are "report cards" that tell employees how well they are performing their jobs and where they need to make improvements.

A good performance review requires experience and skill, but inexperienced supervisors can get help from a broad range of literature on the subject. Some companies also provide formal training programs for their supervisory staffs on employee evaluation and other aspects of supervision.

PLANNING AN AUTOMATED OFFICE

In the last few years American businesses have spent more money on equipment for office workers than for factory workers. That money has been used to purchase computer systems to automate office procedures and streamline the flow of business information.

In recent years the cost of purchasing computer systems has been declining, and computers have become easier to understand and use. Nevertheless, the costs are still high enough and computers are still complex enough that successful companies make it a point to study carefully their automation needs before investing in a computer system. Studies are expected to answer these questions: How much will the system cost? What benefits will it provide? How will the staff react to it? The company that rushes into buying a computer system before it answers these questions risks wasting a substantial investment and losing countless hours of time.

As someone entering the business world, you may one day be involved in helping to plan and/or change the automation in your office. To do this, you need to be aware of the issues and decisions that go into automating an office. You also need to see how automation changes job functions and responsibilities.

Modern business computer systems no longer require such highly technical employees as computer programmers and systems analysts. The need in the future will be for people who understand office functions and procedures. This will create new opportunities for office workers to move up the career ladder into positions where they will be managing electronic offices.

THE BENEFITS OF AUTOMATION

The goal of automation is to increase productivity, either by saving time and money or by enabling businesses to produce more goods or services. In the factory, automation has usually been used to perform a particular task faster than it could be done by hand or to reduce the number of workers needed to perform the task. In the office, too, automation means faster work or fewer people. But it also means doing tasks in new ways. This can result in a reorganization of the office and changes in employees' job functions.

Both kinds of changes are important. If a typist can type twice as fast using a word processor, then that person will be able to produce twice as much work for the company in the same amount of time. The company saves money because it needs only one employee instead of two to perform the same work, and it saves time because letters, orders, and reports can be processed at twice the previous rate.

Changes in job functions can also lead to increased productivity. You have seen throughout this book how automation has changed the functions of secretaries and other office workers by freeing them from repetitious, mundane tasks and by giving them the opportunity to assume management responsibilities. Because these employees can perform more complicated functions, they are much more valuable to the company. Automation has also freed supervisors and managers from performing many routine tasks, and it has speeded up the flow of information processing so that managers can gather information and make decisions more efficiently.

It does not follow automatically that the company that automates will reduce the number of its employees. Automation may eliminate some jobs, and the employees in those jobs may be retrained, laid off, or offered early retirement incentives. What often happens is that because the company's employees can produce more work, the company expands production. Automation makes it possible for the company to reach more customers. It sells more goods or services and generates more income. It may even have to hire more people to help meet the increasing demands for its products.

Automation also enables companies to provide better services for customers. It can greatly increase the speed at which information flows within a company and outside to customers, suppliers, and others with whom the company must interact. This results both in more service and in better quality service to customers.

People in various departments within an organization can have immediate access to the data and information they need to perform their jobs with an automated system (see figure 17.5). Information can be shared and feedback given almost immediately. Many functions that are redundant can be streamlined, increasing efficiency and productivity. Through automation, companies also have access to outside sources of information, such as data banks and information services. All of these factors

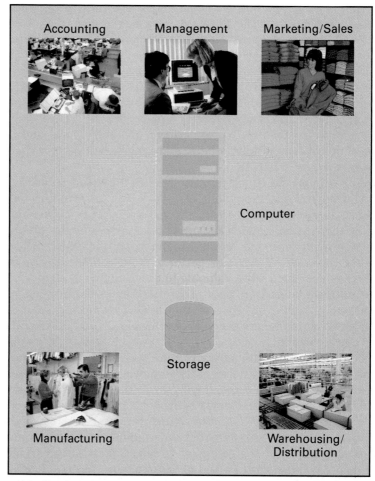

Figure 17.5 Automation allows several tasks to be performed simultaneously. In this example, when accounting processes a purchase order, all other departments can have access to the most up-to-date information on the product.

work together to improve the productivity of the organization.

THE BOTTOM LINE

When a company increases productivity through automation, one of the outcomes should be an improvement in the **bottom line.** Managers have to determine how the **cost-benefit ratio** will affect the bottom line. This is simply business jargon for "How much is it going to cost?" and "How much profit will it generate?" Bottom line means the net profit—the amount of profit remaining after the company has deducted all of its expenses. The term *bottom line* refers to the very last figure—literally the bottom line—on a company's annual financial statement, which always shows the company's net profit for the year.

A cost-benefit ratio is a comparison of the costs of carrying out a plan or operation with the profit or benefit the company can expect to receive. It is a kind of mathematical model that helps management decide whether or not to go ahead with a given proposal. If the ratio is low—that is, if the company can expect a large return for its investment—the project will probably be approved. If the ratio is high—that is, if the profits or benefits are only slightly greater than, equal to, or less than the costs—management will probably decide to shelve the project.

A cost-benefit ratio is a useful tool in making decisions. One problem with it, however, is that it does not include certain intangible benefits. A proposal might, for example, offer improved employee morale or improved client relations, but it is often difficult or impossible to estimate these benefits in monetary terms.

PLANNING FOR AUTOMATION

As you read earlier, people who are planning to automate an office try to answer four basic questions:

1. How much will it cost, not only for installation but also for maintenance and training?
2. What benefits will be derived in time and money saved or in improved services offered customers?
3. How will the staff react?
4. What current systems and procedures will change?

The first two questions are often stated as a combined question: What is the cost-benefit ratio? In planning for office automation, however, it is often better to consider costs and benefits separately. The reason is that it is often difficult to express the potential benefits of automation in specific monetary terms. This is particularly true when a planner is considering new ways of doing things.

To demonstrate the cost-benefit ratio resulting from increasing a keyboardist's speed by 50 percent is relatively easy. It is less easy to specify the cost-benefit ratio resulting from making it possible for a secretary or administrative assistant to access a database or develop a sales graph. Yet in the long run, the company's benefits will probably be greater as a result of the latter changes.

HOW CHANGING TECHNOLOGY AFFECTS PLANNING

Before looking at steps involved in planning office automation, let's first consider how changes in technology have affected the process of planning and implementing a system.

As you have read, automation first entered the business office in the form of huge, expensive, mainframe computers that were used for data processing tasks such as payrolls, inventories, and billing. Not only were they expensive, but they also required special technicians to program and run them. Secretaries, administrative assistants, accountants, and other office workers could not use these computers. They merely provided the necessary data, which was then processed by the newly hired special systems technicians. A host of new jobs appeared in the business world, mostly with the words *systems, programmer,* and *analyst* in their job descriptions.

The financial investment in equipment and staff for these early systems was extremely high, and businesses thought long and carefully before making it. They conducted months-long studies. They hired special consultants to help them decide about equipment or to custom design a system.

The situation today is dramatically different because of the advent of minicomputers and, in particular, microcomputers. Not only are the newer computers inexpensive and powerful, but they can also be used by anyone with a little training. The software programs for today's computers are also less expensive and more powerful. And today's micros can process voice and images as well as text.

Today's computer systems can also perform several different functions at once instead of just one function at a time. Terms such as **multitasking** have been coined to describe these multiple capabilities. Multitasking means that a person using one computer system can use multiple software programs at once; the programs run in the background but are always accessible to the user without quitting one software package to get into another. **Integrated systems** allow for the integration of all software capabilities to all users.

All of these high-tech advances are providing office workers with more power at a lower cost. A company does not need to make a large initial investment when it decides to automate its offices. It does not need to have software programs specifically designed for it; it can buy them off the shelf. And if one program does not work out, the company can get another one. It will not have wasted much money.

This means that in many cases companies no longer need to

hire outside consultants when they decide to automate nor do they need to conduct long-term studies. Secretaries and other office workers can evaluate and recommend software. Who knows better what is needed to perform the tasks? Nor is it necessary for companies to hire squads of systems analysts, programmers, or other specialists, because office workers can operate the sophisticated computers of today with minimal training.

In many fully integrated offices, many of the technical specialists are being phased out as office workers acquire the necessary skills to run the systems. Technical specialists are needed, however, to keep the systems running when problems occur. This change accelerates automation because companies realize that they no longer need to augment their traditional staffs with a host of expensive technicians who could wipe out most, if not all, of the supposed savings from automation.

MAJOR CHALLENGES TODAY

Planners of office automation do face particular challenges today. One has to do with timing and the other with the compatibility of different computer systems within a company.

Timing

Deciding when to automate can be a problem for a company. Computer systems and software programs are improved and upgraded constantly, so it is always tempting to delay automation. Of course, by waiting, the company loses all the potential benefits of automation while a competitor moves ahead and realizes them.

Incompatible Systems

As you learned, some computer systems are often **incompatible**—that is, they cannot communicate with one another. Computer hardware and software have become so inexpensive that middle managers sometimes get their own systems. When this happens, a company can own several different, incompatible systems within the same building. The computer industry is working on ways of overcoming problems of incompatibility.

CHANGING TO A NEW SYSTEM

Although computer systems are much cheaper and easier to program and operate, companies still face a relatively costly and complicated process when they decide to make a changeover from a traditional office to an electronic one. It is true that many companies do not have to hire technical consultants to help them automate, but when they assign their own employees to the task of devising an office automation system, the employees must become at least moderately knowledgeable about computers. Otherwise, they may be overwhelmed by incomprehensible technical jargon and by the great quantity and variety of equipment and software available in today's electronic marketplace.

Companies must give careful thought to automating or replacing an outdated computer system with a new one. They need to choose a system that can carry out all the functions expected of it and that is powerful enough (has enough memory) to meet all of the company's processing needs. If a company chooses the wrong system for its needs, it may be stuck with that system for years to come, or it may lose a sizable investment in time and money and have to automate all over again.

One way companies automate is by conducting a **systems study or systems analysis.** This is a study that focuses on the company's overall system of procedures and functions rather than on individual tasks, although the results will affect the tasks. The study is intended to result in the creation of a complete office automation system capable of performing various functions such as document processing, data processing, graphics production, and interoffice communication. There are eight main steps in the typical system study, beginning with determining the problem.

Determine the Problem

A company must realize that there is something wrong with its current system before it can decide to change to a new system. Members of the company need to determine what the major problems are and what a new system must do to overcome the problems. Determining what is wrong or what the goals of the study are is necessary to begin any systems analysis.

Preliminary Survey

The next step is to identify the need or problem. The people best able to define the need are usually those who will be using the system. Everybody who will be affected by the system should, therefore, be involved, directly or indirectly, in the preliminary survey. One way to do this is to interview each employee to identify specific job tasks (see figure 17.6).

Figure 17.6 Taking a survey of individual jobs tasks is a crucial part of the automation study.

A large company considering ways to automate its offices would need to involve employees from every department. A payroll clerk could suggest ways to automate payroll production. A salesclerk could specify exactly what information he or she needs to include on an order form. Employees in the bookkeeping department would know best what features they would require in a spreadsheet program. This process would continue until the needs of every department and every group of employees are examined and identified.

Office Automation Study

Once needs have been determined and some broad goals established, the next step is to examine the existing system. What is being done, and who is doing it? Why is it being done? This study tracks data such as sales orders or employee records as they go from department to department to see exactly how records are processed and who handles them.

The study is conducted by an office automation committee or team, which is usually made up of a small, representative number of managers and employees. The team should include an administrator whose job it is to handle the paperwork and conduct cost-benefit analyses. The administrator is usually a manager who can make decisions about such things as expenditures and budget allocations.

Another essential member of the team is the **office automation (OA) specialist.** This person knows about automated office systems. He or she is responsible for ensuring compatibility between old and new systems and for explaining the various features of a computer system, such as electronic mail, to the users. The OA specialist also writes the specifications for the new system, works with vendors of computer systems, and oversees the installation of the new system.

The third essential member of the team is the trainer. This person is the users' representative on the committee. It is the trainer's job to generate enthusiasm among the workers for the new system, to explain the system to the users, to arrange for training, and to be available to help the users when they have problems operating the new system.

System Design

Once the office automation study is complete, the team must determine how a computer system can be designed to perform the tasks and functions identified in the systems analysis. It must determine, for example, which employees need document processors, which need data processing equipment, which need communications hardware, and which need letter-quality or graphics printers.

Remember that an automated system not only performs functions faster but also performs functions in different ways. It is up to the automation team to determine, step by step, exactly how the new system will perform each function and how it will change the way that function is performed now. Often the results of the analysis are presented graphically in a **flowchart.** A flowchart uses standard symbols to illustrate the flow of information or work in a system (see figure 17.7).

Consider, for example, the function of preparing and distributing in-house memos. In the traditional office, the process follows the path shown in figure 17.8. A manager dictates a memo to a

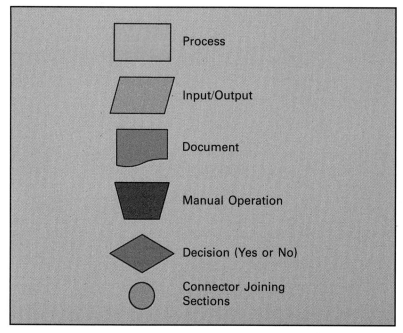

Figure 17.7 These standard symbols are used in flowcharts to depict how information or work flows through a system.

secretary, who transcribes the tape and keys a copy of it. The manager proofreads and approves the memo, and the secretary then makes the required number of copies on a copying machine. Finally, the secretary files a copy of the memo and hand delivers or mails a copy to each recipient.

In the automated office, the process may take different paths, as shown in figure 17.9. Managers may dictate memos, or they may use microcomputers to originate copy. They may either edit, proofread, and file memos themselves or have this done by their secretary. The manager or the secretary can then send the memos instantly by electronic mail to all the recipients. This requires that all recipients have their own terminals, electronic mailboxes, and access codes. They would need to be trained to use the terminals and the electronic mail program. If recipients are located in distant offices, the computer system will have to include telephone modems and communications software.

Notice that in this example some of the secretary's functions of transcribing, keying, copying, and delivering memos have been transferred to the manager and the computer system. As a result, both the manager's functions and the secretary's functions and responsibilities have changed.

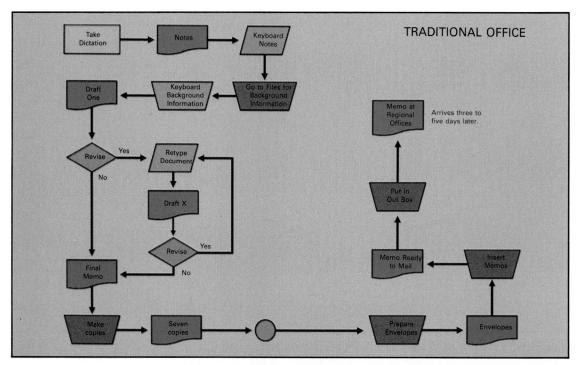

Figure 17.8 In order to determine how automation will alter the performance of a particular task, a flowchart showing the steps followed in a traditional system is created.

To plan an automated system for each function, the automation team must answer many technical questions. These include the following:

• What is the physical layout of the company? Is it contained entirely on one floor of one building, is it spread out over several floors, or is it housed in different buildings?

• What specific equipment is needed at each workstation, in each office, and on each floor, and how can the pieces of equipment be wired or connected to each other?

• How will existing files be transferred to the new media? Some files may need to be transferred from paper to disks; others may be transferred by computer from magnetic tape to disks.

• Which machines will communicate with other machines? How can the old and new systems be made compatible? What communications equipment is required?

• How can the computer's files be protected? Should each workstation have access to every file in the system, or should access be limited to certain users? For example, should access to pay-

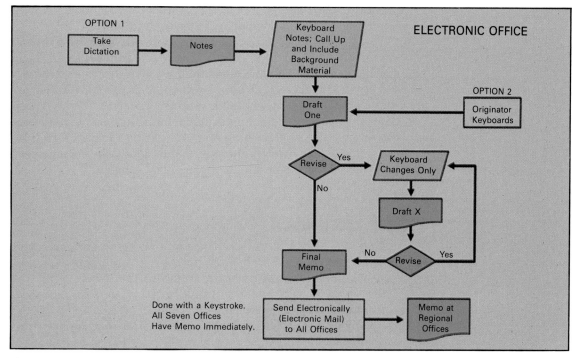

Figure 17.9 A flowchart showing how these same steps can be carried out in an automated system helps the automation specialist analyze the effects of automating the procedure and determine the hardware and software necessary to improve productivity.

roll records be limited only to personnel in the payroll department? What kind of access should each user have? The team may decide that one user may only read a computer file while another may be able to both read it and change it.

• How will the new system change job functions and responsibilities? The clerk whose job has included taking telephone purchase orders and passing them on to other departments for processing by hand may now be required not only to take the orders but also to process them from beginning to end on a computer terminal.

Software Applications Design

Selecting the hardware for a new computer system is only part of the automation team's job. Another major part is selecting the software to be used in the system. Large corporations that still use mainframe computers to carry out applications such as payroll and inventory control probably would have their programmers write programs that allow minicomputers and microcomputers to gain access to these operations. Or, companies may purchase software and apply it to their situation.

The automation team's technical expert can work with the users to help them find the right software and tailor it to meet the specific needs of their business applications. This may mean selecting spreadsheet and data processing programs for the accounting department, choosing graphics programs for the engineering department, buying desktop publishing software for the copying center, and deciding on the right document processing, communications, electronic mail, and database management programs for the general use of the entire company.

Implementation

Once the system is designed, the automation team must oversee its implementation. It must purchase the equipment, supervise its installation, and train employees to use it. First the team prepares **bid specifications,** a list of requirements describing the kind of equipment the company needs and what the company expects the equipment to do. Then it receives and evaluates bids from the vendors who are hoping to sell their system to the company. The team selects the vendor whose bid comes closest in price and features to what it is looking for. Then the team enters into contract negotiations with the vendor. The contract negotiations determine the actual costs, set the requirements for training and maintenance, establish the installation timetable, and so on. The automation team needs to work very closely with the vendor as implementation proceeds. Together they draw up diagrams of each workstation and installation site, detailing requirements for wiring, telephone connections, and cabling, for example. They formulate a training plan so that users are ready to operate the new system as soon as it is installed, and they develop a delivery schedule so that the pieces of equipment can be delivered in stages as each site is prepared and each group of employees completes its training.

Training is an important part of implementation, because an automated system is of little value if the employees will not use it or if they underuse it. The users must fully accept the system and quickly become comfortable using it. Commonly, the vendor trains the company's supervisors to use the new system, and they, in turn, train their employees. The vendor and the software supplier usually provide documentation, consisting of handbooks and manuals, that explains how to use the system and its software.

Maintenance

Nothing is more costly to a company than an automated system that is frequently "down," or not working, particularly when the company or any of its departments cannot function without the system. If an airline's computers are not functioning and it cannot make reservations, customers go to other airlines. If a daily newspaper cannot produce an edition because its computer system is out of commission, it loses thousands of dollars in advertising revenue and newsstand sales. Other kinds of businesses experience similar losses of revenue and customer goodwill when their computer systems are not working for any length of time. Proper maintenance is, therefore, critically important to ensure that breakdowns occur infrequently and that when they do occur, repairs are made as quickly as possible.

When a company purchases a new computer system, it usually asks for a service contract, which is an agreement that the vendor will provide major maintenance service and replacement parts. The vendor might also be required to solve software problems. Large companies may also employ in-house computer service and repair specialists, and smaller companies sometimes designate one or two employees, such as production supervisors, to receive some technical training in computer maintenance from the vendor so that they can solve minor problems quickly. When the vendor and the automation team draw up a maintenance plan, they must take into consideration the need to service and repair equipment in distant branch offices as well as in the main office.

Maintenance also includes special "housekeeping" chores such as periodically purging the computer's memory banks to keep them from becoming overloaded, developing security codes, and even such simple things as making sure all the terminals are turned off at the end of each day. More and more office workers today are undertaking the responsibility for these basic tasks. In large offices one person may be designated and trained to perform the housekeeping function.

Review and Modification

Nothing has changed more rapidly within the last few years than the computer industry. What computers could not do five years ago they do today, and nobody can predict what they will be able to do five years from now. Some companies that automated early on in the electronic revolution have already replaced their computer systems two or three times, and their first

Figure 17.10 After an automated system is implemented, it is monitored by a specialist who recommends revisions based on the needs of the workers and the goals of the organization.

system would seem rather primitive if it were compared with their current equipment.

It will be up to the automation team or to the automation specialist to keep track of changes and advances in computer hardware and software and to recommend improvements for the system when new, more efficient components are developed.

In addition, the automation needs of the company may change from time to time as conditions change. The company may need new machines to help produce a new product, or it may hire more employees and need more workstations. Then the automation team will be responsible for designing the new elements of the system and ensuring that they are compatible with the existing equipment.

 ## MANAGING AUTOMATED OFFICE SYSTEMS

The business office used to be regarded as a place where a series of separate tasks was carried out: dictating, taking dictation, typing, filing, mailing, telephoning, and so on. But office automation has changed the way people look at and describe what occurs in the business office. As we have emphasized throughout this book, the electronic office is now seen as a place where information is processed, and each task is part of IPSOD (input, process, storage, output, distribution), an integrated system to carry out that function.

The way in which people use automation in the business office has also changed. At first, only specially trained personnel operated the large mainframe computers in the data processing department, and they needed technically trained managers to oversee their operations. In the mid-1960s, automated office systems came to be referred to as **management information systems (MIS).** The phrase was intended to stress the idea that managing information was the function of these "keepers of the data."

The development of management information systems created the need for trained personnel to help design and operate them. Colleges and universities began to offer undergraduate and graduate degrees in MIS. These technically trained managers represented a new element in the business office.

Today the movement away from large, centralized automation and toward user-friendly computer systems and purchased software is changing the way information systems are managed. Now microcomputers have become a familiar tool in the office, and virtually everyone works with them to some extent. Businesses no longer need large numbers of technically trained managers. Instead, they need people who can understand office functions and procedures and can adapt automated equipment to perform them.

Operating and managing in an automated office still requires some specialized training, but in many job categories, this training can be acquired on the job or with minimal additional schooling. A secretary, for example, can become a document processing trainer or a supervisor. These jobs require only a little additional training in the same technical skills the secretary already uses to operate his or her document processing equipment. This change is opening up many new career paths for traditional office workers.

SUMMARY

- The three main functions of managers are to plan, to implement, and to evaluate company operations.

- A major task of managers is to make decisions. The basic steps in decision making are defining the problem, gathering information, generating and evaluating options, and choosing an option.

- Two useful tools to use in decision making are brainstorming and modeling.

- The main functions of supervisors are to hire, train, assign, motivate, and evaluate employees.

- Job descriptions explain the functions and tasks of a job, list the minimum qualifications and training for the job, and tell employees who their supervisors are.

- Supervisors need to delegate work to others and to match their employees' abilities and preferences to jobs.

- Supervisors should evaluate employees informally all the time and should hold formal performance evaluations once a year.

- Leadership style is the manner in which managers carry out their functions.

- Management by objectives involves employees in planning and carrying out corporate goals.

- The characteristics of a successful manager include basic job skills, a good self-image, good communication skills, the ability to see the big picture, and initiative and self-motivation.

- The goal of office automation is to increase productivity by saving time and money or by expanding business to generate more income.

- To plan the automation of an office, you must determine how much it will cost, what benefits it will provide, and how the staff will react to it.

- Before a company can automate, it must appoint a team of managers and workers to perform a systems study or analysis.

- In the future, people will need less knowledge about automation and more knowledge of office procedures and functions to manage the electronic office.

VOCABULARY

- long-term planning
- short-term planning
- organization
- evaluating
- team approach
- brainstorming
- modeling

- statement of objectives
- bottom line
- cost-benefit ratio
- multitasking
- integrated systems
- incompatible
- system study or systems analysis

- management by objectives (MBO)
- initial training
- in-service training
- job description
- delegate
- motivate
- office automation (OA) specialist
- flowchart
- bid specifications
- management information systems (MIS)

CHECKING YOUR UNDERSTANDING

1. Describe the four major functions of managers and supervisors. What are the five steps involved in the decision-making function and how do they relate to any process you complete?
2. Describe how brainstorming and modeling can be used in the team approach to management.
3. What skills and abilities are identified with good managers? How can these skills and abilities be used by a manager who practices management by objectives?
4. Describe the types of training you can use within an organization to ready employees for their positions. How can managers contribute to the training process?
5. Part of a manager's or supervisor's duties are to prepare job descriptions. What content is usually contained on a job description? How can a job description help in hiring an employee?
6. After employees have been on the job for a specified time period, they are evaluated. Describe the supervisor's role in employee evaluation. What tools do they use to help them evaluate an employee?
7. As a manager or supervisor you may be involved in the process of automating the entire office or only a part of the office functions. To automate an office you should be able to answer four basic questions. What are these questions? What challenges do you face in answering these questions?
8. Describe a systems analysis. What is the process you would use to conduct a systems analysis?

THINKING THROUGH PROCEDURES

1. Think about a job you have had—paying or nonpaying—and about the person who supervised you. How would you characterize your supervisor's leadership or management style? Write down your thoughts in two columns, with the strengths in one column and the weaknesses in the other. If you had

been in your supervisor's position, what would you have done differently?

2. Find two or three people in your circle of family or friends who have been promoted recently to more responsible jobs in their companies. Ask them what steps they took to move into their new positions and what kinds of problems they encountered when they assumed the new responsibilities. Ask them to tell you how they overcame some of the problems and to explain what they might do differently the next time.

3. With a small group of students in your class, set up a decision-making exercise. As a group, select a "problem" to work on: for example, planning an event or choosing a new computer system for classroom use. Follow the decision-making steps outlined in this chapter, and record each step on a chalkboard. Brainstorm for solutions, evaluate them, and eventually choose one. Make note of the kinds of information your group felt it needed to make a choice. If you could, how would you obtain and analyze that information? Decide and agree on how you would evaluate your choice. Did anyone in the group emerge as a leader? When you have completed the exercise, write down at least three things you learned about decision making by doing this.

chapter **18**

ADVANCING IN YOUR CAREER

■ BUILDING YOUR BUSINESS CAREER

Office support was once a limited career. A good secretary could progress up the career ladder from pool typist to private or executive secretary, or even administrative assistant, but that was about as far as he or she could go. This is not true anymore. Technology not only has changed the way in which office workers perform their jobs but also has vastly increased the opportunities for new jobs and for career advancement.

Today you can enter the business world at an entry-level job such as secretary, data-entry clerk, or word processing operator and move up through the ranks to a specialist, supervisory, or management position. Or once you have gained skills in one company, you can move on to another company that offers better advancement opportunities. If you specialize in one particular area of technology, such as systems analysis or telecommunications, you can join a company that provides these services for businesses, or you can even go into business for yourself.

What you make of your career depends largely on what you put into it. You will not walk into your first job knowing all there is to know about the technology, procedures, and skills we have discussed in this book. Little by little, you will learn these skills, and you can speed up the process by planning your career carefully and by continuing to educate yourself throughout your working life.

This chapter is designed to help you plan your own career. We will discuss the attitudes you must possess to succeed, some of the career paths open to you, and take you step-by-step through the procedures you need to follow to acquire your first job and any subsequent jobs. We will also tell you how to assess your progress as you continue to grow and change in your own chosen career.

ATTITUDES FOR SUCCESS

Businesses are looking for individuals who possess not only knowledge but the communication skills to interact and manage well. As an entry-level employee, you may not always use these skills every day, but when you are hired, managers and supervisors look for those qualities so that there is promise of advancement for you. Once an individual learns the company from the bottom, he or she becomes very valuable. The knowledge these individuals bring to management and supervisory positions is necessary to the continuation of normal business practices.

Throughout this text you have learned to work with technology, people, and procedures. You have developed your knowledge and your skills. Underlying all of this, you must possess and practice professionalism, human relations, and leadership skills.

Professionalism

Part of being a professional means you act and dress according to the situation around you. Professional attributes include those of possessing knowledge, having good oral and written communication skills, understanding the practices and policies of the business, and being able to carry out these practices and policies with good human relations skills.

Think about persons who you think are professional in the way they accomplish their jobs. Executives portray professionalism by being decisive managers and using the team approach to decision making. Administrative assistants portray professionalism by possessing and using their organization and communication skills to accomplish the tasks required of them in the office. Data-entry people portray professionalism by working hard to enter data accurately and understanding the importance of their tasks to the organization as a whole.

Being a professional is an attitude. Any individual can be a professional if he or she possesses knowledge and communication skills that are used and are effective in an office. This attitude is portrayed not only by the way individuals act and carry out their duties but by the way they dress and approach others. Professional individuals understand the need to dress appropriately for an office setting, not as though working is a leisure activity. We will discuss appropriate dress later in this chapter. Along with a professional approach and attitude, good employees use effective human relations skills and are able to fill leadership roles when necessary.

Human Relations

In the previous chapter we discussed the importance of managers using the team approach to decision making. These same ideas are necessary for anyone to carry out effective human relations in the office. For example, two co-workers, Eliza and Richard, both data-entry employees, are working diligently to enter their data accurately by their end-of-day deadline. Richard is interrupting Eliza constantly with small talk. Eliza could be rude and yell at Richard that she is being bothered and does not want to hear these trivial things. Or Eliza can use good human relations skills and politely tell Richard that she would love to hear his stories some other time but she really needs to finish her work today.

People skills, as they are sometimes called, involve the art of motivating others, letting people know when you are happy for their successes, empathetic towards their disappointments, and appreciative of their work. It is the art of using a positive atti-

Figure 18.1 Having good relations with your co-workers is as important as getting along well with your supervisor and clients.

tude in potentially unpleasant situations, such as with Eliza and Richard, and using the correct words with the correct tone at the right time. Motivation of others is necessary for managers and supervisors to be effective at their jobs. The ability to motivate and to initiate new ideas and carry out those ideas can be labeled leadership.

Leadership

As an employee, you will be in a **subordinate** position. This means that you will have others directing your work activities, and that you must carry out those activities assigned to you. Subordinates as well as managers, however, must be leaders. Leaders have the skills to complete their assigned tasks but go one step further and look for ways to do better. Leaders follow through on assigned tasks, take responsibility for the quality of their work, and are team players. Leaders are able to motivate when necessary but are also able to follow when necessary. In your role as an employee, you will use your leadership skills to work productively and improve your working environment.

 # CAREER PLANNING

Right now you are probably ready to start your **job campaign,** or the process of finding a position in a company related to your education and experience. Over the years you have chosen the exciting area of office support to begin your career. You may have consciously set your career goals, or you may now be evaluating your goals and redirecting your life-style. Either way you must be prepared to begin the job campaign process with all the confidence and skill development you have demonstrated in your educational career.

Since you have chosen this means of education, and you are nearly finished, you need to look at ways your career can develop in the future.

 ## SETTING CAREER GOALS

Some people's careers are characterized by careful planning and preparation, while others are shaped by unexpected opportunities and luck. A person's lifetime work history can be called a **career path.** A career path is a progression of jobs or positions that build upon one another as a person develops skills, knowledge, and experience.

A career path may take the form of a career ladder. A **career ladder** involves a logical succession from the initial entry-level position through promotions to various supervisory and managerial levels within a company's organizational structure. When a person wants to take advantage of an opportunity that is not a promotion, he or she might decide to make a **lateral move.** This involves taking a different job at the same level of responsibility and pay as the old one, or at a similar level, in the hope that the new job will provide opportunities for progress along a career path.

Some people's career paths are marked by **career moves—** changes from one department or field to another, sometimes related and sometimes not. For example, someone who has worked for a while in information management might make a career move to marketing. To make a career move, it might be necessary to take a lower-level position in order to get a start in the new area.

The path your own career takes will almost certainly involve a combination of careful planning and sheer chance. There is no way for you to know exactly what the future holds for you, but the planning you do will prepare you to take whatever opportunities come your way. When you think you are ready for a promotion, you can do many things to stand out in a crowd of competitors. You can learn as much as possible about the equipment you operate, you can take courses—for example, in management, accounting, or business administration—and you can develop the interpersonal and managerial skills discussed in earlier chapters. Then when an opportunity is available, you will be ready to step forward and be recognized.

DEVELOPING A PERSONAL PROFILE

Before you can plan a career, you need to take time to assess your background, personality, and life goals. In other words, you need to develop a **personal profile.** You then have to assess the job opportunities and the companies offering them to see how closely you can match your personal profile to the employment requirements. The better the fit, the better your chances of success.

You are more likely to find the right fit if you have a realistic understanding of your abilities and personality. Here are some questions to ask yourself:

• What skills have I learned in my schooling, from previous jobs, and from my hobbies and social activities? (Some examples might include word processing, speaking a foreign language, working with people, writing, doing math, organizing events, and using a computer.)

• What kinds of activities satisfy me, and what kinds of work situations do I seem to like best? (For example, do you like working with people or with things? alone or with a group? Do you like to take responsibility for others, or do you prefer to make an individual contribution? Do you like working with words or with numbers, or do you enjoy a combination of both?)

• What do I hope to accomplish in the short run or in the long run in my life, and what values do I have that might affect the career I choose? (For example, at this time you may be looking for an entry-level position, but what will you want to be doing five or ten years from now? What things hold the highest value for you? money? security? authority? These priorities in your value system will make a difference in the path your career takes.)

Many of your answers to these questions will change as you grow older and your experiences and circumstances change. You may want to start out in a small business office, where you can experience a wide range of office duties, or you may want to work in a large company, where you can specialize in a specific area such as information processing in an advertising agency or medical center. If you are single, you may welcome frequent company transfers so that you can live in different places. If you are married and have a family, you may want to stay in one place.

OFFICE SUPPORT OPPORTUNITIES

Every company, whether it manufactures goods or provides services, has a business office. You may find yourself working for a doctor, a lawyer, an insurance company, a construction contractor, a lumber company, a government agency, a jewelry wholesaler, a school, a bank—any one of thousands of different kinds of businesses and public agencies. The chances are very good that you will be able to match your personal abilities and goals to a company whose product or service interests you.

CAREERS IN TODAY'S OFFICE

What career paths are available in offices, and what kinds of job skills are needed for them? The major categories are de-

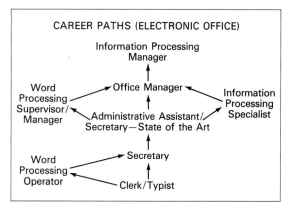

Figure 18.2 The electronic office has opened up new career paths for office workers.

scribed in the pages that follow. Be aware that although they are discussed separately, in today's office you can cross over from one career path or ladder to another (see figure 18.2). Within each category, jobs are listed in order of progression, from entry-level positions to those at the management level. To succeed in each area, you must be well organized, flexible, and attentive to detail, and you must have good communication and adaption skills.

ADMINISTRATIVE SUPPORT

In traditional roles, administrative support workers are mainly secretaries and clerks, who perform all routine secretarial tasks and functions. They range from entry-level secretaries, who do routine information processing, to administrative assistants, who work closely with top managers and oversee the work of other secretaries and assistants. Standard administrative support positions are described below.

Secretary

A secretary is the basic job classification, which is known by several other titles: associate administrative secretary, secretary assistant, level I secretary, and so on. In large organizations several levels exist in this classification, with the title indicating the level. Higher levels represent more experience and ability. At all levels tasks include traditional secretarial duties, such as scheduling, taking and transcribing dictation, processing correspondence, answering telephones, greeting visitors, opening mail, and filing.

Administrative Assistant

The position of administrative assistant requires some traditional secretarial functions, such as processing documents and filing. Reporting to only one principal, a top officer in the organization, means that this individual may also be in charge of maintaining schedules and arranging meetings, helping with research, and overseeing the activities of other office support personnel.

Office Manager

In small, medium, and large organizations an office manager with good technology and managerial skills may be hired to oversee the activities and functions of an office. This person may be in charge of the bookkeepers, data-entry clerks, information management support, and receptionists. In other organizations this person may be in charge of a word processing center or central dictation unit.

Some administrative support positions cross over into managerial duties. The individual is responsible for the work of one principal but may also be responsible for two or more employees who assist in daily activities. This position demands increased skills in creating, retrieving, synthesizing, and making available information and requires knowledge of word and data processing, electronic mail, and electronic records management.

There is a twofold reason for these changes in tasks. First, with routine tasks being automated, administrative support people have time to devote to more creative tasks. Second, the entry of sophisticated equipment into the office increases the value of those operating it. Managers do not have the time to learn to operate the equipment. They rely on administrative support personnel, and the more tasks the electronic equipment performs, the greater the reliance. This translates into greater opportunities for those working in an office support position.

Information Processing Specialist

An information processing specialist is responsible for operating the integrated information system and providing site support to system users and administrators. Emphasis in this position is on coordinating the system to improve communication and information access through the use of software applications. Responsibilities can also include training and administering standards.

Information Processing Manager

An information processing manager is responsible for providing support to those departments involved in the planning, installation, training/use/operation, and maintenance of integrated information processing systems. Primary emphasis is on assistance and support services associated with equipment and software selection, physical installation and arrangement of office workstations, and the development of information schemas and systems. Responsibilities also include training and administering standards to ensure success of the automated office concept.

Word Processing Specialist

The processing of documents on a computer will continue to be an important secretarial function in an electronic office, but in many large companies, word processing has become an entirely separate job category, with many entry-level jobs and levels of advancement. In these companies, the word processing center has replaced the typing pool, and word processing operators have replaced typists. Word processing jobs include the following titles.

Word Processing Trainee A word processing trainee must be able to use word processing software and transfer these skills to another system if necessary. It is imperative that this person have transcription skills and a knowledge of grammar, spelling, formatting, and other basic secretarial skills. Trainees transcribe dictation and process rough drafts and other documents. These employees may be asked to produce, revise, and format lengthy, complicated reports such as legal documents and medical reports and also be skilled at preparing statistical tables. Proofreading and filing/retrieving skills are imperative.

Data-Entry Clerk Also called a keyboard/input operator, a data-entry clerk an entry-level position requires little technical knowledge or experience operating a computer terminal. The data-entry clerk must have good data-entry skills and be able to enter data and figures quickly and accurately. In many companies this position requires employees to work different shifts.

Programmer A programmer must know one or more computer languages and be able to design, write, and test programs so they fit a company's specific needs. Qualities this person must possess include the ability to be logical, organized, and patient.

Systems Analyst A systems analyst works with managers and supervisors to determine their needs and then designs a group of programs to carry out the required functions. This person also designs hardware, trains employees to operate the system, and oversees programmers.

TELECOMMUNICATIONS

Career opportunities in telecommunications are expected to increase as more and more companies integrate their electronic equipment and as the demand for instant communication between offices and between companies continues to grow. People are needed to oversee the sending and receiving of electronic mail, to arrange teleconferences, and to set up and maintain telecommunications networks. The person in this field needs to be a decision maker and problem solver and also needs to be technically oriented. A person could move from any other office career path to telecommunications jobs such as the following.

Technician

A technician helps set up and maintain electronic equipment and provides technical support for teleconferences.

Distribution Services Manager

A distribution services manager supervises the operation of a company's mail system, including facsimile machines, electronic copiers, and computers. Coordination of telecommunications with word processing and data processing activities is one of the main duties of this position.

Telecommunications Manager

A telecommunications manager manages the planning, installation, and day-to-day operation of the telecommunications system and oversees supervisors and technicians.

Figure 18.3, A, B The atmosphere you will be working in and the size of the company are important career considerations. Of the two work environments shown here, which one do you find more appealing?

RECORDS/INFORMATION MANAGEMENT

Secretaries, file clerks, and data processing personnel once kept business records as part of their daily routine, but some electronic offices now maintain separate records centers in which some record-keeping functions are coordinated. The management of records and information involves archiving, filing, handling micrographics, and destroying records. Archiving is the preservation of records for scholarly and historical purposes. Filing is, of course, the process of sorting and storing records. Micrographics involves transforming paper records to microfilm or microfiche for more compact and safer storage. Records/information management personnel also periodically destroy records that are outdated or no longer needed.

Records/information management personnel are usually in charge of paper, computerized, film, and optical records. Their jobs generally include database management, that is, maintaining, updating, and managing a company's computerized databases. Some of the jobs in records/information management include the following.

Records and Information Technician

A records and information technician is knowledgeable in the maintenance of specialized records systems such as medical records, engineering documentation, personnel records, etc. This person's duties can include assisting systems analysis, establishing and maintaining files, updating inventories, maintaining operating procedures, and preparing records for transfer. Other clerical duties may be assigned as well. This position usually requires an associate degree or work experience in the records area.

Micrographics Technician

The duties of a micrographics technician include maintaining equipment, procedures, and controls necessary to support micrographics operations, including quality control, indexes, and production. To become a micrographics technician, you must have a diploma or associate degree, with emphasis or knowledge in micrographics.

Senior Micrographics Clerk

The senior micrographics clerk receives and prepares documents for microfilming, operates microfilming equipment, reviews and inspects developed film, is responsible for filming nonstandard documents, maintains production logs, performs routine user maintenance of equipment, assists with special projects, and ensures disposal of source documents according to procedures.

Records Supervisor

A records supervisor is responsible for overseeing the workers who maintain a central records file. With specialized knowledge of common filing errors, this person helps retrieve lost or missing files. A files supervisor also oversees the periodic disposal of obsolete files, in accordance with company guidelines and legal requirements.

Records and Information Manager

A records and information manager is responsible for managing long-range plans and resource projections. This person develops procedures with regard to basic organization policies, determines future personnel and equipment needs, establishes procedures for systems analysis, and may work with vendors and contractors in meeting the goals of the company. This is a managerial job that usually requires four years of college and a degree. A records manager is involved in all phases of information management and has the ultimate responsibility for seeing that files are organized efficiently and that they are reviewed for transfer and/or destruction periodically. Many records managers are certified by ARMA, the Association of Records Managers and Administrators. Certification is based on specific training and a demonstration of competency in the field of records management.

Archivist

An archivist is more likely to exist in government offices, libraries, and educational institutions than in business organizations. Archivists determine which records should be preserved, arrange the records, and take precautions to protect the records from environmental damage.

Forms Manager

A forms manager oversees the types, quantity, and quality of forms generated in an organization.

If you want further information on these or other careers in information management, consult a current edition of the *Occupational Outlook Handbook* or research careers in your placement center.

 # JOB APPLICATION PROCESS

You have set some career and personal goals and have given thought to the kind of business that interests you. Now it is time to find a job. Here are the steps you will need to follow to find a job:

- Determine your career and entry-level employment goals.
- Research companies that have these positions.
- Prepare a résumé.
- Prepare a letter of application or inquiry.
- Complete required documentation, such as application forms, transcript requests, references requests.
- Obtain an interview.
- Follow up on the interview.

At the end of process, either you or the employer will decide if this is the right job for you. If it is not, then you begin the process again.

DETERMINE YOUR GOALS

Before you can begin searching for prospective employers, you need to set some short- and long-term goals for yourself. Short-term goals include an entry-level position, and long-term goals include where you want to be in five or ten years. You must also search inside yourself and determine how you function and what makes you the worker you are. If you are a self-starter, then maybe you are able to begin in a position that requires less direction. If you believe you succeed better with some direction, then your first job needs to reflect this. If you are not aware of your goals and your work style, then you may not succeed at your first position. Success at this stage is an important part of your career plan.

Write down your goals, list your strengths and weaknesses, and make a decision as to what type of position you want to pursue based on this knowledge.

RESEARCH COMPANIES AND POSITIONS

There are many places where you can look for prospective entry-level positions and employers, starting right at your school. Some of them are described following.

School Placement Services

Many schools offer placement services, and employers may even come to your school to meet prospective applicants and to describe the kinds of jobs they have to offer. Find out where your school's placement office is, and visit it regularly. Usually, the placement office maintains a bulletin board on which job announcements and visits by company recruiters are posted. Your school placement office will not find you a job, but it can help you write a résumé, line up references, and research potential employers. Many placement offices will keep copies of students' credentials on file and send them to prospective employers at the students' request.

Employment Agencies

An employment agency is in the business of bringing job hunters and companies in search of personnel together. It attempts to match a job hunter's education, work experience, and employment preferences to the needs of the companies that come to it for referrals. Employment agencies that place office workers are almost always fee-paid agencies; that is, they charge the prospective employer, not the job hunter, a percentage of the employee's salary for the first year. That fee does not come out of the employee's salary. If you find an agency that requires you to pay a fee, you may want to do more research.

Temporary Employment Agencies

One way to enter the job market is to sign up with a temporary employment agency that supplies clerical workers and word processing operators to businesses for short periods of time. If you work for a temporary service, you gain valuable on-the-job experience, you learn how to operate different kinds of computer systems, and you get to see how different business offices function.

If you go to an agency that does both permanent and temporary placements, it can put you into a temporary job while it lines up employment interviews for you. Sometimes you can also find a permanent job with a company that has employed you in a temporary position and likes your performance.

Newspapers

The help-wanted ads in newspapers are a very good source of employment opportunities. Get into the habit of reading the classified advertisements for job listings. Large-city newspapers often have extensive listings grouped together in categories such as *business, education, professional, office,* and *clerical.* Employers often purchase display advertisements describing their company and the career opportunities and benefits they offer. Reading these ads helps you gain an impression of companies for which you might like to work.

Networking

Often people find jobs because they hear of job openings from friends or acquaintances. This form of job seeking is called **networking** because it involves using the connections you have with people to advance your career. The advantage of word-of-mouth contacts is that your source may be able to answer many of your questions about the job and describe frankly the company and your prospective co-workers. The friend might also know someone at the company and be able to put in a good word for you. Another advantage of word of mouth is that you might hear of a job opening before it is advertised.

Blind Letters and Calls

You might find a job by sending your résumé with a cover letter inquiring about a position to a company for which you want to work. Try to follow up the letter with a visit to the personnel office. This could be a good way to introduce yourself to a prospective employer, who may think of you if a job opening occurs. Once in a while, but rarely, a company may be looking for new talent and create a job opportunity if the right individual comes along. Showing this kind of initiative in seeking a job could generate a positive interest in you.

PREPARE A RÉSUMÉ

A **résumé** is a brief summary of your educational and employment history, as well as a means to express your special skills and abilities.

Your résumé should be clearly written and well organized. Avoid vague, flowery phrases, and make sure your spelling, grammar, and punctuation are correct. If possible, keep your résumé to one page. Some employers only scan résumés and will not take the time to read a long résumé.

You may prepare your résumé with word processing software, or you may use desktop publishing software for a more professional look. If you prepare it, you can tailor each résumé to a particular employer and the job opportunity you are seeking, but you will have to edit and print out a new résumé each time you apply for a job. Always use good quality paper and a laser printer. If you do not have this equipment available, have your résumé printed by a professional printer. Many times they will give you the data disk of the résumé after they have completed the printout. If you use this approach, you will not be able to alter the résumé to fit each employment opportunity. Whichever way you produce your résumé, avoid ornate typefaces or over-dramatic layouts that make the résumé difficult to read.

Employers use resumes to screen job applicants so that they do not waste valuable time interviewing job hunters who do not possess the education, training, or experience they need for a specific job. For example, a manager who needs to hire a computer programmer can sort through a pile of résumés quickly and pick out the applicants who list training or experience in programming. The manager may then arrange interviews with several of those applicants. Using résumés to screen job seekers not only saves the manager's time but also saves you the time and expense of interviewing for jobs for which you are not qualified.

Résumés usually contain the following information (see the example in figure 18.4).

Name and Address

Include the address you are currently living at. If you have another permanent address, include it because you may not be at your present address for very long.

David A. Diaz

1632 Hillside Ave.
Rockford, IL 61109
(815) 555-2805

POSITION SOUGHT:

Administrative Assistant

EDUCATION:

East Chicago Community College, Chicago, IL
Office Education Training Program (Graduation Pending June 1987)
Specialized in Business courses and attained:

1. Typewriting speed, 60 wam; shorthand speed, 120 wam.
2. An understanding and operating knowledge of transcribing machines, the IBM Personal Computer, and business applications software.
3. A working knowledge of electronic calculators.
4. An understanding of human relations in dealing with coworkers, superiors and subordinates.

Maintained a B average.

WORK EXPERIENCE:

VANGUARD INSURANCE COMPANY, 4500 Michigan Avenue, Chicago, IL 60653
♦ <u>Secretary/Assistant Office Manager</u> - September 1990 to present.
♦ Supervisor: Mrs. Anna Robinson. Telephone: (312) 555-9530, Extension 419.

McCARTHY'S CATERING, 93 West Mill Road, Rockford, IL 61104.
♦ <u>Kitchen aid</u> - September 1988 to June 1990.
♦ Supervisor: Mr. Maurice Doher. Telephone: (815) 555-4987, Extension 2167.

OTHER EXPERIENCE AND ACTIVITIES:

Member of Chicago Chapter of Illinois Office Education Association.
Chairperson of Future Business Leaders of America Fund-Raising Drive to raise $2000 for club activities.
Member of Illinois chapter of Phi Beta Lambda.

REFERENCES:

Mr. Richard Loo, Office Manager, Vanguard Insurance Company, 4500 Michigan Avenue, Chicago, IL 60653, (312) 555-9530.

Ms. Jennifer Best, Dean, East Chicago Community College, 4398 West 22 Street, Chicago, IL 60616, (312) 555-9208.

Figure 18.4 This is an example of a commonly used résumé format.

Job Objective

In a study of Fortune 500 companies, they were asked if a career objective or job objective was important to list on a résumé. The majority of companies stated that a job objective is helpful to them in hiring employees.

Employment History

You can list your employment history either in reverse chronological order or in descending order of importance. If you choose reverse chronological order, list the last job you held first, the second-to-last job next, and so on. If you choose to list your jobs in order of importance, list the job in which you exercised the most authority, earned the highest salary, or held the most responsibility first, then the next most important job, and so on. Your employment history should tell you which presentation is likely to make the best impression on a prospective employer.

Always list the starting and ending dates for each job along with the name of the company, address, and telephone number; the position you held; and a brief explanation of your responsibilities if they are not self-evident from the job title.

Educational Background

Starting with the highest level of school attended, give the date of graduation from each school, the names of the schools, your majors, and the degrees or diplomas earned.

If you attended a college, vocational school, or graduate school but did not graduate, state that you attended the school and give the dates. You can also list the courses you took if they seem relevant to the job you are seeking. Because each person's education is different, you may also want to include major projects or activities you succeeded at in school. Include those items that show your ability to communicate verbally and in writing and show your leadership or organizational skills.

Accomplishments

Give the names of any professional or school organizations you belong to and any offices you hold or have held. Include activities you have participated in and the contribution you made to the organization. Also list any honors you have received for professional, academic, or athletic achievements. Carrying out the duties of a club officer, graduating in the top 10 percent of your class, or joining professional organizations demonstrates your determination to excel and your ability to shoulder responsibility.

Special Abilities and Skills

Can you speak Spanish? Were you the editor of your college paper? Can you operate a video camera? These abilities may give you an advantage over your competition for the job you are seeking.

References

It is up to you to decide whether you want to list references on your résumé. Some people list the names and addresses of three or more professional and educational references; others state that references are available upon request. References may be former employers or supervisors if you have previous work experience, or they may be teachers, guidance counselors, and advisers if you have just completed your schooling.

Always check with the people you intend to list as references beforehand to be sure that they are willing to be listed and that they will recommend you without reservation to a prospective employer. If you have the slightest doubt about whether a person will give you a good report, do not list that person as a reference. You may also obtain letters of recommendation from your references. Keep copies of these in a folder, and take them with you to job interviews, but do not include them with your résumé. Or your school placement office will keep these references on hand with your other credentials and send them to employers upon your request.

PREPARE A LETTER OF APPLICATION OR INQUIRY

Once you have located a prospective employer and prepared a résumé, your next task is to prepare a cover letter to accompany your résumé. There are two types of cover letters. The first is an **application letter.** This form of letter is written when you know there is a position available, and you are applying for it. The other is a **letter of inquiry.** Write this type of letter when you do not know if a position is available, and you want to find out what possibilities there are in this company. In either case, the cover letter explains which job you are applying for, highlights your qualifications for the job, and highlights or expands on the information on your résumé. The cover letter is your chance to make a short sales pitch for yourself. It should lead the employer's attention to the résumé by making direct reference to it (see the example in figure 18.5).

If you are replying to a help-wanted ad, mention the advertisement in your cover letter, and state when and where it appeared. Then explain in one brief paragraph why you feel your education and employment background qualify you for the job. The entire letter should be no more than three or four paragraphs long. The major purpose of the letter is to get an interview so you can further explain how your qualifications fit the position.

If the ad asks you to state your salary requirements, find out what the general salary range is for the job. Your placement of-

1632 Hillside Ave.
Rockford, IL 61109

April 29, 1992

Ms. Anne Jacobs
General Manager
World-Wide Tours
7800 Olive Drive
Downers Grove, IL 60515

Dear Ms. Jacobs:

Will you please consider me an applicant for the administrative assistant position that you
advertised in the April 27 Evening Star. My enclosed resume will support my belief that
I am qualified to handle the job.

I will be graduated from East Chicago Community College on June 16, 1992, and will be
ready for full-time employment anytime after that date. While in college, I maintained a
perfect attendance record and a B average. During my senior year, I have been able to
acquire on-the-job experience as an assistant office manager/secretary for the Vanguard
Insurance Company. Here my duties include taking dictation, transcribing, handling
routine correspondence, and managing the administrative records for the office. In this
position, I have discovered an aptitude and liking for administrative work, and I hope to
pursue this interest in business.

As you will note from my resume, I have participated actively in professional
organizations. Probably the most challenging activity was chairing a successful campaign
to raise $2000 for the Future Business Leaders of America club. Professional involve-
ments, teamwork, and responsibility have become more significant to me because of such
activities.

Will you please allow me a personal interview? If you wish, you may call me at
(815) 555-2805 after 4:30 p.m.

Sincerely yours,

David A. Diaz

Enclosure

**Figure 18.5 A good cover letter should make the employer want to look
at your résumé.**

fice or employment agency, published career guidebooks, and
professional associations should be able to help you find the appropriate salary range. Use that range as a guide to arrive at a
range that would be reasonable on the basis of your current salary and your qualifications and experience. If you ask for too
much, your application may be rejected before you even get an
interview.

The cover letter is also the place to provide information such
as temporary addresses or telephone numbers and to ask for an
interview. If you must travel to a distant city for an interview,
you may want to arrange several interviews in that city over a
one- or two-day period. In your cover letter, tell the company
when you expect to be in the area and ask if it would be possible
to schedule an interview then.

COMPLETE REQUIRED DOCUMENTATION

Some companies ask job seekers to fill out an application form as well as submit a résumé. If you are asked to fill out an application form, read it through first, and then fill it out carefully. Companies often use application forms to judge job seekers' thoroughness and their ability to follow directions. In this case neatness does count. You may also be asked to submit letters of reference or a copy of your educational transcript. Check with your registrar to learn the process they use for sending out transcripts to employers.

Job applicants are often asked to take one or more skills or aptitude tests. The company may ask you to type a sample letter to determine your typing speed. If you are not familiar with the equipment, the tester should allow you a warm-up period. You may also be asked to take a transcription or notetaking test so the company can test your skills. Some companies also test applicants on their writing and mathematical skills.

The employment application may ask you personal questions about such things as age, race, gender, and marital status. Some companies request a birthdate. You are not required by law to answer such questions. You are also not legally required to take any psychological or lie detector tests the company may request. You will have to decide for yourself what to do in these situations. You can simply leave an objectionable question unanswered on the application form, and if you wish to avoid a test, try to decline as gracefully as possible. Be aware, however, that your refusal to answer a question or take a test is likely to reduce your chances of obtaining the job.

OBTAIN AN INTERVIEW

Some companies like to have their human resources departments conduct preliminary interviews and then follow up with an interview by the supervisor for whom the job seeker would work. When you fill out an application or when you attend an interview, you should be shown a job description (see figure 18.6). A job description describes the tasks and functions of a job, the qualifications required, and the accountability or reporting relationships. As you read through the job description, write down any questions that occur to you so that you can get answers to them during the employment interview. The job description is your best measure of how closely your background and career goals match the job to be done.

POSITION DESCRIPTION

Job Title ___Technology Assistant_____

Department ___Management Information Systems___ Location___6th Floor_____

Manager: Name ___Ann Jordan_____ Title___Manager, Technology Services___

1. MAJOR FUNCTION:

Primary emphasis is on using the interactive capabilities of the system to improve the coordination and efficiency of document preparation, storage, and retrieval. The integrated information system may be resident on a local or wide area network, or disk-based at each secretarial station. This position reports to management and in some cases works with the information processing specialist as well.

2. SPECIFIC DUTIES: % Time

1. Establishes station-specific procedures for information   5%
   processing functions, including: document formats,
   electronic file management, document distribution and
   controls, and use and operation of equipment.

   Defines forms and document formatting.

   Develops electronic filing procedures.

   Develops and defines procedures for information/records
   management, determining how informtion will be archived
   and stored.

   Defines document distribution methods and controls.

   Develops procedures for use and operation of equipment.

2. Utilizes new and/or advanced interactive capabilities of   5%
   the integrated information system to improve the efficiency of office functions.

   Maintains a working knowledge of software capabilities.

   Uses new features of software and integrated software
   as appropriate.

3. Maintains the equipment inventory system and prepares   5%
   reports based on data base analyses.

   Uses data base system to build inventory files.

Figure 18.6 Seeing a job description will help you explain how your skills match the requirements of the job.

Preparing for the Interview

The first thing to do to prepare for a job interview is research the company. You can find out about a company from newspaper and magazine articles, business directories, and your local chamber of commerce. Your public library should have back copies of newspapers and magazines from your local community and larger metropolitan areas. In the library's reference section you can find several directories such as *Standard and Poor's Register of Corporations, America's Corporate Families,* and the *Thomas Register of American Manufacturers.*

These books contain information about the products and services a company provides, its annual revenues, the number of employees, its divisions and subsidiaries, the names of its corporate officers, and the stock exchanges that list the company's stock if it is a publicly owned corporation. All of this information will help you form a mental picture of the company so you can ask intelligent and informed questions at your job interview. Similar directories are also available on law firms and doctors. If the company is not publicly owned, then you may have to do some primary research by calling individuals in the company and finding out what type of business it is, who their customers are, how large the business is, and its growth potential.

Next write down all the questions you have about the job, about salary and fringe benefits, and about company policies. The interviewer will probably answer many of these questions during the course of the interview. Then you can ask any questions that have been left unanswered at the end.

Once you have learned as much as you can about the company and determined which questions you plan to ask at the interview, also spend some time trying to anticipate the questions the interviewer is likely to ask you and prepare suitable answers. Questions such as the following are appropriate:

1. Tell me something about yourself.
2. What makes you a good employee?
3. What are your strengths? weaknesses?
4. Why did you choose the school you are at for your program?
5. What types of equipment and software are you familiar with?
6. What are your document processing skills?
7. What do you plan to be doing five years from now?
8. What type of work environment do you function well in?
9. Are you willing to relocate?
10. Hypothetical questions that put you in situations you must solve.

Hypothetical questions may relate to human relations situations such as in the case stated earlier, where data-entry personnel were in a conflict. The interviewer may say, "You are working to meet a deadline. You co-worker is constantly interrupting you to discuss things other than work-related issues. How do you handle this situation?"

Write out your answers to these questions and practice them verbally in front of a mirror. You will be able to determine what your body language is telling the interviewer as well as what your words are saying. The more prepared you are with the answers, the more organized, competent, and professional you will be to the interviewer.

The Interview

The employment interview is usually the first time you are seen by a company representative. First impressions are important, so dress appropriately, be well groomed, and be on time. Image is important and rightly so. When going for a job interview, consider your image. This is not to say that image should replace substance as the measure of a person. It is to say that image—the way you present yourself—is an effective way to communicate. When dressing for an interview, consider what you wish to communicate about yourself.

What you wear should be natural for you *in the situation*. Jeans may be natural to you—but not in a job interview situation. You know from television commercials that companies spend millions of dollars creating an image that will engender trust and confidence. Your prospective employer will be looking for someone with these qualities as well as someone who indicates a serious interest in the job by his or her appearance.

Interview questions such as those described are intended to both ascertain your skills and abilities and explore your personality to determine whether you will fit in with the company team and with the manager's leadership style. Interviewers may ask you to cite specific examples of projects you have completed.

One particularly tough question is the question of salary. Usually, the interviewer will tell you what the company expects to pay for the position, but sometimes an interviewer will ask you what salary you want or expect. If you expect to be asked about salary, prepare for the question beforehand by following the same steps we discussed in the section on cover letters. You can also simply tell the interviewer that you would be willing to accept the prevailing salary for the position.

When it is your turn to ask questions, keep in mind that the questions you ask also reveal something about your personality. Asking questions can make a good impression. It shows that you are interested and aware. Be sure to ask questions about the duties and responsibilities of the position, travel requirements, whom you will report to, how long the position has been available, how many people were in the position in the last three or four years, and other questions that help you understand more about the company. This is your time as well as the company's time to ascertain whether this position is right for you.

Figure 18.7 A good interviewer tells you about the job and the company, asks questions about you, and gives you a chance to ask questions as well.

When the interview is over, you need to know what the next steps should be. Employers usually interview several applicants before they make a job offer, so you will probably have to wait one or two weeks before you can learn whether you have the job. The interviewer should tell you whether he or she will call or write to you and how long you can expect to wait. If you are offered a job at the interview, you can ask for a short time to think about the job offer if you wish.

FOLLOWING UP THE INTERVIEW

Get as much information as possible before accepting a job with a company. Questions about salary, benefits, working hours, and other company policies must be worded tactfully in the interview situation. Many companies provide written brochures to answer many of these questions; however, you may also wish to discuss them with the human resources person who handles your position (rather than with the immediate supervisor).

Evaluating the Position

In order to evaluate the position and determine if it and the company are right for you, you should consider the answers you receive to the following questions.

- What will my hours of work be? Will I have regular lunch hours and breaks?

- If I work overtime, will I be paid, or will I receive compensatory time off?

- May I expect to have an accurate job description so that I will know exactly what is expected of me?

- When will I be eligible for a vacation, and how much vacation time will I receive each year?

- Will I be required to join a union or professional association as a condition of employment?

- What is the salary range for the job, and how often could I expect to receive a raise?

- What is the company's policy regarding sick days, personal leave days, and holidays?

- What fringe benefits will I receive? Is there a medical insurance, dental, eyeglass, or prescription plan?

- Is there a pension plan, and will I be able to contribute to it?

- Does the company have an employee credit union?

- What is the company's policy regarding maternity and paternity leave? Does the company provide day-care facilities for the children of employees?

- Does the company have a stock purchase or profit-sharing plan?

- Does the company pay bonuses, and how does an employee earn a bonus?

- Will the company pay tuition for employees who take job-related courses, and does it offer any in-service training or seminars?

- Does the company provide free parking for employees?

Evaluating the Interview

As soon as you can after the interview, evaluate your own performance. Make a list of the things you feel you did right and the things you would do differently at another job interview. Even if you have to go through several job interviews before you are offered a position, you will not have wasted your time. Each interview is a learning experience. The more familiar you become with the job interview, the more relaxed and confident you will be. Here are some questions to ask yourself:

- Did I prepare questions and research the company beforehand?

- Did I remember to bring reference letters, work samples, and any other requested documents to the interview?

- Was I on time for the interview?

- Did I talk too much or too little?

- Did I answer the interviewer's questions honestly and completely?

- Did I dress appropriately?

- Did I display any nervous behavior such as fidgeting, giggling, or forgetting things I wanted to say?

- If I handled any questions badly, how would I answer them differently the next time they are asked?

- Was I courteous at all times?

Other Follow-up Activities

Another follow-up task is to write down any details about the job that you want to remember, such as salary, hours, duties, and so on. Now that you know more about the job, you have to decide whether you want to accept it if it is offered to you. Consider whether the position matches your background and goals. Ask yourself how the company lets you know what it expects of you, how you will be evaluated, and who will evaluate you. Also ask yourself whether the company can provide you with the career path you have chosen. Will it provide educational assistance and offer career development opportunities?

Send the interviewer a brief thank-you note, but avoid calling or writing before the decision deadline to inquire about the status of your application. After the deadline it is acceptable to call or write to ask when a decision will be made. This shows that you are still interested in the job.

Making the Decision

As you look at several job possibilities, you may find it difficult to sort them all out and concentrate on the most desirable. A useful tool to help you organize your priorities is a decision-making matrix. You can make one of these easily.

A matrix is a grid on which you list your job possibilities ver-

DESIRED JOB CHARACTERISTICS

	Salary (6)	Fringe Benefits (4)	Challenge (5)	Opportunity (7)	Prestige (3)	Location (1)	Hours (2)	Totals
Job option 1			✔	✔	✔			15
Job option 2	✔	✔				✔	✔	13
Job option 3	✔		✔		✔			14

Figure 18.8 A decision-making matrix such as this one is a simple device you can create to help you in selecting the best job option to pursue.

tically on the left and the characteristics you desire in a job horizontally on the top (see figure 18.8). Rate the job characteristics according to how important you feel they are to you. Give the least important characteristics a "1" and the next least a "2." If you have identified seven characteristics, as shown in the illustration, the most important will have a value of "7." Opposite each option, check the appropriate box. If the job meets your salary goal, put a check there. Then add the value for the boxes checked. The total values can help you make your decision. If there is a tie, you can add other characteristics.

The company may offer you the job while you still have interviews scheduled with several other companies or while you are waiting to hear about a job that you would prefer. The company making the job offer may be willing to wait a short while for you to decide. You may consider calling the other company to tell the supervisor or human resources manager that you have received an offer and need to make a decision. In that case the second company might be willing to make a job offer also, or it might not. In any event, the decision is yours. Once you have made it, stick to it.

Sometimes an interviewer will tell you that you are not suited for the job you have applied for. Try not to take the rejection personally, and continue to be polite, because you never know when the company will have a position for which you are suited. Do not be afraid to turn down a job offer if you decide that your interests, background, and skills do not fit well or if you are not confident that you can do the job.

ADVANCING ON THE JOB

Getting a job is one accomplishment; getting ahead in the job is an even more important achievement. We said at the beginning of this chapter that your career is what you make of it. You can put in your eight hours every day and do only what is expected of you, or you can seek new challenges and opportunities to grow. To do that, you need to become as competent as you can in your present job. Study your superiors and co-workers so that you can begin to develop interpersonal and management skills. Learn all you can about the equipment you operate and the procedures of the office, and take on administrative support responsibilities. If you can accomplish all of these goals, you will make yourself a valued employee, and you may even be picked to take the **fast track.** People are said to be on the fast track when they are singled out as potential management material and given rapid promotions.

POTENTIAL GROWTH

Many businesses have tools designed to help employees develop and grow on the job. These tools are job descriptions, which you have previously read about, and performance appraisals. Job descriptions define the job. They identify exactly what it is the employee must do. Performance appraisals are conducted by supervisors with employees. They are intended to monitor performance so an employee can eliminate weaknesses and improve strengths.

At first glance, it might seem to you that job descriptions and performance appraisals are solely management tools to make sure you do the work. While it is true they could be solely used in this way, they are also intended to protect employees and help them develop. If the tasks you are expected to do are clearly spelled out and agreed to, you are protected from whims or arbitrary actions of supervisors. This protection is increased if you are given periodic performance evaluations based on your job description.

If you do not get a periodic evaluation, ask for one. Seek an appropriate time to discuss with your supervisor the scope and responsibilities of your job and how you are responding to them. Also ask what areas need improvement and what you can do to increase your chances of being promoted.

A clear job description is necessary to ensure effective evaluation of potential. If one does not exist for your position, developing one could be a useful exercise and increase your understanding of your job and what it requires from you.

GROWING PROFESSIONALLY

To grow professionally, you need to keep up with the changes and developments in your field. Your company may be willing to pay for your membership in a professional organization or for a subscription for one or more professional publications. Even if you have to pay for these things yourself, you will probably find that they are worth the expense. Professional organizations and periodicals keep you informed of new equipment and procedures. They provide contacts, advice on common problems, and ideas you can use to make your job easier and more interesting.

Some professional organizations you might be interested in joining include Professional Secretaries International, the National Association of Executive Secretaries, and the Association of Records Managers and Administrators. There are organizations for supervisors and managers such as the Association of Information Systems Professionals, the Administrative Management Society, and the National Association of Office Managers, and there are also many groups for people who perform specific business functions such as data processing and accounting. You can find out more about these and other professional associations by consulting the *Encyclopedia of Associations* in the reference section of your local library.

Professional associations usually publish their own newsletters and periodicals, which you receive when you enroll as a member. You can learn a great deal about the industry you work for from reading these publications. Reading to keep up with the changes in your company's business and in your own field is essential if you hope to advance in your career. You can also keep informed by subscribing to newspapers and magazines such as *Modern Office Technology, The Office,* the *Wall Street Journal, Business Week,* and *Fortune.*

Some professional organizations offer certification programs, which enable you to demonstrate your competence in your profession. The largest and best-known certification program is the Certified Professional Secretary certificate program, which is offered by Professional Secretaries International (PSI). PSI gives a certificate to candidates who pass a two-day examination in six business areas, including accounting, law, administration, and technology. PSI and other organizations also offer courses and seminars to their members to improve their secretarial skills. Many companies pay tuition and grant time off from work so that their employees can attend these seminars and courses.

ONGOING EDUCATION

If you cannot attend a course or seminar offered by a professional organization, you may want to seek out classes on your own. As you advance up your career ladder, you are likely to discover that professional advancement involves lifelong learning. Many successful people find that they must return to school repeatedly throughout their working lives to retrain themselves for new careers, to keep up with technological advances in their fields, or just to grow in their own careers and explore other career options.

Day or evening courses are available for adults in most four-year colleges, community colleges, vocational schools, and high schools. Many privately operated trade schools offer courses in legal and medical secretarial training, computer programming and electronics, and a wide variety of other careers.

When you begin to assume administrative support and supervisory functions, you may want to take courses in management, business law, business administration, telecommunications, accounting, computer applications, and even psychology. You may have taken several of these courses already as part of your program. In that case you may just want to take the courses you

Figure 18.9 Keeping your technological skills up-to-date is an area where you can take the initiative to get the necessary training.

missed, or you may want to take refresher courses in some subjects. This does not mean that you have to return to school on a full-time basis or run yourself ragged trying to work and carry a heavy load of classwork at the same time. You can take one or two courses a year or every couple of years or proceed at any other pace that is comfortable for you. Part-time courses are usually fairly inexpensive at public schools and community colleges, and your employer may be willing to pick up some or all of the costs.

Adult education can be an enjoyable and relaxed experience because you no longer have to compete for grades. If you pay for your own courses, no one needs to know or cares whether you pass or fail a course except you. And you will probably be very interested in the courses you take because you can apply what you are learning directly to your employment experience.

REASSESSING CAREER GOALS

After you are in a position for a while, you may feel the need to reassess your career goals. It is normal for people to discover that they have new ideas about their careers after they have held a position for awhile. Sometimes this happens because they learn more about themselves and their abilities on the job. Sometimes they discover a new interest. You may initiate the reassessment of your goals. You might also be helped in the process by your company. To reassess your career, it might be a good idea to ask yourself again the questions you asked when you first considered your career. Have the answers changed? If so, how? How would you reprioritize the job characteristics on your decision-making matrix?

In the course of a performance evaluation, your supervisor may be able to advise you on career directions by commenting on your strengths and weaknesses. Your supervisor may suggest a career path you could follow, advise you on what you need to know, and even suggest courses you could take to prepare for your next opportunity.

You also need to consider whether you want to continue on a traditional career path or branch out into a specialty. A traditional path might begin with a secretarial job that leads to the positions of administrative assistant, office supervisor, and manager of office services, in that order. You can stay on a path like this, or you can decide to retrain yourself for any one of a number of specialized jobs. If you decide to pursue an office technology career, you could become an information processing manager or get additional training to become an office automation specialist or trainer. You could become a legal or medical secretary, or you could become a secretary in a research laboratory, where your duties would include preparing documents containing many unusual scientific symbols and words. Sometimes secretaries become familiar enough with their companies' products to move into another career in the same business. A secretary in a plastics manufacturing company could become a salesperson, for example.

If you are in a job where you operate a variety of electronic equipment, you may discover that you have a flair for working with technology. You could become a specialist in one of the technical areas, such as computer programming or telecommunications. Since many of these technical areas are related, it is often possible to move from one career path to another with only minimal additional training. If you specialize in document processing, for example, you could go from being a supervisor to selling, installing, or repairing word processing equipment. You could even become a self-employed consultant who helps companies plan and install office automation systems.

After you reevaluate your career goals and explore the opportunities your company has to offer, you may decide that you want a career change or a change in assignments that requires new skills and knowledge. You will probably need to do some reading off the job or take some courses to prepare yourself for your new job.

MAKING A CHANGE

Once you are ready for a career change, you must begin the job-hunting process all over again. This time it can begin with your own company. Many companies have a regular policy of recruiting and promoting from within, and they will post new job openings in the personnel office or on an employees' bulletin board. If, after a reasonable amount of time has passed, there are no opportunities for advancement at your present company, you will have to look outside the company for a new position.

Go through the same steps of preparing a résumé, getting interviews, and following up, only this time you have more experience, and you will feel more self-confident.

Once you have obtained a new job, you need to resign gracefully from your present job. Inform your supervisor of your resignation as soon as possible, and provide a written letter of resignation if it is requested. The following is an example of a letter of resignation.

Dear Mr. Brooks:

Please accept my resignation as executive secretary for the Research Department effective June 10, 19—.

Since I plan to move to Denver, Colorado, on July 1, I will need a few weeks to get things ready and packed. Prior to my leaving, I will be happy to train my replacement if you wish.

Thank you for the opportunity to work with your Research Department. This job allowed me to expand my experience and thus become a more efficient secretary. My replacement has much to look forward to!

Respectfully yours,

Common practice is to give at least two weeks' notice so your employer can begin searching for your replacement. Make sure you are reimbursed for any benefits, such as pension contributions and unused vacation days, that are due you. Even if you have been unhappy in your present job, maintain good relations with your employer and co-workers until you leave. You may need them in the future for references or professional contacts.

ATTITUDES FOR CONTINUED SUCCESS

In the first part of this chapter, we talked about careers in office automation and the qualifications for those jobs. Recall that many of the jobs require flexibility, good communication skills, and initiative. As you grow on the job past your entry-level position, you will discover that your future progress depends more and more on your attitude and human relations skills than on the basic job skills that enabled you to land a job in the first place.

Your willingness to work with a team, your ability to cooperate, and good communication skills will help you get along with your co-workers. Initiative, self-motivation, and enthusiasm will show your supervisor that you have leadership potential. Curiosity, a willingness to learn, and flexibility will enable you to acquire new skills and grow in your career.

If you maintain an interest in new technological developments and if you are willing to accept changes and try new procedures, you will keep pace with the rapid changes to come, no matter what career you choose. Good Luck!

SUMMARY

- A career path is a person's work history. It consists of vertical moves up a career ladder or lateral moves to another department or field.

- To choose the right career path, first understand your own personality, abilities, and goals.

- The number of information processing jobs will continue to increase over the next ten years.

- When job hunting, look for a prospective employer through your school placement services, through employment agencies, in newspaper ads, through friends and contacts, and by sending blind letters and making calls.

- Résumés usually contain your identification, work history, and educational background and a list of achievements and interests, skills and abilities, and references.

- To apply for a job, send your résumé and a cover letter to the employer. You may have to fill out an application form and take various tests.

- Always research the company and list any questions you want to ask when preparing for an interview.

- During the interview, the interviewer will tell you about the job, ask you questions about yourself, and give you a chance to ask questions as well.

- After the interview, evaluate yourself and determine what you would do differently the next time.

- To get ahead in a job, become as competent as you can, learn about the equipment you use, take on administrative support duties, and develop management skills.

- Join professional organizations and read job-related newspapers and magazines to grow professionally.

- Also expect to take various educational courses from time to time as you advance on the job.

- If you decide to change your career path, you will have to retrain for a new career and begin job hunting all over again.

- Job advancement often depends on positive attitudes such as cooperativeness, initiative, and flexibility.

VOCABULARY

- subordinate
- job campaign
- career path
- career ladder
- lateral move
- career move
- personal profile
- networking
- résumé
- application letter
- letter of inquiry
- fast track

CHECKING YOUR UNDERSTANDING

1. Career planning is an ongoing process. List the traits you need to consider in preparing a personal profile. Using this list, write your own personal profile.
2. List the careers that are available in the administrative support, telecommunications, or records management area. Refer to your personal profile and determine which of these careers you would be inclined to pursue.
3. Describe the steps you would use to find a job. What are specific agencies that can help you find a job?
4. What is the purpose of an application letter and résumé? Do they serve the same purpose or different purposes? What types of information should be included in a résumé and in an application letter?
5. What is the purpose of a job interview? What can you expect to happen during an interview?
6. What should you consider when you evaluate your performance at a job interview? How will this evaluation help you?
7. What activities can you participate in that will help you advance in your career?
8. Describe some of the things you will have to consider in reassessing your career goals when you are ready to move forward in your career.

THINKING THROUGH PROCEDURES

1. Prepare a basic résumé. Use figure 18.5 as a sample, but organize it to highlight information about you. Once you have it drafted, type it, making sure that it has impeccable spelling, grammar, and punctuation. Then get together with a friend, and have that person critique your résumé. Ask him or her to develop possible interview questions based on what your résumé says. Does your résumé make it possible for you to get

across the most important information about you? If it does not, rewrite it.

2. For a couple of weeks in a row, read the classified advertisements for job openings. On Sunday read the display advertisements for career opportunities. Write down the positions you think you might be interested in if you were job hunting. Pick one company and one job opening, and analyze them carefully. Research the company: learn the answers to the questions posed in this chapter, and use all the local sources of information available to you. Write the information down. Then analyze the job to discover what skills and qualifications might be required in the job. Write those down. Compare your résumé with what you know about the company and the job. How good is the fit? Finally, write a cover letter, using figure 18.6 as a guide. What can you say about yourself that would make an employer want to look at your résumé?

3. Use desktop publishing software to create a final version of the résumé you just drafted. Also prepare your own letterhead to be used with your letter of application. The letterhead should include your return address.

4. You may already have a good idea about what you would like to do in your future work. By inquiring among your friends, family, or professors at school, get the name of someone who has a position similar to the one you think you are interested in having. Call and make an appointment with that person, explaining that you would like to talk with her or him about the work the person does and the preparation required for it. Be sure to explain that you are not asking for a job but are only exploring career options. When you meet the person, ask what the work is like. What is most likable and least likable about it? What qualifications does the job require? What is the person's background, and what skills does the person have? What advice would he or she give someone entering the same career? Be sure to take notes. When the meeting is over, compare the answers you got to your questions with your life and career goals and the résumé you prepared. How do all these things compare? Make a list of the qualifications you already have; write down the ones you must still acquire.

UNIT 7: THE PROBLEM SOLVING PROCESS

Part A:

Your current job is administrative support specialist to the teleconference planning manager at Hofaker Telecommunications. When the position of office supervisor for the technology support staff was announced, you decided to apply for the job. You found out that the job involves supervising the staff members who are responsible for providing customers with on-site support of their teleconferencing systems.

You realize that it has been five years since you evaluated yourself and your career goals. Using the problem solving checklist as a guide, describe the process you would use to prepare yourself to apply for this position. Review the job description that appears on page 501 and analyze your qualifications. Determine what skills and abilities you acquired in your current position and the personal attributes you have that would make you successful in this supervisory position.

PROBLEM SOLVING CHECKLIST

DEFINE THE WORKPLACE PROBLEM

What are the abilities and skills necessary to be an office supervisor? What is the process for applying for the position?

ANALYZE THE WORKPLACE PROBLEM

What skills and abilities do you have that qualify you for the position? What are your strengths and weaknesses? What job search materials are needed?

PLAN YOUR PROCEDURE

Are your job search materials up-to-date? Have you listed your goals and objectives? Have you defined your strengths and weaknesses? Have you anticipated interview questions and answers?

IMPLEMENT YOUR PROCEDURE

Are you following the guidelines for the application process? Are you ready for the interview?

EVALUATE YOUR RESULTS

Did you follow the job search guidelines and submit all necessary documentation?

Did you evaluate the interview process? Did you get the job?

Part B:

To prepare for the interview, you need to anticipate the questions that will be asked. You know that you will be asked about your ability to manage your work, solve problems, and work with others. You are also aware that your methods of organizing, planning, and following through will be important factors in the interviewer's decision. Looking back at all you have learned about management, problem solving, and decision making, list the questions you might be asked and the experience, knowledge, or skill that would fit into answering each question.

PROBLEM SOLVING CHECKLIST

DEFINE THE WORKPLACE PROBLEM

What skills and abilities are necessary to be an office supervisor?

ANALYZE THE WORKPLACE PROBLEM

What skills and abilities do you have that make you qualified for the position? What previous job experience do you have that is related to the duties of the position?

PLAN YOUR PROCEDURE

What information do you have that can be used to anticipate the interview questions?

IMPLEMENT YOUR PROCEDURE

What questions will be asked about your management style, decision-making ability, human relations skills, communication skills, knowledge of office procedures, and ability to solve problems? What situations have you been in that exhibited your abilities in these areas?

EVALUATE YOUR RESULTS

Have you answered all the questions fully and honestly? Have you practiced the answers orally? Have you prepared for the necessary job campaign materials and selected your wardrobe for the interview?

Glossary

Account A record of financial transactions.

Account receivable The amount to be collected from customers to whom goods and services are sold on credit.

Accounting software Programs used to carry out basic accounting tasks, such as payroll, inventory, and invoicing.

Active records Records that must be kept in the office because they are used regularly.

Affidavit A sworn, written statement of fact.

Ageism Discrimination against others because of their age.

Agenda A listing of the activities or the order of business for a meeting.

Agreement A legally enforceable understanding or arrangement between two or more parties.

Analog signals Electrical waves that are transmitted over telephone lines.

Answer A legal document responding to the notification of a lawsuit.

Answering machine A device that answers a telephone automatically and records incoming and outgoing messages.

Answering service A reception and message-taking service that takes calls and receives packages for businesses.

Aperture card A card with a rectangular hole that holds only one microform image.

Application letter A letter written from the standpoint of knowing a position is available and applying for it.

Applications software program Programmed instructions that make a computer execute a required task.

Appointment A time set aside for two people to discuss an issue.

Appraisal of records An analysis to determine the type of record and its worth to the company.

Archive An off-site storage location for inactive files.

Artificial intelligence Programs that simulate the reasoning of the human mind by, to a limited extent, applying judgment inference in addition to calculating data.

ASCII American Standard Code for Information Interchange, the most widely used coding system to represent data. Data converted to ASCII code can be read by most manufacturers' equipment.

Attitude The beliefs and feelings that cause people to react in a certain way toward an object, a person, a situation, an event, or an idea.

Audio teleconference A telephone conference using telecommunications technology to link two or more people in separate locations.

Automatic collator See Collator

Automatic document feed The ability to feed one sheet at a time automatically from a stack of originals placed in a feeder tray.

Automatic Teller Machine (ATM) A computer terminal with a keypad that enables the user to instruct the machine to complete banking transactions.

Automation *See* Office automation.

Backup copy A duplicate copy of stored electronic files.

Balance The total funds contained in an account.

Balance sheet A financial statement that shows the company's total assets and liabilities.

Bank draft A check used to transfer large sums of money against one bank's account into another bank.

Baud rate The speed at which a modem transmits data.

Bid specifications A list of requirements describing the kind of equipment the company needs and what the company expects the equipment to do.

Binder A machine that fastens pages together into a book.

Body language Nonverbal communication that depends on behavior such as gestures, facial expressions, and posture.

Boilerplate Preprinted sections of written documents that are used when the same information has to be processed repeatedly.

Bottom line 1. The net profit; the amount of profit remaining after all expenses have been deducted. 2. The last figure on a company's annual financial statement.

Brainstorming The process in which a manager exchanges ideas freely with the staff.

Budget A company's plan of expenditures and income for a given period of time.

Business record Any documentation of a business transaction.

Bylaws The written policies and procedures of an organization.

Calendaring software A program used for maintaining appointment schedules.

Capital expense budget A budget that shows long-range expenditures for new facilities, equipment replacement, land purchases, and mortgages.

Caption 1. The title that appears on the guide tab of a file folder. 2. The words under which a document is filed.

Career ladder A series of successive steps that marks the stages of a person's work history.

Career move A change in a person's career path; moving from one department or field to another.

Career path The progression of jobs that forms a person's work history.

Cashier's check A check that is guaranteed by the bank.

Cell The part of a spreadsheet where the columns and rows intersect to define the area in which data is entered.

Cellular mobile telephone Telephone that transmits signals via microwave transmission technology rather than wires or cables, enabling it to be carried from one location to another for use.

Centralized dictation system A dictation/transcription setup in which dictation is received in a centralized location to be transcribed.

Centralized reprographics center A type of copy center most commonly found in offices that makes heavy use of reprographics and where many different kinds of equipment are located and operated by specialists.

Centralized storage system A storage system in which manual or electronic files are stored in a location that is accessible to all the workers who need the information.

Centrex system A phone switching system in which users can choose between dialing directly and using the operator's assistance.

Certified check A check drawn against a company checking account and certified by a bank teller.

Chain of command The hierarchy of levels of management within an organization.

Character printer An impact printer that prints one character at a time.

Charging out A procedure for borrowing files.

Charter airline Airlines that handle special flight requests.

Check register A log in which the number, date, and amount of each check are recorded, as well as the payee's name and the reason for payment.

Chronological file A loose-leaf binder or file folder for storing copies of each piece of outgoing correspondence, always in chronological order.

Coding 1. Highlighting or writing a caption on a paper record or naming an electronic file. 2. Writing a computer program.

Collator A device that puts copies of the pages of a multipage document into the correct order.

Combination unit A desktop dictation machine that can record dictation and play it back for transcription.

Command Keystrokes that activate software program functions.

Command-driven program A program that uses commands rather than menus to perform functions.

Communicate To send, or distribute, information to others.

Communication The process by which information is sent by a sender and understood by a receiver.

Communications software Software that enables computers to send and receive information.

Commuter airline A company that provides air transportation between a major airport and a smaller airport or between major airports that are not far apart.

Compatibility The ability of one kind of computer to accept and process disks or tapes prepared on another type of computer.

Complaint A legal document that sets forth the basis for a lawsuit.

Computer-assisted retrieval (CAR) A process of automatic microform retrieval that uses an electronic index.

Computer chip *See* Microprocessor.

Computer graphics Pictorial representations of data, such as graphs or charts, on a computer screen.

Computer language Instructions, coded to be understood by a computer, that tell a computer what to do (for example, Cobol, BASIC).

Computer-output microform (COM) Normal, printed computer output reduced to microform by a special output device.

Computer programmer An individual who writes computer programs.

Computer system The different hardware and software components that are required to operate a computer.

Conference A formal meeting at which the primary objective is to exchange information.

Conference call A telephone call involving three or more people in different locations.

Confidentiality The ability to keep information private.

Configuration The setup of electronic equipment.

Consecutive numeric system A filing system that uses consecutive numbers: 1, 2, 3, and so on.

Contract A legally enforceable understanding or arrangement between two or more parties.

Control code A binary language that represents each letter, number, and symbol.

Control unit The part of the computer's processing unit that causes the system to carry out program instructions.

Convenience copier Copy machine situated close to the employees' work area so that it might easily be used for small copying jobs.

Convention A formal meeting at which members of a large professional group or organization elect officers, establish policies, conduct business, and exchange information of interest to the membership.

Copyright laws Laws that protect the ownership of published material.

Cost-benefit ratio A comparison of the costs of carrying out a plan or operation with the profit or benefit the company can expect to receive.

Court order A formal instruction issued by a judge to a party in a lawsuit to do or stop doing a specific action.

Creation The origination of data and information.

Cross-reference A message that refers you to another location for the file you are searching for.

Cursor A lighted indicator on a computer monitor that can be moved to different locations for inputting data.

Cursor control keypad The portion of an electronic keyboard that controls the movement (up, down, left, right) of the cursor on the computer screen.

Database A stored collection of data on a particular subject.

Database management A computer software application used for entering, organizing, storing, and retrieving data in formats and orders specified by the user.

Data communications The exchange of data between computers.

Data manipulation Reorganizing data to show different aspects of the same information.

Data processing 1. The application of a programmed sequence of operations upon numerical data. 2. A general description of computer operations.

Deadline A specified date on which a task must be completed.

Decentralized dictation system A dictation and transcription setup in which individuals give and transcribe dictation at their own workstations.

Decentralized storage system A storage system in which each worker maintains his or her own manual or electronic files.

Decision-support tools *See* Productivity tools.

Decode To detect and interpret a message.

Delegate To assign tasks to members of the staff or other employees.

Departmental budget The items from a company's operating and capital budgets that pertain to an individual department.

Deposit slip A bank form on which to record the date and amount of cash or a check being deposited.

Desktop publishing Composition software used for designing and laying out the pages of printed documents.

Digital Relating to information represented by a code made up of digits.

Digital camera A special camera wired to a computer that converts photographic images into computer signals.

Digital scanner A device that scans charts, maps, and blueprints and converts them into digital data so that they can be reproduced on a computer screen.

Digital signals Electrical pulses that can be read by a computer.

Direct deposit transfer Automatic transfer of an employee's pay from the company's account to the employee's bank account.

Directory A listing of designated storage areas on a storage medium, used to locate electronic files.

Direct outward dialing A feature of computerized telephone switching systems that allows users to make outside calls directly by dialing an access number first.

Dishonored check A check that the bank cannot collect on either because it was altered, misdated, or made out incorrectly or because there were not sufficient funds in the drawer's account to cover it.

Disk drive A device that contains a small electromagnetic head that is capable of reading and writing information on a disk.

Disk operating system (DOS) *See* Operating system software

Disk tutorial A lesson, recorded on a disk and displayed on a computer screen, that explains procedures and programs.

Disposition The last stage of the life cycle of a record.

Distribute To send, or communicate, information to others.

Distribution/communication The movement of data or processed information from one location to another by manual or technological means.

Documentation The instruction manuals and other reference materials that explain a computer system or software.

Document-based management system (DBMS) Optical disk technology used to store large volumes of active or inactive files.

Dot-matrix printer An impact printer that forms characters by projecting tiny metal bristles or pins in patterns, producing draft-quality output.

Downloading Transferring information received over a communications network to a software program so that it can be printed out or processed at an individual workstation.

Electronic calculator A machine that performs basic mathematical functions automatically.

Electronic calendar A computerized system for recording appointments, setting up meetings, and scheduling other daily, weekly, or monthly activities.

Electronic file Documents stored electronically on tape or disks.

Electronic mail The distribution of messages in soft copy form.

Electronic mailbox A program that permits computers to send, store, and receive messages.

Electronic message *See* Electronic mail.

Electronic network *See* Network.

Electronic notebook A tabletlike input device that converts handwriting to machine-readable text characters.

Employee assistance programs Company programs that help employees deal with work-related problems, such as job-related stress, job training, retirement, and investment counseling.

Encode To create a message and send it to a receiver.

Endorsement The payee's signature on the back of a check authorizing it to be cashed or deposited.

Ergonomics The study of how the physical work environment affects workers and job performance.

Ethics A value judgment of right and wrong in any given situation or circumstance.

Evaluation The review of business plans and their implementation to determine whether they have been successful.

Executable file The commands written into a software program that enable it to run on a computer system.

Expenditure The amount of money spent to operate a business.

Expense account A form that businesses use to reimburse employees for using their own money to meet business expenses or to account for cash advances they receive.

Expense report A form on which employees formally report, on a regular basis, all their business expenses to their employers.

Expert systems Software programs that use artificial intelligence to simulate the human thought process. *See also* Artificial intelligence.

External modem A modem that is attached to a computer by a cable and to a telephone by a standard telephone cord.

Facsimile machine An electronic device that scans printed documents, converting words or images on them into signals that are transmitted over telephone lines, and receives printed documents by converting the signals into words or images and reproducing them on paper.

Facsimile transmission A method of immediate electronic transfer of information by the use of a facsimile machine or a fax board.

Fast track Rapid advancement in job positions.

Fax board A circuit board within a computer that provides the capability to send and receive documents through facsimile transmission without first producing a hard copy.

File-drawer guides A paper divider used to separate file folders in drawers.

File folder A folder used to organize papers in file drawers and cabinets.

File-guide caption *See also* Caption.

Floppy disk A device used to store computer data, made of a flat, double-sided sheet of pliable plastic that is magnetically treated and coated in a protective vinyl jacket.

Flowchart A step-by-step graphic description of a process or operation.

Footer A line of identifying information that appears at the bottom of a page of text.

Formal meeting A meeting that is held either within the office or at another location, usually with a large number of people in attendance and with formal speeches or presentations.

Format 1. A procedure that prepares a floppy disk for use in an operating system. 2. The arrangement of information on a page.

Form letter A letter with preprinted paragraphs.

Function A series of operations or responsibilities involved in carrying out work.

Function keys Keys on a keyboard that are used to input commands, which control a specific processing function.

Garbage in, garbage out *See* GIGO.

General journal A list in chronological order of each business transaction in which money is received or spent.

General ledger A record of financial business transactions, grouped according to account.

GIGO "Garbage in, garbage out," an expression that means if what is input into a computer is wrong, what comes out will also be wrong.

Grammar checker A feature available in some word processing packages that checks for some common grammatical errors.

Graphic/presentation software Programs that produce charts, graphs, and other forms of illustrations.

Graphic user interface (GUI) A utility program that lets the user select menu options using graphically based icons.

Gross pay The amount of pay before any deductions are made.

Groupware *See* Project management software.

Guaranteed reservation A hotel reservation in which the hotel guarantees that the room will be held as long as necessary. Payment is usually required whether or not the room is used, unless cancellation is requested.

Handwriting recognition *See* Electronic notebook.

Hard copy Computer output in a permanent, visually readable form, usually on paper.

Hard disk A high-volume storage device made of rigid plastic, aluminum, or ceramic and magnetically treated.

Hardware The physical components of a computer system.

Header A line of identifying text that appears at the top of a page.

Hierarchy An organizational structure in which top management controls all aspects of the organization through a "chain of command" decision-making process that follows specified levels of authority.

Horizontal relationships In the workplace, refers to interaction with co-workers.

Hygienes Specific elements of a job—pay, advancement potential, status, work conditions, and interpersonal relationships—that can affect a worker's motivation by their absence or presence.

IBM PC-compatible A computer's capability of running MS-DOS, that is, Microsoft disk operating systems.

Icons Picture symbols that are used to identify software commands.

Important records Records that should be retained for five to seven years.

Inactive records Records that may be moved to inactive storage or discarded because they are no longer used regularly.

Income statement A statement that shows a business's net income or loss within a given period of time.

Incompatible Unsuitable for use together.

Industrial Age The period of time when the American economy was based on the production of goods.

Informal meeting A meeting that takes place in an office or conference room at which discussions of everyday business activities occur.

Information Age The period of time beginning in the 1970s, when the American economy shifted from production of goods to a dependence on service-oriented businesses that rely heavily on the exchange of information.

Information management (system) The function of organizing and controlling all aspects of business records, from their creation, protection, and use to their storage and ultimate disposal.

Information processing The combination of word processing, data processing, communication, voice, and imaging technology.

Information processing cycle The process through which all information in the office environment flows, defined in stages as input, processing, storage, output, and distribution/communication.

Initial training The training of new employees.

Input 1. The entering of data into the computer. 2. The data entered into the computer.

In-service training The retraining of employees.

Integrated information processing The use of hardware and software that allows the user to perform various information processing tasks simultaneously or using the same piece of equipment.

Integrated software A package or series of software programs for several applications that are designed to work together.

Interactive A method of exchanging information by computer in which users carry on a dialogue by inputting their comments and reading the responses.

Internal modem A modem located on a circuit board inside of a computer.

International company A company that has business operations in several different countries.

Interoffice mail The mail exchanged between people who work at the same location or at the company's branches.

Inventory Products or other items that a company must store.

Invoice A form used to request payment for goods or a service.

IPSOD Acronym signifying the stages of processing information in the electronic office: input, process, storage, output, distribution.

Itinerary A list of travel arrangements that includes departure and arrival times, flight or train numbers, hotel addresses and telephone numbers, and other details.

Jargon Specialized technical language not normally used in everyday communication.

Jet lag The fatigue and confusion that result from flying across several time zones.

Job campaign The process of finding a position in a company related to education and experience.

Job description The expected skills and responsibilities of an employee.

Keyboard The most commonly used input device using an alphanumeric set of keys, a ten-key numerical pad, and various function keys and other keys for keying text, figures, and commands.

Key operator The person in an office responsible for photocopier maintenance.

Key system A type of telephone switching equipment using phones equipped with keys or buttons that represent different telephone lines.

Labor-intensive Relating to tasks that require many work hours to complete.

Laptop computer A small, portable microcomputer with many of the same capabilities as a desktop-sized personal computer.

Laser disk A durable, nonmagnetic storage medium of great capacity that uses laser beams to burn tiny holes into the metal of the disk.

Laser printer A high-speed printer that uses a combination of electronics and photography to produce high-quality originals.

Lateral move A sideways step on a career path.

Law blank A printed legal form with blanks to be filled in with information supplied by a supervisor or from source documents.

Leading The amount of space between lines on a printed document.

Letterhead Stationery printed with a heading, usually including the company name and/or logo, as well as the address.

Letter of inquiry A letter written when you do not know a position is available, requesting information about possible positions.

Light pen A pen-shaped, light-sensing input device used to "write" or "draw" on a computer screen.

Line item A category of expenditures or income that is given a separate line in a budget.

Local area network (LAN) A privately owned communication system connecting a company's computers; usually located within a small area, such as in one building.

Log on To "sign in" with an individual identification code, which must be entered into the computer before access is authorized.

Long-term goal An objective to be reached within a specific timeframe, from several months to several years.

Long-term planning Refers to projects that take a year or more to implement.

Mailgram A combination of a telegram and a letter.

Mailmobile An interoffice mail system with a mailcart that follows a magnetic track on the floor automatically and is programmed to stop at various points for collection.

Mainframe A powerful computer with large storage capacities, capable of processing vast quantities of information quickly.

Main memory *See* Random access memory.

Maintenance The stage in the life cycle of a record during which it is stored for retrieval.

Management by objectives (MBO) A style of management in which workers meet with managers periodically to discuss objectives.

Management information systems (MIS) Automated office systems.

Manual distribution A system in which people rather than electronic machines carry information from one place to another.

Matrix management An organizational structure in which the lines of reporting go across lines of responsibility as well as up and down lines of authority.

Meeting A gathering of two or more people to discuss a common goal.

Memory 1. Where information is stored in a computer; it can be either permanent (ROM) or temporary (RAM) storage. 2. The capacity of a computer to store information.

Mental filters The unique elements in a person's mind—ideas, facts, attitudes, emotions, experience, and memories—that interpret (or decode) messages in an individual way and trigger a response.

Message The information exchanged between a sender and receiver in the communication process.

Microcomputer A small computer also called a desktop computer or personal computer.

Microfiche Flat sheets of easy-to-use film that can hold hundreds of pages of micrographic images, arranged in rows and columns.

Microfilm jacket A clear plastic sheet, sealed to form horizontal slots, that holds short strips of microfilm.

Microform reader A machine into which microfilm is inserted to be read.

Microprocessor The circuits or computer chips inside of the computer that receive data from the input devices, carry out the processing instructions, and send the results to output devices.

Modeling Setting up a formula or model to forecast the possible outcome of a decision.

Money order A bank check, usually issued for amounts under $250.00.

Motion A proposal for action made during a formal meeting.

Motivate To help employees perform their tasks with enthusiasm and initiative.

Mouse A hand-operated device that controls the cursor and is used to input processing commands without the use of a keyboard.

MS-DOS The disk operating system developed by the Microsoft Corporation.

Multitasking The capability of using more than one software program at once.

Net pay The amount of pay remaining after deductions are made.

Network Computer systems linked by electronic cables, telephone lines, and satellite communications devices.

Networked system *See* Networking.

Networking 1. The linkage of computers to one another through special communications lines or telephone lines so that data and information can be transmitted electronically from one system to another. 2. Making contacts with friends or acquaintances in order to advance your career.

Notarize The stamping of a signed document by a notary public.

Notary public A person commissioned by a state government to verify signatures on documents for legal purposes.

Notetaking A rapid writing system based on the alphabet or symbolic shorthand symbols.

Numeric data Numbers.

Numeric keypad The portion of an electronic keyboard with keys for each of the ten Arabic digits.

Office automation The use of computers and other electronic equipment to perform office tasks that were previously performed by people.

Office automation (OA) specialist The person responsible for overseeing the implementation of an electronic office system and for explaining the various features of a computer system to its users.

Office landscaping A flexible arrangement of office space using movable partitions (rather than fixed walls) to provide economical workstations.

Office politics The interaction of individuals dealing with business matters outside of the formal channels of communication.

Official Airline Guide (OAG) An up-to-date listing of airline flight information—available in print or electronic form.

On-line information services Companies that, for a fee, provide access to particular types of information from their data banks to meet the needs of their subscribers.

Operating budget A statement that lists the expected income and costs of the day-to-day operations of a company.

Operating system software Software needed to operate the internal functions of the computer. Also known as the disk operating system (DOS).

Optical disk *See* Laser disk.

Organization The way in which a business divides responsibilities among its departments and divisions and how it assigns various tasks and functions to employees and structures its chain of authority or command.

Originator The creator of a dictated document.

Output Processed data that can be displayed on the computer screen or printed out as a paper document.

Owner's equity The amount of the owner's financial interest in the company.

Paging device A small, portable device that alerts the person carrying it when someone is trying to reach him or her; also called a beeper.

Parliamentary procedure The rules that structure a formal meeting.

Participative approach A modern management technique in which employees are consulted and involved in the decision-making process.

Passport An official government identification document that grants citizens permission to travel abroad.

Password A personal code used by an individual to identify himself or herself to the central computer.

Password system A log-on security procedure that requires a user of a networked computer system to enter a code (password) before gaining access to files stored on the system.

Peripherals Equipment such as printers, modems, scanners, and terminals that can be added to the CPU.

Personal information software Programs used for individually designed needs, such as personal calendars, notebooks, and address books.

Personal profile An assessment of background, personality, and life goals.

Petty cash A small cash fund kept by most offices to pay for small day-to-day expenses.

Photocopier A machine that duplicates documents from an original page to another page.

Point-of-sale transfer Use of a bank identification card to transfer funds directly from a bank to a store's account.

Pointer An arrow or other symbol on the computer screen that indicates the movement and action of the mouse when a mouse is used for input.

Portable computer *See* Laptop computer.

Postage meter A machine, licensed by the U.S. Postal Service, that prints postage fees on gummed strips of paper that are used as stamps.

Posting The process of transferring data from a journal to a ledger.

Power of attorney Legal authorization for one person to act as an agent for another.

Prejudice An adverse or harmful opinion based on a generalization or stereotype about an individual or group of people.

Printer The output device that produces a paper copy of processed information.

Printout Text or copy printed out on paper by a computer.

Priority A certain level of urgency or importance.

Private branch exchange (PBX) A type of telephone switching equipment that requires the central switching station for all the telephone extensions connected to the system.

Procedure A set of defined steps that compose the elements for completing a task.

Processing 1. To organize data into useful information. 2. The organization and calculation of words and numbers by a computer.

Productivity 1. The ability to perform work at an increased rate of speed and/or with fewer employees. 2. Improved efficiency in the workplace and better quality of output.

Productivity tools A variety of business applications (such as database management, spreadsheets, or graphics) that can be used on a computer.

Professional conference planner Service that specializes in planning large-scale conventions and conferences.

Programmable key A key on a computer keyboard that can be custom programmed by the user.

Programming language The codes used to write computer programs.

Programming software The instructions or programs implanted in the circuits of the central processing unit of a computer, enabling it to carry out processing functions.

Project budget Log of expenses for individual programs of a company, for example, an advertising campaign or film project.

Project management software A program used for long-term project planning.

Protocol 1. A set of rules or procedures that allows different models of computers to communicate clearly with one another. 2. The exchange of predetermined signals in a specific sequence.

Quorum The number of people required by the group before a vote can be taken.

Racism Discrimination against others because of their race.

Random access memory (RAM) 1. Computer memory in which data is temporarily stored and from which it can be retrieved by the user. 2. The amount of data a computer can store, measured in kilobytes (K).

Read only memory (ROM) Preprogrammed information that is permanently stored by the manufacturer in the computer's memory and that cannot be changed by the user.

Receiver One who detects and interprets a message.

Records Pieces of important information that, collectively, make up a database.

Records center A room or designated area where records are stored.

Records/information management The organization and control of business records; developing systems to store, protect, retrieve, use, and dispose of records.

Records inventory A survey of files to determine how many exist, who uses them, where they are stored, and in what form.

Reminder facilities A feature of an electronic time management system in which a reminder indicator (of a meeting, commitment, project, and so on) is displayed automatically on the computer screen at the exact time and date for which it is set.

Reprographics system Equipment used to duplicate and collate paper copies of documents.

Resolution 1. A formal expression of opinion or intention. 2. The sharpness of the picture on a computer screen.

Restrictive endorsement An endorsement that sets conditions such as "for deposit only" to a specific account.

Résumé A brief summary of a person's educational and employment history used by employers to screen job applicants.

Retention schedule A schedule that lays out a timeline for how long records will be kept.

Revenue The amount of cash received by a company.

Rider A separate sheet of paper attached to a legal document to add necessary space.

Rough draft A preliminary copy of a document on which corrections and editing changes are made.

Satellite Communications device that orbits the earth and transmits signals beamed to it from localities around the globe.

Scanner An electronic device that can "read" text, images, and bar codes and transfer them into a computer system.

Schedule A timetable for a project that indicates the sequence of work and sets deadlines.

Scrolling function The movement of soft copy vertically and horizontally on a computer monitor to allow the user to view different portions of a document.

Self-esteem Confidence and pride in oneself.

Seminar *See* Conference.

Sender One who creates and transmits a message.

Sensory receiver A body part or mechanical device that receives and interprets stimuli.

Sexism Discrimination against others because of their gender.

Short-term goal A goal to be reached within a short period of time.

Short-term planning A schedule for business projects that can be carried out within a few weeks or months.

Shredder A machine that cuts up paper and other materials so that they cannot be pieced back together.

Signal 1. Stimulation from an individual's environment; something a person sees, hears, tastes, smells, or feels. 2. An electronic pulse used to transmit information.

Soft copy Computer output displayed on a computer monitor.

Software A set of instructions, or programs, directing the operation of a computer.

Source documents Various base forms (such as purchase orders, bills, checkbook stubs, invoices, and credit agreements) used to record accounting information.

Speakerphone A telephone device that amplifies a call so that many people can hear it at once; widely used for audio teleconferences.

Spellchecker An electronic dictionary used with word processing software.

Spreadsheet 1. Ruled accounting paper on which figures are entered in columns and rows. 2. Graphic applications software that presents figures in a grid format on the computer screen.

Stand-alone system A microcomputer; a self-contained workstation with all the equipment and processing power it needs to operate independently.

Statement of objectives A description of the goals or objectives that an employee is expected to accomplish.

Stock *See* Inventory.

Stop-payment order A request to a bank to withhold payment on a check that was written against an account.

Storage The recording of information so that it can be recalled for later use.

Store To save information permanently on a medium that can be read by a computer system or in paper form.

Stress The body's response to change and stimulation.

Subordinate An employee who takes direction from another and has work assigned to him or her.

Subpoena An order to appear at a trial or hearing to testify.

Supercomputer The most powerful type of computer, with the largest storage and processing capacity of all computers.

Systems analyst A computer specialist who determines how computer data processing can be applied to specific functions.

Systems study or **systems analysis** A study that focuses on the company's overall system of procedures and functions, rather than on individual tasks.

Tact A sense of what to do or say to avoid offending or embarrassing people.

Task A specific work activity.

Team approach An approach to management whereby managers and supervisors do not make decisions in isolation; they ask for input from staff.

Telecommunications Technology that allows information to be transmitted over telephone lines or through satellite linkage.

Telecommuting Using computers and telephone equipment to work at home instead of at the office.

Teleconference A conference among people at different locations electronically linked by audio and/or visual connections.

Telephone transfer Transferring funds or investments by a telephone transaction.

Teletypewriters Keyboard devices with printers that can send and receive messages over telephone lines.

Template A plastic or cardboard plate that fits over the panel of function keys on an electronic computer keyboard; used as a guide to the function keys of a particular program.

Temporary memory *See* Random access memory.

Terminal-digit system A filing system that uses numbers specifically assigned to classify records into groups; the last number (terminal digit) indicates where to start looking for the file.

Theory X and theory Y Two competing claims on whether people naturally avoid work or actually are fulfilled by their jobs.

Thesaurus A book that lists words and their synonyms (different words that have nearly the same meaning).

"Things-to-do" facility A feature of an electronic time management system in which a list of items that the user needs to be reminded about at a specific time is stored electronically for future viewing on the computer screen as needed.

Tickler file A follow-up file, arranged by day of the month, that serves as a daily reminder of tasks that must be acted upon.

Time management Planning, organizing, and using time effectively.

Time sharing Simultaneous access by many users to a shared central computer facility.

To do/did list A list of prioritized activities.

Transcript A word-for-word record of everything said during a meeting; a written or printed copy.

Travel and entertainment (T&E) report *See* Expense report.

Traveler profile questionnaire Questions used to determine specific needs of a traveler.

Traveler's check A form that is used like cash; purchased from a bank or express company and payable only when signed by the owner; used by travelers because it is safe to carry.

Travel preference form A record of an individual's travel preferences.

Turnaround time The time from when a task is assigned to when it is expected to be completed.

Tutorial Lessons on how to use a software application, usually supplied on a disk by the software vendor.

Ultrafiche Flat sheets of film that hold miniaturized images that are even smaller than those on microfiche; ultrafiche can only be produced by an expensive photographic process.

Unimportant records Records that can be discarded because they are not useful.

Uploading Transferring information to a communications software file so that it can be sent out through a wide area network.

Useful records Records that are usually retained for one to three years.

Utilities Programs that assist in the operation of hardware and software applications.

Vendor A person or company that produces and sells computer software equipment.

Vertical relationships In the workplace, relationships with managers and supervisors to whom an individual is a subordinate.

Video input A device that can capture an image being recorded by a video camera and transfer it to a medium that can be read by a computer system.

Video teleconference The use of closed-circuit television to allow people in widely separated locations to hold a meeting without traveling.

Virus A hidden computer program that can be introduced inadvertently into the computer circuitry, causing random system malfunctions.

Visa A permit granted by the government of a country to allow foreigners to enter the country.

Visitor's log A record of office visits, including the name, time, date, and purpose of each visit.

Vital records Permanently kept records that are vital to the company.

Voice input Direct input of verbal data into the computer without the use of a keyboard.

Voice mail An electronic message system that uses a telephone linked to a voice-activated computer.

Wide area network (WAN) A communication system that employs satellites, telephone lines, microwaves, and dedicated communications channels to connect computer systems in widely separated locations.

WMRM (Write Many Read Many) Optical disk storage technology that allows data to be stored, changed, and deleted.

Word processing 1. Using a computer to create, edit, revise, format, or print out text. 2. The organizing of words by a computer.

Word processing software Software used to input, process, store, edit, and revise documents.

Wordwrap The feature on a word processor that returns the carrier to the left margin automatically as copy is entered; sometimes called automatic carrier return.

Workstation The area in the electronic office that incorporates all the equipment, furnishings, and accessories needed to perform one's work.

WORM (Write Once Read Many) An optical disk storage system that allows the storage of information only once on a disk and retrieved many times.

Appendix 1: Letter Styles

Block Style

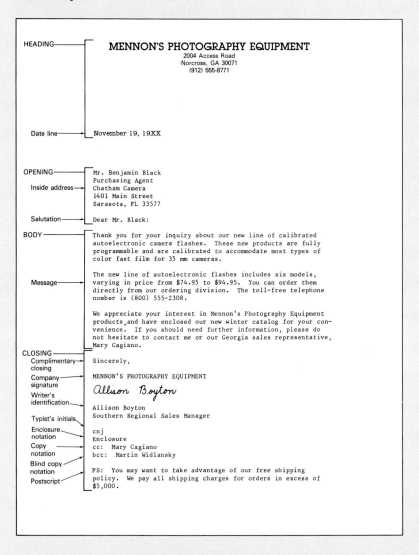

HEADING

MENNON'S PHOTOGRAPHY EQUIPMENT
2004 Access Road
Norcross, GA 30071
(912) 555-8771

Date line → November 19, 19XX

OPENING

Inside address →
Mr. Benjamin Black
Purchasing Agent
Chatham Camera
1401 Main Street
Sarasota, FL 33577

Salutation → Dear Mr. Black:

BODY

Thank you for your inquiry about our new line of calibrated autoelectronic camera flashes. These new products are fully programmable and are calibrated to accommodate most types of color fast film for 35 mm cameras.

Message

The new line of autoelectronic flashes includes six models, varying in price from $74.95 to $94.95. You can order them directly from our ordering division. The toll-free telephone number is (800) 555-2308.

We appreciate your interest in Mennon's Photography Equipment products and have enclosed our new winter catalog for your convenience. If you should need further information, please do not hesitate to contact me or our Georgia sales representative, Mary Cagiano.

CLOSING

Complimentary closing → Sincerely,

Company signature → MENNON'S PHOTOGRAPHY EQUIPMENT

Allison Boyton

Writer's identification →
Allison Boyton
Southern Regional Sales Manager

Typist's initials → cnj

Enclosure notation → Enclosure

Copy notation →
cc: Mary Cagiano
bcc: Martin Widlansky

Blind copy notation →

Postscript → PS: You may want to take advantage of our free shipping policy. We pay all shipping charges for orders in excess of $5,000.

Modified-Block Style

ILLINOIS OFFICE TECHNOLOGIES, INC.
3200 South Michigan Avenue
Chicago, IL 60611
(312) 555-8700

August 22, 19XX

Ms. Diane Nelson
Advertising Manager
Business Network Supplies Center
220 Delaware Avenue
Buffalo, NY 14202

Dear Ms. Nelson:

Would you please send me your current office supplies catalog
and price list? I am in charge of our company's reference
center and receive requests from my coworkers for office
supplies and equipment catalogs.

May I be put on your mailing list so that I will receive new
catalogs as they are available?

Sincerely,

ILLINOIS OFFICE TECHNOLOGIES, INC.

David P. Weinstein

David P. Weinstein
Reference Center Associate

pd

Modified-Block Style with Indented Paragraphs

113 Oak Street
Ridgewood, NJ 07451
April 3, 19XX

Mr. William Chang
Personnel Director
The New Jersey Sentinel
315 Terrace Avenue
Hackensack, NJ 07604

Dear Mr. Chang:

    Your advertisement for a well-rounded student with organizational skills for a summer word processing job was posted in the guidance center of Carlton Business School, where I am a student. I believe I am the student for whom you are looking. Let me explain why.

    As the enclosed resume illustrates, I am about to receive an associate's degree from Carlton, where I have been an honor student. My course of study has included not only shorthand and transcription, which, I'm sure you'll agree, are important skills, but also experience on most word processing equipment. In addition, for the last summer, I worked as a word processing operator at Hines & Crawford, a law firm in my home town of Ridgewood. I believe both my educational background and my work experience will help me satisfy the requirements for the job you need to fill this summer.

    I can begin work any time after June 15.

    You can reach me at 555-5165 any day after 4 p.m. May I have a personal interview at your convenience?

            Sincerely,

            Brenda Coleman

            Brenda Coleman

Enclosure

Simplified Style

STETSON'S EDUCATIONAL AMUSEMENTS
718 Stadium Drive
San Antonio, TX 78412
(512) 555-7355

February 17, 19XX

Tots & Teddy Bears
Nursery Schools, Inc.
116 West 3rd Street
Tulsa, OK 74103

NURSERY SCHOOL EDUCATIONAL PRODUCTS

Tots & Teddy Bears Nursery Schools are synonymous with excellence in preschool education--we know a lot about you! Because we're interested in the same thing as you, we want you to get to know more about us.

Stetson's Educational Amusements is an internationally respected developer and marketer of educational toys. Our staff of educators and instructional designers develops toys especially helpful to preschoolers, ages 2 to 5. You'll find our pegboards, musical instruments, and, yes, even our computers, in every state domestically and in 41 countries internationally.

We must be doing something right, as you are! In order that you might join forces with us in the important area of early education, I've enclosed our new catalog of preschool products. Won't you call us, toll free, at (800) 555-4447, to help your preschoolers learn that thinking is fun? Each day's delay could mean a more difficult job for you and your staff without Stetson's Educational Amusements to help you.

Amy D'Angelo

AMY D'ANGELO - ADVERTISING AND PRODUCTION DIRECTOR

cnj
Enclosure

PS: For a limited time only, we are offering first-time customers, <u>absolutely free</u>, a bonus of two 6' x 8' wall hangings on learning numbers and the alphabet the visual (easy) way! Offer free until May 1.

Appendix 2:
Report Parts

Outline Format

```
REPORT OF THE OFFICE EQUIPMENT COMMITTEE


  I.  PURPOSE OF STUDY - PHOTOCOPIER NEEDED


 II.  SCOPE OF STUDY

        A.  Copying needs - by department
        B.  Equipment available


III.  PROCEDURES

        A.  How much copying do we do?
            1.  Volume
            2.  Paper sizes used
            3.  Capabilities used
            4.  How many machines?  What kinds?
            5.  Changes projected?
        B.  Machines tested
            1.  Capabilities
            2.  Performance
            3.  Costs for leasing or buying
            4.  Service contracts available
        C.  User reactions - by department


 IV.  FINDINGS


  V.  RECOMMENDATIONS AND CONCLUSIONS
```

Title Page

```
            COMPARISON AND ANALYSIS OF
              NEW-PRODUCT REVENUE

             1984, 1985, and 1986




                  Prepared by

                Michael Muller
              Director of Marketing

              January 31, 19XX




                  Prepared for

     General Management and Stockholders
            of Bronson Laboratories
```

Table of Contents

TABLE OF CONTENTS

I. Summary 1

    A. Purpose 2
    B. Scope 3
    C. Objective 3

II. Identification of New Products,
     1984-1986 4

III. Markets for New Products 6

IV. Market Success for New Products 8

V. Revenue Generated from New Products, ... 12

VI. Conclusions and Recommendations 15

Appendixes 17

Bibliography 19

Index 21

Appendix 3:
Proofreader's Symbols

PROOFREADERS' MARK	DRAFT	FINAL COPY
⌄ Insert a comma	a large⌄old house	a large, old house
⌄ Insert an apostrophe	my children's car	my children's car
⌄⌄ Insert quotation marks	he wants a "loan"	he wants a "loan"
= Insert a hyphen	a first=rate job	a first-rate job
	ask the cöowner	ask the co-owner
‒‒ OR ⊥/M Insert a dash or change a hyphen to a dash	Success⌃at last! Here it is⊥cash!	Success‒‒at last! Here it is‒‒cash!
___ Insert underscore	an issue of Time	an issue of Time
⨍⨎ Delete underscore	a very long day	a very long day
( ) Insert parentheses	left today(May 3)	left today (May 3)
¶ Start a new paragraph	¶ If that is so	If that is so
⧉ Indent 2 spaces	Net investment in ⧉ tangible assets	Net investment in tangible assets
⊐ Move to the right	$38,367,000⊐	$38,367,000
⊏ Move to the left	⊏ Anyone can win!	Anyone can win!
= Align horizontally	Bob Muller TO⨍	TO: Bob Muller
‖ Align vertically	‖ Jon Peters Ellen March	Jon Peters Ellen March

PROOFREADERS' MARK	DRAFT	FINAL COPY
ss [Single-space	ss [I have heard / he is leaving.	I have heard / he is leaving.
ds [Double-space	ds [When will you / have a decision?	When will you / have a decision?
+1 l #→ Insert 1 line space	Percent of Change / +1 l # → 16.25	Percent of Change / 16.25
−1 l #→ Delete (remove) 1 line space	Northeastern / −1 l #→ regional sales	Northeastern regional sales
⌒ Delete space	to⌒gether	together
# Insert space	It⌃may⌃be	It may not be
⌒ Move as shown	it is (not) true	it is true
⌒ Transpose	beleivable	believable
⌒ Spell out	(is it) so	it is so
	② years ago	two years ago
	16 Elm (St.)	16 Elm Street
⌃ Insert a word	How much⌃is it?	How much is it?
ℐ or — Delete a word	it may not be true	it may be true
⌃ or ⋏ Insert a letter	temperature	temperature
ℐ or ⌄ Delete a letter and close up	commitment to buy	commitment to buy
⌒ Add on to a word	a real⸌ly good day	a really good day
ℐ or / Change a letter	this superℓedes	this supersedes
ℐ or — Change a word	and if you won't	but if you can't
.... Stet (don't delete)	I was very glad	I was very glad
/ Lowercase a letter (make it a small letter)	₣ederal ₲overnment	federal government
≡ Capitalize	Janet L. greyston	Janet L. Greyston
⌄ Raise above the line	in her new book⌄	in her new book*
⌃ Drop below the line	H2SO4	H$_2$SO$_4$
⊙ Insert a period	Mr⊙ Henry Grenada	Mr. Henry Grenada

Appendix 4:
Address Abbreviations

Two-Letter State and Territory

Alabama	AL
Alaska	AK
Arizona	AZ
Arkansas	AR
American Samoa	AS
California	CA
Colorado	CO
Connecticut	CT
Delaware	DE
District of Columbia	DC
Federated States Micronesia	FM
Florida	FL
Georgia	GA
Guam	GU
Hawaii	HI
Idaho	ID
Illinois	IL
Indiana	IN
Iowa	IA
Kansas	KS
Kentucky	KY
Louisiana	LA
Maine	ME
Marshall Islands	MH
Maryland	MD
Massachusetts	MA
Michigan	MI
Minnesota	MN
Mississippi	MS
Missouri	MO
Montana	MT
Nebraska	NE
Nevada	NV
New Hampshire	NH
New Jersey	NJ
New Mexico	NM
New York	NY
North Carolina	NC
North Dakota	ND
North Mariana Islands	MP
Ohio	OH
Oklahoma	OK
Oregon	OR
Palau	PW
Pennsylvania	PA
Puerto Rico	PR
Rhode Island	RI
South Carolina	SC
South Dakota	SD
Tennessee	TN
Texas	TX
Utah	UT
Vermont	VT
Virginia	VA
Virgin Islands	VI
Washington	WA
West Virginia	WV
Wisconsin	WI
Wyoming	WY

Directional Abbreviations

North	N
East	E
South	S
West	W
Northeast	NE
Northwest	NW
Southeast	SE
Southwest	SW

Street Suffixes

Alley	ALY	Heights	HTS
Annex	ANNEX	Highway	HWY
Arcade	ARC	Hill	HL
Avenue	AVE	Hills	HLS
Bayou	BYU	Hollow	HOLW
Beach	BCH	Inlet	INLT
Bend	BND	Island	IS
Bluff	BLF	Islands	ISS
Bottom	BTM	Isle	ISL
Boulevard	BLVD	Junction	JCT
Branch	BR	Key	KY
Bridge	BRG	Knolls	KNLS
Brook	BRK	Lake	LK
Burg	BG	Lakes	LKS
Bypass	BYP	Landing	LNDG
Camp	CP	Lane	LN
Canyon	CYN	Light	LGT
Cape	CPE	Loaf	LF
Causeway	CSWY	Locks	LCKS
Center	CTR	Lodge	LDG
Circle	CIR	Loop	LOOP
Cliffs	CLFS	Mall	MALL
Club	CLB	Manor	MNR
Corner	COR	Meadows	MDWS
Corners	CORS	Mill	ML
Course	CRSE	Mills	MLS
Court	CT	Mission	MSN
Courts	CTS	Mount	MT
Cove	CV	Mountain	MTN
Creek	CRK	Neck	NCK
Crescent	CRES	Orchard	ORCH
Crossing	XING	Oval	OVAL
Dale	DL	Park	PARK
Dam	DM	Parkway	PKY
Divide	DV	Pass	PASS
Drive	DR	Path	PATH
Estates	EST	Pike	PIKE
Expressway	EXPY	Pines	PNES
Extension	EXT	Place	PL
Fall	FALL	Plain	PLN
Falls	FLS	Plains	PLNS
Ferry	FRY	Plaza	PLZ
Field	FLD	Point	PT
Fields	FLDS	Port	PRT
Flats	FLT	Prairie	PR
Ford	FRD	Radial	RAD
Forest	FRST	Ranch	RNCH
Forge	FRG	Rapids	RPDS
Fork	FRK	Rest	RST
Forks	FRKS	Ridge	RDG
Fort	FT	River	RIV
Freeway	FWY	Road	RD
Gardens	GDNS	Row	ROW
Gateway	GTWY	Run	RUN
Glen	GLN	Shoal	SHL
Green	GRN	Shoals	SHLS
Grove	GRV	Shore	SHR
Harbor	HBR	Shores	SHRS
Haven	HVN	Spring	SPG
		Springs	SPGS
		Spur	SPUR

Square	SQ	Turnpike	TPKE
Station	STA	Union	UN
Stream	STRM	Valley	VLY
Street	ST	Viaduct	VIA
Summit	SMT	View	VW
Terrace	TER	Village	VLG
Trace	TRCE	Ville	VL
Track	TRAK	Vista	VS
Trail	TRL	Walk	WALK
Trailer	TRLR	Way	WAY
Tunnel	TUNL	Wells	WLS

Index

A

Account, 483
Accounting, 482-487
  software for, 112
Accounts payable, 481, 488
Accounts receivable, 481, 487
Administrative Assistant, 8, 17-19, 313, 349, 550
Administrative support function, 18-19
Administrative support specialist, 18
Address abbreviations, 604-607
Address label, 393
Address preparation guide, 389
Ageism, 154
Agreements, 491
Airborne, 384
Airlines, 281
Aldus Corporation, 112
Aldus Pagemaker, 112, 383
American Standard Code for Information Interchange (ASCII), 392, 396
Analog signals, 66
Analog waves, 248
Answering machine, 245, 255
Answering service, 255
Aperture card, 449
Applications software, 94, 97, 535-536
  accounting, 112
  budgeting, 465
  calendaring, 108
  communications, 397
  design, 537-538
  desktop publishing 45, 111-112
  grammar checker, 374
  graphics, 102
  programs, 99
  project management, 45, 108, 109, 202
  scheduling, 221
  spreadsheet, 45, 102
  types of, 100
  word processing, 44, 99
Appointment schedules, 290
Archivist, 555
ARMA (Association of Records Managers and Administrators), 431
Arithmetic-logic unit, 74
Artificial intelligence, 113

ASCII (American Standard Code for Information Interchange), 392, 396
Association of Records Managers and Administrators (ARMA), 431
AT&T (American Telephone and Telegraph), 246, 396
ATM (Automatic teller machine), 373, 374
Attitude, 150, 153, 165, 545, 547
Audience, 134
Audio teleconference, 268
Automatic call back, 252
Automatic payment/Electronic funds transfer (EFT), 477
Automatic route selection, 253
Automatic teller machine (ATM), 473-474
Automation, 10
Automation, office (*see* Office automation)

B

Backup, 48
Balance sheet, 482
Bank draft, 476
Banking, 474
  account balance, 478
  accounts, 476
  ATM, 373-374
  balance reconciliation, 479
  by mail, 476
  computer transfers, 477
  EFT, 477
  night depositories, 476
  payments, 476, 479
  point of sale transfers, 477
  statements, 479
Basic job skills, 513
Basic office skills, 20-23
Baud rate, 393
BDP (Business Data Processing), 32
Bid specification, 536
Blind letters, 558
Block format, 332
Block style, 328, 595
Body language, 126, 136, 137, 143
Boilerplate, (*See also* Mail/merge) 362
Bottom line, 526
Brainstorming, 509-510

Budgets, 461-464
  software for, 466
Bulletin board service, 394
Business Data Processing (BDP), 32
Business language, 133, 135
Business letters (*see* Letters)
Business trips (*see* Travel)
Bylaws, 218, 221

C

Cable, 249
Calculator, 91
  electronic, 83-84
Calendar, 178, 182
  electronic, 198, 209, 223
  evaluation, 177
  manual, 203
Calendaring software, 108
Call accounting, 253
Call forwarding, 252
Call reduction, 256
Call waiting, 253
Canceled check, 479-480
Canon, 384
Capital expense budget, 463
Career development, 26
Career ladder, 546
Career path, 546
Career planning, 546-556
Careers, 543-580
Carnegie, Dale, 155
Cash advance, 292
Cellular phone, 79, 245
Central processing unit (CPU), 74, 95
Centralized data base, 17
Centralized storage system, 429
Centrex system, 251
Chain of command, 158
Charter airline, 281
Charts, 103, 340
Check register, 475-476
Checks, 476
Chronological file, 436
Chips, 91
Circuit board, 66, 74
Circuits, 74
Clipboard, 369
Command, 100
Communication, 31, 125, 138, 205, 209
  audience, 134
  business, 142

Communication *(continued)*
  checklist, 132
  formal, 141
  informal, 139-140, 156
  listening *(see* Listening skills)
  message preparation, 132
  methods, 131
  miscommunication, 125, 137
  nonverbal, 137
  office, 197
  oral, 125, 132
  person-to-person, 139-142, 143
  preparing for, 129
  purpose, 130
  signals, 127
  telephone techniques, 141
  written *(see* Written
    Communications)
  (See also Letters; Reports)
Communication components, 79-81,
    91
  facsimile machine *(see* Facsimile
    machine)
Communication/distribution of
    information, 10, 12, 36-37,
    49-52, 381
  incoming mail procedures, 404,
    411
  traditional mail, 384, 412, 414
  electronic mail, 37
  electronic methods, 390-399
  facsimile transmission, 51
  mail-room practice, 388
  manual methods, 384
  processing mail, 400-404
  transmission media, 394-396
Communications devices 79
  (See Communications components)
Communications satellite, 396
Communications skills, 514
Communications software, 393
Communications tools, 109-111
Commuter airline, 280
Compatibility, 97
Components, computer, 70-82
Compuserve, 394
Computer-aided transcription, 83-84
Computer-assisted retrieval (CAR),
    451
Computer chips, 74
Computer conferences, 235
Computer data signal, 248
Computer graphics, 48, 105
Computer input microfilm (CIM),
    452
Computer output microfilm (COM),
    451
Computer components, *(See also*
    Components, computer), 70-82
  configuration, 66
  control codes, 393

Computer components *(continued)*
  data communication systems, 66,
    80
  data transfer, 248
  hardware *(see* Hardware), 63, 70
  input components, 71-73, 91
  laptop, 65
  mainframe, 64, 90
  microcomputer, 19, 65, 90
  minicomputer, 64, 90
  portable, 65
  protocols, 392
  sharing, 68
  software *(see* Software)
  standalone systems, 66
  storage, *(see* Disk drive; Floppy
    diskette, Hard disk; Memory)
  supercomputer, 64
  systems, 63
Conference call, 51, 245, 252
Conferences, 213, 216, 217, 231
  budget, 231
  computer, 234
  electronic, 51
  evaluation/follow up, 237
  recording, 234
  reporting, 237
  registration, 233
  site selection, 232
  speakers, 233
  teleconference *(See*
    Teleconference)
  video teleconference *(See* Video
    teleconferences)
  (See also Conventions; Meetings)
Configuration, 66
Contracts, 491
Control unit, 74
Controlling, 505
Conventions, 216, 231 *(See also*
    Conferences; Meetings)
Copyright laws, 361
Corporate Travel Department, 279
Correspondence *(See* Letters)
Cost-benefit ratio, 526
Courier mail services, 387
Court order, 493
CPU (Central processing unit) 74,
    95
  memory, 77
Creative thinking, 24, 25
Credit agreements, 465-466
Credit cards, 292, 466
Credit transactions, 464-466
Cursor, 72, 103

D

Data bank, 359
Database, 16, 359

Database management, 100-102
Data communications, 91
  (See also Facsimile transmission;
    Local area network)
Data communication services, 79,
    91
Data communication systems, 66,
    80
Data gathering, 130
Data input *(See* Input)
Data processing, 32
  accounting and *(see* Accounting)
dBase IV, 101
Deadlines, 187
Dealer support, 116
Decision making, 507-508
  factors in, 52
  function, 52
Decoding, 126
Dedicated phone line, 79
Deming, Dr. W. Edwards, 148
Deming's philosophy, 165
Departmental budget, 463
Deposit slip, 472
Desktop publishing, 45, 111-114,
Dictation, 320, 350
  machine, 352
  centralized system, 354
  process, 320
  shorthand machines, 355
  taking, 353
  transcribing, 352
Dictation/transcription systems,
    81-82, 91
Digital facsimile machine, 361
Digital signals, 66, 248
Direct deposit transfer, 471
Directory, 46
Dishonored check, 482
Disk, 49, 373
Disk operating system (DOS), 46,
    97
Disk drive, 75
  (See also Floppy diskette; Hard
    disk)
Displaywriter (IBM), 99
Distribution/communication of 10,
    12, 36-37, 49-52
  information *(See* Communication/
    distribution of information)
Distribution Services Manager,
    552
Document processing, 309, 347 *(see
    also* Editing)
  merging, 362
Documentation legal *(see* Legal
    documentation)
DOS (Disk operating system), 46, 97
Dot matrix printer, 77
Dow Jones, 394
Download, 359, 396

E

E-mail, 110, 111, 323
EBCDIC (Extended Binary Coded Decimal Interchange Code), 396
Editing, 357, 374
EDP (electronic data processing), 32
EFT (electronic funds transfer) 477
Electronic calculators, 83
Electronic calendar, 198, 223
Electronic cottage, 147
Electronic data processing (EDP), 32 (see also Computers, Data processing; Word processing)
Electronic dictionary, 373, 375
Electronic distribution, 384, 390
Electronic file, 35, 357, 382, 384
Electronic filing, 406
Electronic funds transfer (EFT), 477
Electronic manuals and help facilities, 115
Electronic mail, 37, 49-51, 110, 111, 323, 359, 390, 397, 404
Electronic mailbox, 391, 404
Electronic messaging, 37
Electronic notebook, 357
Electronic office, 1, 314 (See also Office automation)
Electronic reminder system (See Tickler file)
Electronic spreadsheet software, 102
Electronic storage and retrieval, 75 (see Microforms) (See also Disk drive; Floppy diskette; Hard disk; Memory)
Electronic typewriter, 83, 84, 364, 382
Electronic workstation, 61, 63
Employee assistance programs, 164, 165
Employee evaluations, 506
Employment agencies, 557
Encoding, 126
Endless loop, 354
Endorsement, 472
Ergonomics, 84
Evaluation, 506
Executable file, 365
Expenditures, 461
Expense reports, 298, 464
    forms, 299
    records, 298
Expert systems, 113
Extended Binary Coded Decimal Interchange Code (EBDCIC), 392

F

Facsimile machine, 12, 80, 396-397
Factors in selecting technology, 51

Facsimile transmission, 51
Fax board, 81
Federal Communications Commission, 395
Federal Express, 384
Feedback, 129, 132, 137
Fiber optic cable, 249
Files, 35
Filing, 436
First Publisher, 112
Floppy diskette, 75, 91
Flowchart, 532
Framework, 107
Function, 5, 8
Function key, 71
Furniture and equipment design, 84-86
Funds, 291

G

Garbage in, garbage out (GIGO), 23
General journal, 480, 482
General ledger, 484
GIGO (garbage in, garbage out), 23
Goal setting, 25
Grammar checker, 374
Graphics, 340
    computer, 45, 103
Graphics/presentation software, 103
Graphic user interface (GUI), 107, 368
Gross pay, 469
GUI (graphic user interface), 107, 368

H

Handwriting recognition device, 73, 91, 358
Hard copy, 14, 35, 77, 382, 384
Hard disk, 75, 91
Hardware, 63, 70
    output devices (see Output; Reprographics)
    (see also Data communications; Floppy diskette; Hard disk; Memory)
Harvard Graphics, 104
Herzberg's motivation Hygiene theory, (see Motivation)
Hewlett Packard, 384
Hiring, 516
Horizontal relationships, 151
How to Win Friends and Influence People, 155
Human relations, 146, 545
    skills, 155

I

IBM (International Business Machines), 34, 97, 107

Icons, 107
Income statement, 482
Industrial Revolution, 508
Information Age, 3-4
Information management, 421-497 (See also Filing)
Information processing, 11, 12, 31, 34, 347
    communication/distribution (see Communication/distribution of information)
    input (see Input)
    output (see Output; Reprographics)
    storage, 31, 34 (See also Electronic storage and retrieval; Filing systems)
Information processing cycle, 37-40, 381
Information processing manager, 551
Information processing specialist, 550
Initiative, 515
Input, 10, 12, 41-43, 370
    boilerplate, 362
    components, 71-73, 91
    devices for (see Input components)
    dictation (see Dictation)
    digital facsimile, 361
    download, 359
    electronic mail, 359
    optical character reader (OCR), 72, 360
    upload, 359
    (See also Input components, Electronic storage and retrieval)
Input components, 71-73, 91
    facsimile machine, 12, 80, 396-397
    handwriting recognition device, 73, 91, 358
    keyboard, 71, 91
    light pen, 73, 91
    mouse, 71, 91
    optical character reader (OCR), 72, 360
    scanner, 34, 72, 91
    voice input, 73, 91
Input devices, (see Input components)
Integrated software, 105
Integrated systems, 528
Integrated technology, 37
Internal Revenue Service (IRS), 482
International company, 294
Internet, 394
Interoffice mail, 388
Interoffice memo, (See Memorandums)
Interpersonal skills, 26

Interviewing, 564
Inventory, 467
Invoices, 487
IRS (Internal Revenue Service), 482
Itinerary, 280, 290

J

Jet lag, 284
Job application process, 556-572
Job campaign, 546
Job description, 519-520
Job hunting (*see* Job application
    process)
Journal (*see* General journal)

K

Key system, 245
Keyboard, 71, 91

L

LAN (local area network), 68, 80,
    90, 390
Laser printer, 78
Lateral move, 547
Law blank, 489
Leadership, 511, 513, 546
    MBO, 512
    (*See also* Management practice;
        Motivation; Supervision)
Leading, 370
Legal documentation, 491-495
Letter-quality printer, 78
Letters, 326
    block style, 328, 595
    business (*see* Business letters)
    form, 329, 596
    indented paragraphs, 597
    simplified style, 598
    (*See also* Memorandums)
LEXIS, 69
Light pen, 73, 91
Line item, 462
Line spacing, 370
Listening skills, 23, 136-137
Litigation, 493
Local area network (LAN), 68, 80,
    90, 390
Long-term planning, 504
Lotus 1-2-3, 102, 103, 107

M

Macintosh, 107
Machine dictation, 352
Magnetic Tape Selectric Typewriter
    (MT/ST), 34
Magnetic tape storage, 75
Mailgram, 398-399
Main memory, 75
Mainframe, 90

Management, personal, 25, 27
Management by Objectives (MBO),
    512
Management information system
    (MIS), 539
Management practice, 503-542
    brainstorming, 509-510
    decision making (*see* Decision
        making)
    leadership, 511, 513
    MBO, 512
    modeling, 510
    planning, 504-505
    (*See also* Leadership; Supervision)
Management style, 509
Manual distribution, (*see*
    Communication/Distribution
    of information, manual
    methods)
Maslow's hierarchy of needs, (*see*
    Motivation)
MCI, 247
Media mix, 452
Megatrends, 146
Meetings, 221-229
    evaluation, 241
    notetaking, 230-231
    project team, 217
    project team, 217
    refreshments, 230
    seminars, 217
    staff, 216
    supplier/client, 217
    support duties, 230
    taperecording, 231
    transcripts, 231
    types of, 217
    workshops, 217
    (*See also* Conferences;
        Conventions; Seminars;
        Workshops)
Memo, interoffice (*see*
    Memorandums)
Memo report, 340
Memorandums (Memos), 323
Memory, 75, (*see also* Disk drive;
    Floppy diskette; Hard disk;
    RAM; ROM)
Mental filter, 126, 127, 128, 133,
    137
Merging, 362
Messages, 132
Messenger service, 387
Microcomputer, 19, 65, 90
Microfiche, 449
Microforms, 447
Micrographics (*see* Microforms)
Micrographics technician, 554
Microimage, 451 (*see also*
    Microforms)
Microprocessors, 74, 91

Microsoft Corporation, 107
Microsoft Excel, 103
Microsoft Windows, 105, 368
Microsoft Word, 99
Microsoft Works, 107
Microwave transmission, 79,
    394-395
Minicomputer, 64, 90
Minutes, 221, 238, 239
Miscommunication, 125, 127, 137
Modified block format, 329, 596, 597
Mobile phone, 79
Modeling, 510
Modem, 66, 80, 91, 111, 248, 359,
    393
Money orders, 472, 476
Monitor, 77, 91
Morenot, 104
Motivation, 25, 508, 515, 520
Mouse, 71, 91, 107
MS-DOS (microsoft disk operating
    system), 97, 107, 383
MT/ST (Magmatic Tape Selectric
    Typewriter), 34
Multimate, 99
Multitasking, 528

N

Naisbitt, John, 146
Net pay, 469
Networked systems, 49
Networks, 68, 248-249 (*See also*
    Local area network; Wide
    area network)
Networking, 14, 558
NEXIS, 69
Nonelectronic scheduling system,
    (*See* Calendars, manual)
Nonverbal communication, 137-138
Norton Utilities, 99
Notary public, 494
Notetaking, 350

O

OCR (optical character reader) 72,
    360
Office automation, 4, 524
    ergonomics in (*see* Ergonomics)
    functions, 5, 8
    system study for, 530
    word processing and (*see* Word
        processing)
Office automation (OA) specialist,
    532
Office communication, 197-212
Office landscaping, 86
Office manager, 550
Office politics, 156, 165
Office supplies, 88-89
Office worker, 347

Official Airline Guide (OAG), 280, 281, 609
Official Railway Guide, 286
On-line information services, 69, 359
Operating system software, 96-97
  MS-DOS, 97, 107, 383
  OS/2, 107
  Windows, 107
Optical character reader (OCR), 72, 360
Oral communication, 125, 132, 143
  listening, 143
  speaking, 23
  voice control, 134
Organizational structure, 14-17
Organizing, 505
Originator, 81
OS/2, 107
Outline, 338
Output, 10, 12, 14, 48-49, 381
  hard copy 14, 35
Output components, 77, 91 *(see also* Monitor; Printer)
Output devices *(see* Output components)
Overnight mail, 387
Oversensitivity, 154
Owner's equity, 482

P

Page size, 370
Paging device, 255
Paradigm Reference Guide, 368
Parliamentary procedure, 215, 221
Participative approach, 148, 165
Passport, 294, 365
Password, 47
Payee, 472
Payroll, 469-471
PBX (Private Branch Exchange), 245
Performance appraisal *(See* Employee evaluation)
Personal profile, 547-548
Petty cash, 468-469
Photocopier, 83
Placement services, 557
Planning, 108-109
Plotter, 79
Point-of-sale transfer, 477
Pointer, 72
Postage meter, 409
Posting, 484
Postscript, 383
Power of attorney, 492
Powerpoint, 104
Prejudice, 154
Printers, 77, 91, 383
  laser, 78

Printers *(continued)*
  letter-quality, 78
  plotters, 79
Printout, 77
Private Branch Exchange (PBX), 245
Problem solving skills, 24
Procedure, 5, 8
Processing, 10, 12, 31-34, 43-46, 91
Processing components, 74, 95
  central processing unit (CPU), 74
Procom, 393
Prodigy, 394
Productivity, 5, 508
  tools, 45, 99
Professional conference planners, 213
Professionalism, 544
Programmable key, 71
Programmer, 95
Programming language *(See also* Software), 94
Programming software, 95, 97
Project budget 463
Project management software, 45, 108, 202
Proofreading, 319, 357
  symbols, 602-603
Public Relations Publications, 342
Purchase orders, 488

Q

Quality *(see* Deming's philosophy), 149
Quark Express, 112
Quorum, 221, 239

R

RAM (random access memory), 34, 75, 368
Racism, 154
Random access memory (RAM), 34, 75, 368
RCA, 396
Records, 554-555
  inventory, 424
Records management *(see* Information management)
Reference materials, 89
Registration, 233
Reports, 337, 599 *(see also* Memo reports)
Reprographics, 91
  hardcopy, 17
  printers *(see* Printers)
  (see also Output)
Reprographics systems components, 82-83
Restrictive endorsement, 474
Retrieval, 47, 75
Resume writing, 559

Revenues, 461
Rider, 490
Robert's Rules of Order, Newly Revised, 215, 216
Routing slip, 403

S

Satellite, 79
Scanner, 34, 72, 91
Scheduling *(see* Time Management)
Secretary, 549
Self-esteem, 25
Seminars *(see* Conferences), 215, 216
Senior micrographics clerk, 555
Sensory receiver, 127
Sexism, 266
Short-term planning, 504
Shorthand, 350
  machine, 350
Signals, 127
  analog, 66
  digital, 66
Simplified format 598
Smartware, 107
Soft copy, 14, 34, 382, 386
Software, 44, 94
  accounting, 112
  applications *(see* Applications software)
  documentation, 115
  electronic manuals, 116
  help facilities, 116
  integrated, 105
  operating systems, 96-97
  project management, 45, 109
  types of, 99
  user groups, 116
  word processing, 44, 99
  vendor support, 115
Speaker phone, 268
Speaking, *(see* Oral communications) 23
Speed dialing, 252
Spelling checker, 373, 375
Spreadsheets, 45, 102
Sprint, 247
Stop payment order, 476
Storage, 10, 12, 31, 34, 46, 87
  floppy disks, 75, 91
  hard disk, 75, 91
  (See also Electronic storage and retrieval; Filing systems)
Storage components 75, 76, 91
Storage systems, 427
Stress, 162, 349
Strunk, William Jr., 318
Subordinate positions, 546
Subpoena 493
Super computer, 64

Supervision, 516-524
  employee evaluation, 521-522
  hiring, 516
  job description, 519-520
  training, 517
  (*See also* Leadership;
    Management approaches)
Symphony 107
System design, 532
System study, 530
Systems analyst, 95

T

Table of contents, 601
Task, 5, 8
Team approach, 509
Telecommunications, 245
  (*See also* Data communications)
Telecommuting, 269
Teleconference, 142, 143, 235, 268
  audio, 268
  video, 51, 269
Telegraph, 390
Telephone, 79, 235, 245
  answering machine, 245
  cellular, 79, 245
  centrex system, 251
  conference call, 51, 247
  key system, 245
  lines, 66, 69, 79, 80
  mobile, 79
  PBX, 245
  speaker phone, 268
  systems, 91
  telecommuting (*see*
    Telecommuting)
  teleconference (*see* Teleconference)
  voice mail, 245, 256-257
Telephone features, 251-254
Telephone techniques, 245, 257-258
Telephone transfers, 477
Teletypewriter (TTY), 397
Telex, 390, 397-398
The Elements of Style, 318
Thesaurus, 374
Time management, 169-189, 193
  calendars (*see* Calendars)

Time management *(continued)*
  deadlines, 187
  schedule, 178
Time zones, 608
Title page, 600
Toastmasters, 233
Traditional mail, (*see*
    Communication/distribution
    of information, manual
    methods)
Training, 517-518
Transcript, 229
Transcription, 320
Travel agency, 278
Travel arrangements, 275-305
Travel and Entertainment expense
    report, 298
Traveler's checks, 292, 472
Travel documents, 294
Travel preference forms, 277
Traveler's profile questionaire, 276
Turnaround time, 313
TWX, 397-398
Typewriter, 91
  electronic, 83-84, 364, 382

U

Ultrafiche, 450
U.S. Postal Service, 384, 385-387,
  398
  address preparation guide, 389
  ZIP Code, 408
Unisys Corporation, 97
Upload, 359, 396
User groups, 116
Utility program, 99

V

Vendor support, 116
Ventura Publisher, 112
Vertical relationships, 152
Video display terminal (VDT) (*see*
    Cathode-ray tube)
Video input device, 73, 91
Video teleconference, 51, 269

Virus, 99, 365
Visa, 295
Visicalc, 103
Voice input device, 73, 91
Voice mail, 51, 79, 111, 245

W

Wellness programs, 164
Western Union, 396, 397, 398
White, E.B., 318
Wide area network (WAN), 68, 80,
  90, 392
Windows, 107 (*see also* Operating
    systems)
WMRM (Write many, read many),
  446
WordPerfect, 99
Word processing, 17, 32, 34, 44, 99
  software for, 99
Word processing specialist, 551
Work area, 86
Workflow, 10, 12
Workstation, 63, 81-84, 89, 90, 91
Write-protect tab, 367
Writing, 312 (*see also*
    Communications; Business
    letters; Letters; Reports)
Writing process, 313 (*see also*
    Communication/distribution
    of information)
Written communications, 125,
    312-318
  memorandums (memos) (*see*
    Memorandums)
  letters (*see* Letters)
  reports (*see* Reports)
  public relations publications
    (*see* Public relations
    publications)

X

Xerox, 396

Z

Zenith, 97
ZIP Code, 408